Guitar Reference Guide

SCALES

By Joe Charupakorn

ISBN 1-57560-245-8

PREFACE

From the pentatonic riffs of the blues to the sinuous lines of bebop, the blistering licks of rock to the fleet-fingered runs of classical, scales form the foundation for music. Scales provide the resources for harmony and melody, and give these elements order, logic, and a sense of inevitability. Scales also play a vital role in the technical development of any instrumentalist and are a requisite study for all serious musicians.

This book presents the most thorough collection of scales ever published for guitar. Each scale is displayed in one-, two-, and three-octave versions with several fingering options. Beginning and intermediate guitarists should first master the major and minor scales and their modes, plus the blues scale and the pentatonic major and minor scales—all over the fretboard with different fingerings and in different keys—then learn other scales as the need arises, or when curiosity strikes. Advanced guitarists will want to expand their knowledge with the more esoteric scales and fingerings presented here.

Keep in mind, however, that scales are not music. Scales are only tools—very important tools—that, with careful study and a patient, open-minded approach, will exponentially increase your creative options and significantly broaden your tonal palette.

—Joe Charupakorn

ABOUT THE AUTHOR

Joe Charupakorn is a guitarist, composer, and author. He earned a Master of Fine Arts in Composition from Purchase Conservatory of Music at the State University of New York, where he graduated Magna Cum Laude. Joe has also studied privately with many musical heavyweights—including jazz pianists Richie Beirach and Mike Longo, guitar legend Mike Stern, and contemporary classical composer Ruth Schonthal. He has performed around the world, in places such as Amsterdam, Nice, Barcelona, and Bangkok, and is currently active as a guitarist, composer, and teacher in the New York metropolitan area.

ACKNOWLEDGMENTS

I'd like to thank Arthur Rotfeld and Toby Wine, my editors, for their insight, patience, and guidance; Robert Papp for assistance in designing the scale pages; and my family and friends for their unconditional support.

CONTENTS

Part I: Introduction to Scales

Basic Scale Theory 4
Modes 4
Pentatonic Scales 5
Symmetrical Scales....................5
Scale Formula Chart 6

Part II: Playing Scales on the Guitar

Reading Scale Diagrams....................8
Position-Based Fingerings....................8
Three-Notes-Per-String Fingerings 9
Position-Based Fingerings Starting on All Scale Degrees, and
Three-Notes-Per-String Fingerings Starting on All Scale Degrees....................10
Four-Notes-Per-String Fingerings 10
The Scales....................11

Part III: Scales in Standard Notation

The Scales....................152

PART I: INTRODUCTION TO SCALES

Basic Scale Theory

Scales

A scale is a series of notes, organized sequentially, beginning and ending on a given tonic, or root. From the initial tonic, any combination of steps can be added until the tonic is reached again, thus forming a scale.

The twelve notes used in Western music form what is known as the *chromatic scale*. From these twelve notes, we can create other scales using step patterns, by dividing the octave into combinations of half steps (H), our smallest interval, and whole steps (W), which are equivalent to two half steps.

The step pattern for the major scale is W W H W W W H.

Another approach to creating scales is to use *scale formulas*. A scale formula shows the degrees of a given scale as they relate to the degrees of a major scale. This approach provides an accurate account of the function of each note in the scale and is essential in styles such as jazz, where knowledge of the relationship of each note to the given harmony (as chords are derived from scales) is necessary.

Major scale formula	1	2	3	4	5	6	7	8
C major	C	D	E	F	G	A	B	C
Natural minor scale formula	1	2	♭3	4	5	♭6	♭7	8
C natural minor	C	D	E♭	F	G	A♭	B♭	C

Modes

A mode, like a scale, is a series of notes, organized sequentially, beginning and ending on a given root. Modes, however, are derived from a *parent scale*, such as the major scale (which is also known as the Ionian mode). A mode contains the exact same notes as its parent scale, but simply begins and ends on a different note. For example, if we take the notes of a C major scale (C D E F G A B C), but start and end the scale on D, we get the D Dorian mode (D E F G A B C D). Although the notes of a mode and its parent scale are exactly the same, each note has a different tonal relationship and gravitational pull to its respective root. All modes can be learned this way. Here's a chart to help you memorize the order. Remember all of these modes contain the same notes, they just start in a different place. (Note: Though shown in the key of C, you can replace the note names with the note names from any other major scale.)

C Ionian (Major)
D Dorian
E Phrygian
F Lydian
G Mixolydian
A Aeolian (Natural Minor)
B Locrian

Modes can also be constructed by using the step pattern or the scale formula approaches outlined in the "Scales" section.

Here's how you can construct D Dorian using this step pattern approach.

Dorian = W H W W W H W

D Dorian =	D		E		F		G		A		B		C		D
		W		H		W		W		W		H		W	

Here's how you can construct D Dorian using the scale formula approach.

Dorian = 1 2 ♭3 5 6 ♭7

D Dorian =	D	E	F	G	A	B	C	D
	1	2	♭3	4	5	6	♭7	8

Pentatonic Scales

Pentatonic scales are five-note scales (*penta* means five) that are used primarily for creating melodies. Though often heard in folk and Asian music, pentatonic scales—specifically the pentatonic minor and pentatonic major—are also the most widely used scales in blues and rock guitar.

Symmetrical Scales

Symmetrical scales are built upon a repeating interval pattern that terminates at the octave. These scales lack a sense of key center or tonality, as every symmetrical scale has several possible tonics. Because of their repetitive design, these scales are among the easiest to memorize and visualize.

Scale Formula Chart

Name	**Formula**	**Step Pattern**	**Tonic 7th Chord**	**Extensions†**
Chromatic Scale				
Chromatic Scale	1 ♯1 2 ♯2 3 4 ♯4 5 ♯5 6 ♯6 7	H H H H H H H H H H H H		
Major Scale and its Modes				
Ionian (Major)	1 2 3 4 5 6 7	W W H W W W H	maj7	9, 11*, 13
Dorian	1 2 ♭3 4 5 6 ♭7	W H W W W H W	m7	9, 11, 13
Phrygian	1 ♭2 ♭3 4 5 ♭6 ♭7	H W W W H W W	m7	♭9*, 11, ♭13
Lydian	1 2 3 ♯4 5 6 7	W W W H W W H	maj7	9, ♯11, 13
Mixolydian	1 2 3 4 5 6 ♭7	W W H W W H W	7	9, 11*, 13
Aeolian (Natural Minor)	1 2 ♭3 4 5 ♭6 ♭7	W H W W H W W	m7	9, 11, ♭13
Locrian	1 ♭2 ♭3 4 ♭5 ♭6 ♭7	H W W H W W W	m7♭5	♭9*, 11, ♭13
Melodic Minor Scale and its Modes				
Melodic Minor	1 2 ♭3 4 5 6 7	W H W W W W H	m(maj7)	9, 11, 13
Dorian ♭2	1 ♭2 ♭3 4 5 6 ♭7	H W W W W H W	m7	♭9*, 11, 13
Lydian Augmented	1 2 3 ♯4 ♯5 6 7	W W W W H W H	maj7♯5	9, ♯11, 13
Lydian ♭7	1 2 3 ♯4 5 6 ♭7	W W W H W H W	7	9, ♯11, 13
Mixolydian ♭6 (Hindu)	1 2 3 4 5 ♭6 ♭7	W W H W H W W	7	9, 11*, ♭13
Aeolian ♭5	1 2 ♭3 4 ♭5 ♭6 ♭7	W H W H W W W	m7♭5	9, 11, ♭13
Super Locrian	1 ♭2 ♭3 ♭4 ♭5 ♭6 ♭7	H W H W W W W	7♭5	♭9, ♯9, ♭13
Harmonic Minor Scale and its Modes				
Harmonic Minor	1 2 ♭3 4 5 ♭6 7	W H W W H W+H H	m(maj7)	9, 11, ♭13
Locrian ♮6	1 ♭2 ♭3 4 ♭5 6 ♭7	H W W H W+H H W	m7♭5	♭9*, 11, 13
Ionian ♯5	1 2 3 4 ♯5 6 7	W W H W+H H W H	maj7♯5	9, 11*, 13
Dorian ♯4	1 2 ♭3 ♯4 5 6 ♭7	W H W+H H W H W	m7	9, ♯11, 13
Phrygian Dominant	1 ♭2 3 4 5 ♭6 ♭7	H W+H H W H W W	7	♭9, 11, ♭13
Lydian ♯2	1 ♯2 3 ♯4 5 6 7	W+H H W H W W H	maj7	♯9, ♯11, 13
Super Locrian 𝄫7	1 ♭2 ♭3 ♭4 ♭5 ♭6 𝄫7	H W H W W H W+H	°7	♭9, ♭4*, ♭13,
Harmonic Major Scale and its Modes				
Harmonic Major	1 2 3 4 5 ♭6 7	W W H W H W+H H	maj7	9, 11*, ♭13
Dorian ♭5	1 2 ♭3 4 ♭5 6 ♭7	W H W H W+H H W	m7♭5	9, 11, 13
Phrygian ♭4	1 ♭2 ♭3 ♭4 5 ♭6 ♭7	H W H W+H H W W	7	♭9, ♯9, ♭13
Lydian ♭3	1 2 ♭3 ♯4 5 6 7	W H W+H H W W H	m(maj7)	9, ♯11, 13
Mixolydian ♭2	1 ♭2 3 4 5 6 ♭7	H W+H H W W H W	7	♭9, 11*, 13
Lydian Augmented ♯2	1 ♯2 3 ♯4 ♯5 6 7	W+H H W W H W H	maj7♯5	♯9, ♯11, 13
Locrian 𝄫7	1 ♭2 ♭3 4 ♭5 ♭6 𝄫7	H W W H W H W+H	°7	♭9, 11, ♭13

* Extension usually omitted. † Naturally occuring extensions (above the 7th).

Name	Formula	Step Pattern	Tonic 7th Chord	Extensions†

Pentatonic and Blues Scales

Name	Formula	Step Pattern	Tonic 7th Chord	Extensions†
Blues	1 ♭3 4 ♭5 5 ♭7	W+H W H H W+H W	m7	11
Pentatonic Major	1 2 3 5 6	W W W+H W W+H	6	9
Pentatonic Minor	1 ♭3 4 5 ♭7	W+H W W W+H W	m7	11
Major ♭2 Pentatonic	1 ♭2 3 5 6	H W+H W+H W W+H	6	♭9*
Major ♭6 Pentatonic	1 2 3 5 ♭6	W W W+H H W+W	major triad	9, ♭13
Minor 6 Pentatonic	1 ♭3 4 5 6	W+H W W W W+H	m6	11
Minor 7♭5 Pentatonic	1 ♭3 4 ♭5 ♭7	W+H W H W+W W	m7♭5	11
Whole Tone Pentatonic	1 3 ♯4 ♯5 ♭7	W+W W W W W	7♯5	♯11
Banshiki-Cho	1 ♭3 4 ♭6 ♭7	W+H W W+H W W	m7(no 5th)	11, ♭13
Hirajoshi	1 2 ♭3 5 ♭6	W H W+W H W+W	minor triad	9, ♭13
Iwato	1 ♭2 4 ♭5 ♭7	H W+W H W+W W	7sus4♭5	♭9
Kokin-Chosi	1 ♭2 4 5 ♭7	H W+W W W+H W	7sus4	♭9
Kumoi	1 2 ♭3 5 6	W H W+W W W+H	m6	9
Naka Zora	1 ♭2 4 5 ♭6	H W+W W H W+W	sus4 triad	♭9, ♭13
Pelog	1 ♭2 ♭3 5 ♭6	H W W+W H W+W	minor triad	♭9, ♭13
Ritsu	1 2 4 5 6	W W+H W W W+H	sus4 triad	9, 13
Ryūkyū	1 3 4 5 7	W+W H W W+W H	maj7	11*
Shimo-Chidori	1 3 ♯4 5 7	W+W W H W+W H	maj7	♯11

Symmetrical Scales

Name	Formula	Step Pattern	Tonic 7th Chord	Extensions†
Augmented	1 ♯2 3 5 ♯5 7	W+H H W+H H W+H H	maj7♯5	♯9, 5
Diminished Half/Whole	1 ♭2 ♯2 3 ♯4 5 6 ♭7	H W H W H W H W	7	♭9, ♯9, ♯11, 13
Diminished Whole/Half	1 2 ♭3 4 ♭5 ♯5 6 7	W H W H W H W H	m(maj7)♭5	9, 11, ♯5, 13
Whole Tone	1 2 3 ♯4 ♯5 ♭7	W W W W W W	7♭5	9, ♭13

Bebop Scales

Name	Formula	Step Pattern	Tonic 7th Chord	Extensions†
Bebop Dominant	1 2 3 4 5 6 ♭7 7	W W H W W H H H	7	9, 11*, 13
Bebop Major	1 2 3 4 5 ♯5 6 7	W W H W H H W H	maj7	9, 11*, 13
Bebop Tonic Minor	1 2 ♭3 4 5 ♯5 6 7	W H W W H H W H	m(maj7)	9, 11, 13
Bebop Minor	1 2 ♭3 4 5 ♯5 6 ♭7	W H W W H H H W	m7	9, 11, 13

Exotic Scales

Name	Formula	Step Pattern	Tonic 7th Chord	Extensions†
Eight-Tone Spanish	1 ♭2 ♭3 3 4 ♭5 ♭6 ♭7	H W H H H W W W	7♭5	♭9, ♯9, 11*, ♭13
Enigmatic	1 ♭2 3 ♯4 ♯5 ♯6 7	H W+H W W W H H	maj7♯5	♭9, ♯11, ♯13
Gypsy	1 2 ♭3 ♯4 5 ♭6 ♭7	W H W+H H H W W	m7	9, ♯11, ♭13
Hungarian	1 ♯2 3 ♯4 5 6 ♭7	W+H H W H W H W	7	♯9, ♯11, 13
Hungarian Minor	1 2 ♭3 ♯4 5 ♭6 7	W H W+H H H W+H H	m(maj7)	9, ♯11, ♭13
Leading Whole Tone	1 2 3 ♯4 ♯5 ♯6 7	W W W W W H H	maj7♯5	9, ♯11, ♯13
Lydian Minor	1 2 3 ♯4 5 ♭6 ♭7	W W W H H W W	7	9, ♯11, ♭13
Major Locrian	1 2 3 4 ♭5 ♭6 ♭7	W W H H W W W	7♭5	9, 11*, ♭13
Marwa	1 ♭2 3 ♯4 6 7	H W+H W W+H W H	maj7(no 5th)	♭9*, ♯11, 13
Neapolitan Major	1 ♭2 ♭3 4 5 6 7	H W W W W W H	m(maj7)	♭9*, 11, 13
Neapolitan Minor	1 ♭2 ♭3 4 5 ♭6 7	H W W W H W+H H	m(maj7)	♭9*, 11, ♭13
Oriental	1 ♭2 3 4 ♭5 6 ♭7	H W+H H H W+H H W	7♭5	♭9*, 11, 13
Prometheus	1 2 3 ♯4 6 ♭7	W W W W+H H W	7(no 5th)	9, ♯11, 13
Prometheus Neapolitan	1 ♭2 3 ♯4 6 ♭7	H W+H W W+H H W	7(no 5th)	♭9, ♯11, 13
Todi	1 ♭2 ♭3 ♯4 5 ♭6 7	H W W+H H H W+H H	m(maj7)	♭9*, ♯11, ♭13

PART II: PLAYING SCALES ON THE GUITAR

Reading Scale Diagrams

The scales in this book are presented in diagram form. These diagrams represent a portion of the guitar neck and show note locations and fingerings. The perspective of the diagrams is as if you are facing a guitar with its headstock pointing to your left (see the diagram below). The horizontal lines represent frets and the vertical lines represent strings. (Note: The 6th string is the thickest, lowest-sounding string.) The dots indicate the note location *and* the fingering. The scale's tonic is always shown as a white dot.

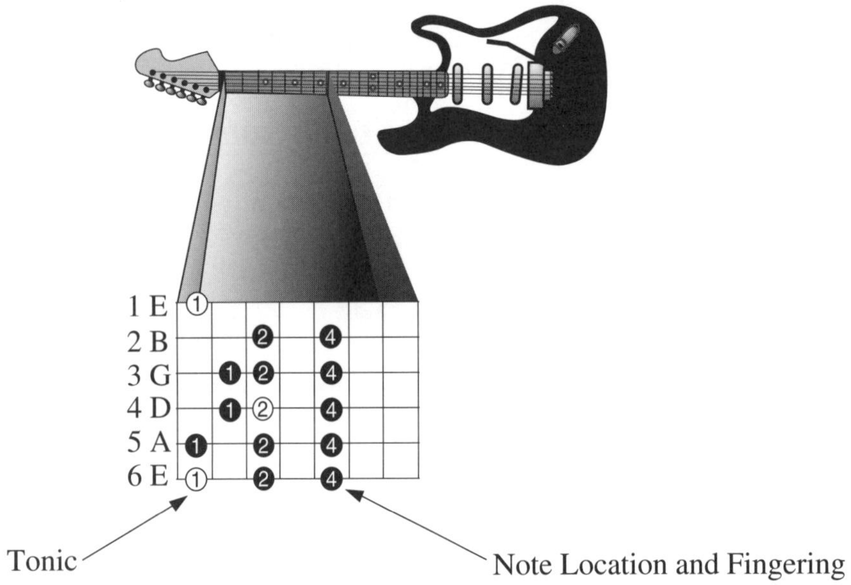

Position-Based Fingerings

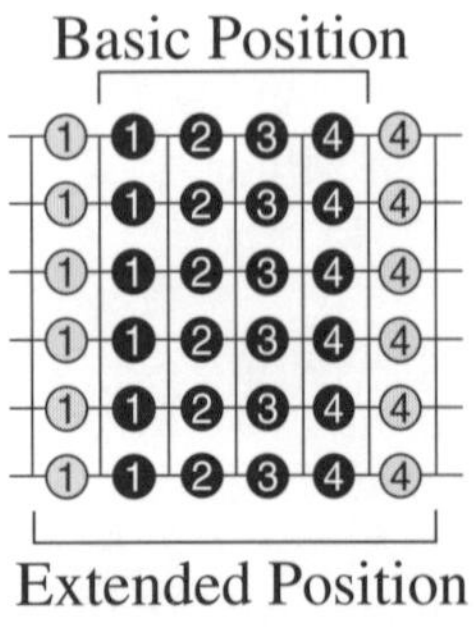

Position-based fingerings allow you to cover a two-octave range without moving your hand out of position. Generally, although not written in stone, a position on the guitar covers a six-fret range across all six strings with each finger assigned to one or two frets. The first finger covers the first two frets and the pinkie covers the last two. The third and fourth notes are covered by the second and third fingers. *The position is named by the fret played by the first finger that is adjacent to the fret assigned to the second finger.*

The advantage of this approach is that there is never any doubt concerning the fingering of a note. The disadvantage is that there is not always a uniform amount of notes per string, which can cause confusion with picking strokes.

Three-Notes-Per-String Fingerings

Three-notes-per-string fingerings are commonly employed when speed and precision are desired. This approach is geared toward moving up and down the fingerboard rather than staying in position. In seven- and eight-note scales, each string covers the distance of a 3rd; the first finger and pinkie are always used to begin and end on each string, with either the second or third finger covering the middle note. On any given string, there are only a few combinations of finger patterns possible within the range of a 3rd:

Within a minor 3rd

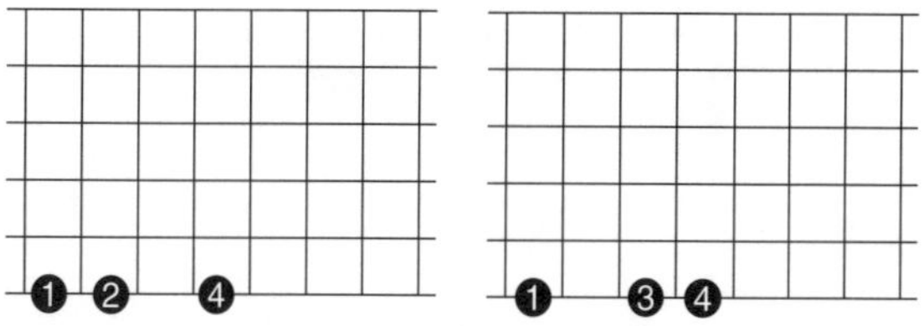

Within a major 3rd

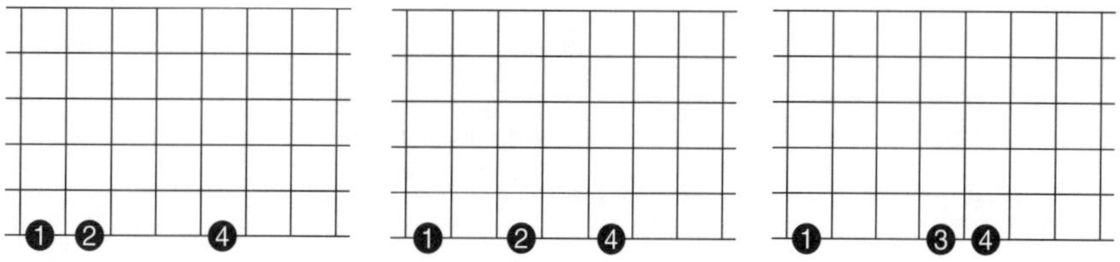

When using this technique on scales with fewer notes such as pentatonic and six-note scales, the range of a single string can increase to a 4th. Here are the possible finger combinations:

Within a perfect 4th

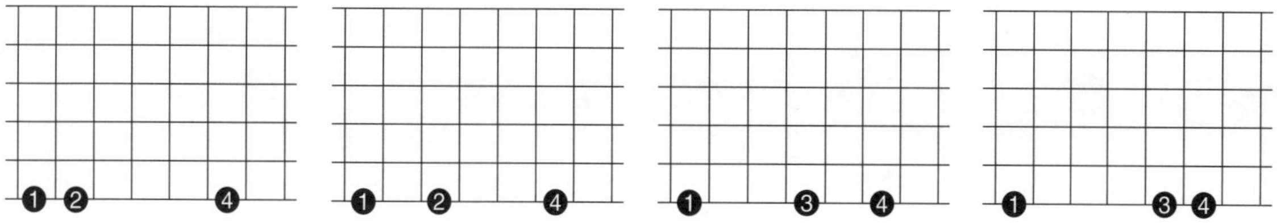

Within an augmented 4th

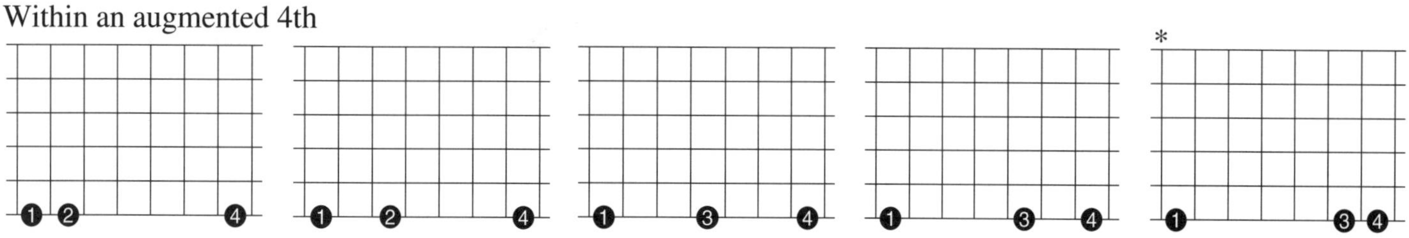

*Uncommon

Because there is a uniform number of notes from string to string and the note patterns are easy to visualize, many guitar techniques that require consistency in articulation, such as alternate picking and legato playing (via hammer-ons and pull-offs), can be easily accomplished.

Position-Based Fingerings Starting on All Scale Degrees, and Three-Notes-Per-String Fingerings Starting on All Scale Degrees

The "Position-Based Fingerings Starting on all Scale Degrees" and "Three-Notes-Per-String Fingerings Starting on all Scale Degrees" diagrams display fingerings for a given scale beginning with each degree as the lowest note. The first diagram shows the root as the lowest note and starting point. Each subsequent diagram begins on the next scale step up from the previous one.

Notice how each fingering overlaps with the next. Visualizing each fingering with awareness of its relationship to its adjacent fingerings, as well as to the whole fretboard, will help expedite fretboard mastery.

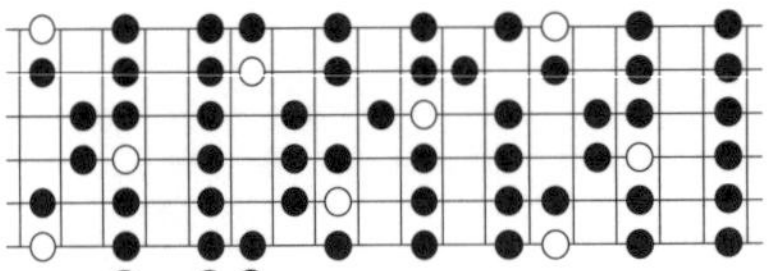

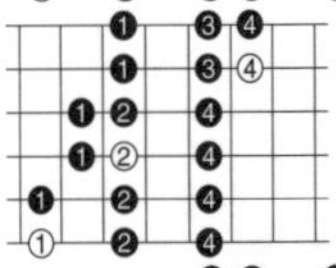

Starting on the root

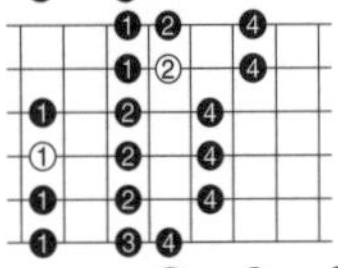

Starting on the 2nd

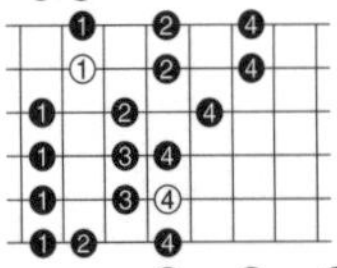

Starting on the 3rd

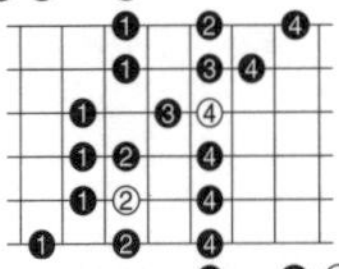

Starting on the 4th

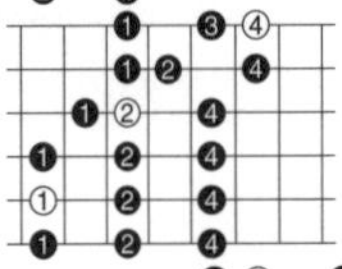

Starting on the 5th

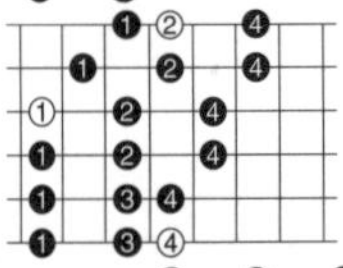

Starting on the 6th

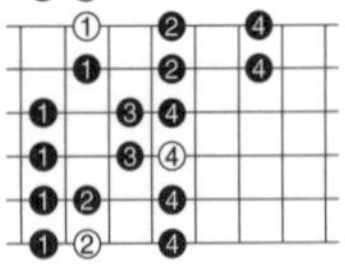

Starting on the 7th

Four-Notes-Per-String Fingerings

Four-notes-per-string fingerings allow you to cover a wide range of notes with a minimum of string changes. This approach is particularly useful for legato playing where a smoother, horn-like articulation is desired.

The fingerings provided use all four fingers on a single string and are shown beginning on every string except the first. Some of these fingerings are challenging and may require a bit of stretching. If you find the stretches too difficult, try an extended three-notes-per-string approach. You can either use your pinkie for the last two notes (with a slide into the last note), or your first finger for the first two notes (with a slide into the second note) and the three-notes-per-string fingerings for the other notes.

Pinkie Slide

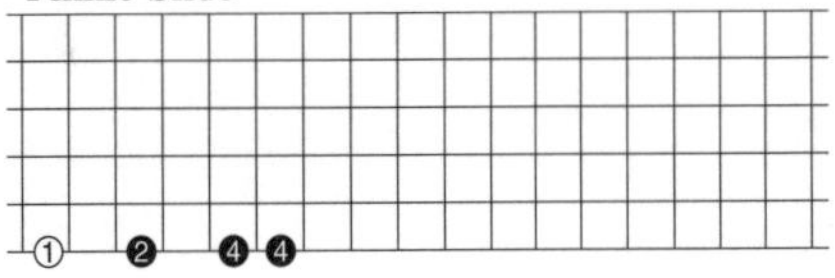

First-Finger Slide

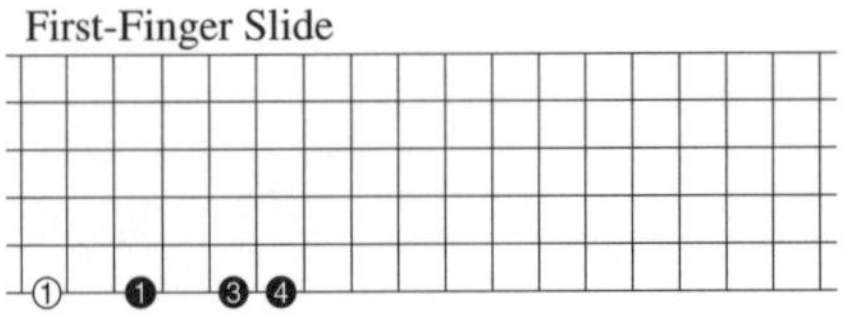

The Scales

Chromatic Scale 12

Major Scale and its Modes 14
Ionian (Major) 14
Dorian 16
Phrygian 18
Lydian 20
Mixolydian 22
Aeolian (Natural Minor) 24
Locrian 26

Melodic Minor Scale and its Modes 28
Melodic Minor 28
Dorian ♭2 30
Lydian Augmented 32
Lydian ♭7 34
Mixolydian ♭6 (Hindu) 36
Aeolian ♭5 38
Super Locrian 40

Harmonic Minor Scale and its Modes 42
Harmonic Minor 42
Locrian ♮6 44
Ionian ♯5 46
Dorian ♯4 48
Phrygian Dominant 50
Lydian ♯2 52
Super Locrian 𝄫7 54

Harmonic Major Scale and its Modes 56
Harmonic Major 56
Dorian ♭5 58
Phrygian ♭4 60
Lydian ♭3 62
Mixolydian ♭2 64
Lydian Augmented ♯2 66
Locrian 𝄫7 68

Pentatonic And Blues Scales 70
Blues 70
Pentatonic Major 72
Pentatonic Minor 74
Major ♭2 Pentatonic 76
Major ♭6 Pentatonic 78
Minor 6 Pentatonic 80
Minor 7♭5 Pentatonic 82
Whole Tone Pentatonic 84
Banshiki-Cho 86
Hirajoshi 88
Iwato 90
Kokin-Chosi 92
Kumoi 94
Naka Zora 96
Pelog 98
Ritsu 100
Ryūkyū 102
Shimo-Chidori 104

Symmetrical Scales 106
Augmented 106
Diminished Half/Whole 108
Diminished Whole/Half 110
Whole Tone 112

Bebop Scales 114
Bebop Dominant 114
Bebop Major 116
Bebop Tonic Minor 118
Bebop Minor 120

Exotic Scales 122
Eight-Tone Spanish 122
Enigmatic 124
Gypsy 126
Hungarian 128
Hungarian Minor 130
Leading Whole Tone 132
Lydian Minor 134
Major Locrian 136
Marwa 138
Neapolitan Major 140
Neapolitan Minor 142
Oriental 144
Prometheus 146
Prometheus Neapolitan 148
Todi 150

Chromatic Scale

Scale Tones

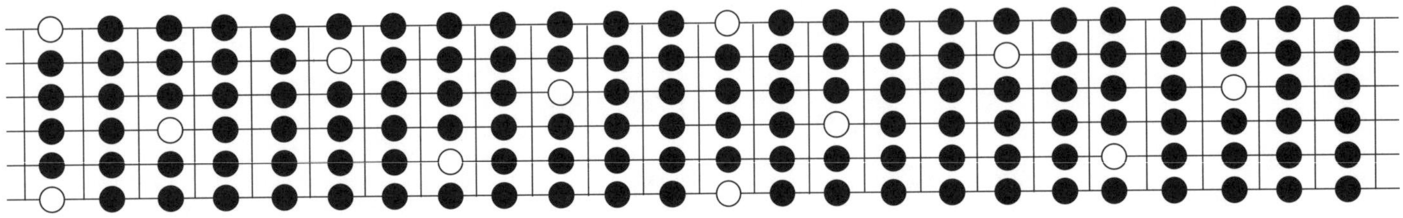

One-Octave Fingerings

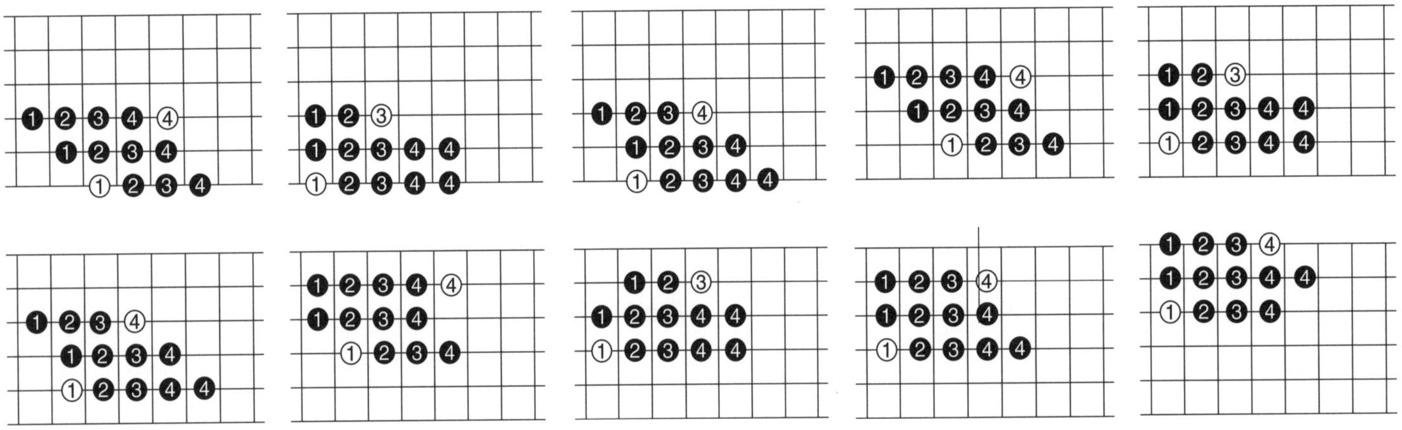

Two-Octave Fingerings

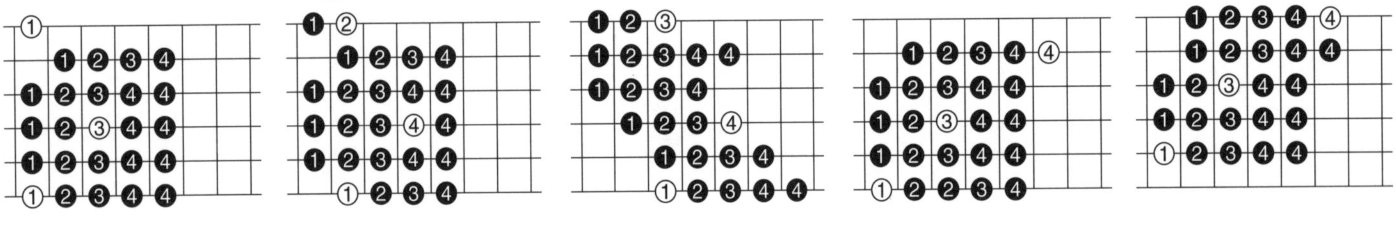

Three-Octave Fingering

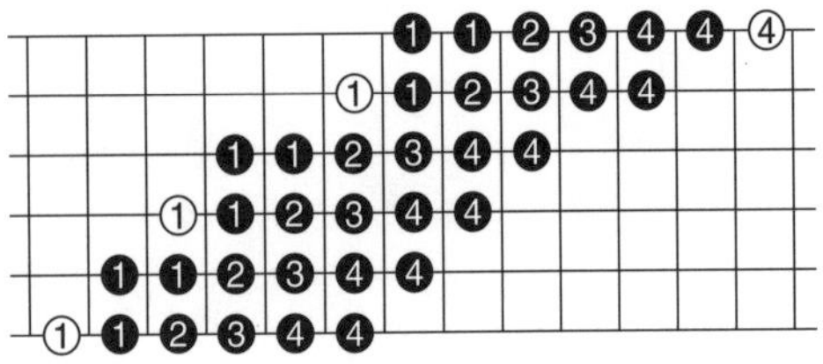

Four-Notes-Per-String Fingerings

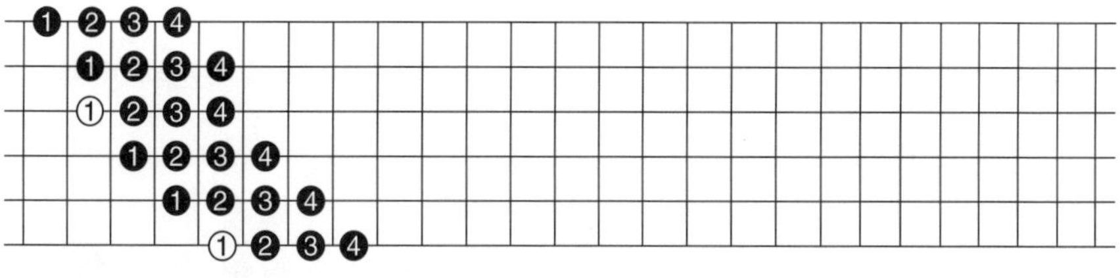

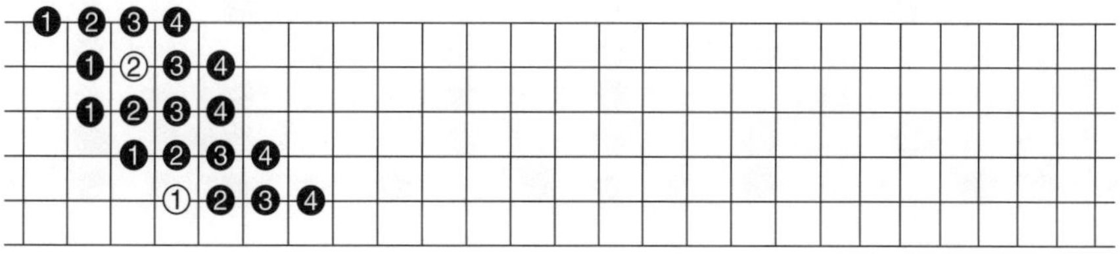

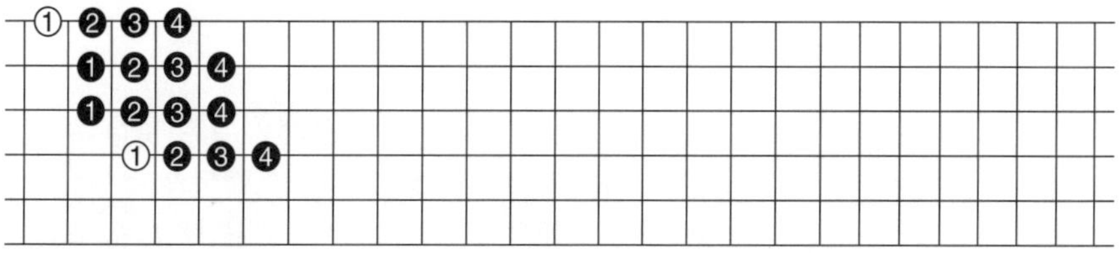

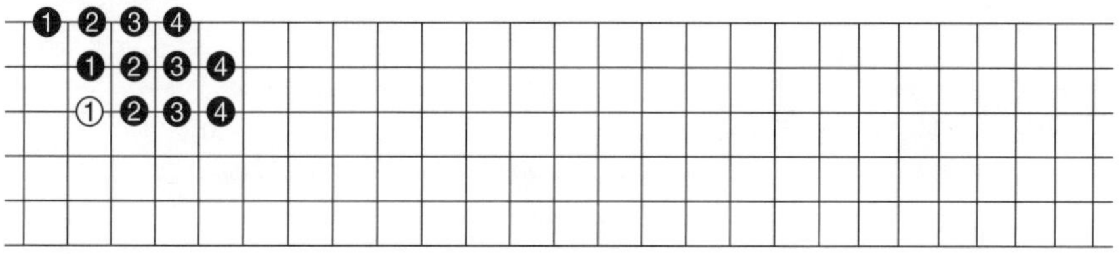

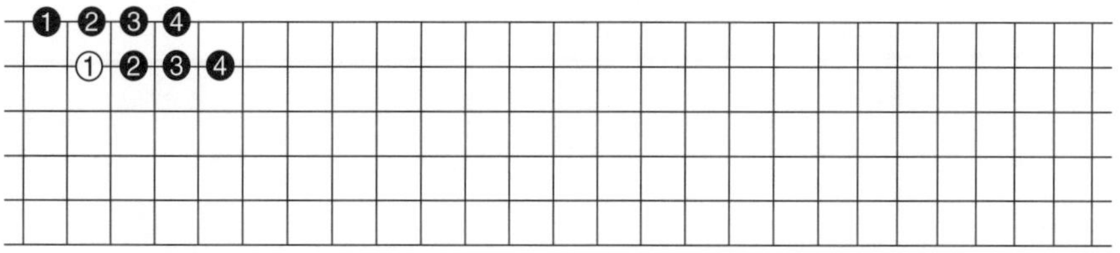

Ionian (Major)

Scale Tones

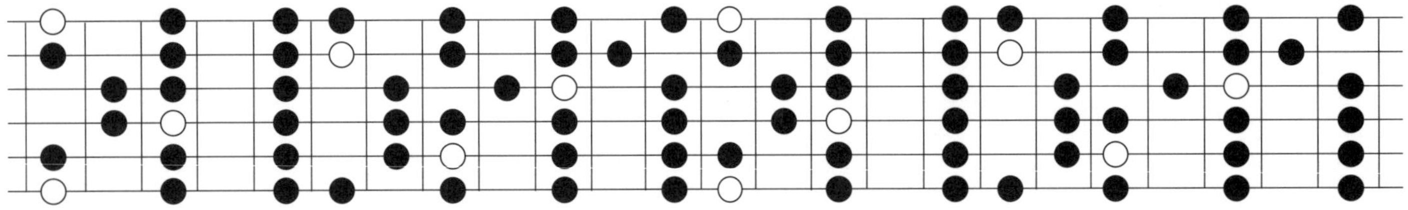

One-Octave Fingerings

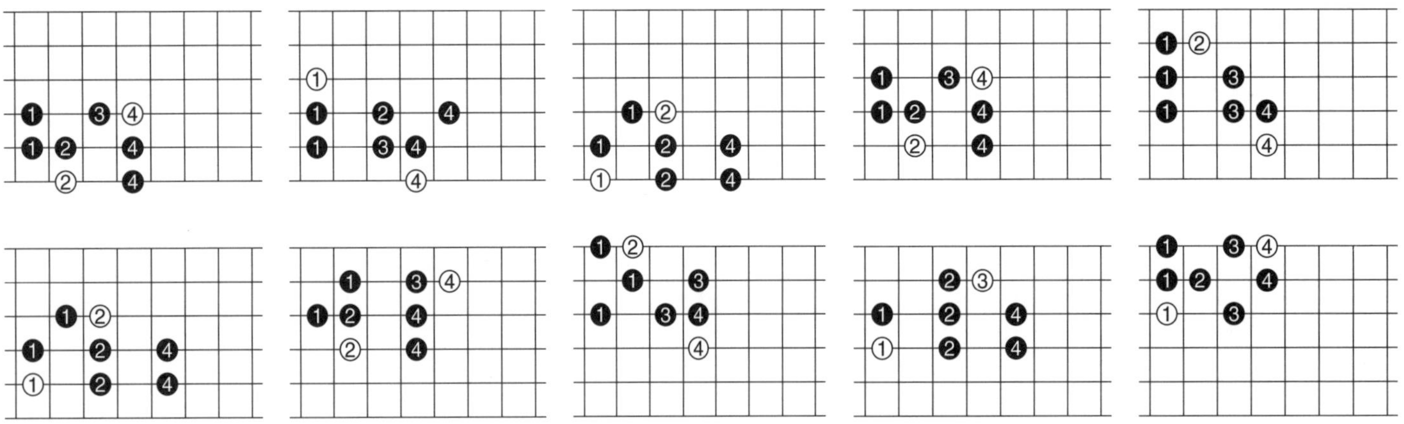

Two-Octave Fingerings

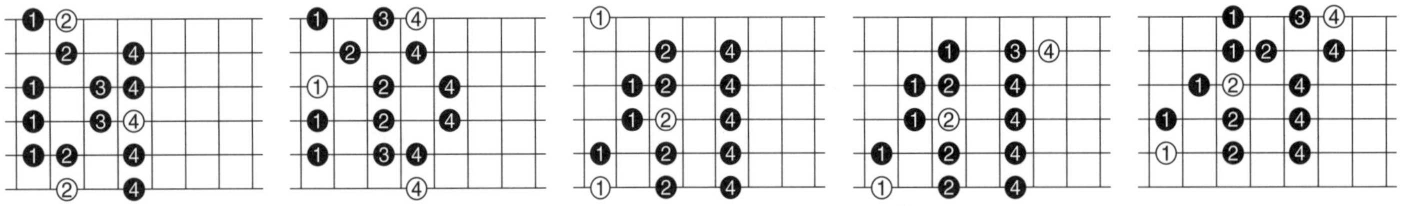

Three-Octave Fingerings

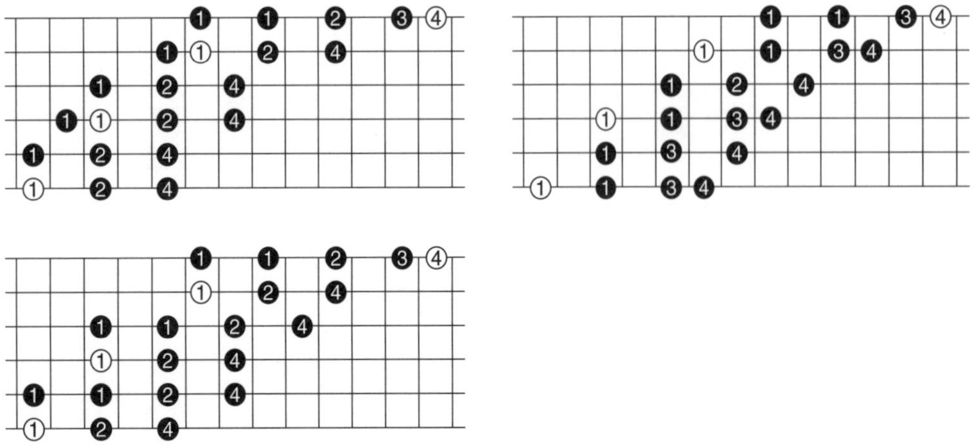

Position-Based Fingerings, Starting on all Scale Degrees

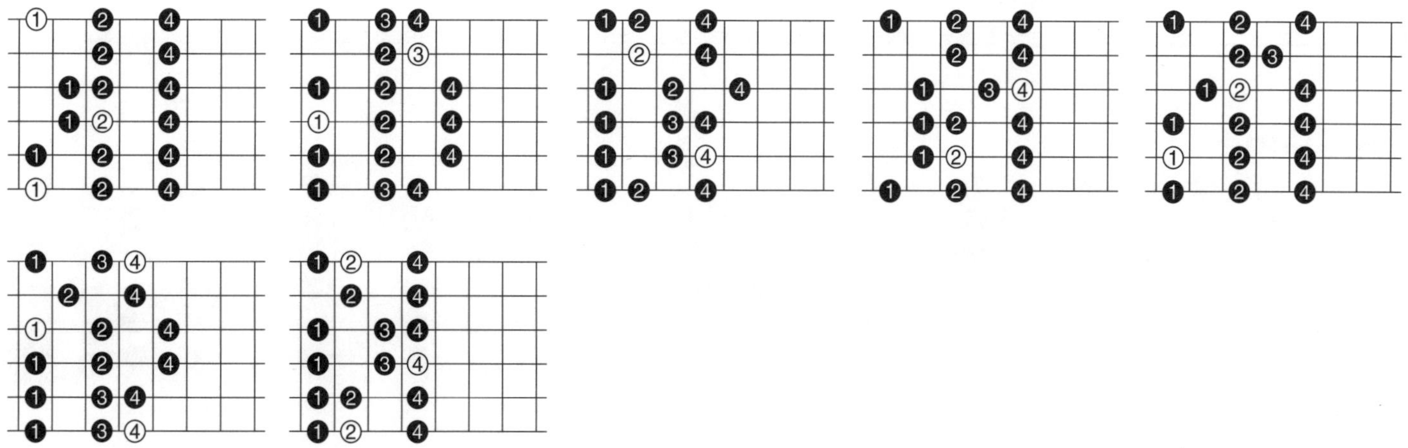

Three-Notes-Per-String Fingerings, Starting on all Scale Degrees

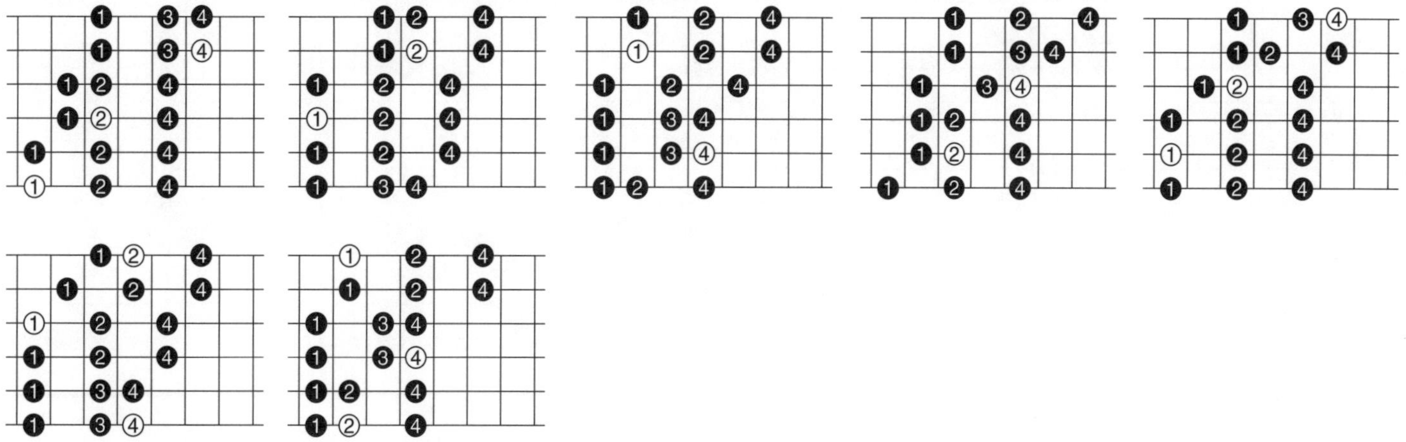

Four-Notes-Per-String Fingerings

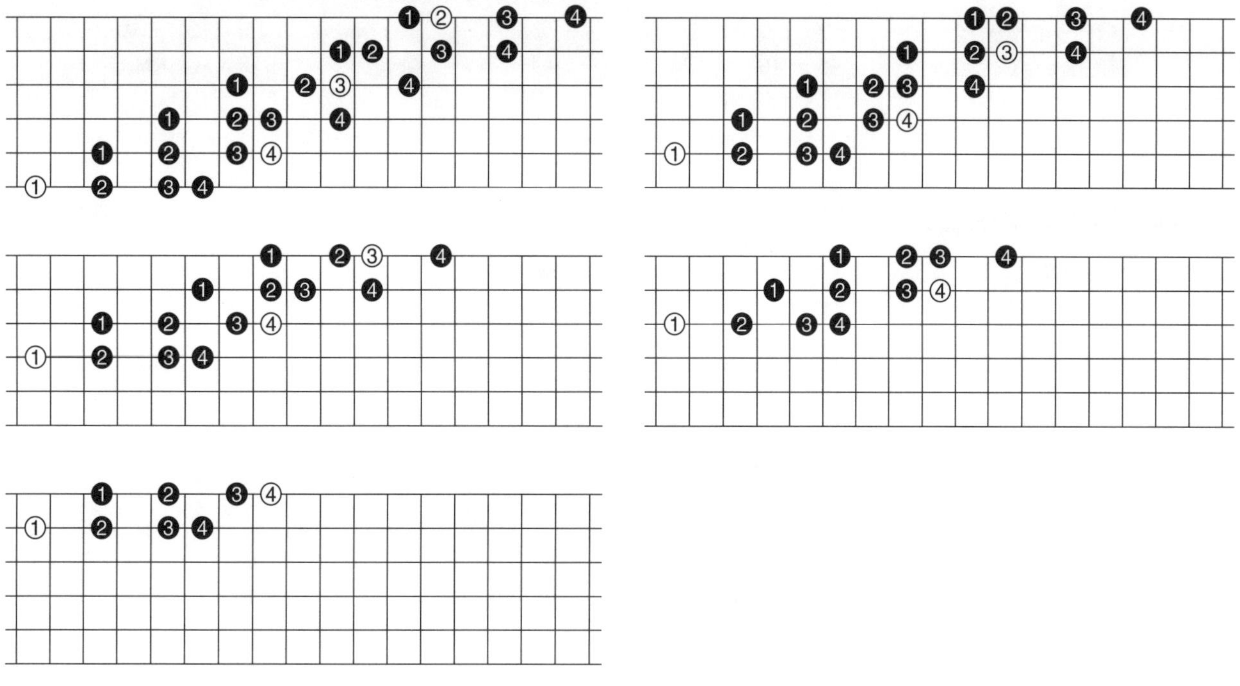

Dorian

Scale Tones

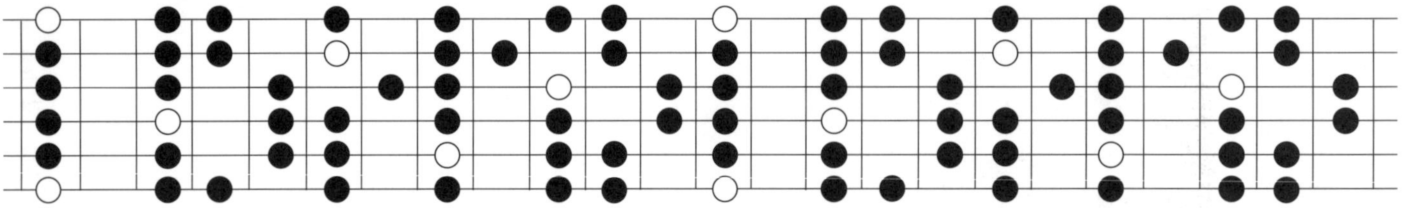

One-Octave Fingerings

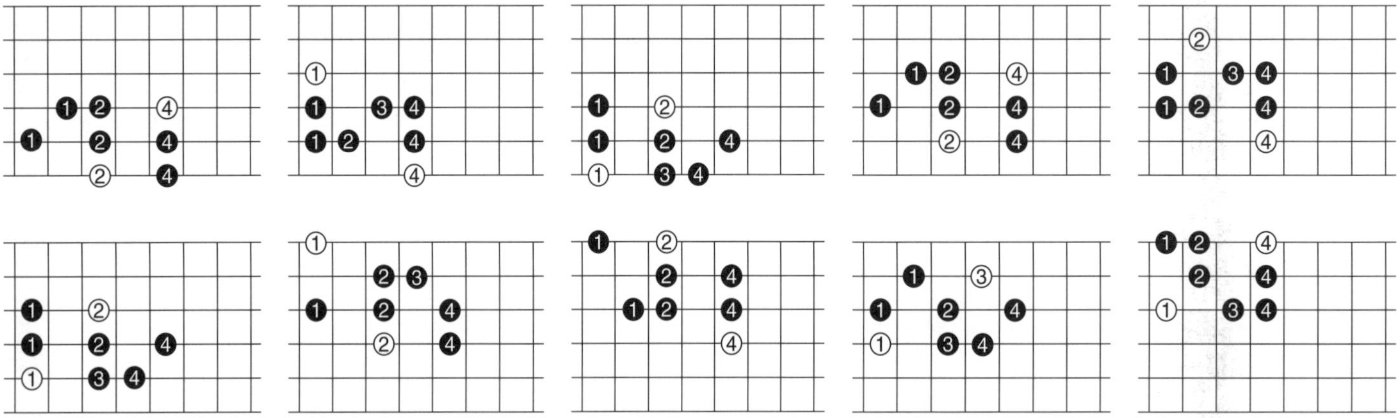

Two-Octave Fingerings

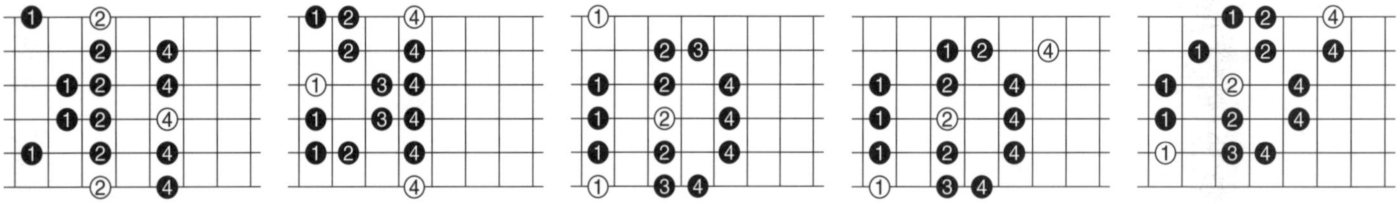

Three-Octave Fingerings

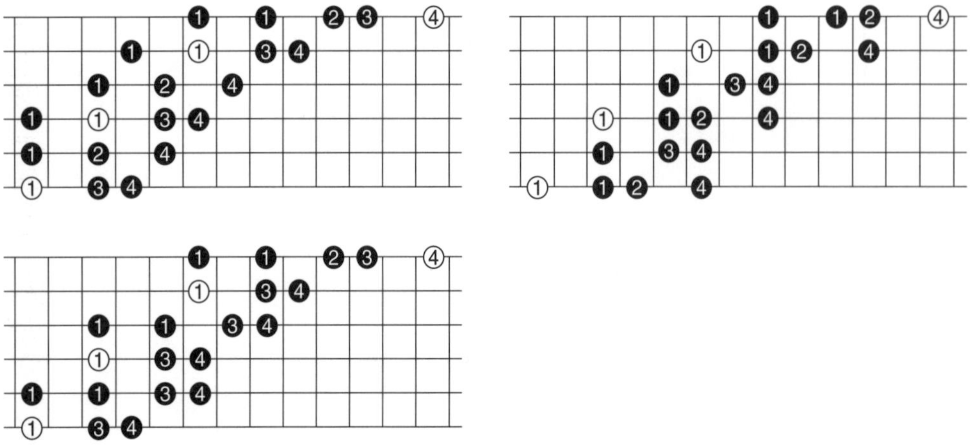

Position-Based Fingerings, Starting on all Scale Degrees

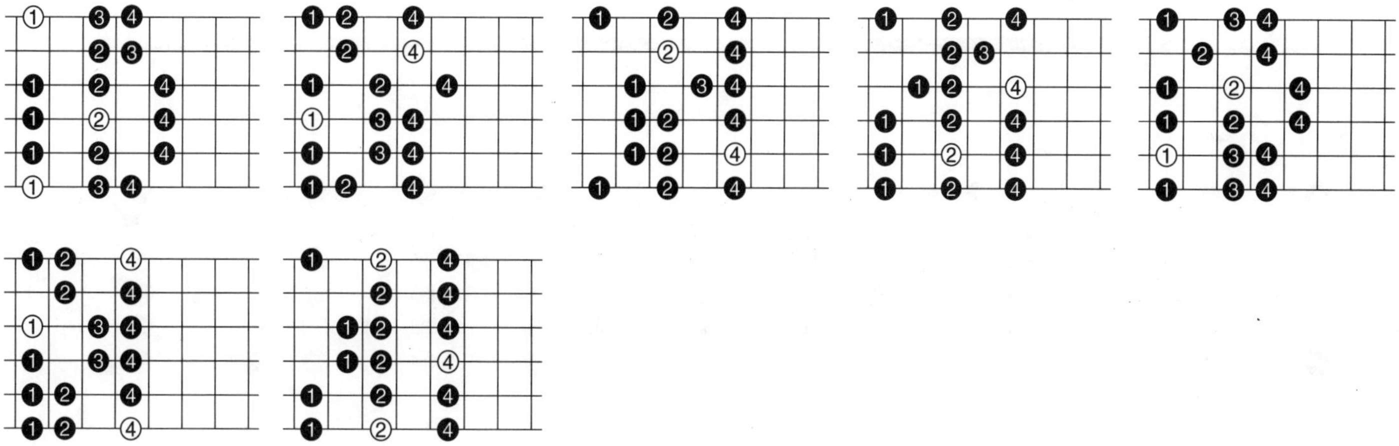

Three-Notes-Per-String Fingerings, Starting on all Scale Degrees

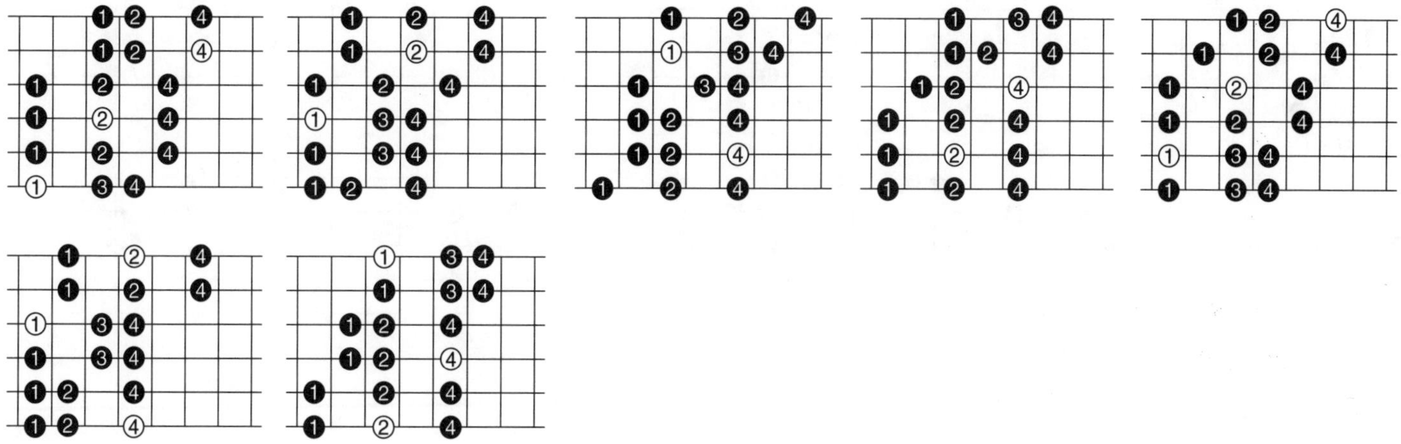

Four-Notes-Per-String Fingerings

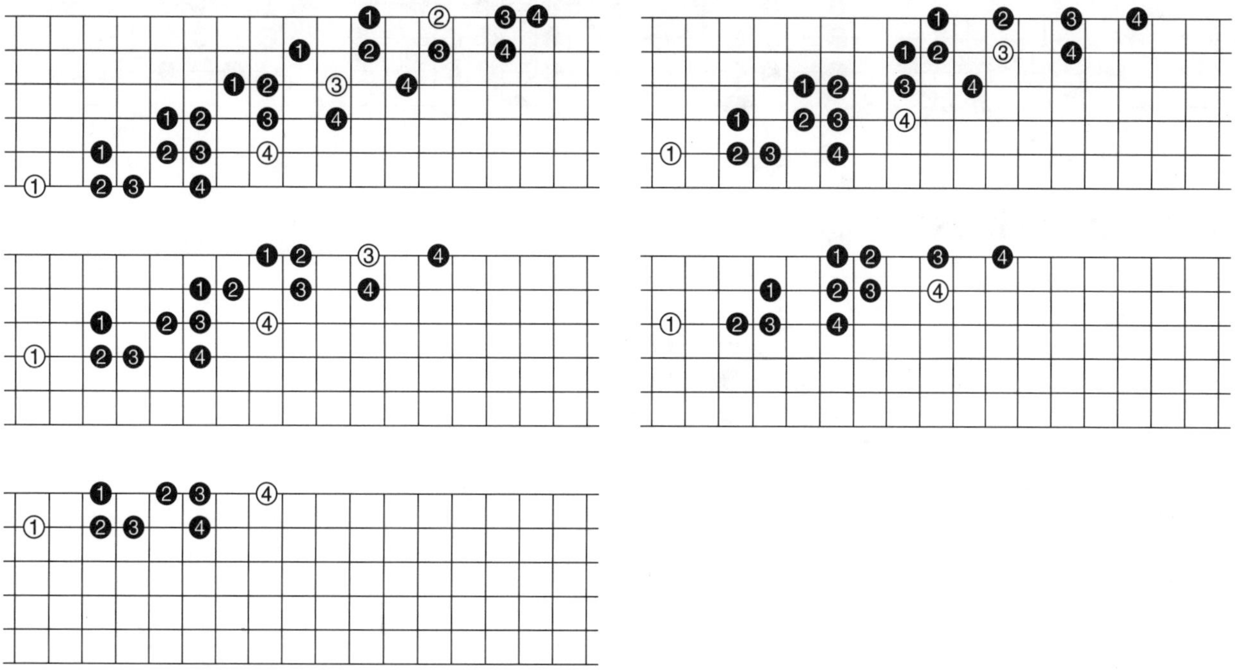

Phrygian

Scale Tones

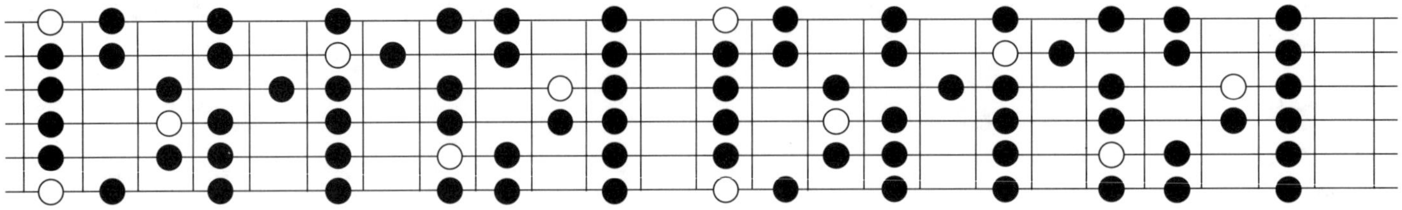

One-Octave Fingerings

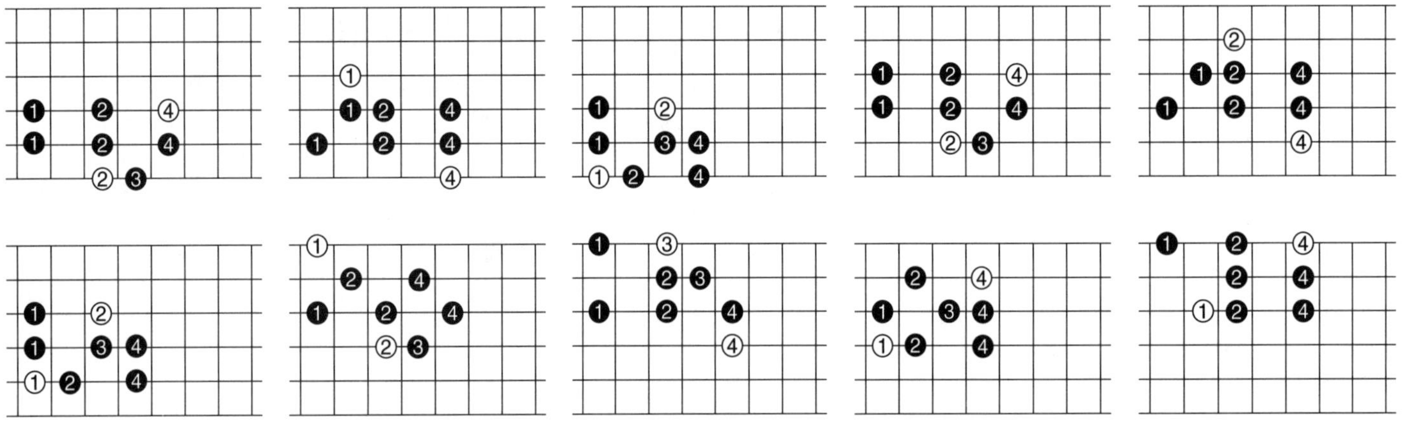

Two-Octave Fingerings

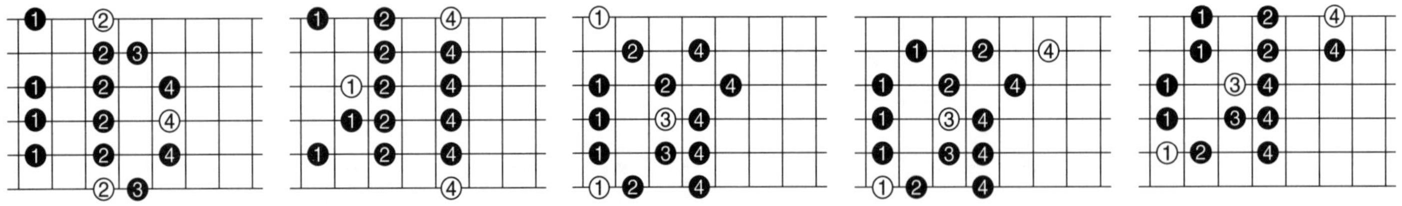

Three-Octave Fingerings

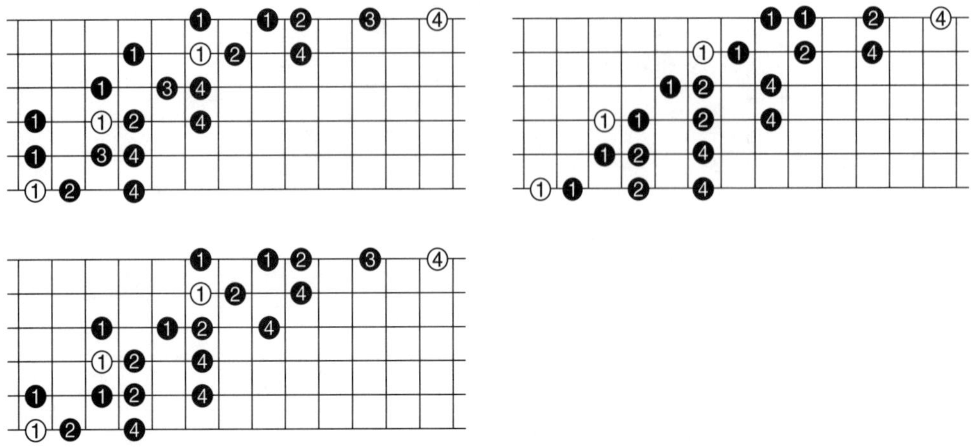

Position-Based Fingerings, Starting on all Scale Degrees

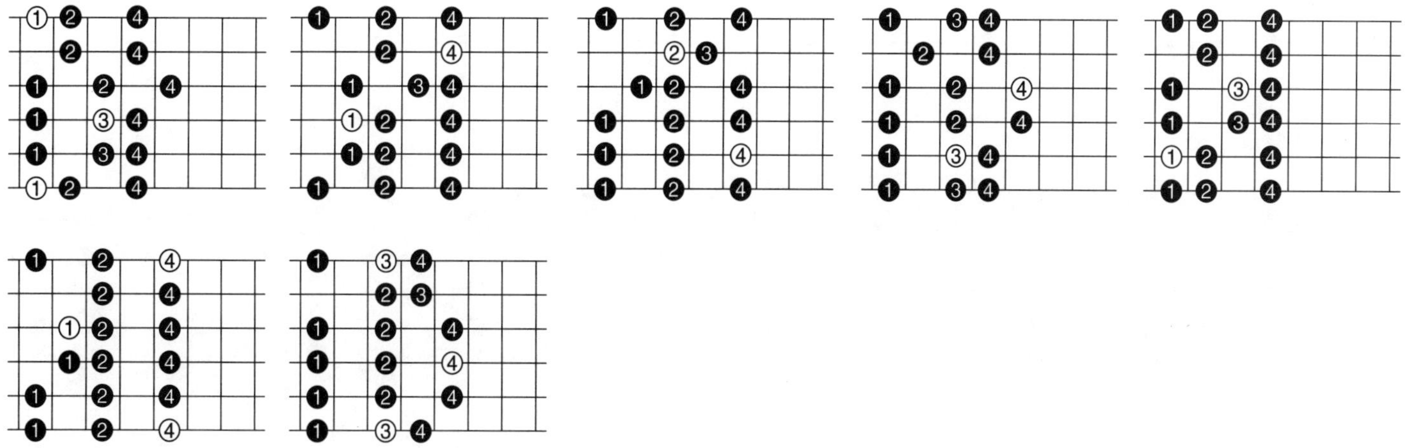

Three-Notes-Per-String Fingerings, Starting on all Scale Degrees

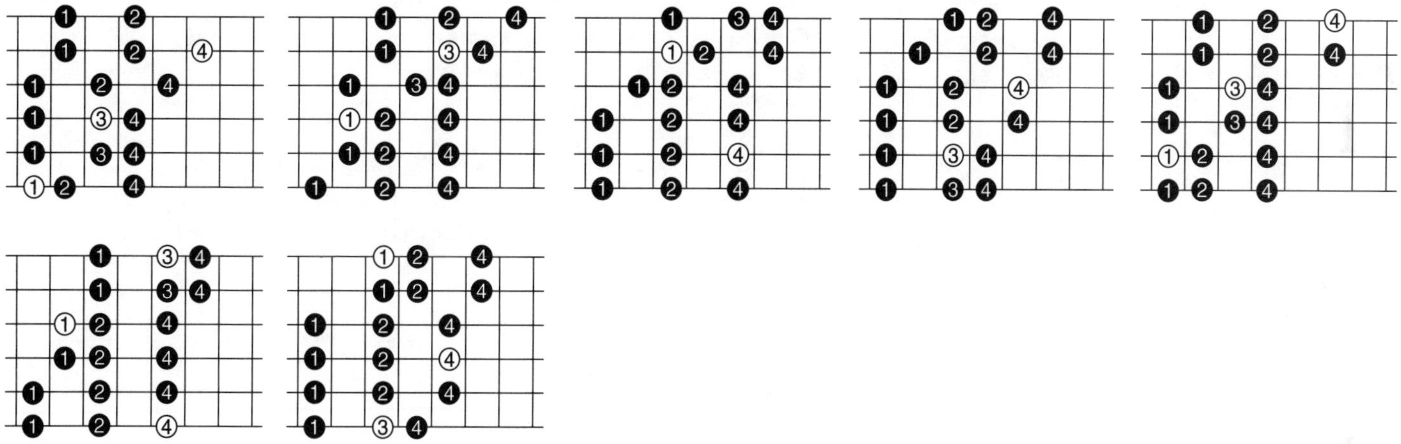

Four-Notes-Per-String Fingerings

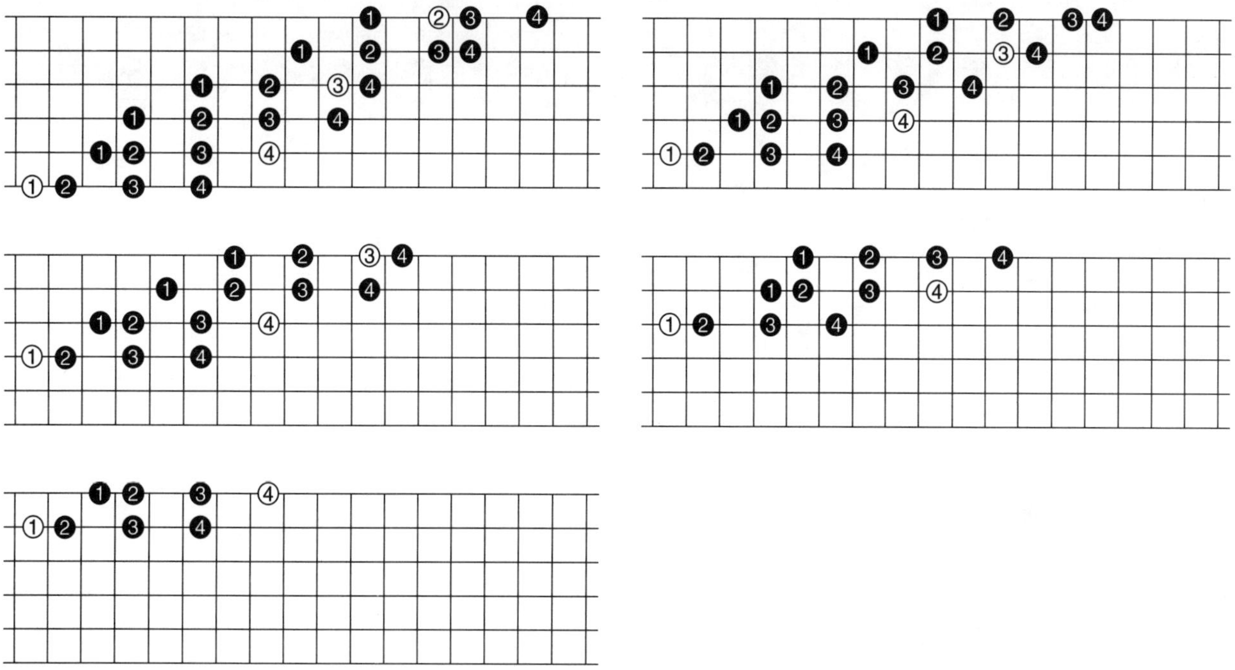

Lydian

Scale Tones

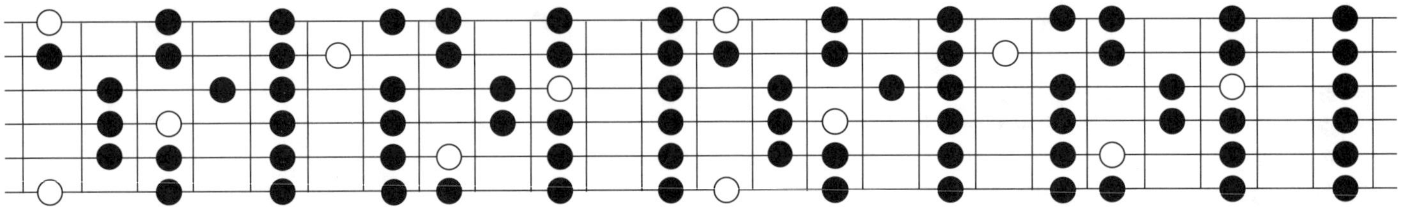

One-Octave Fingerings

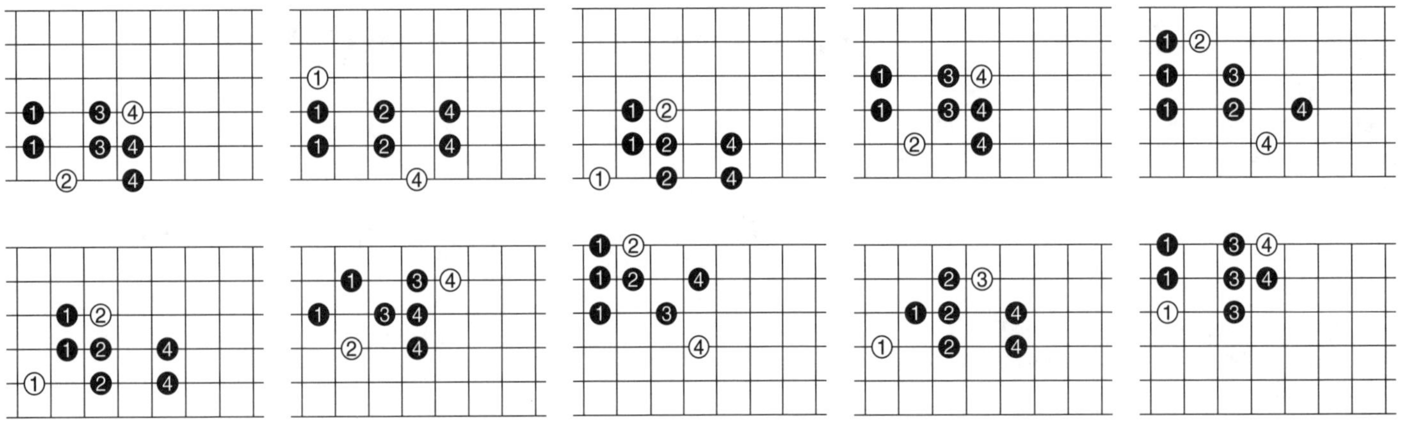

Two-Octave Fingerings

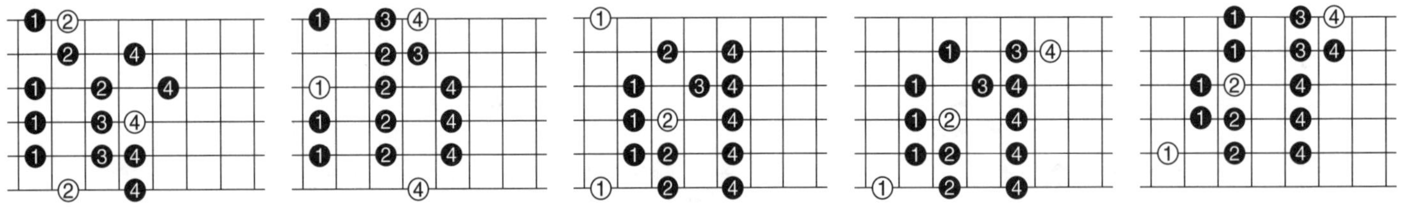

Three-Octave Fingerings

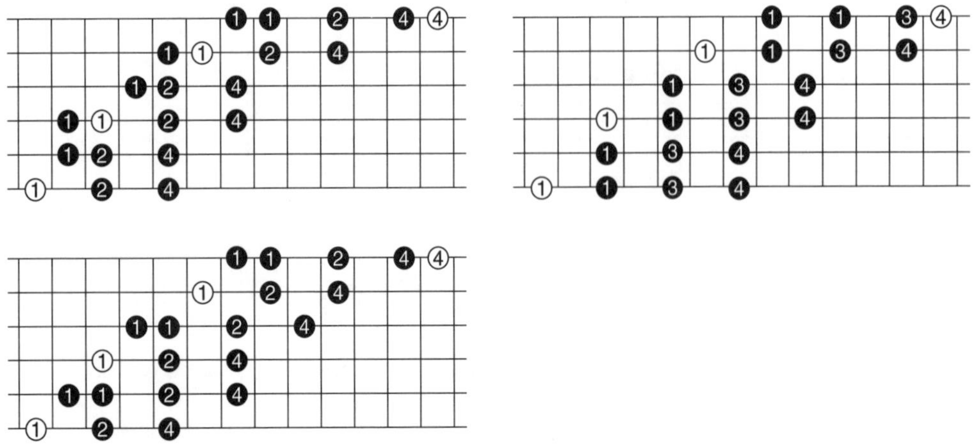

Position-Based Fingerings, Starting on all Scale Degrees

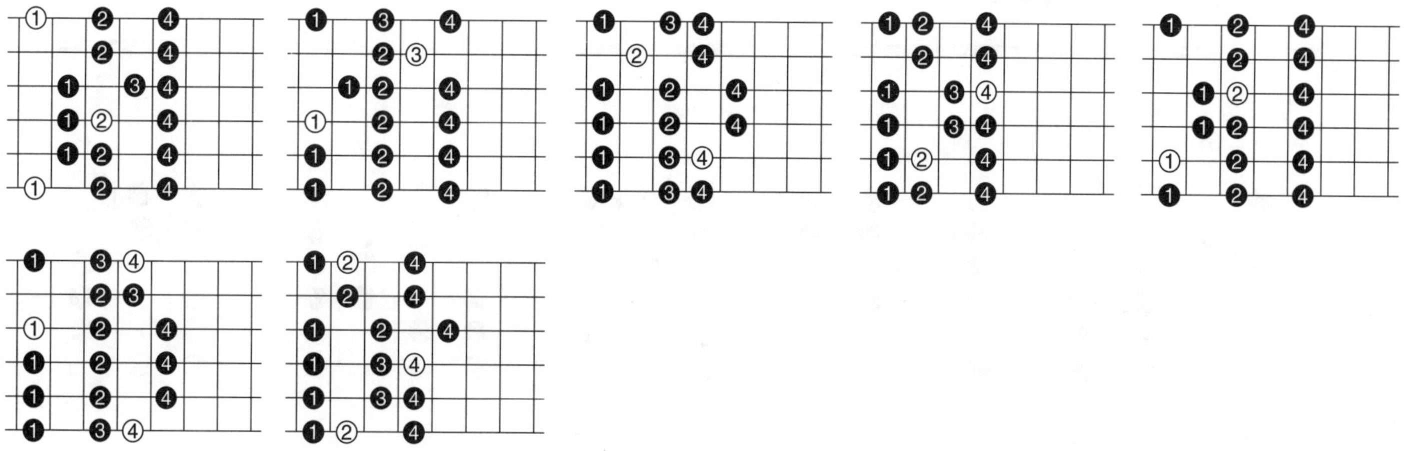

Three-Notes-Per-String Fingerings, Starting on all Scale Degrees

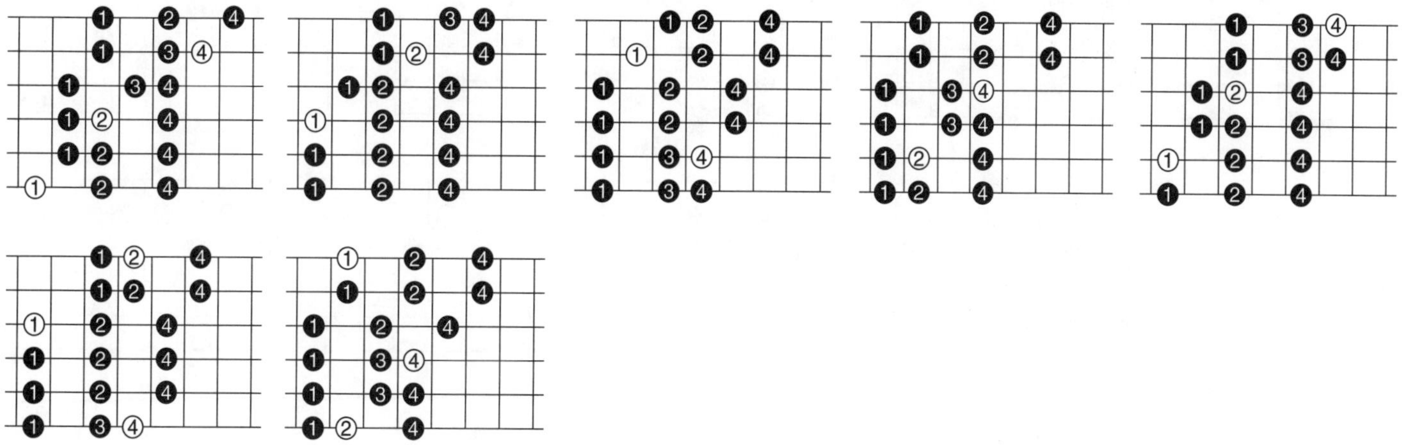

Four-Notes-Per-String Fingerings

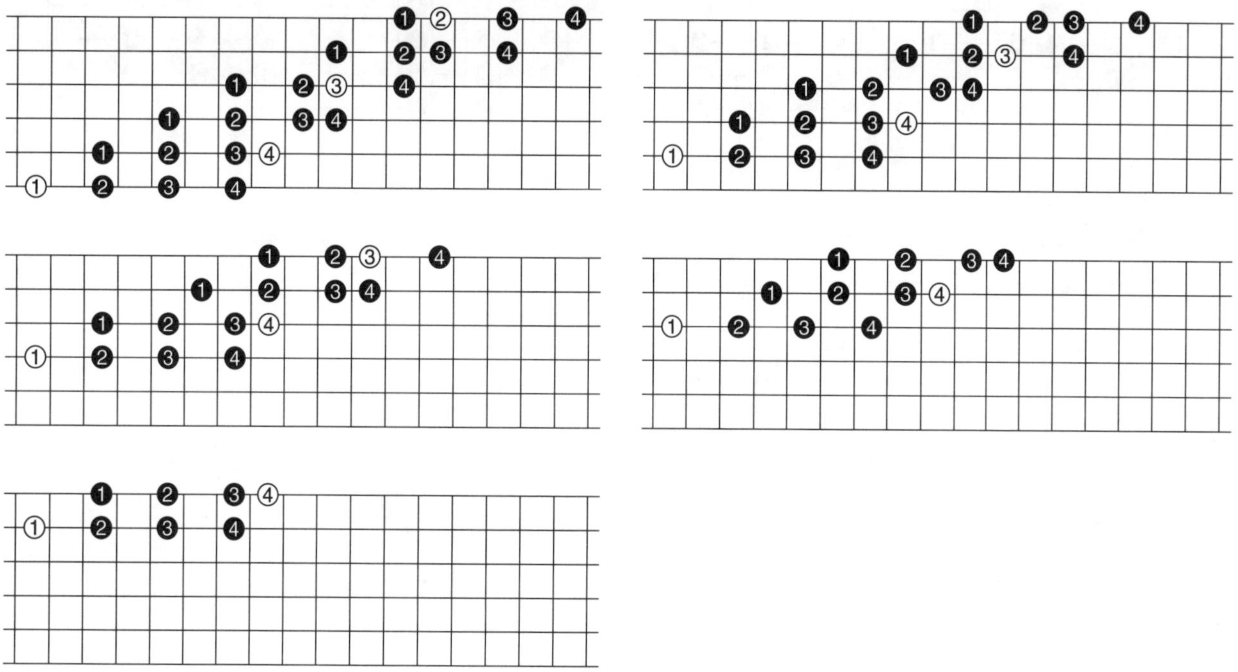

Mixolydian

Scale Tones

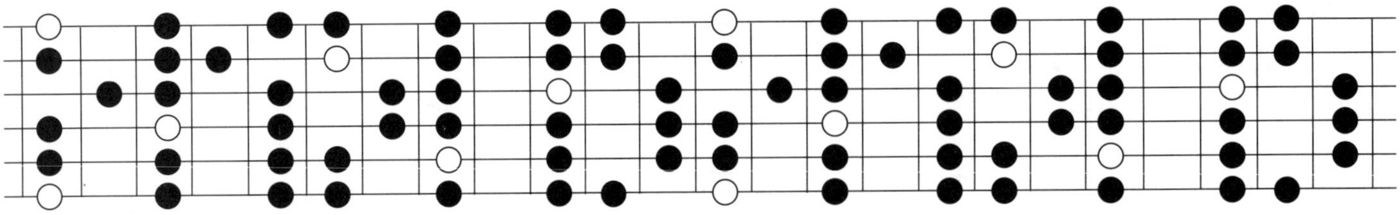

One-Octave Fingerings

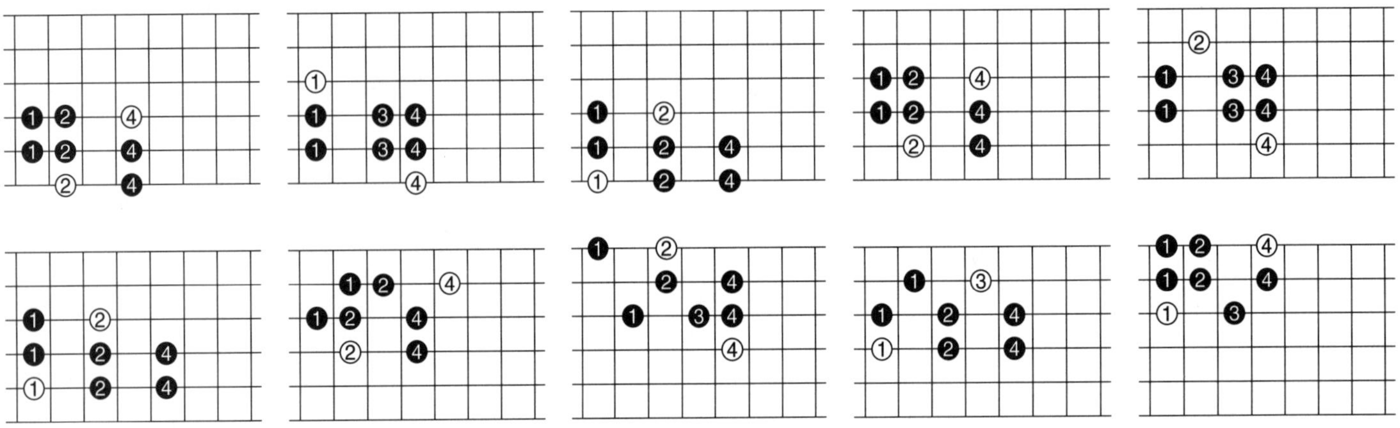

Two-Octave Fingerings

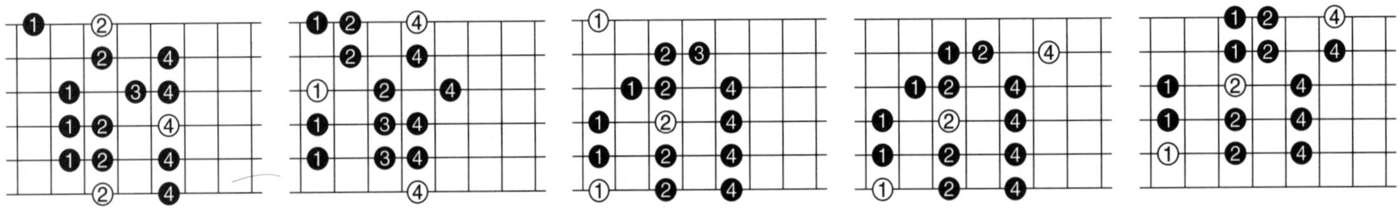

Three-Octave Fingerings

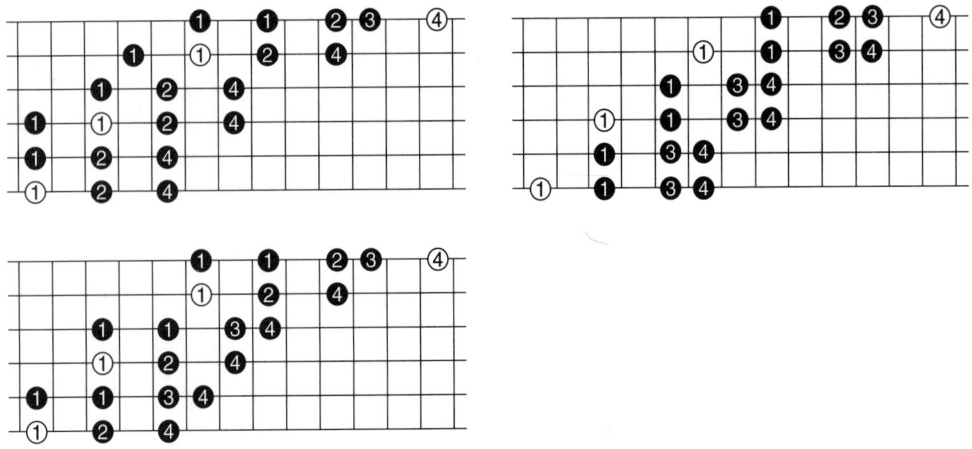

Position-Based Fingerings, Starting on all Scale Degrees

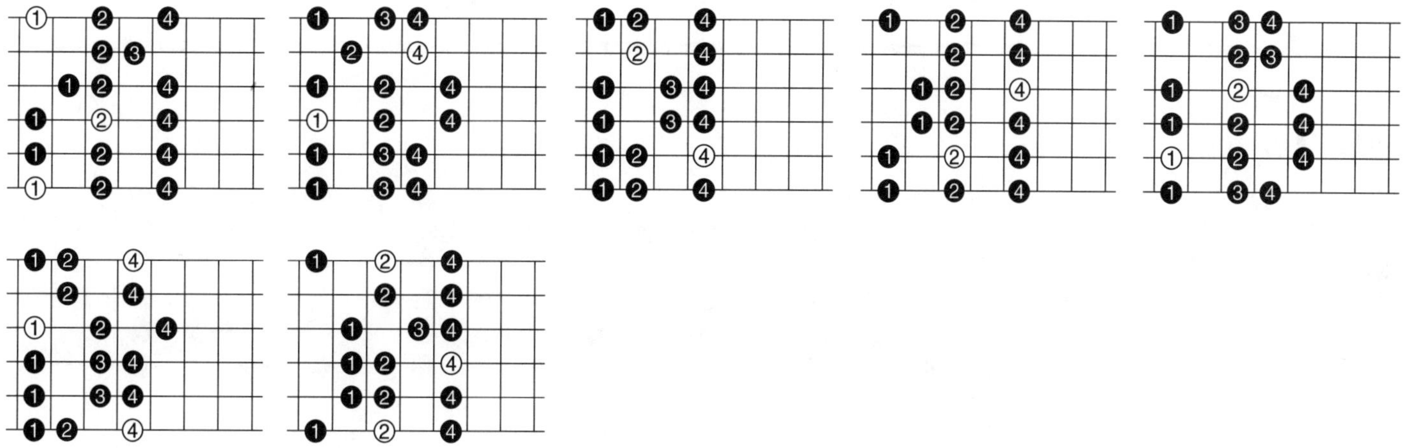

Three-Notes-Per-String Fingerings, Starting on all Scale Degrees

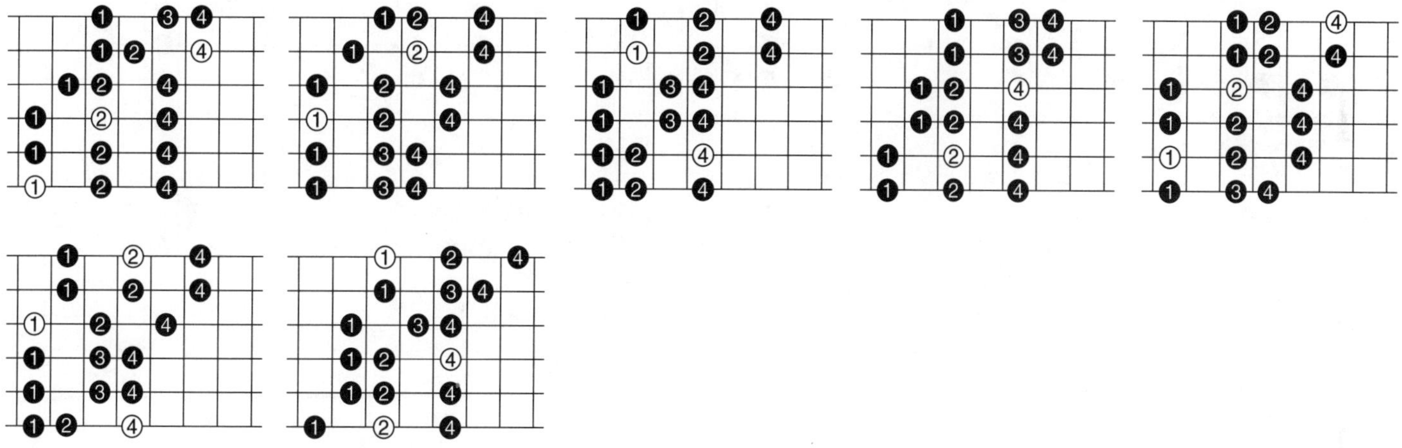

Four-Notes-Per-String Fingerings

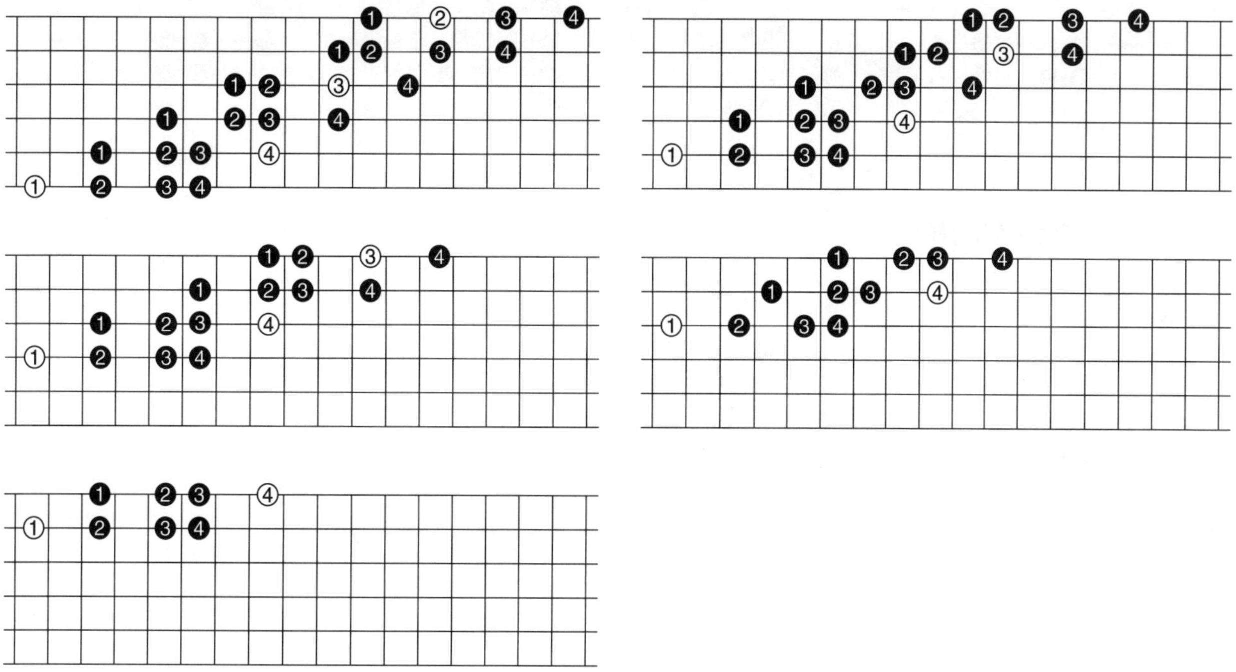

Aeolian (Natural Minor)

Scale Tones

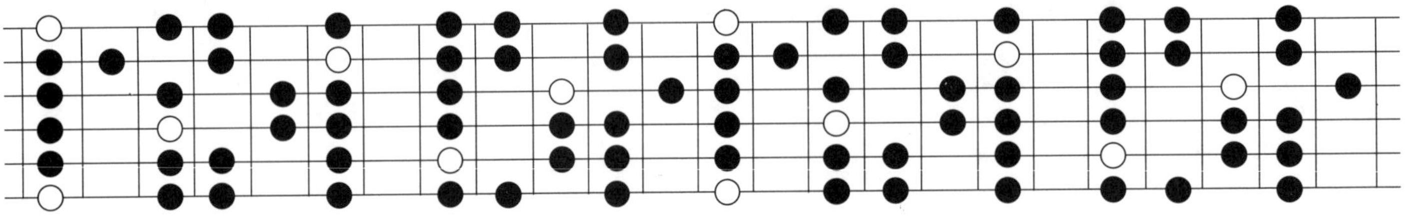

One-Octave Fingerings

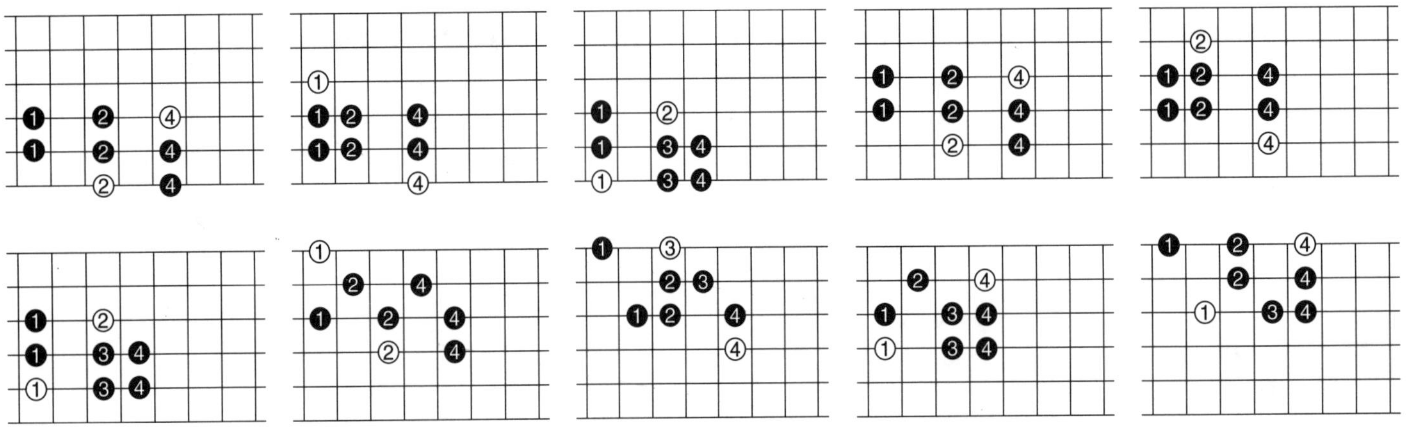

Two-Octave Fingerings

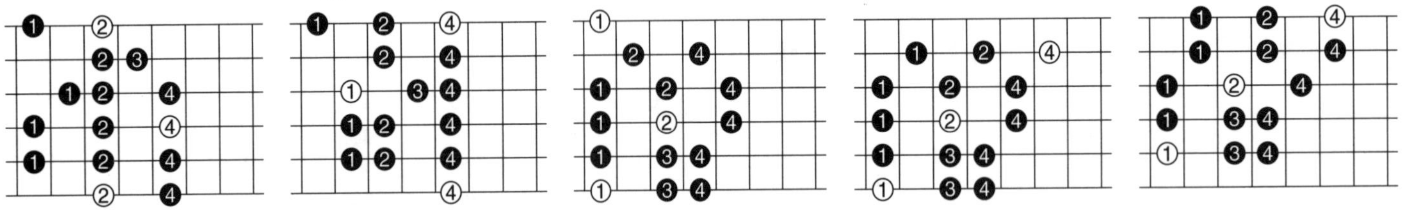

Three-Octave Fingerings

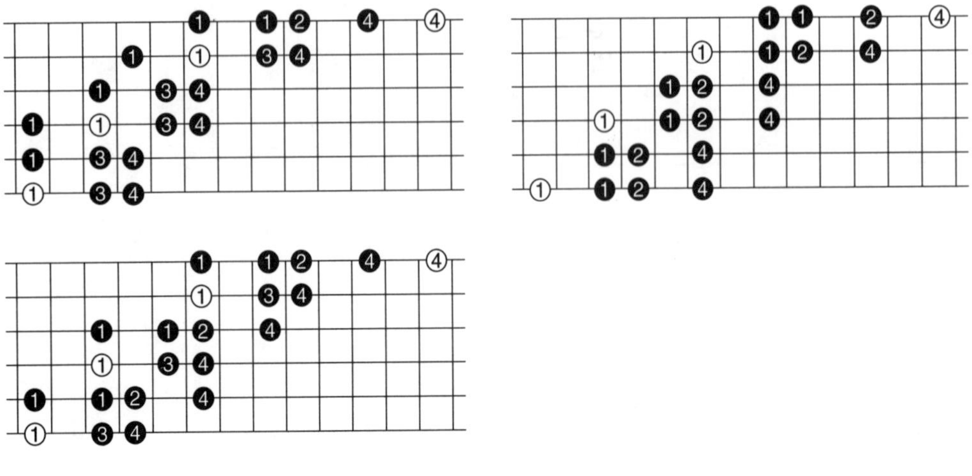

Position-Based Fingerings, Starting on all Scale Degrees

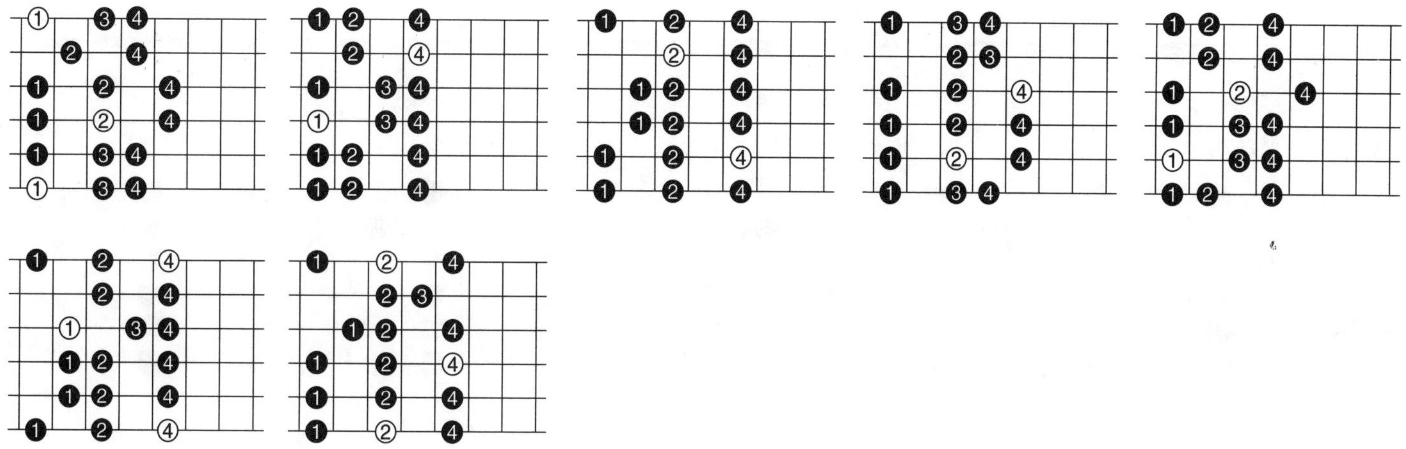

Three-Notes-Per-String Fingerings, Starting on all Scale Degrees

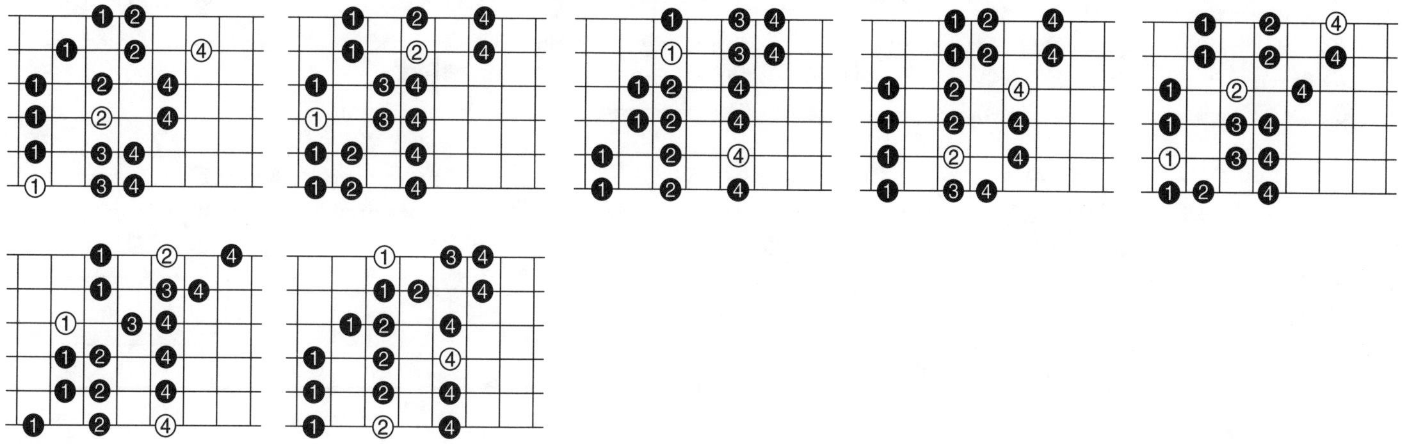

Four-Notes-Per-String Fingerings

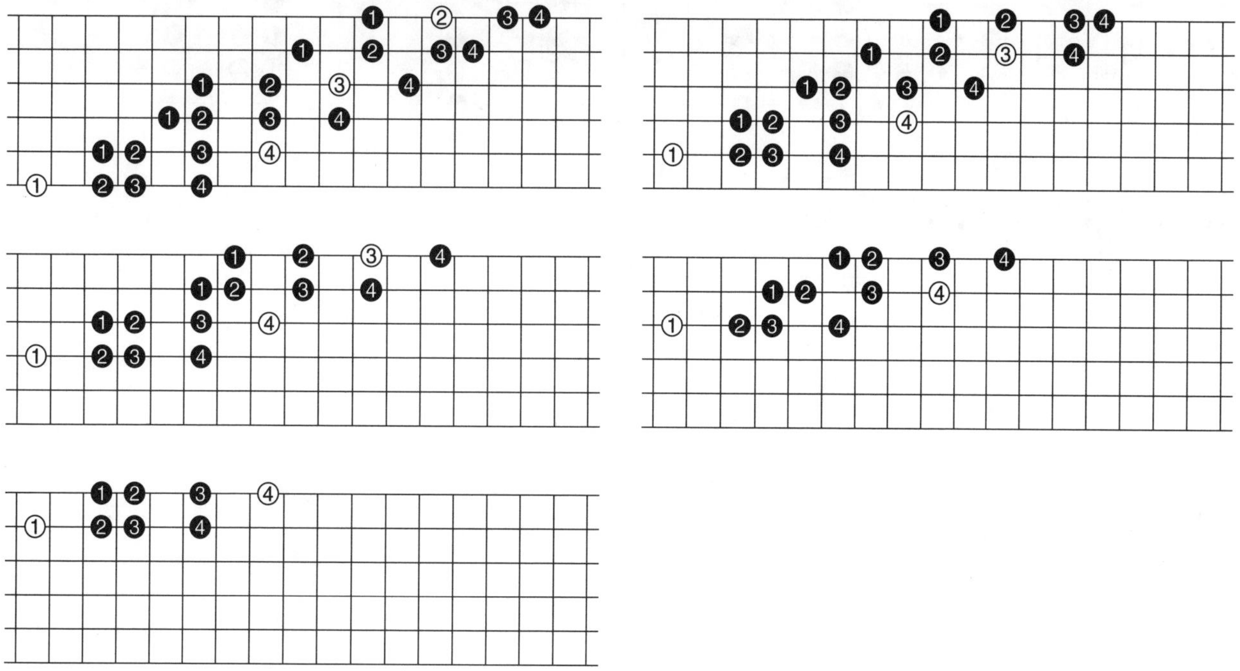

Locrian

Scale Tones

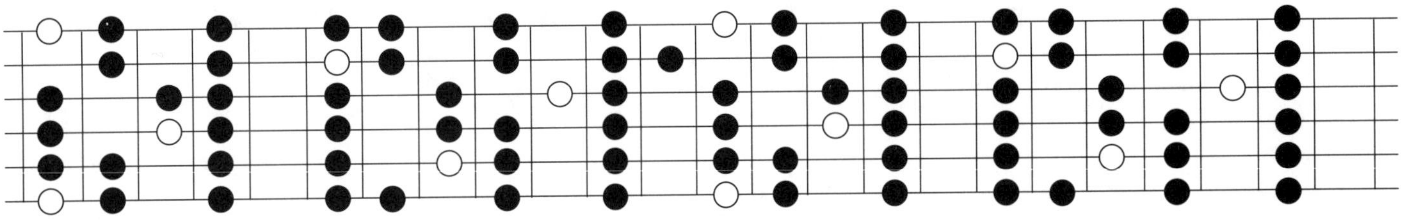

One-Octave Fingerings

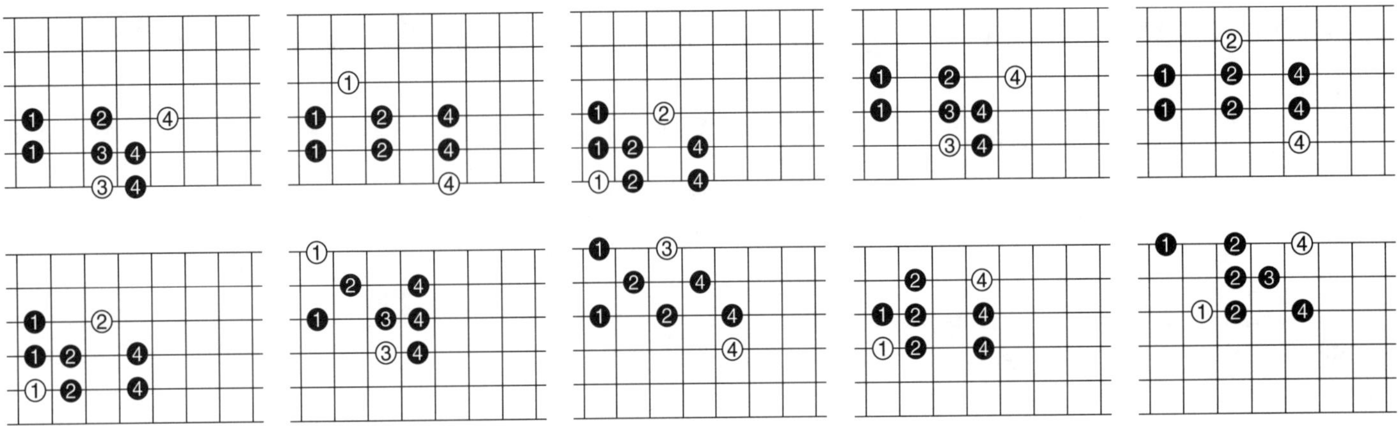

Two-Octave Fingerings

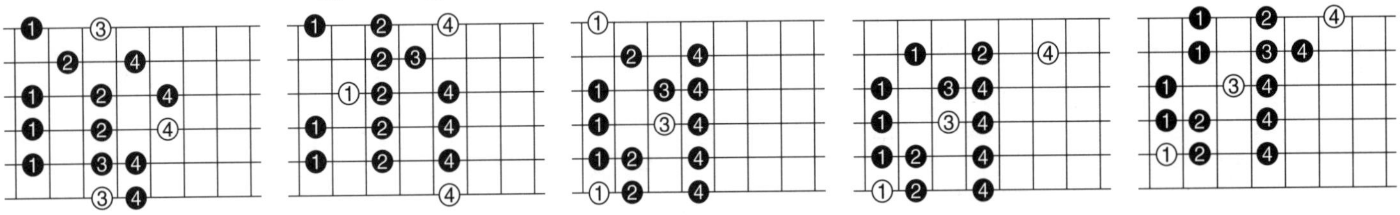

Three-Octave Fingerings

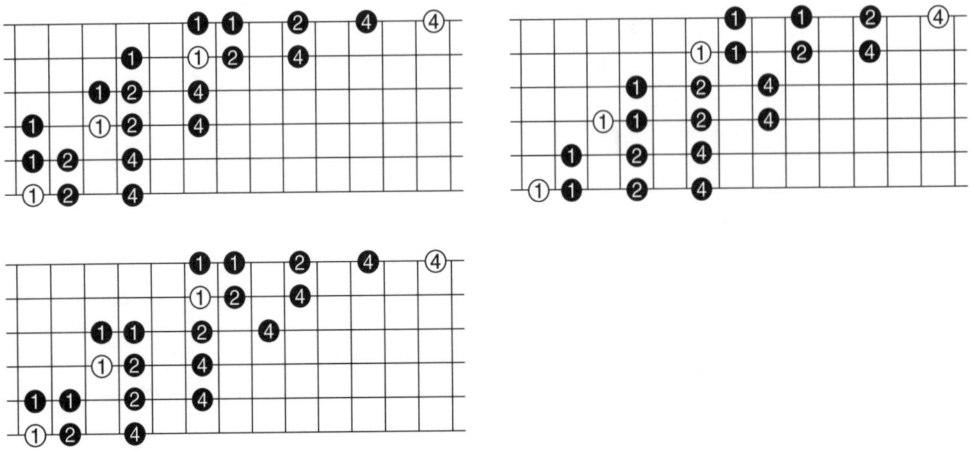

Position-Based Fingerings, Starting on all Scale Degrees

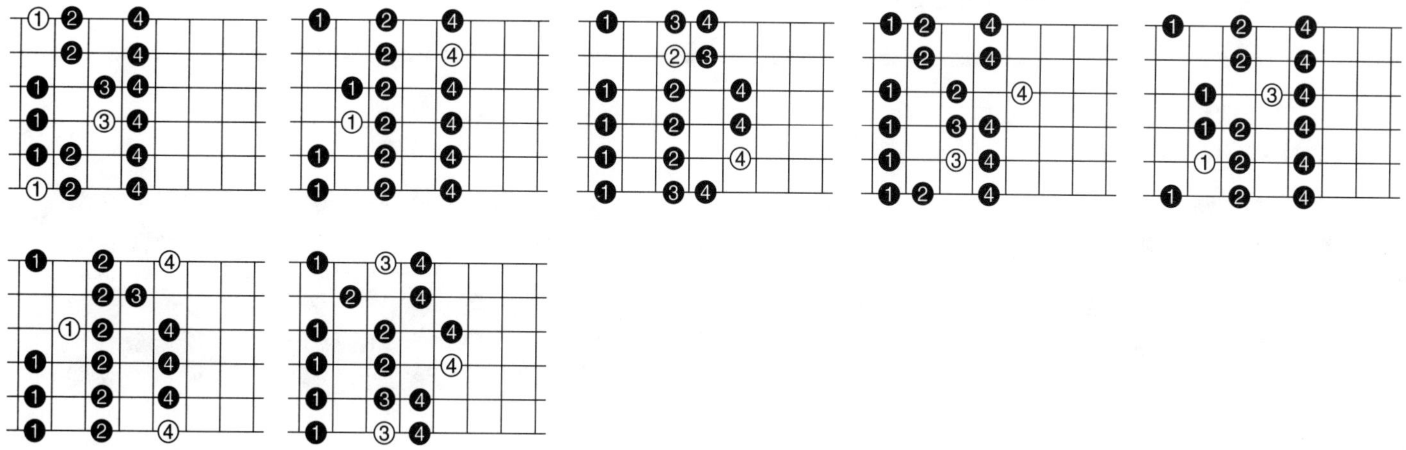

Three-Notes-Per-String Fingerings, Starting on all Scale Degrees

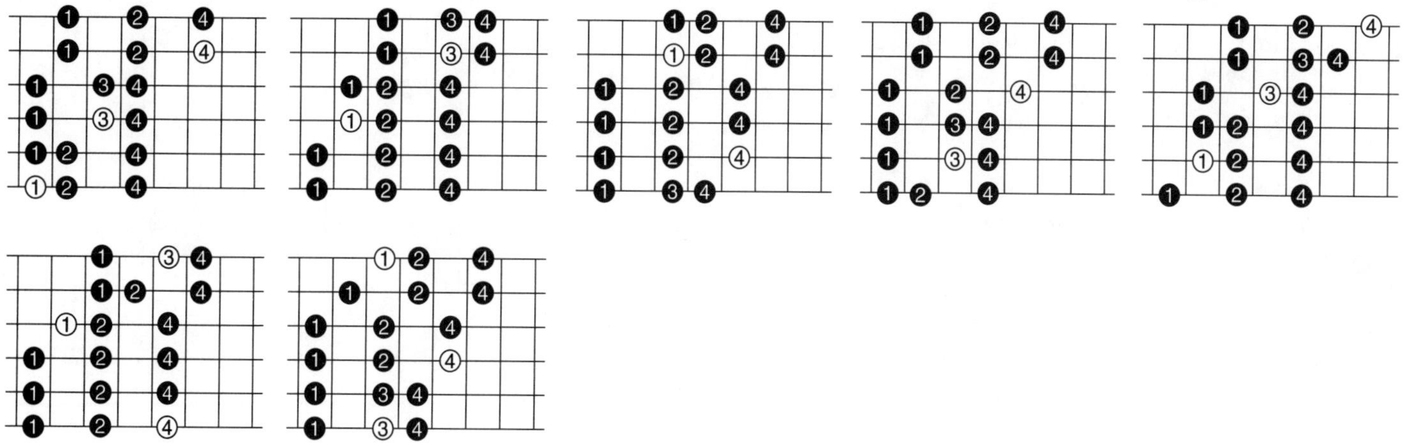

Four-Notes-Per-String Fingerings

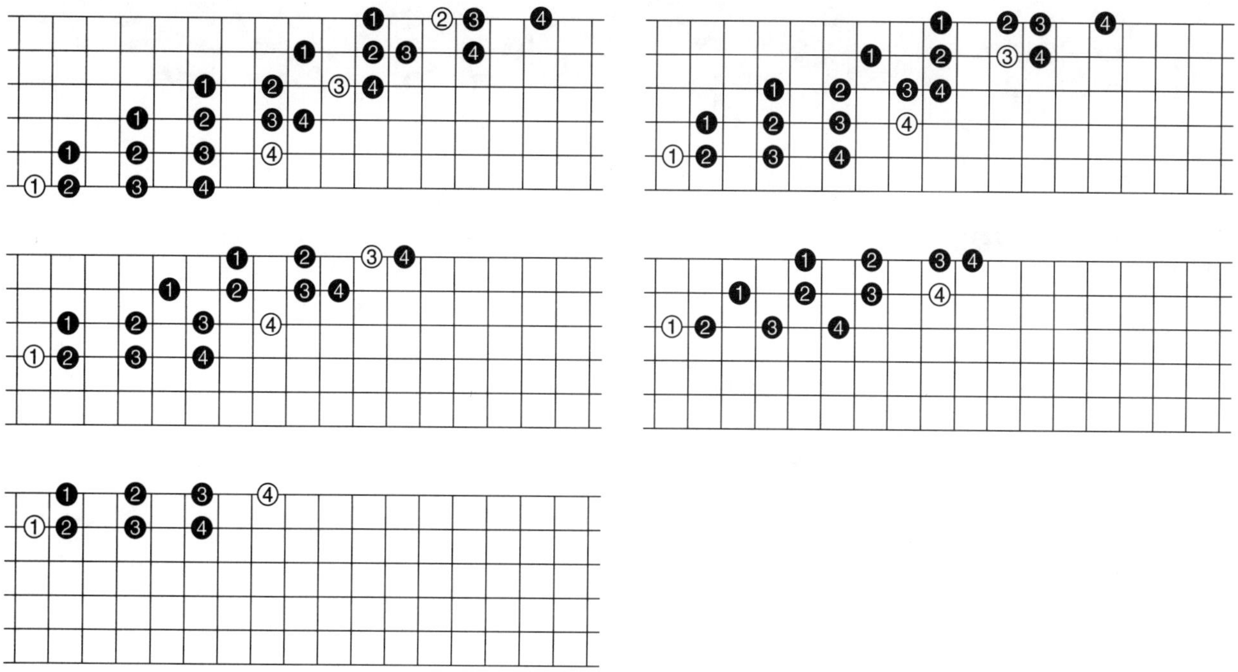

Melodic Minor

Scale Tones

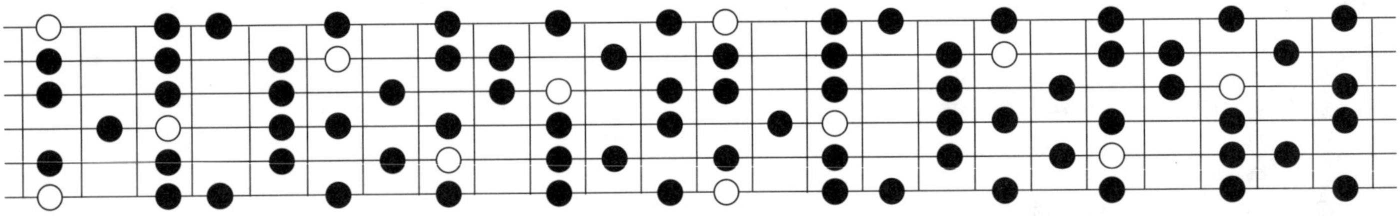

One-Octave Fingerings

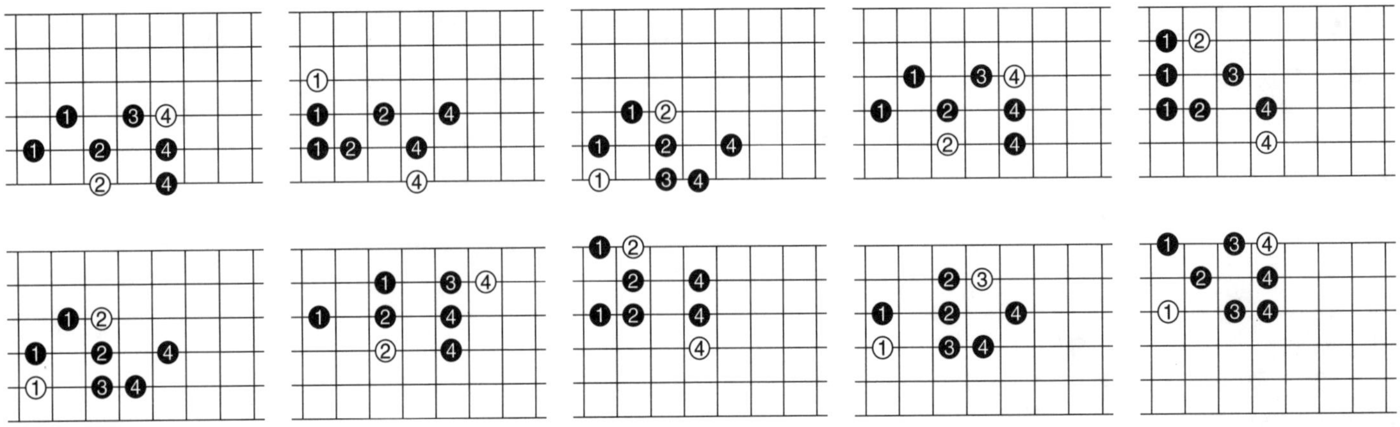

Two-Octave Fingerings

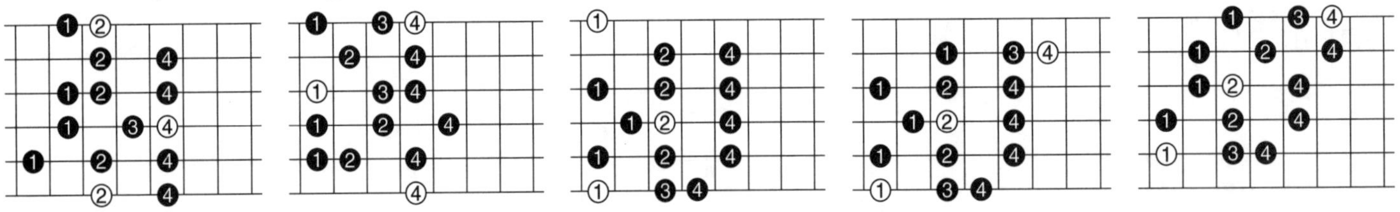

Three-Octave Fingerings

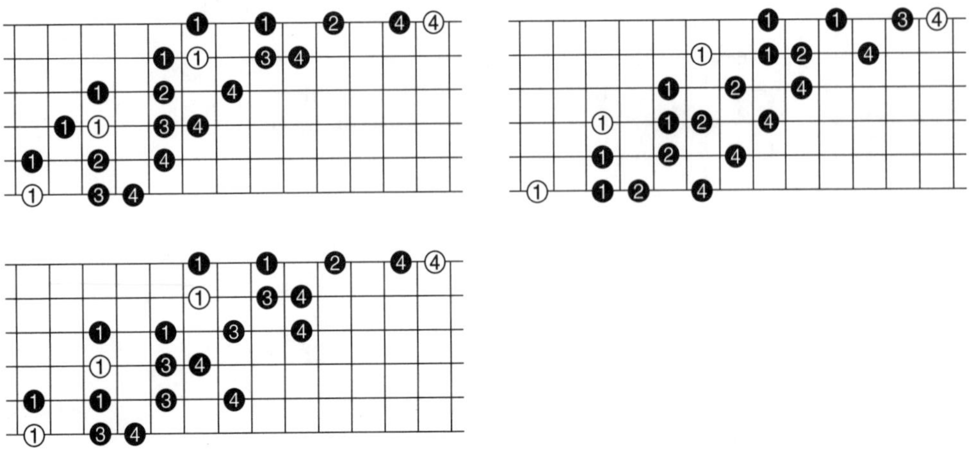

Position-Based Fingerings, Starting on all Scale Degrees

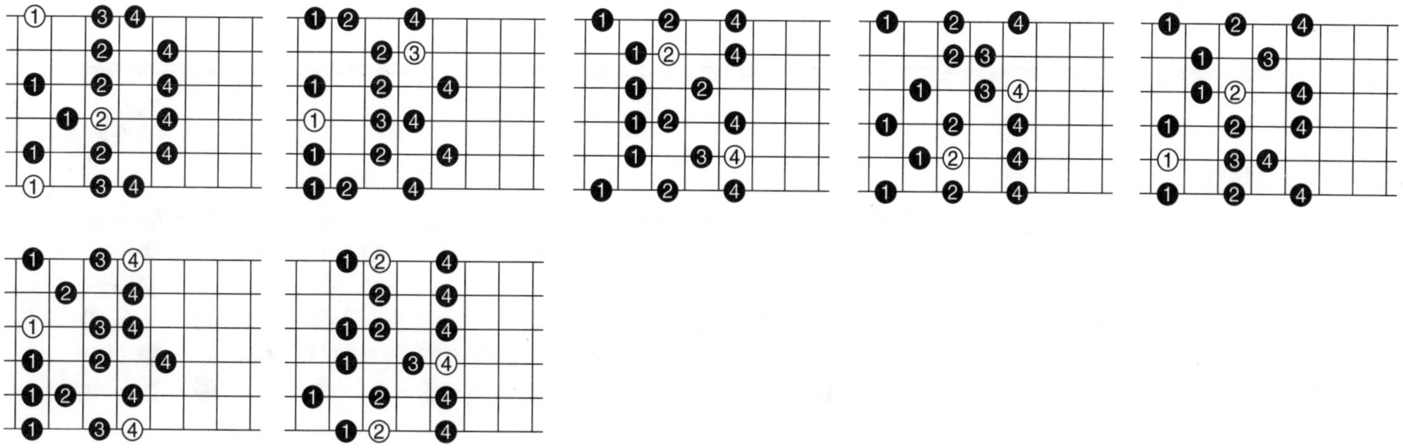

Three-Notes-Per-String Fingerings, Starting on all Scale Degrees

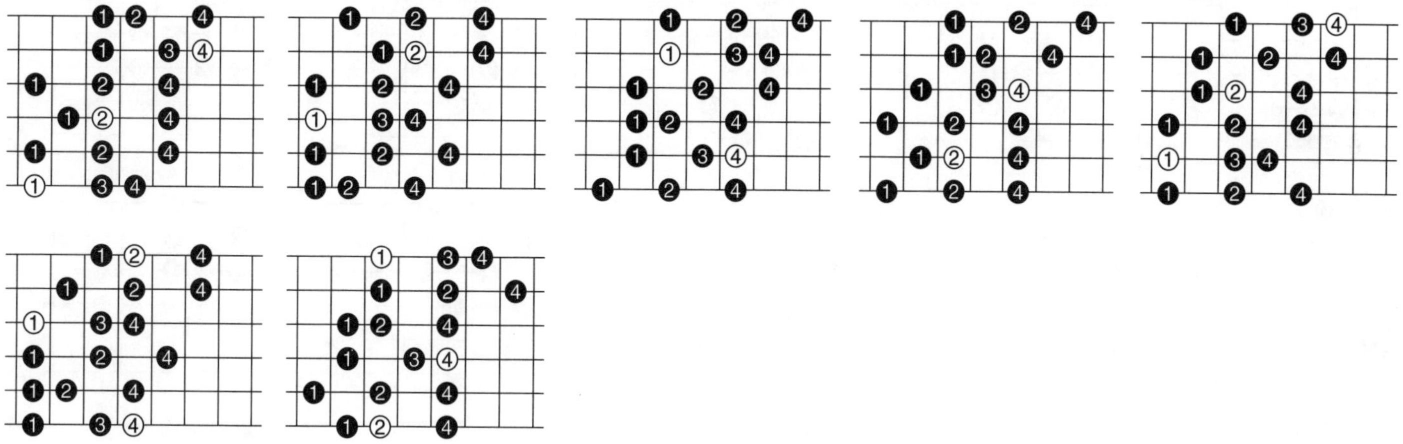

Four-Notes-Per-String Fingerings

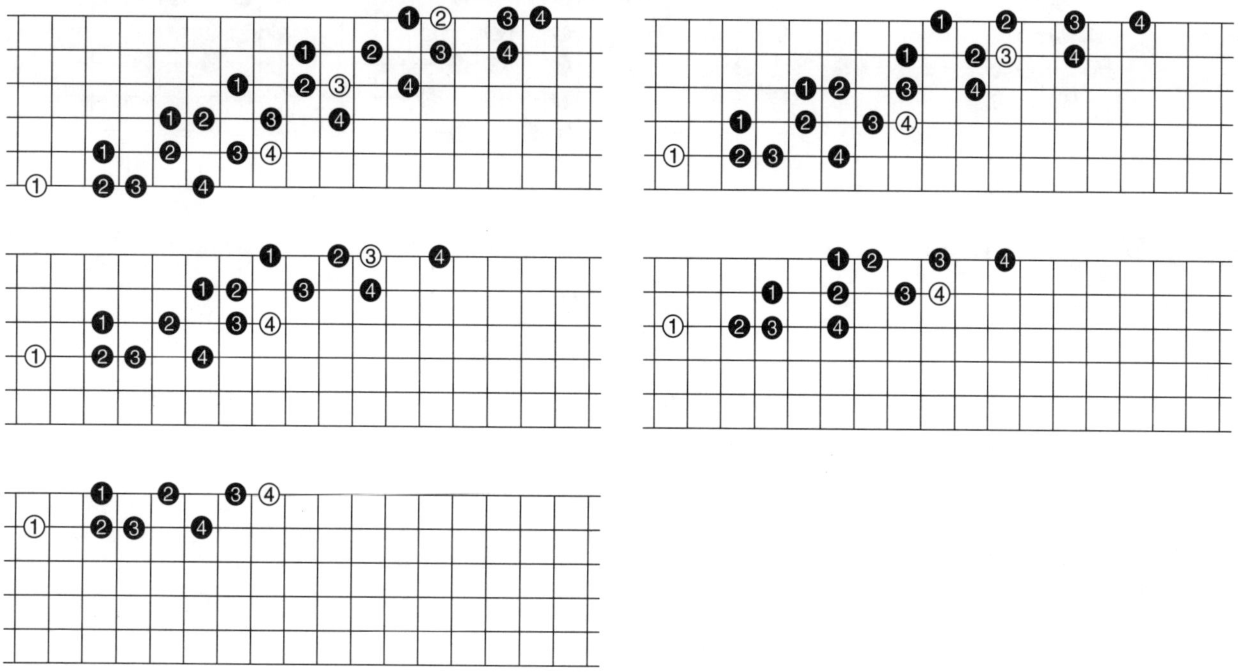

Dorian ♭2

Scale Tones

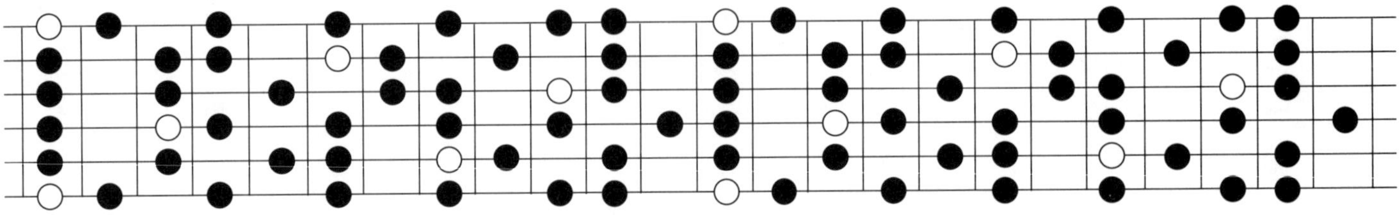

One-Octave Fingerings

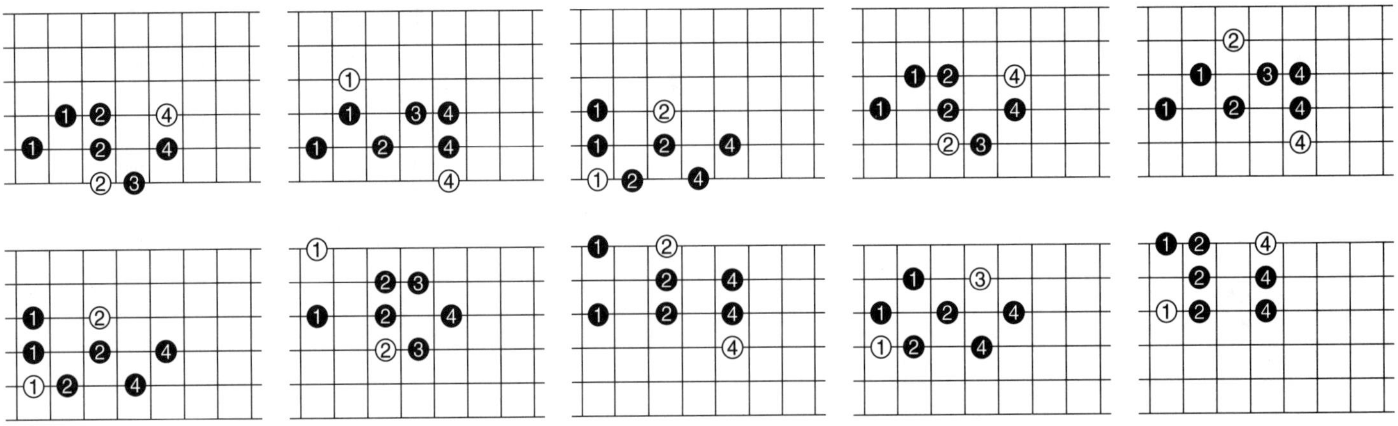

Two-Octave Fingerings

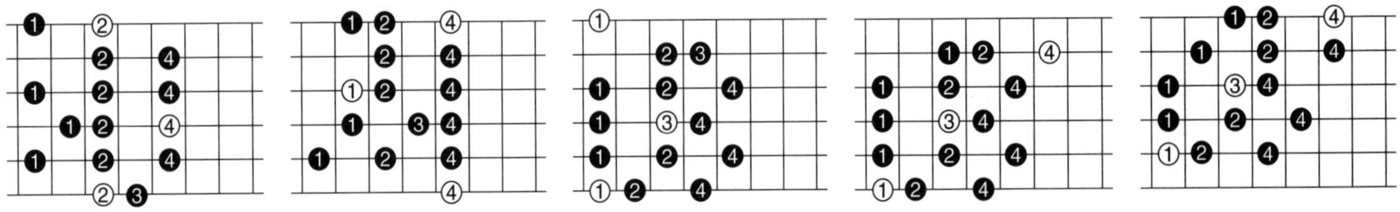

Three-Octave Fingerings

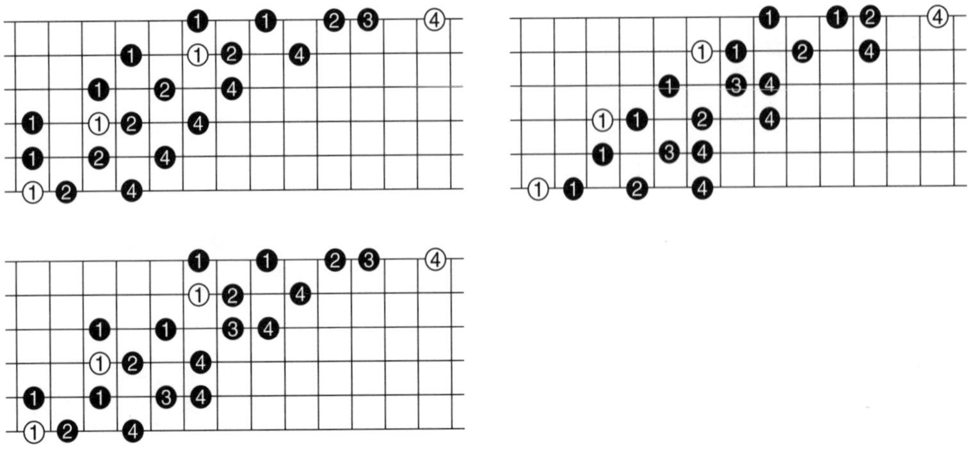

Position-Based Fingerings, Starting on all Scale Degrees

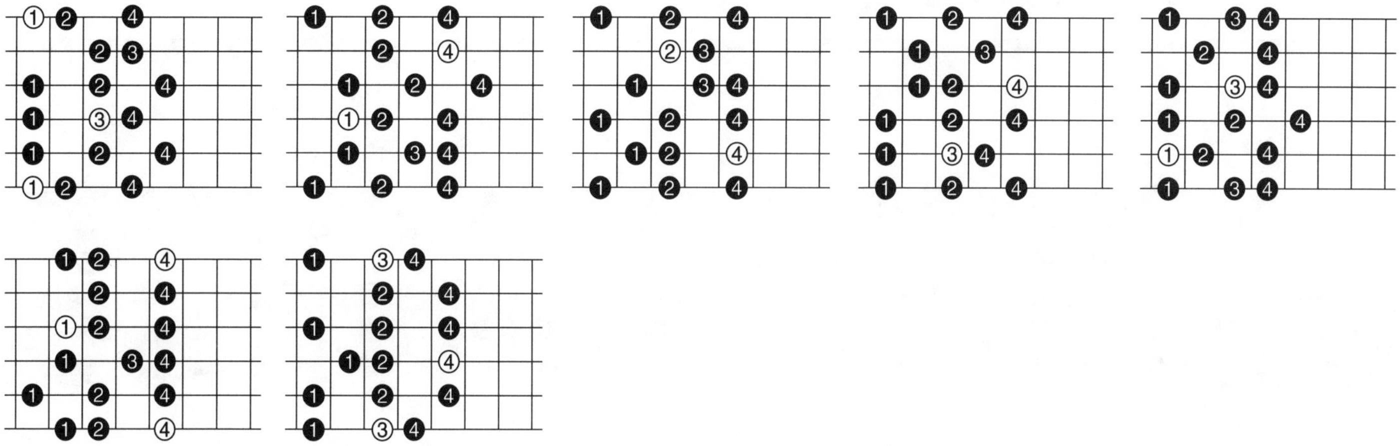

Three-Notes-Per-String Fingerings, Starting on all Scale Degrees

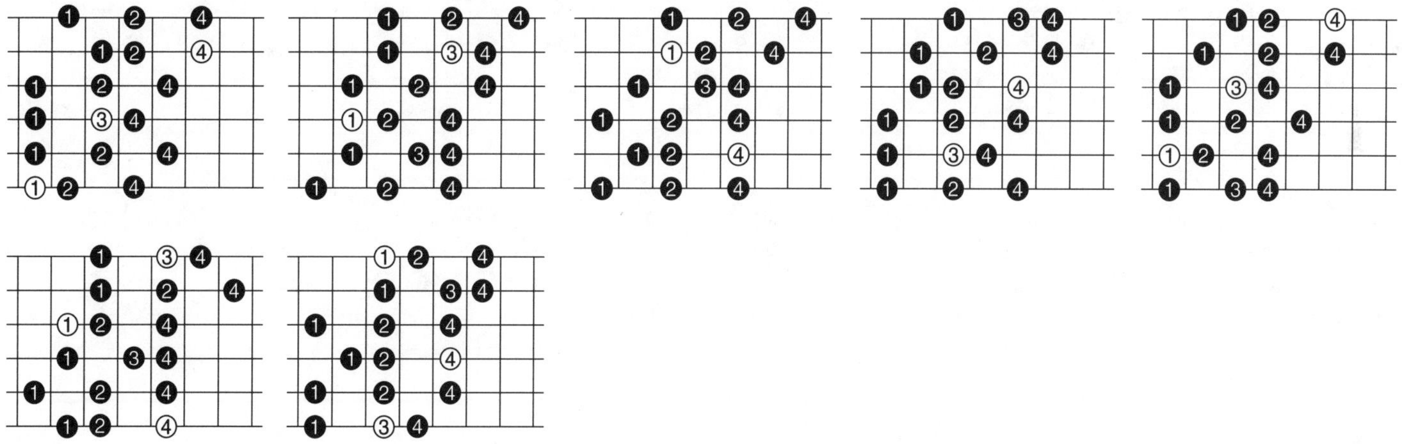

Four-Notes-Per-String Fingerings

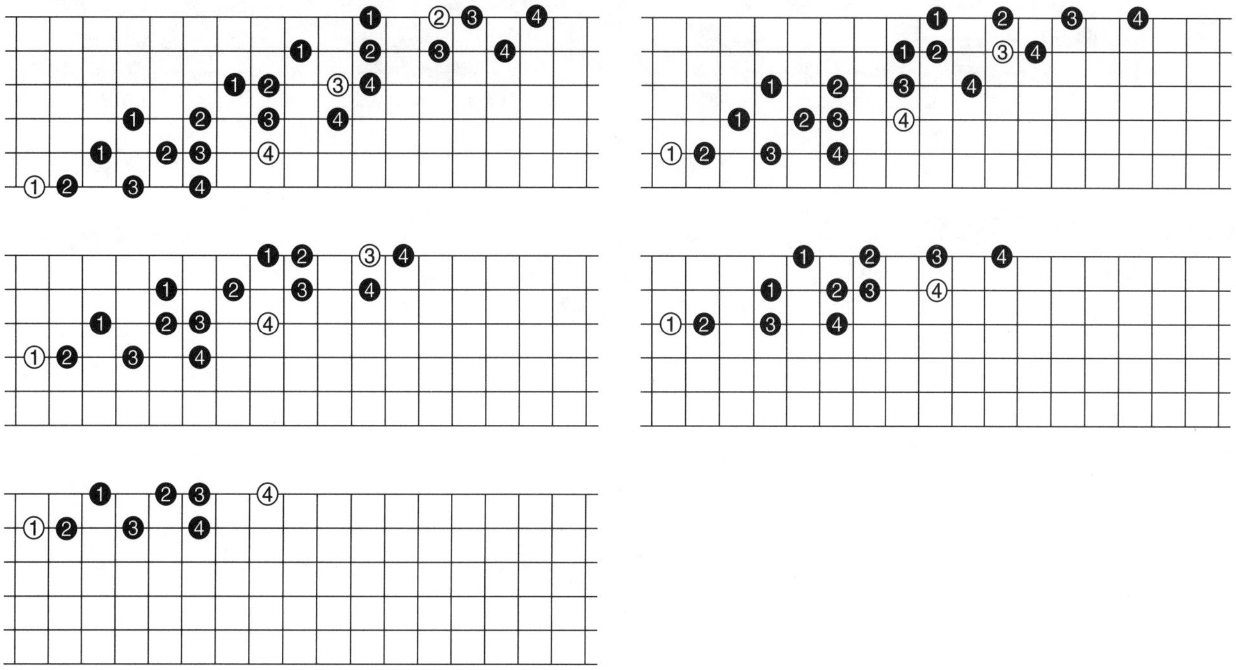

Lydian Augmented

Scale Tones

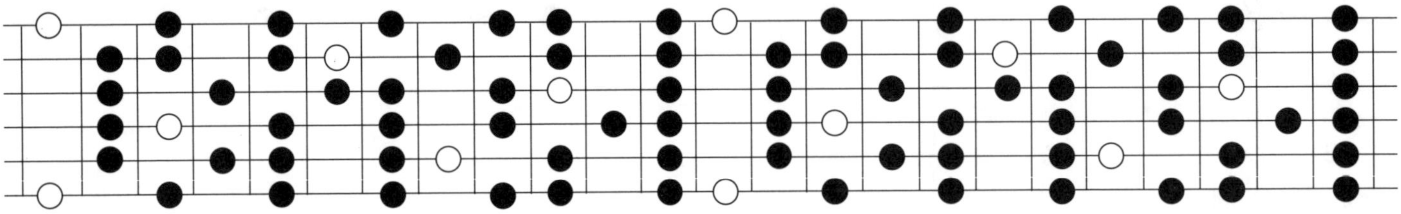

One-Octave Fingerings

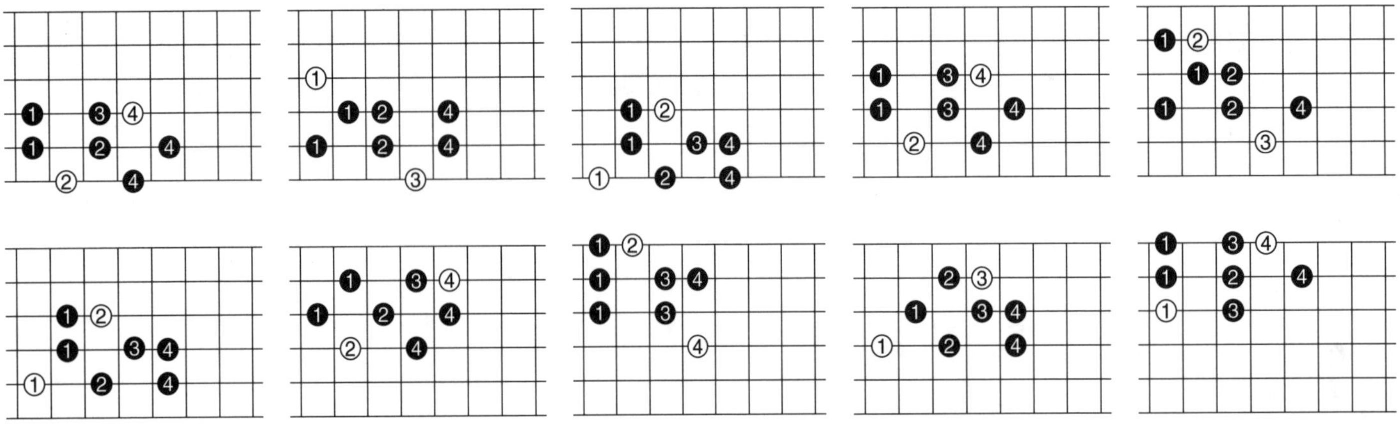

Two-Octave Fingerings

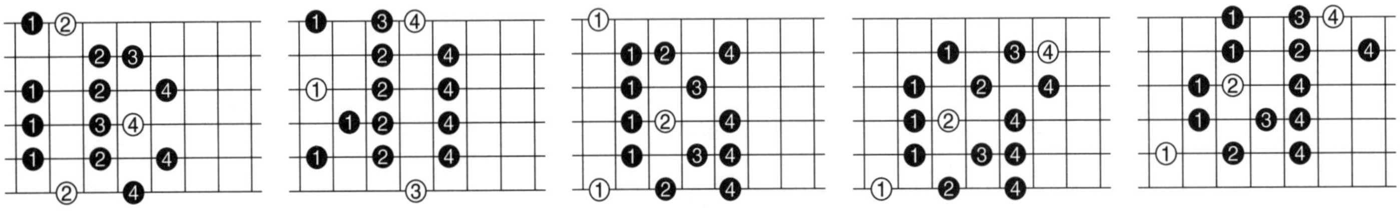

Three-Octave Fingerings

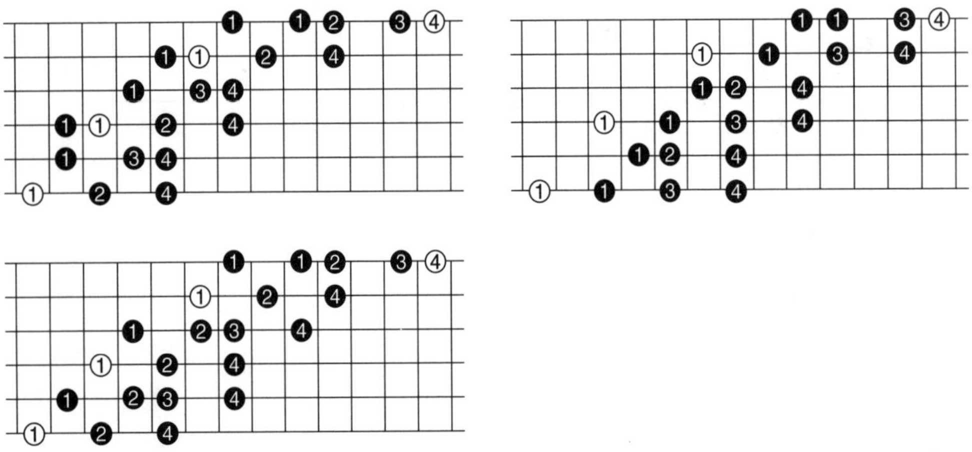

Position-Based Fingerings, Starting on all Scale Degrees

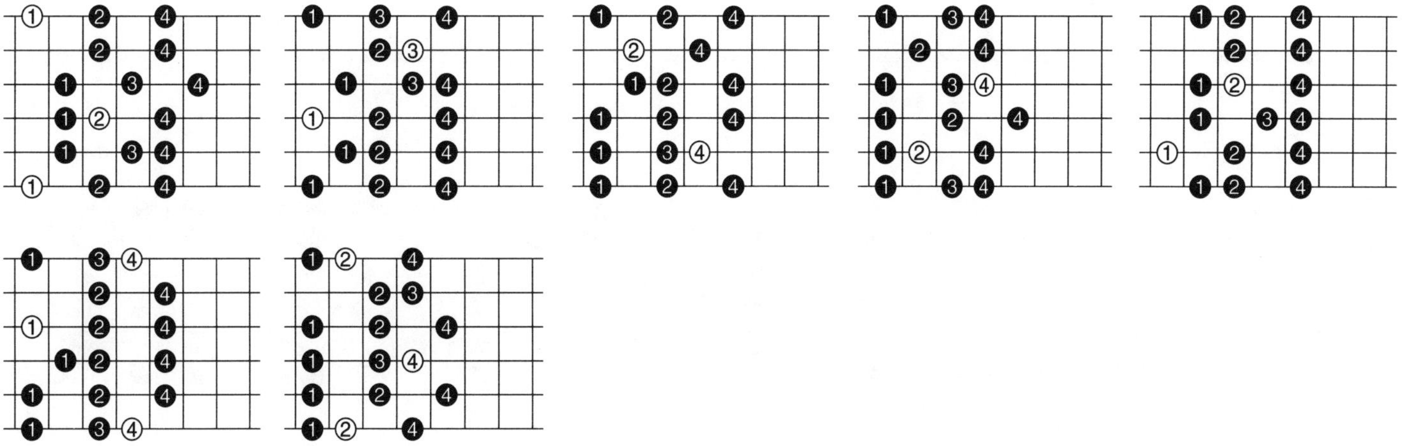

Three-Notes-Per-String Fingerings, Starting on all Scale Degrees

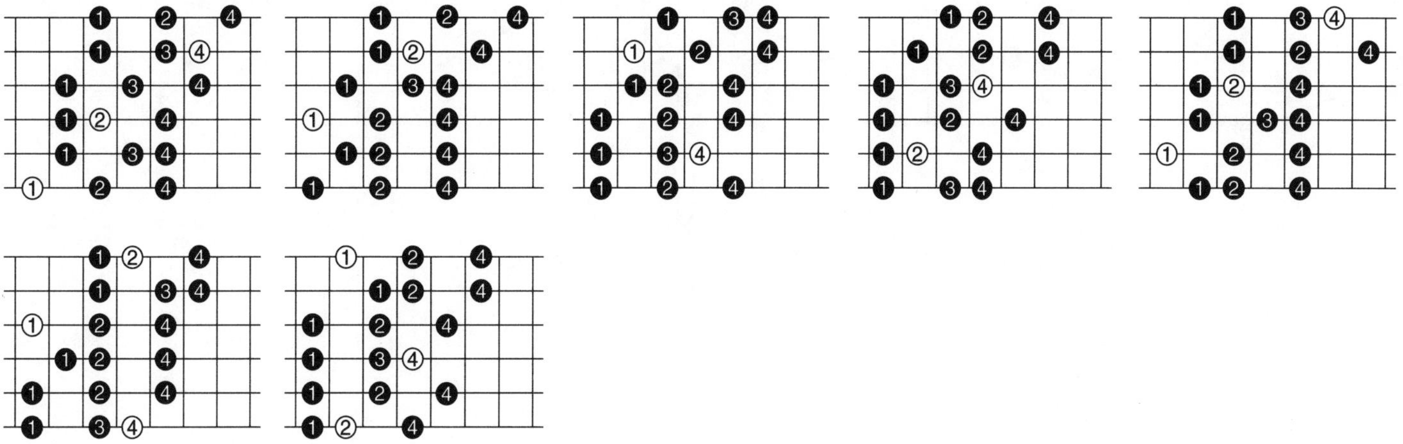

Four-Notes-Per-String Fingerings

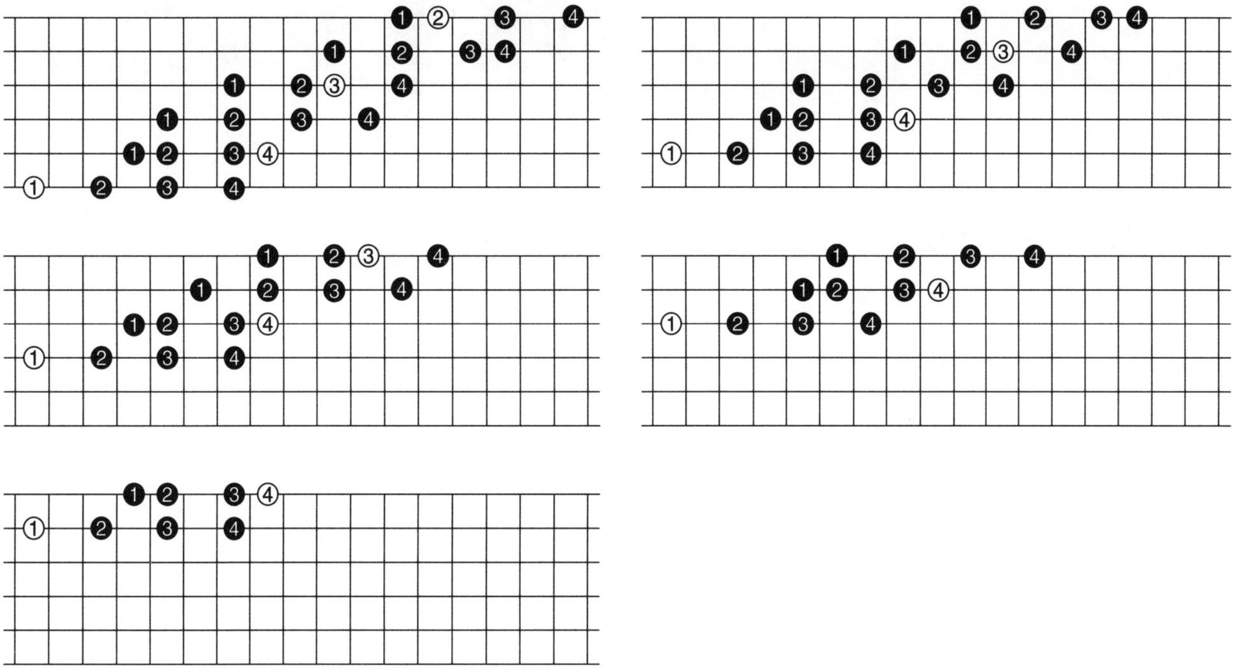

Lydian ♭7

Scale Tones

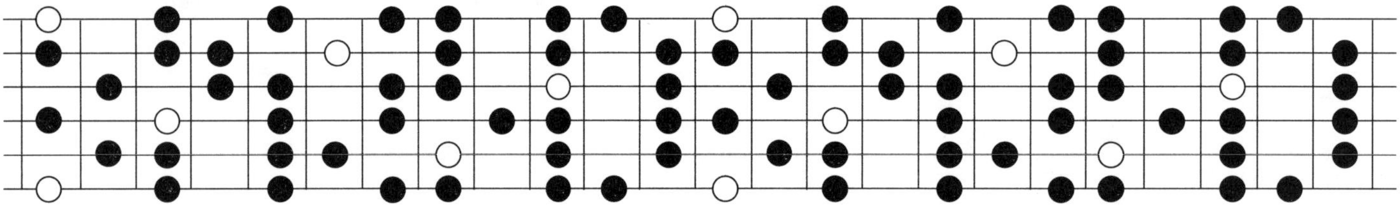

One-Octave Fingerings

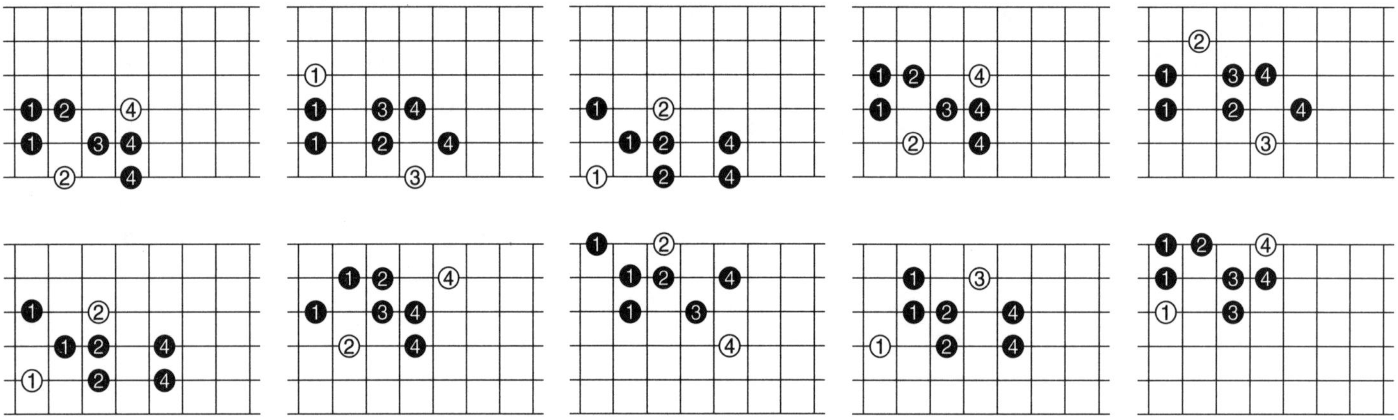

Two-Octave Fingerings

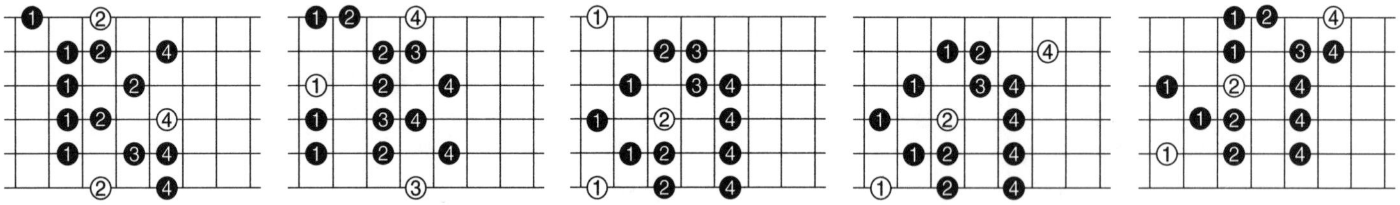

Three-Octave Fingerings

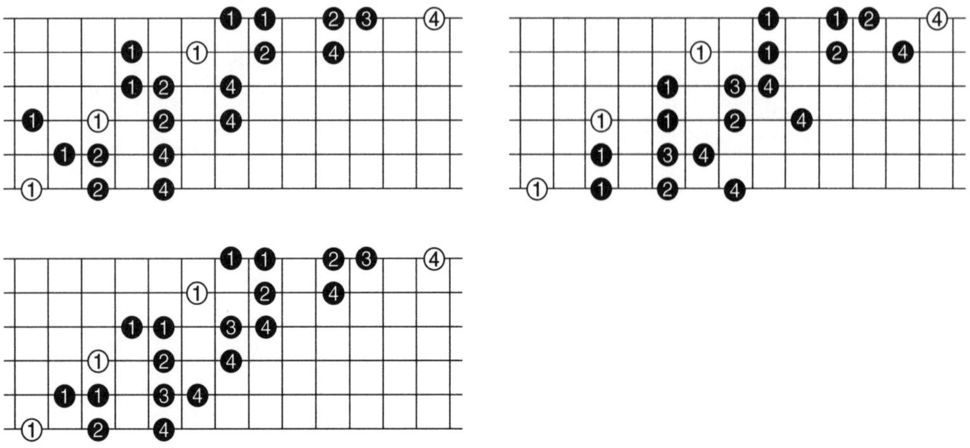

Position-Based Fingerings, Starting on all Scale Degrees

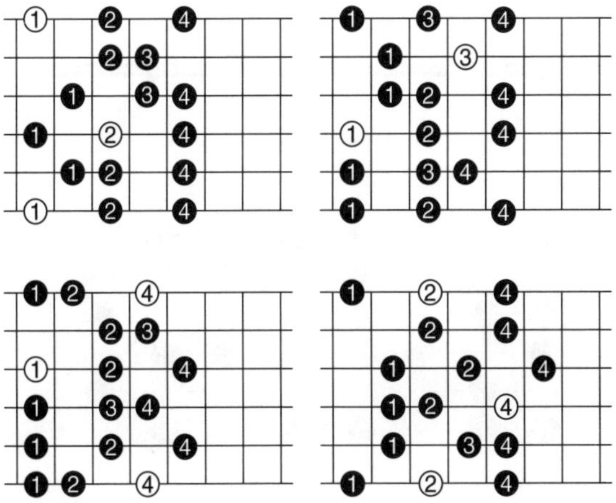

Three-Notes-Per-String Fingerings, Starting on all Scale Degrees

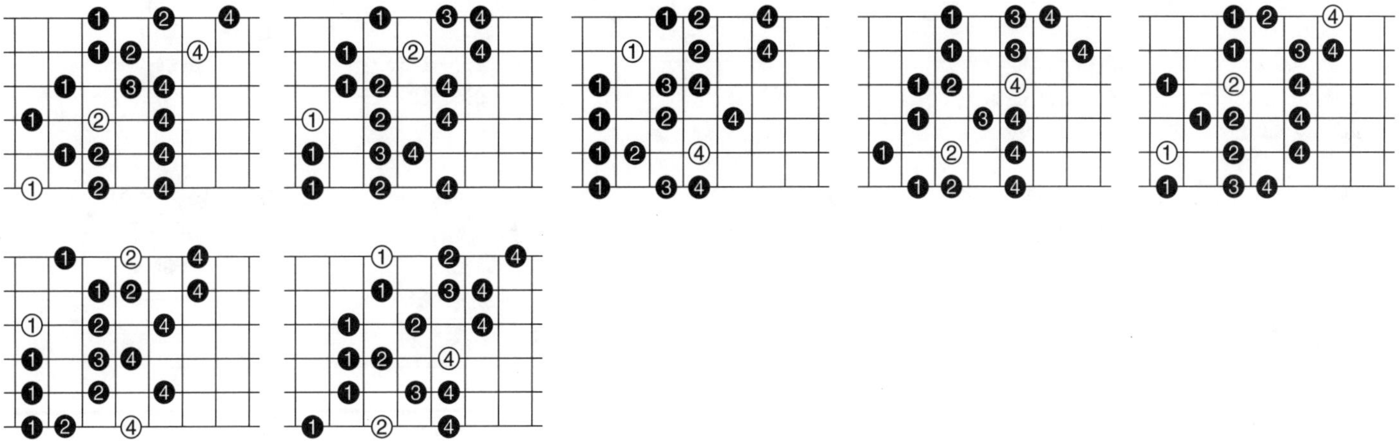

Four-Notes-Per-String Fingerings

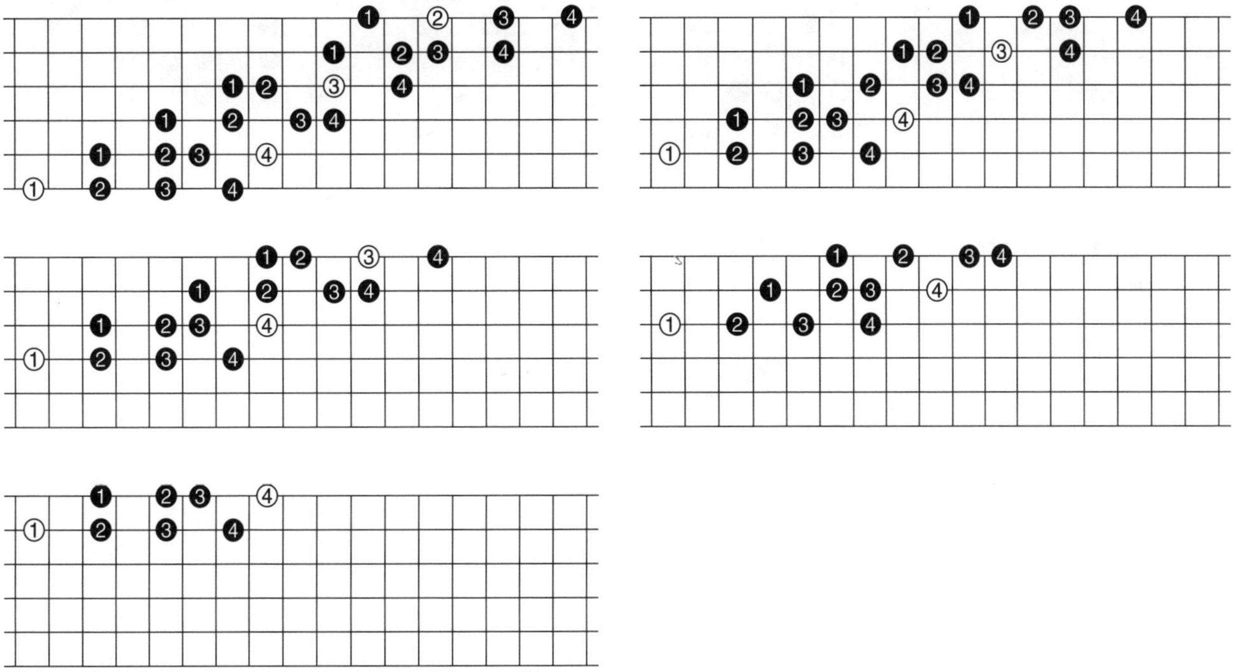

Mixolydian ♭6 (Hindu)

Scale Tones

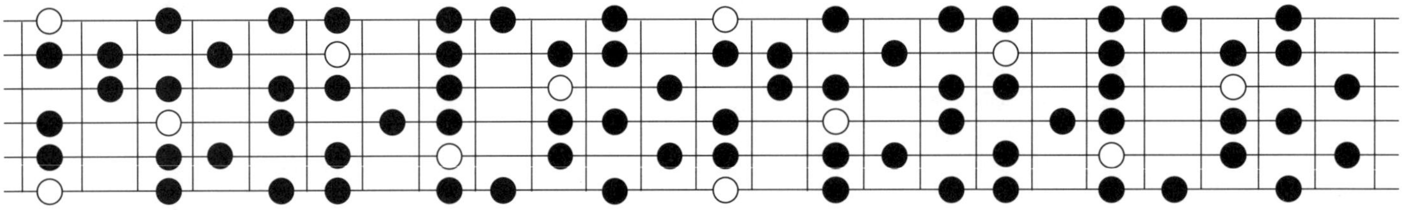

One-Octave Fingerings

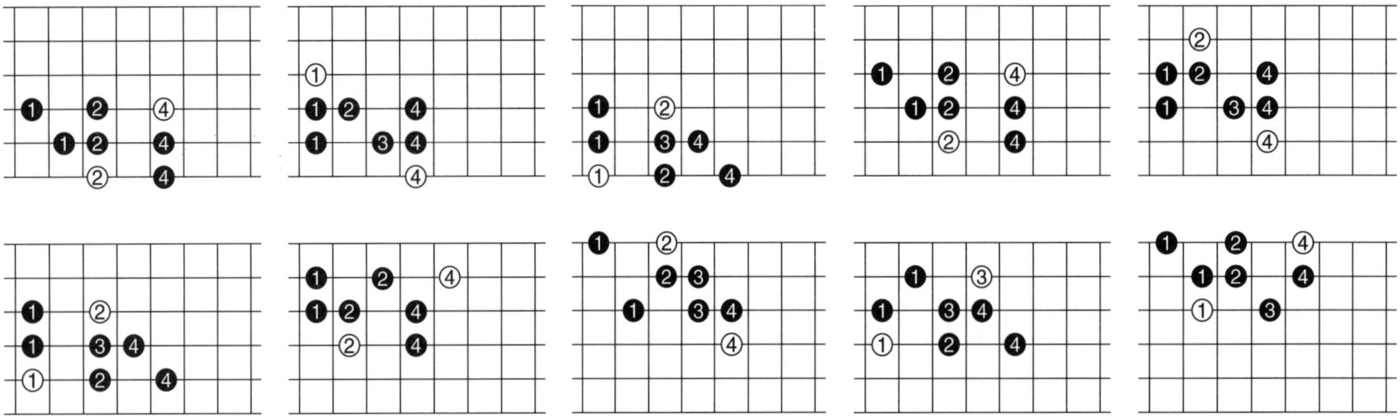

Two-Octave Fingerings

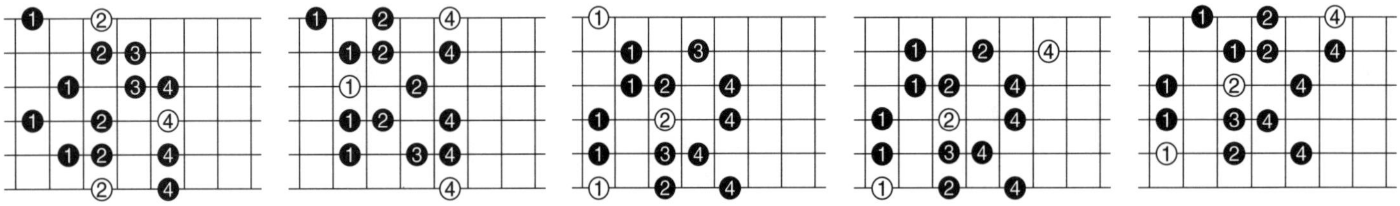

Three-Octave Fingerings

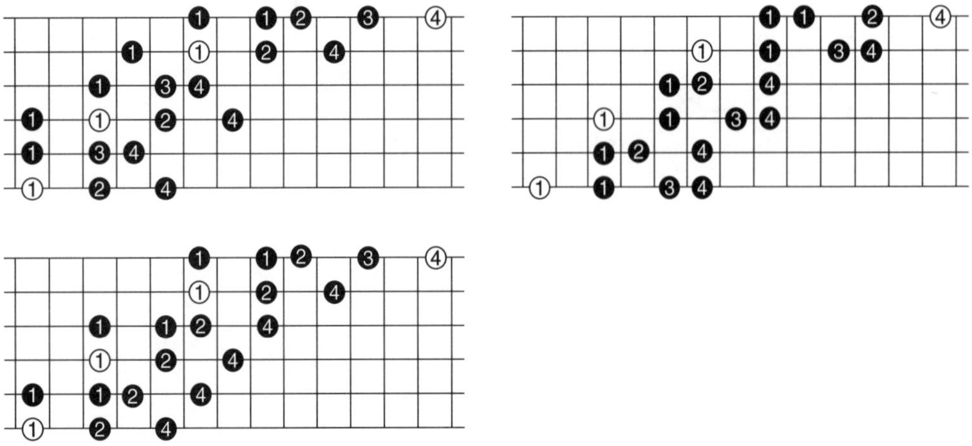

Position-Based Fingerings, Starting on all Scale Degrees

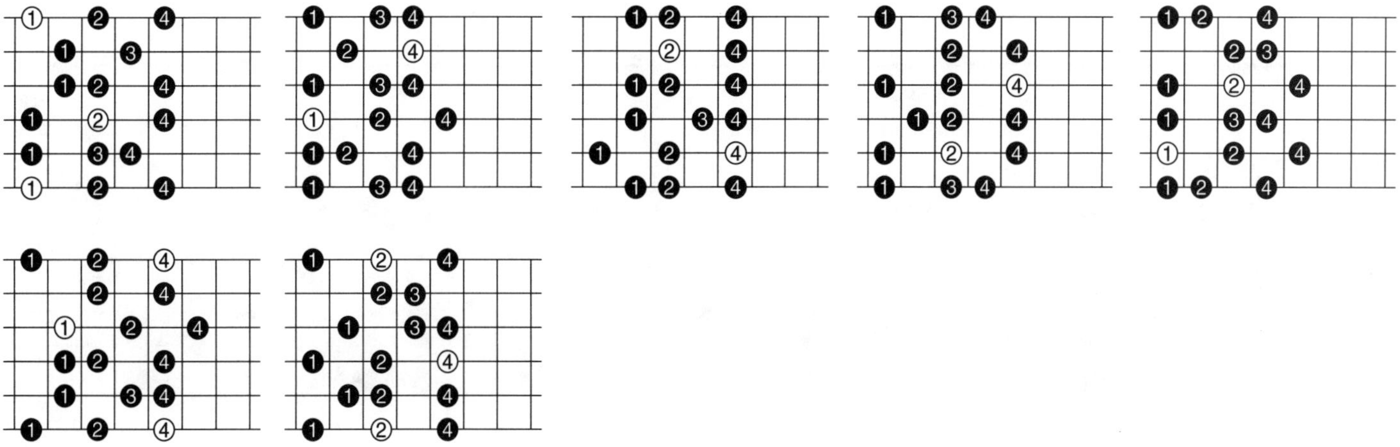

Three-Notes-Per-String Fingerings, Starting on all Scale Degrees

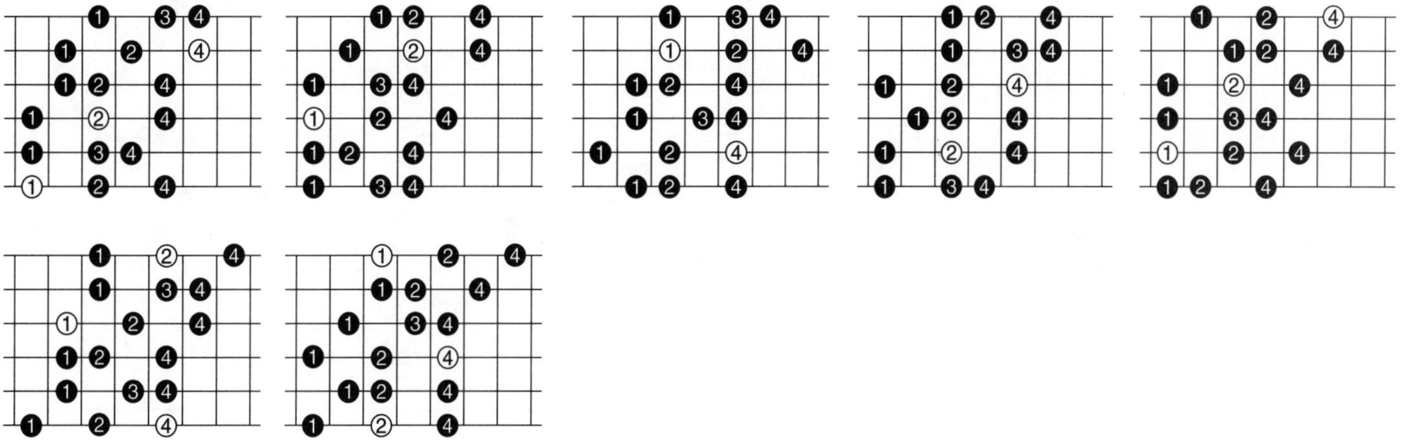

Four-Notes-Per-String Fingerings

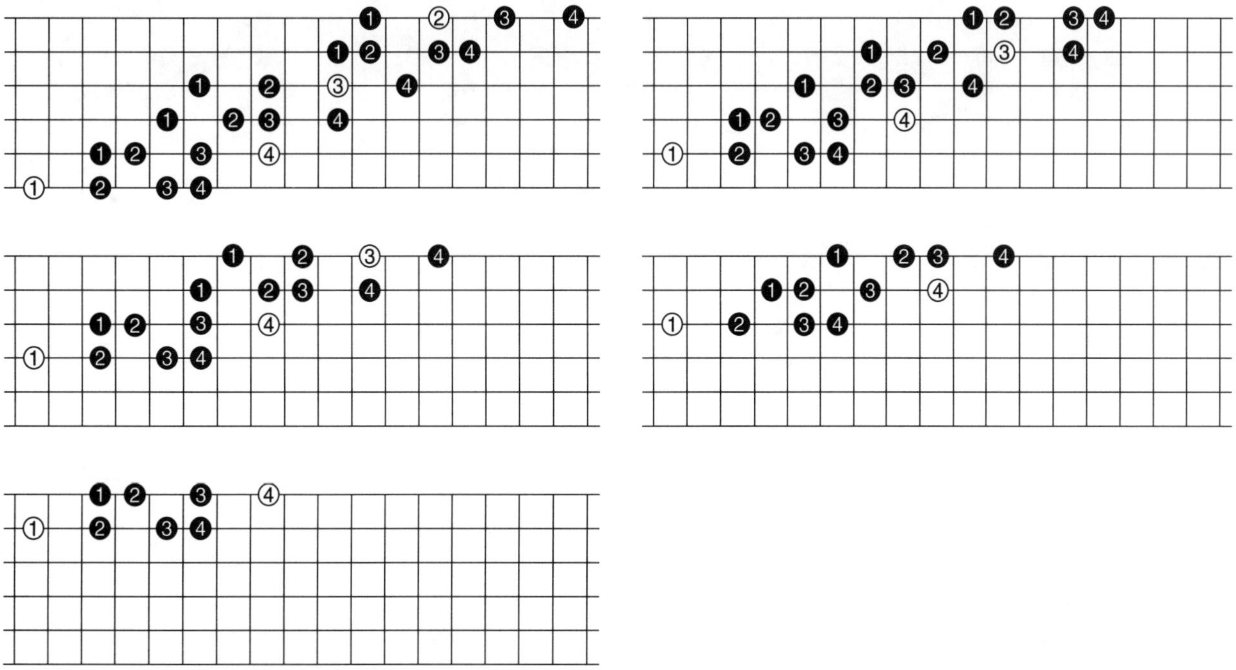

Aeolian ♭5

Scale Tones

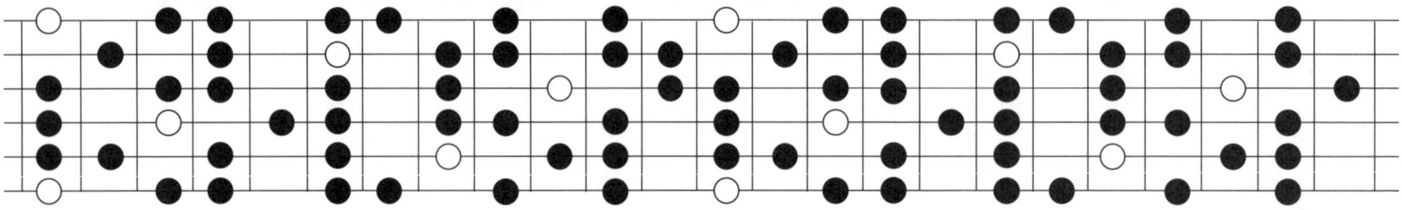

One-Octave Fingerings

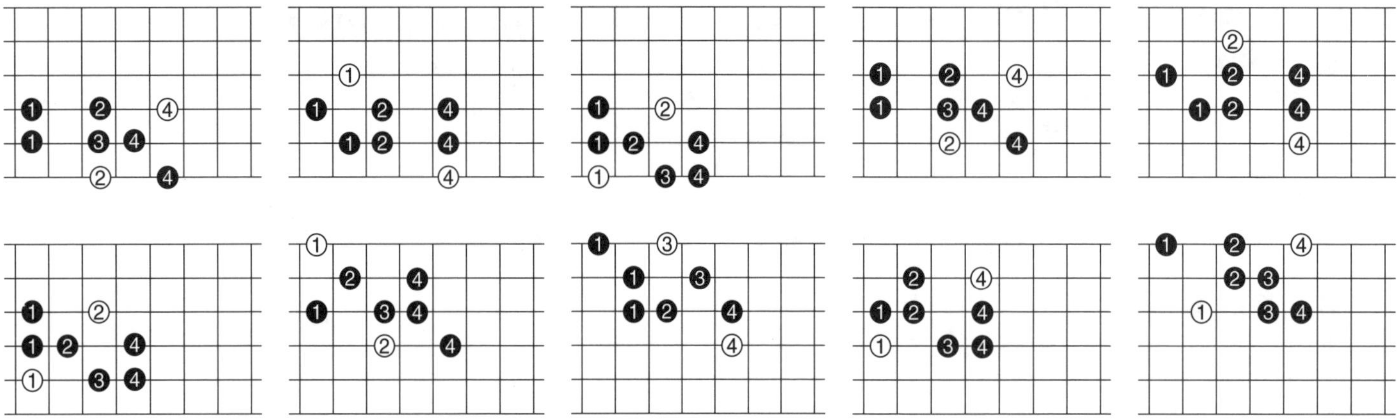

Two-Octave Fingerings

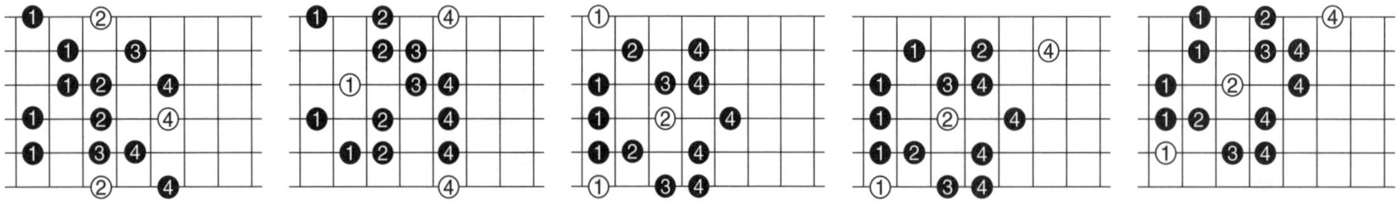

Three-Octave Fingerings

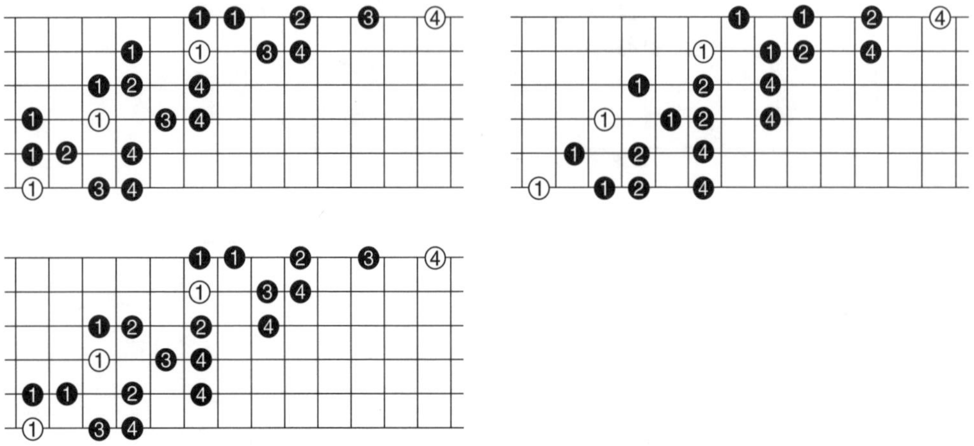

Position-Based Fingerings, Starting on all Scale Degrees

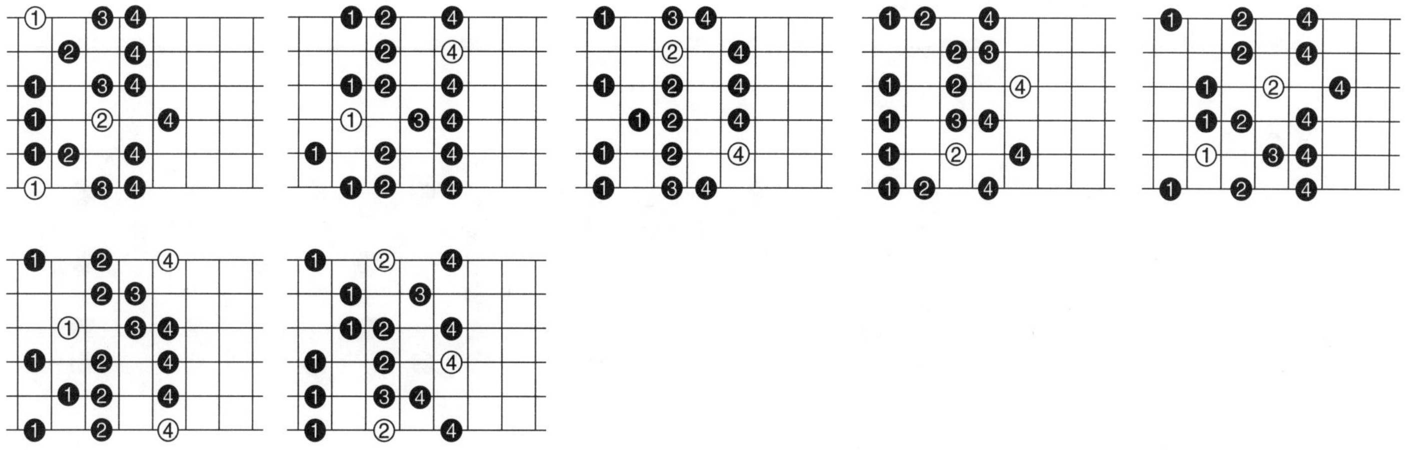

Three-Notes-Per-String Fingerings, Starting on all Scale Degrees

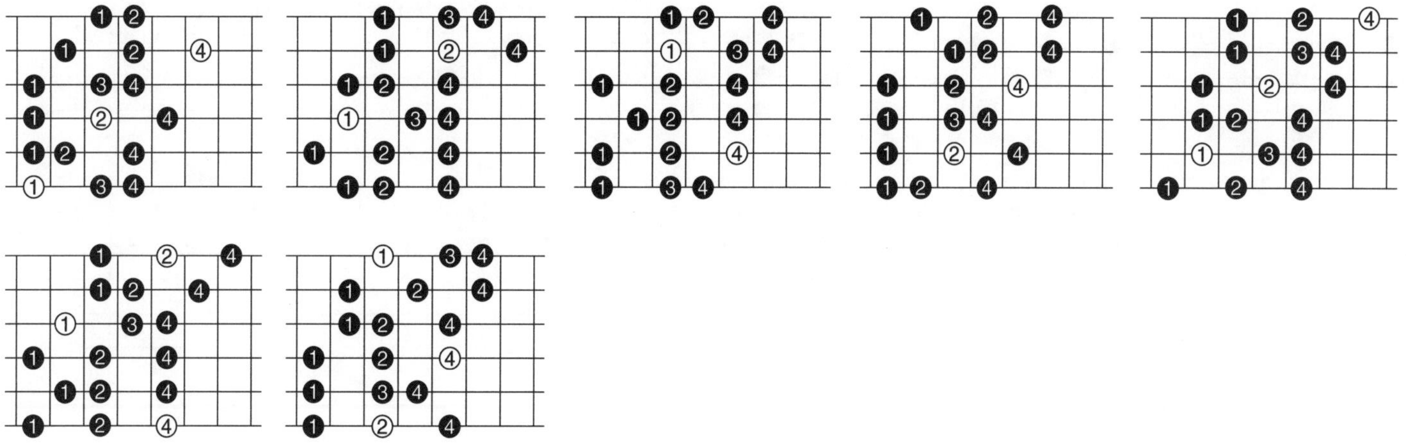

Four-Notes-Per-String Fingerings

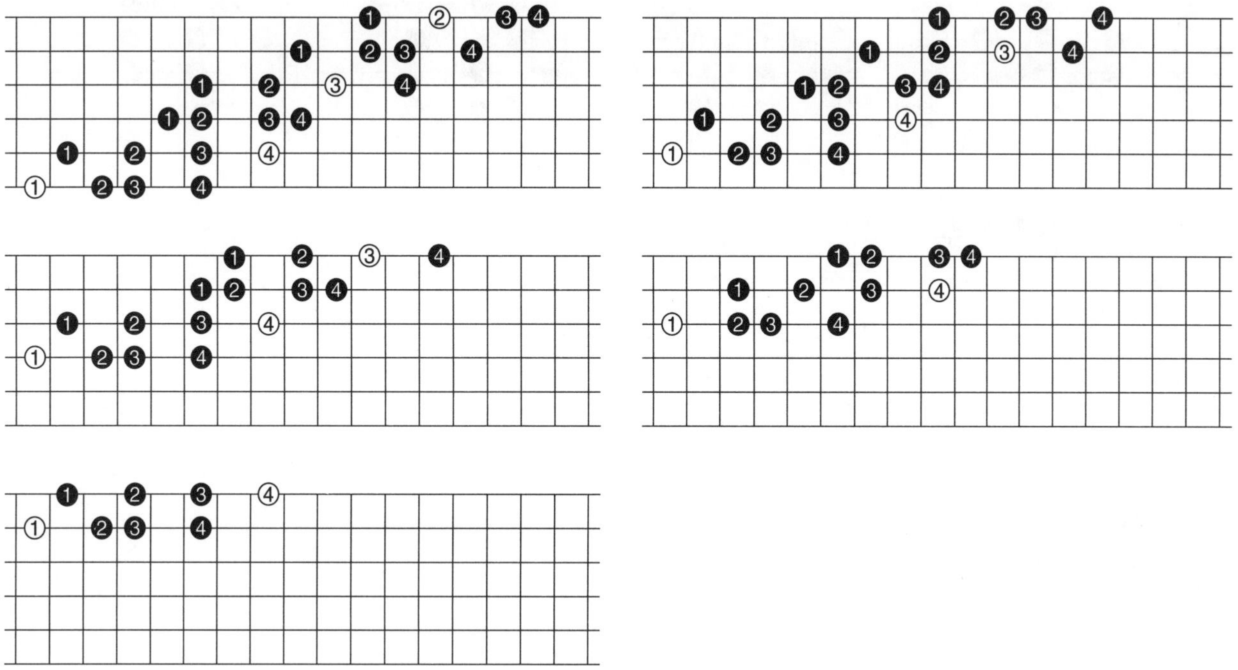

Super Locrian

Scale Tones

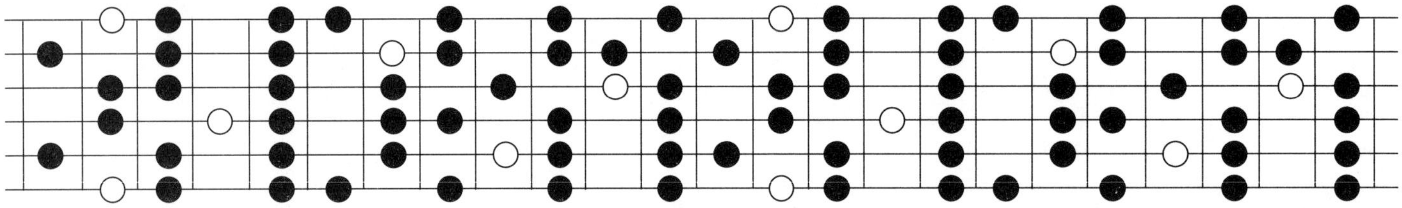

One-Octave Fingerings

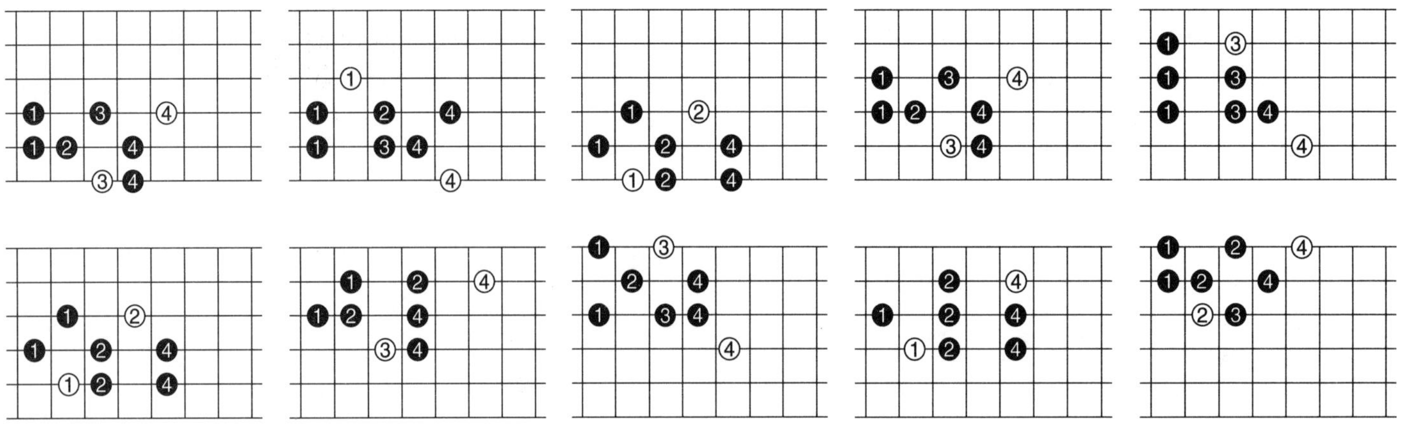

Two-Octave Fingerings

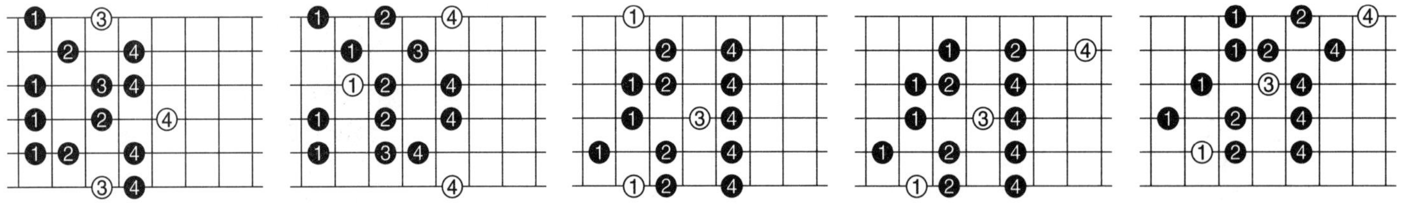

Three-Octave Fingerings

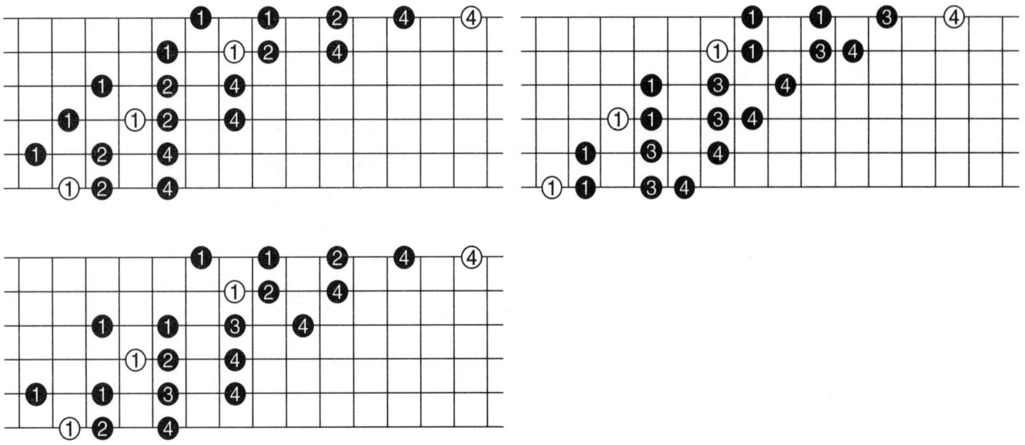

Position-Based Fingerings, Starting on all Scale Degrees

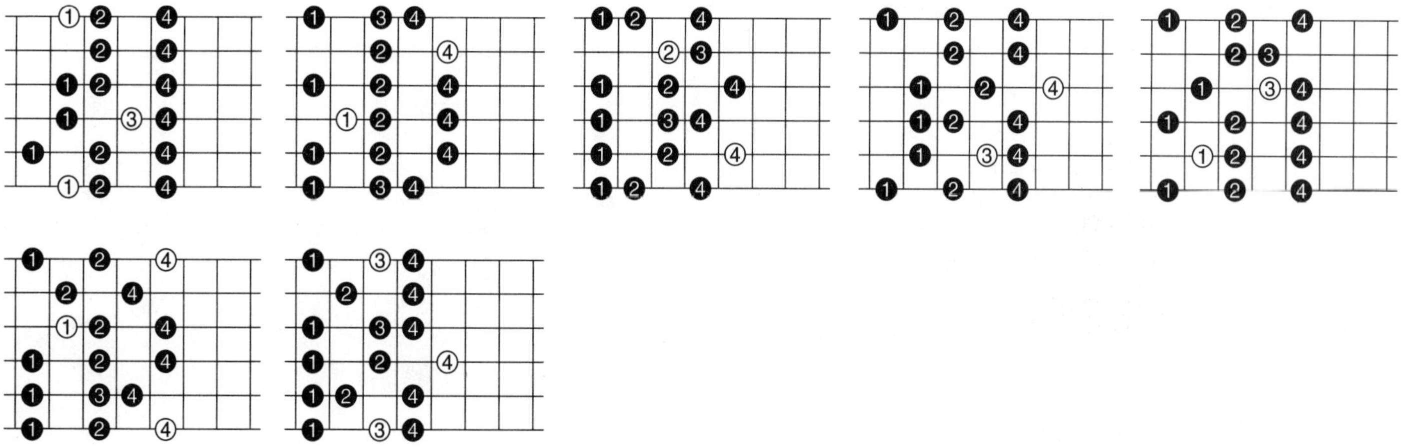

Three-Notes-Per-String Fingerings, Starting on all Scale Degrees

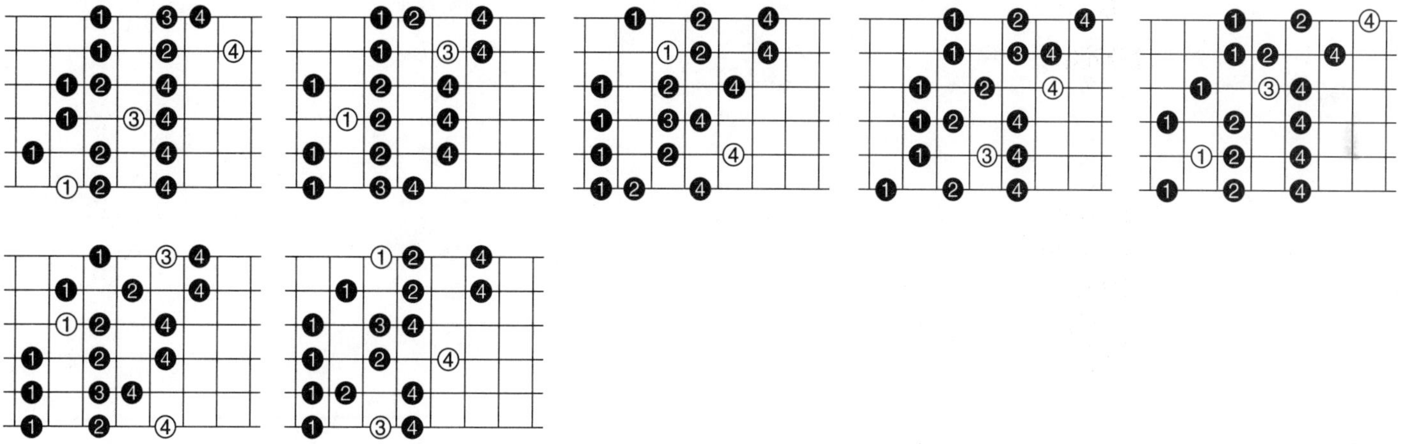

Four-Notes-Per-String Fingerings

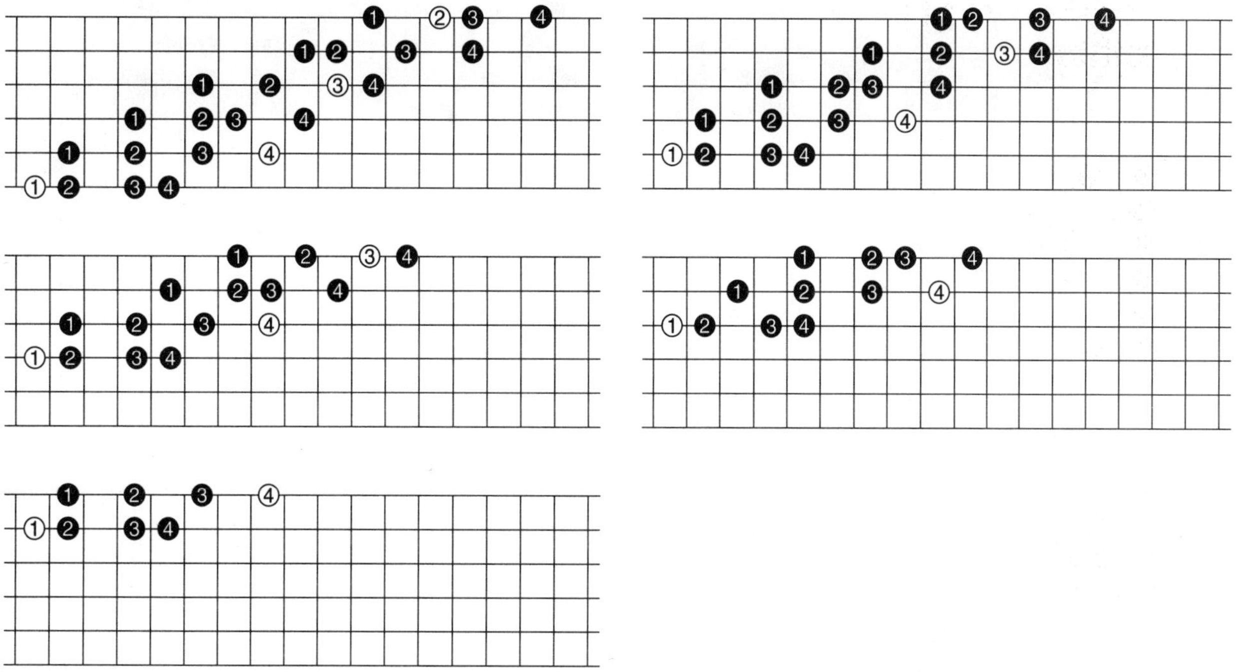

Harmonic Minor

Scale Tones

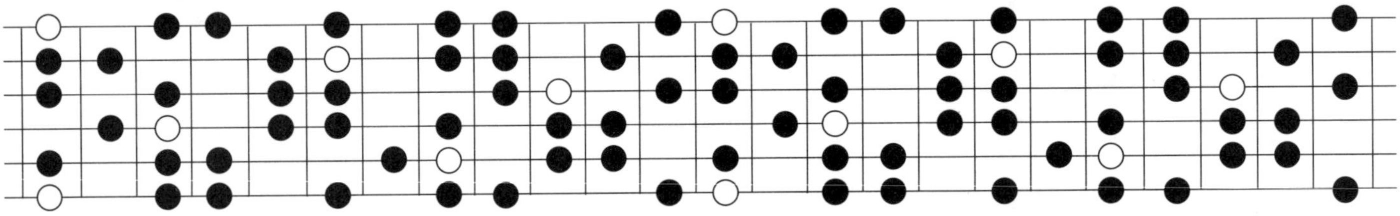

One-Octave Fingerings

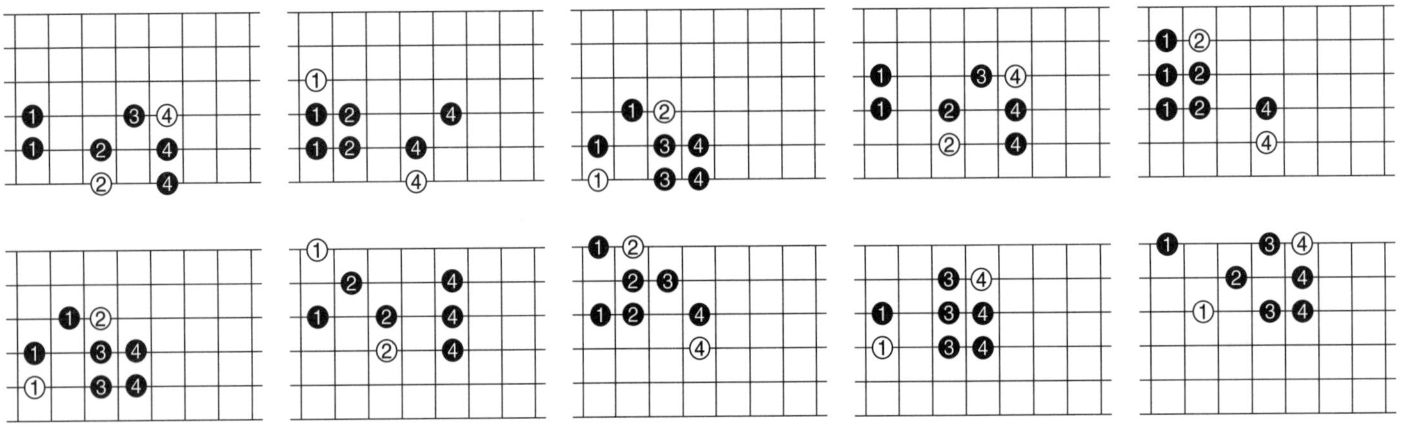

Two-Octave Fingerings

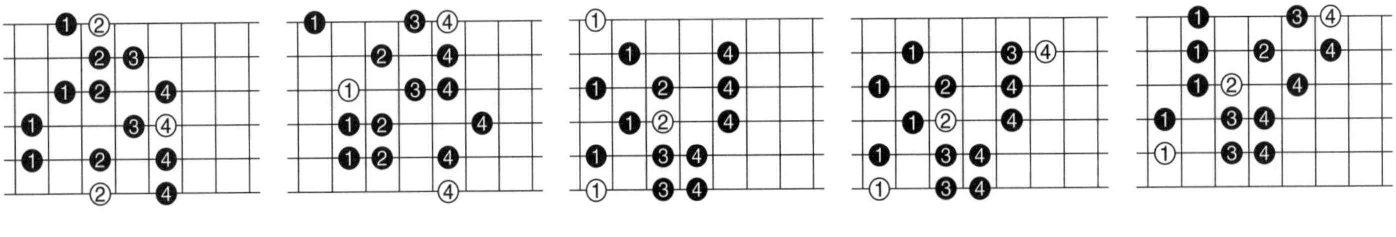

Three-Octave Fingerings

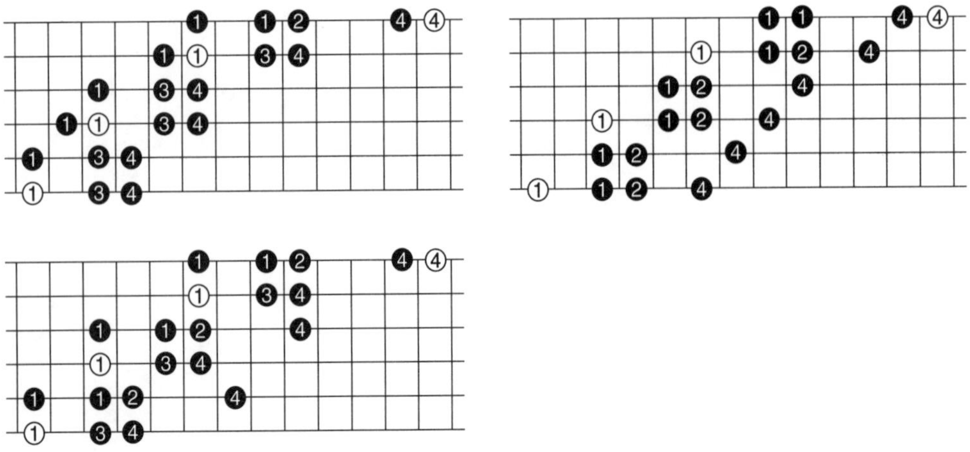

Position-Based Fingerings, Starting on all Scale Degrees

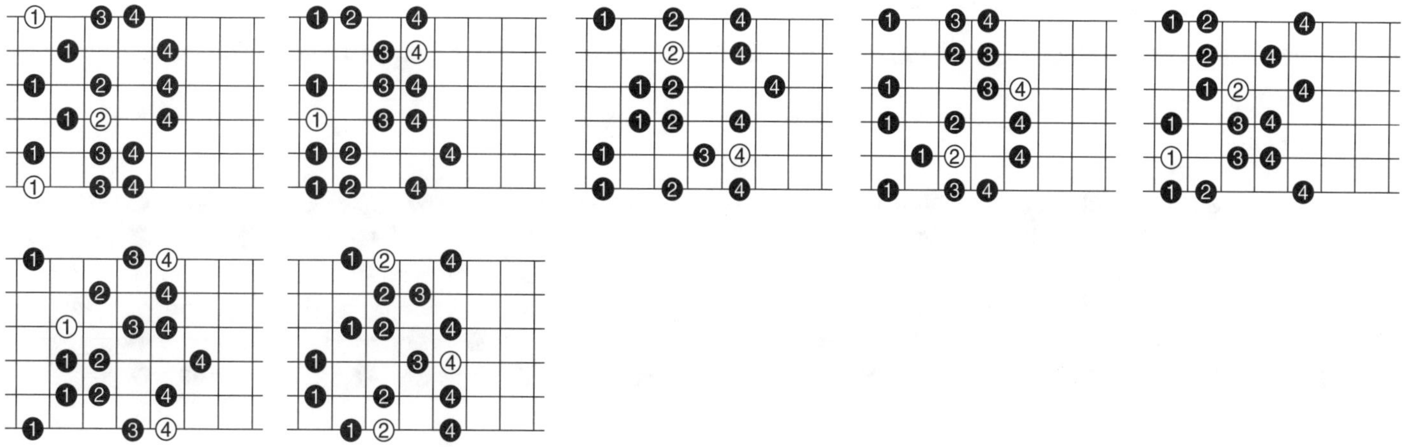

Three-Notes-Per-String Fingerings, Starting on all Scale Degrees

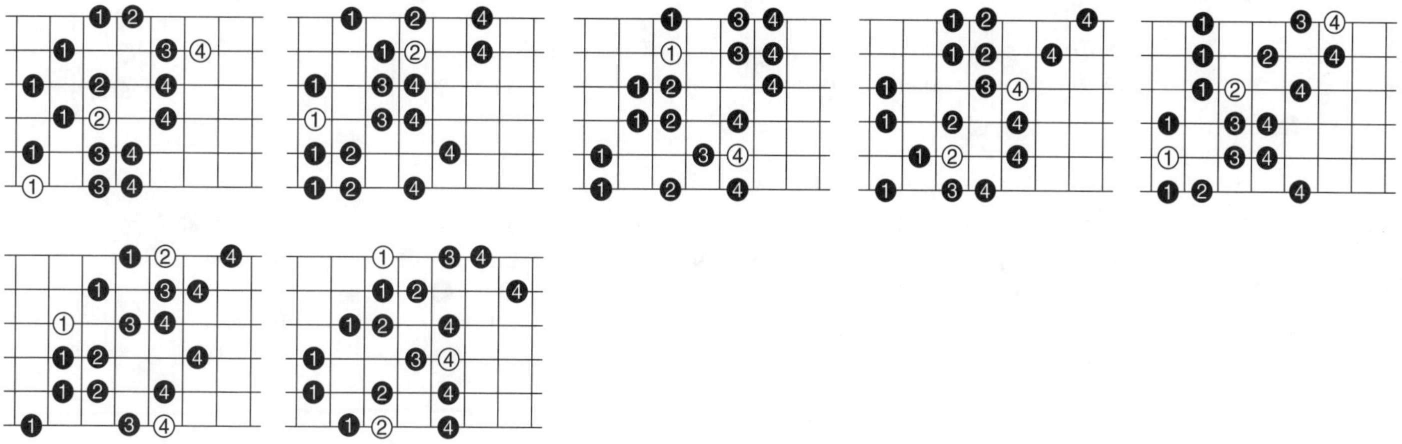

Four-Notes-Per-String Fingerings

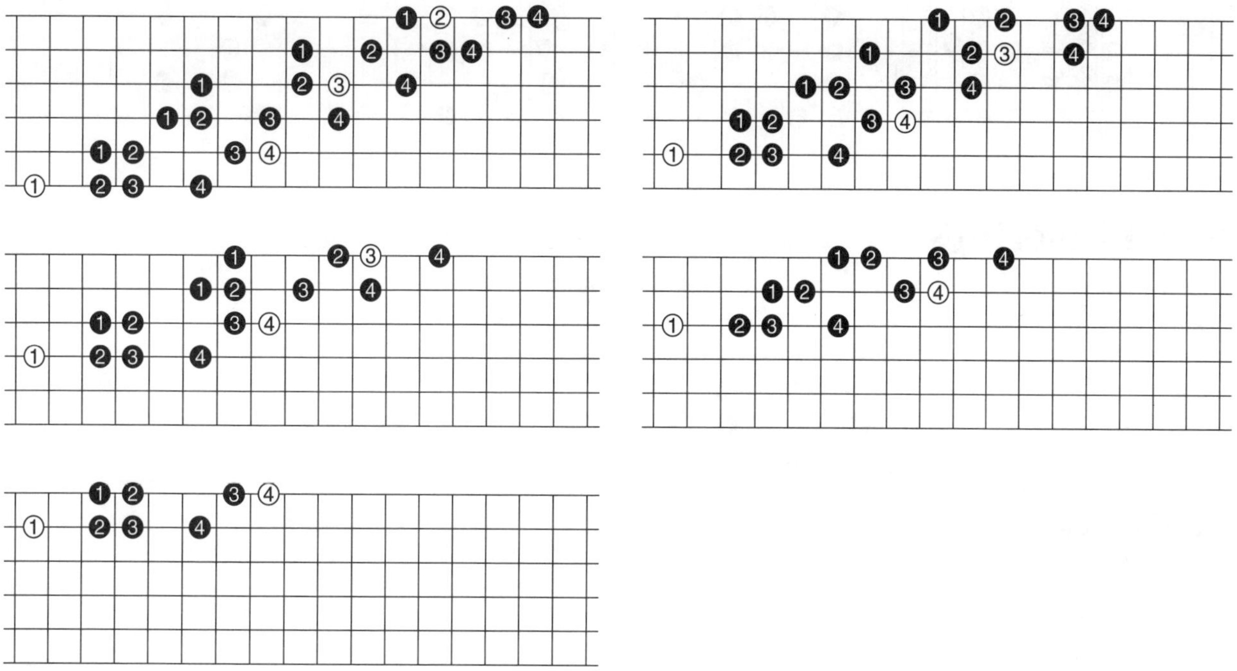

Locrian ♮6

Scale Tones

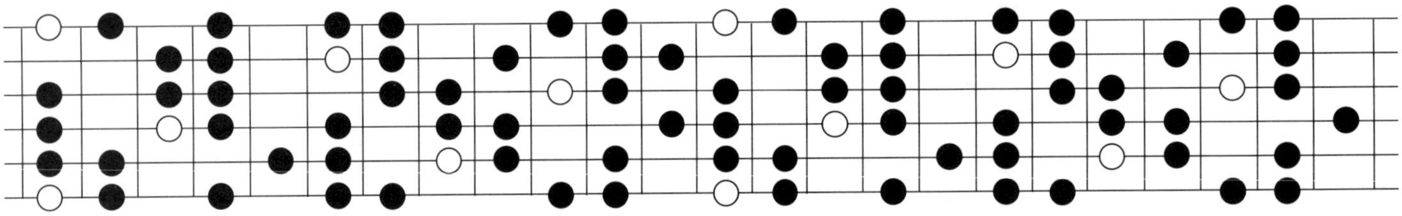

One-Octave Fingerings

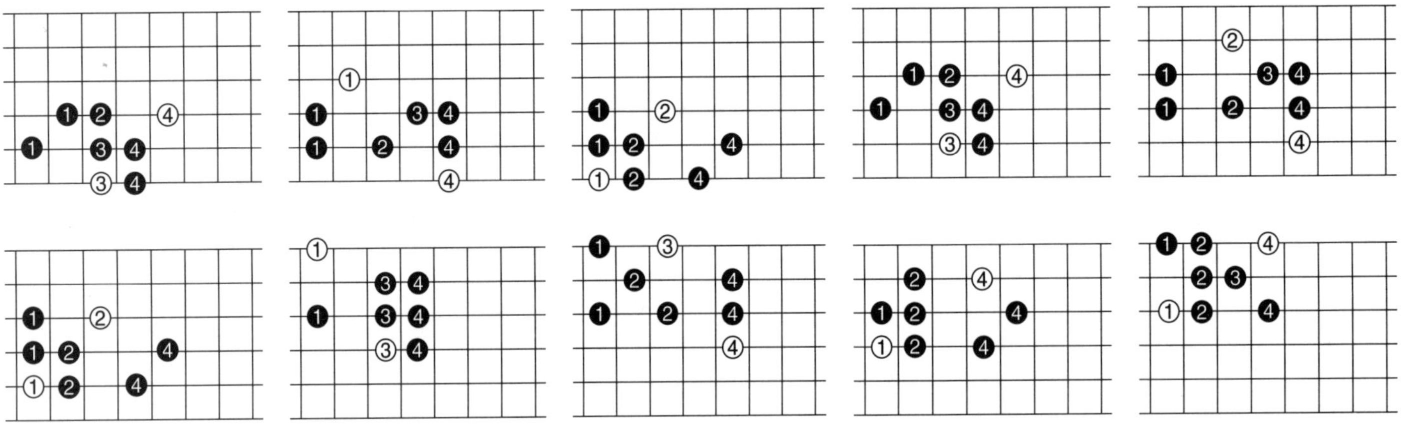

Two-Octave Fingerings

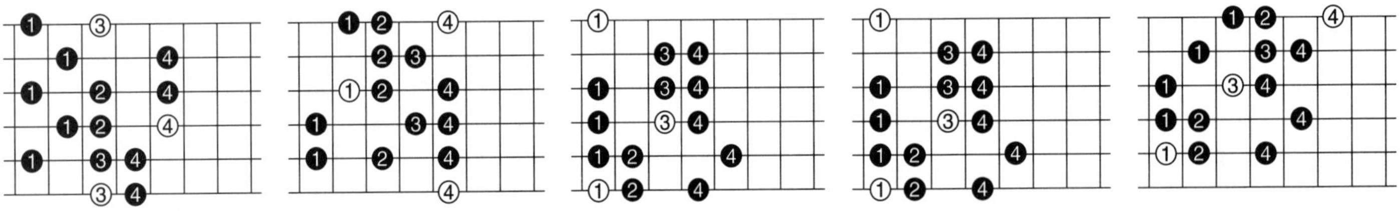

Three-Octave Fingerings

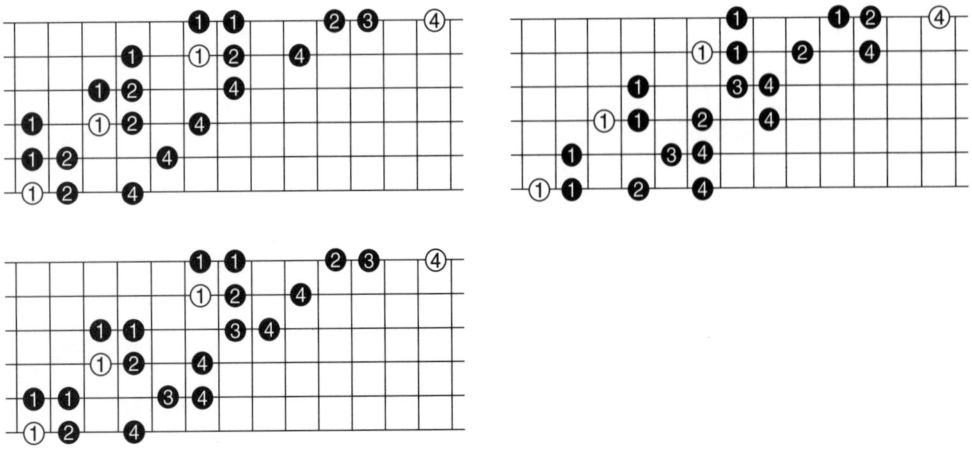

Position-Based Fingerings, Starting on all Scale Degrees

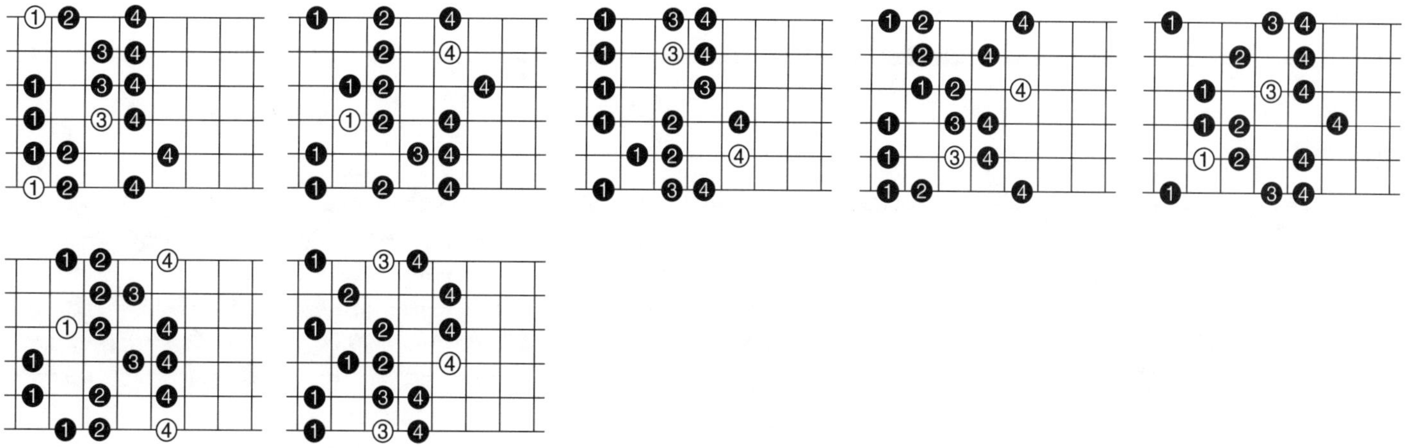

Three-Notes-Per-String Fingerings, Starting on all Scale Degrees

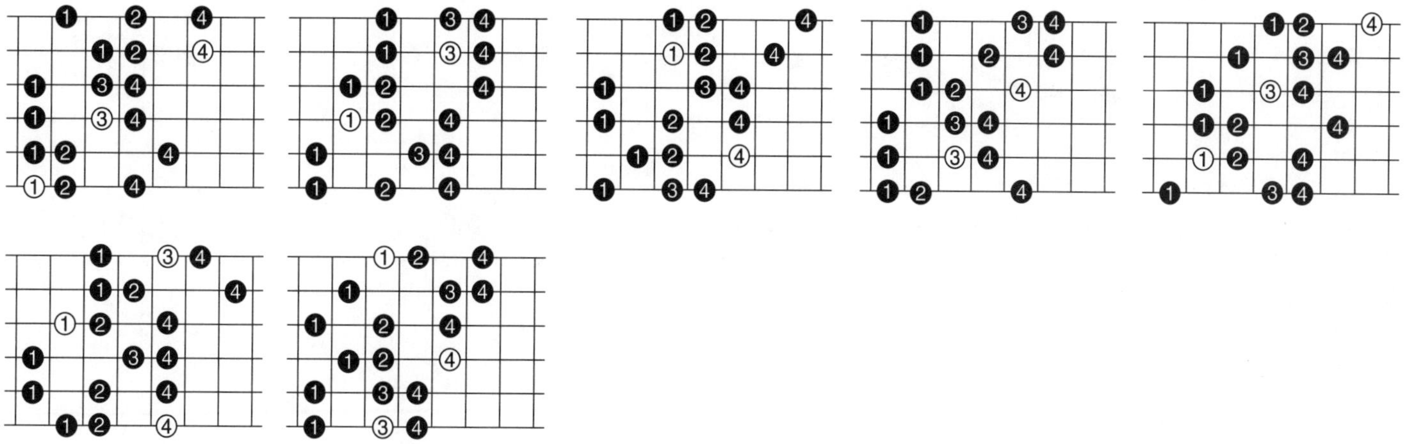

Four-Notes-Per-String Fingerings

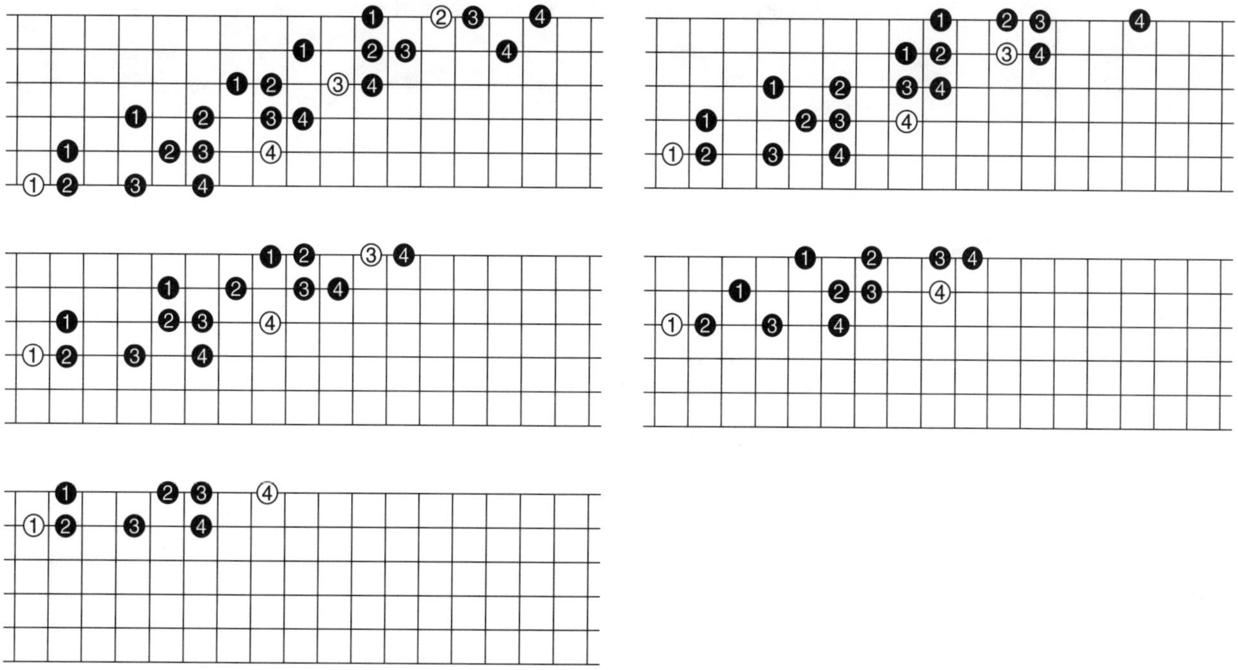

Ionian ♯5

Scale Tones

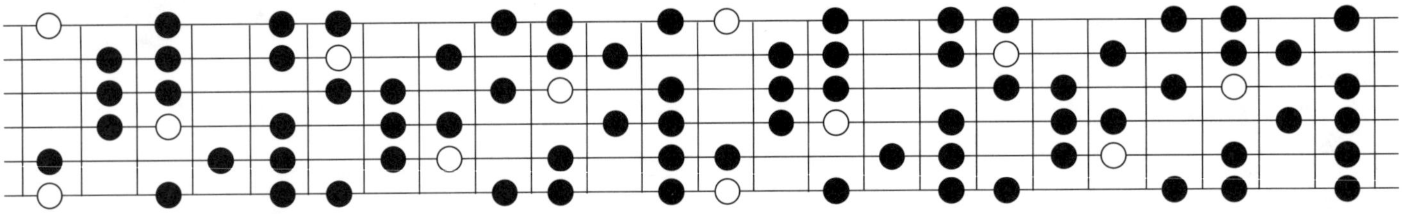

One-Octave Fingerings

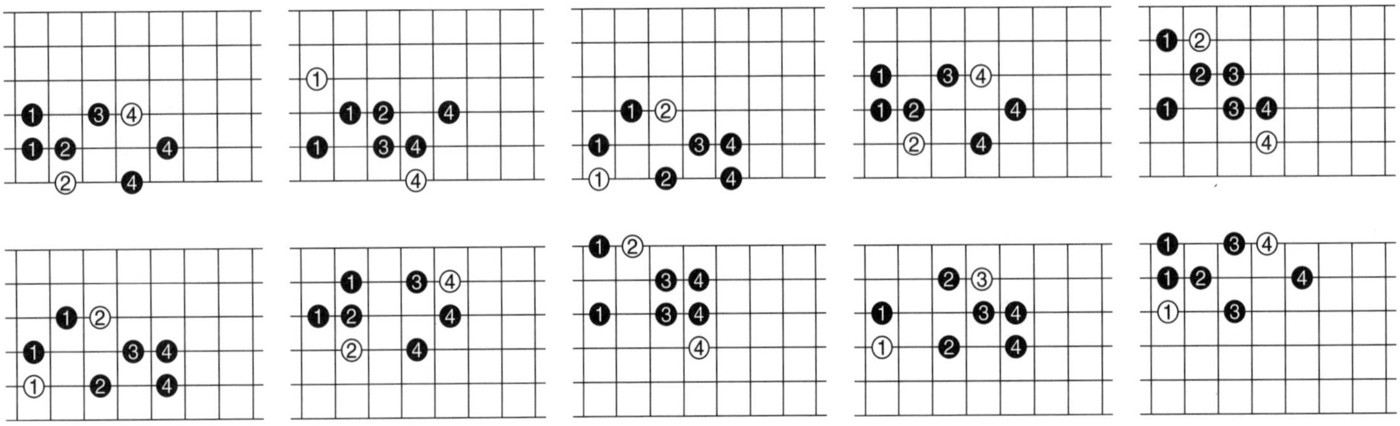

Two-Octave Fingerings

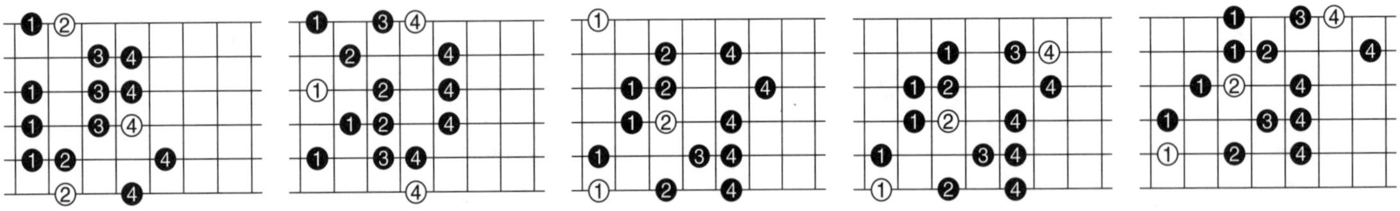

Three-Octave Fingerings

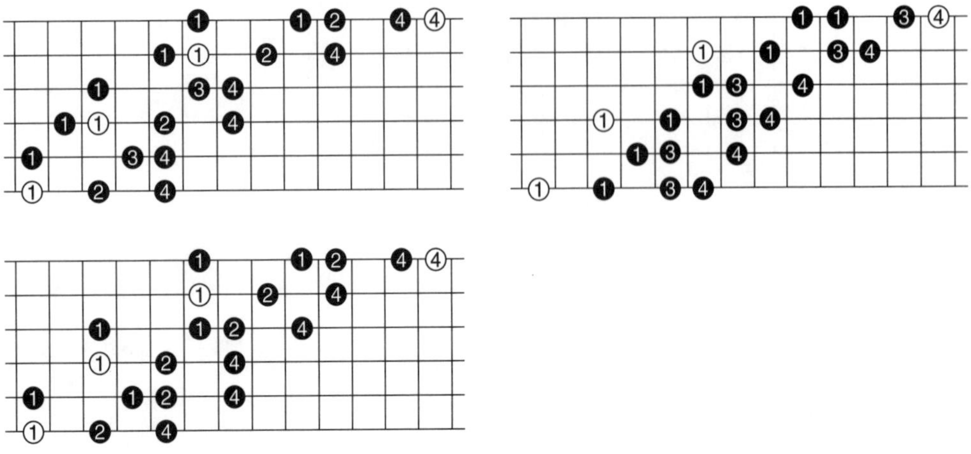

Position-Based Fingerings, Starting on all Scale Degrees

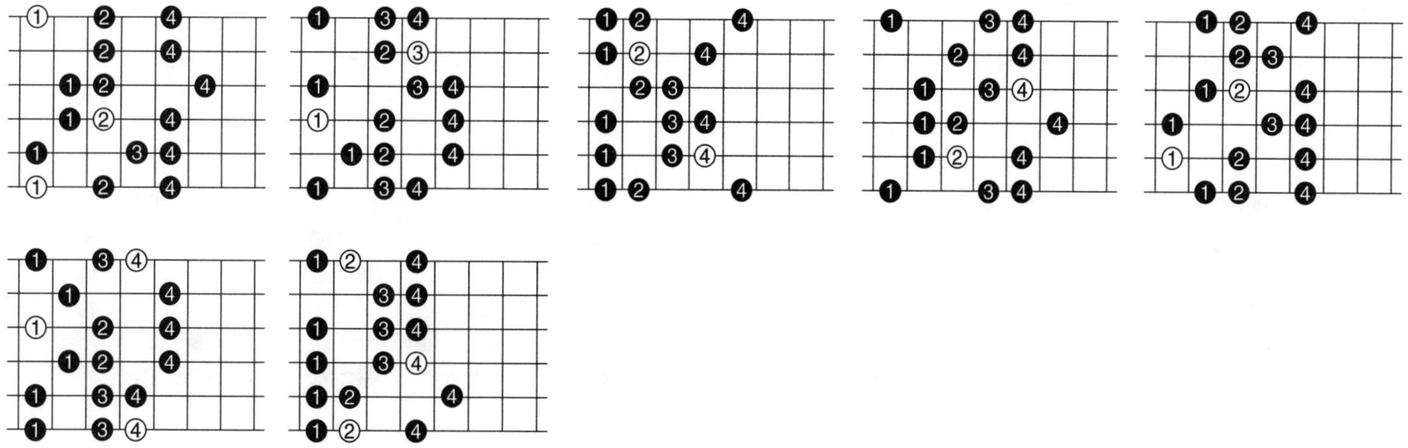

Three-Notes-Per-String Fingerings, Starting on all Scale Degrees

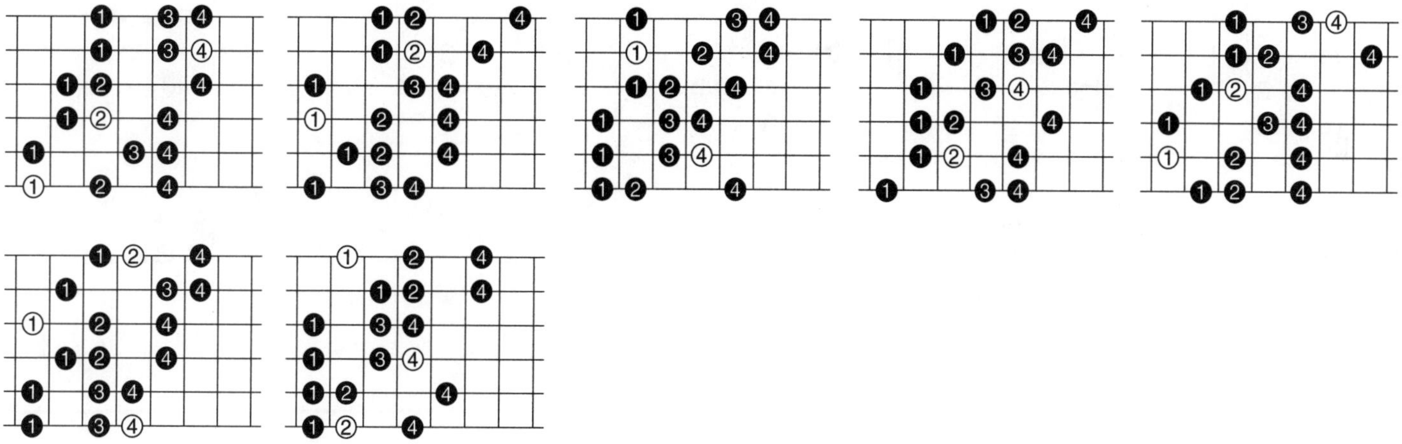

Four-Notes-Per-String Fingerings

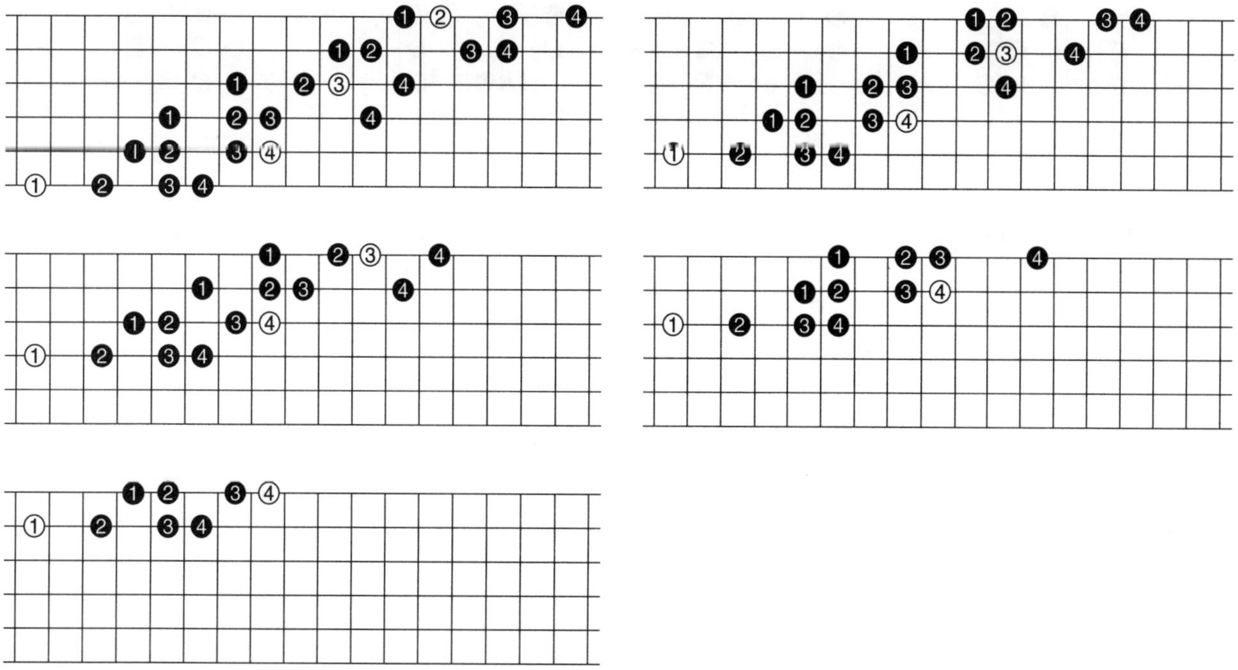

Dorian ♯4

Scale Tones

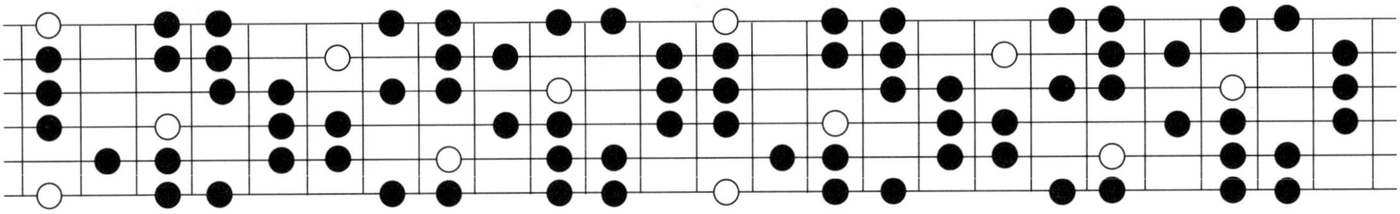

One-Octave Fingerings

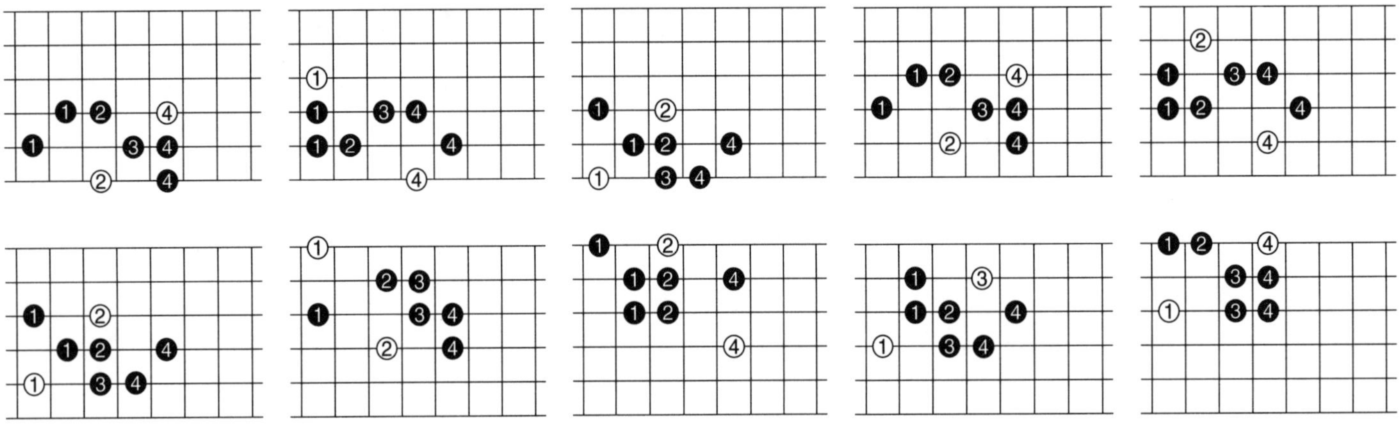

Two-Octave Fingerings

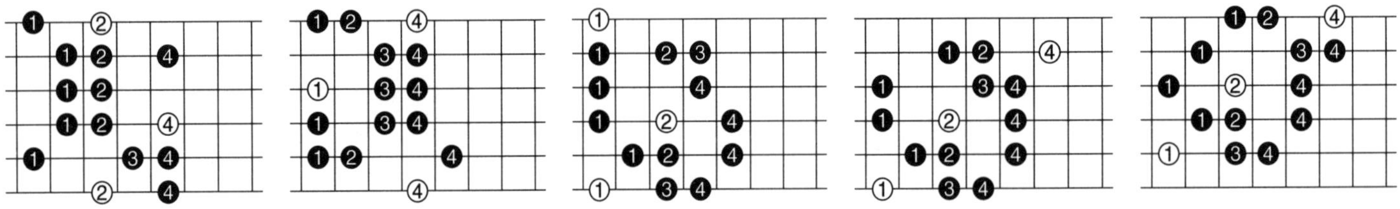

Three-Octave Fingerings

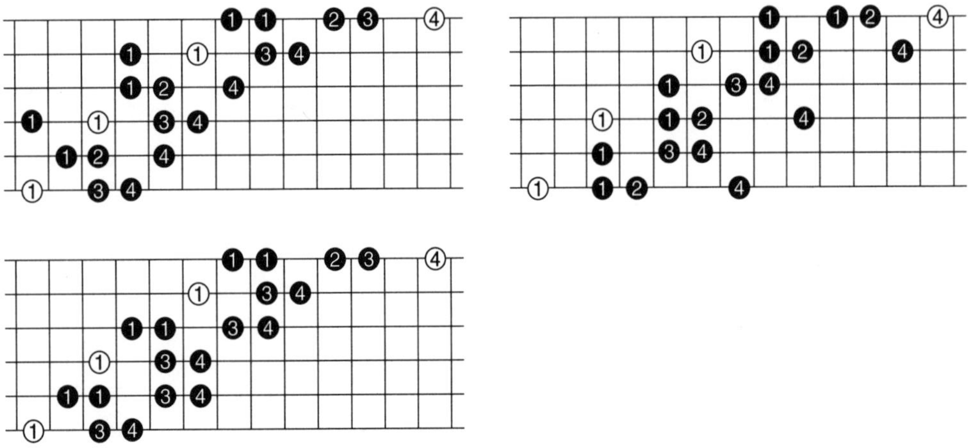

Position-Based Fingerings, Starting on all Scale Degrees

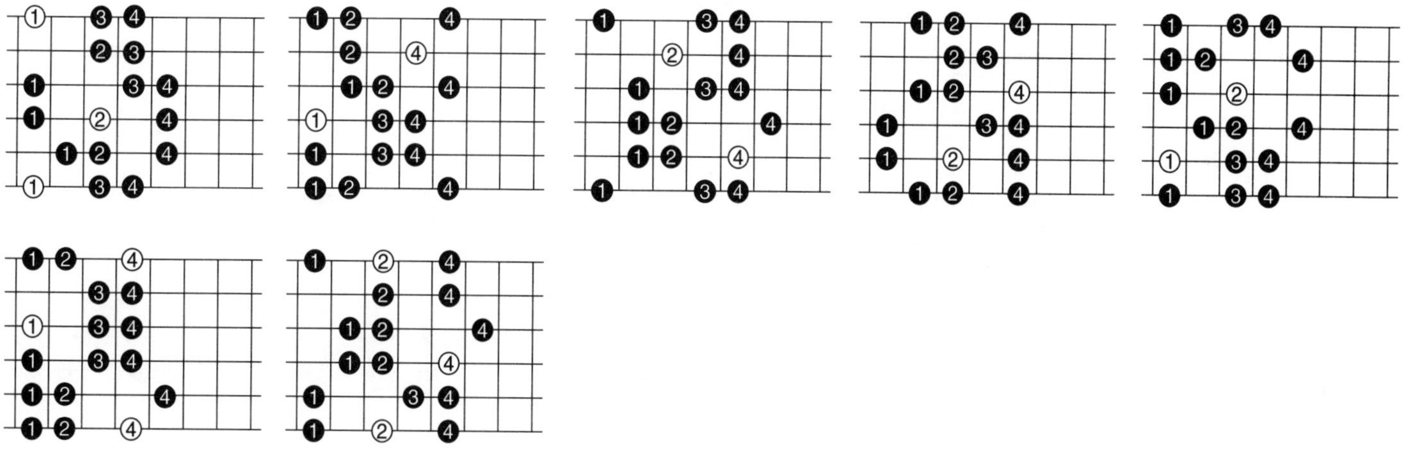

Three-Notes-Per-String Fingerings, Starting on all Scale Degrees

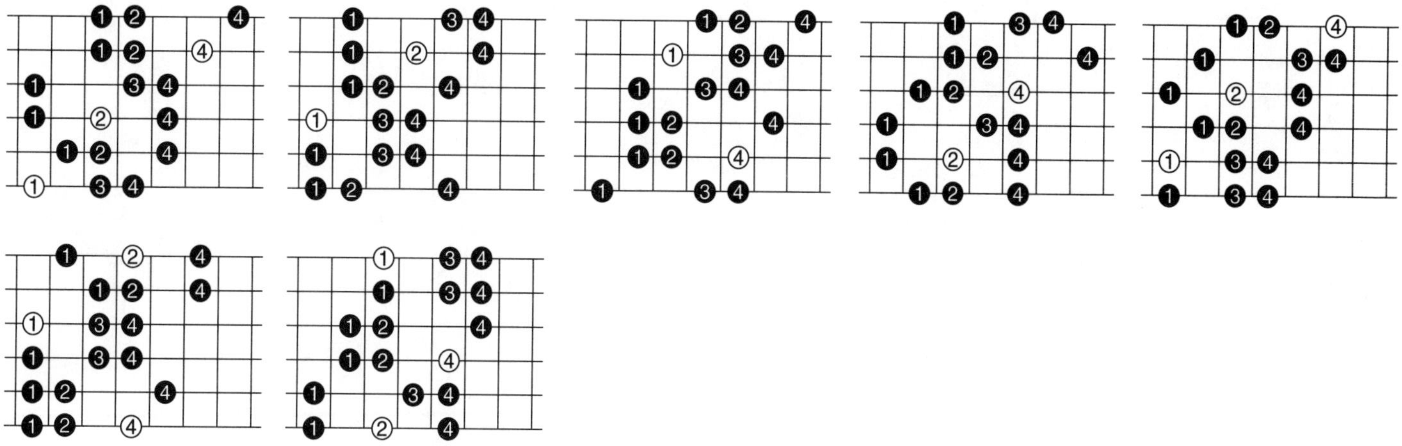

Four-Notes-Per-String Fingerings

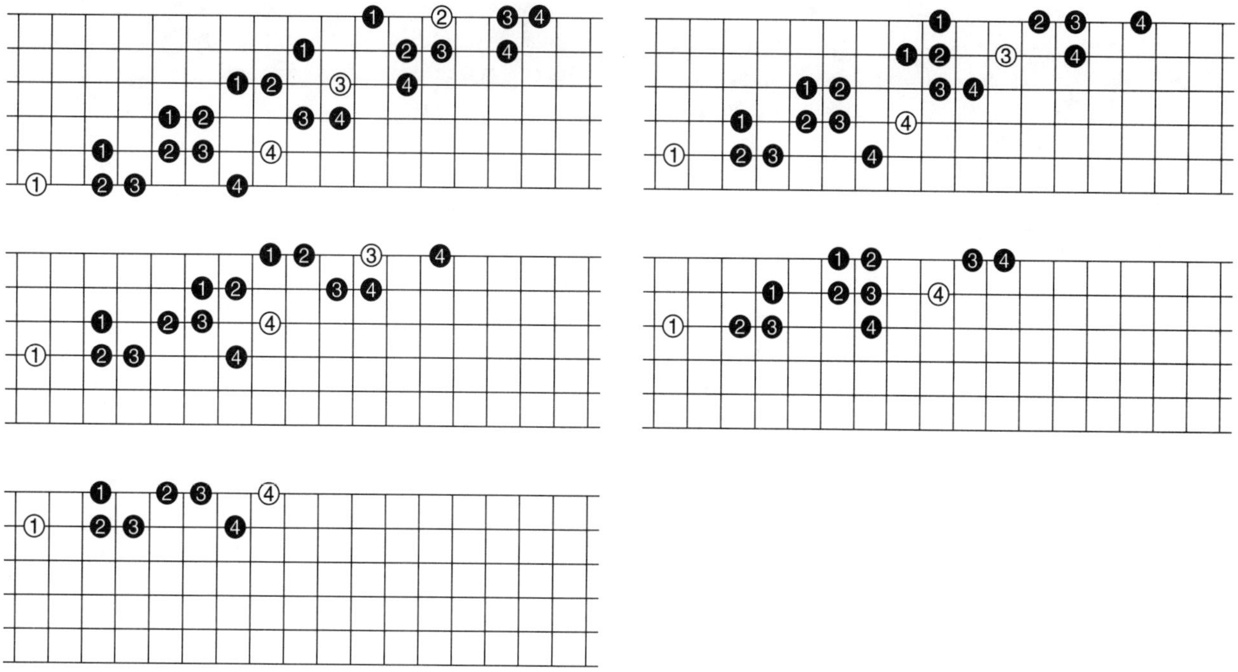

Phrygian Dominant

Scale Tones

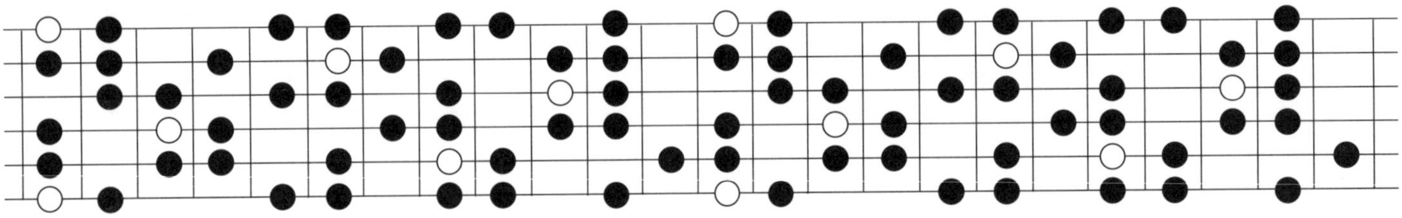

One-Octave Fingerings

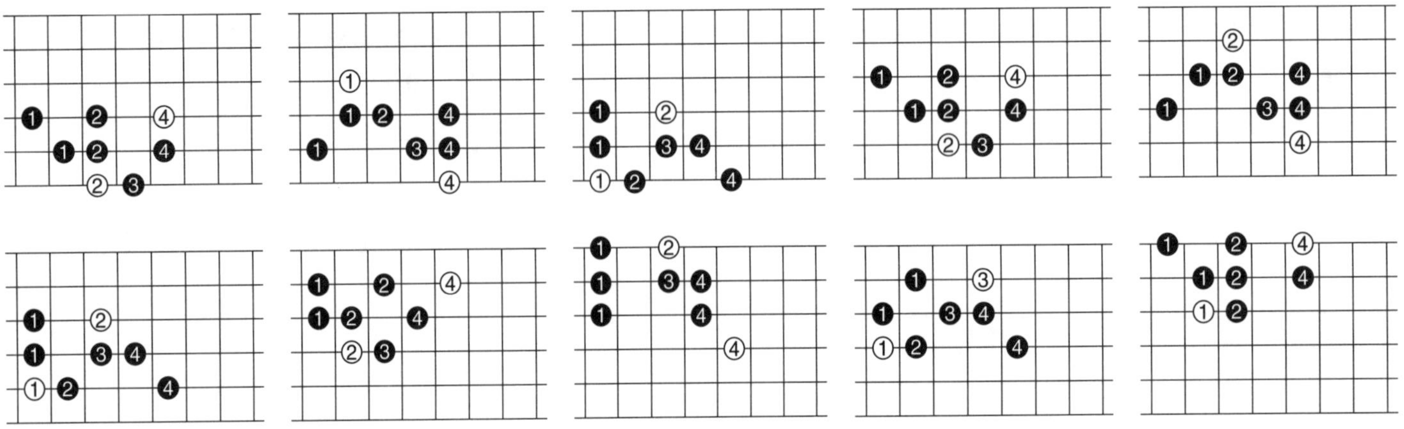

Two-Octave Fingerings

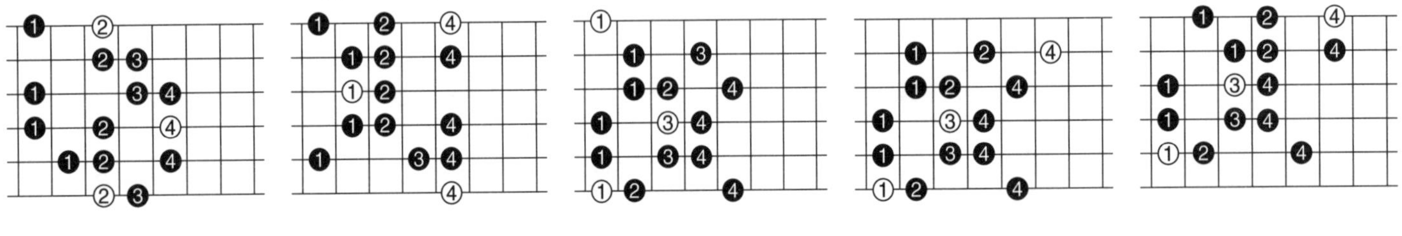

Three-Octave Fingerings

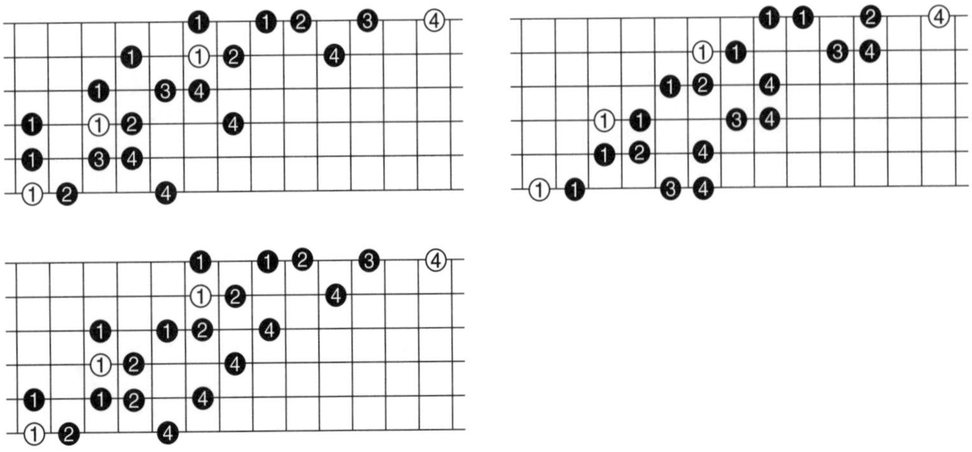

Position-Based Fingerings, Starting on all Scale Degrees

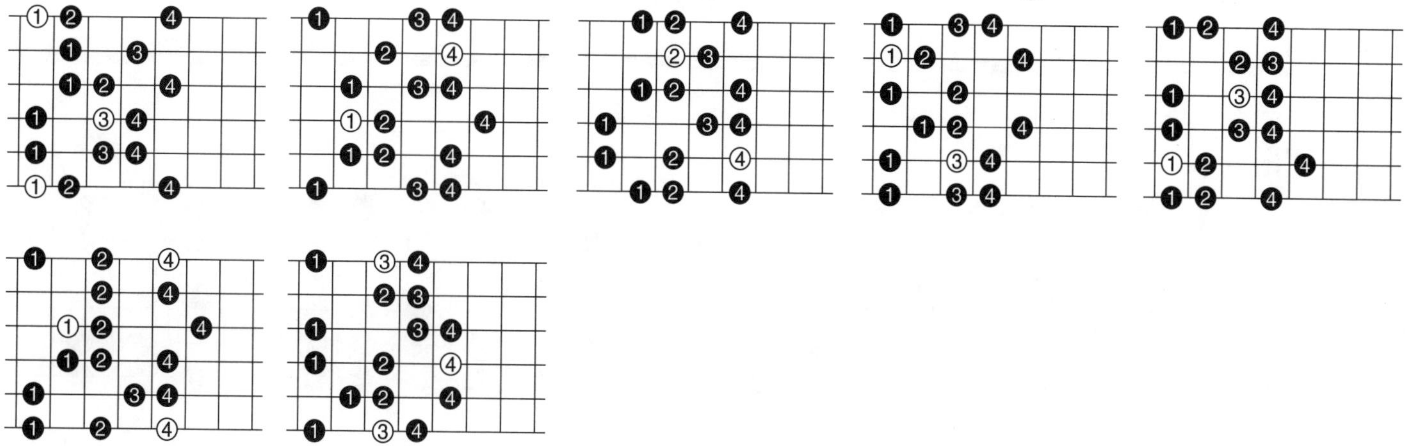

Three-Notes-Per-String Fingerings, Starting on all Scale Degrees

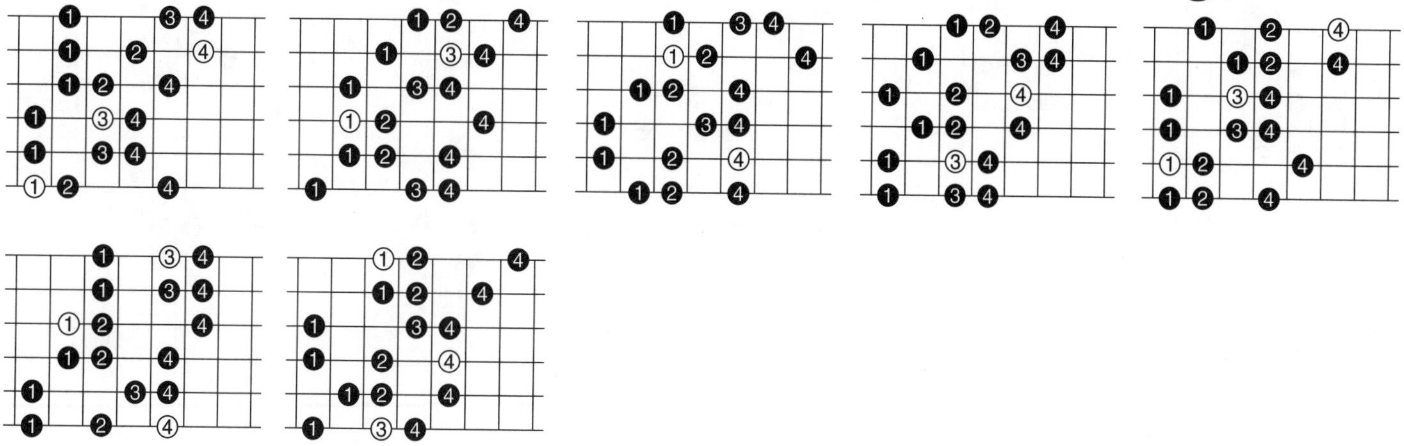

Four-Notes-Per-String Fingerings

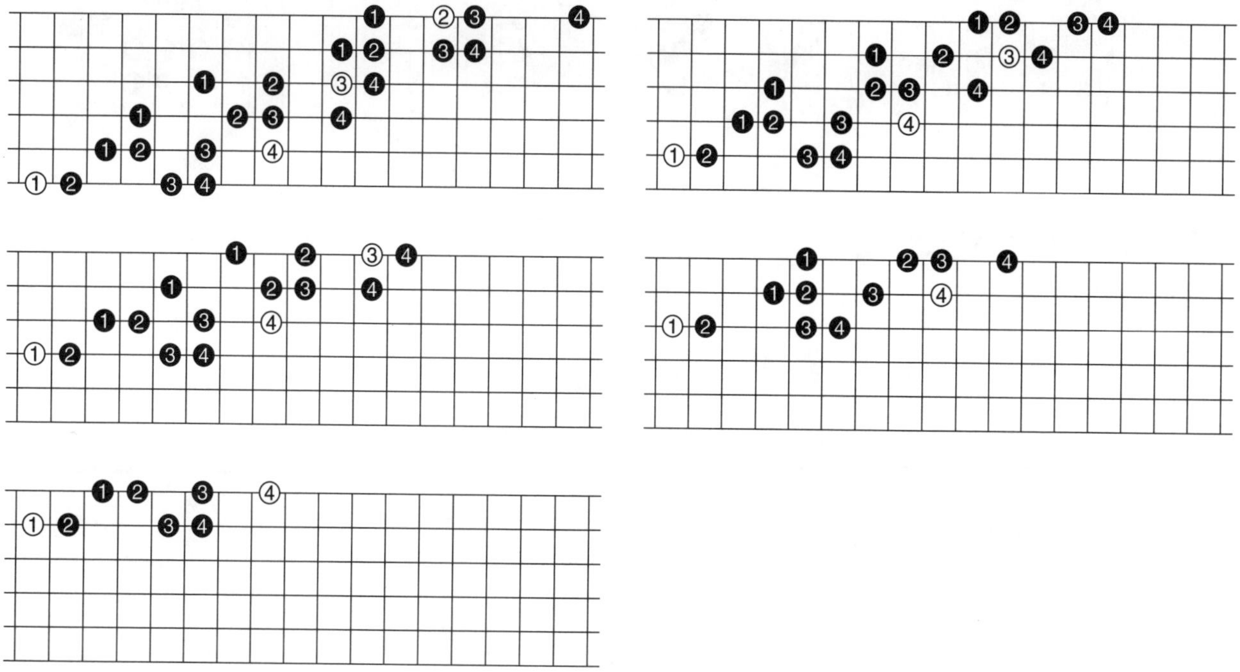

Lydian ♯2

Scale Tones

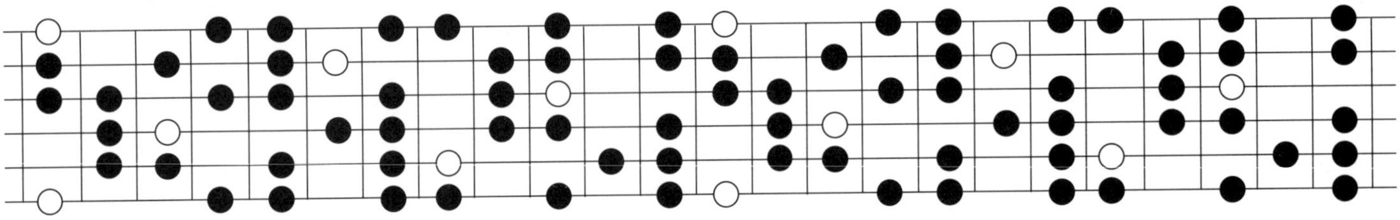

One-Octave Fingerings

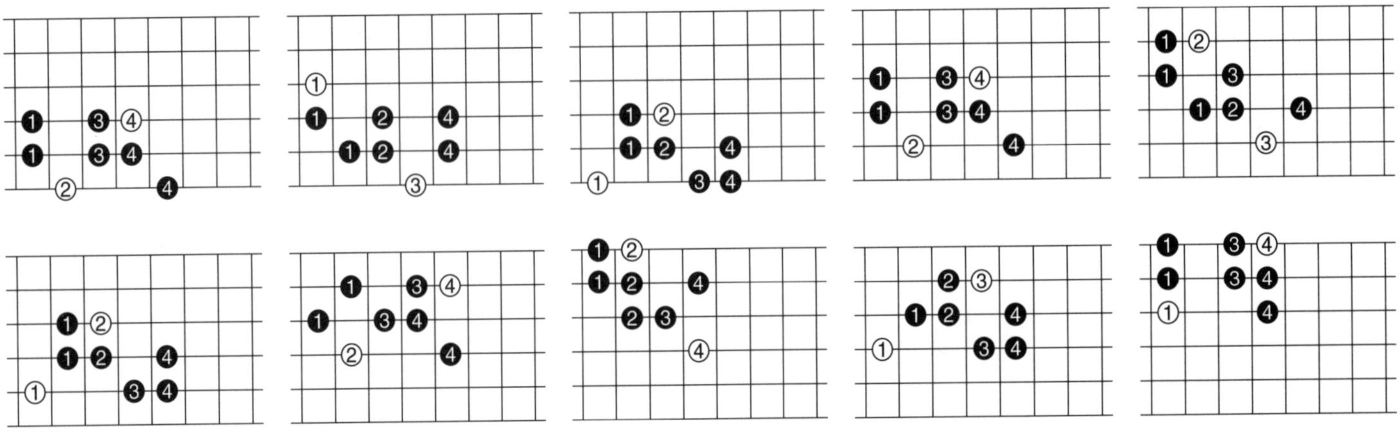

Two-Octave Fingerings

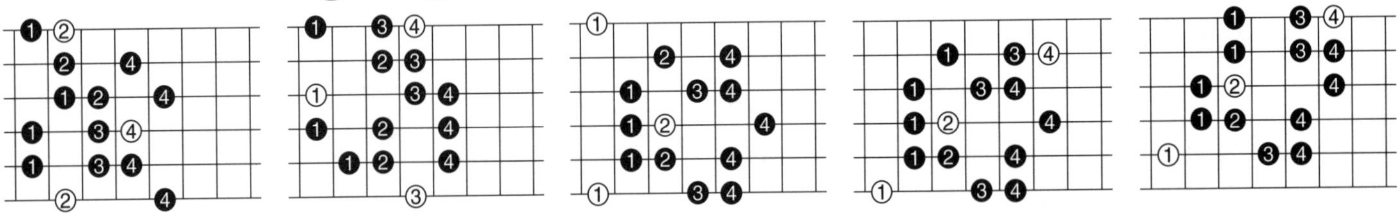

Three-Octave Fingerings

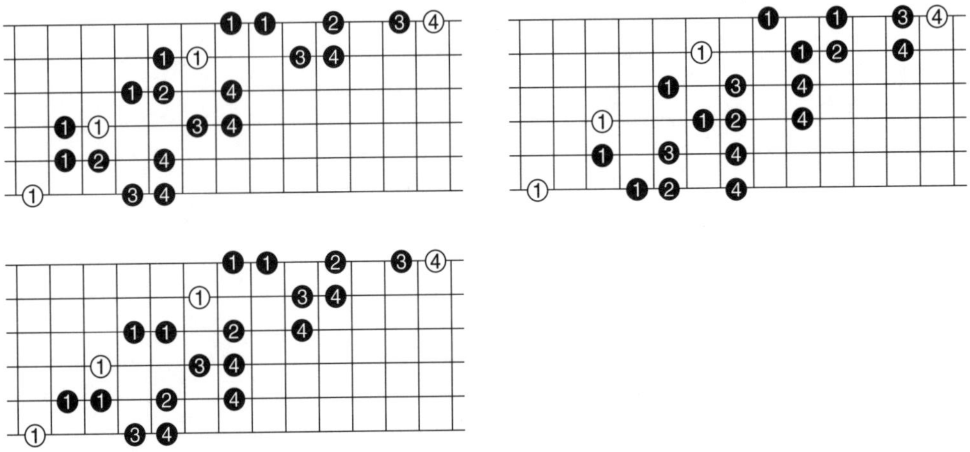

Position-Based Fingerings, Starting on all Scale Degrees

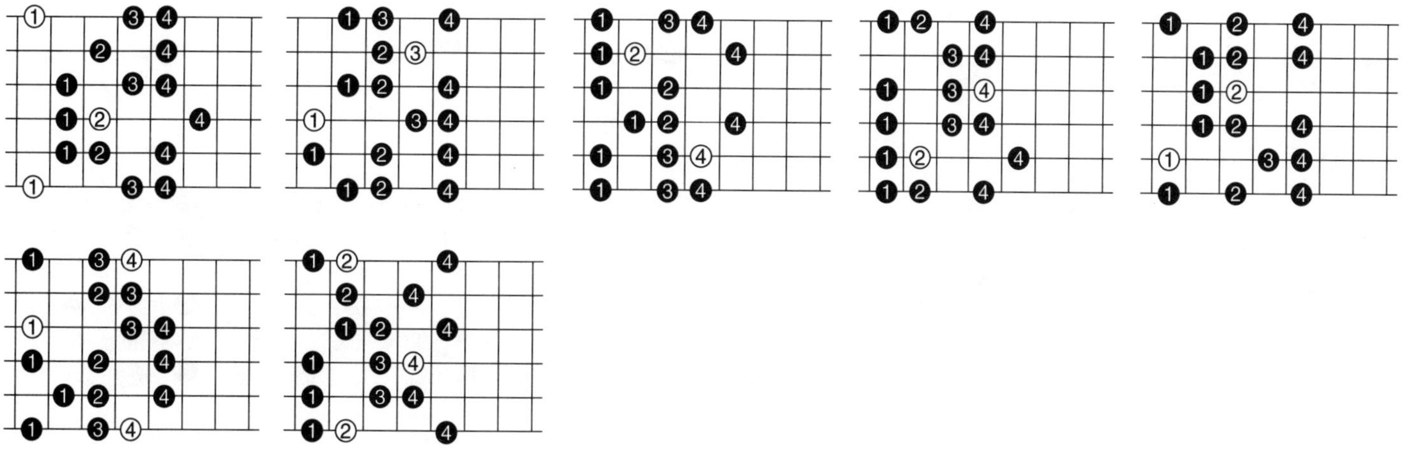

Three-Notes-Per-String Fingerings, Starting on all Scale Degrees

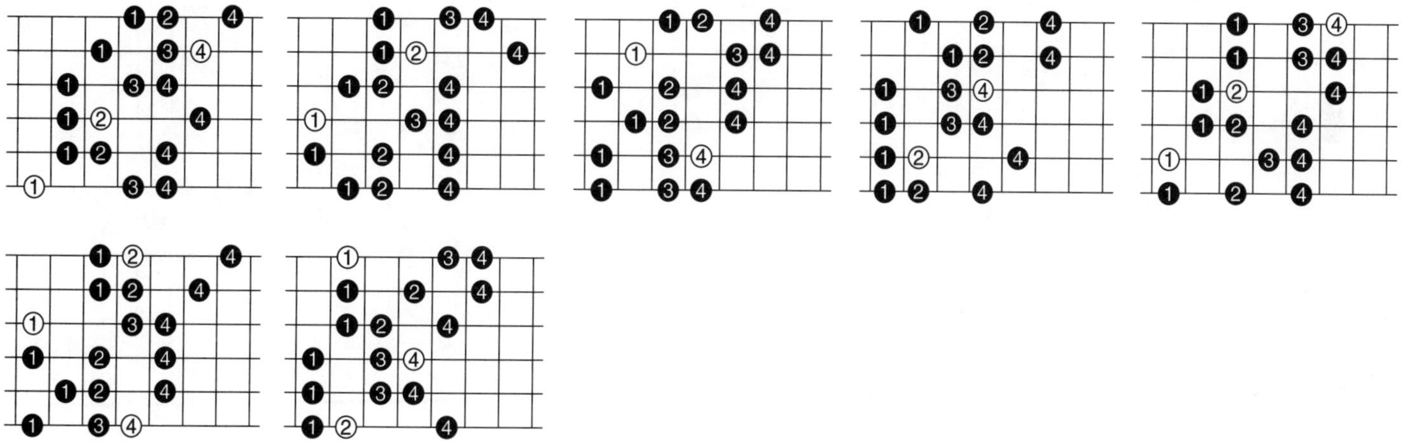

Four-Notes-Per-String Fingerings

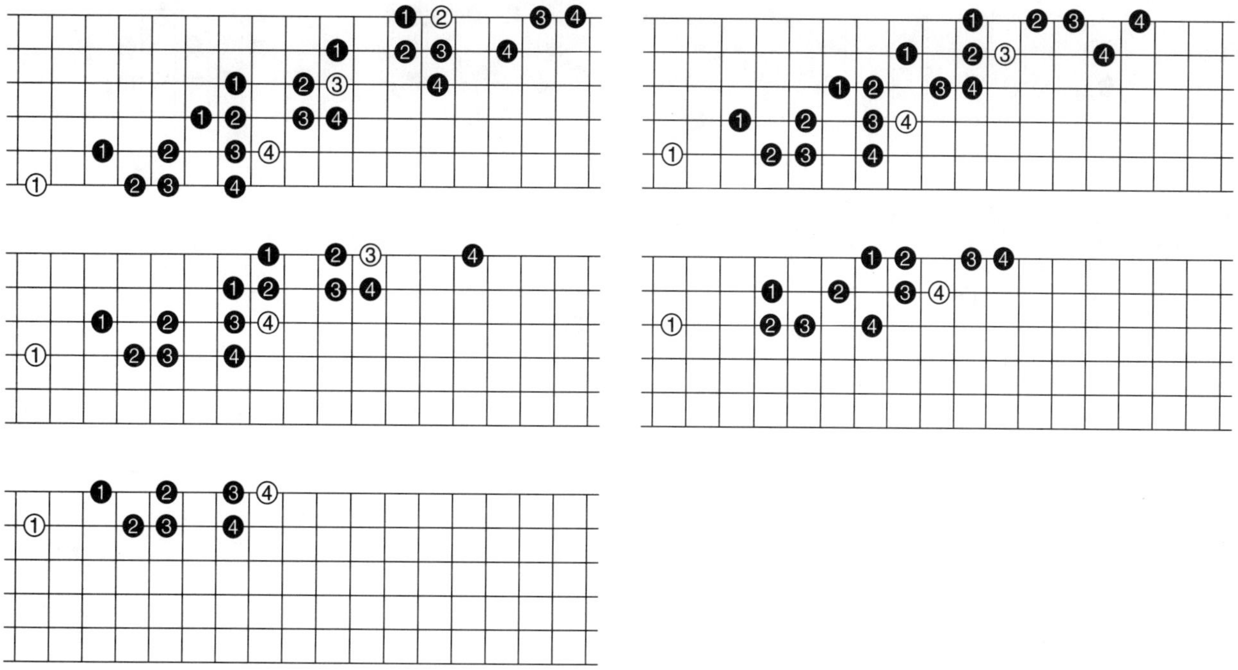

Super Locrian 𝄫7

Scale Tones

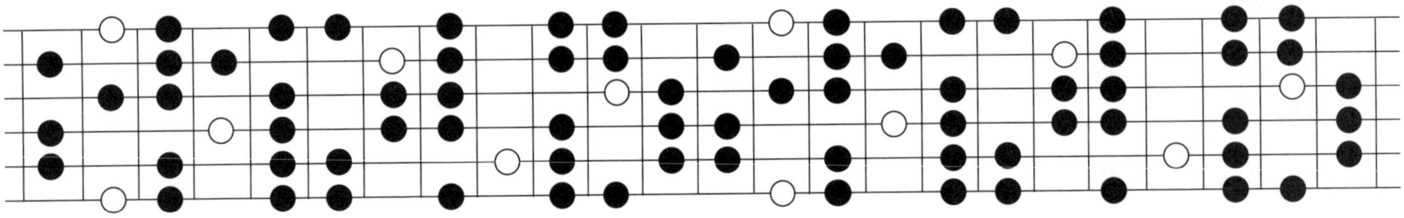

One-Octave Fingerings

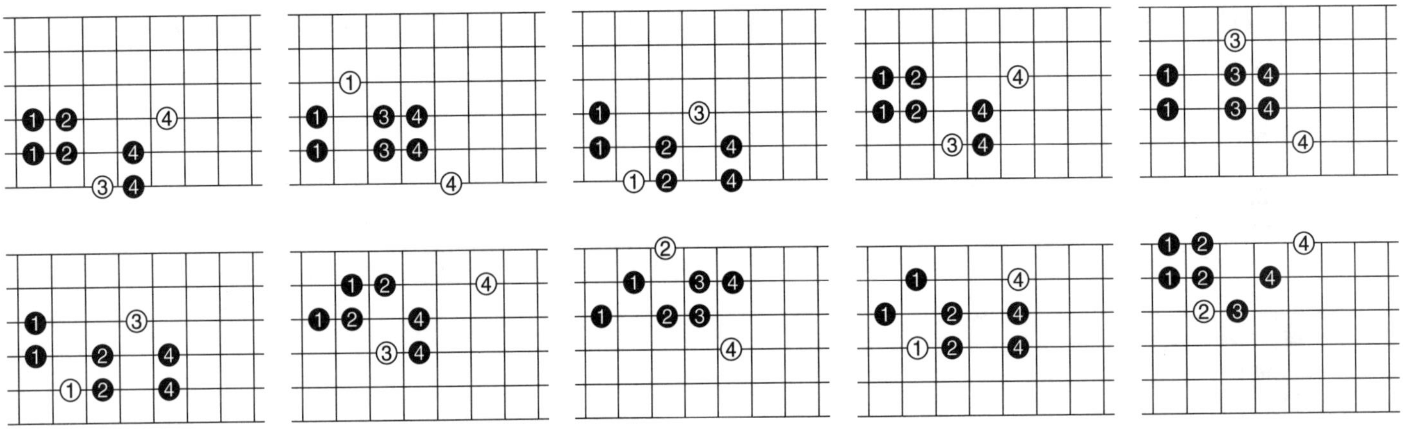

Two-Octave Fingerings

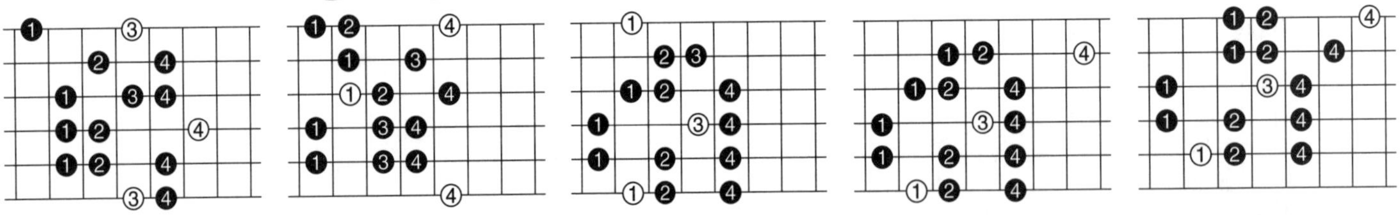

Three-Octave Fingerings

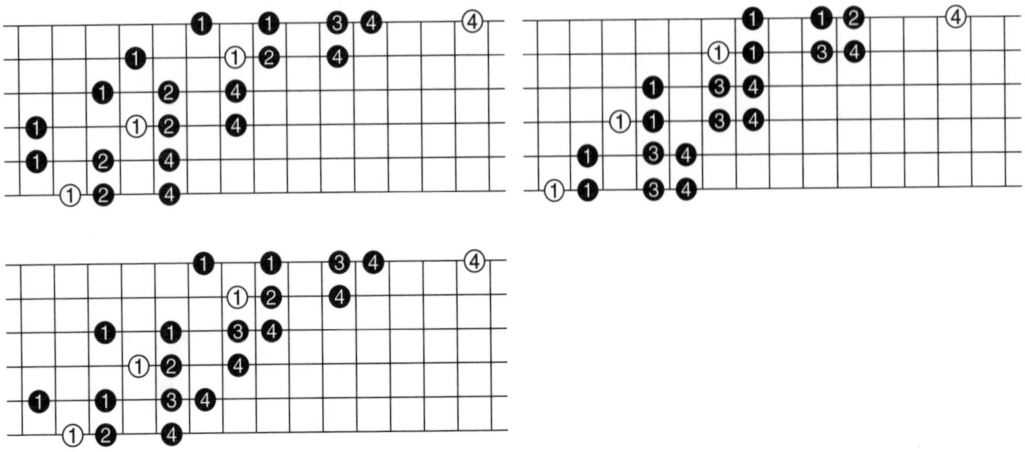

Position-Based Fingerings, Starting on all Scale Degrees

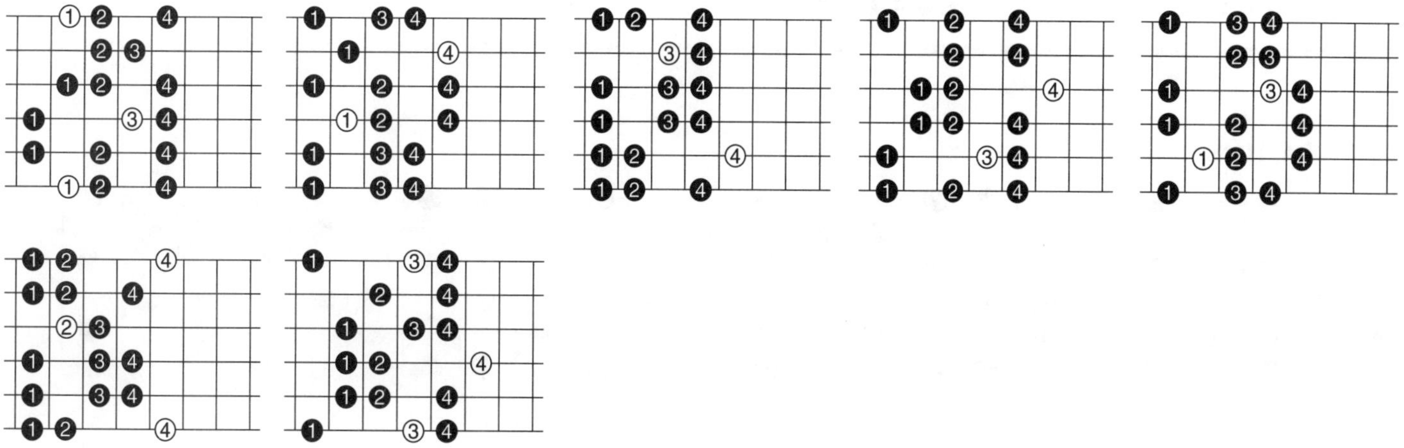

Three-Notes-Per-String Fingerings, Starting on all Scale Degrees

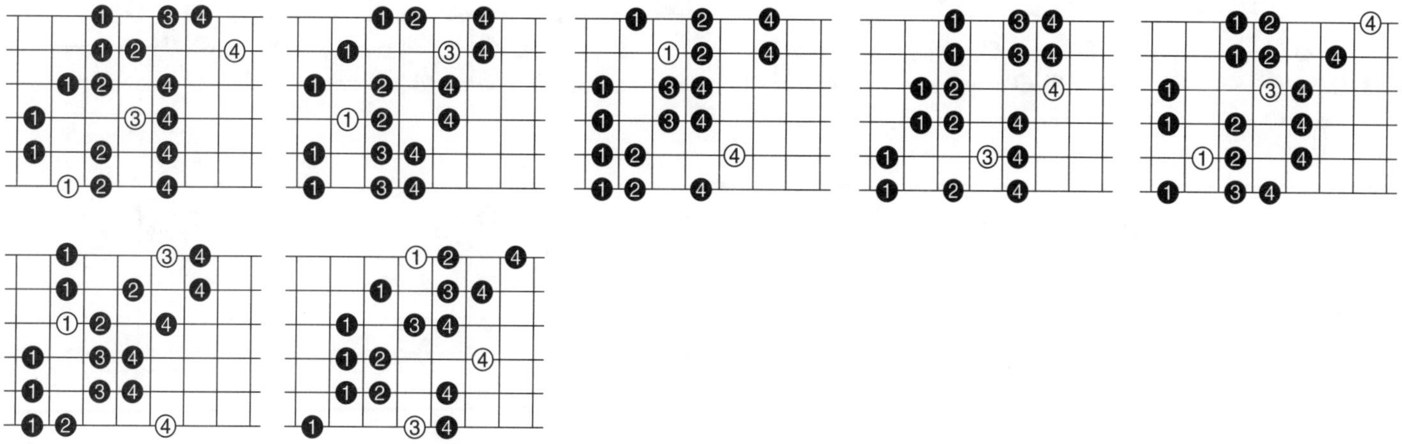

Four-Notes-Per-String Fingerings

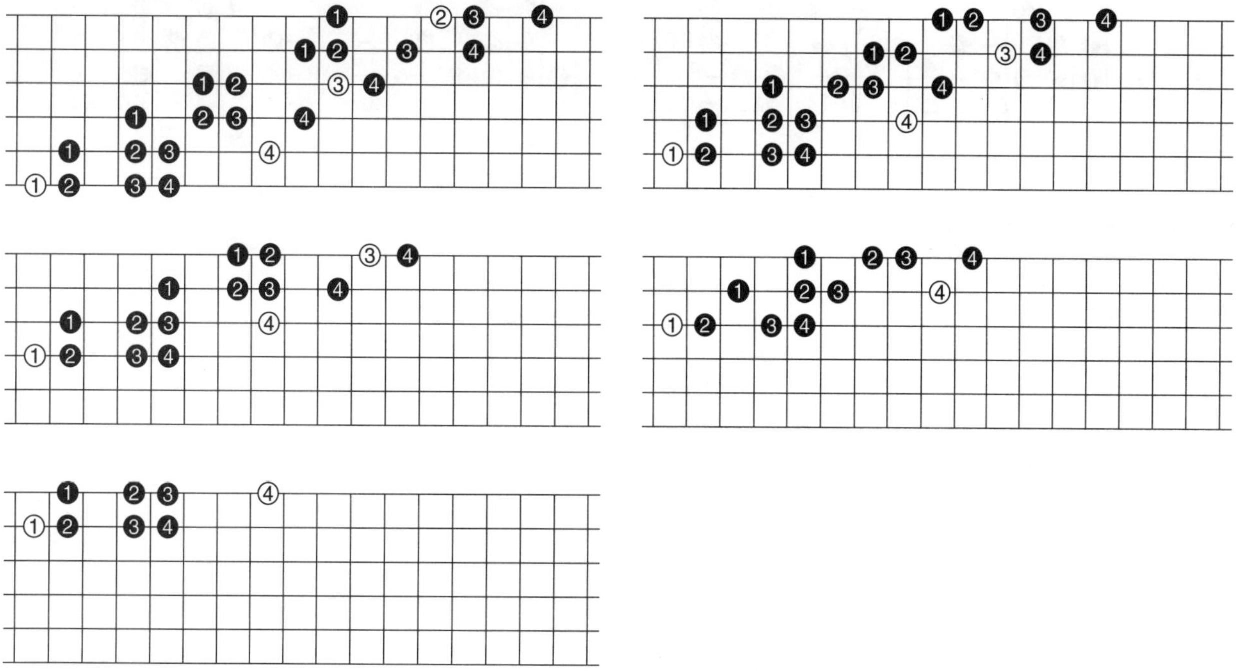

Harmonic Major

Scale Tones

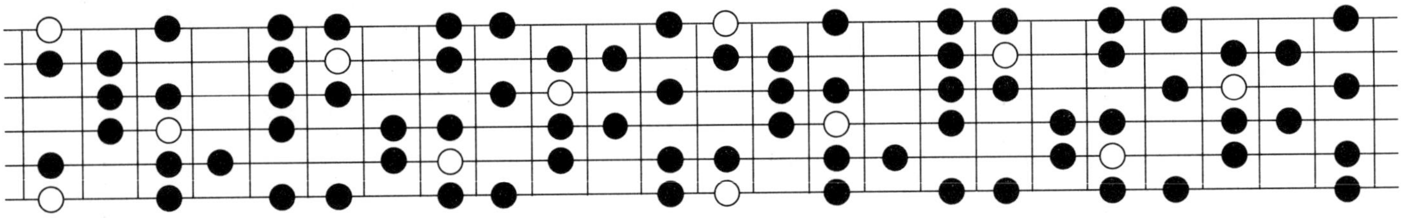

One-Octave Fingerings

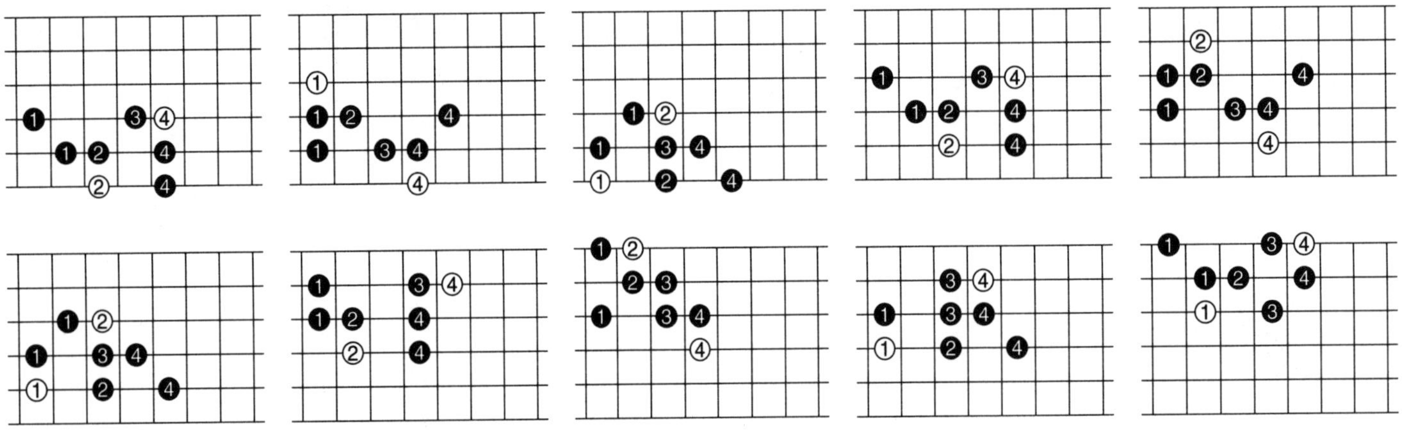

Two-Octave Fingerings

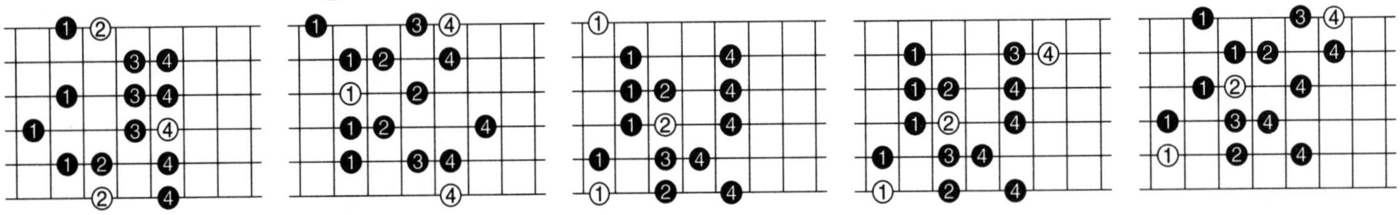

Three-Octave Fingerings

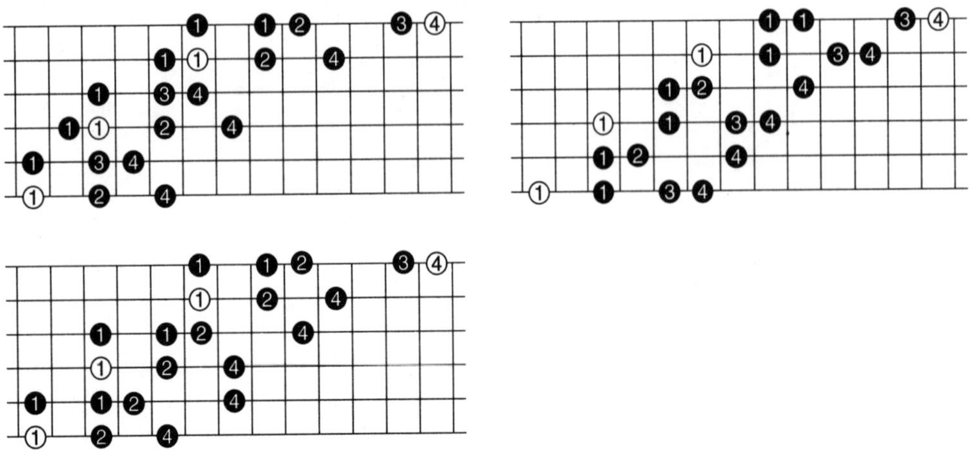

Position-Based Fingerings, Starting on all Scale Degrees

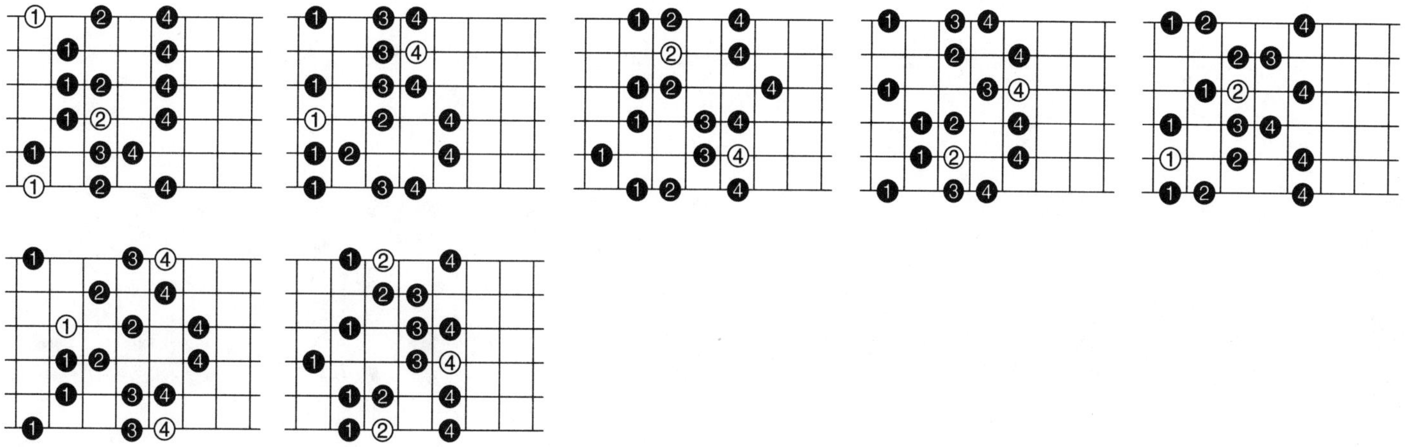

Three-Notes-Per-String Fingerings, Starting on all Scale Degrees

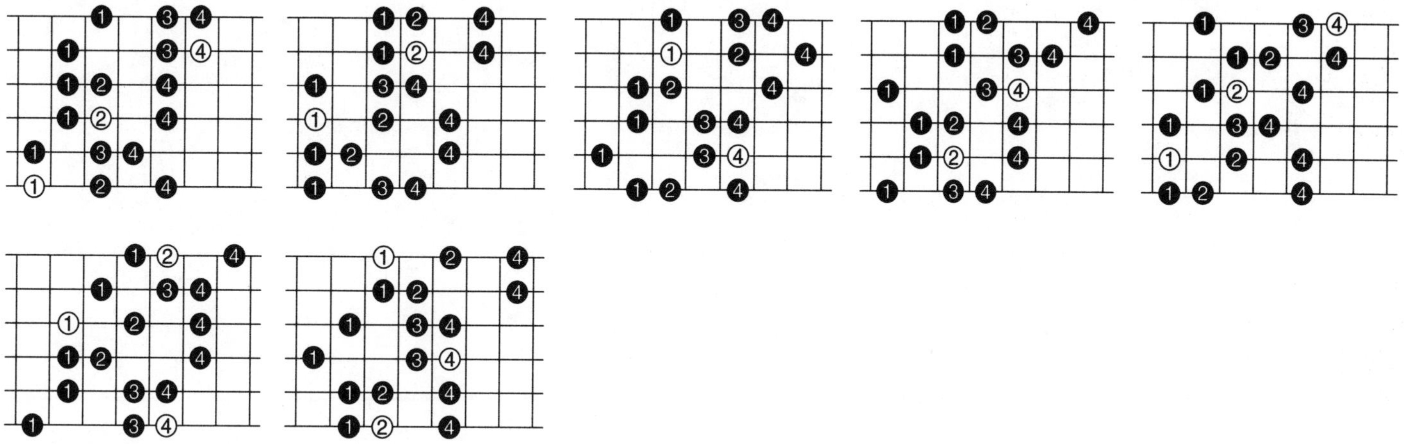

Four-Notes-Per-String Fingerings

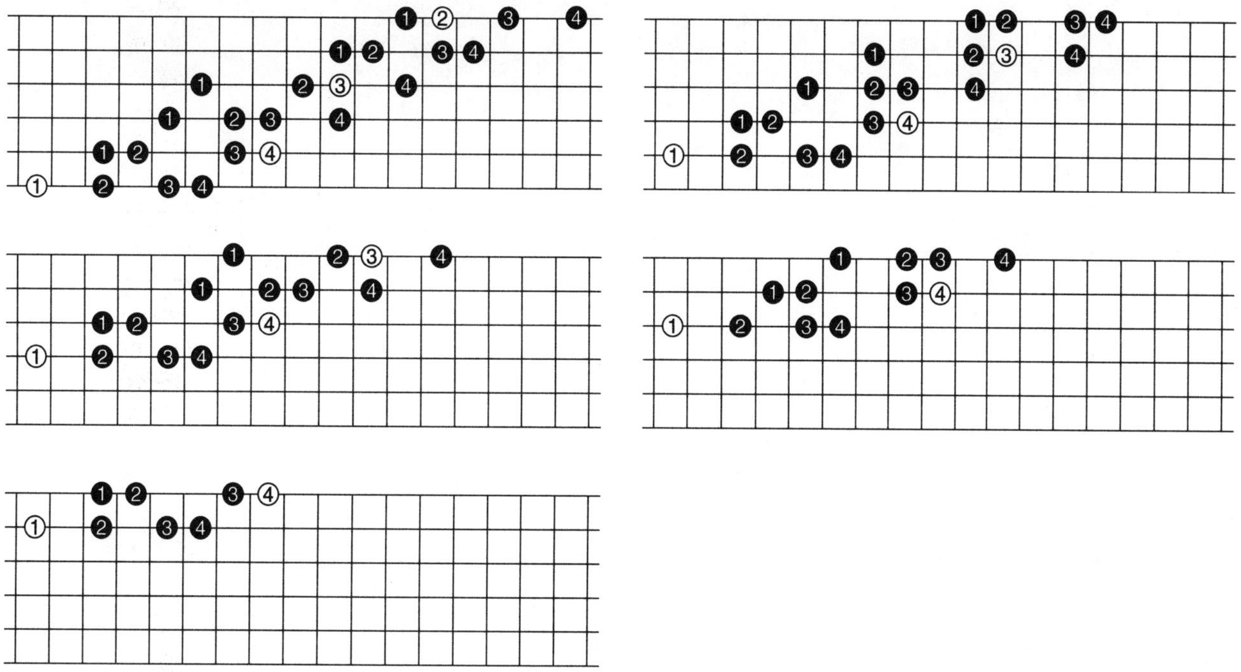

Dorian ♭5

Scale Tones

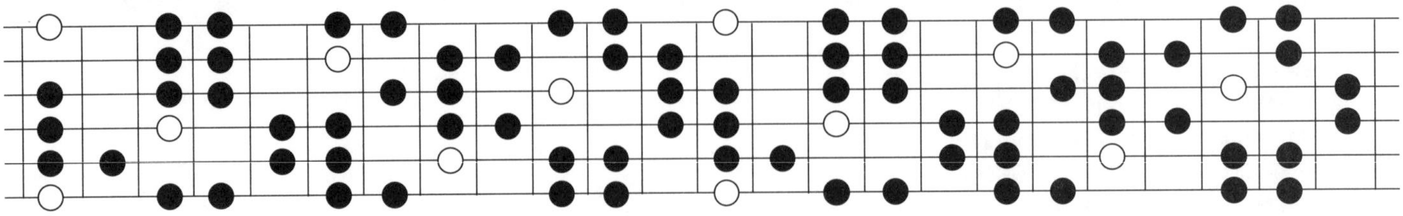

One-Octave Fingerings

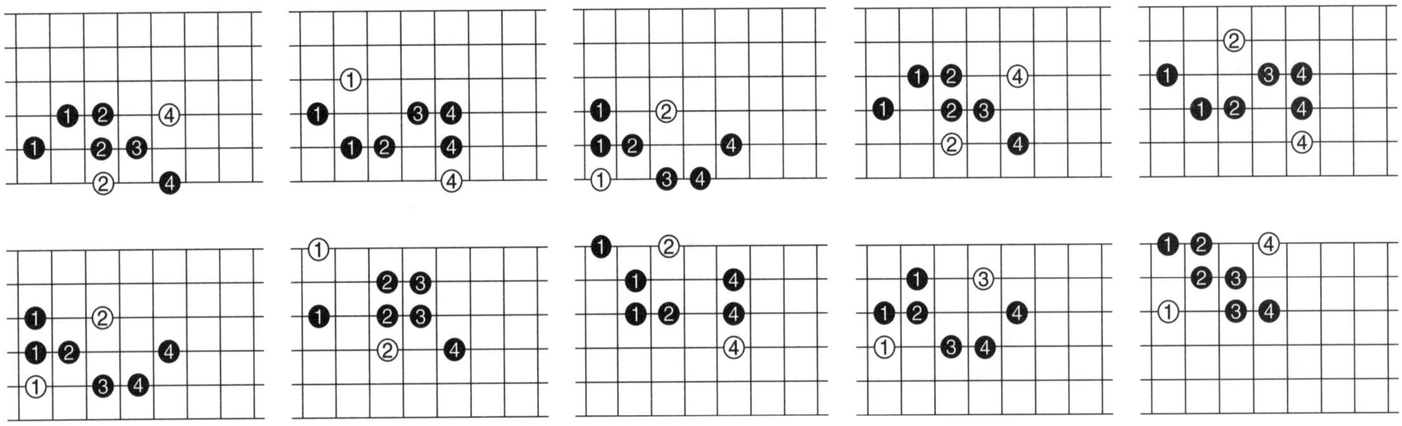

Two-Octave Fingerings

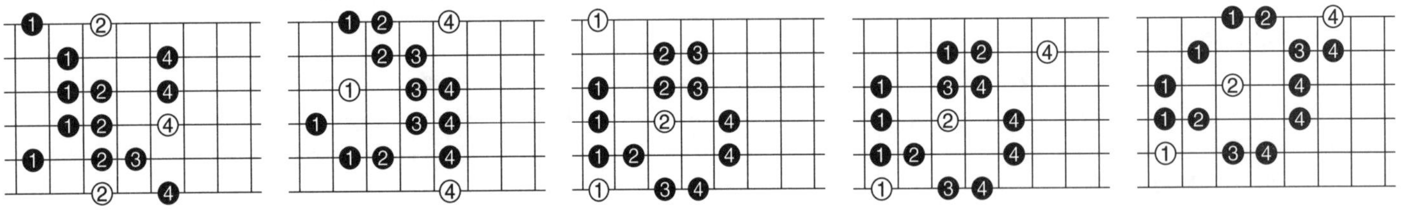

Three-Octave Fingerings

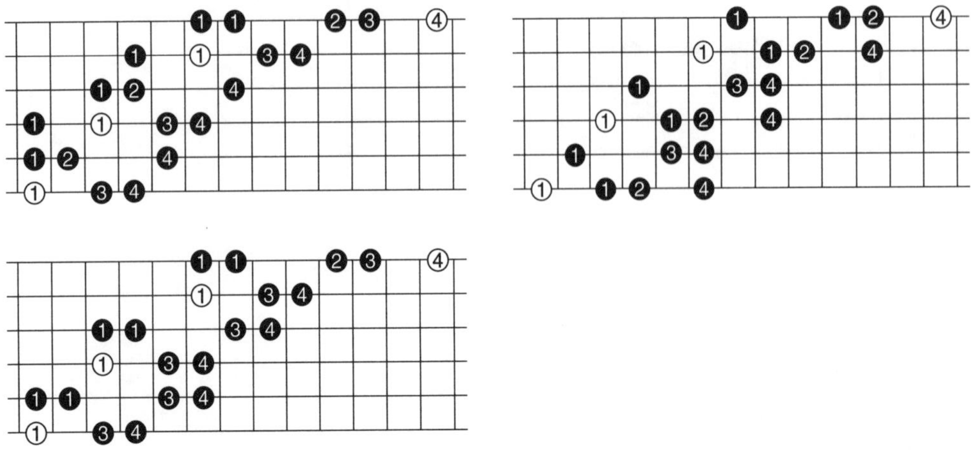

Position-Based Fingerings, Starting on all Scale Degrees

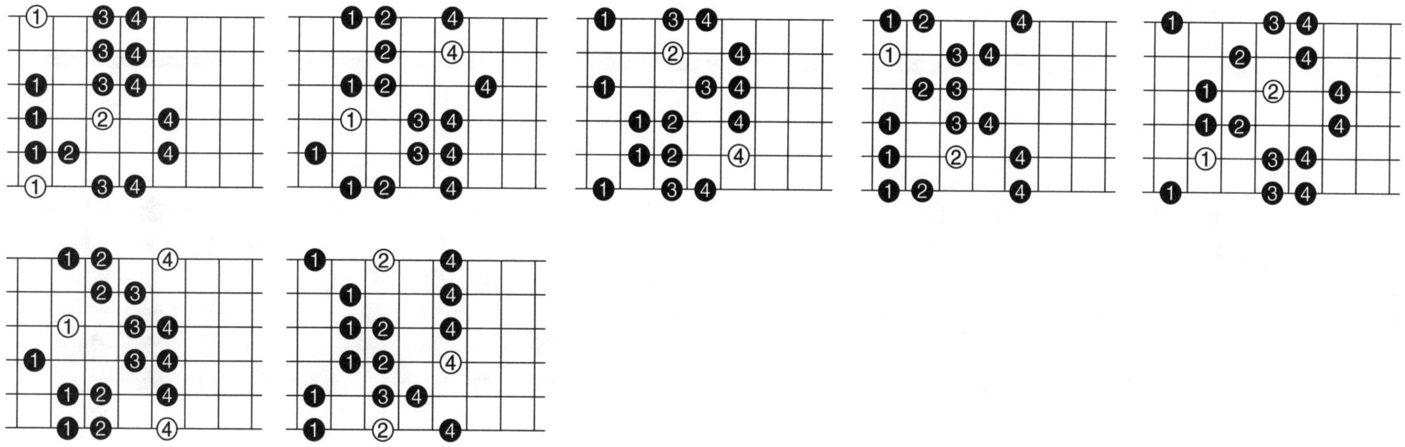

Three-Notes-Per-String Fingerings, Starting on all Scale Degrees

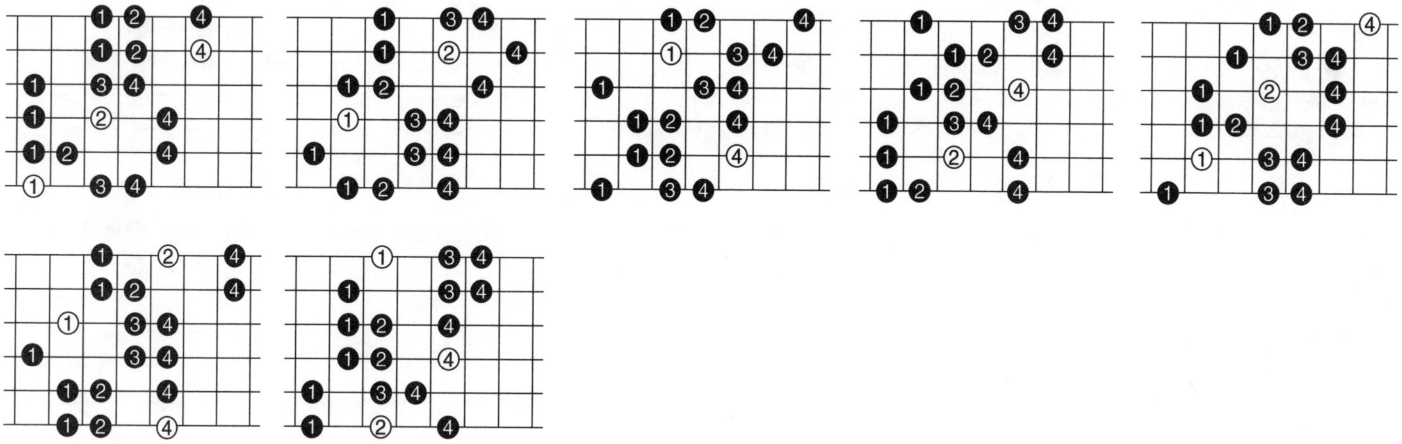

Four-Notes-Per-String Fingerings

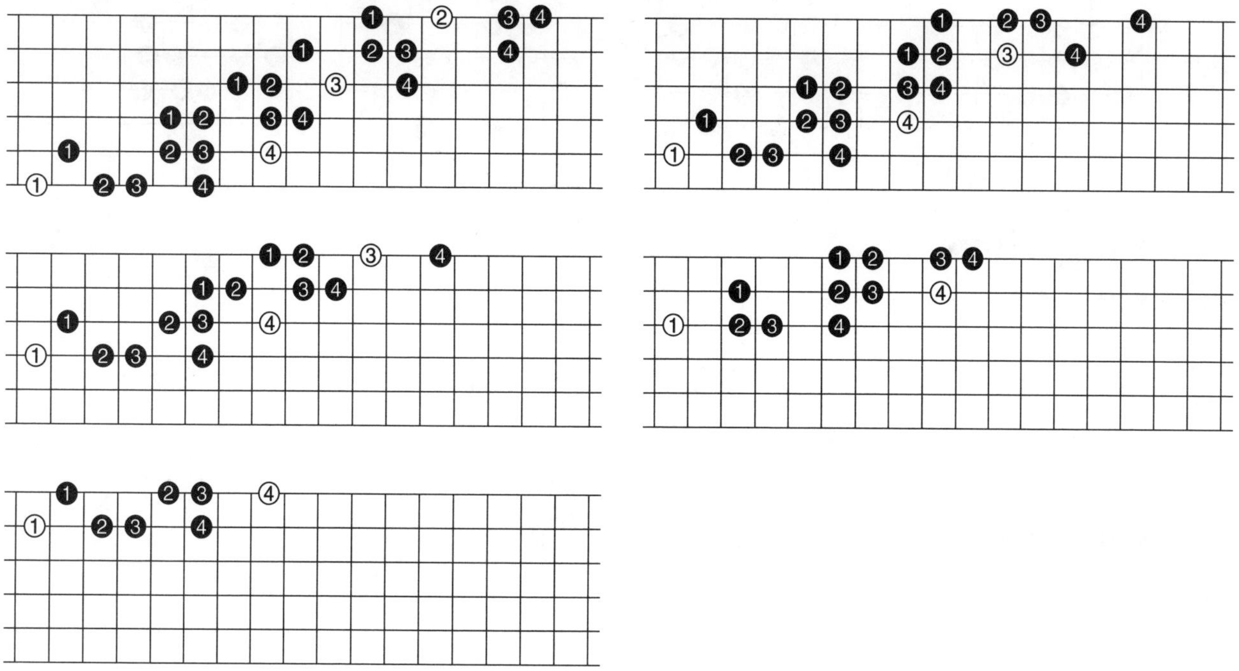

Phrygian ♭4

Scale Tones

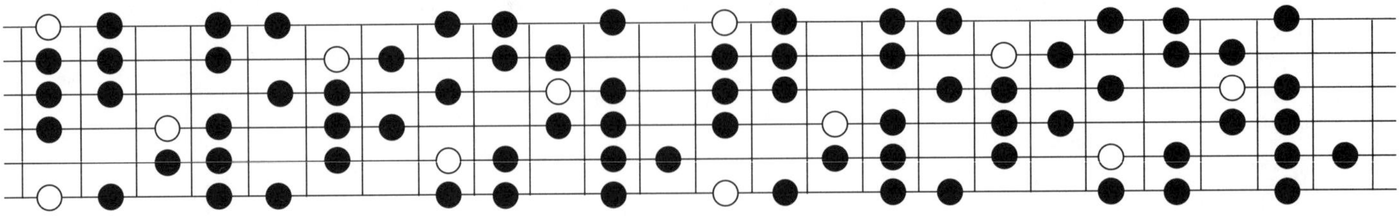

One-Octave Fingerings

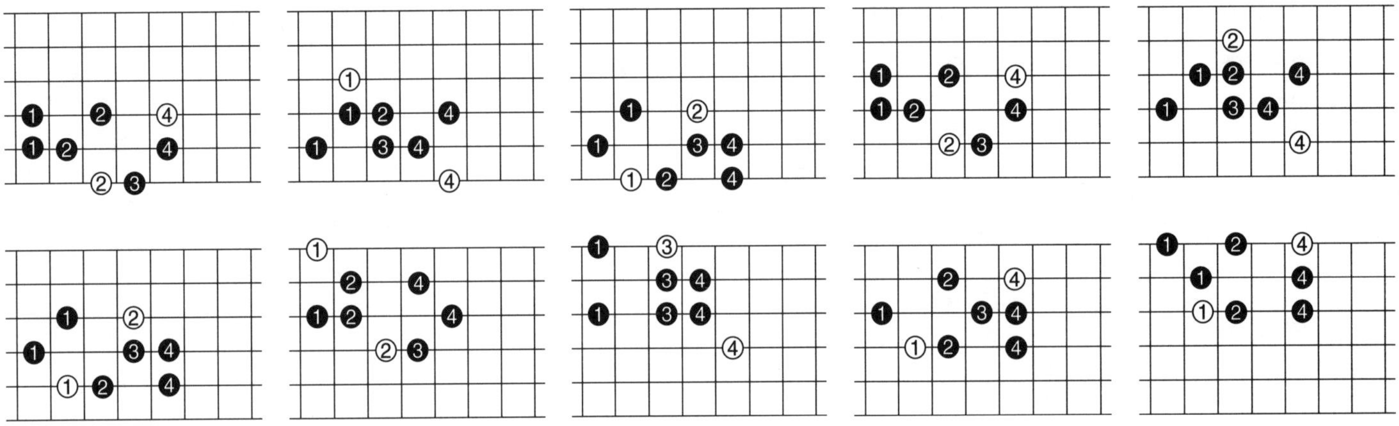

Two-Octave Fingerings

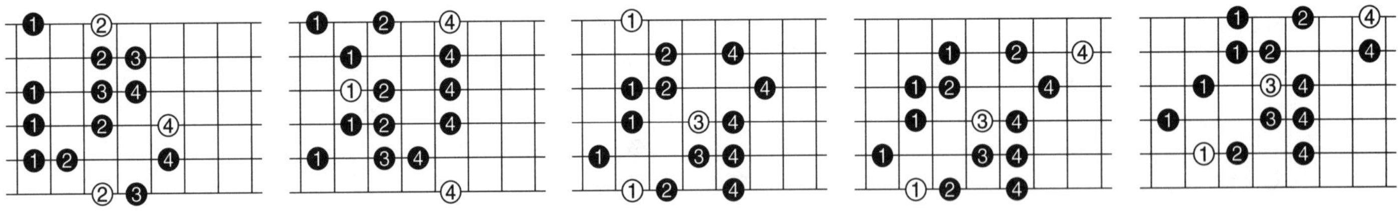

Three-Octave Fingerings

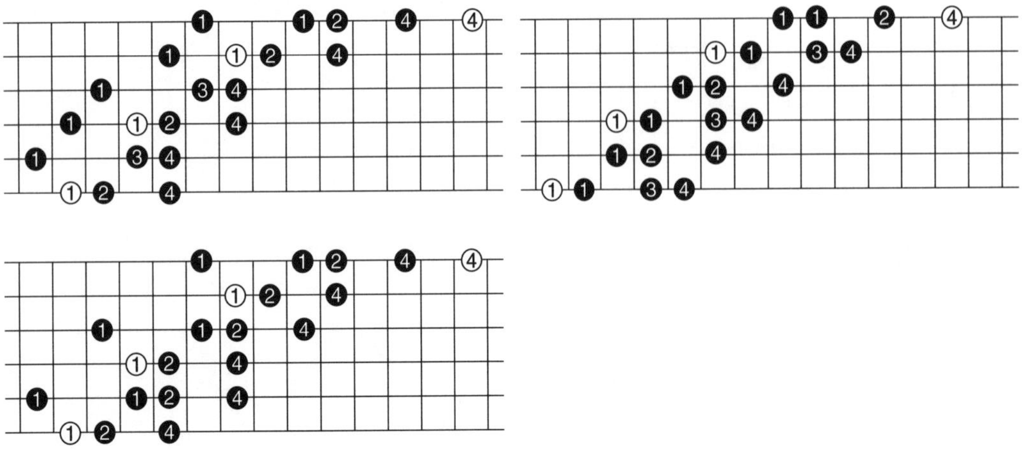

Position-Based Fingerings, Starting on all Scale Degrees

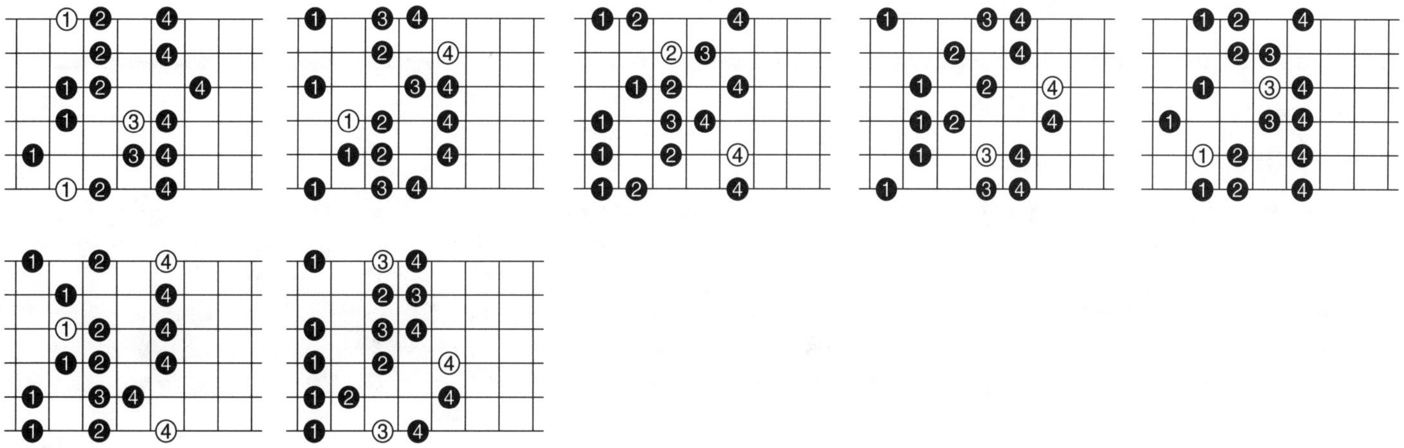

Three-Notes-Per-String Fingerings, Starting on all Scale Degrees

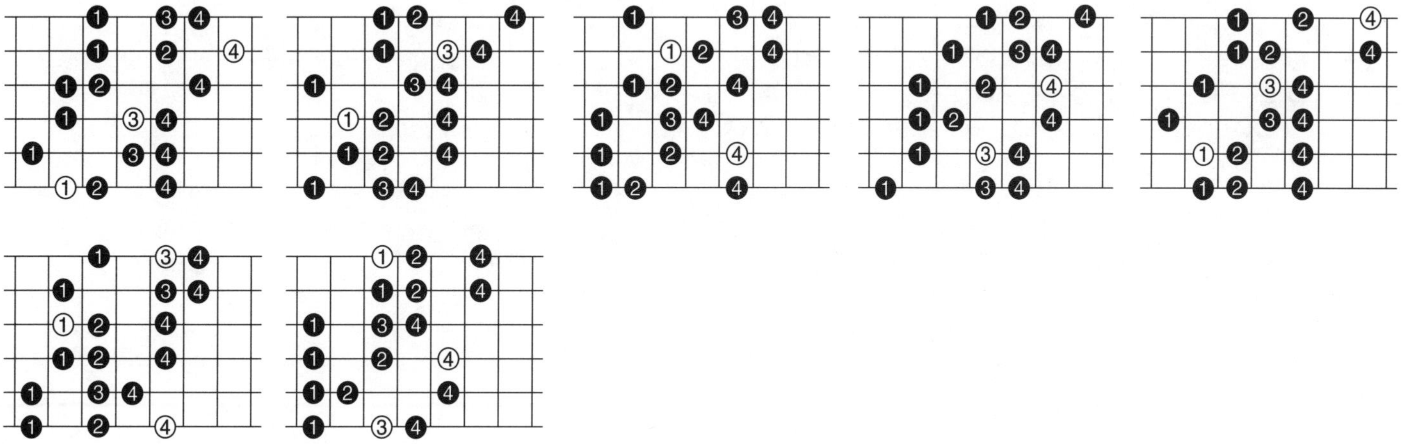

Four-Notes-Per-String Fingerings

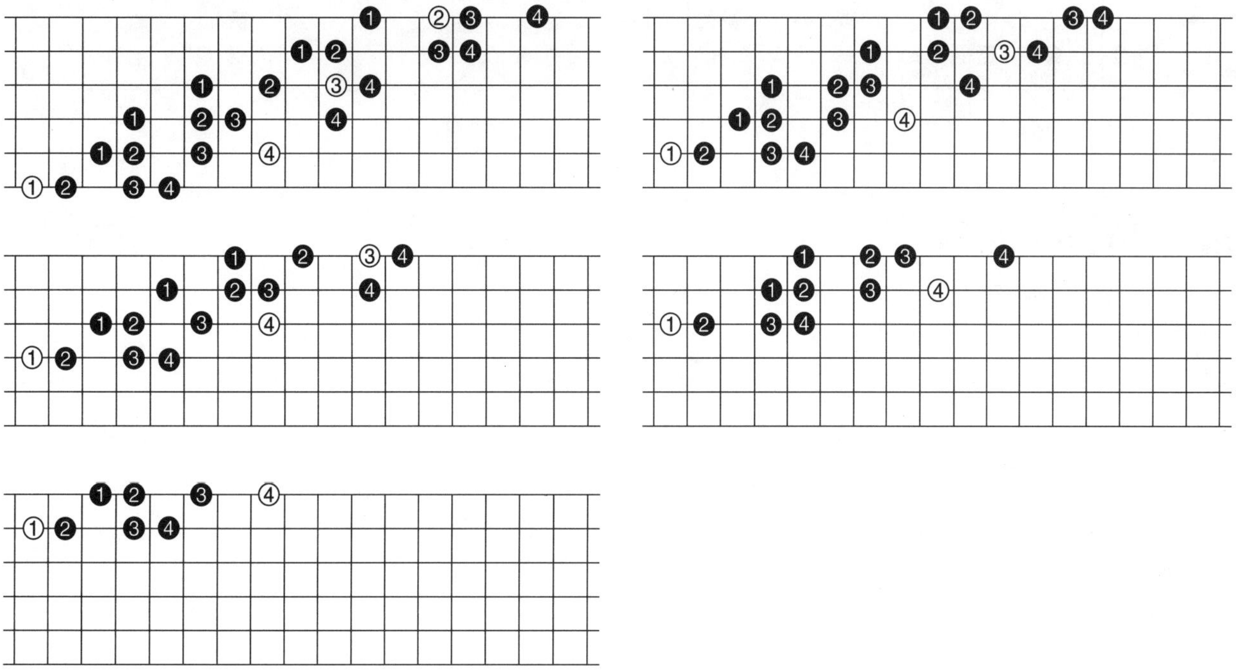

Lydian ♭3

Scale Tones

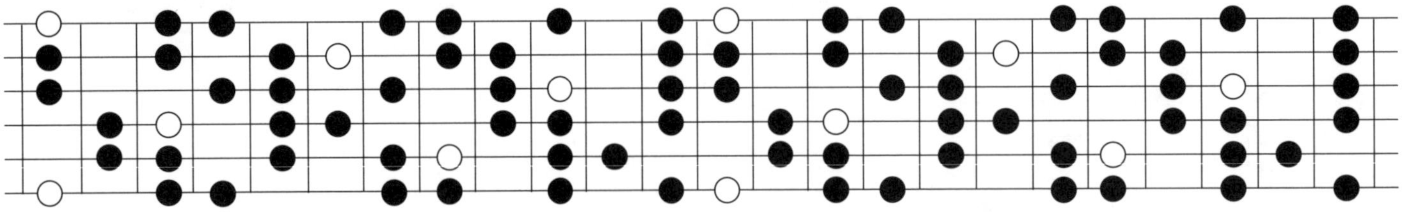

One-Octave Fingerings

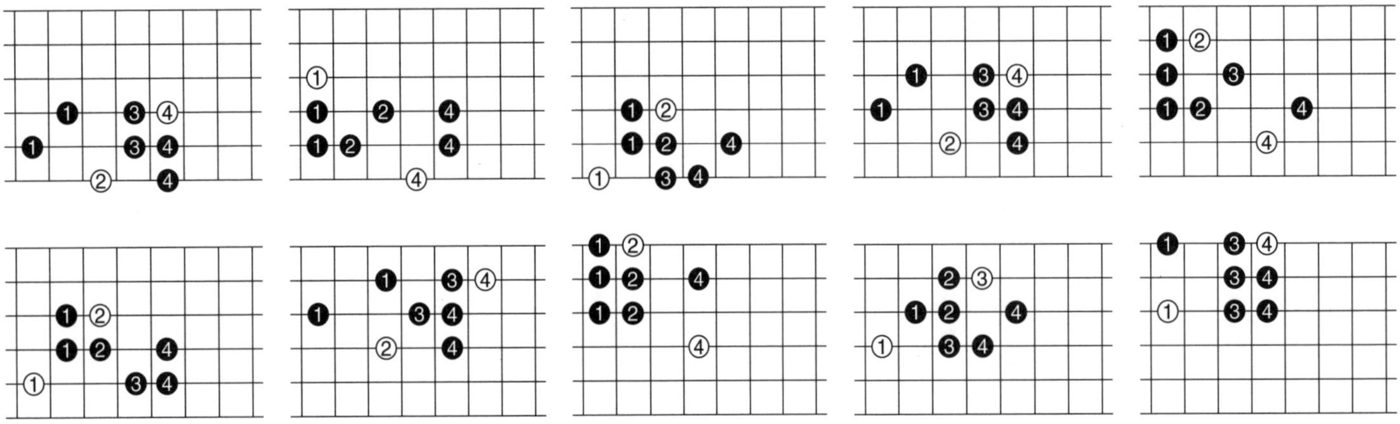

Two-Octave Fingerings

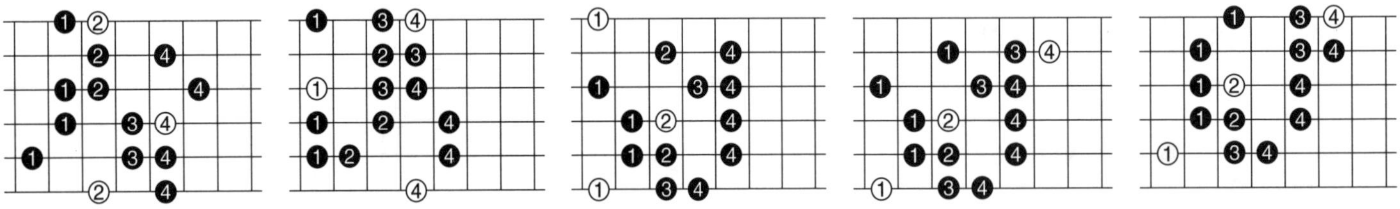

Three-Octave Fingerings

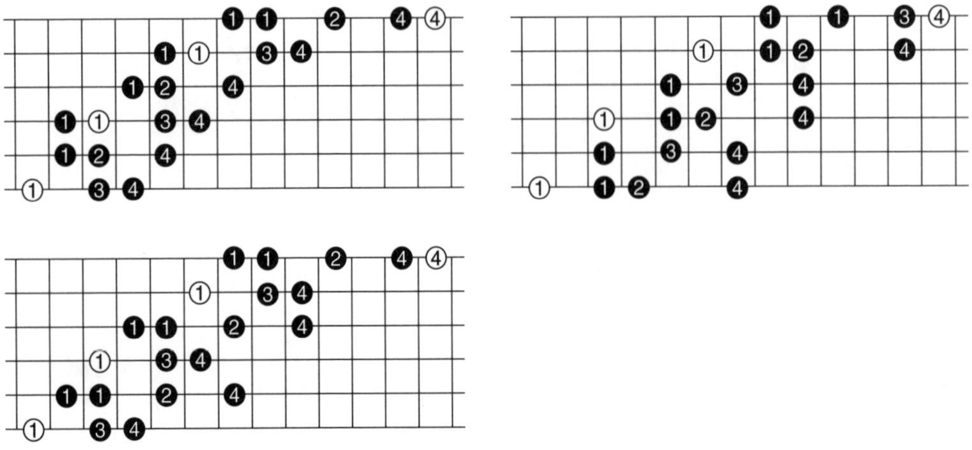

Position-Based Fingerings, Starting on all Scale Degrees

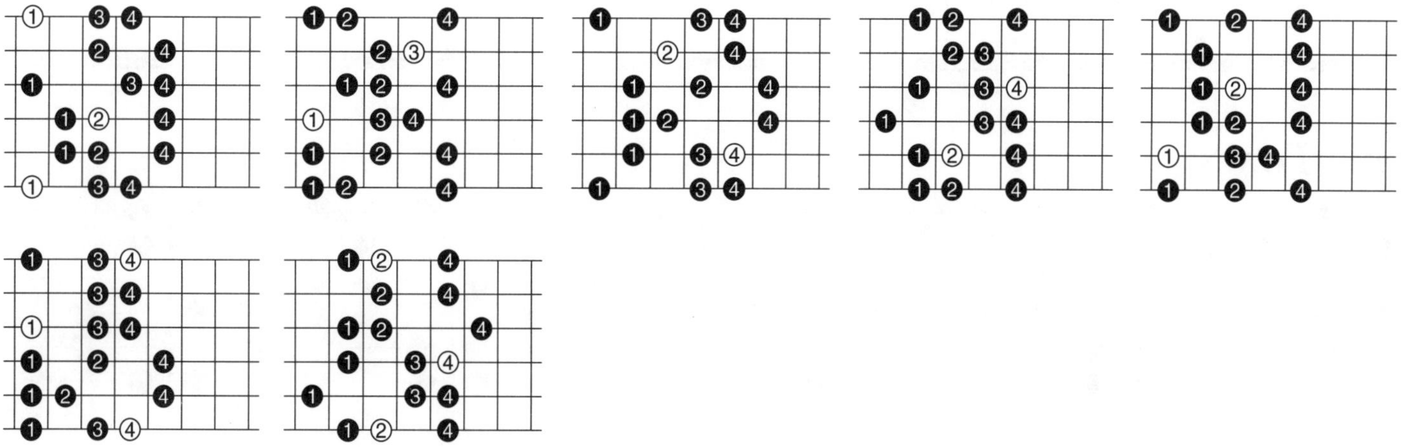

Three-Notes-Per-String Fingerings, Starting on all Scale Degrees

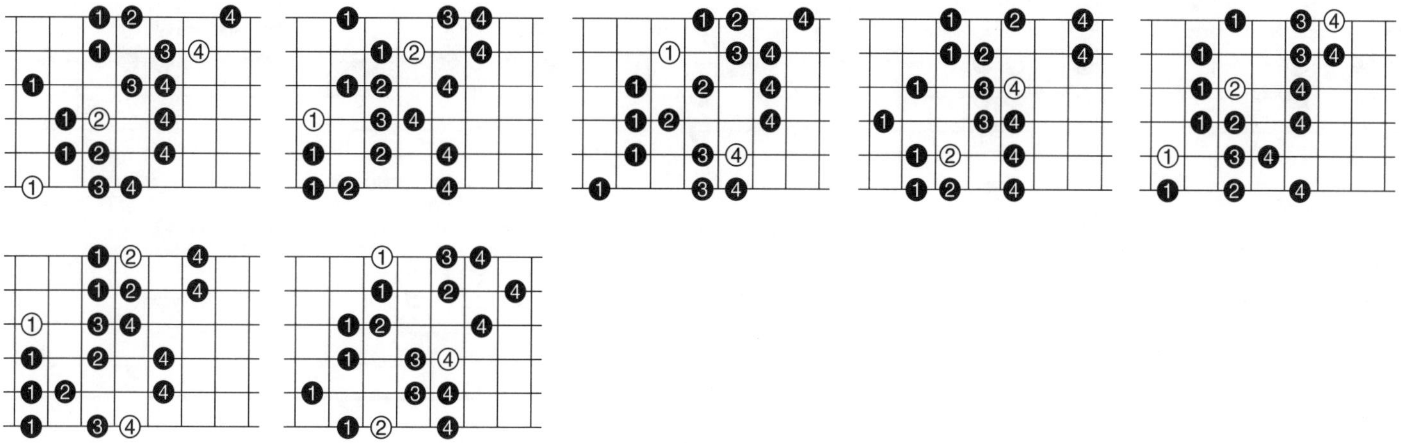

Four-Notes-Per-String Fingerings

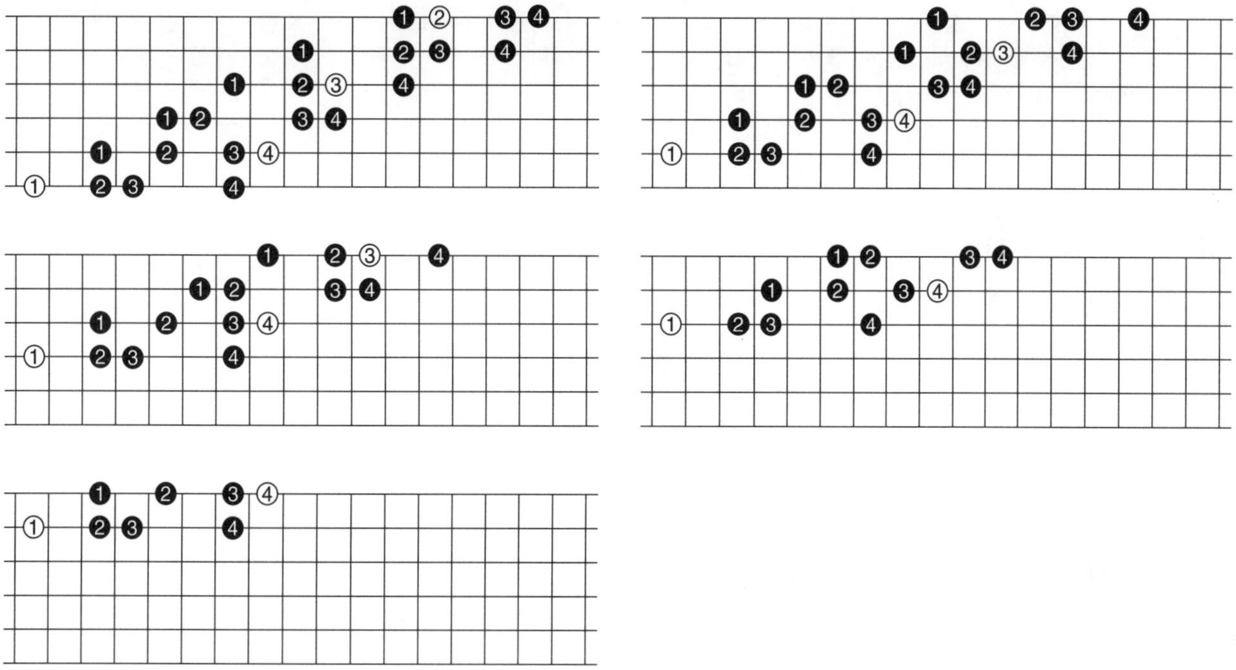

Mixolydian ♭2

Scale Tones

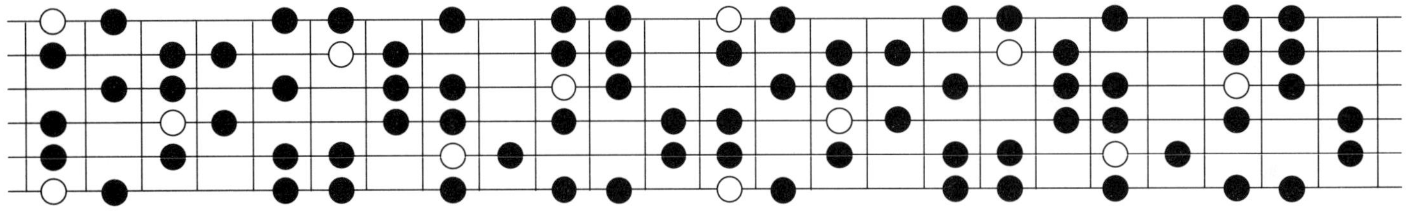

One-Octave Fingerings

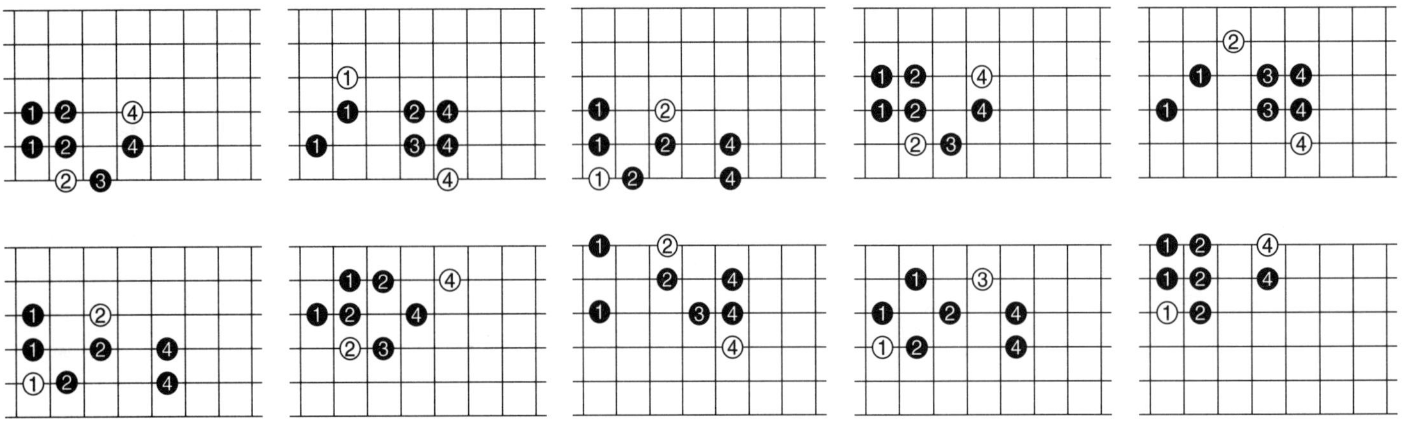

Two-Octave Fingerings

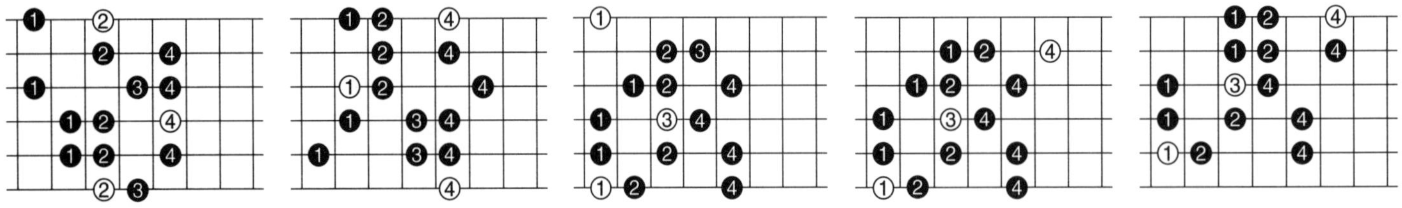

Three-Octave Fingerings

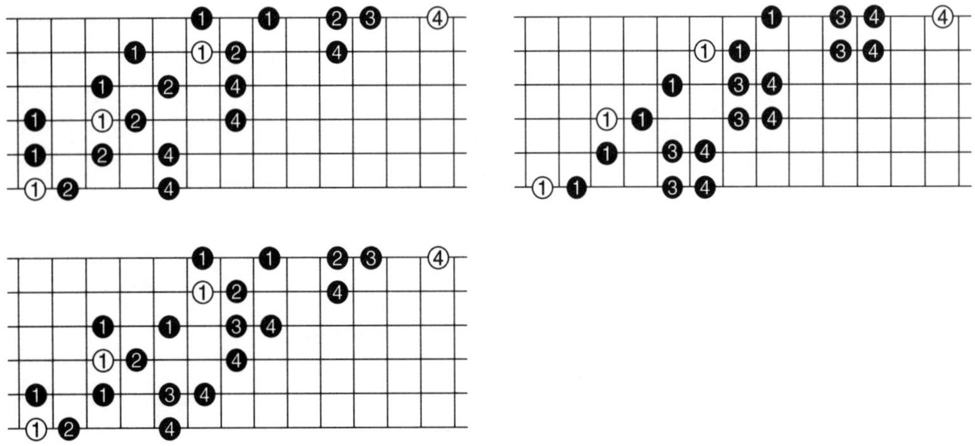

Position-Based Fingerings, Starting on all Scale Degrees

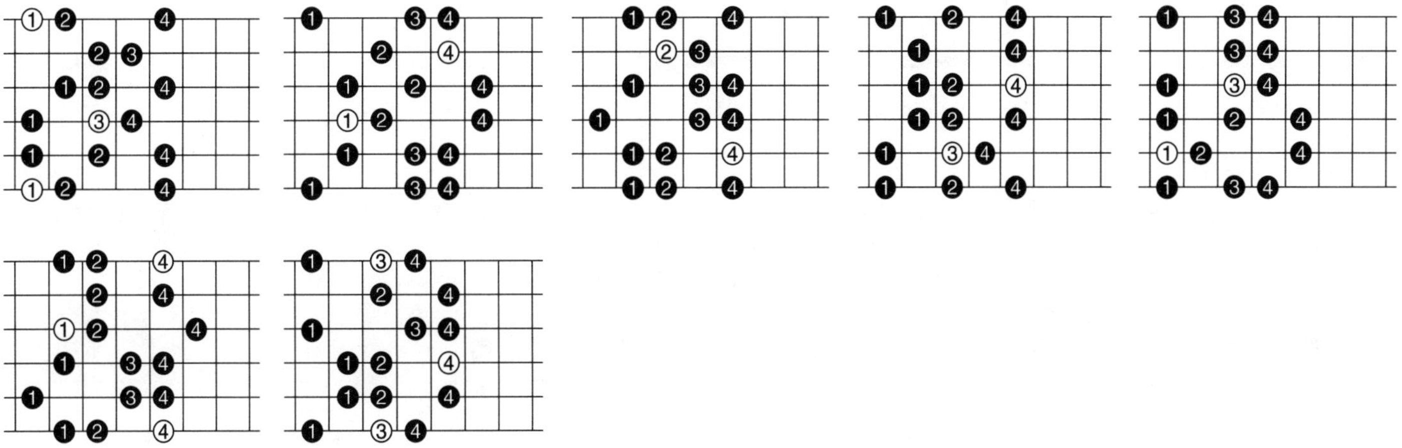

Three-Notes-Per-String Fingerings, Starting on all Scale Degrees

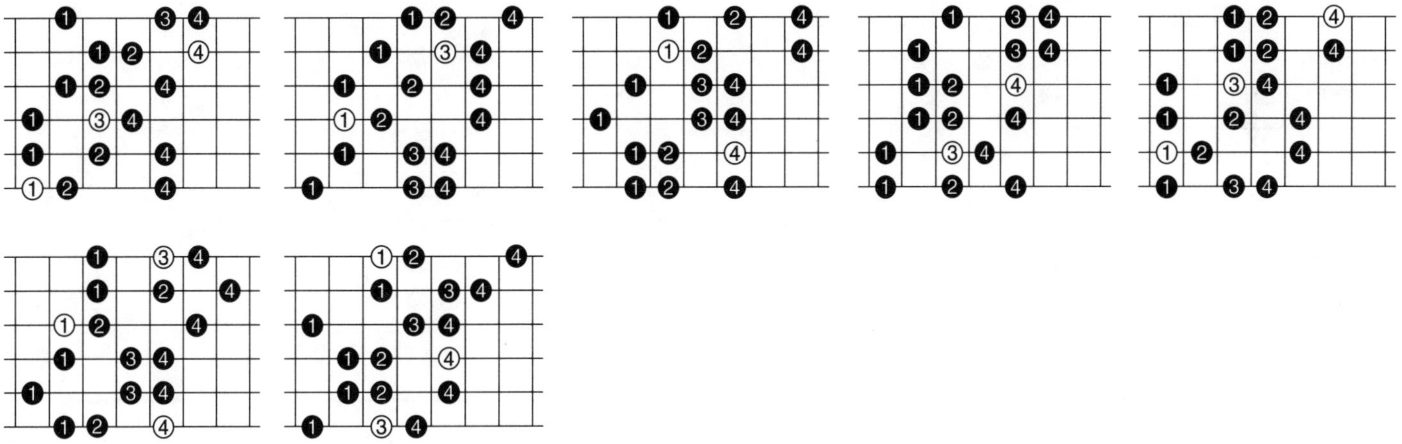

Four-Notes-Per-String Fingerings

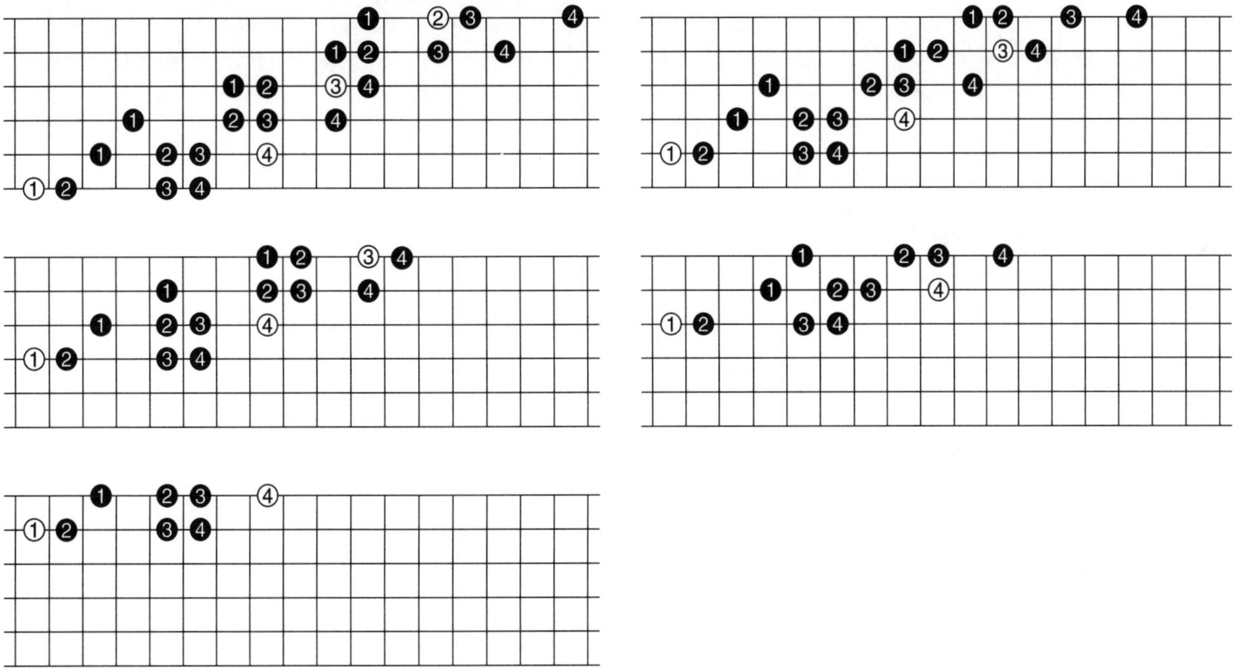

Lydian Augmented ♯2

Scale Tones

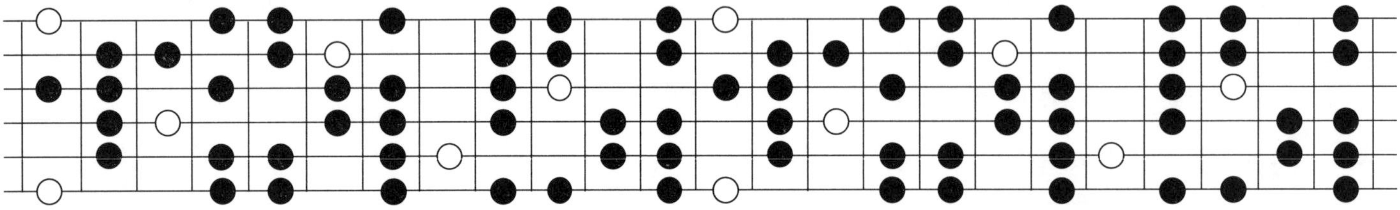

One-Octave Fingerings

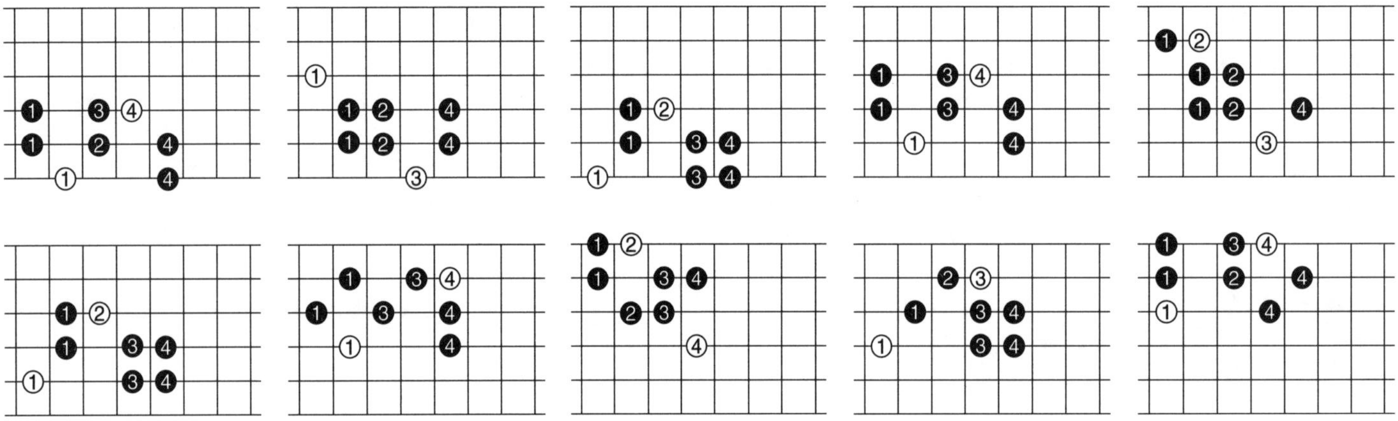

Two-Octave Fingerings

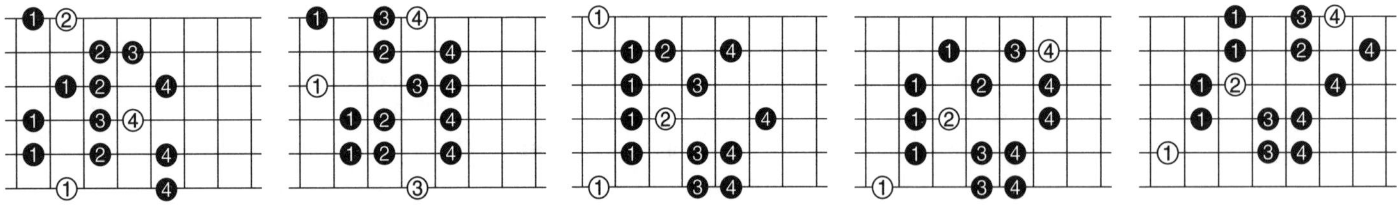

Three-Octave Fingerings

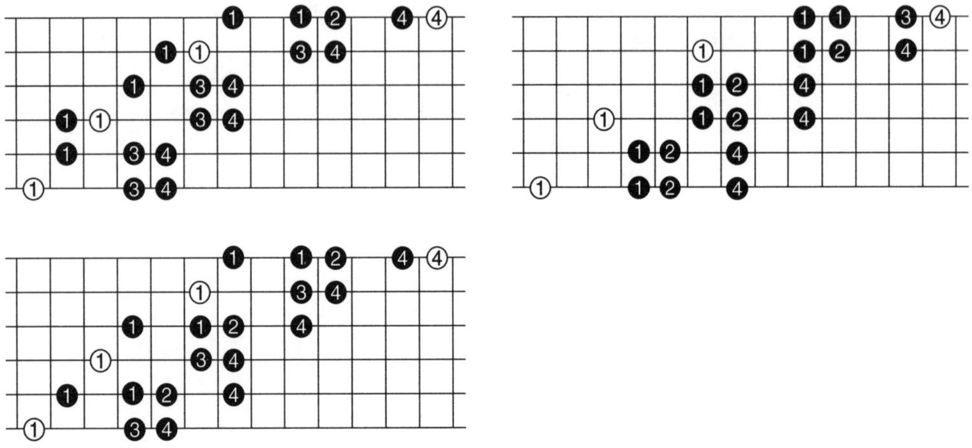

Position-Based Fingerings, Starting on all Scale Degrees

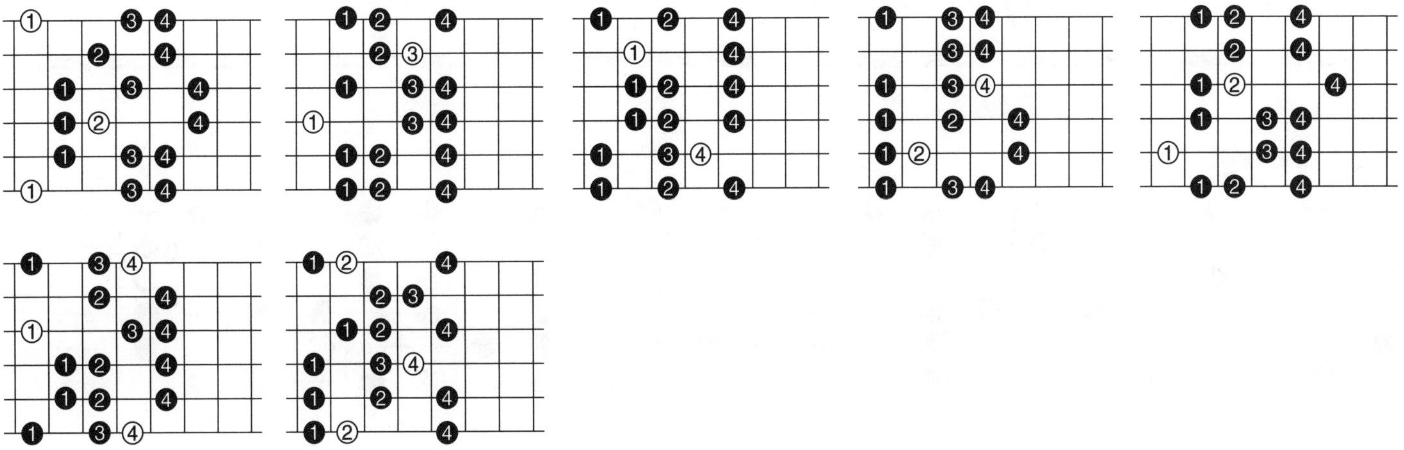

Three-Notes-Per-String Fingerings, Starting on all Scale Degrees

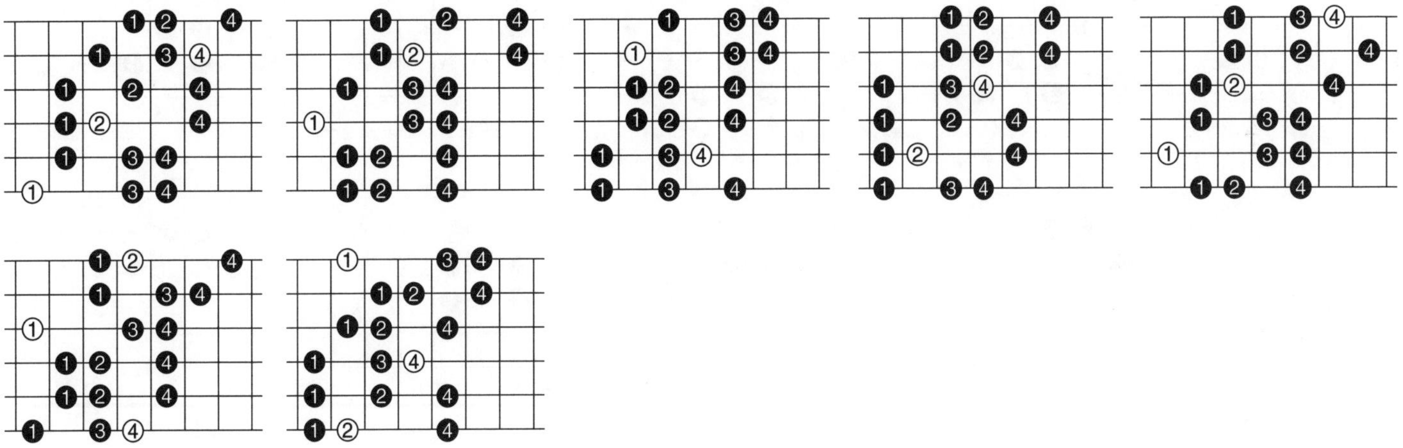

Four-Notes-Per-String Fingerings

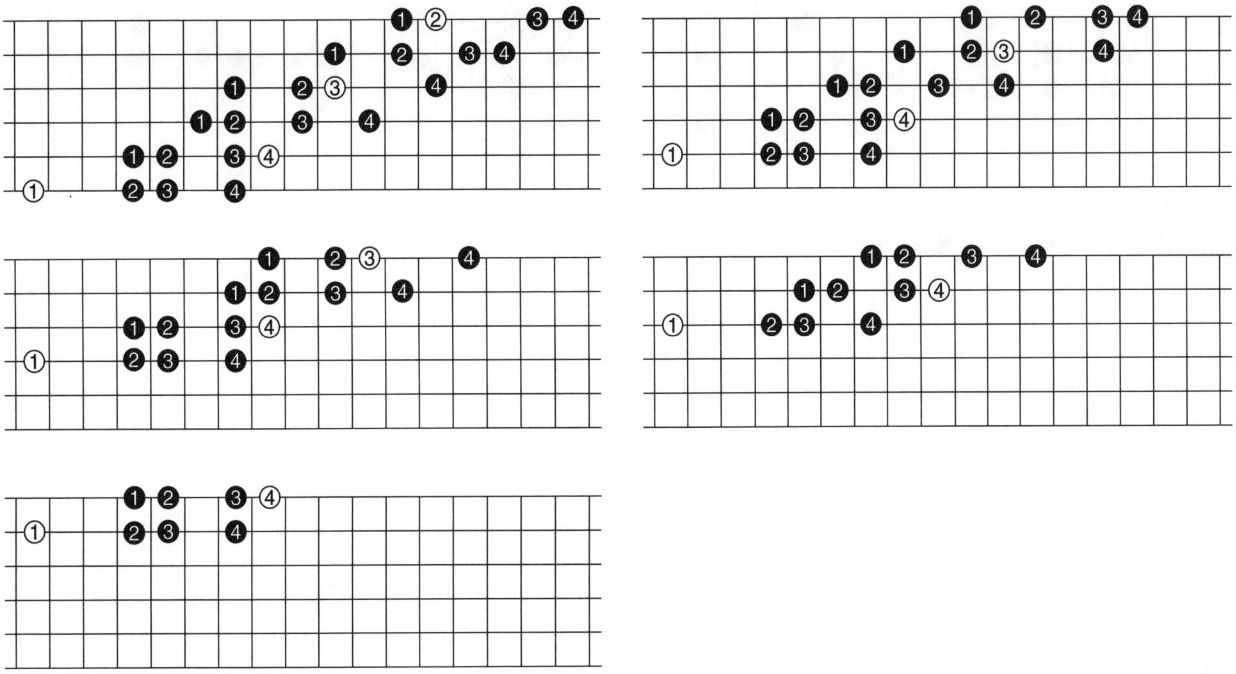

Locrian 𝄫7

Scale Tones

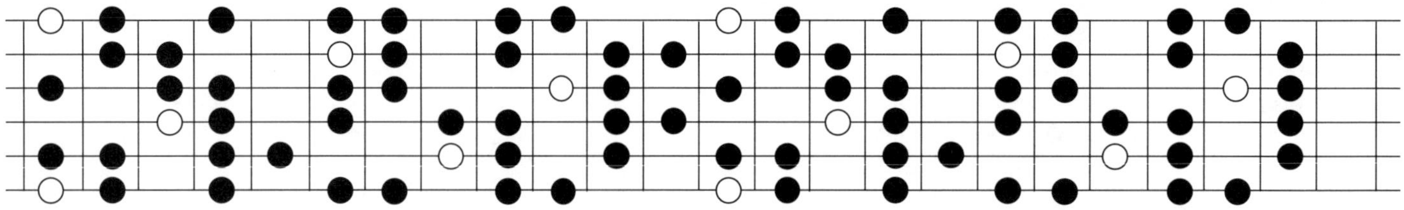

One-Octave Fingerings

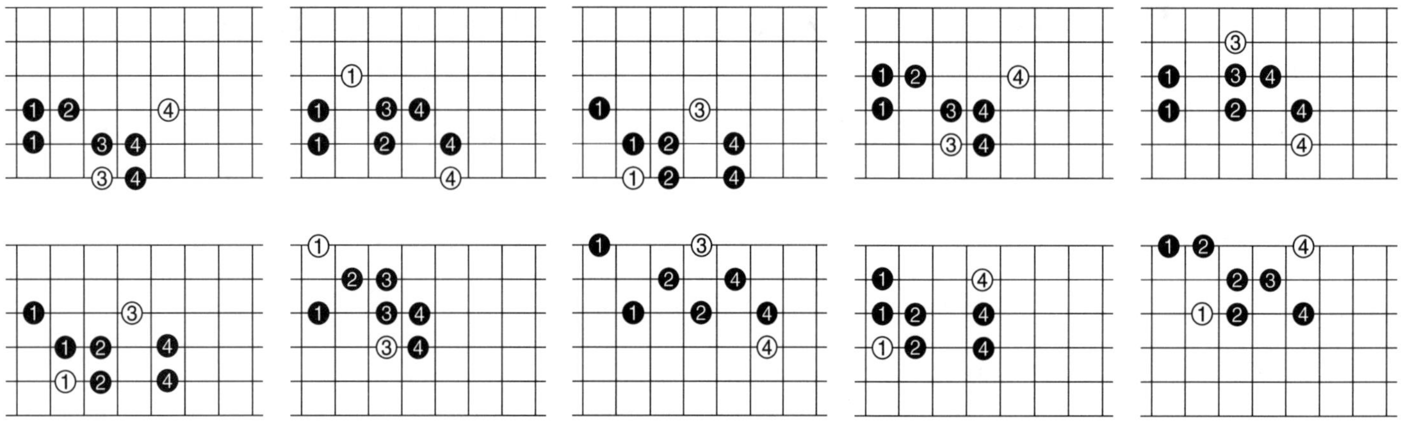

Two-Octave Fingerings

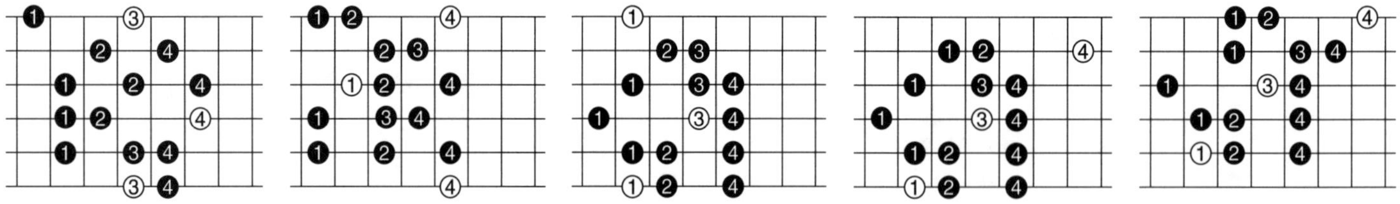

Three-Octave Fingerings

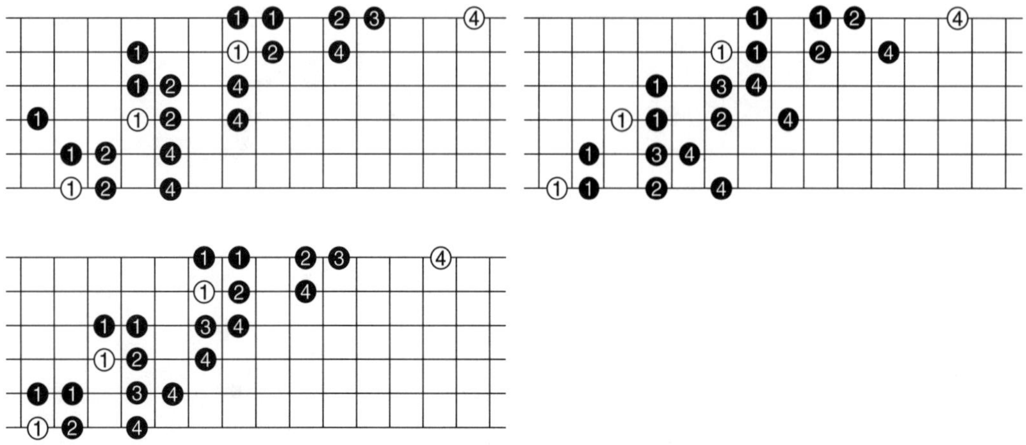

Position-Based Fingerings, Starting on all Scale Degrees

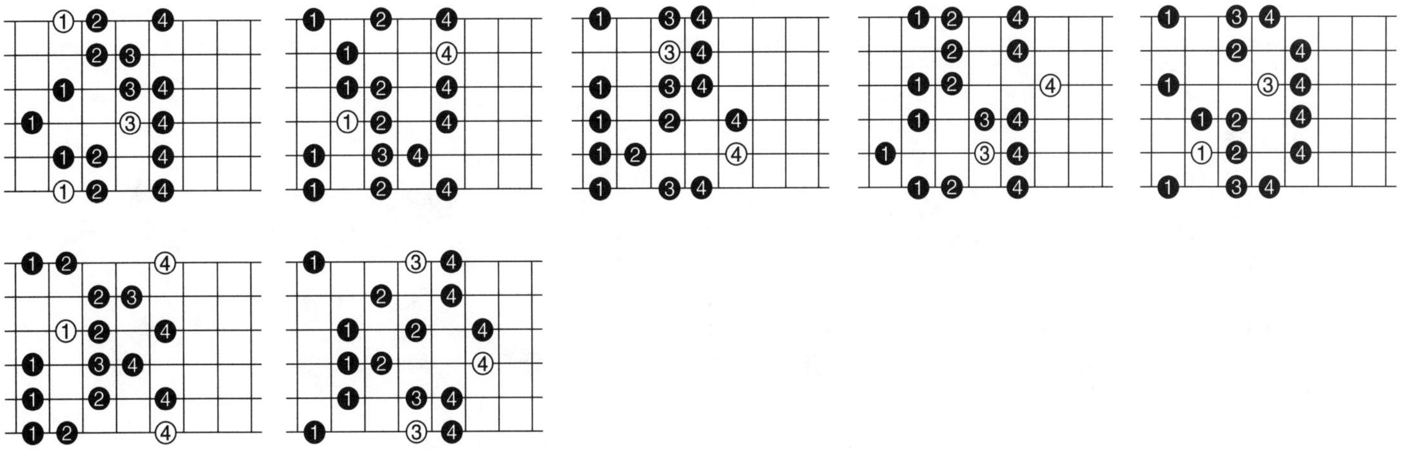

Three-Notes-Per-String Fingerings, Starting on all Scale Degrees

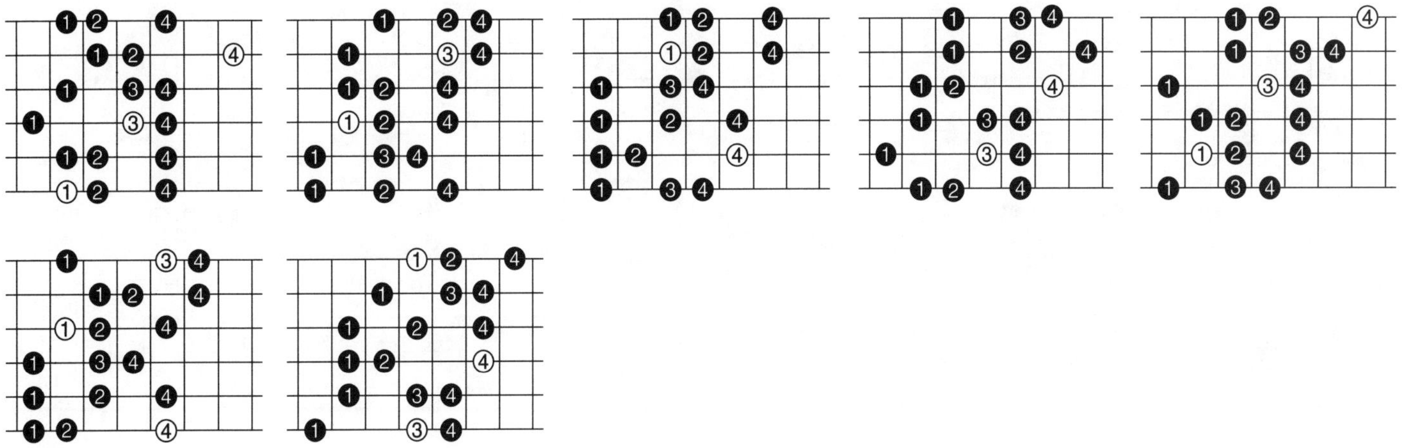

Four-Notes-Per-String Fingerings

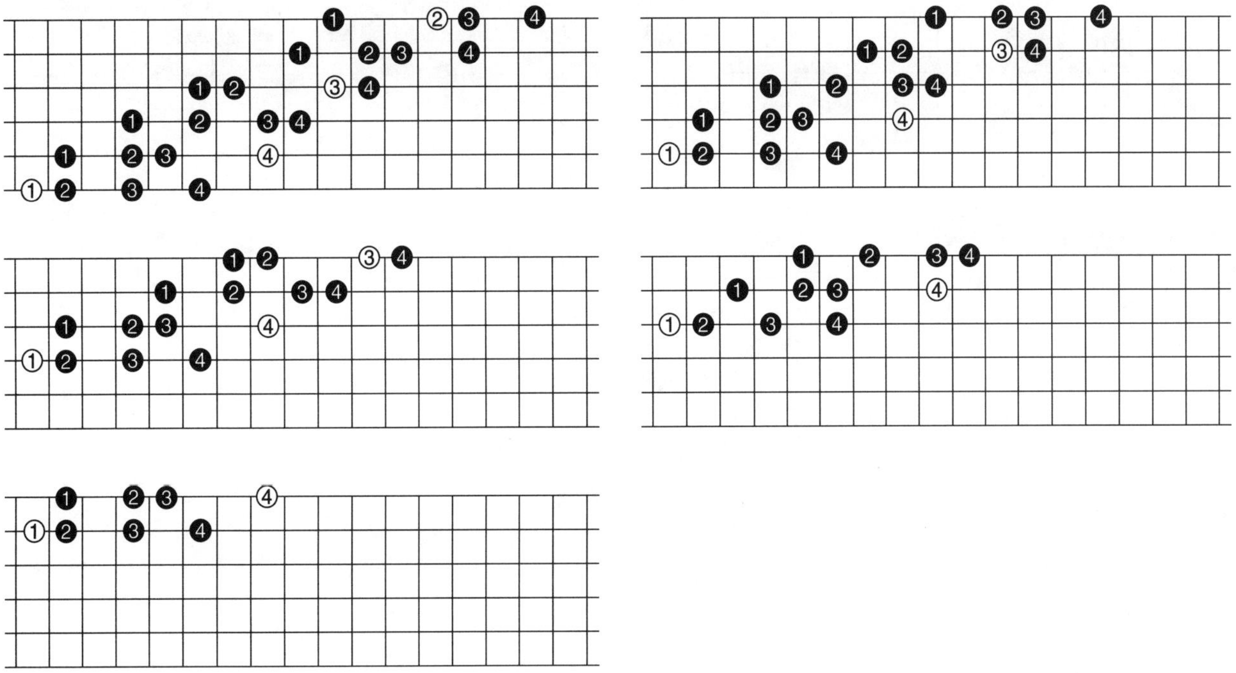

Blues

Scale Tones

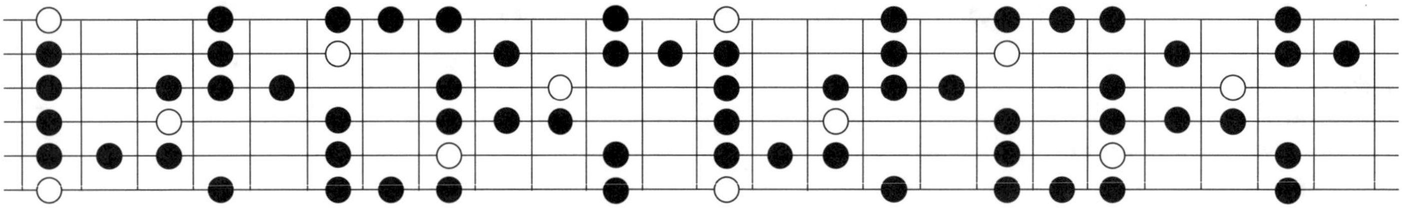

One-Octave Fingerings

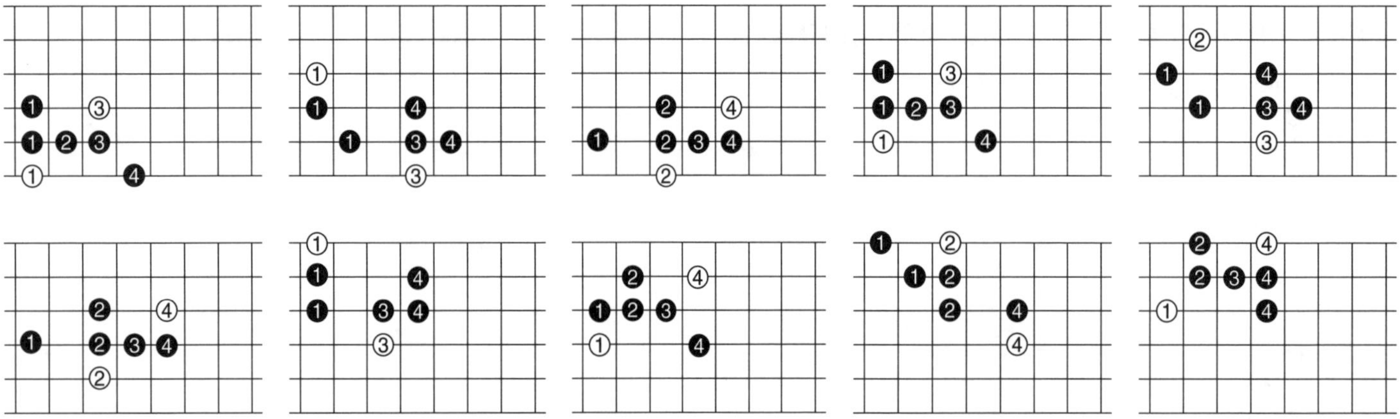

Two-Octave Fingerings

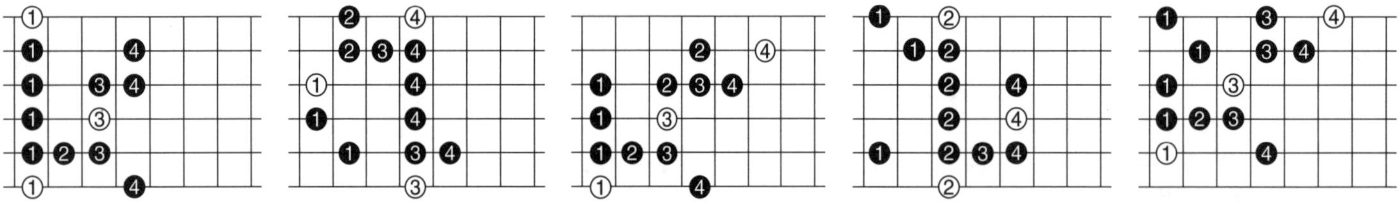

Three-Octave Fingerings

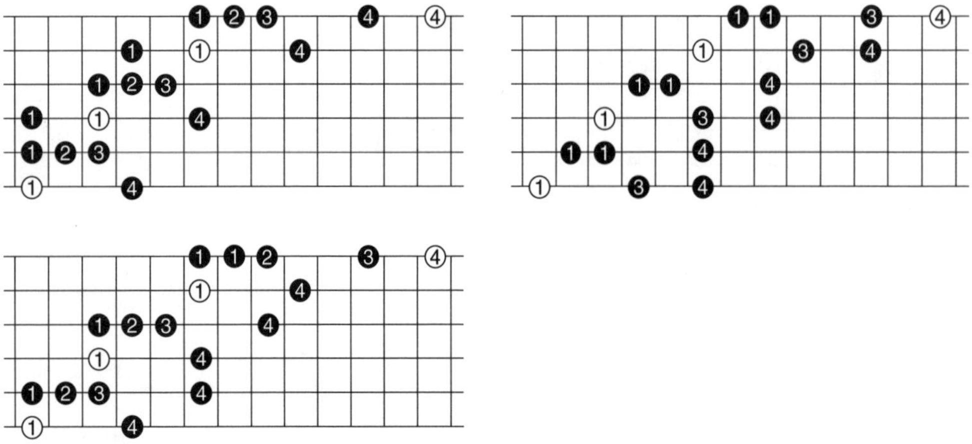

Position-Based Fingerings, Starting on all Scale Degrees

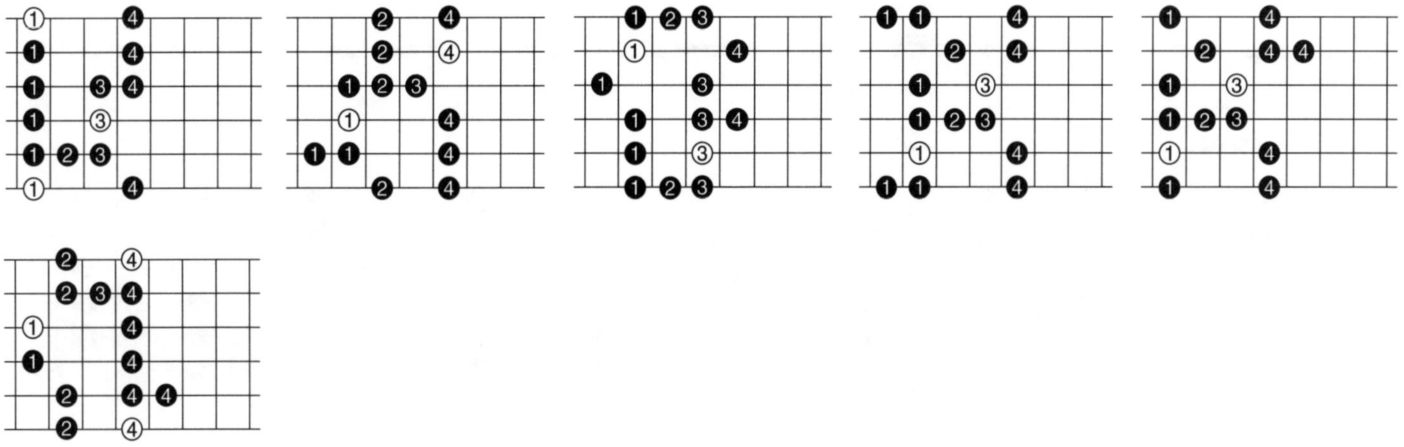

Three-Notes-Per-String Fingerings

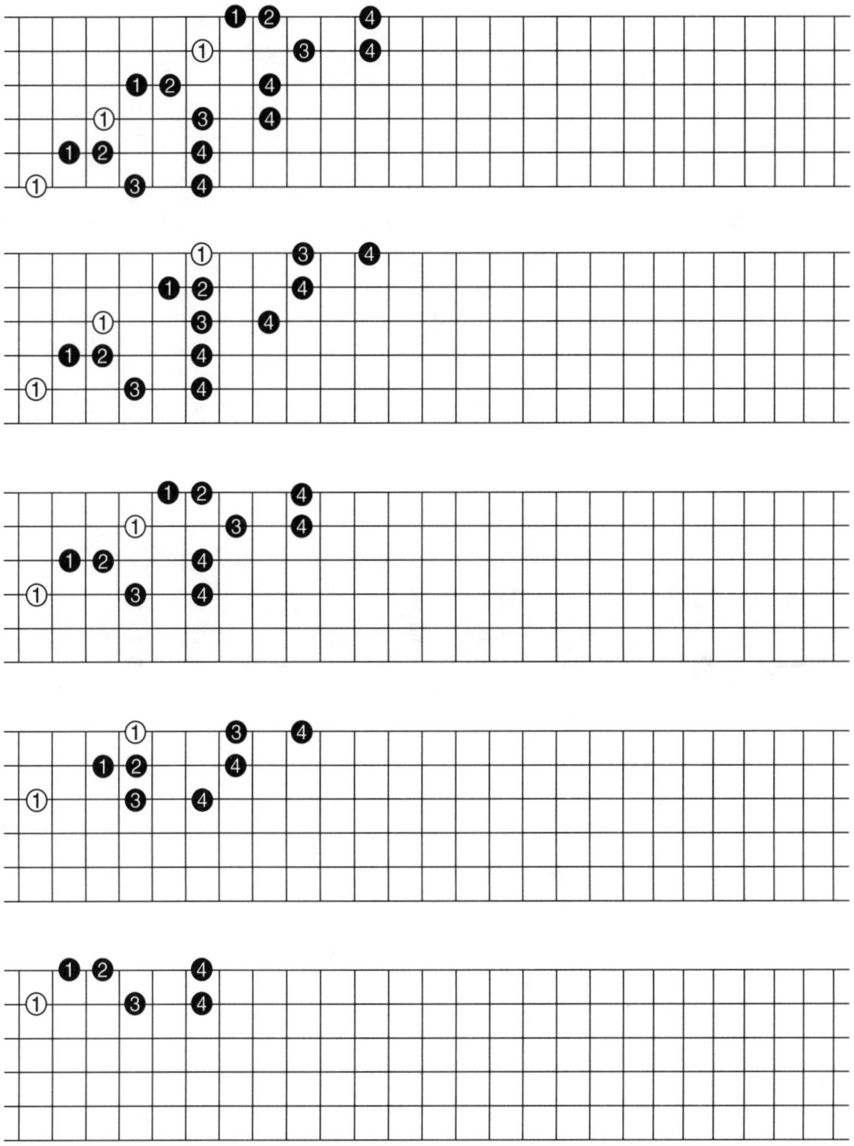

Pentatonic Major

Scale Tones

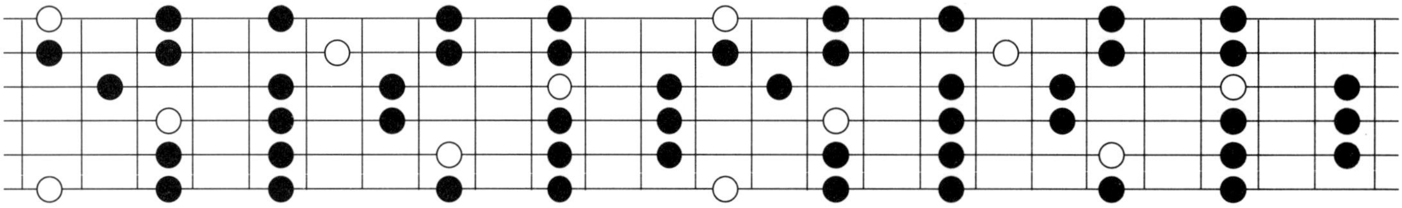

One-Octave Fingerings

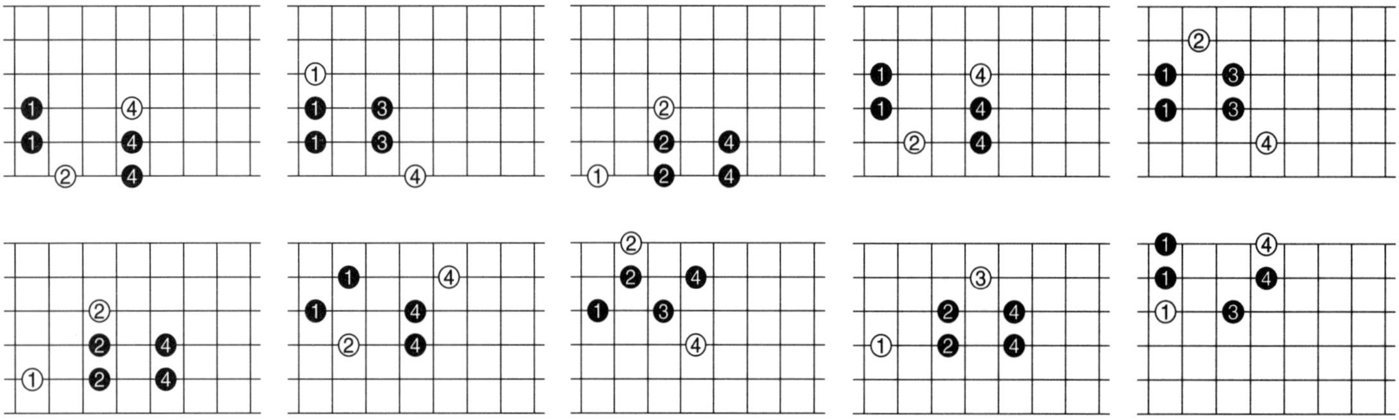

Two-Octave Fingerings

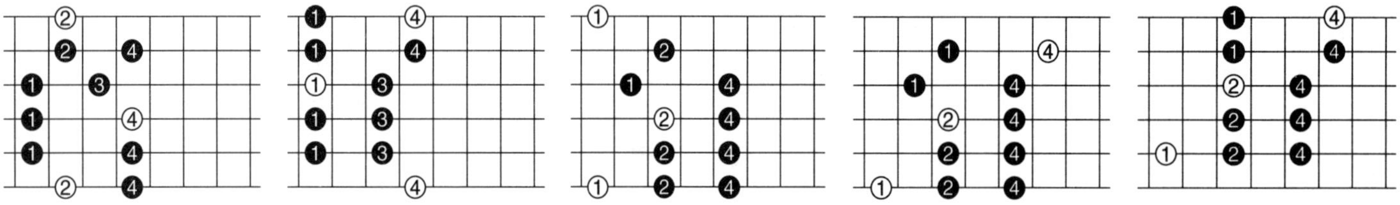

Three-Octave Fingerings

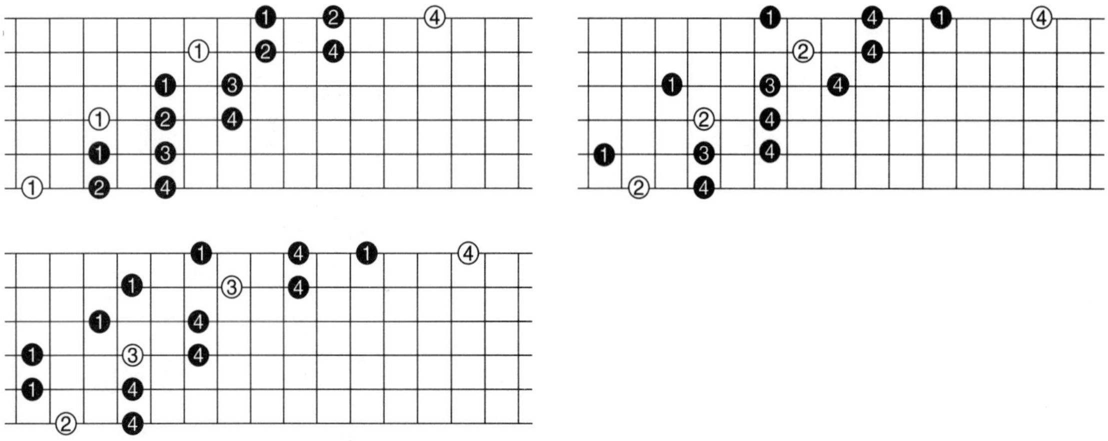

Position-Based Fingerings, Starting on all Scale Degrees

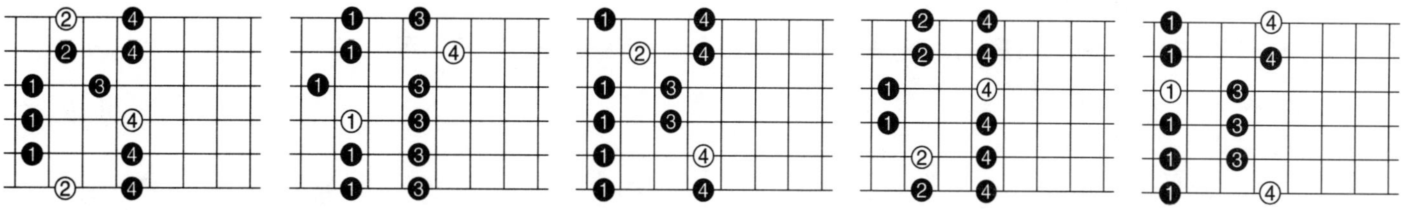

Three-Notes-Per-String Fingerings

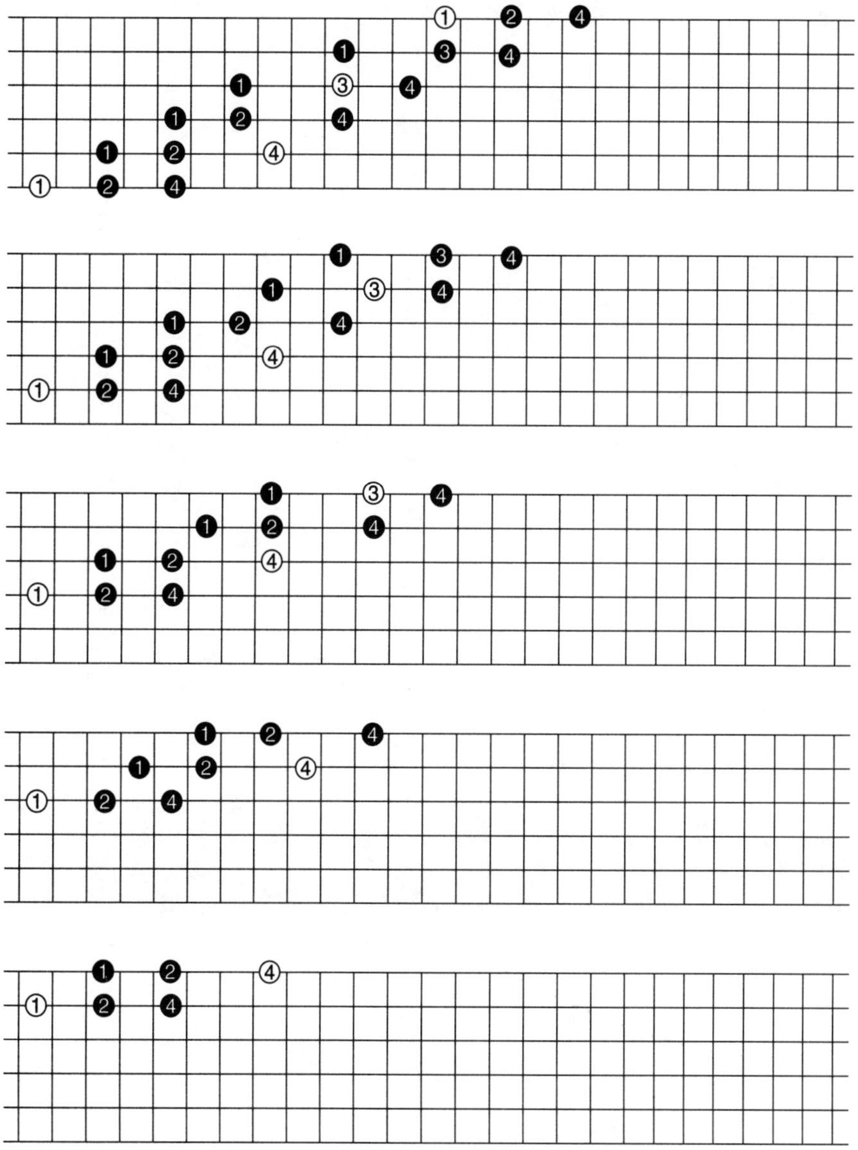

Pentatonic Minor

Scale Tones

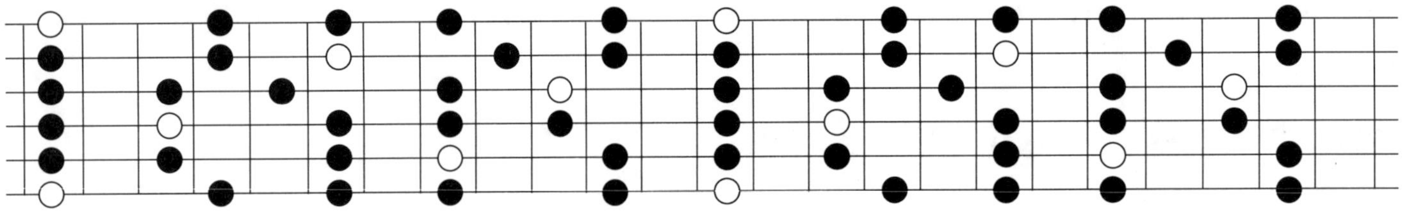

One-Octave Fingerings

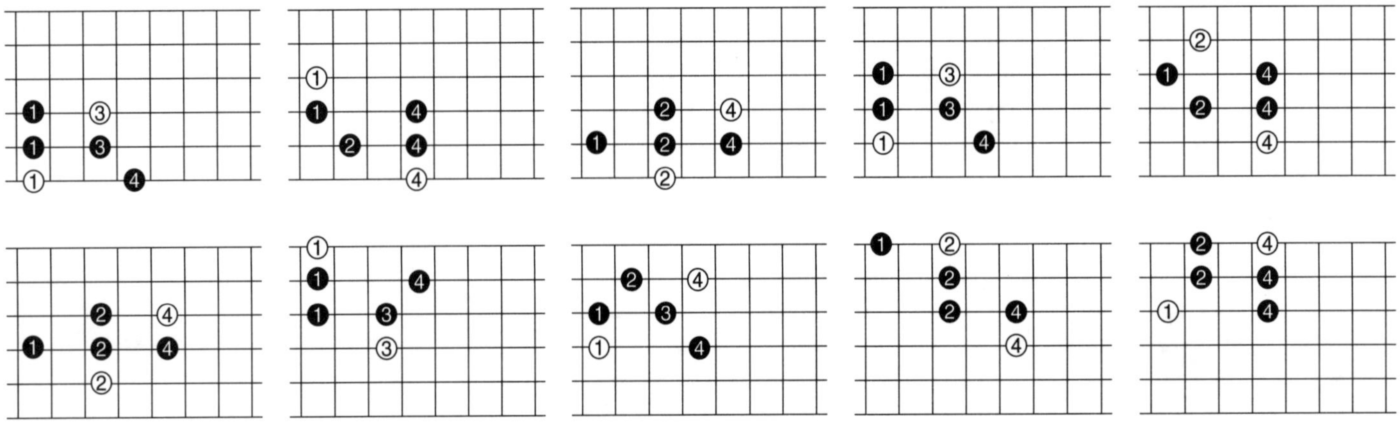

Two-Octave Fingerings

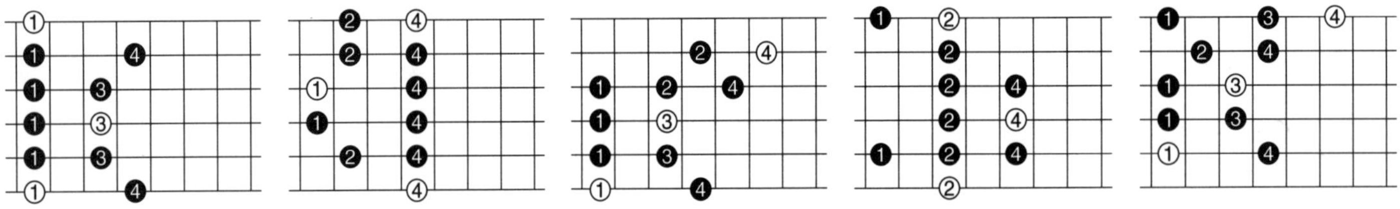

Three-Octave Fingerings

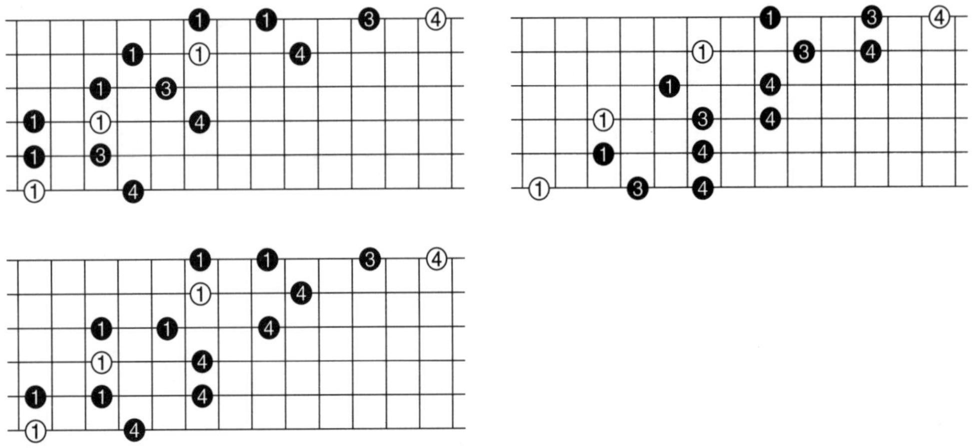

Position-Based Fingerings, Starting on all Scale Degrees

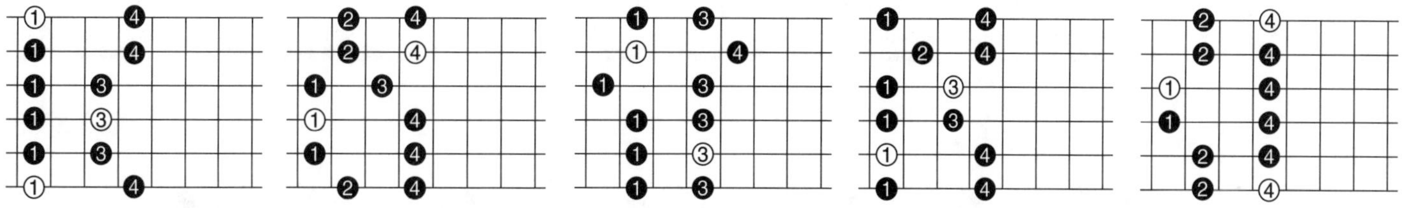

Three-Notes-Per-String Fingerings

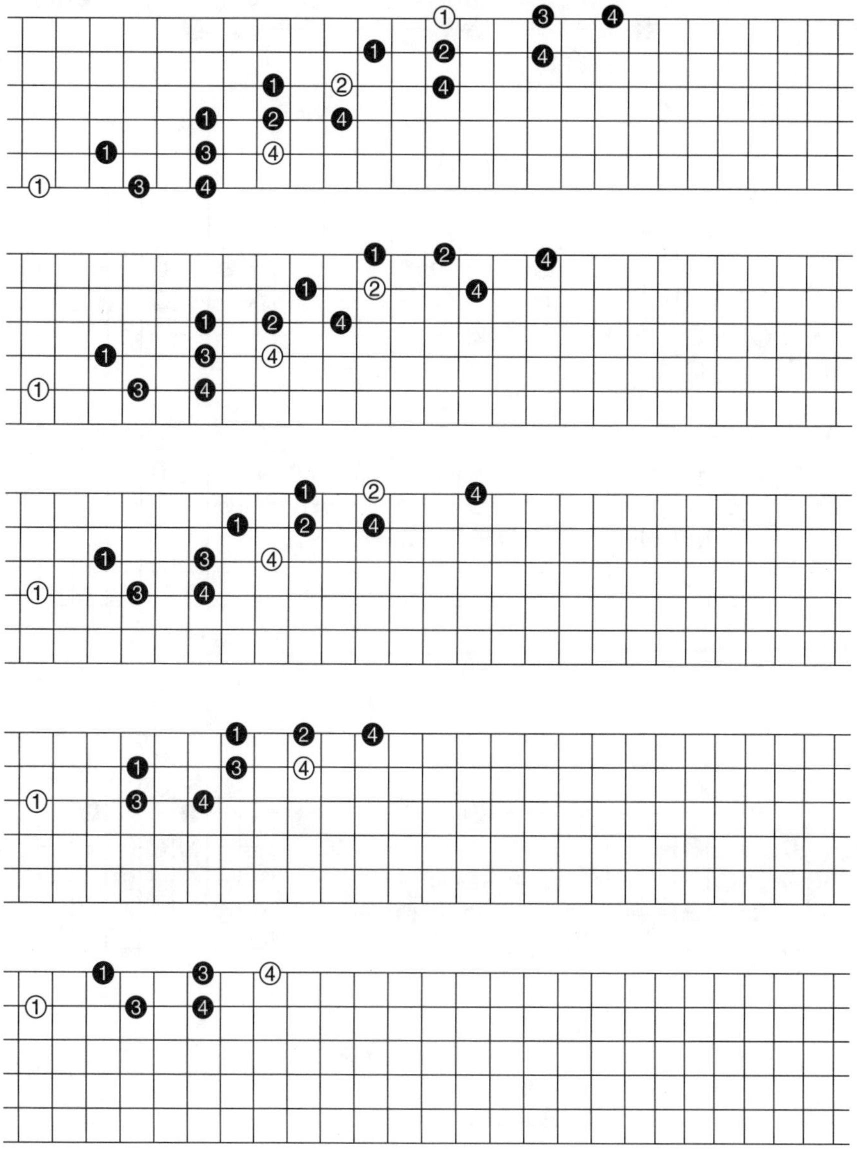

Major ♭2 Pentatonic

Scale Tones

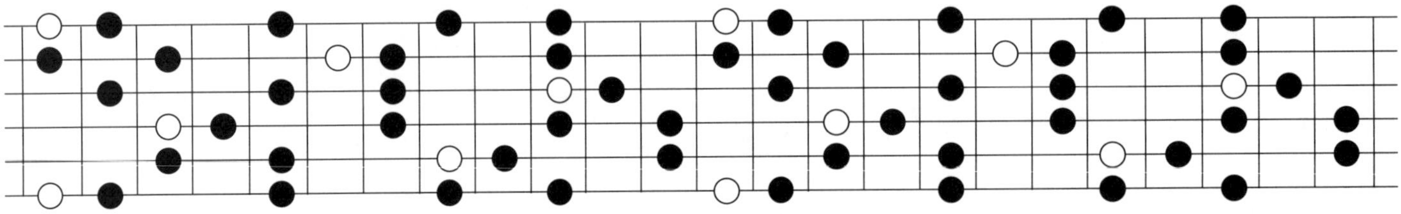

One-Octave Fingerings

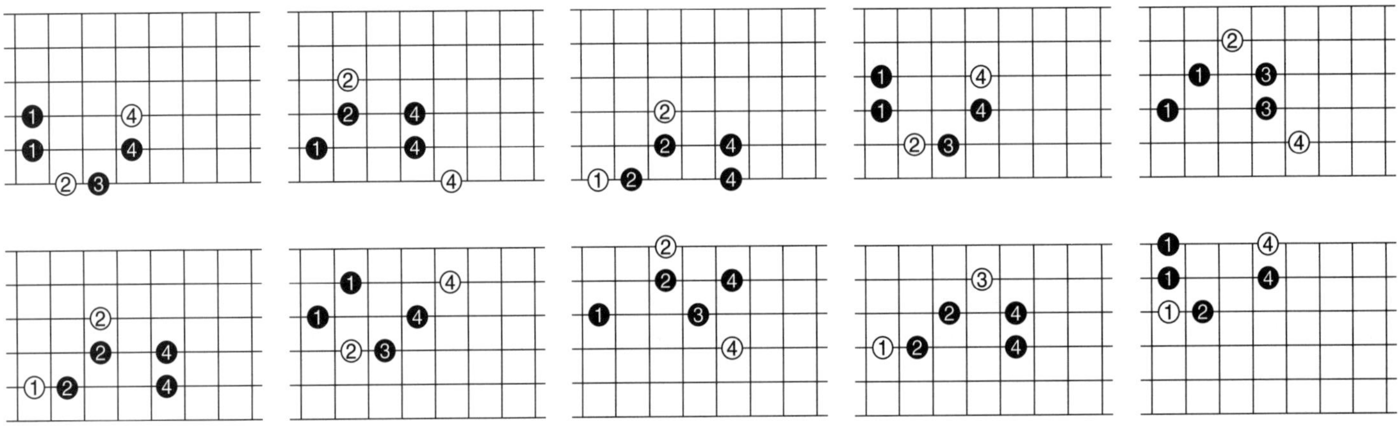

Two-Octave Fingerings

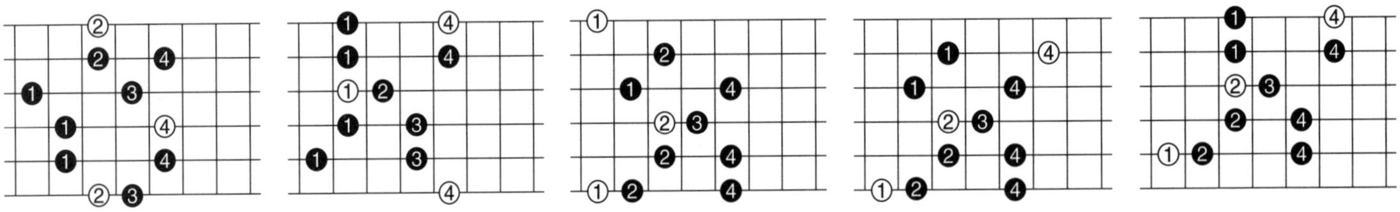

Three-Octave Fingerings

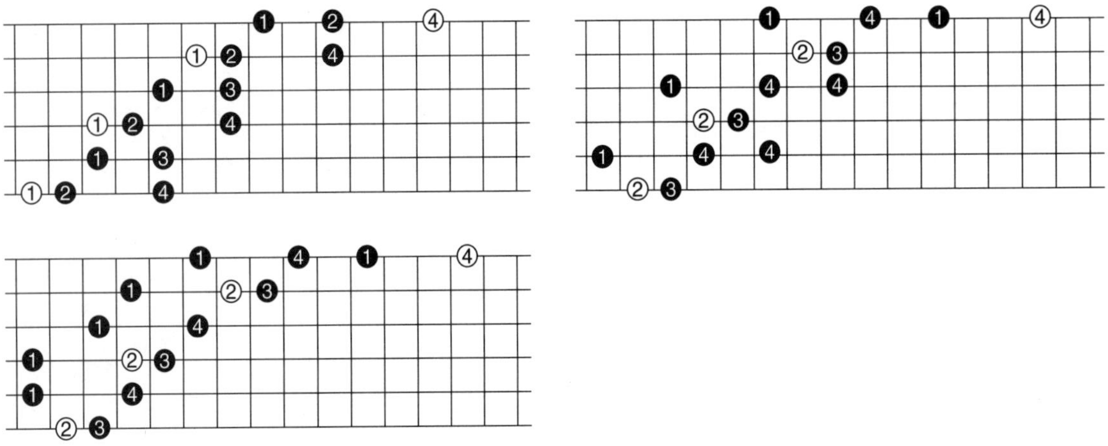

Position-Based Fingerings, Starting on all Scale Degrees

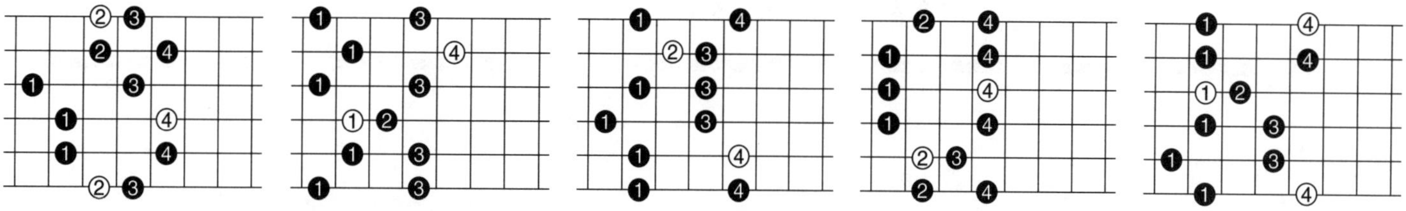

Three-Notes-Per-String Fingerings

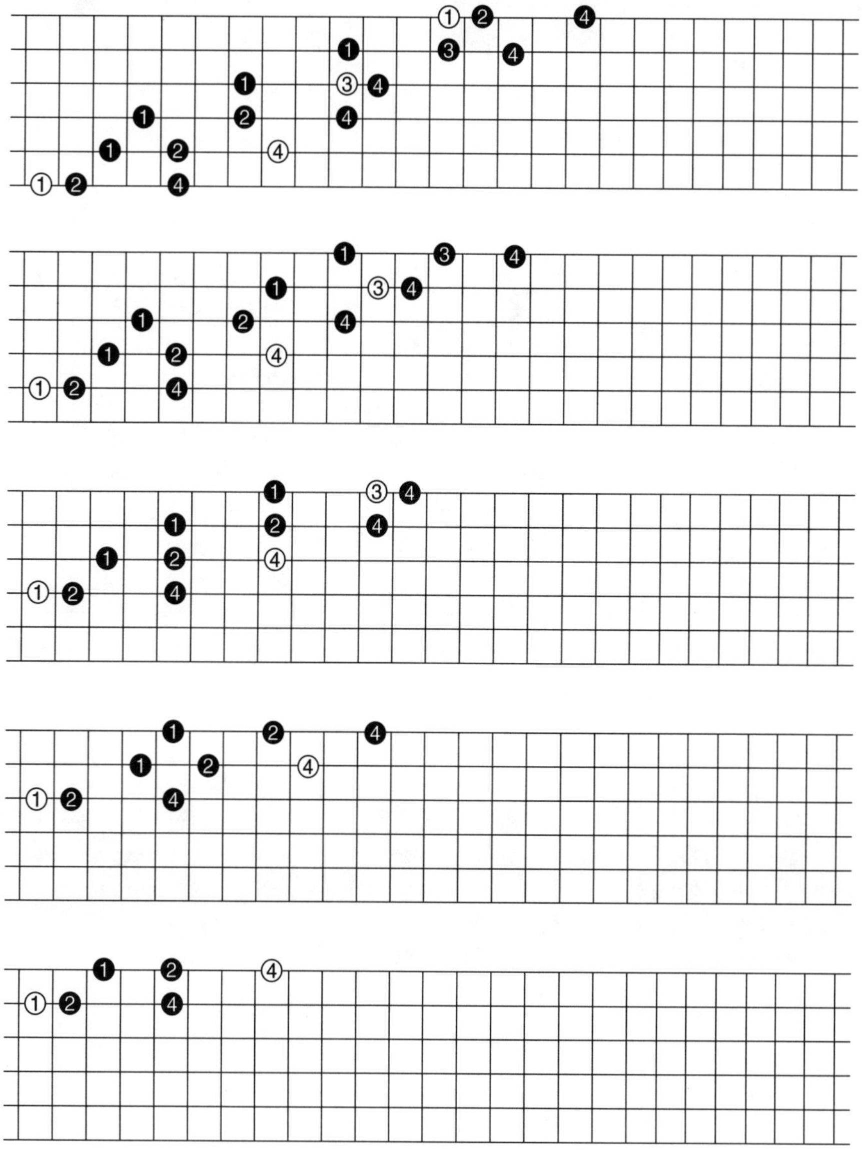

Major ♭6 Pentatonic

Scale Tones

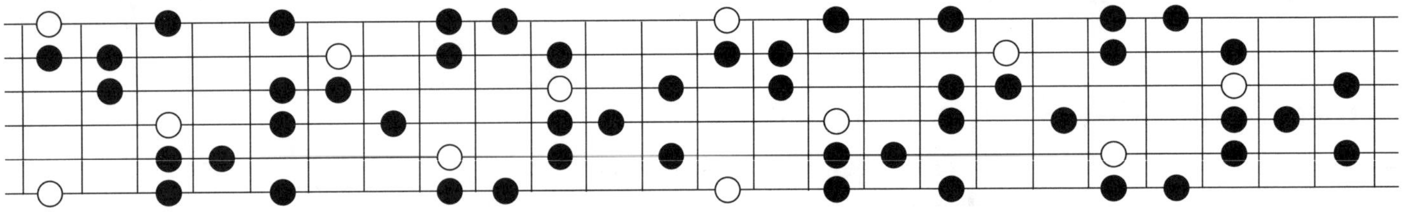

One-Octave Fingerings

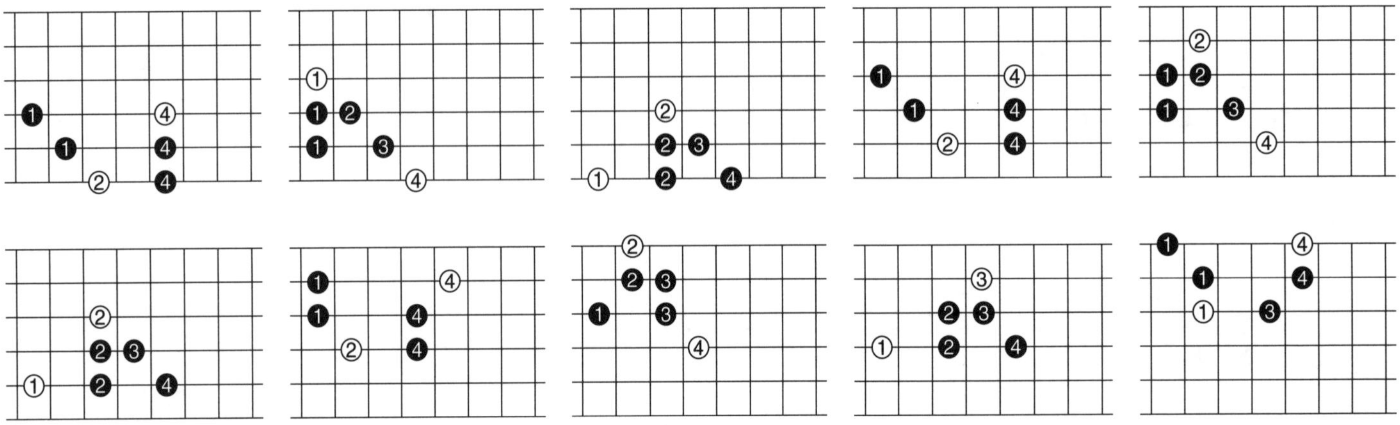

Two-Octave Fingerings

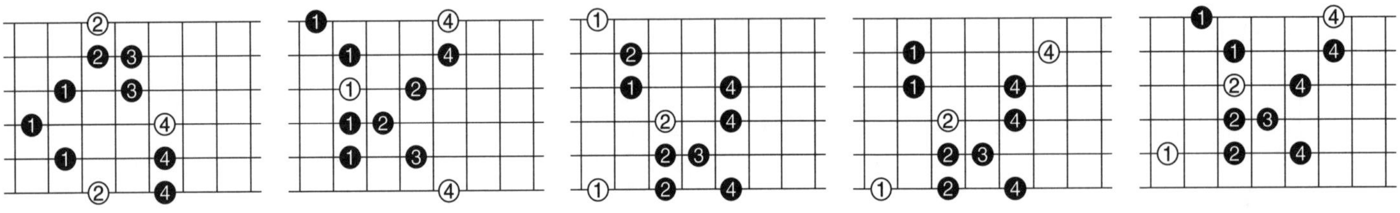

Three-Octave Fingerings

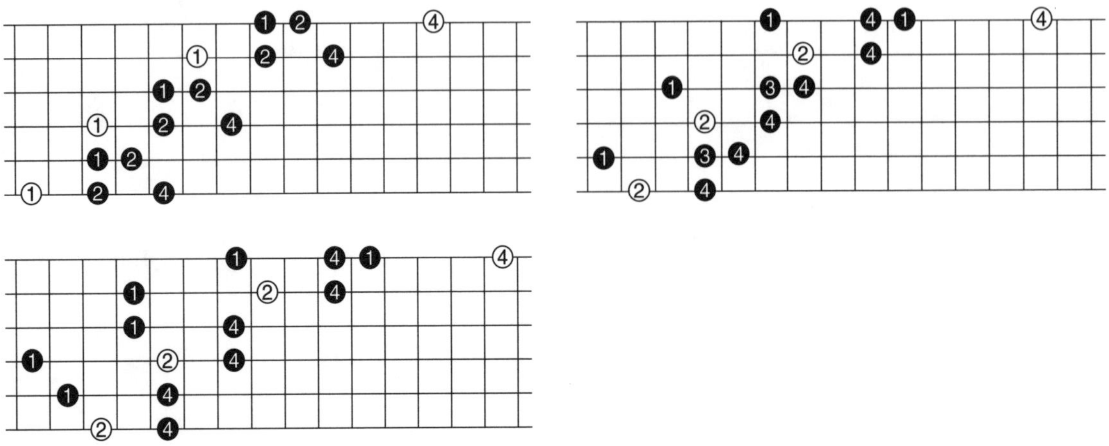

Position-Based Fingerings, Starting on all Scale Degrees

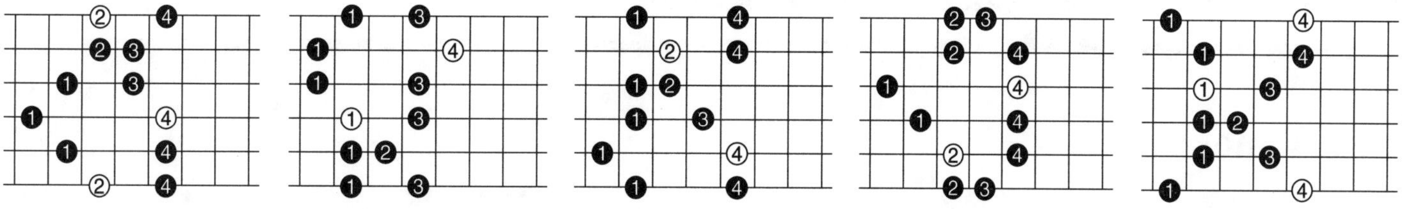

Three-Notes-Per-String Fingerings

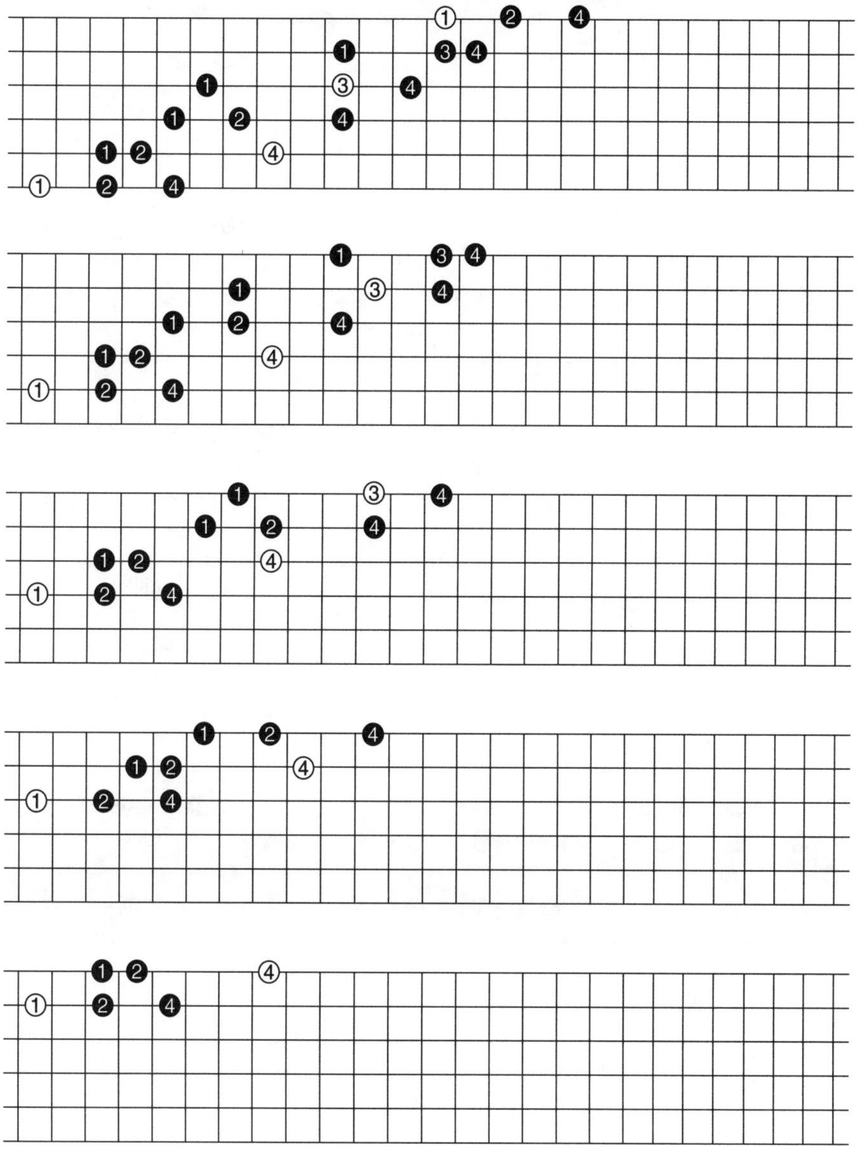

Minor 6 Pentatonic

Scale Tones

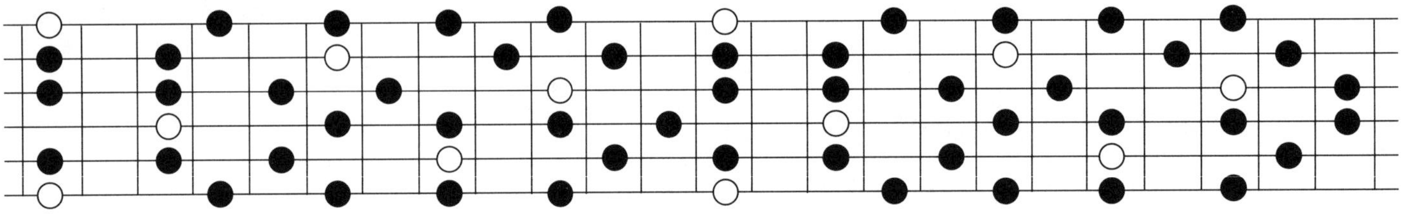

One-Octave Fingerings

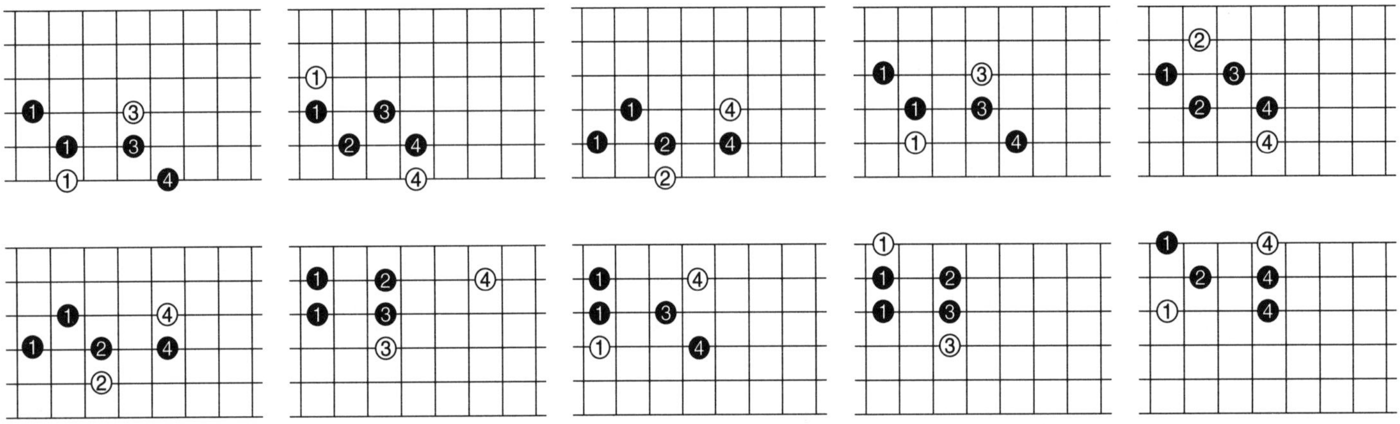

Two-Octave Fingerings

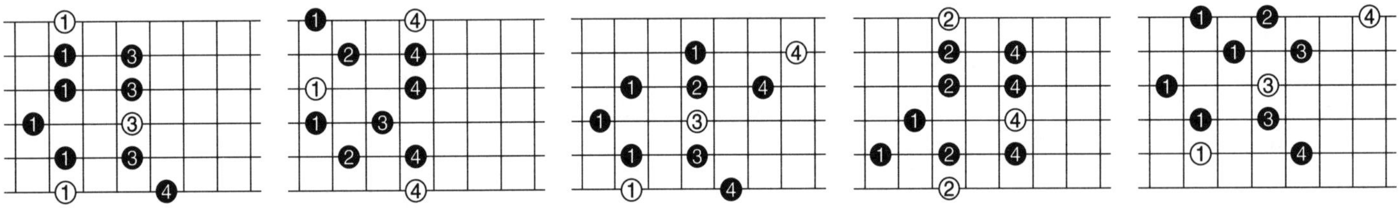

Three-Octave Fingerings

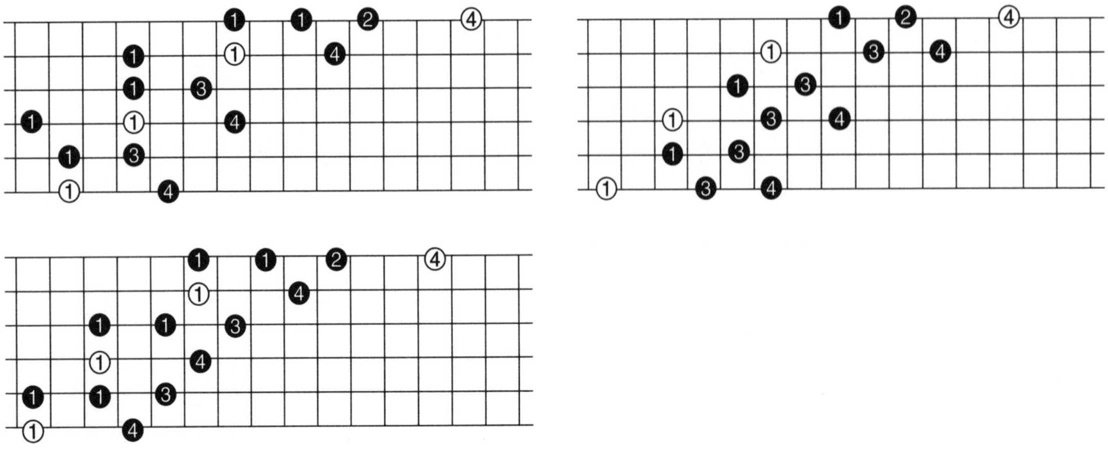

Position-Based Fingerings, Starting on all Scale Degrees

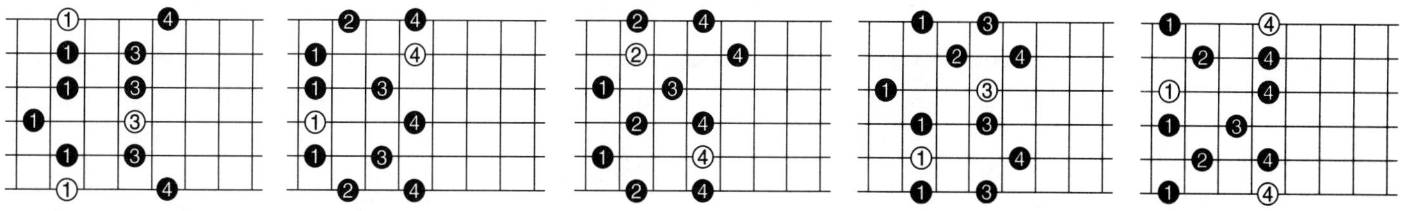

Three-Notes-Per-String Fingerings

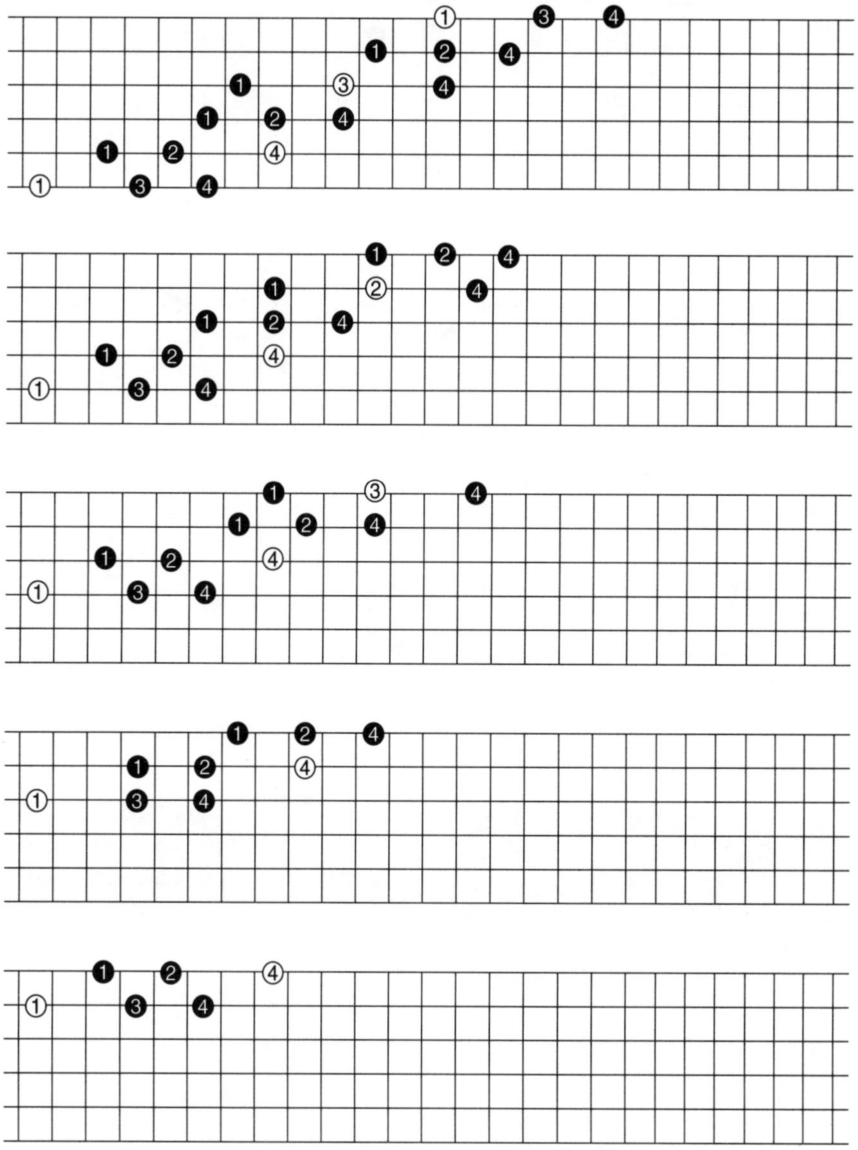

Minor 7♭5 Pentatonic

Scale Tones

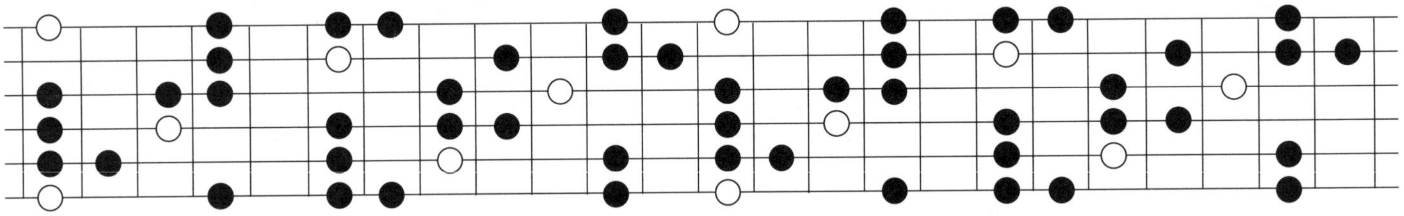

One-Octave Fingerings

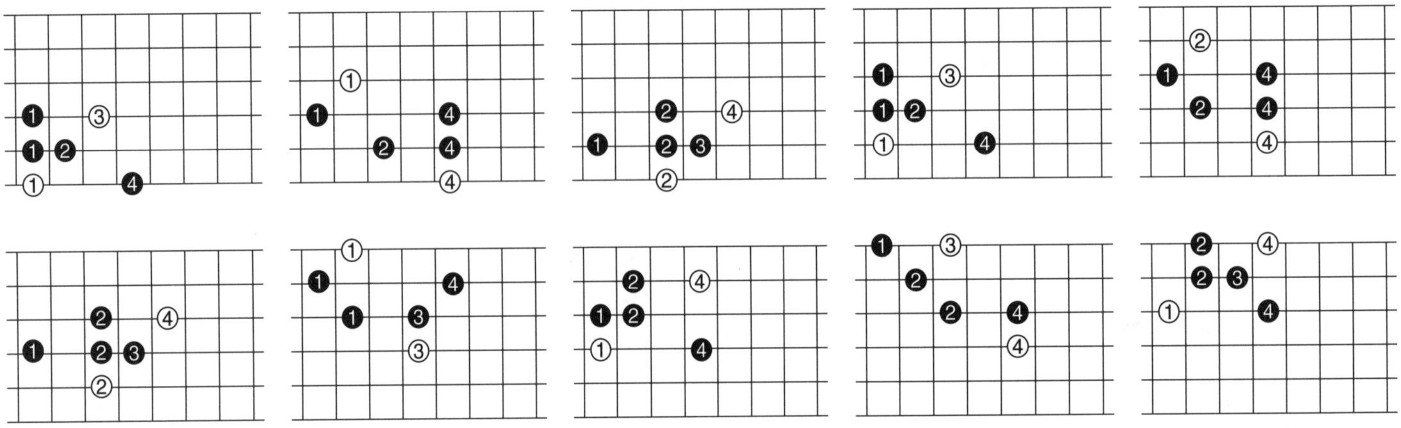

Two-Octave Fingerings

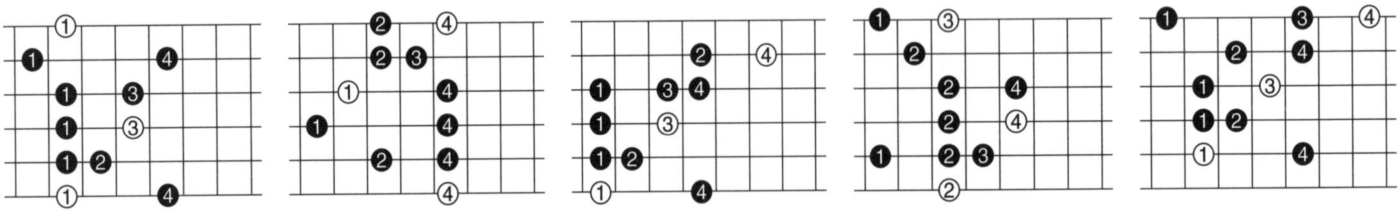

Three-Octave Fingerings

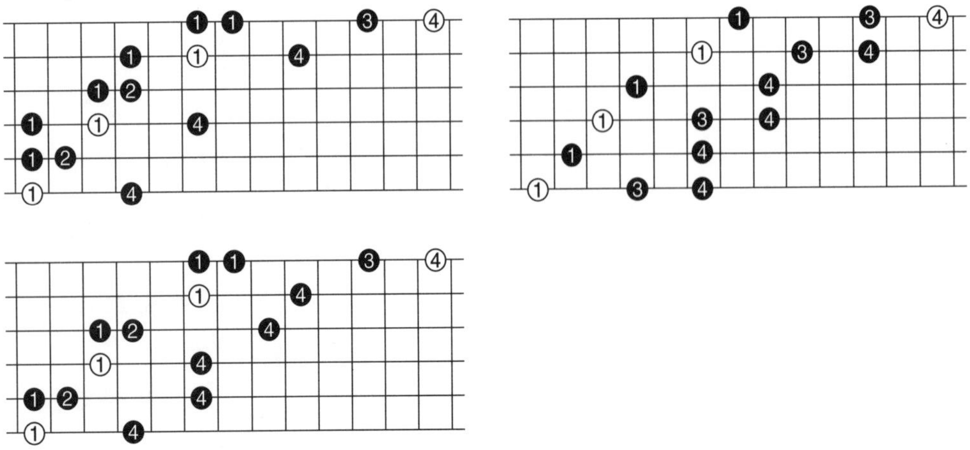

Position-Based Fingerings, Starting on all Scale Degrees

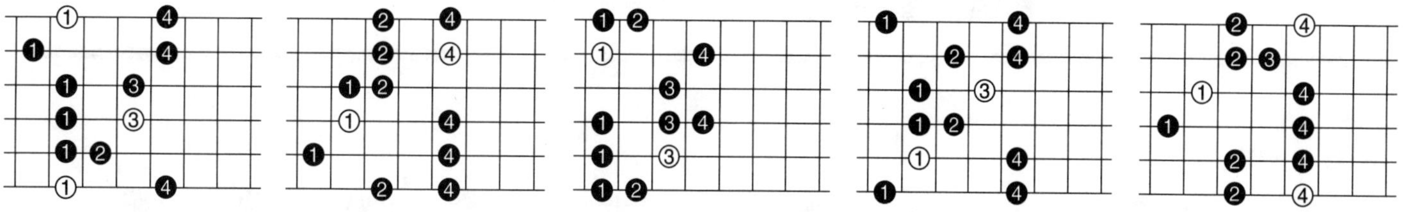

Three-Notes-Per-String Fingerings

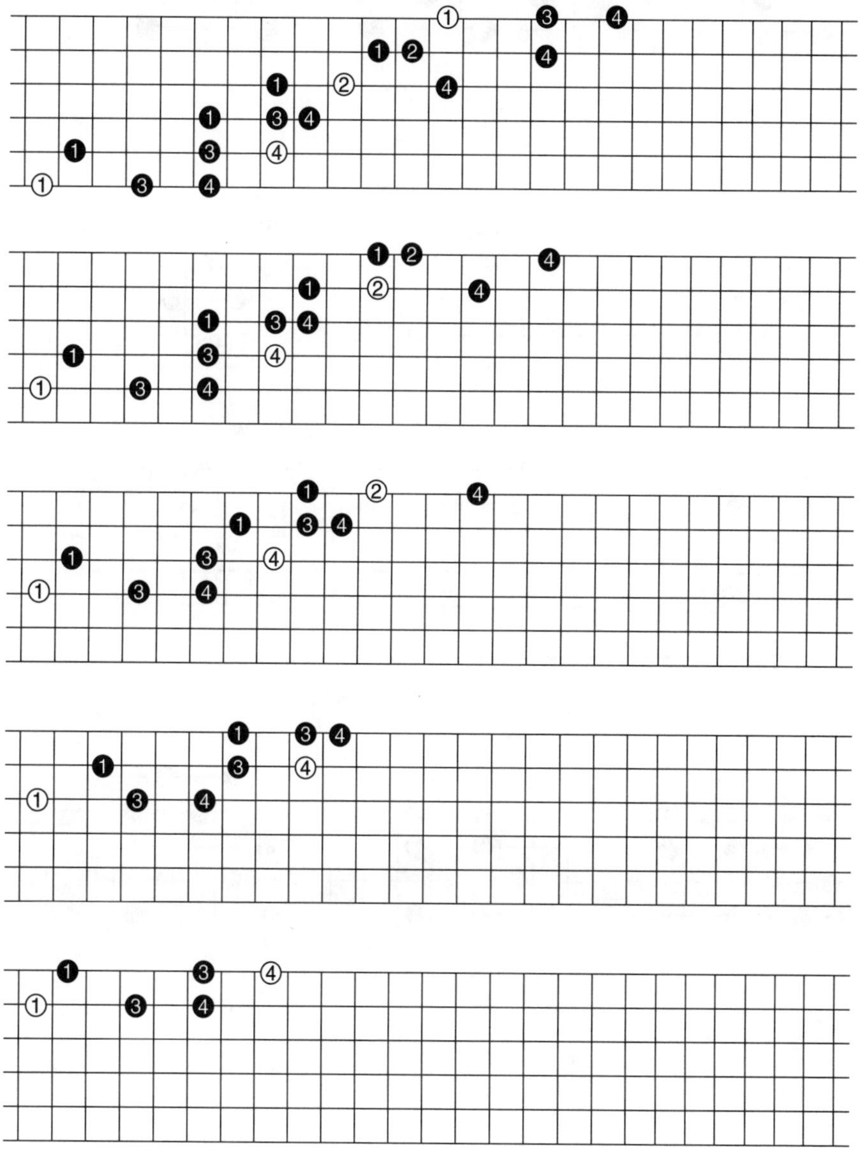

Whole Tone Pentatonic

Scale Tones

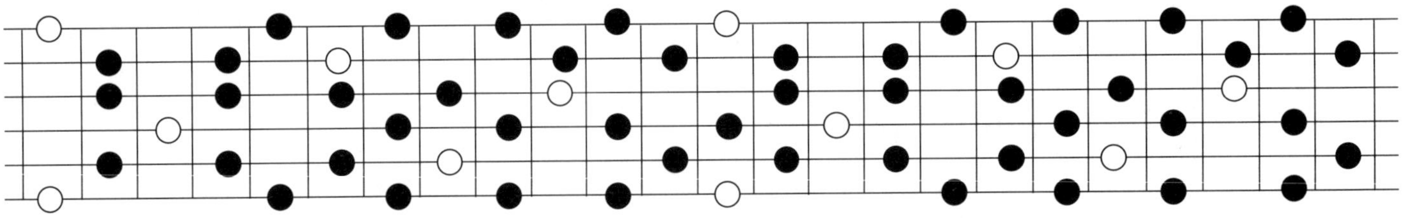

One-Octave Fingerings

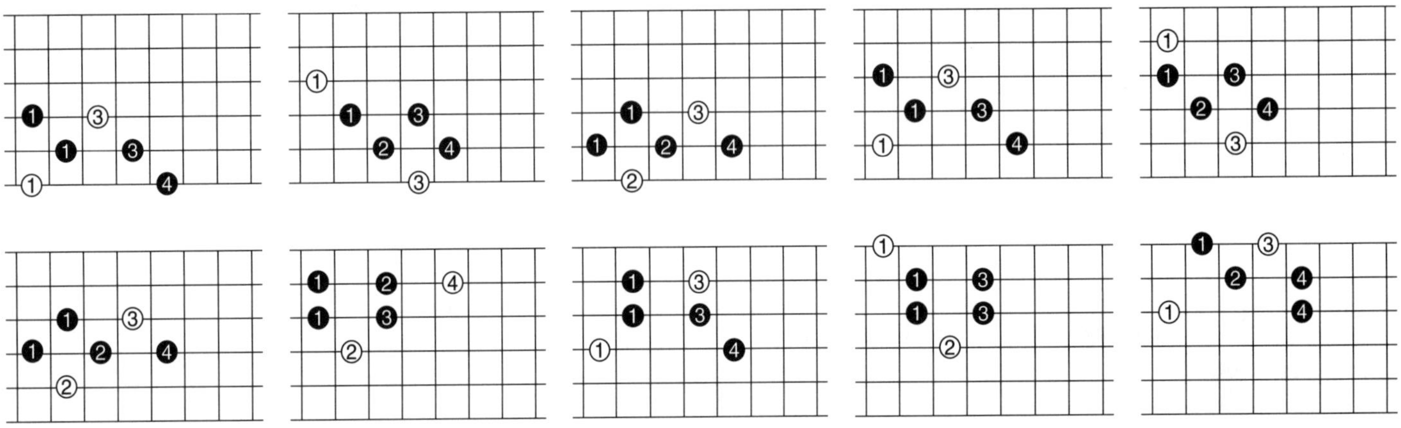

Two-Octave Fingerings

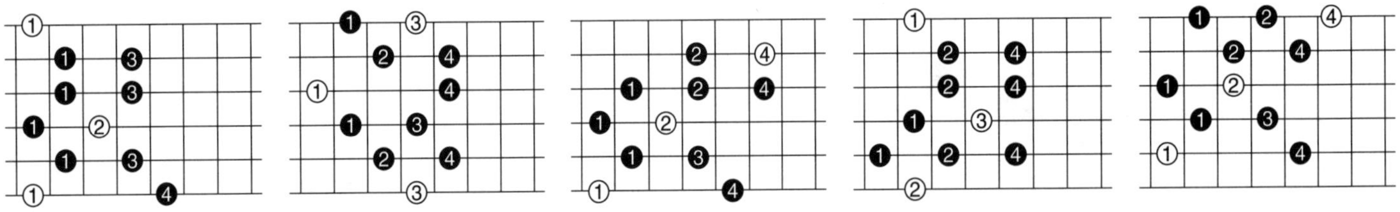

Three-Octave Fingerings

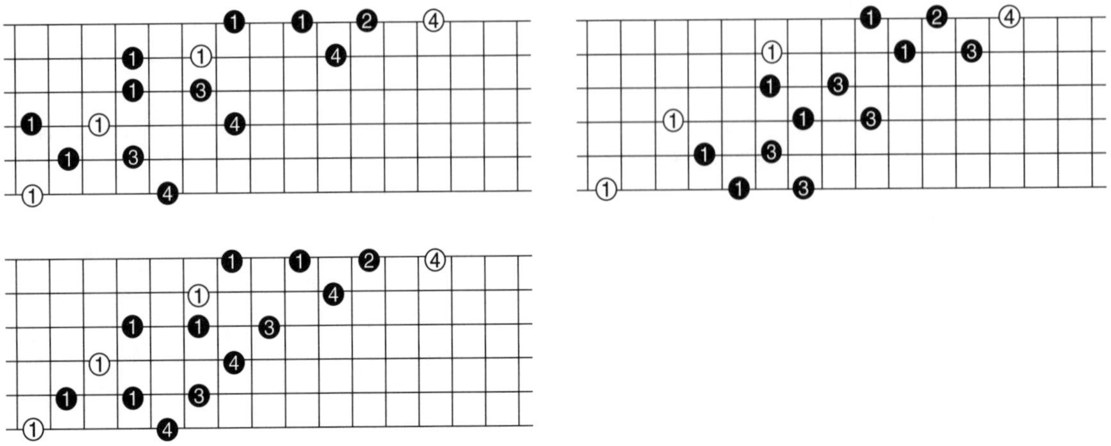

Position-Based Fingerings, Starting on all Scale Degrees

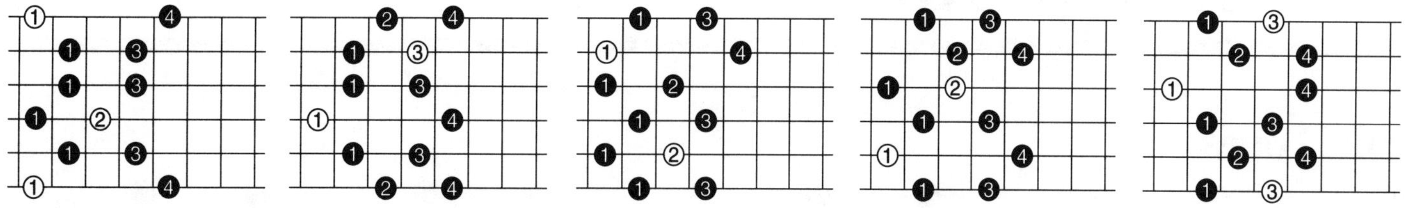

Three-Notes-Per-String Fingerings

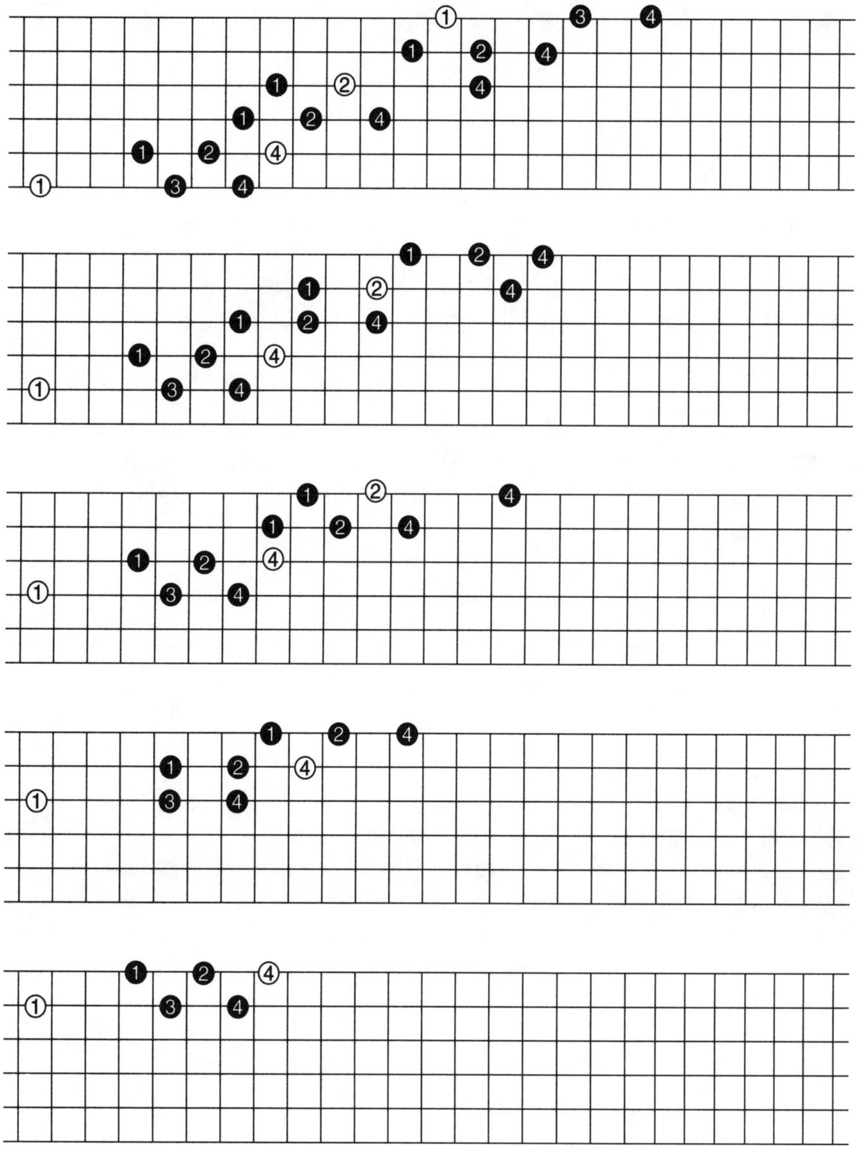

Banshiki-Cho

Scale Tones

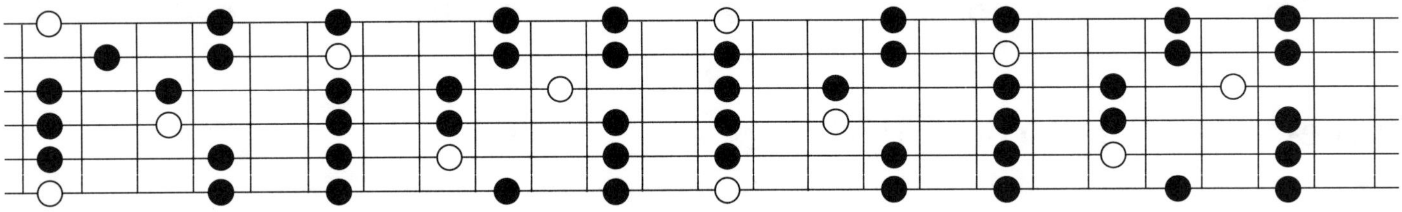

One-Octave Fingerings

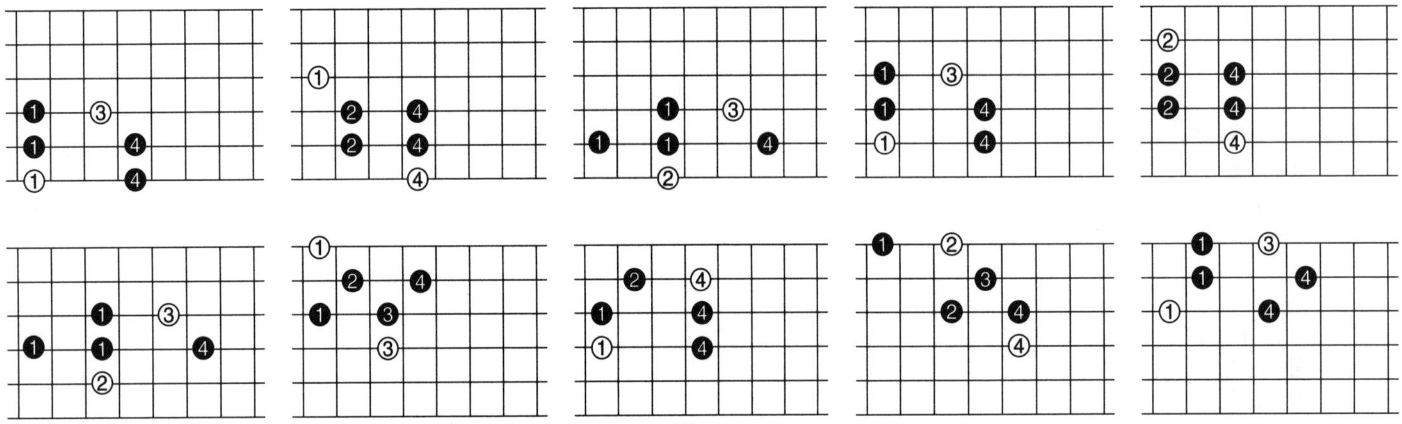

Two-Octave Fingerings

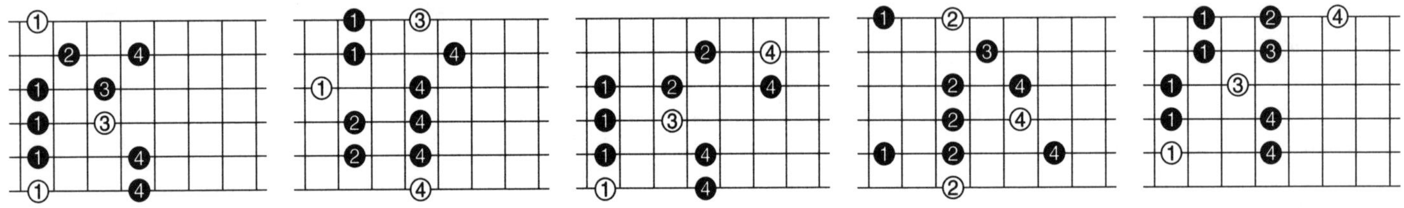

Three-Octave Fingerings

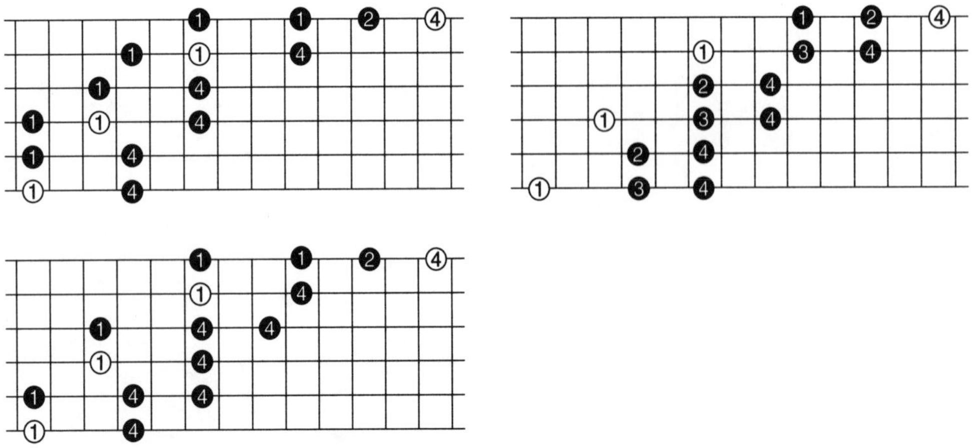

Position-Based Fingerings, Starting on all Scale Degrees

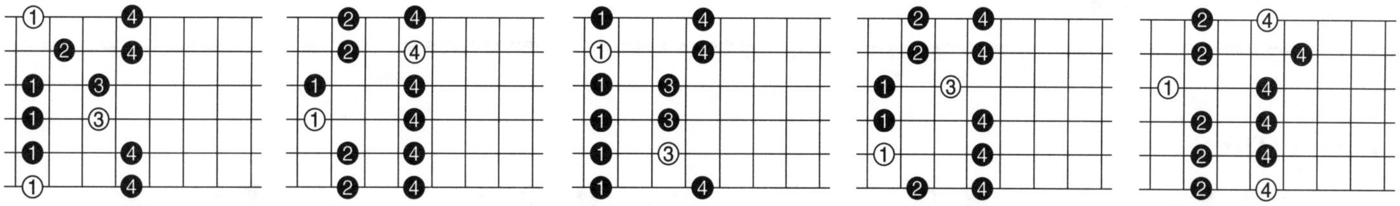

Three-Notes-Per-String Fingerings

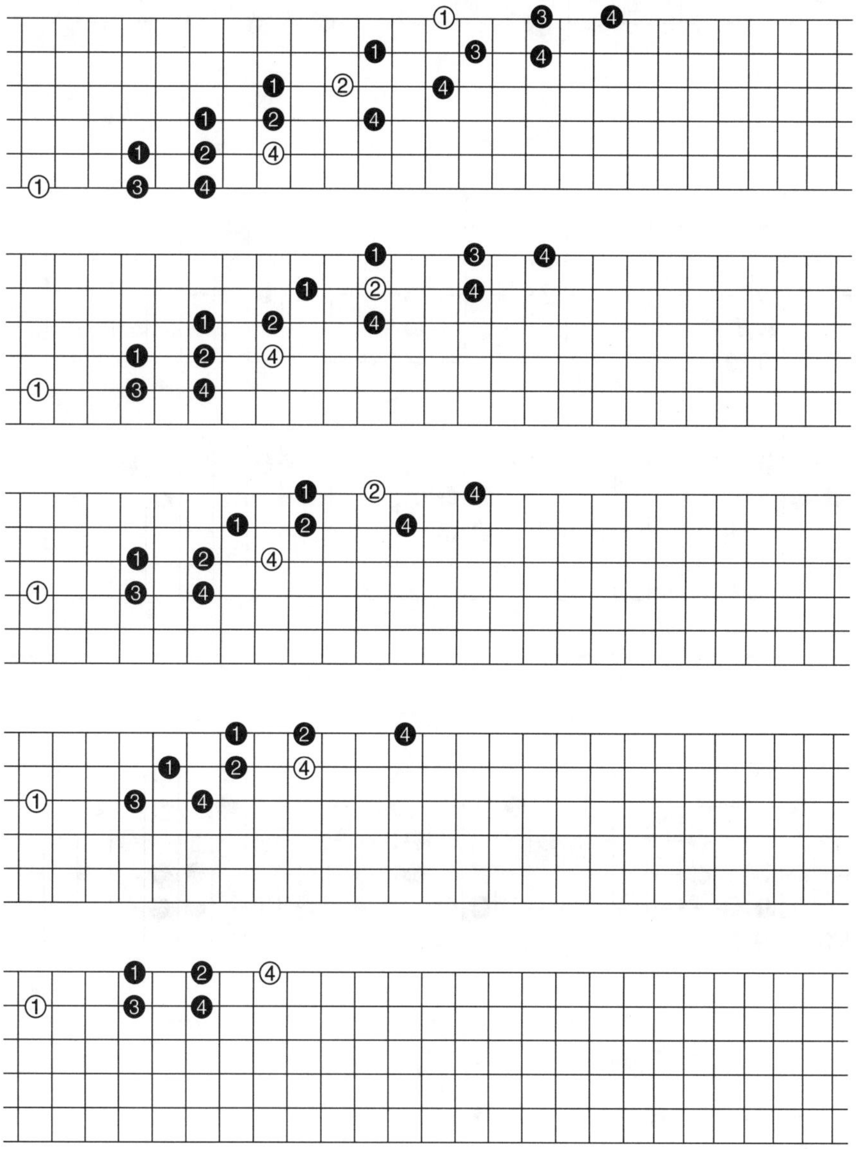

Hirajoshi

Scale Tones

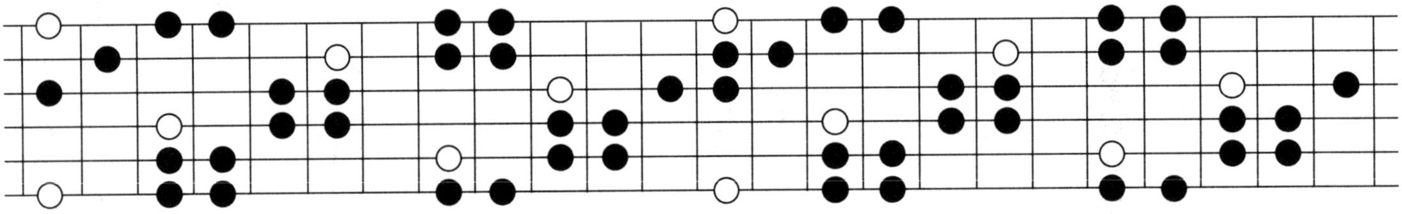

One-Octave Fingerings

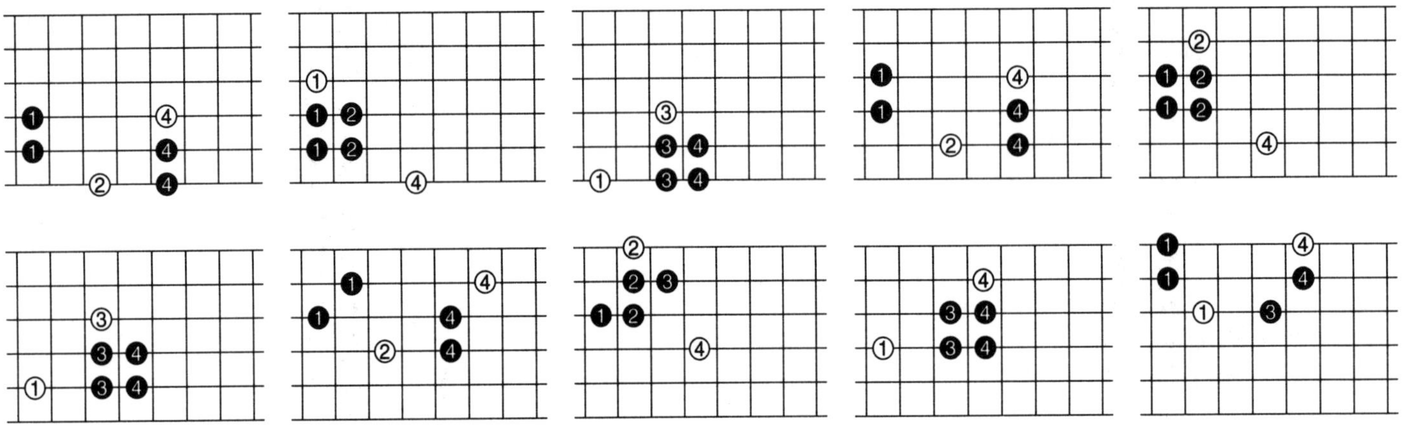

Two-Octave Fingerings

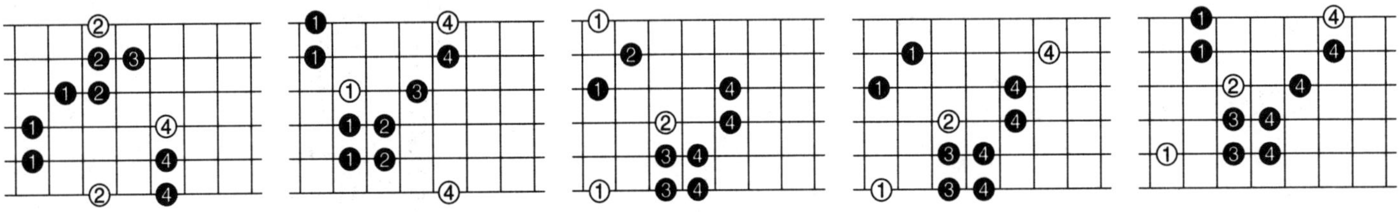

Three-Octave Fingerings

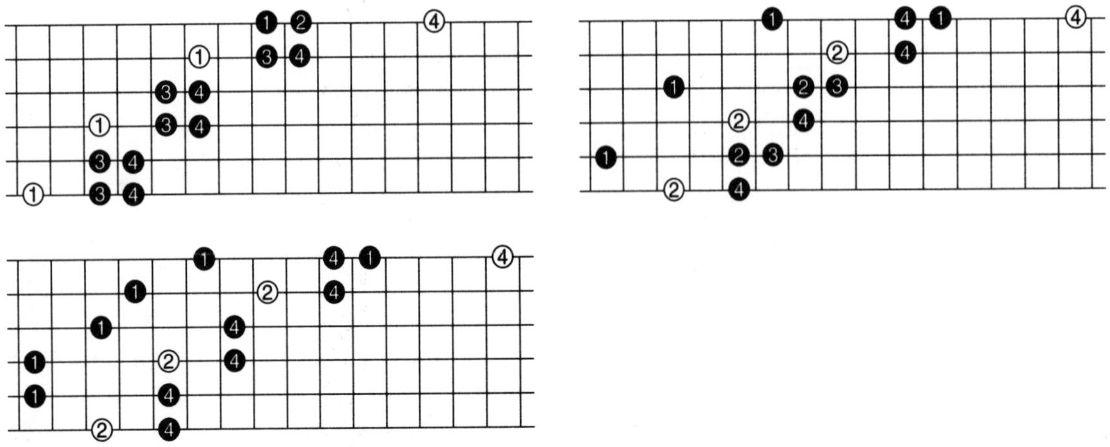

Position-Based Fingerings, Starting on all Scale Degrees

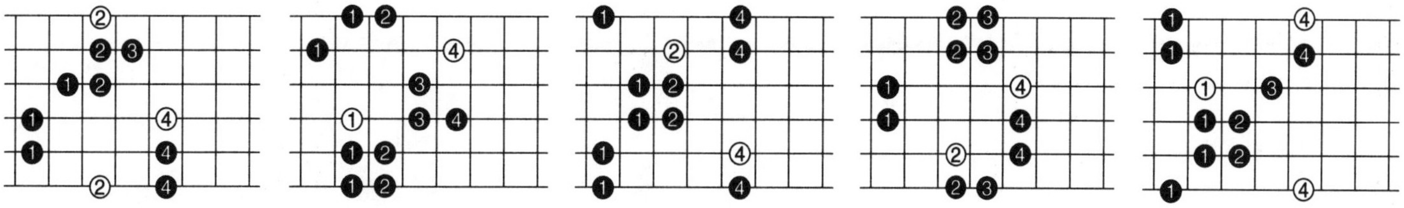

Three-Notes-Per-String Fingerings

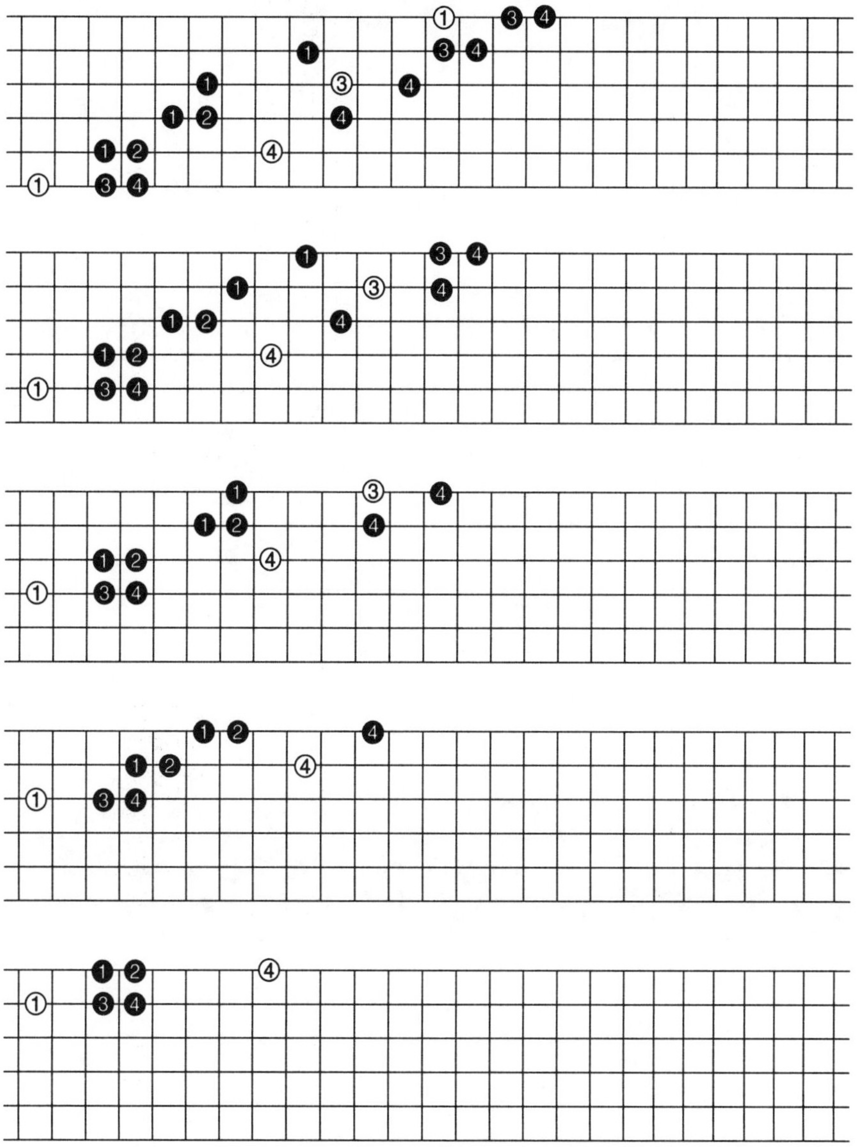

Iwato

Scale Tones

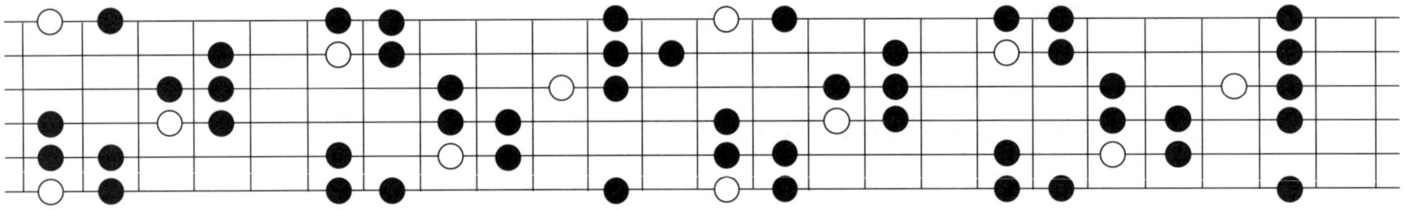

One-Octave Fingerings

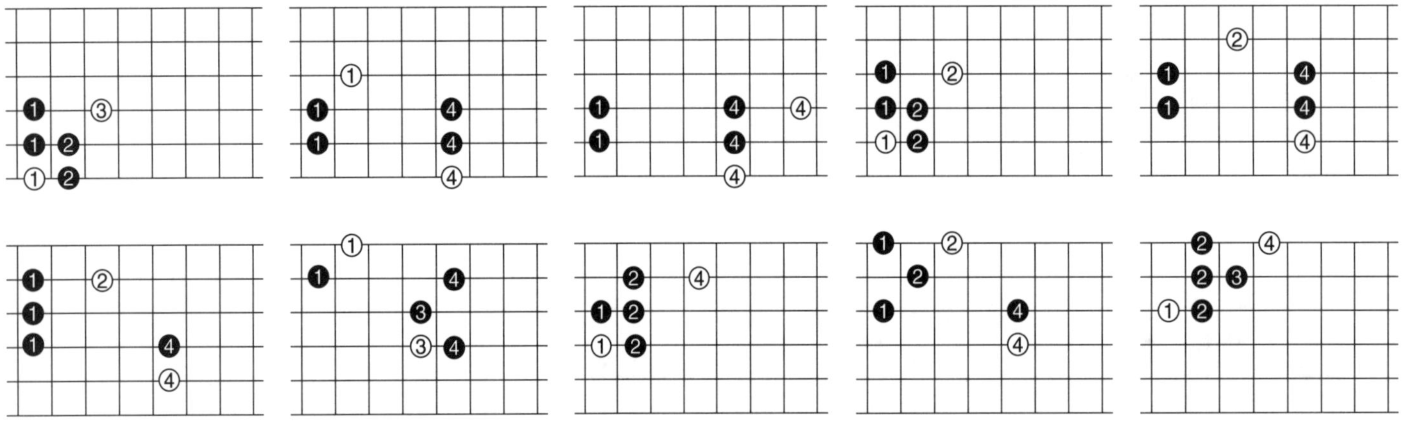

Two-Octave Fingerings

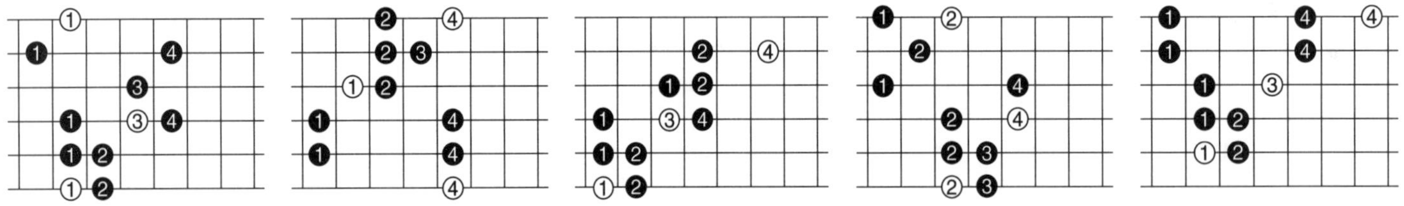

Three-Octave Fingerings

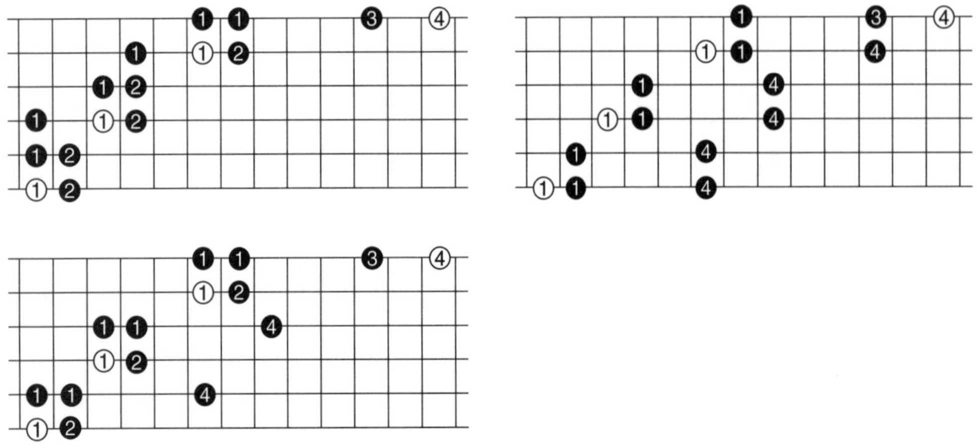

Position-Based Fingerings, Starting on all Scale Degrees

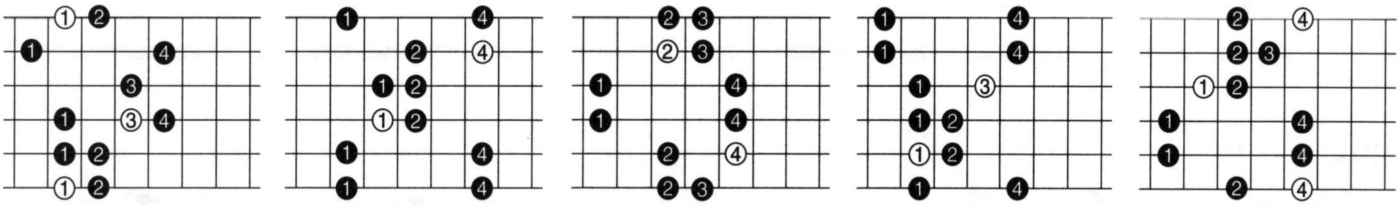

Three-Notes-Per-String Fingerings

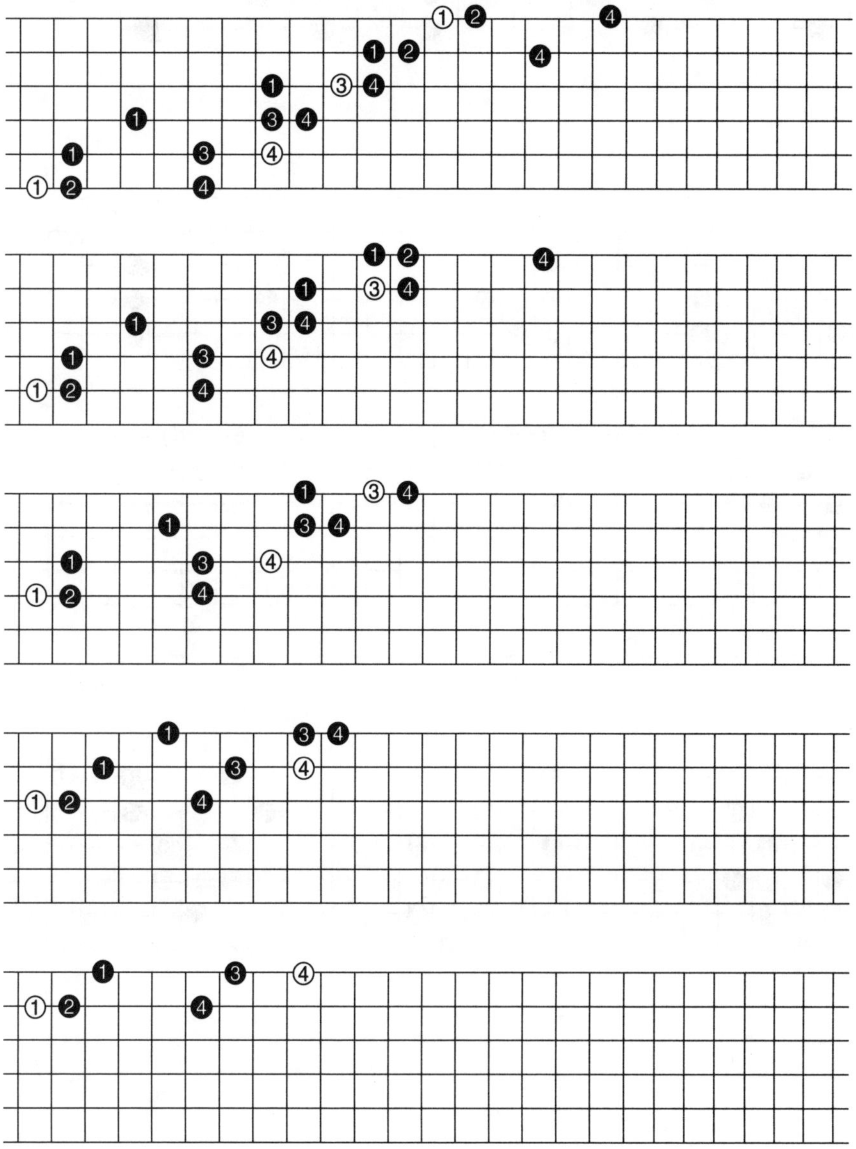

Kokin-Chosi

Scale Tones

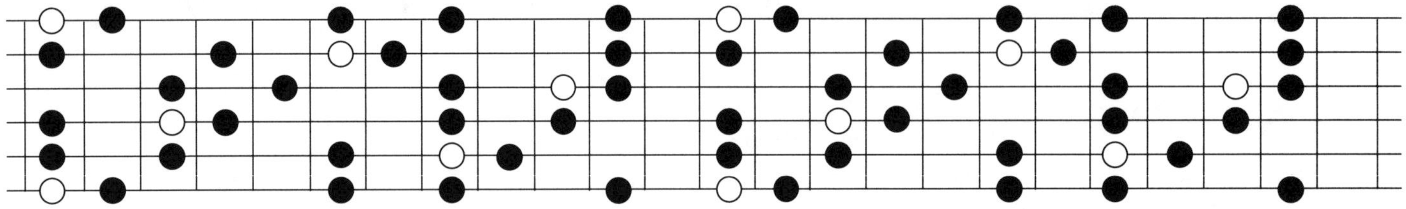

One-Octave Fingerings

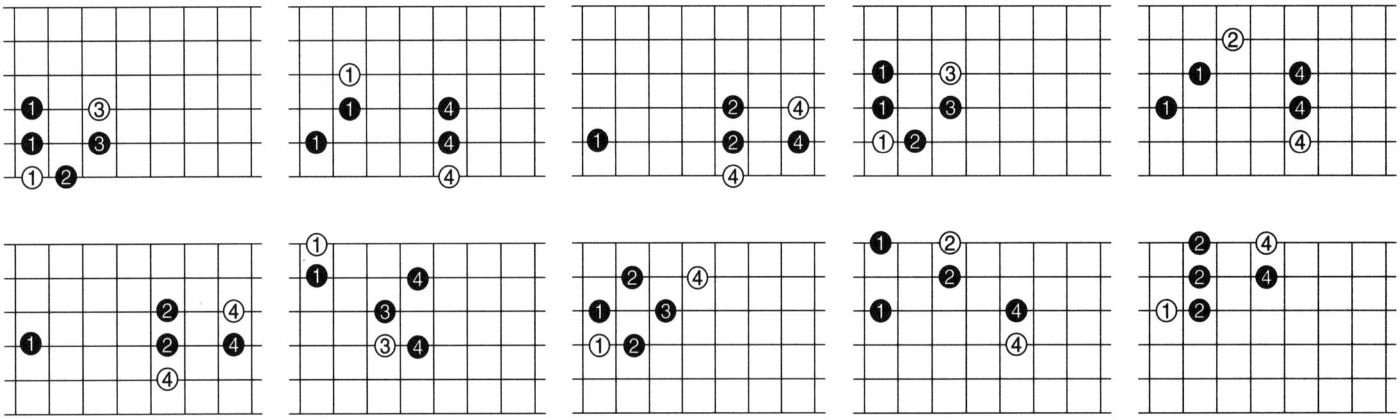

Two-Octave Fingerings

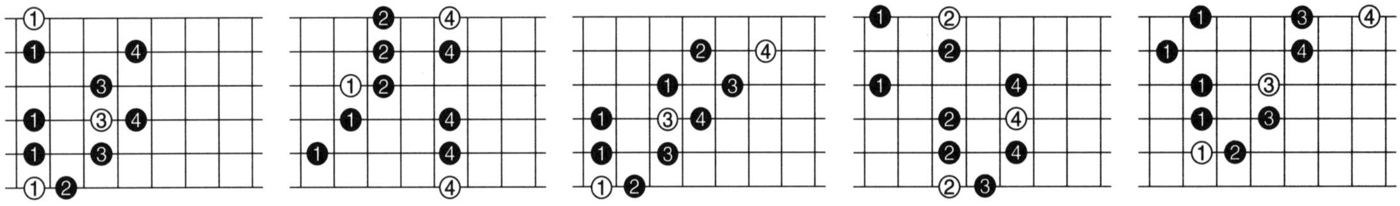

Three-Octave Fingerings

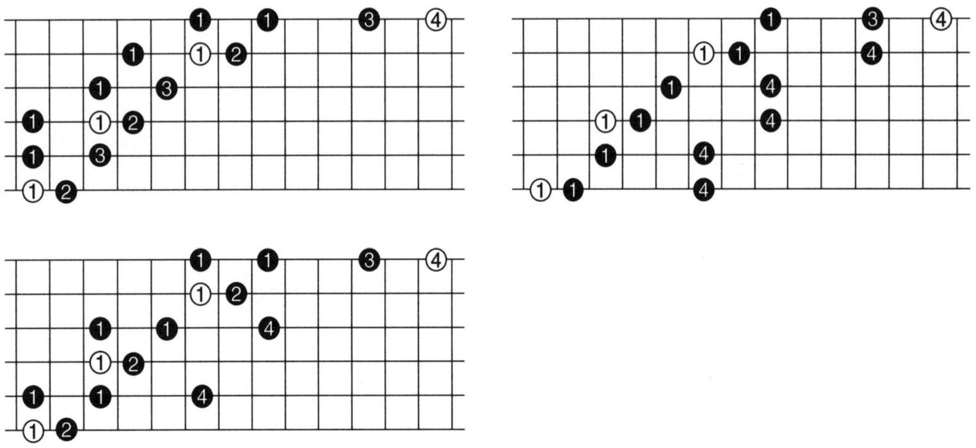

Position-Based Fingerings, Starting on all Scale Degrees

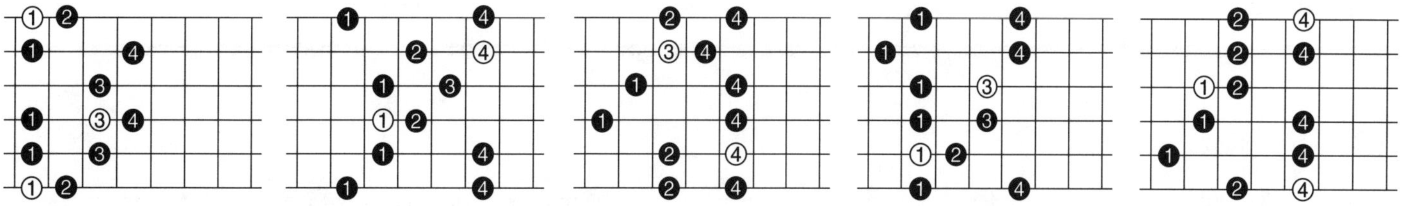

Three-Notes-Per-String Fingerings

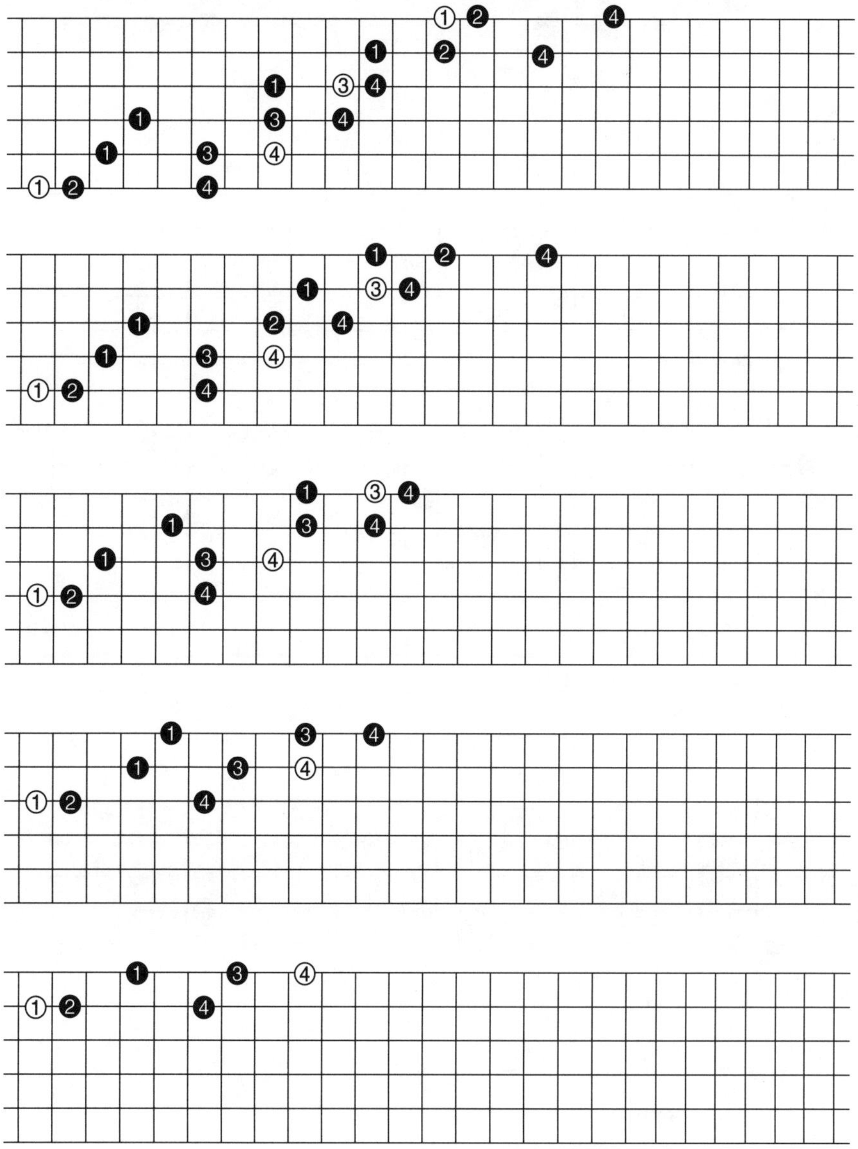

Kumoi

Scale Tones

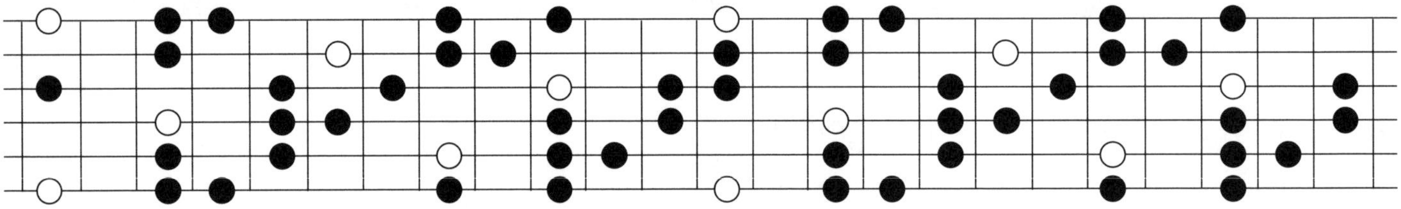

One-Octave Fingerings

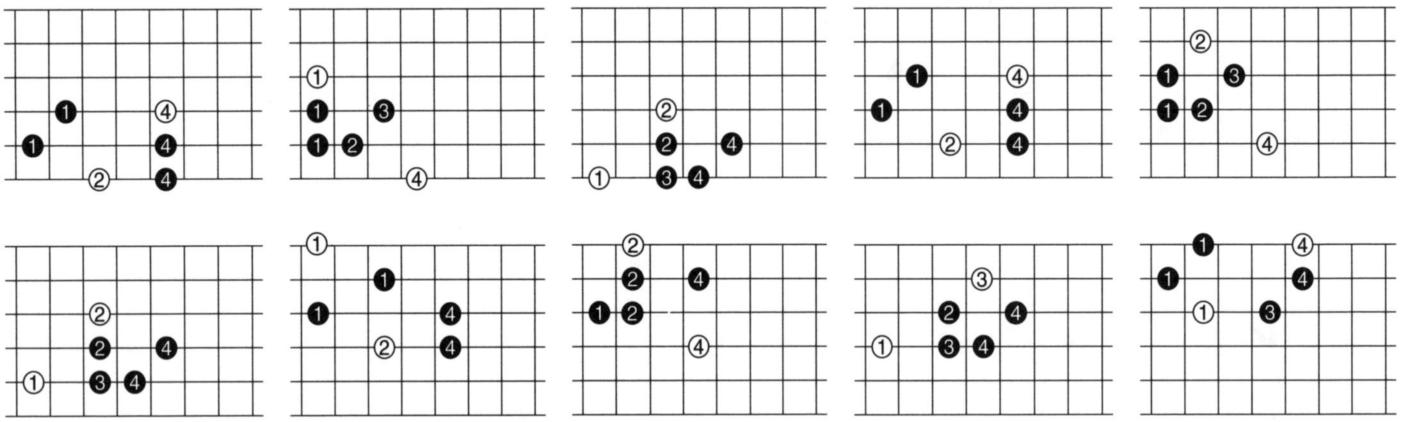

Two-Octave Fingerings

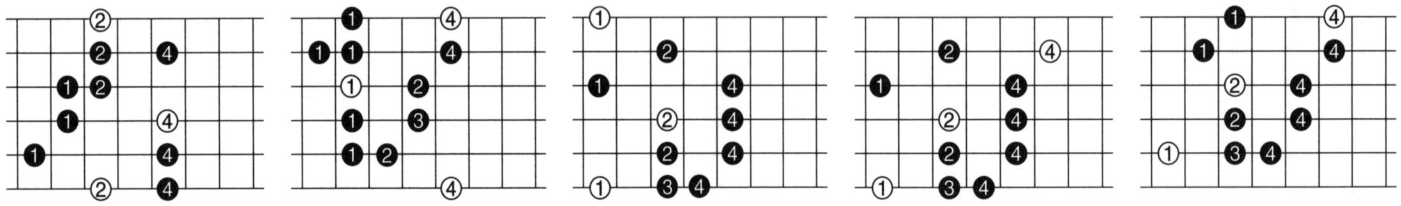

Three-Octave Fingerings

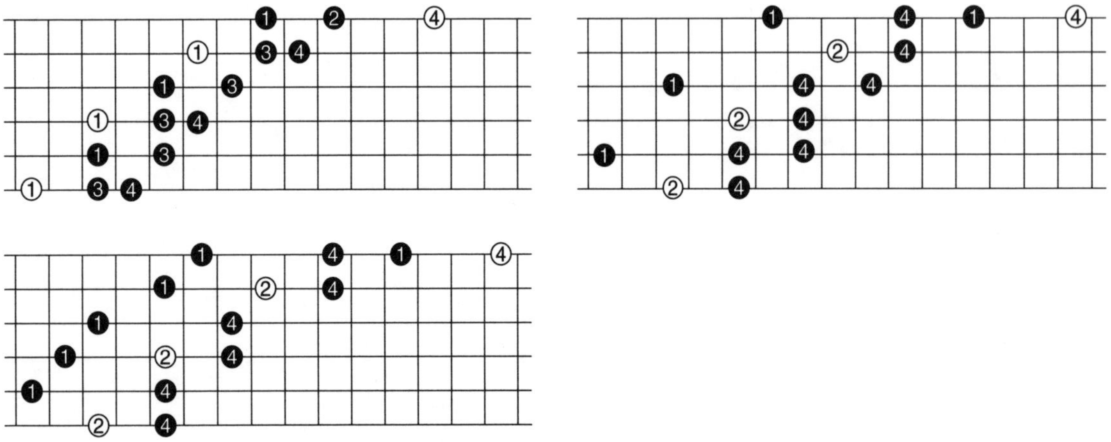

Position-Based Fingerings, Starting on all Scale Degrees

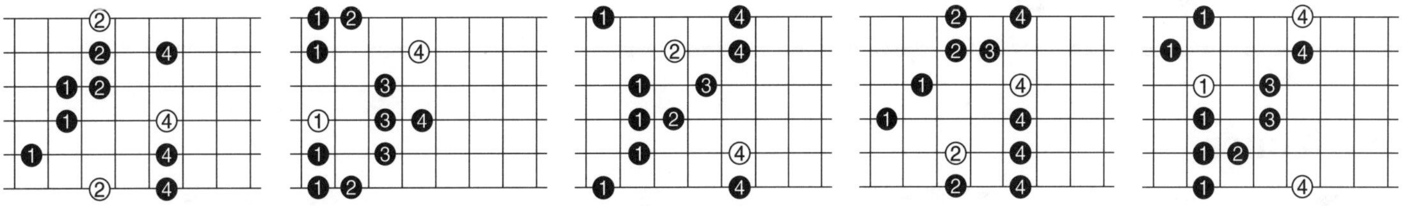

Three-Notes-Per-String Fingerings

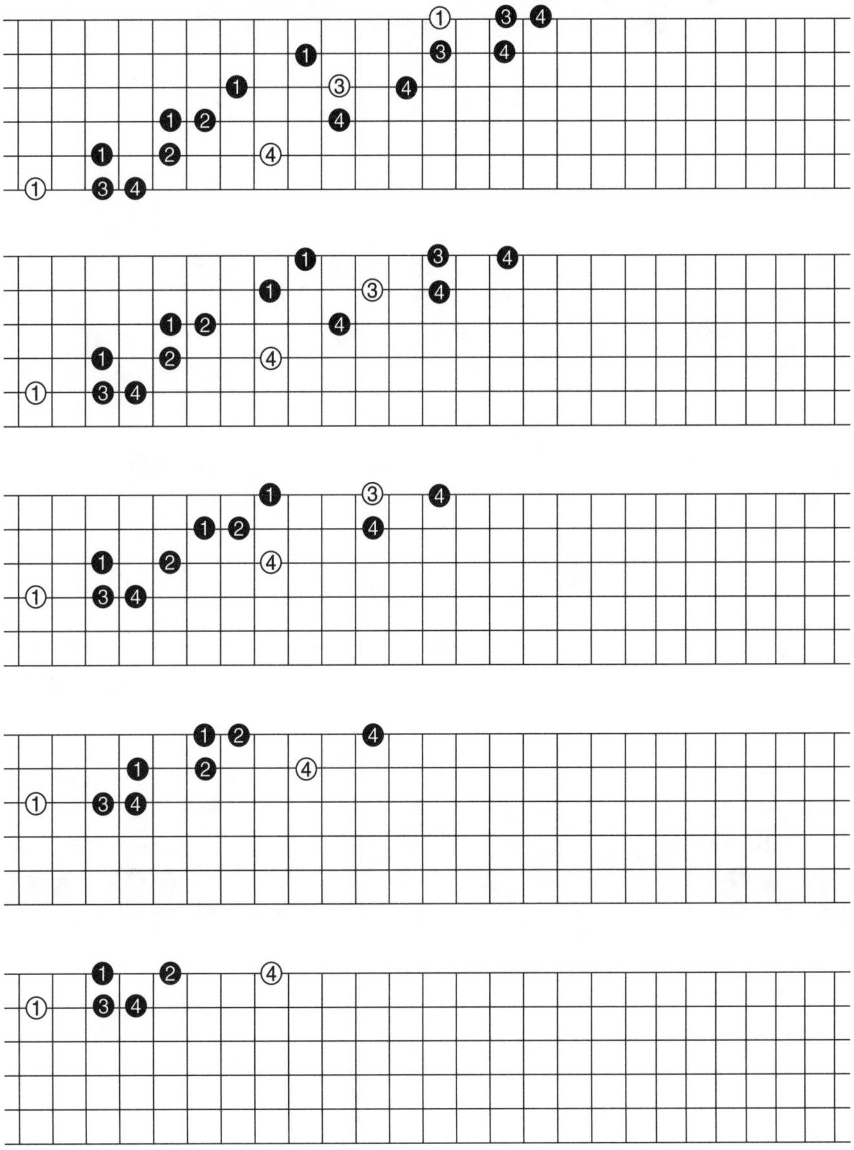

Naka Zora

Scale Tones

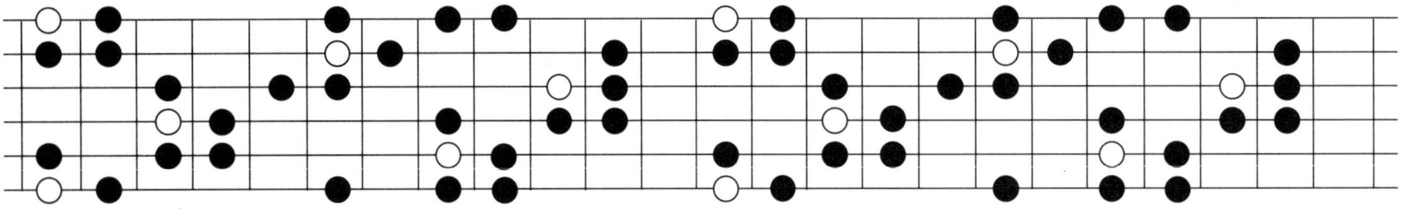

One-Octave Fingerings

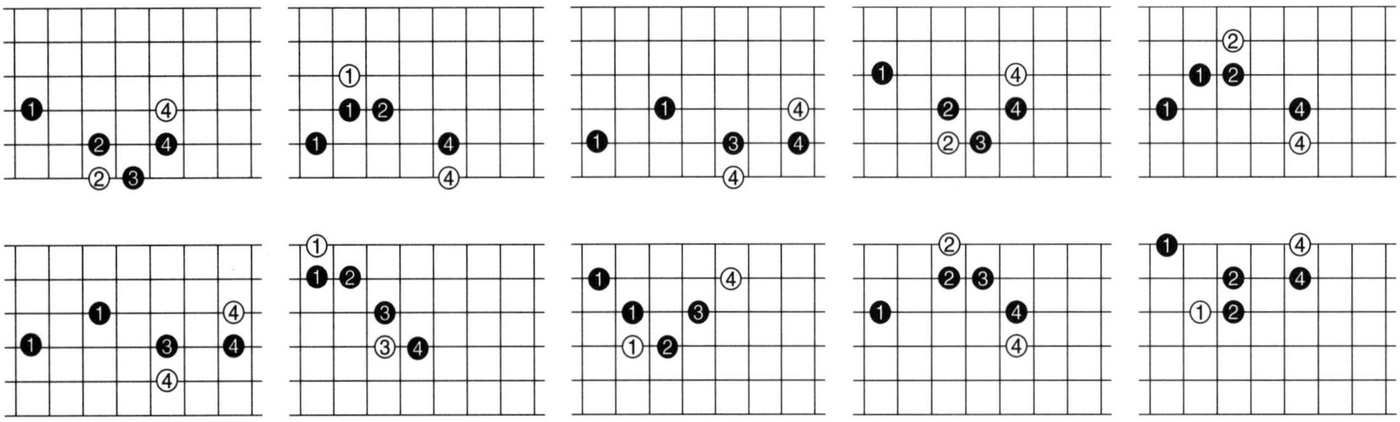

Two-Octave Fingerings

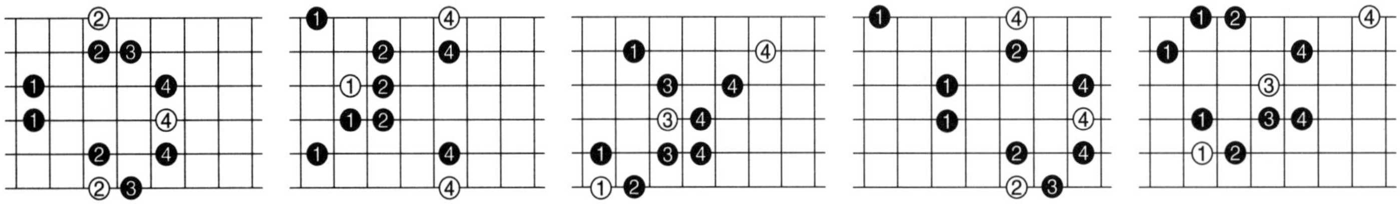

Three-Octave Fingerings

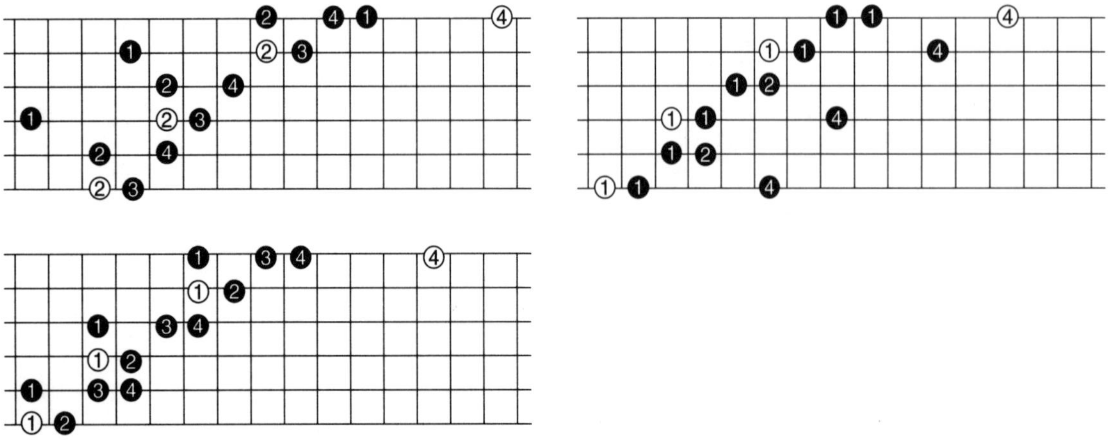

Position-Based Fingerings, Starting on all Scale Degrees

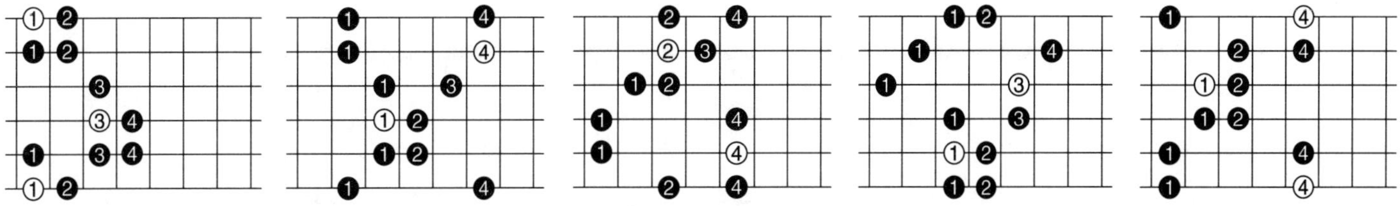

Three-Notes-Per-String Fingerings

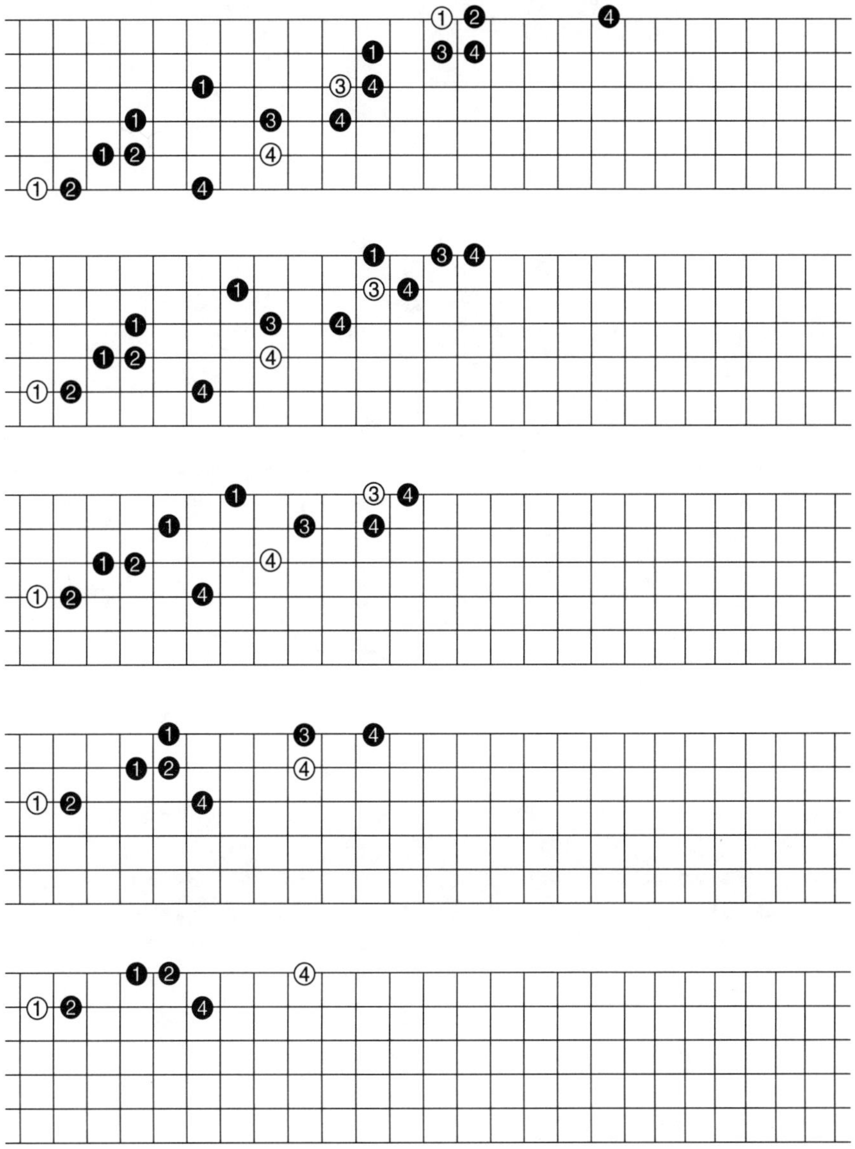

Pelog

Scale Tones

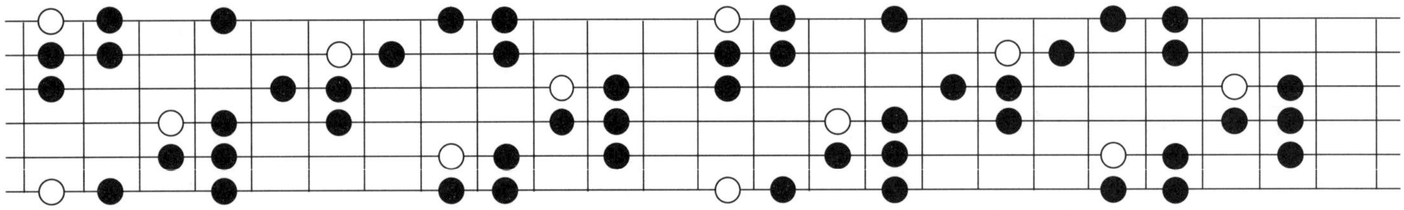

One-Octave Fingerings

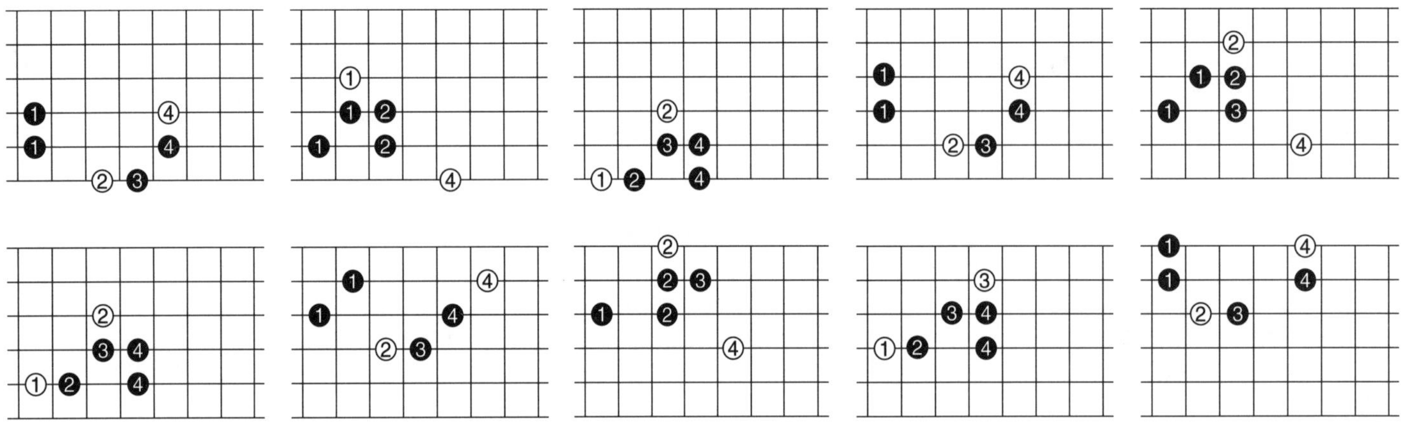

Two-Octave Fingerings

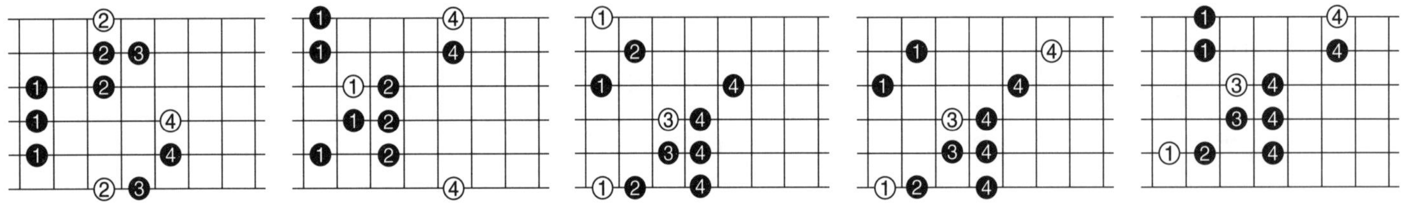

Three-Octave Fingerings

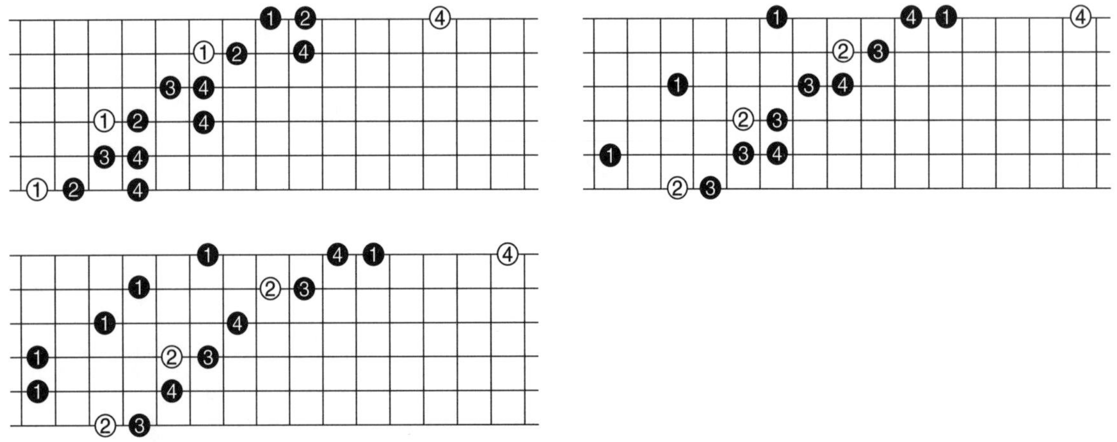

Position-Based Fingerings, Starting on all Scale Degrees

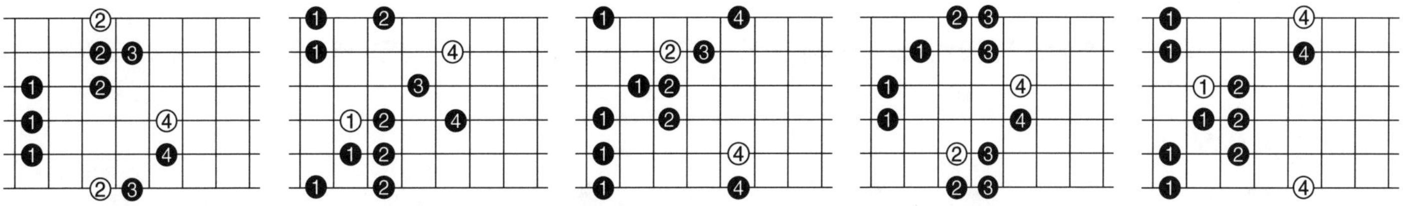

Three-Notes-Per-String Fingerings

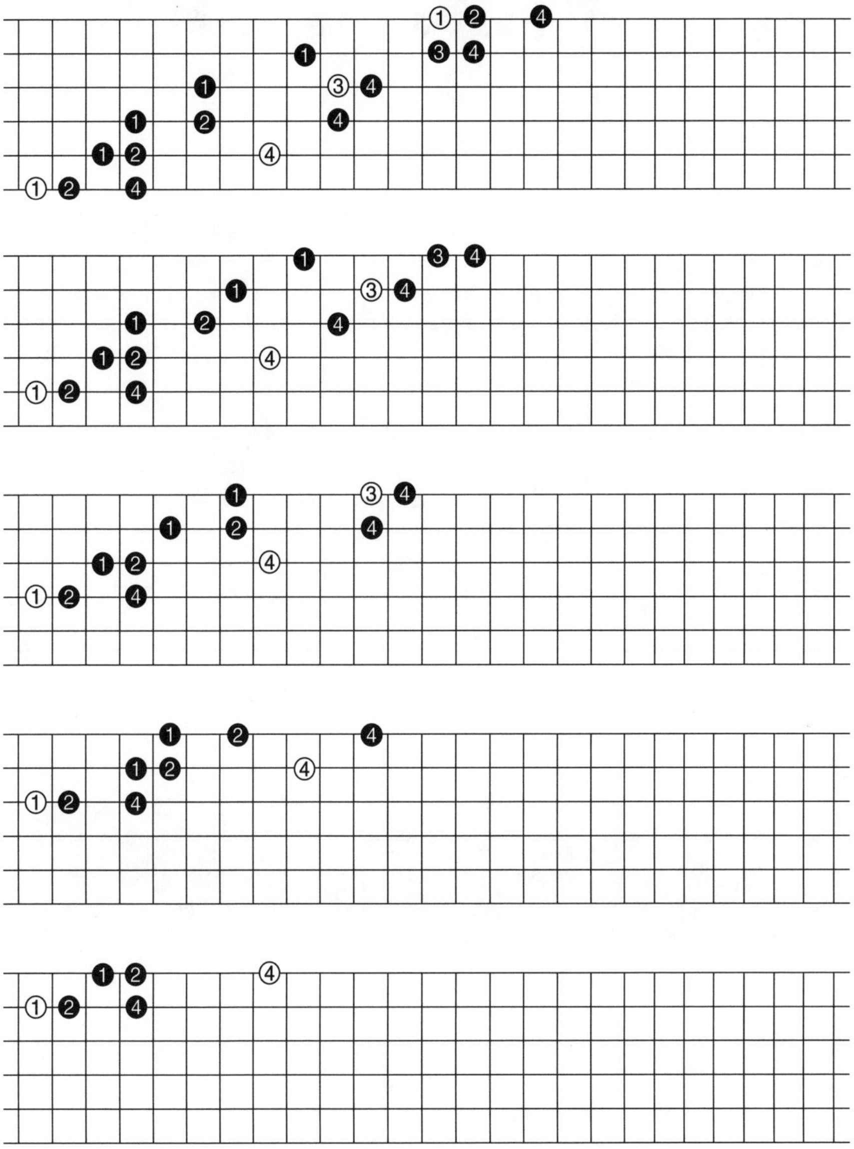

Ritsu

Scale Tones

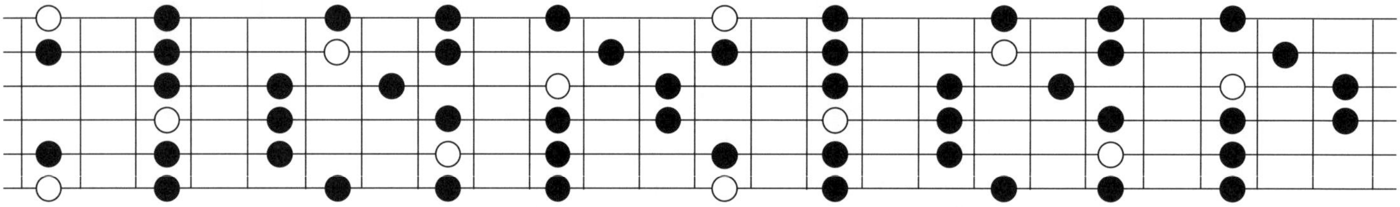

One-Octave Fingerings

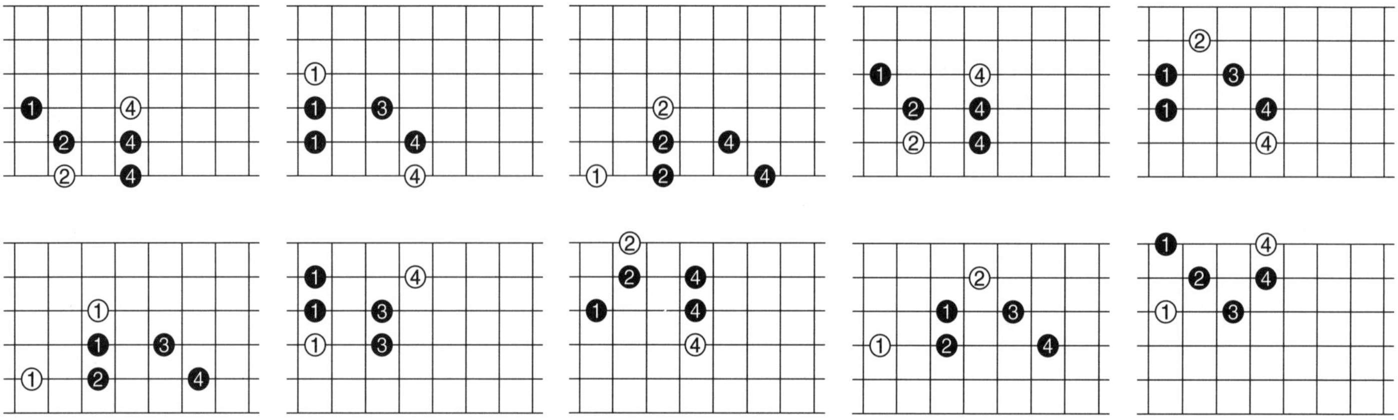

Two-Octave Fingerings

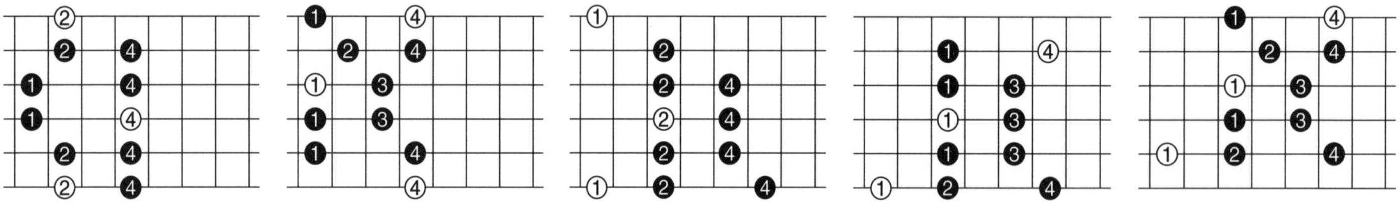

Three-Octave Fingerings

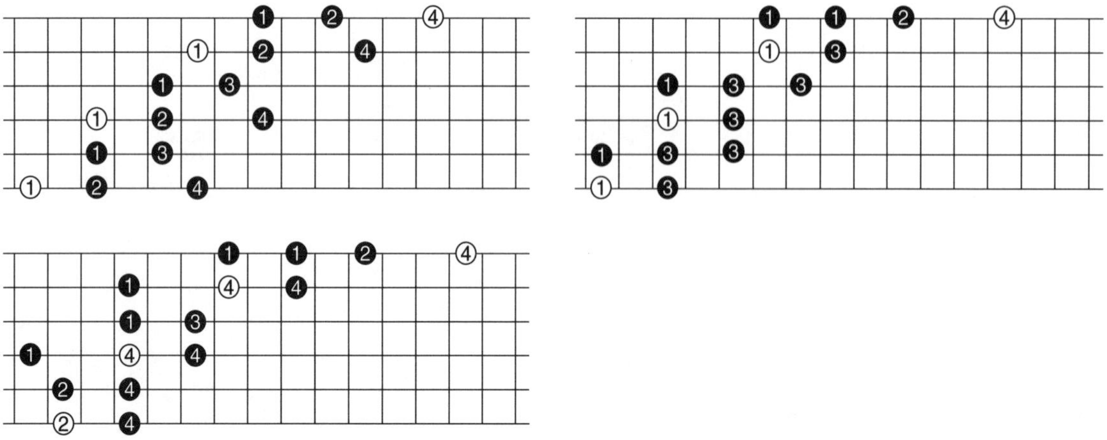

Position-Based Fingerings, Starting on all Scale Degrees

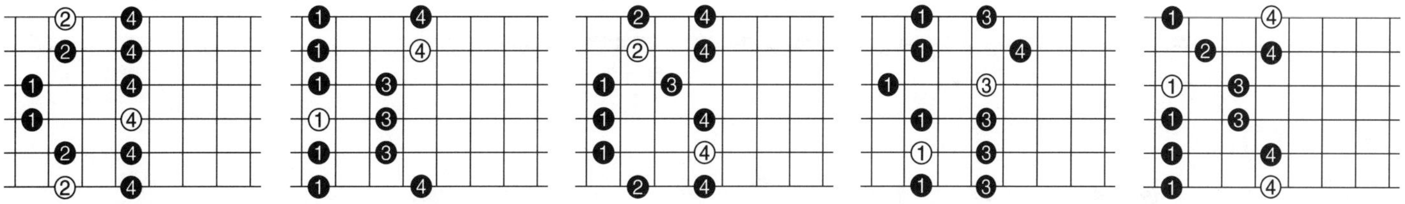

Three-Notes-Per-String Fingerings

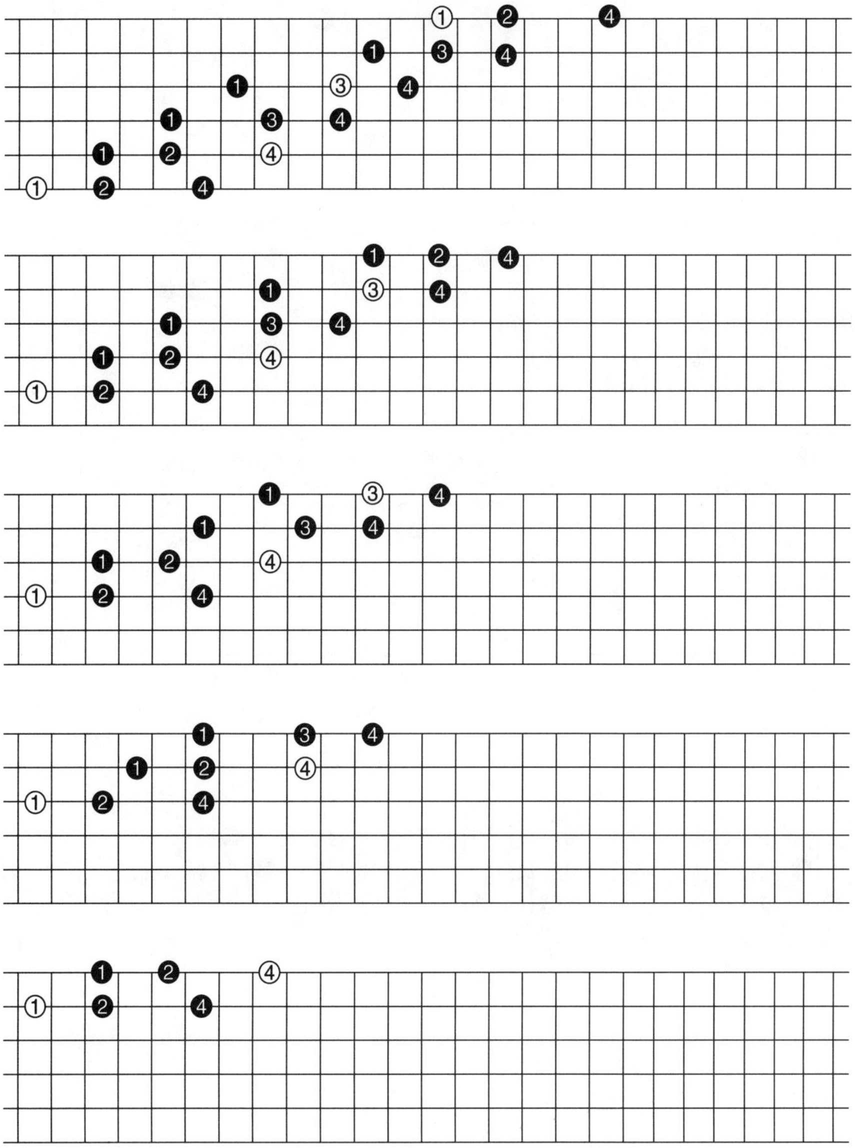

Ryūkyū

Scale Tones

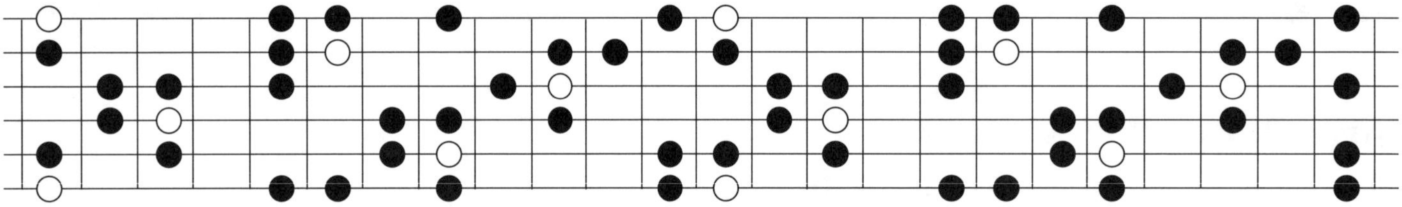

One-Octave Fingerings

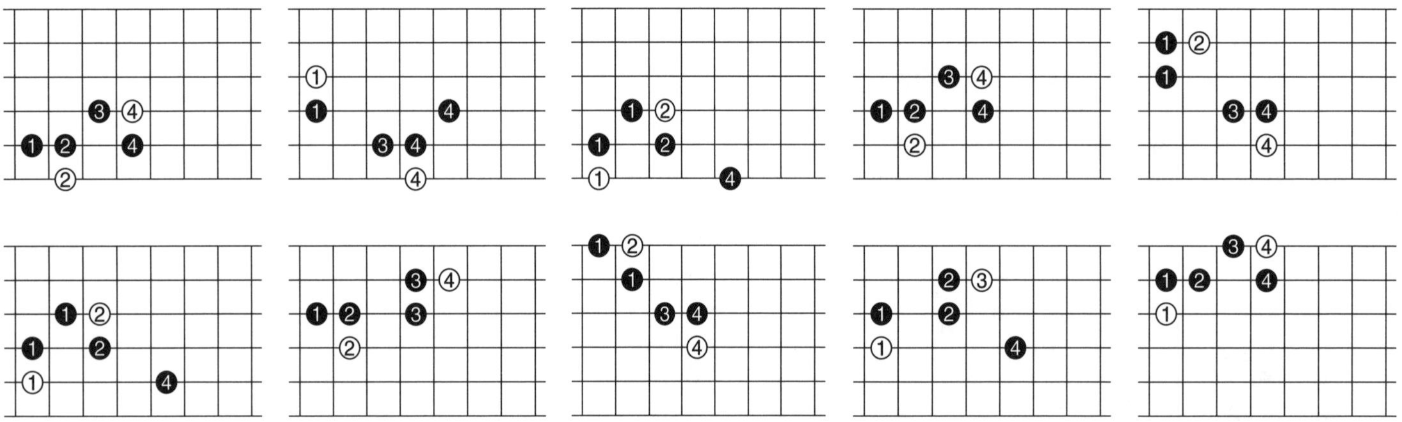

Two-Octave Fingerings

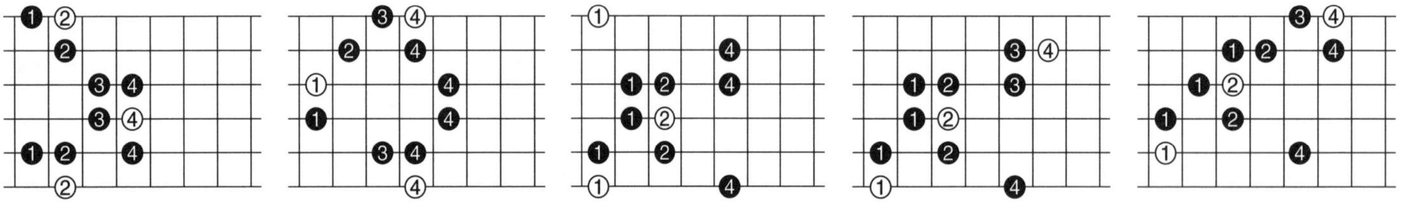

Three-Octave Fingerings

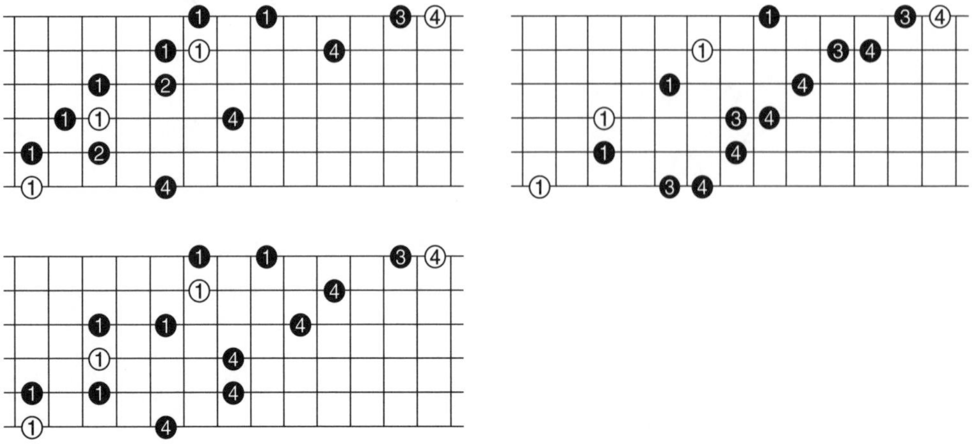

Position-Based Fingerings, Starting on all Scale Degrees

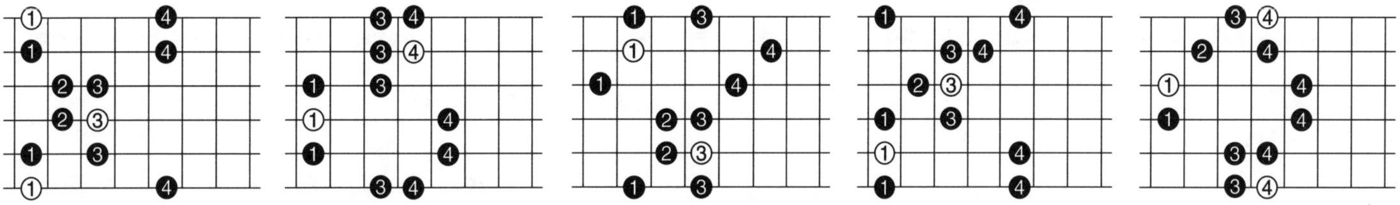

Three-Notes-Per-String Fingerings

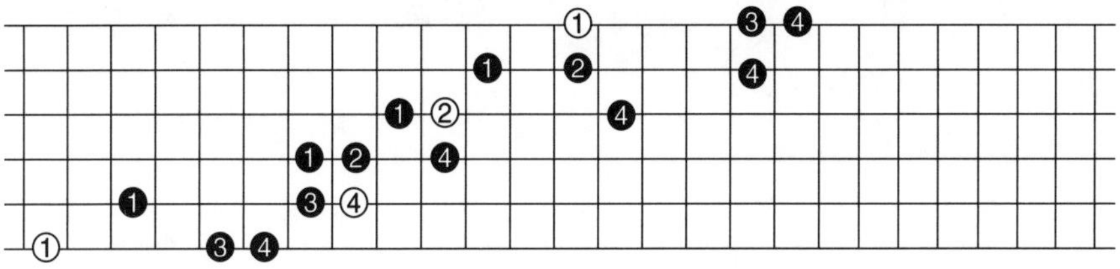

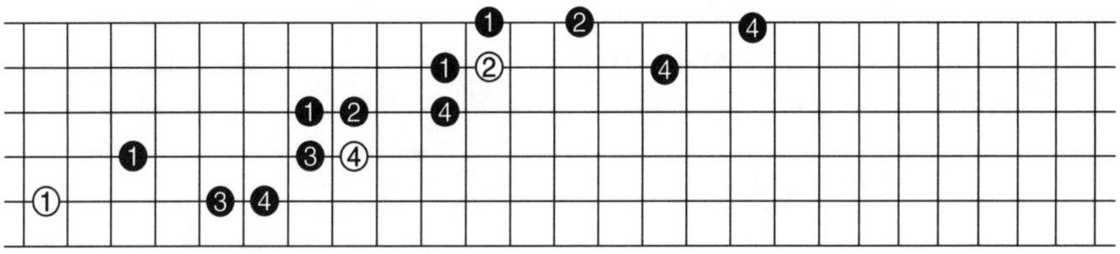

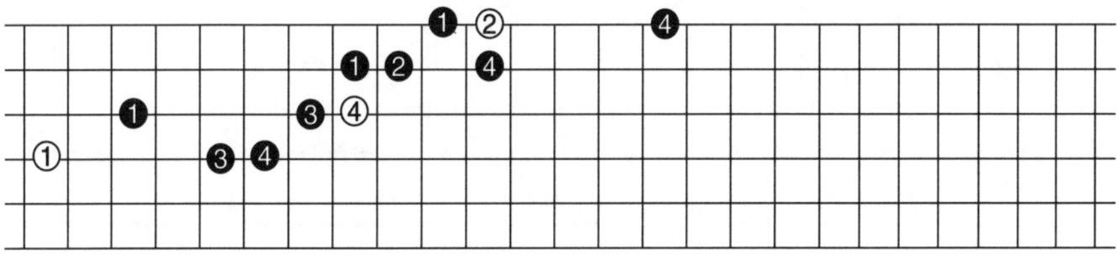

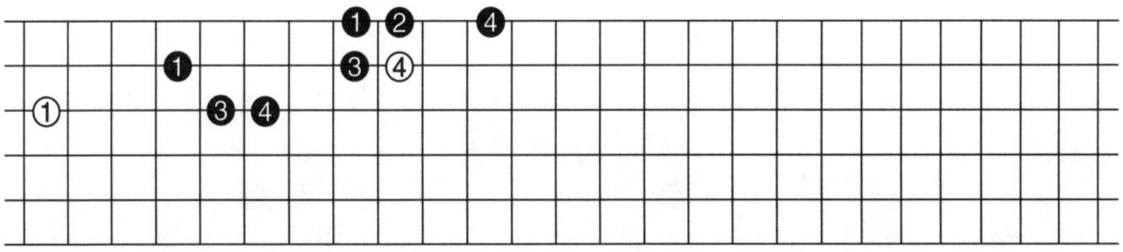

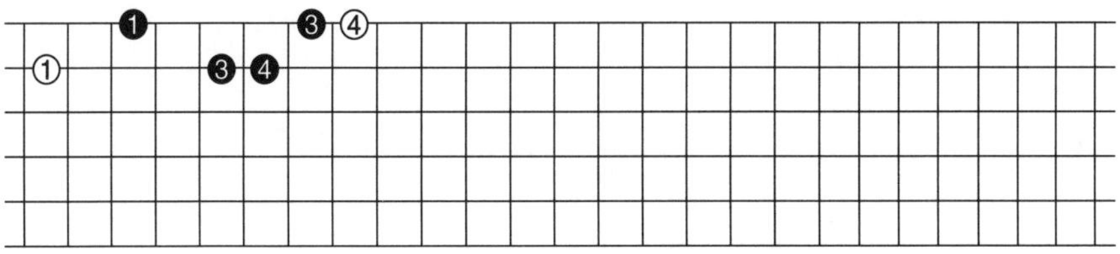

Shimo-Chidori

Scale Tones

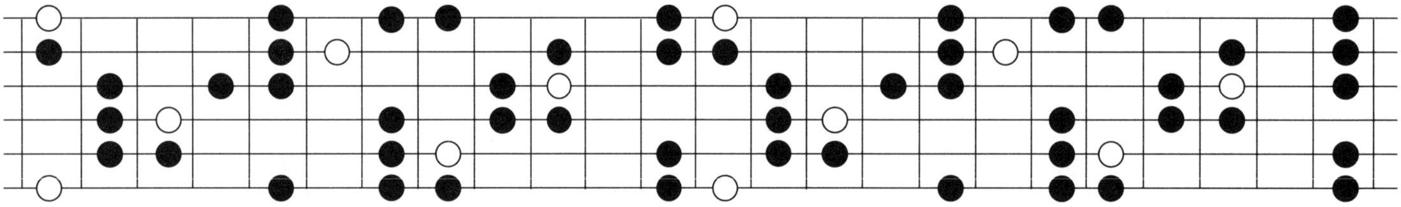

One-Octave Fingerings

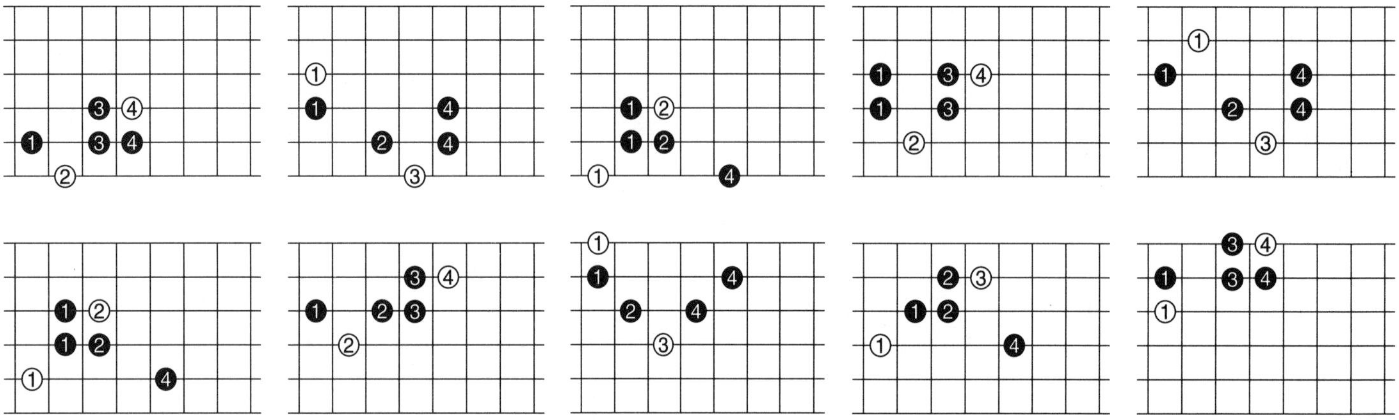

Two-Octave Fingerings

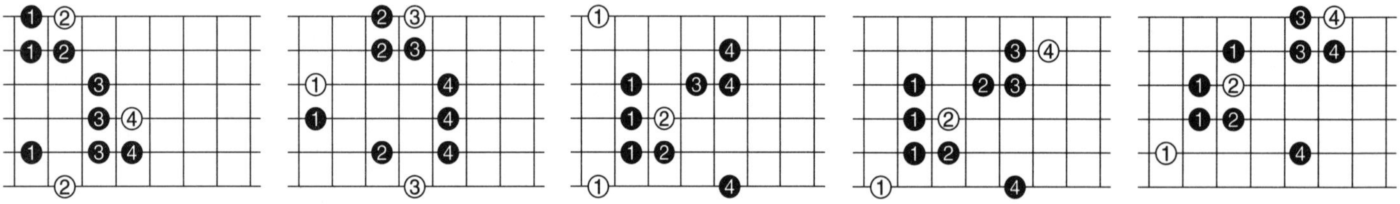

Three-Octave Fingerings

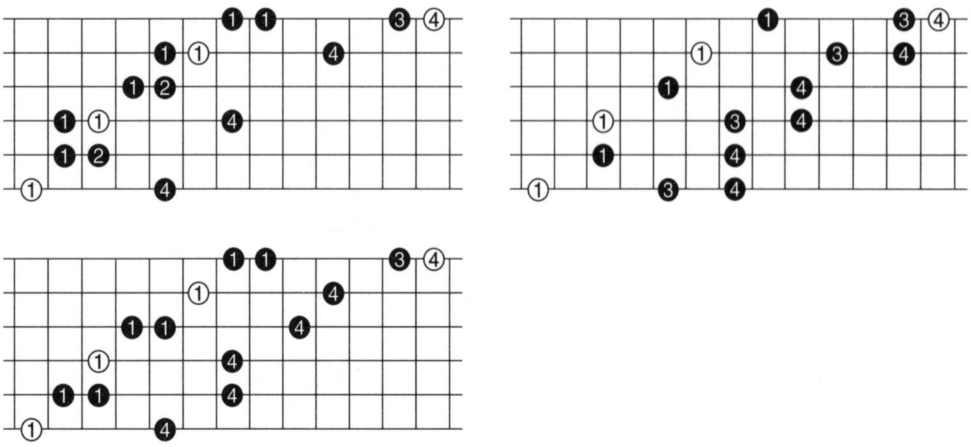

Position-Based Fingerings, Starting on all Scale Degrees

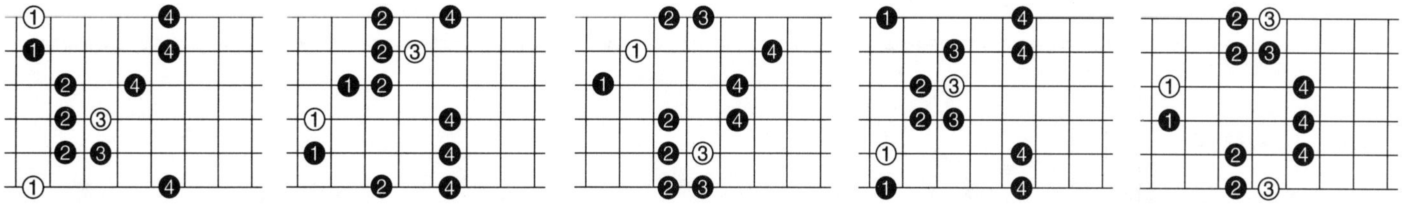

Three-Notes-Per-String Fingerings

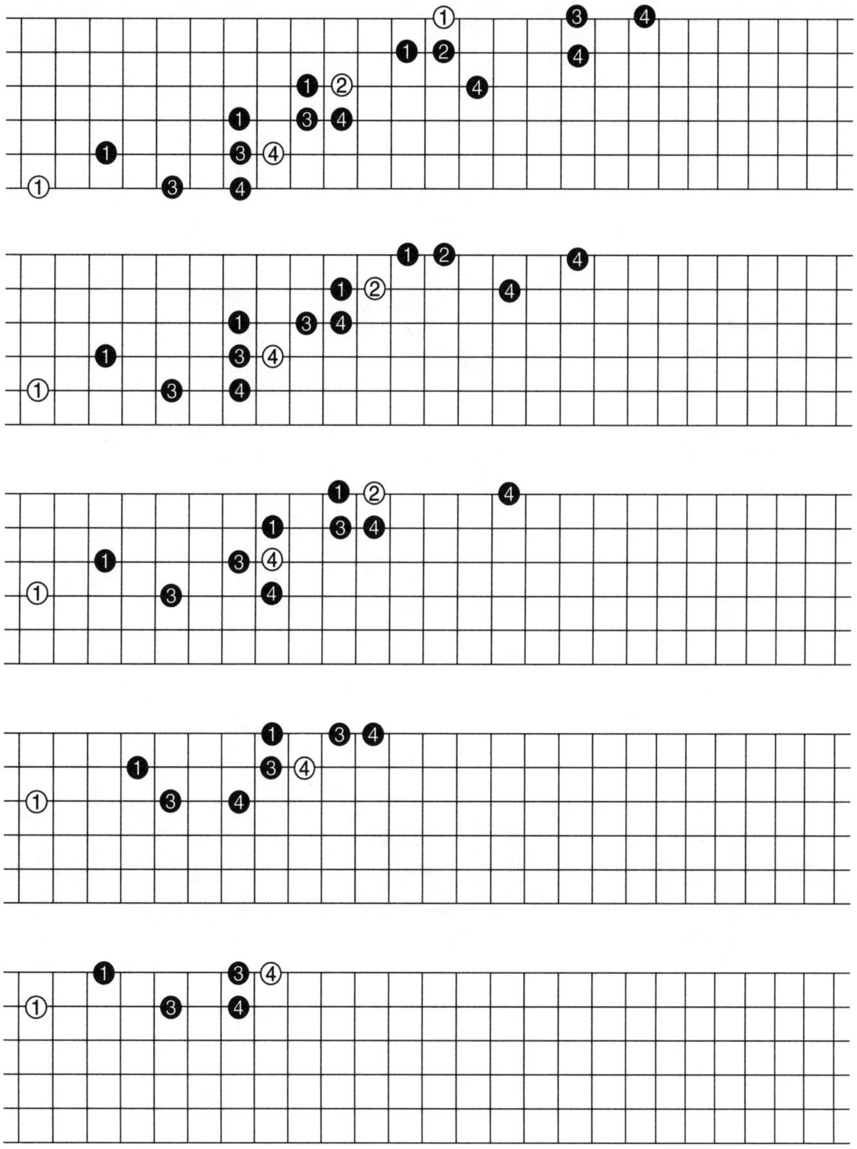

Augmented

Scale Tones

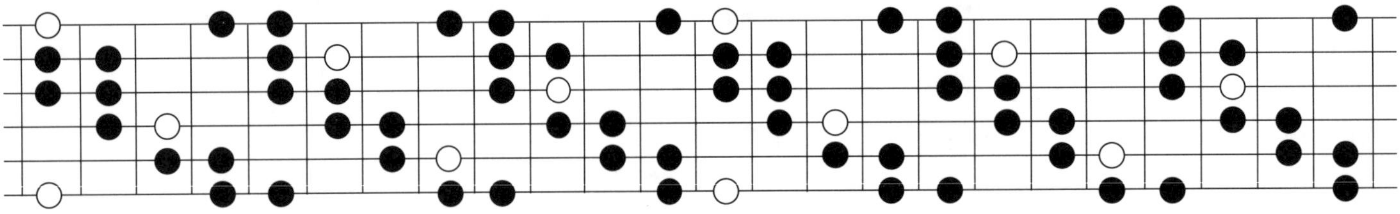

One-Octave Fingerings

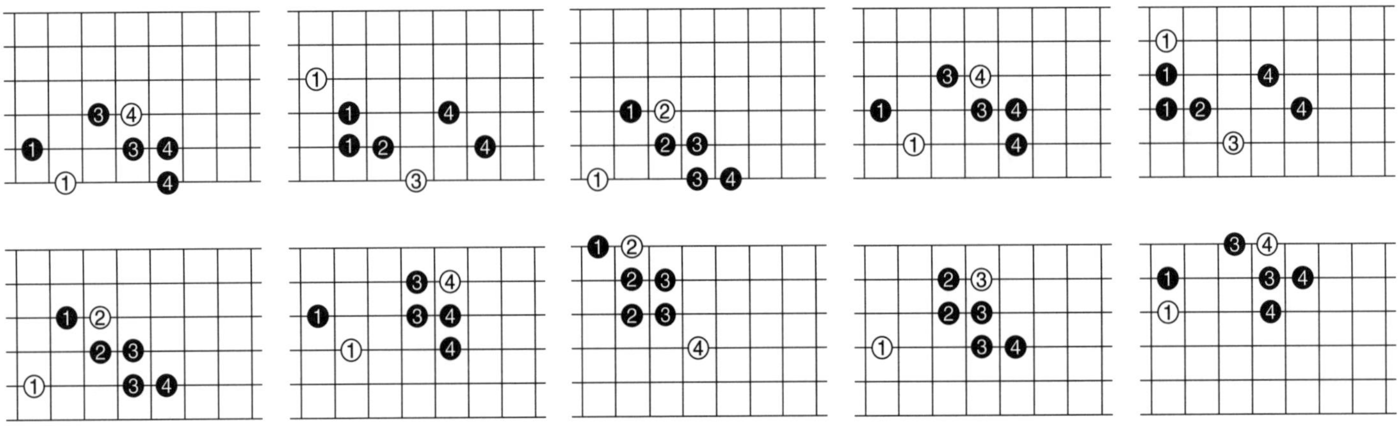

Two-Octave Fingerings

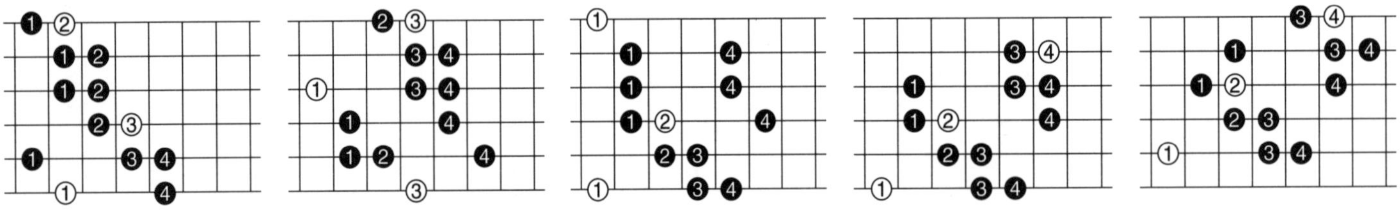

Three-Octave Fingerings

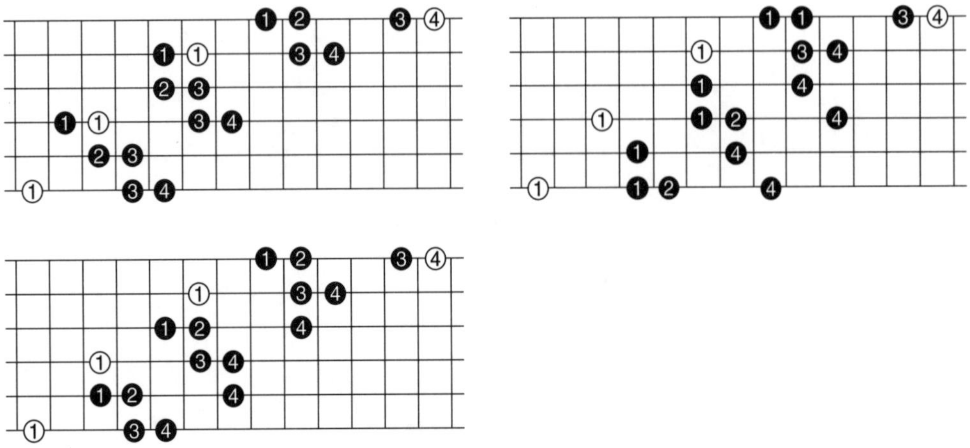

Position-Based Fingerings, Starting on all Scale Degrees

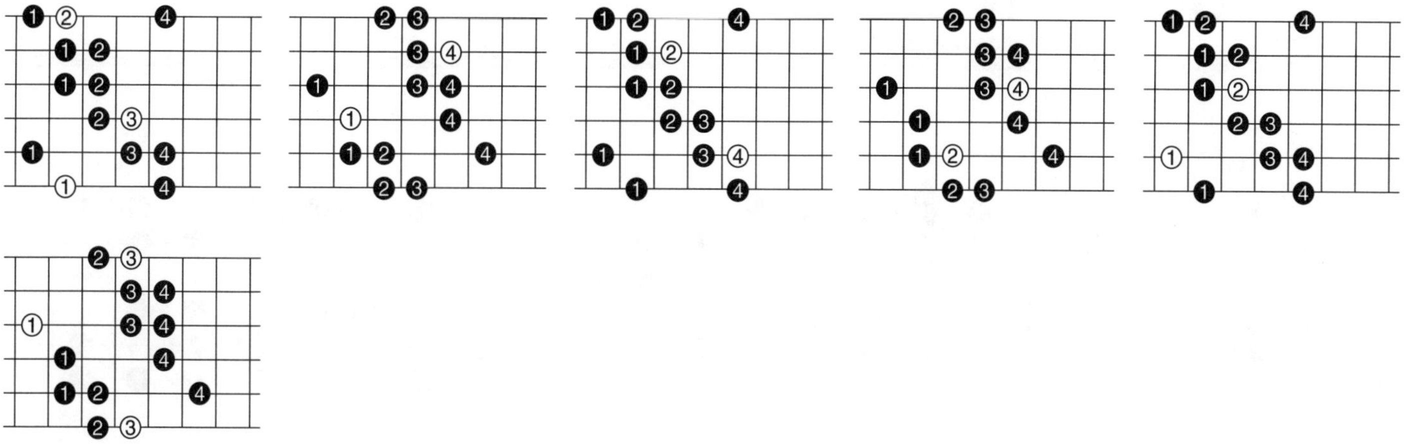

Three-Notes-Per-String Fingerings

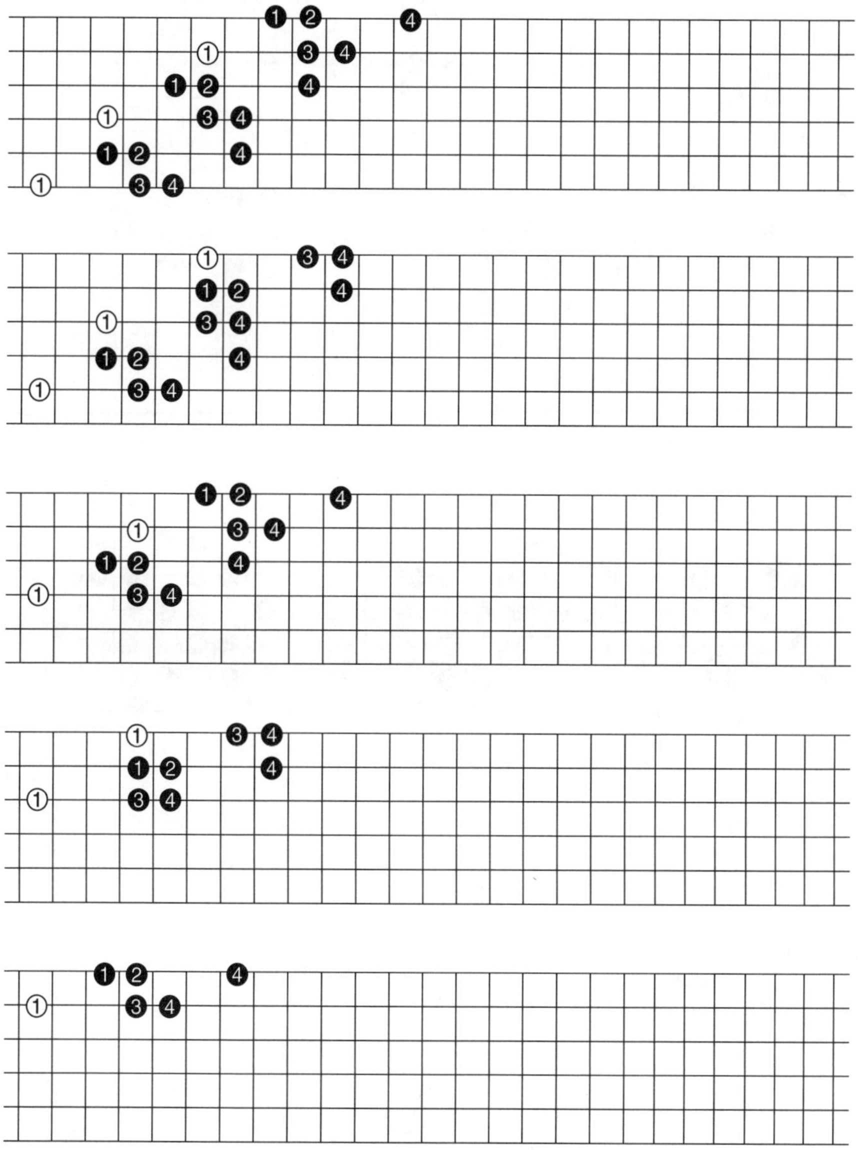

Diminished Half/Whole

Scale Tones

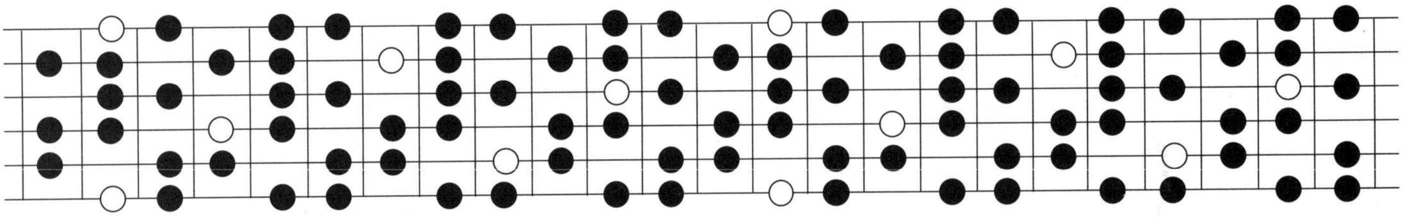

One-Octave Fingerings

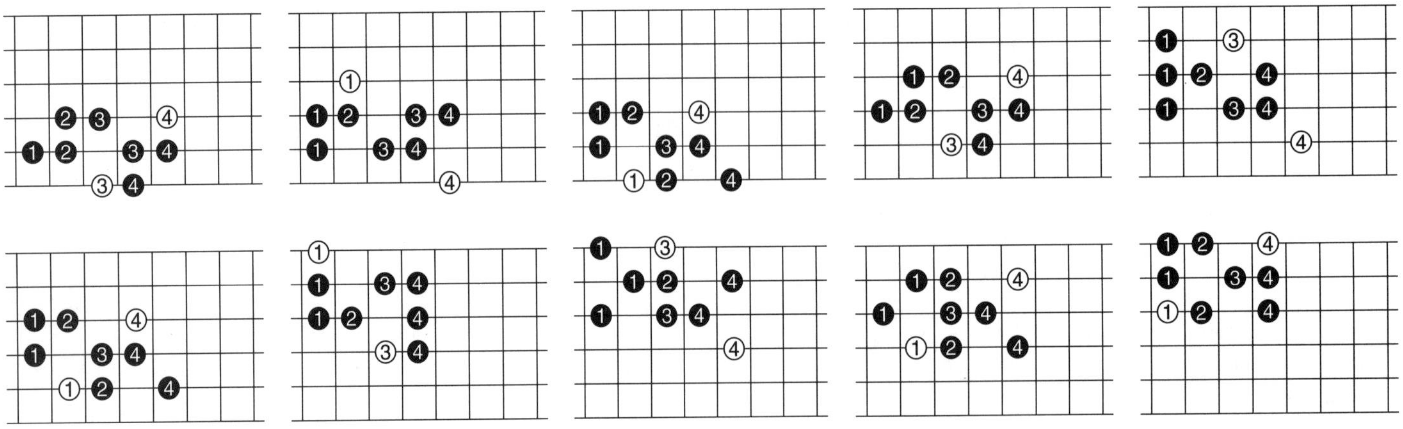

Two-Octave Fingerings

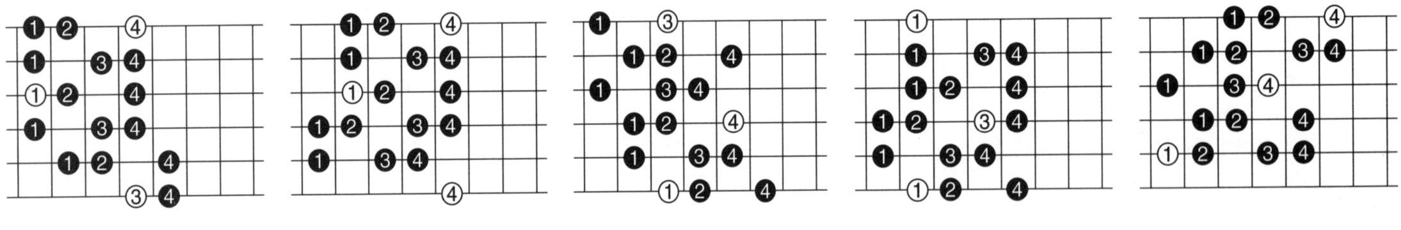

Three-Octave Fingerings

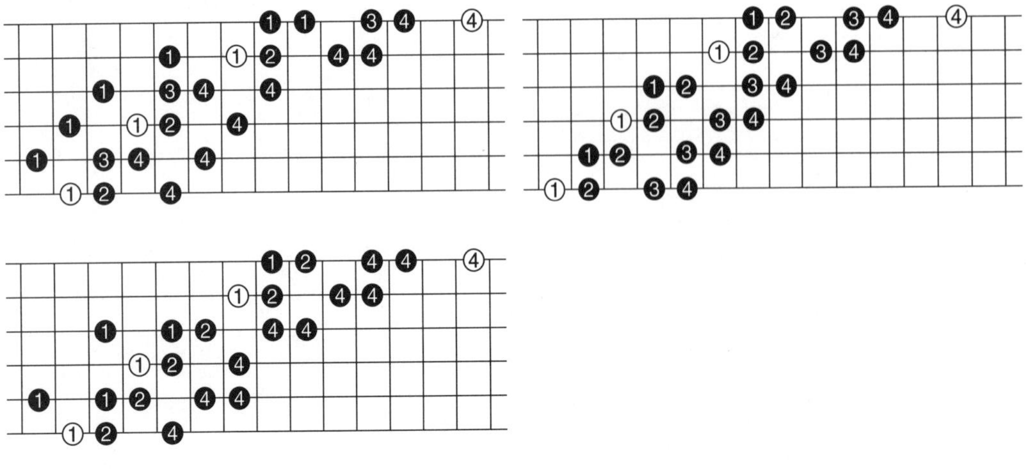

Position-Based Fingerings, Starting on all Scale Degrees

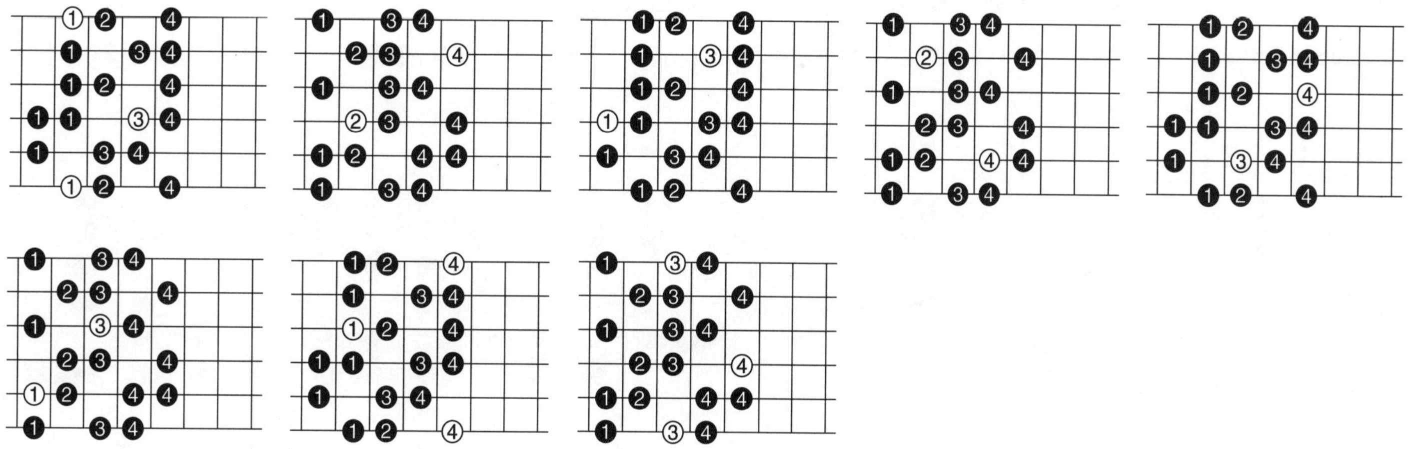

Three-Notes-Per-String Fingerings, Starting on all Scale Degrees

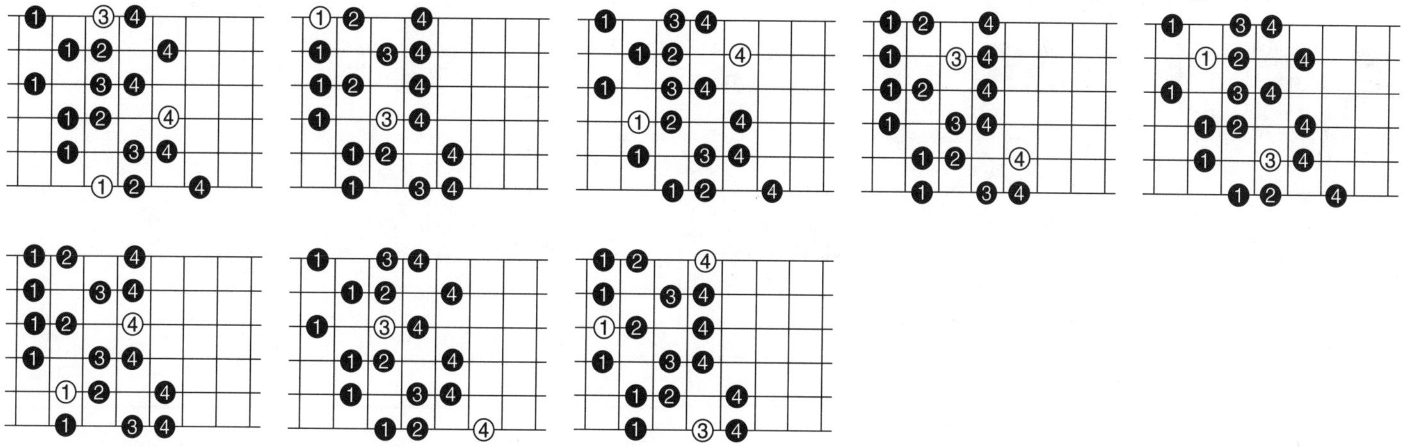

Four-Notes-Per-String Fingerings

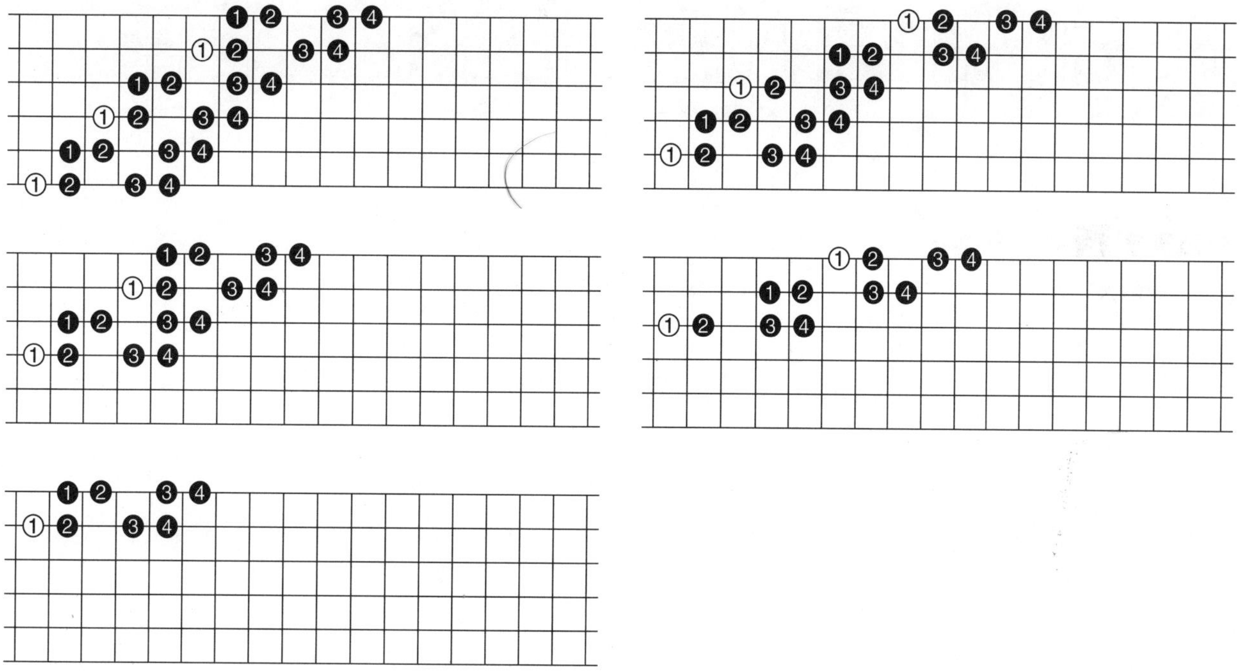

Diminished Whole/Half

Scale Tones

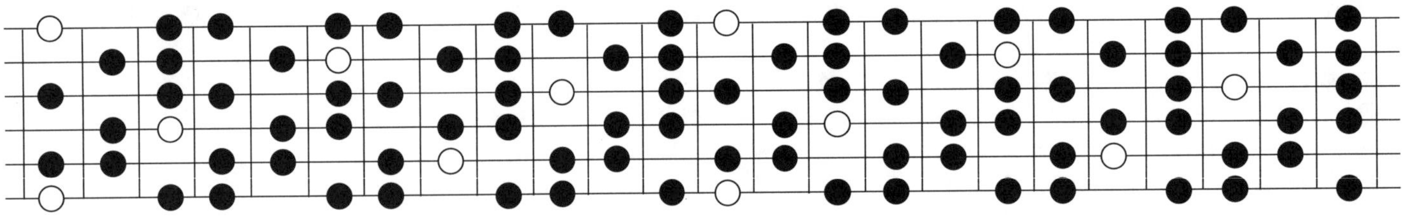

One-Octave Fingerings

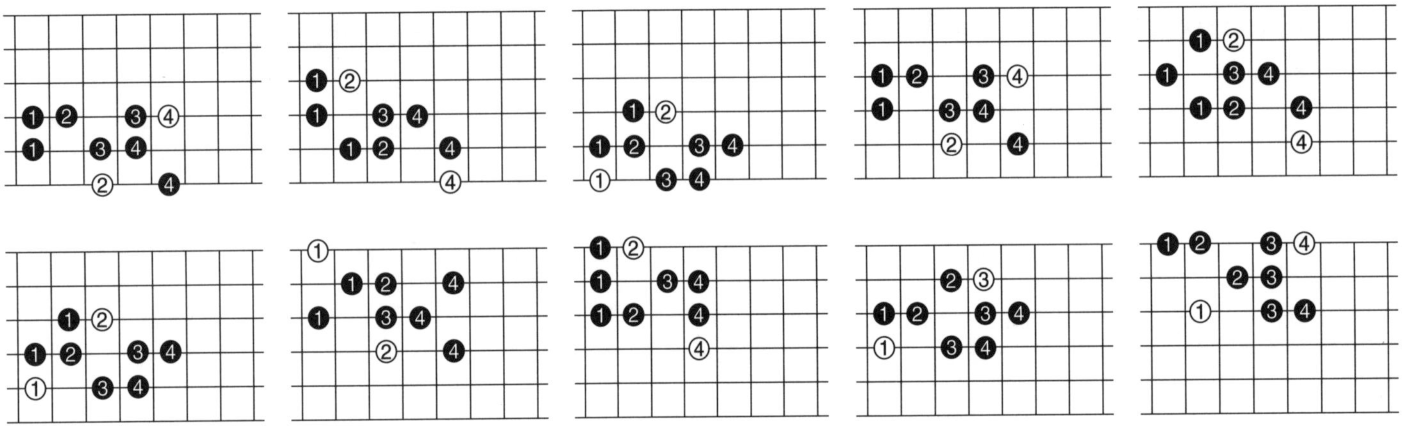

Two-Octave Fingerings

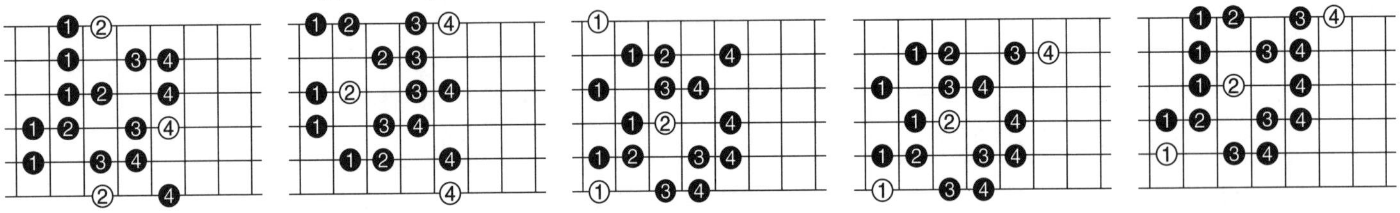

Three-Octave Fingerings

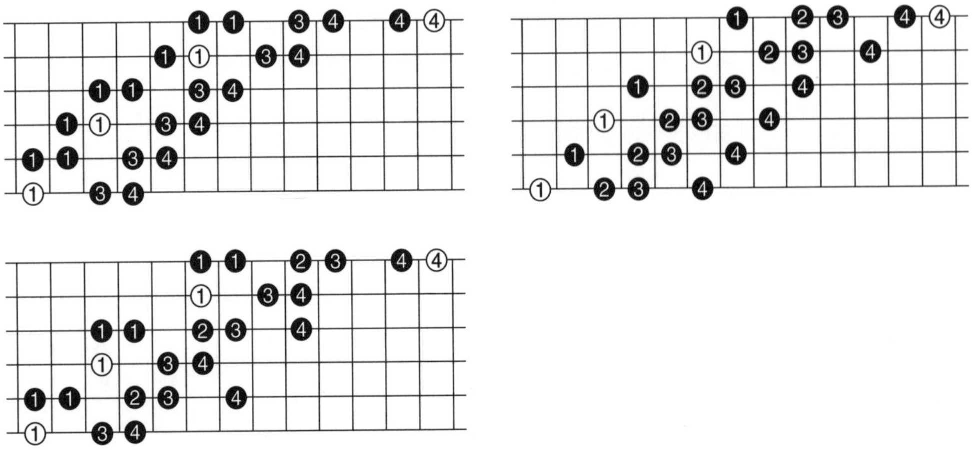

Position-Based Fingerings, Starting on all Scale Degrees

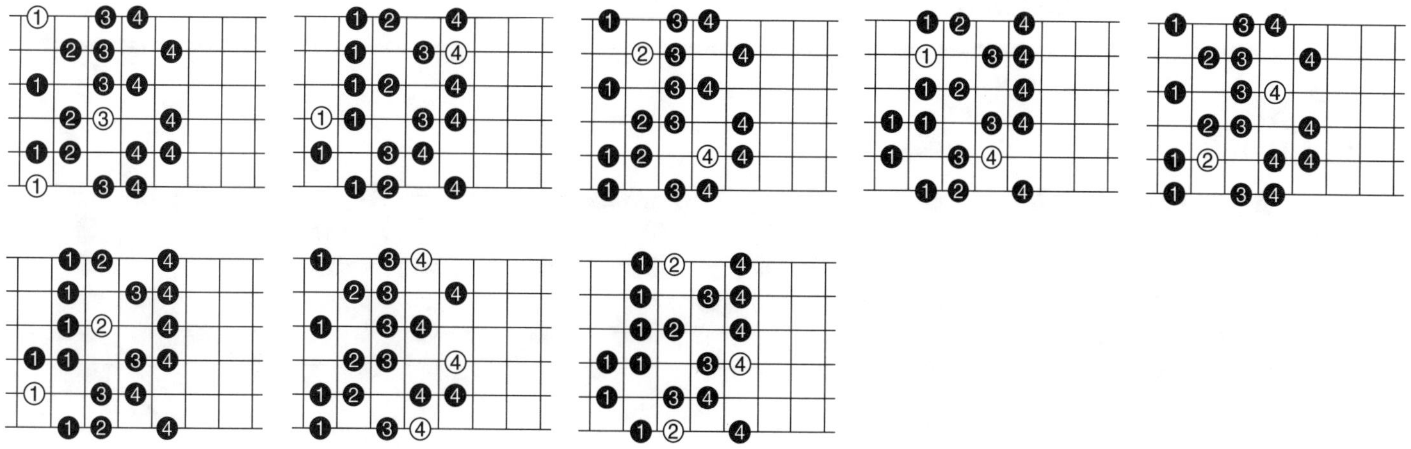

Three-Notes-Per-String Fingerings, Starting on all Scale Degrees

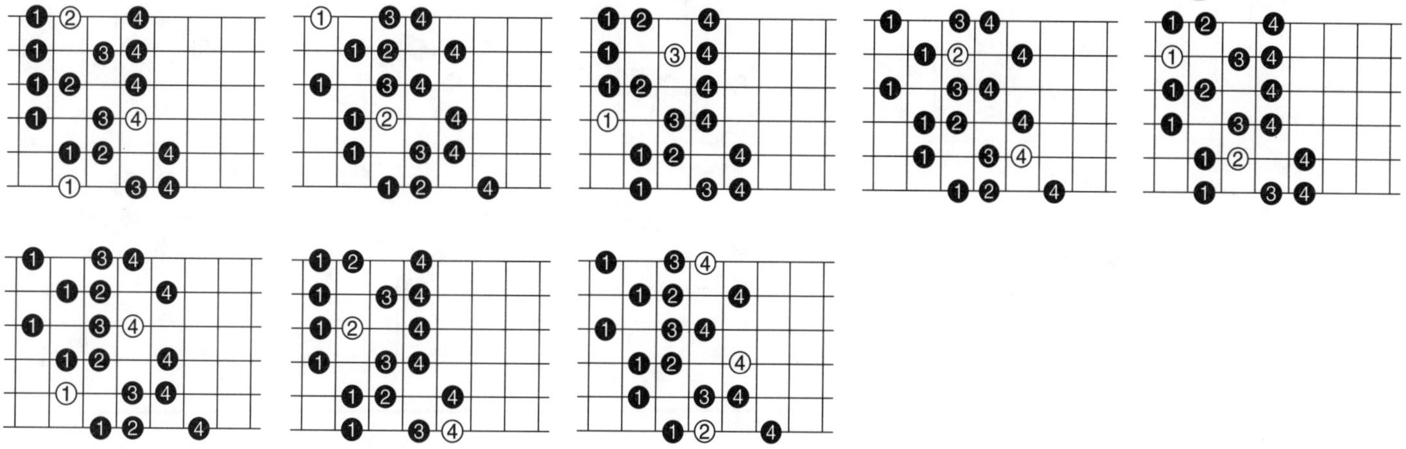

Four-Notes-Per-String Fingerings

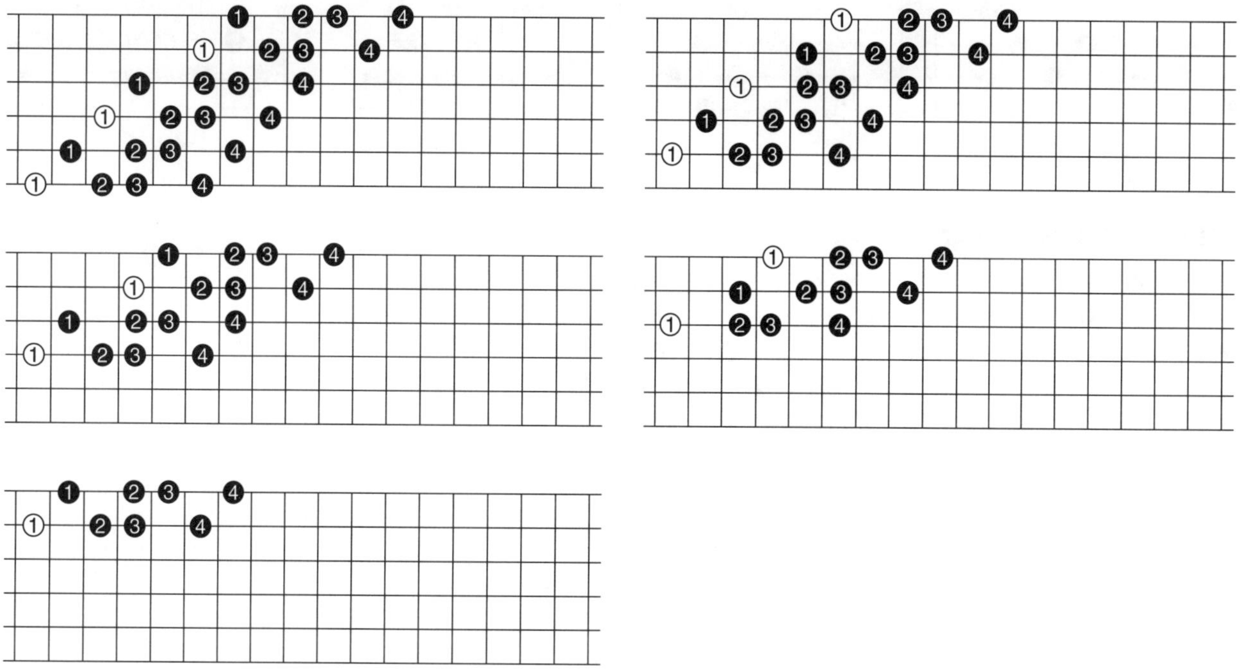

Whole Tone

Scale Tones

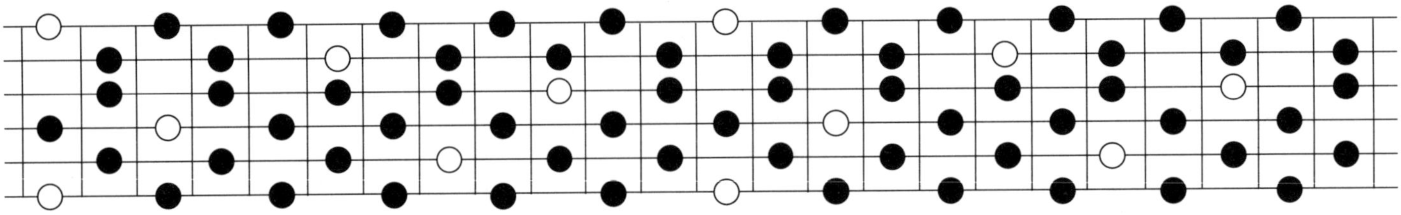

One-Octave Fingerings

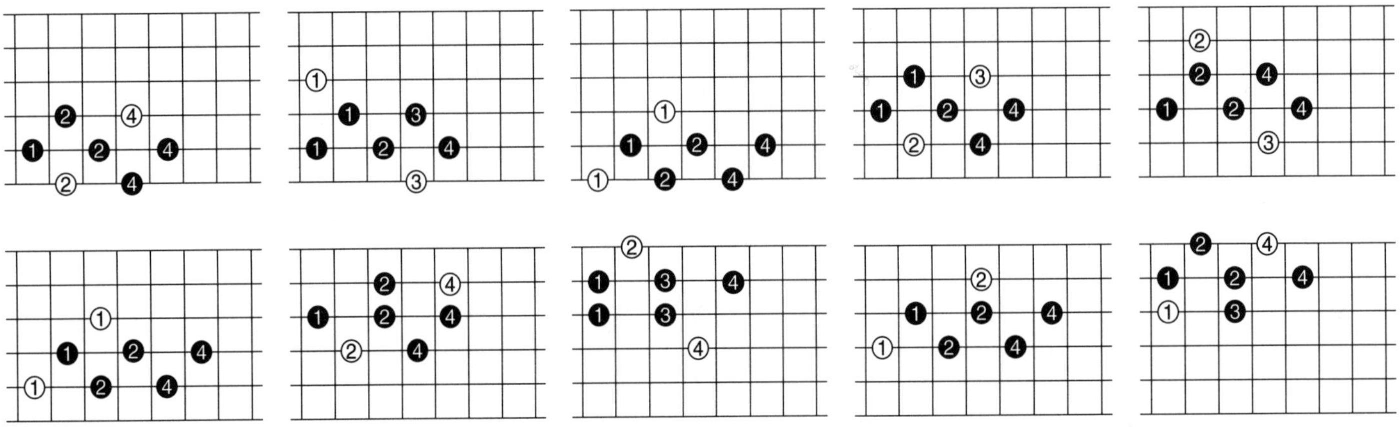

Two-Octave Fingerings

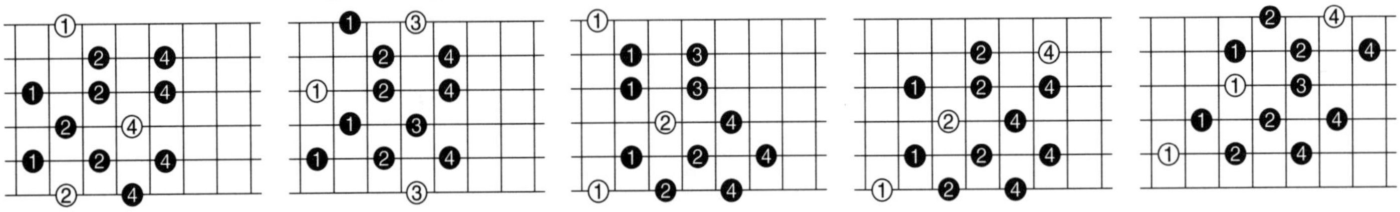

Three-Octave Fingerings

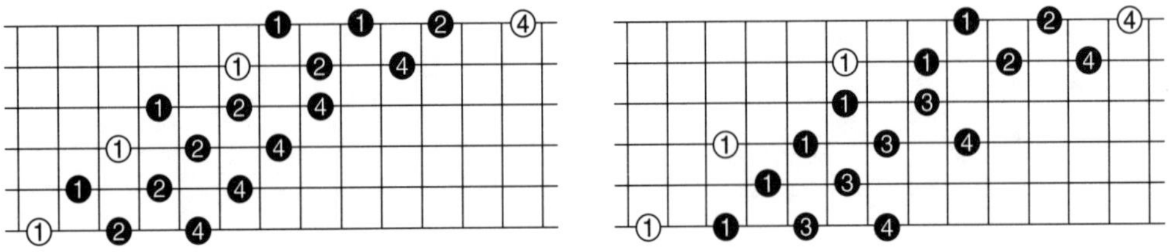

Position-Based Fingerings, Starting on all Scale Degrees

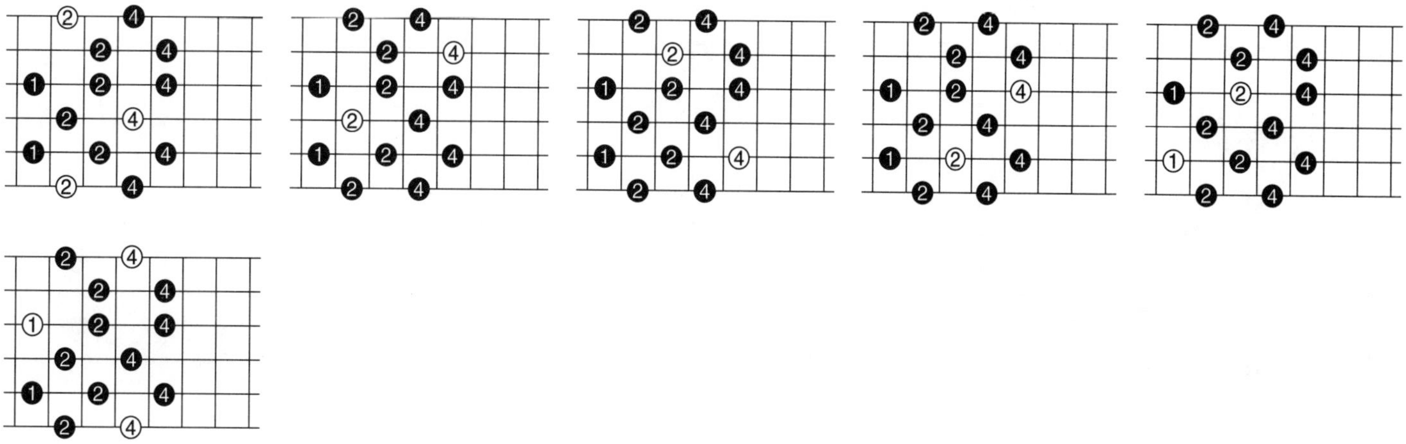

Three-Notes-Per-String Fingerings

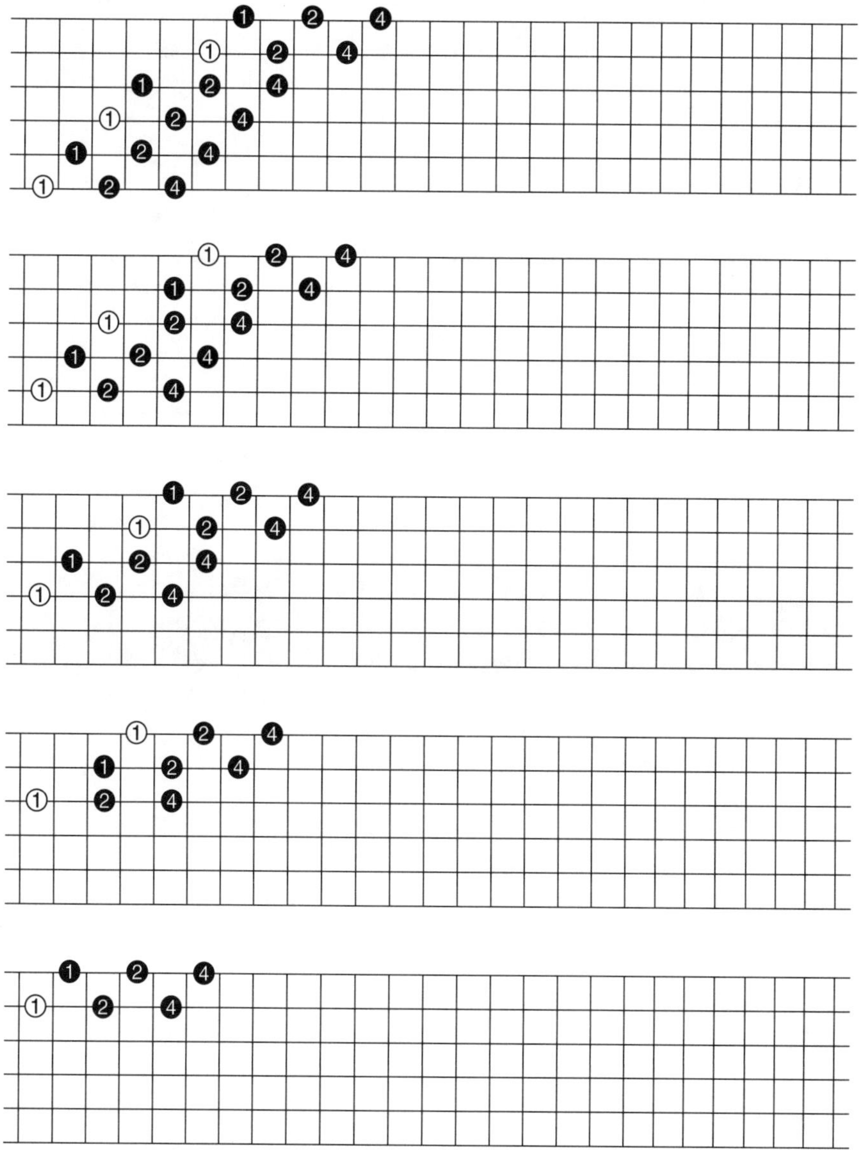

Bebop Dominant

Scale Tones

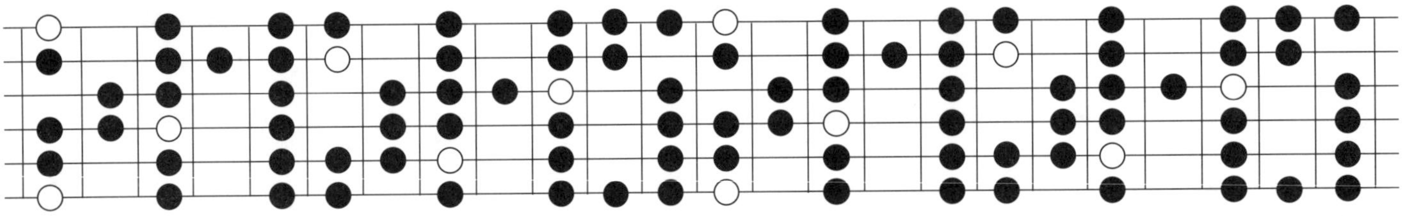

One-Octave Fingerings

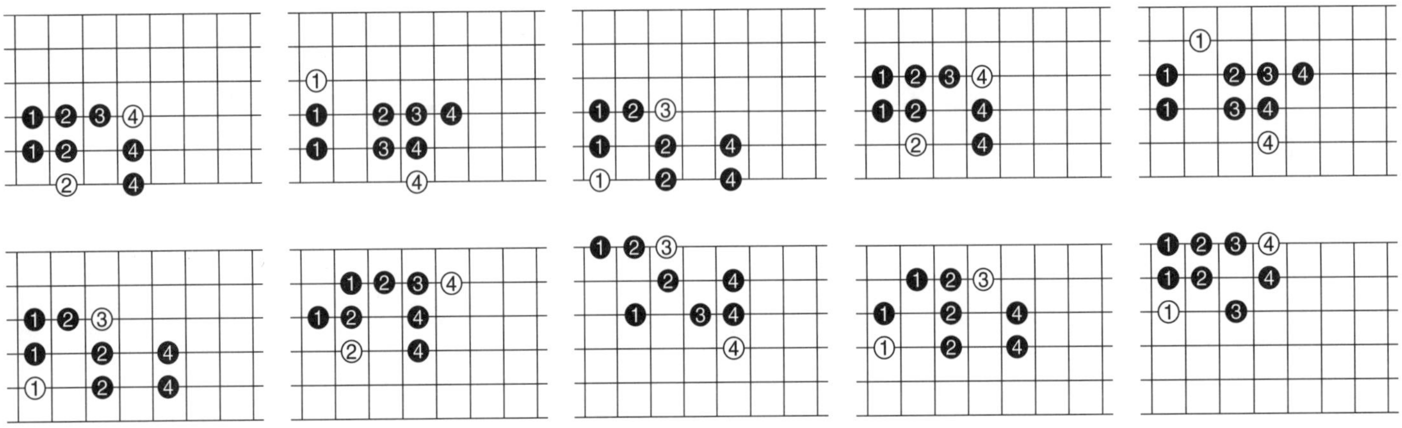

Two-Octave Fingerings

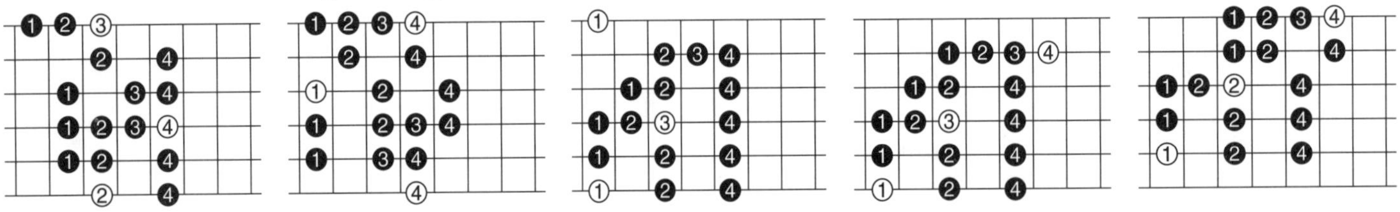

Three-Octave Fingerings

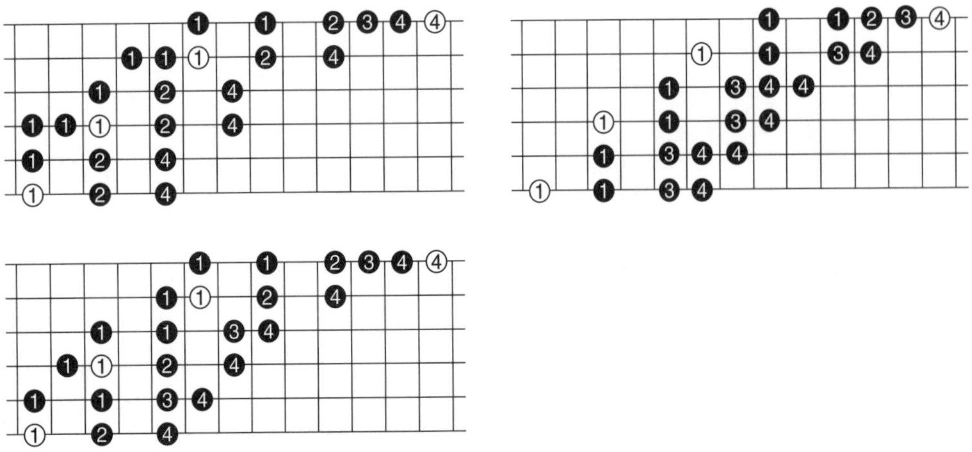

Position-Based Fingerings, Starting on all Scale Degrees

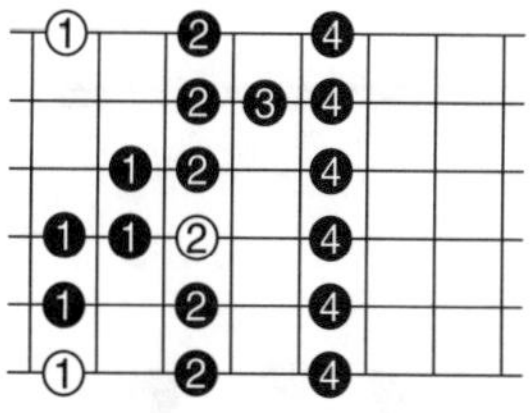
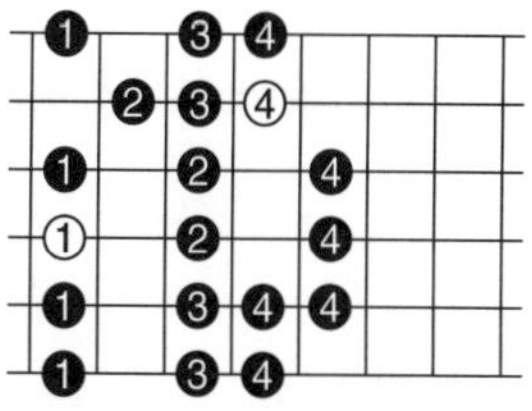
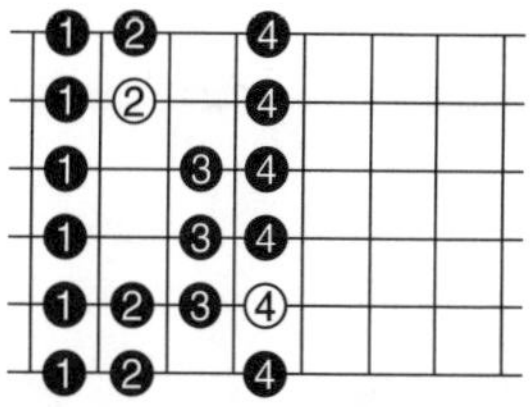
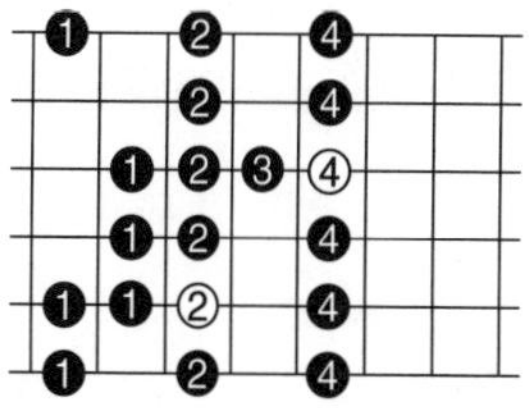
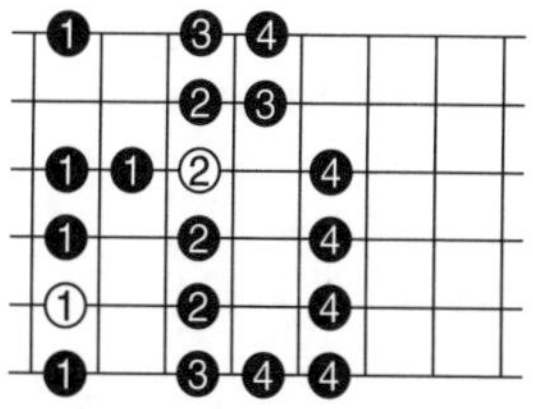
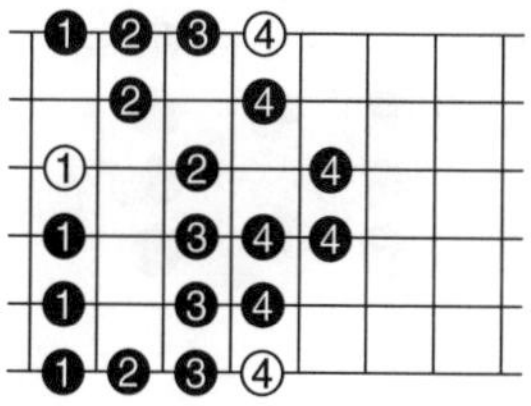
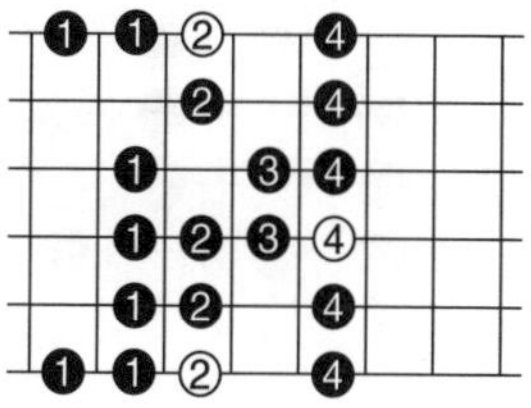
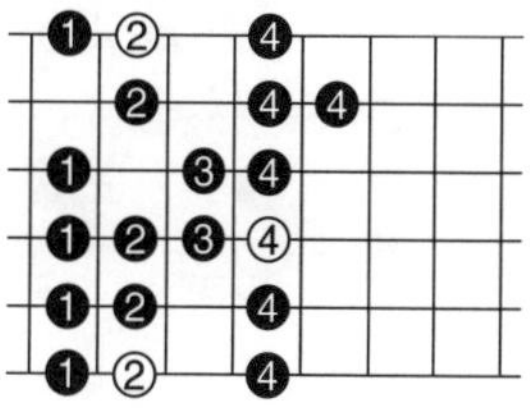

Three-Notes-Per-String Fingerings, Starting on all Scale Degrees

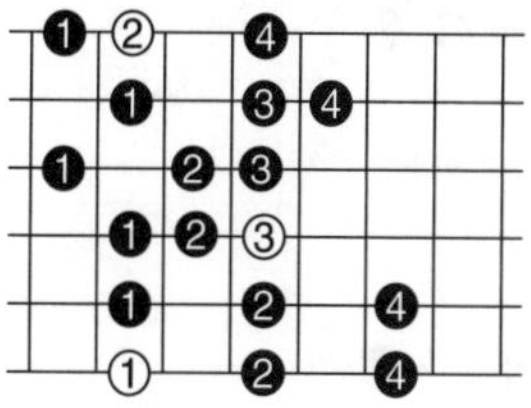
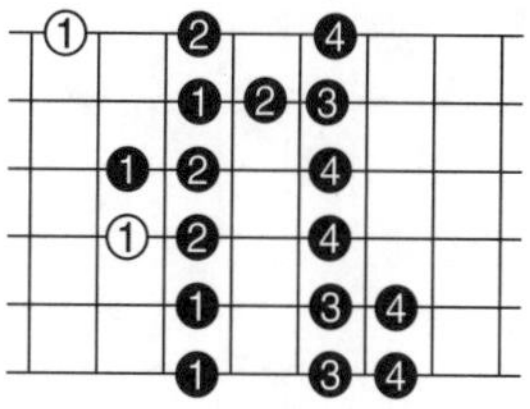
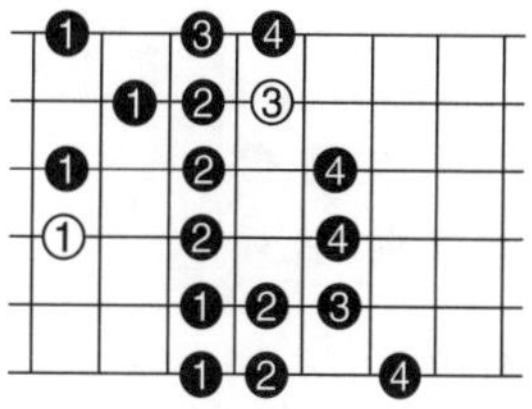
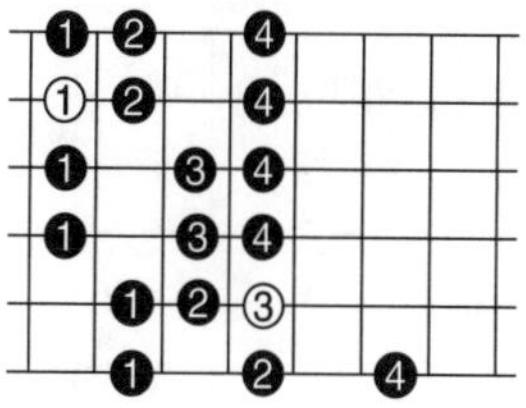
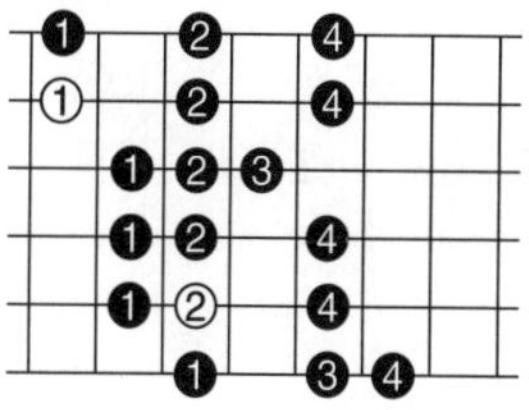
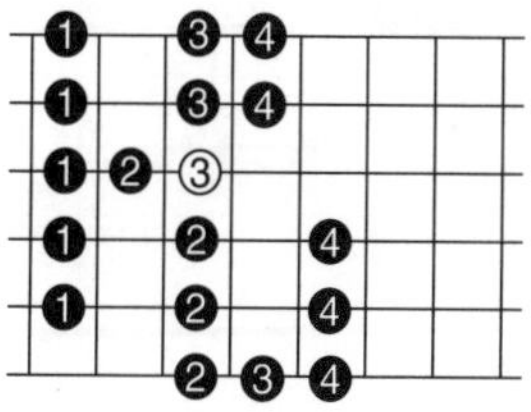
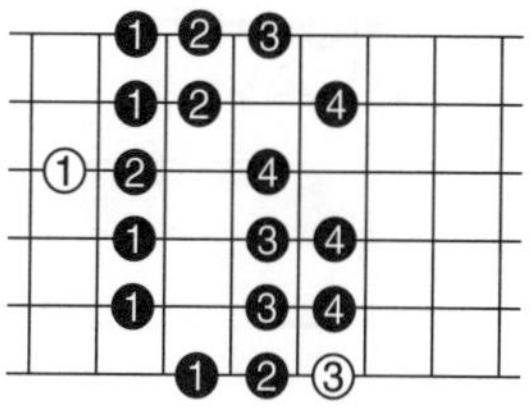
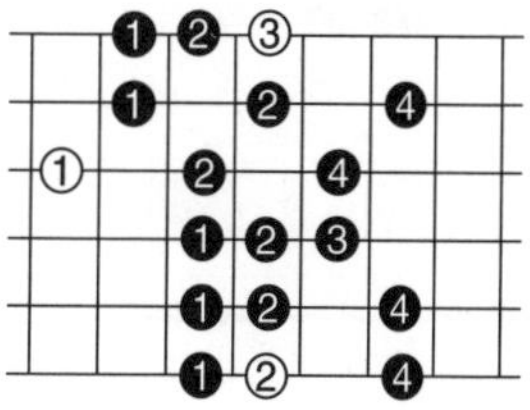

Four-Notes-Per-String Fingerings

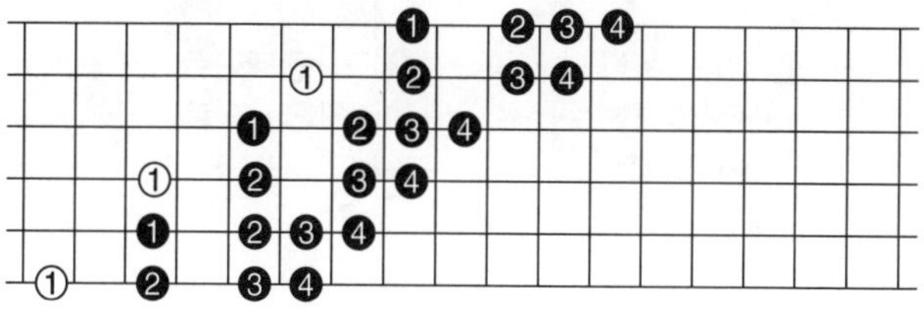
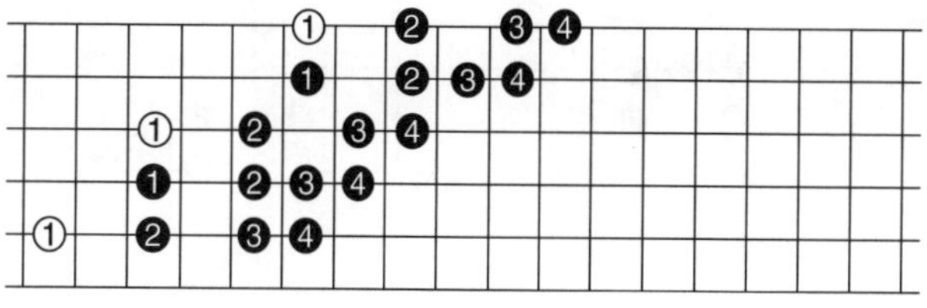
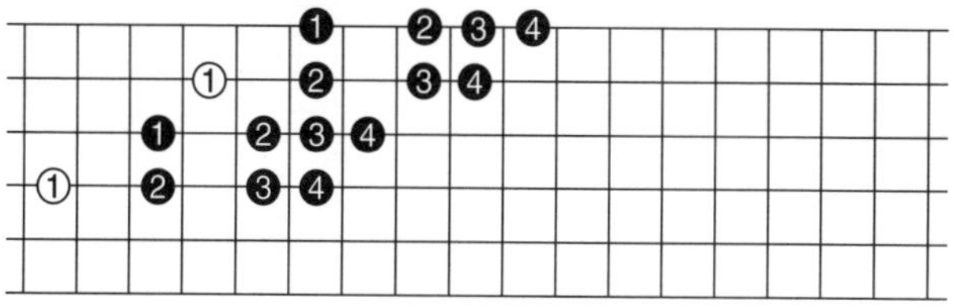
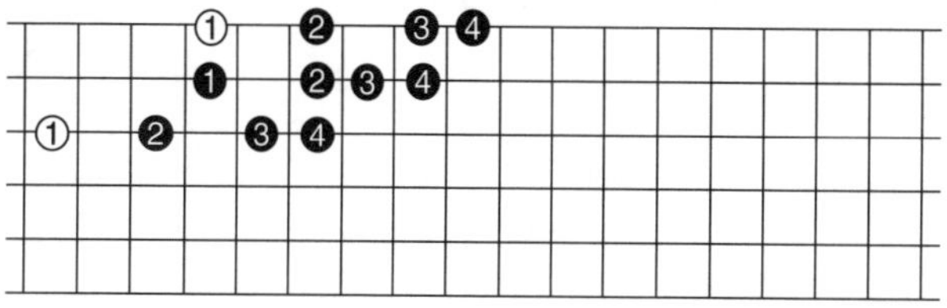
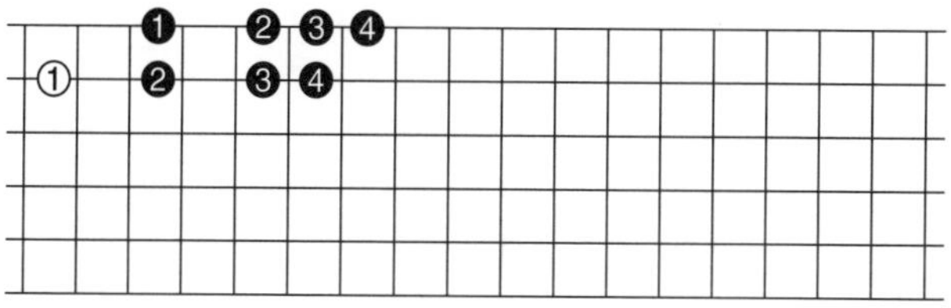

Bebop Major

Scale Tones

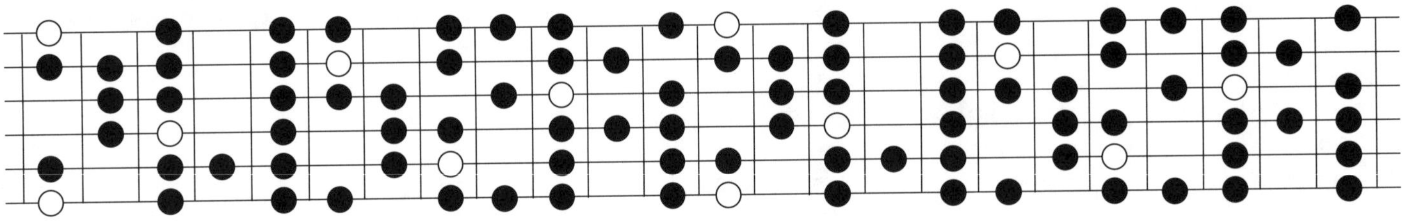

One-Octave Fingerings

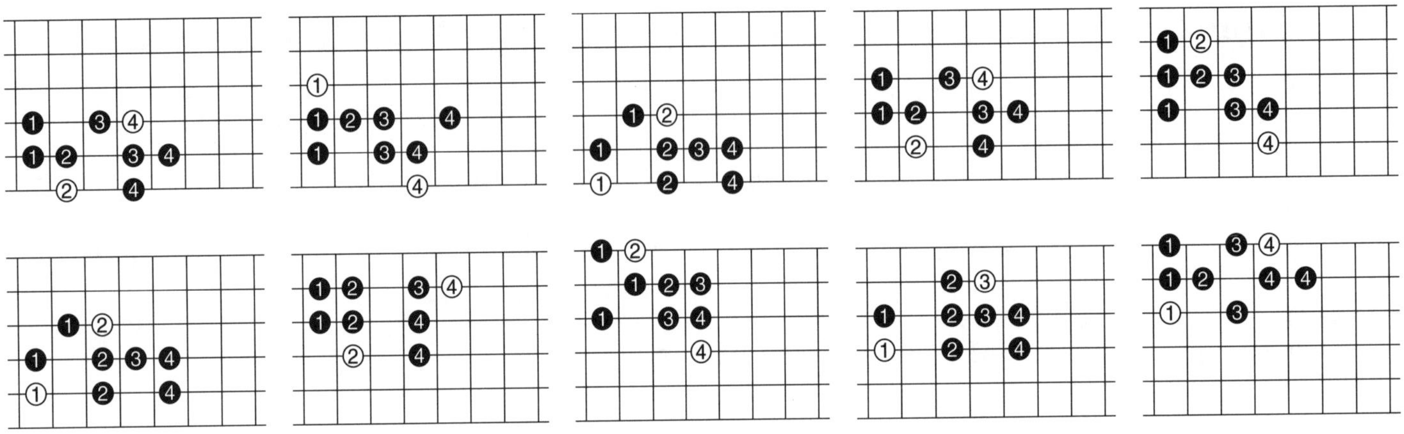

Two-Octave Fingerings

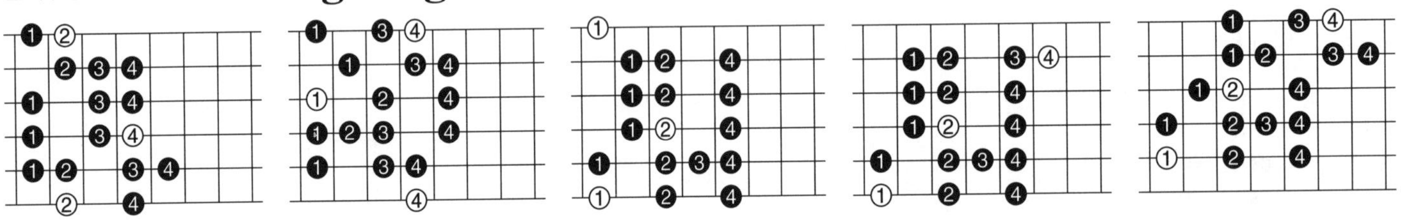

Three-Octave Fingerings

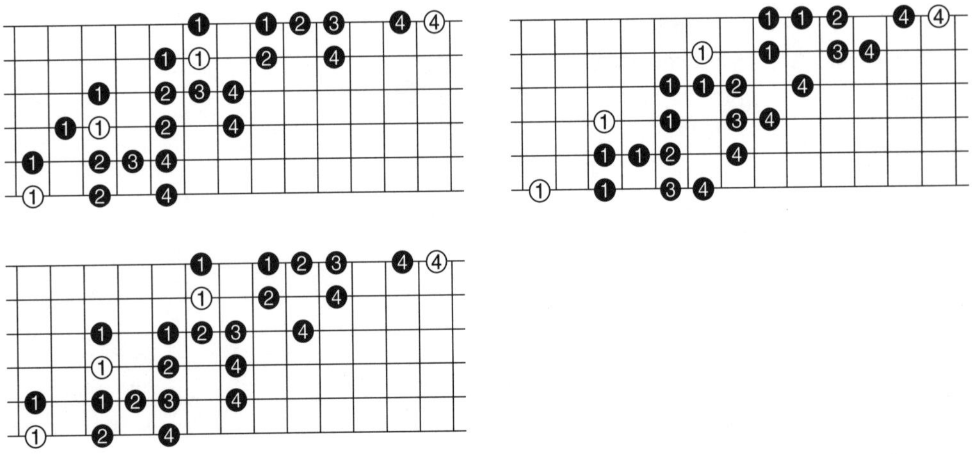

Position-Based Fingerings, Starting on all Scale Degrees

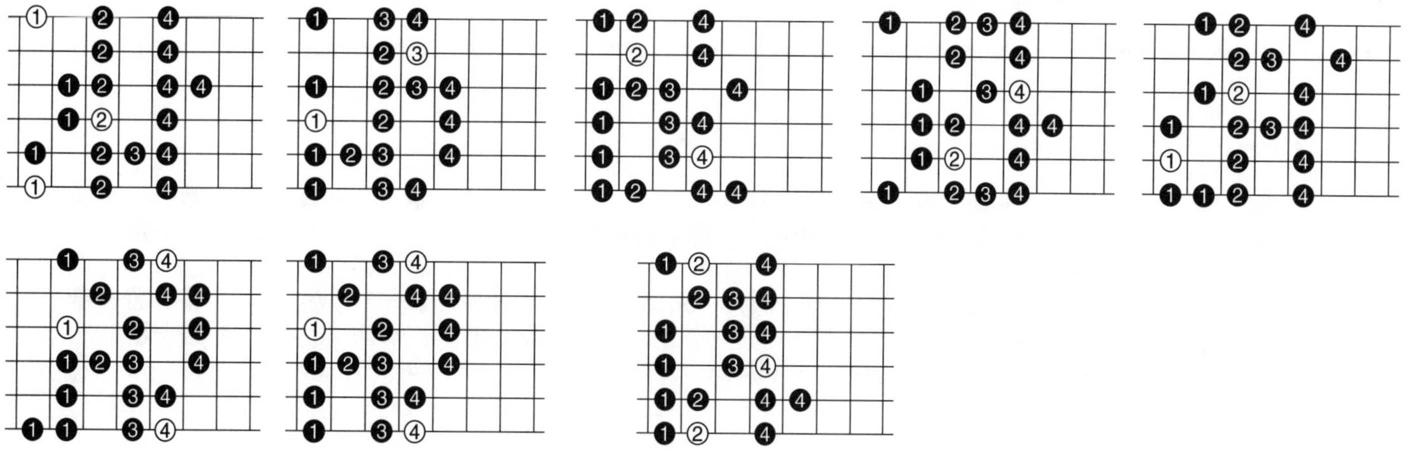

Three-Notes-Per-String Fingerings, Starting on all Scale Degrees

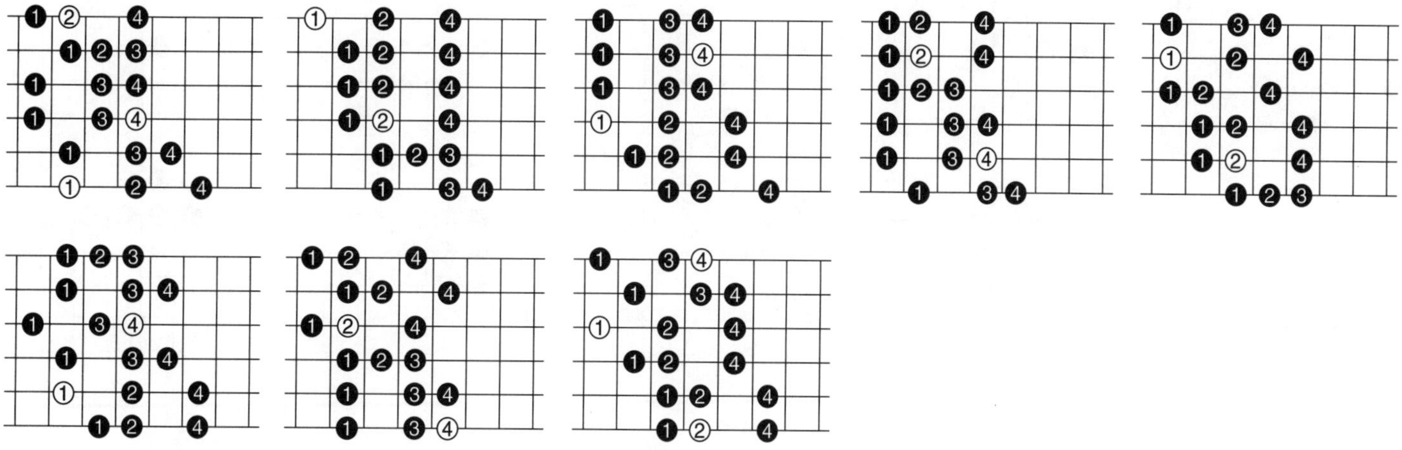

Four-Notes-Per-String Fingerings

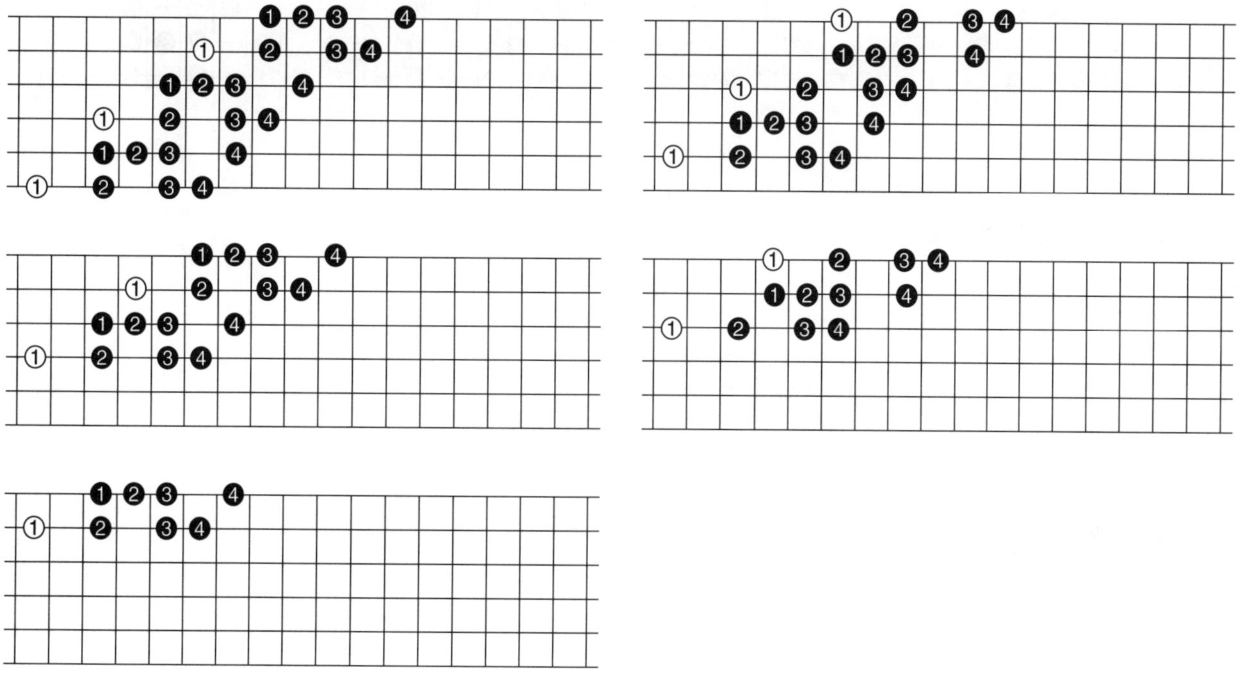

Bebop Tonic Minor

Scale Tones

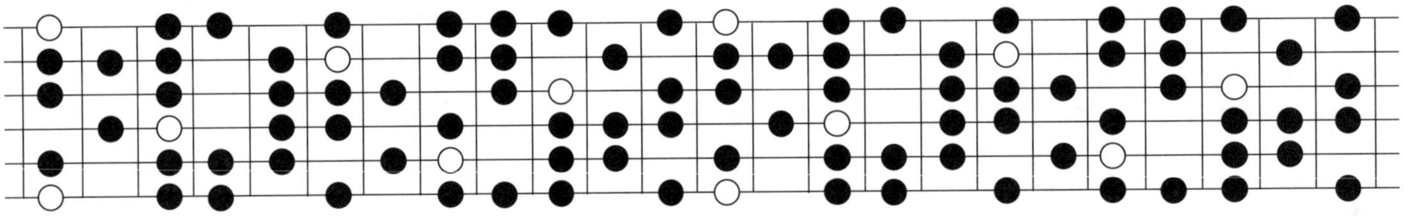

One-Octave Fingerings

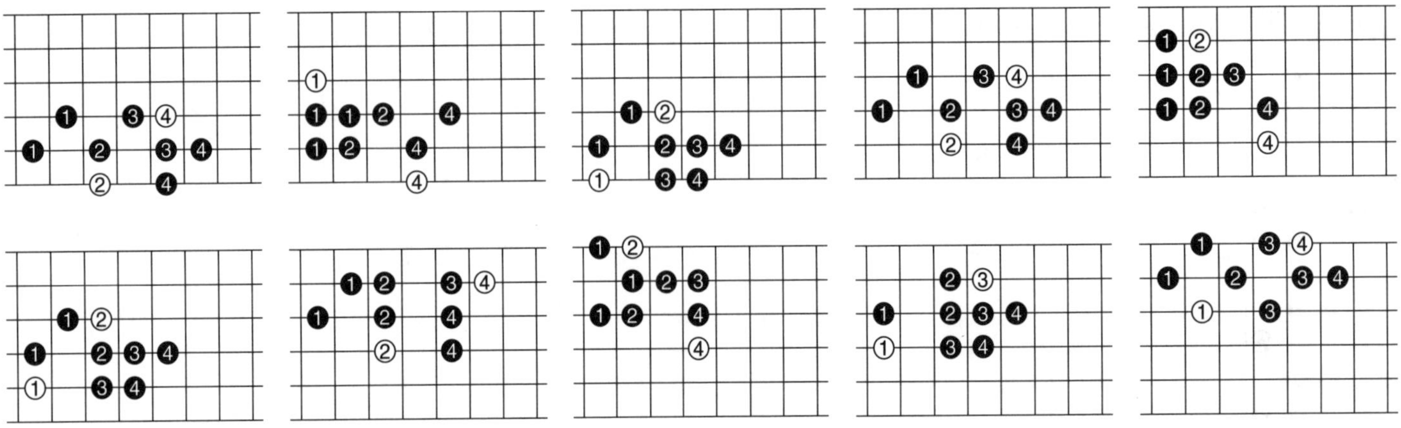

Two-Octave Fingerings

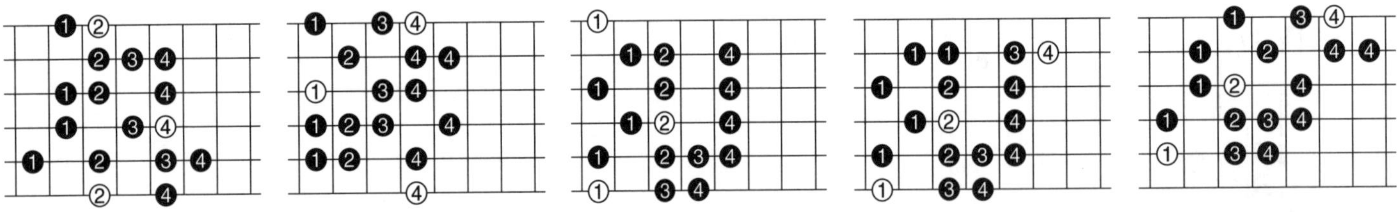

Three-Octave Fingerings

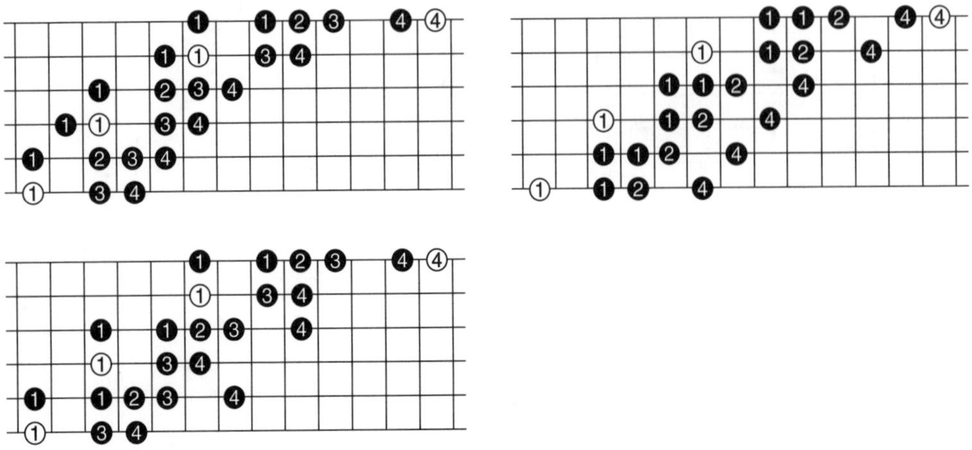

Position-Based Fingerings, Starting on all Scale Degrees

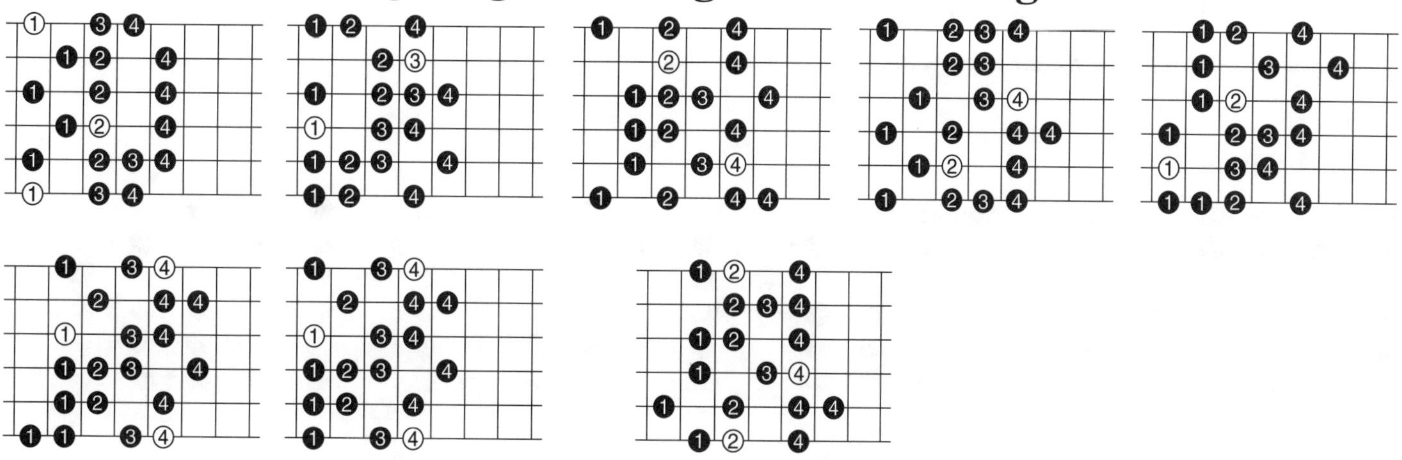

Three-Notes-Per-String Fingerings, Starting on all Scale Degrees

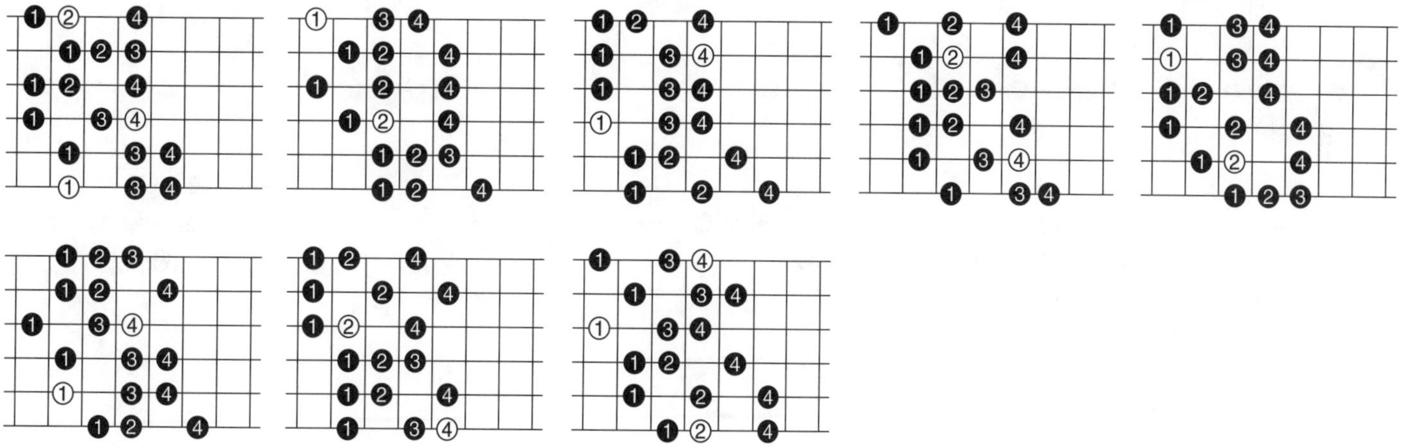

Four-Notes-Per-String Fingerings

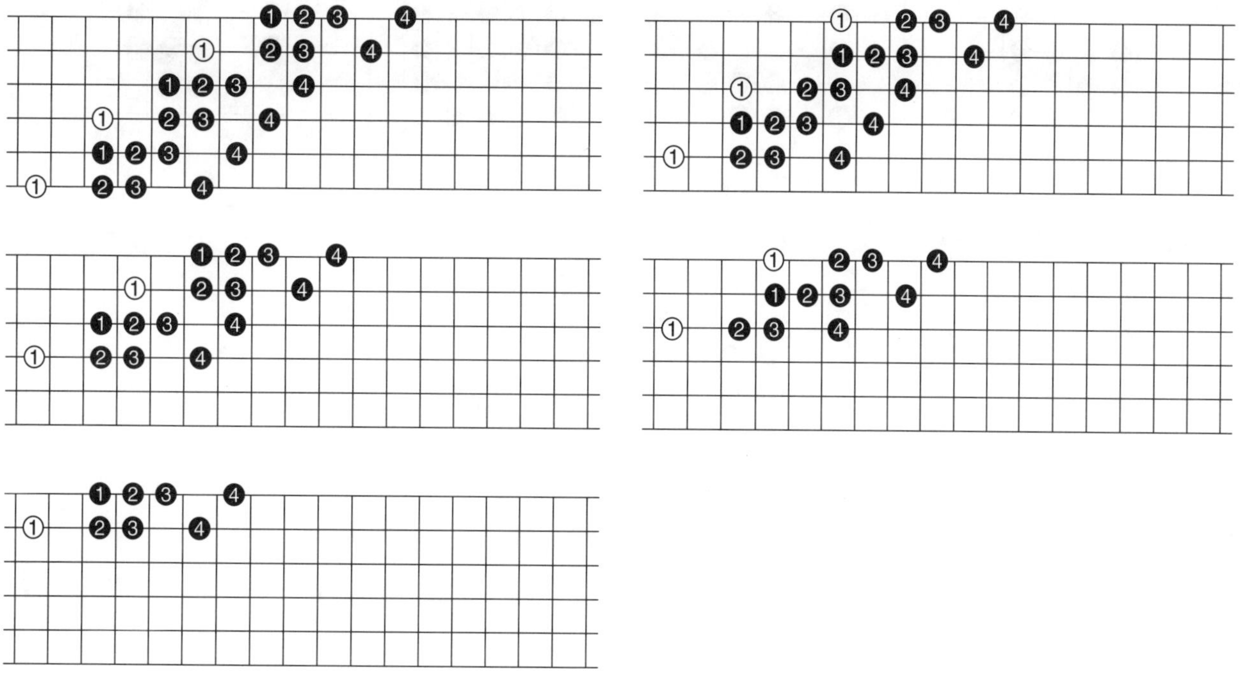

Bebop Minor

Scale Tones

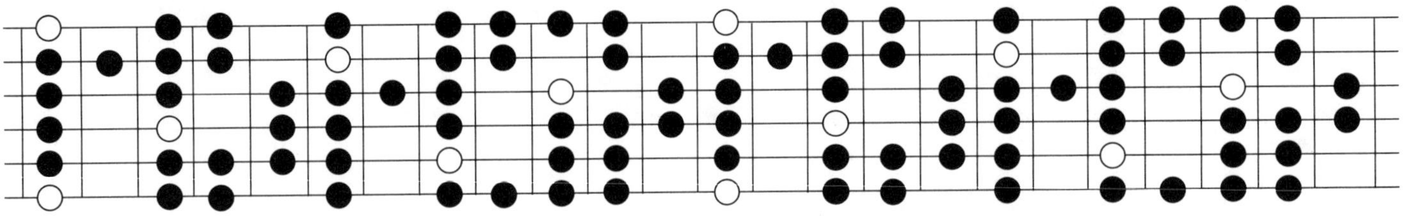

One-Octave Fingerings

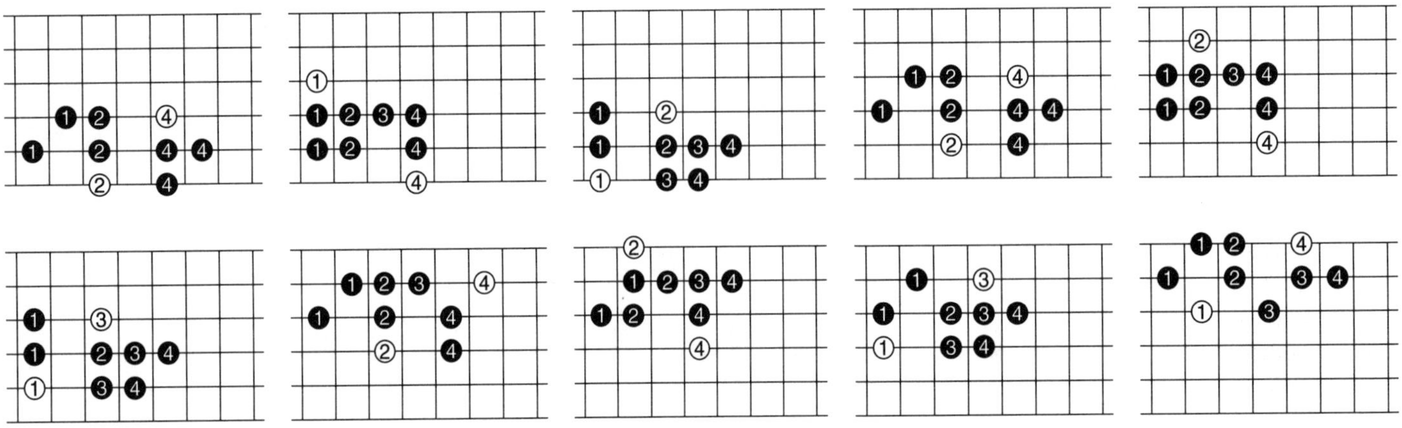

Two-Octave Fingerings

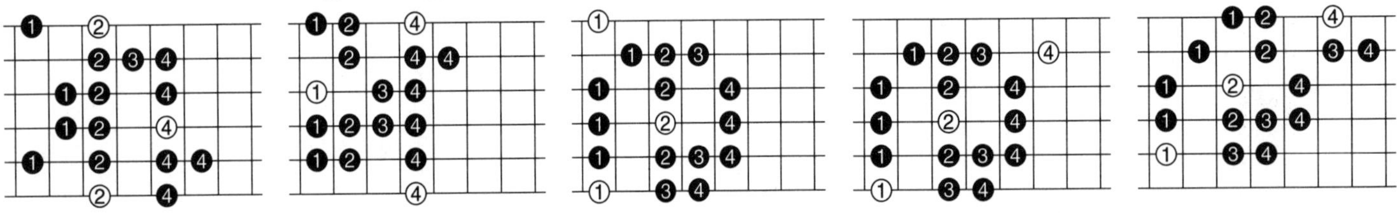

Three-Octave Fingerings

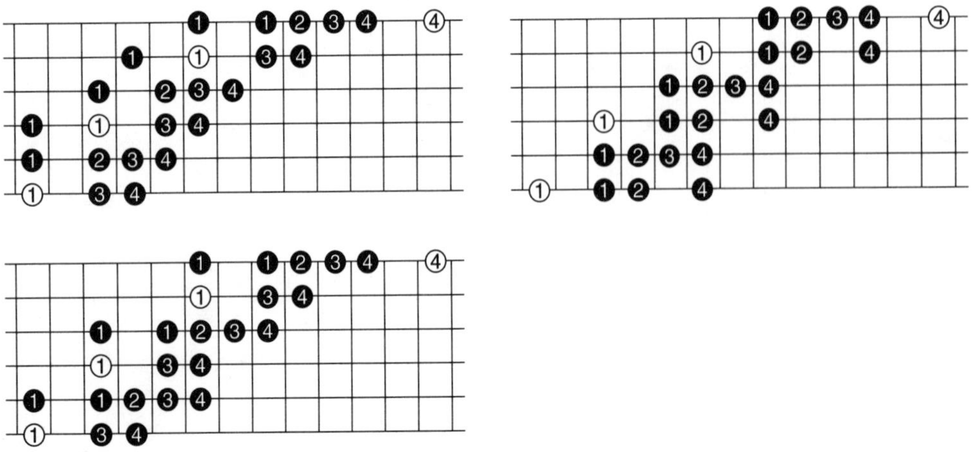

Position-Based Fingerings, Starting on all Scale Degrees

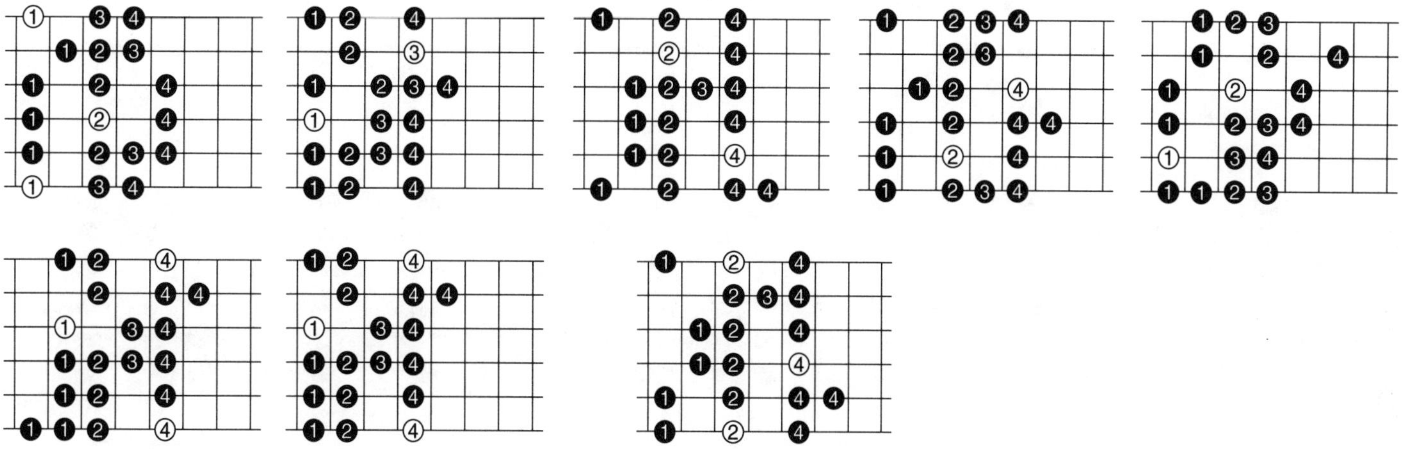

Three-Notes-Per-String Fingerings, Starting on all Scale Degrees

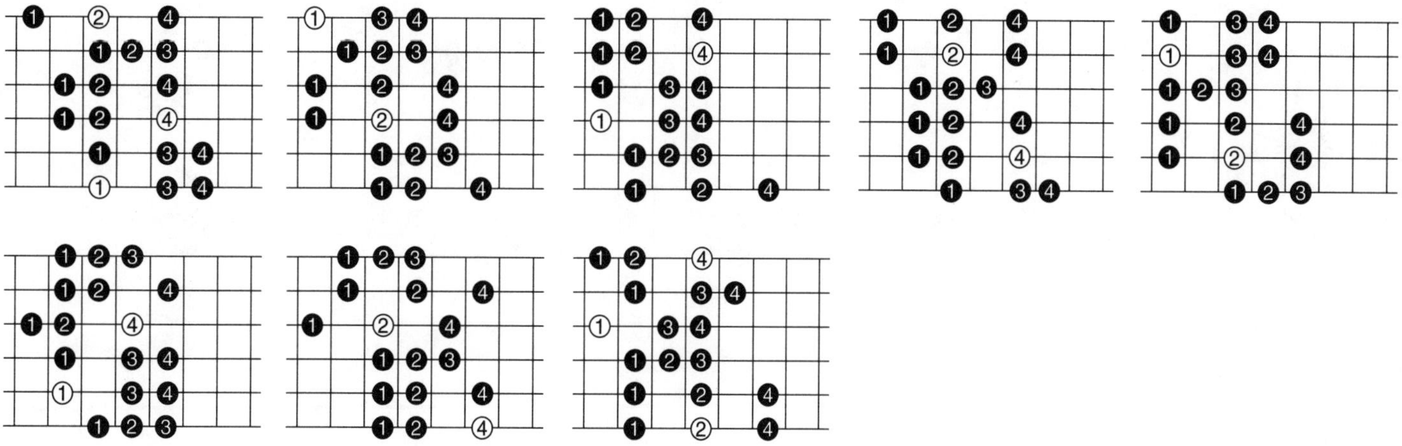

Four-Notes-Per-String Fingerings

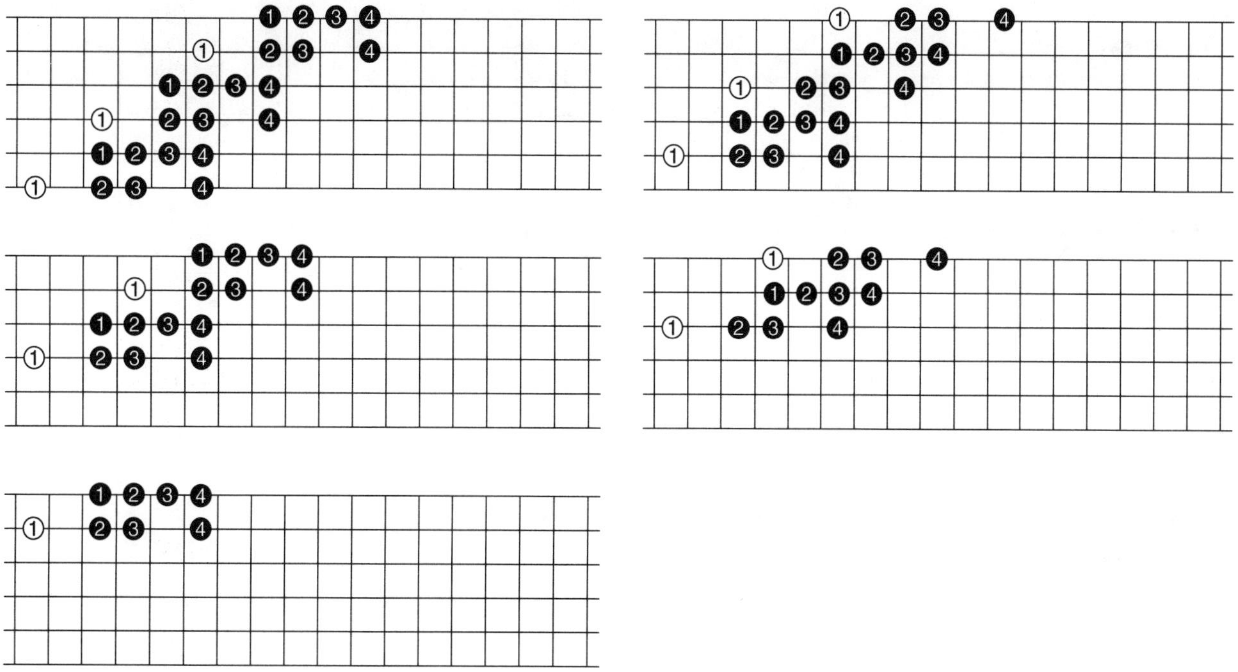

Eight–Tone Spanish

Scale Tones

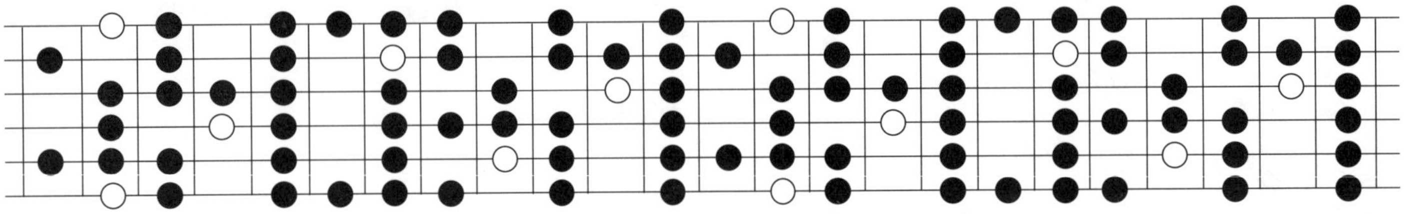

One-Octave Fingerings

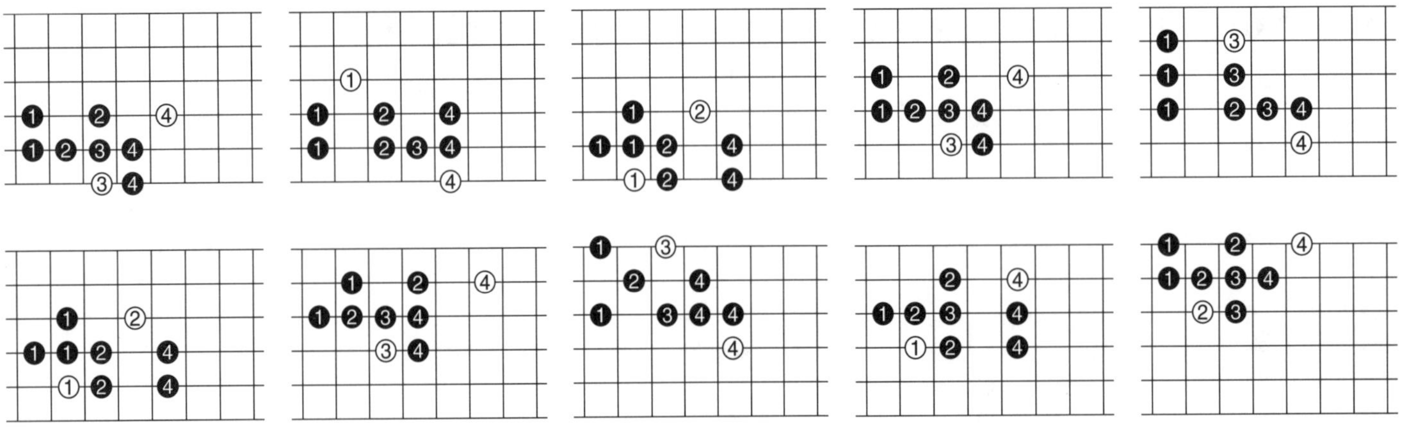

Two-Octave Fingerings

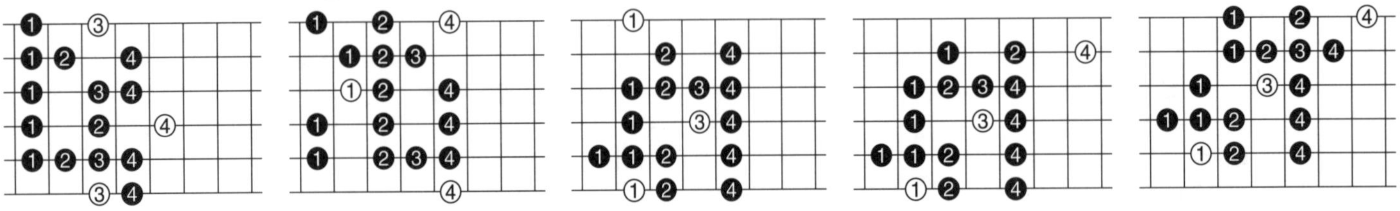

Three-Octave Fingerings

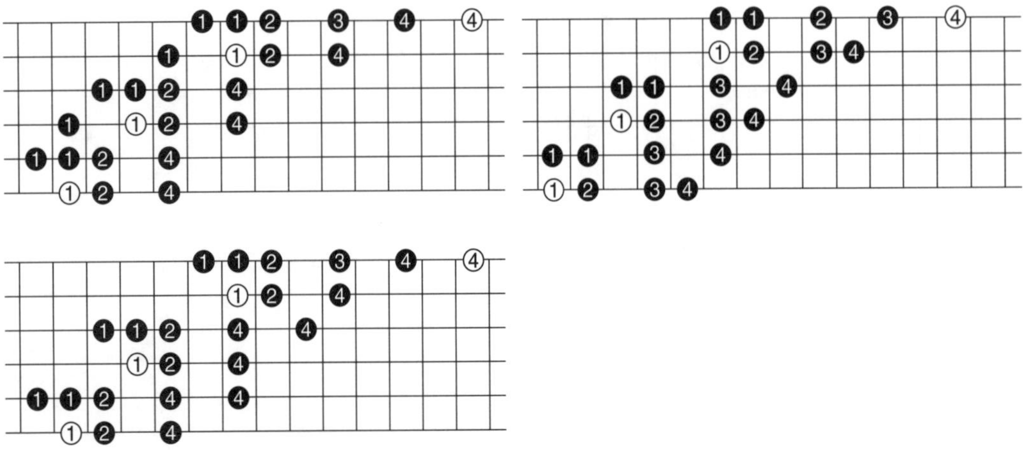

Position-Based Fingerings, Starting on all Scale Degrees

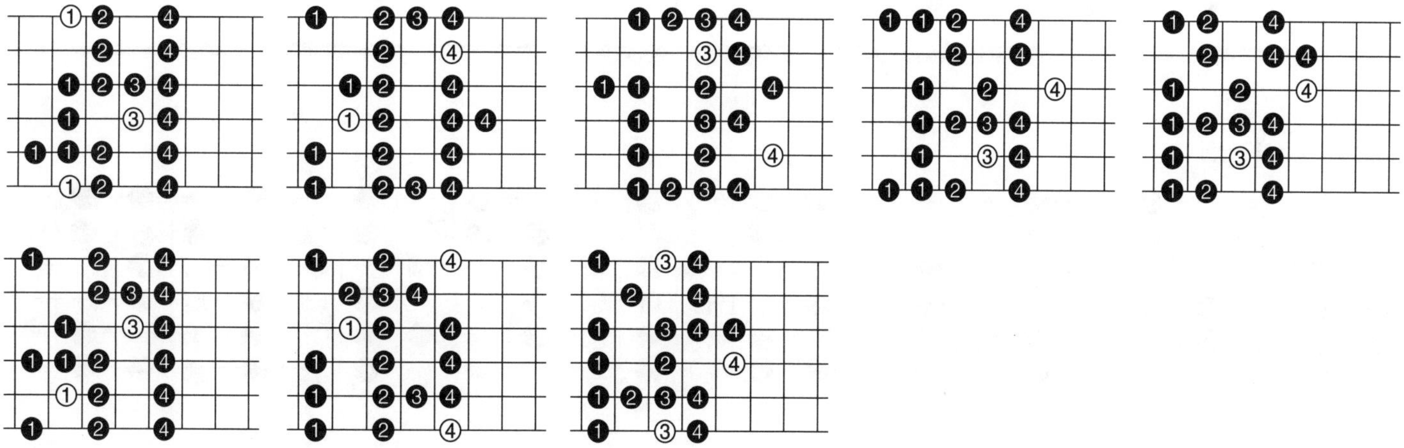

Three-Notes-Per-String Fingerings

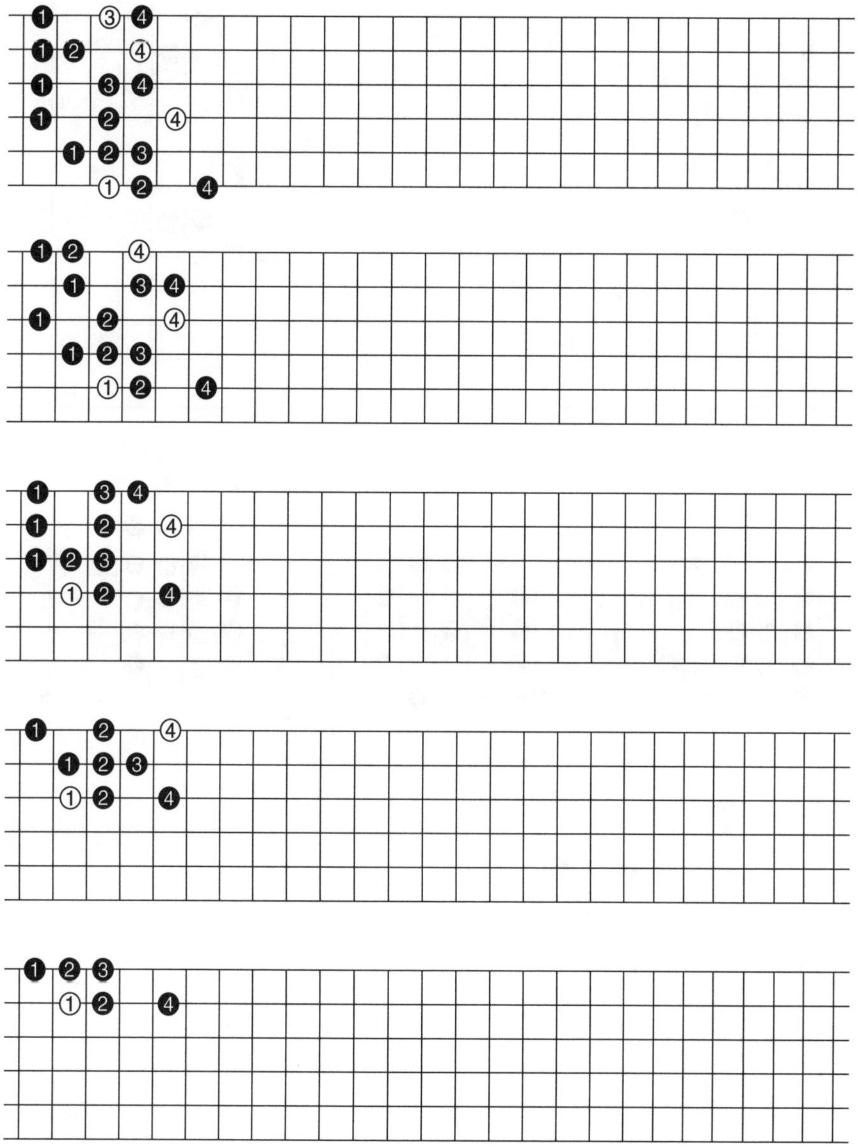

Enigmatic

Scale Tones

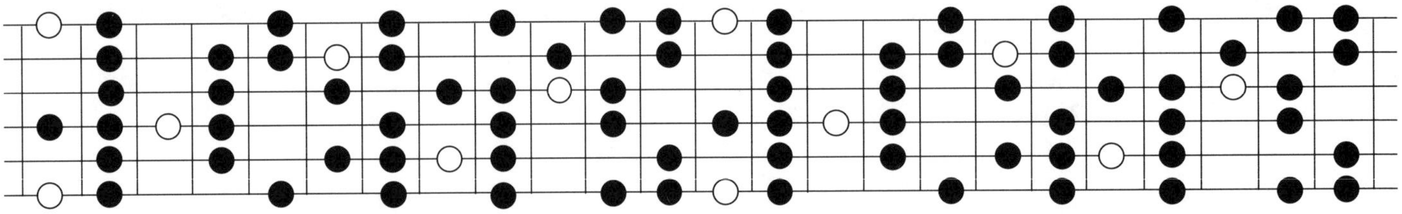

One-Octave Fingerings

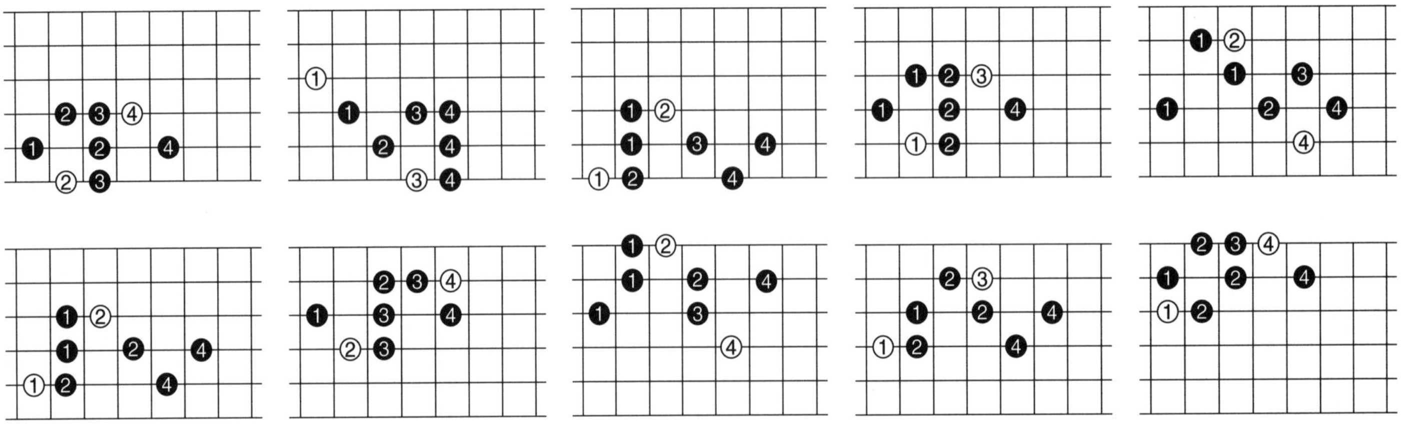

Two-Octave Fingerings

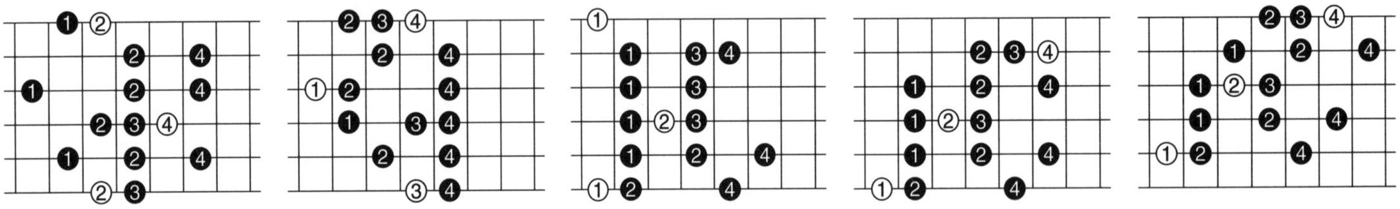

Three-Octave Fingerings

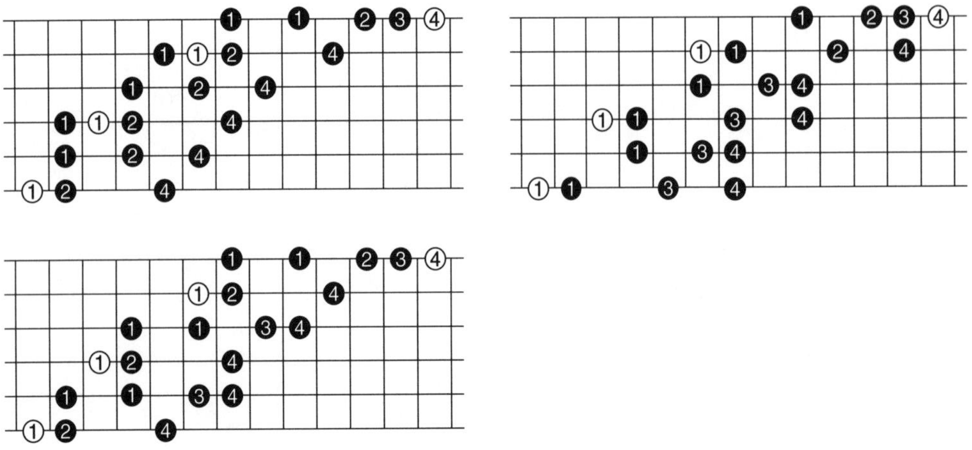

Position-Based Fingerings, Starting on all Scale Degrees

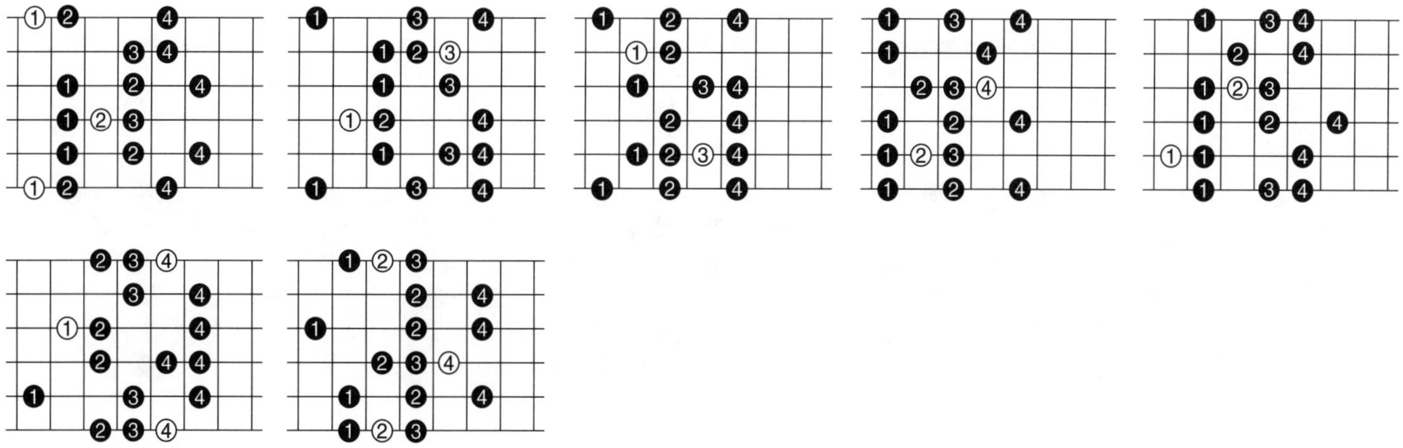

Three-Notes-Per-String Fingerings

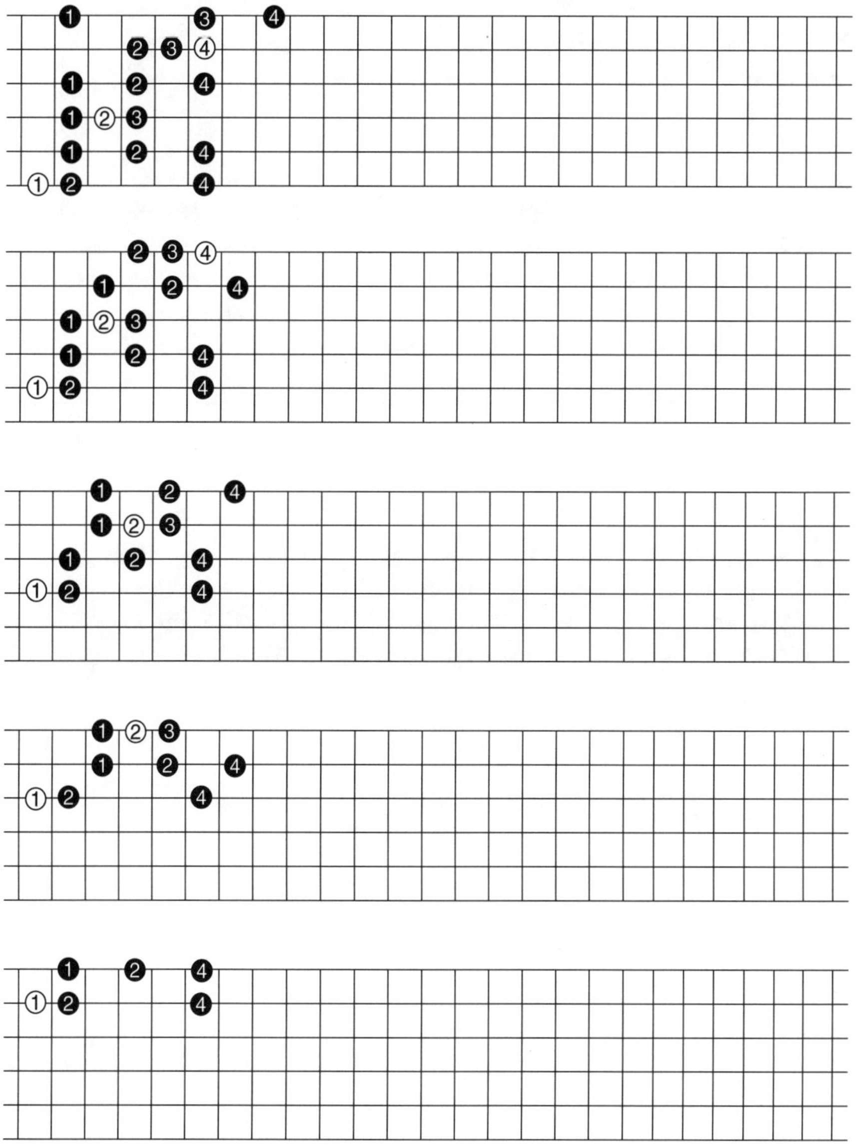

Gypsy

Scale Tones

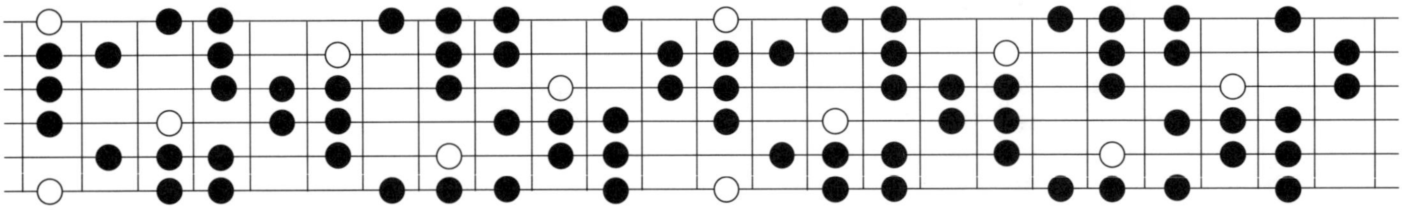

One-Octave Fingerings

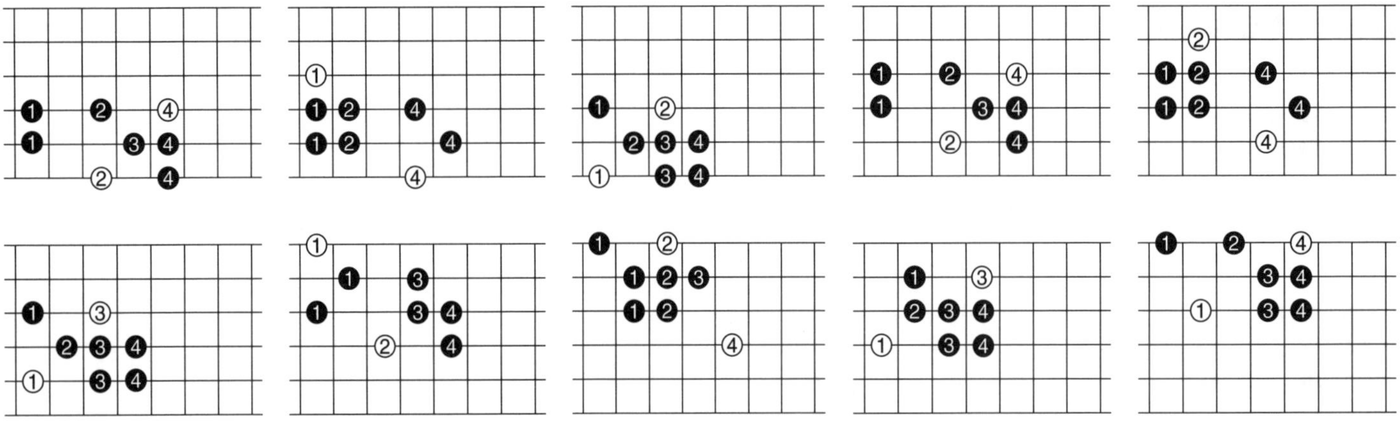

Two-Octave Fingerings

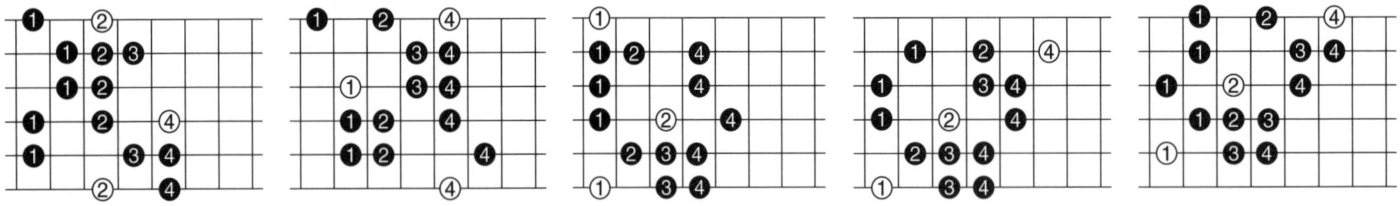

Three-Octave Fingerings

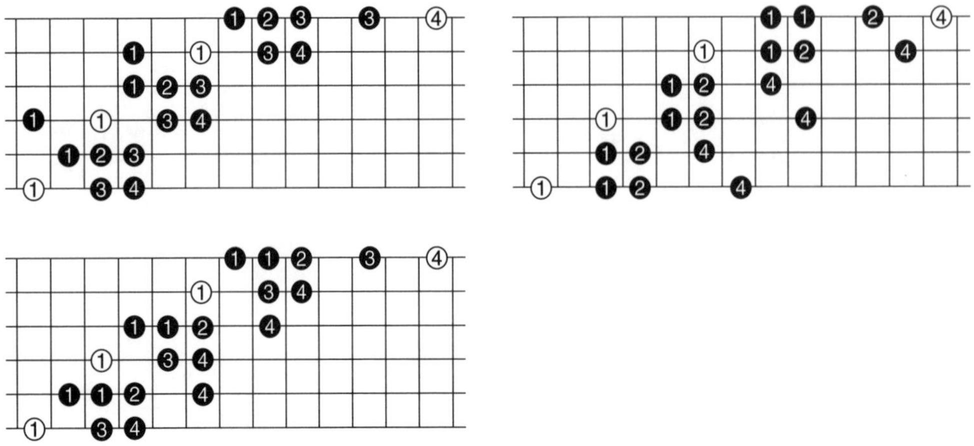

Position-Based Fingerings, Starting on all Scale Degrees

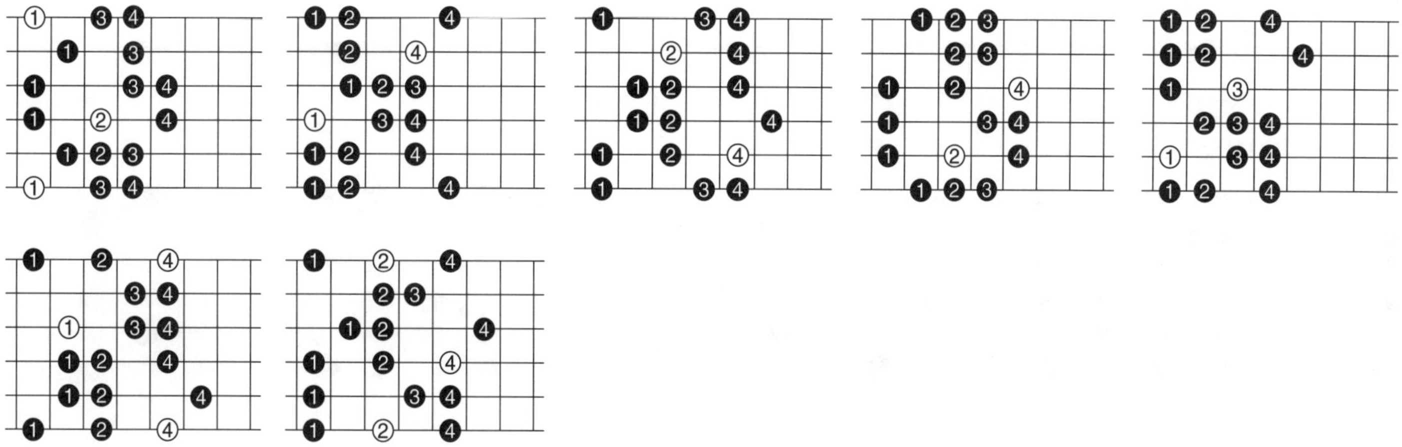

Three-Notes-Per-String Fingerings, Starting on all Scale Degrees

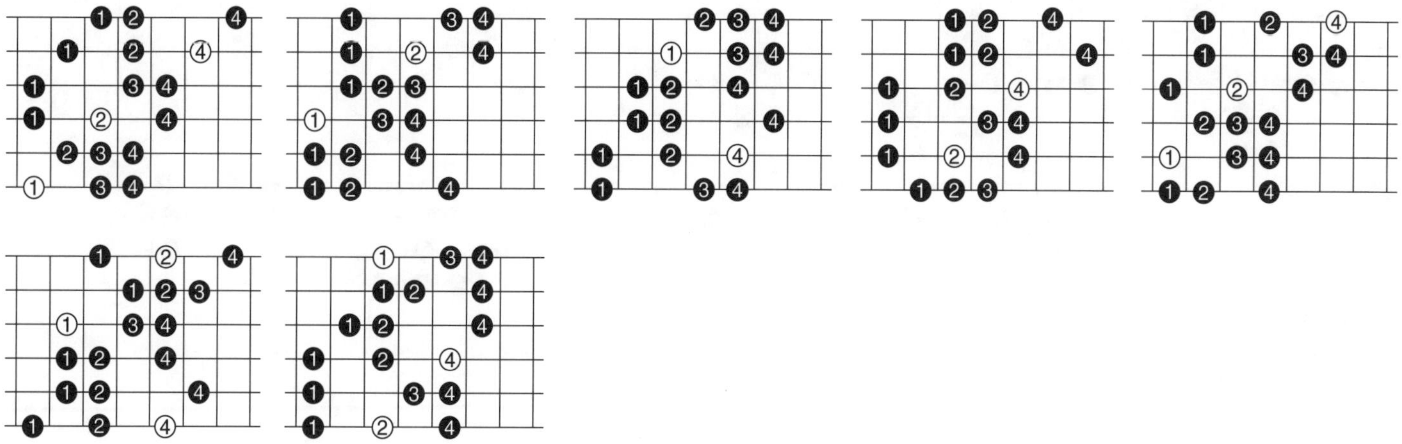

Four-Notes-Per-String Fingerings

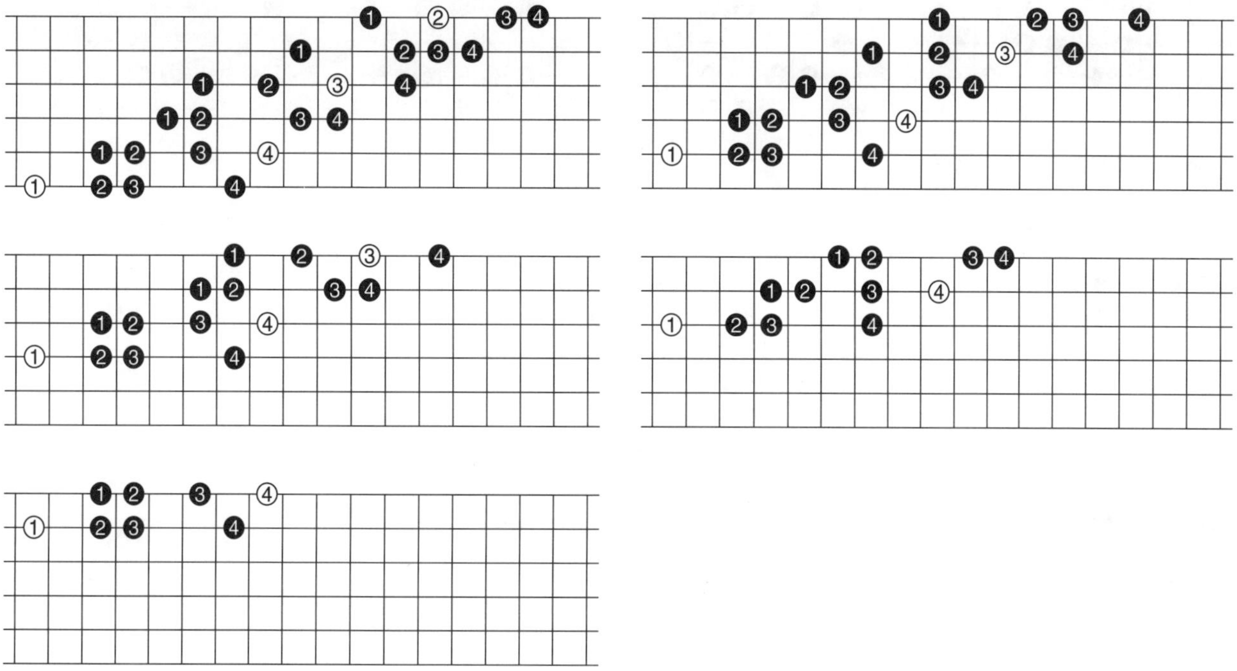

Hungarian

Scale Tones

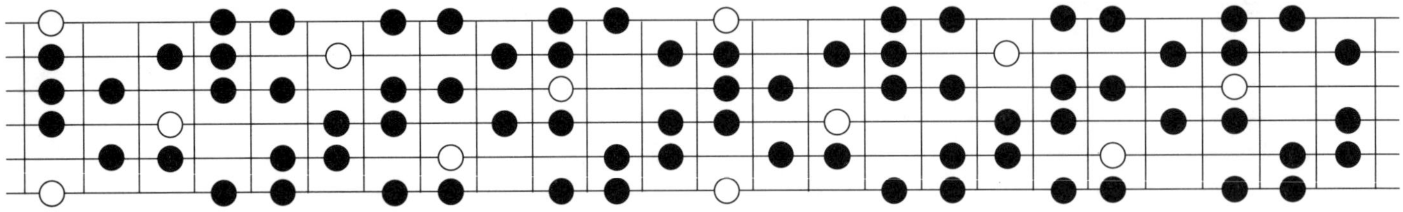

One-Octave Fingerings

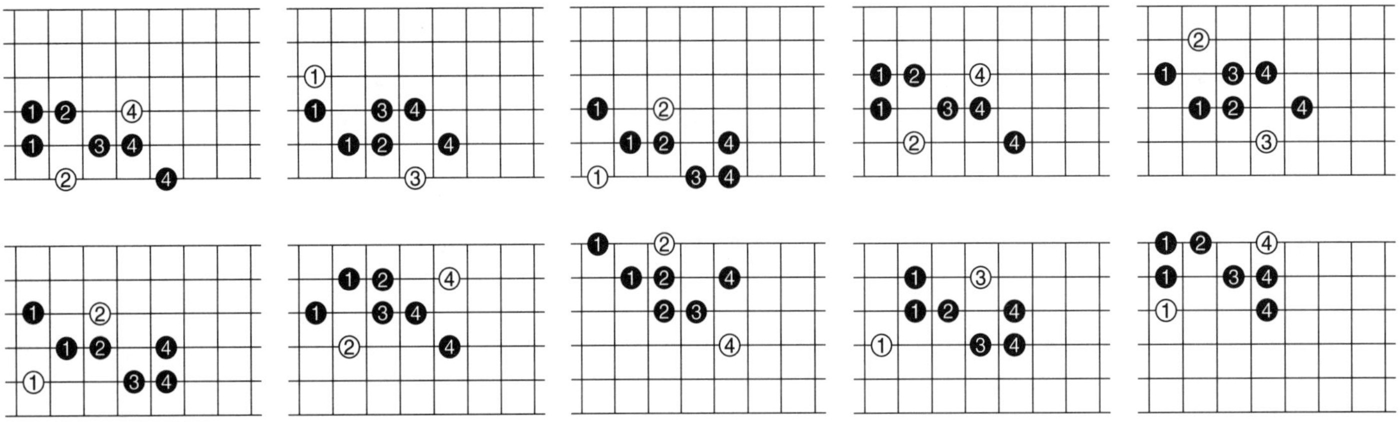

Two-Octave Fingerings

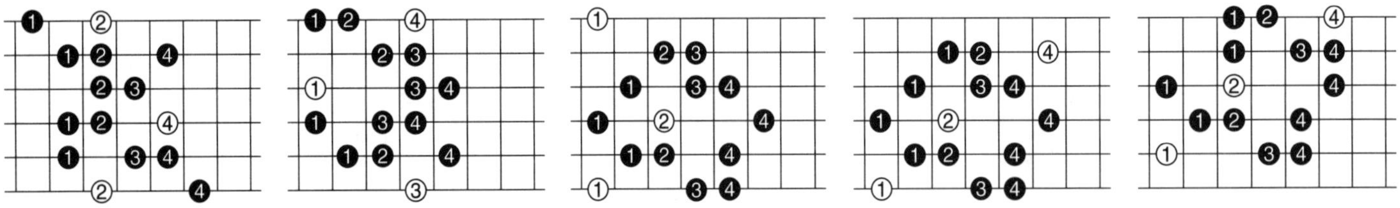

Three-Octave Fingerings

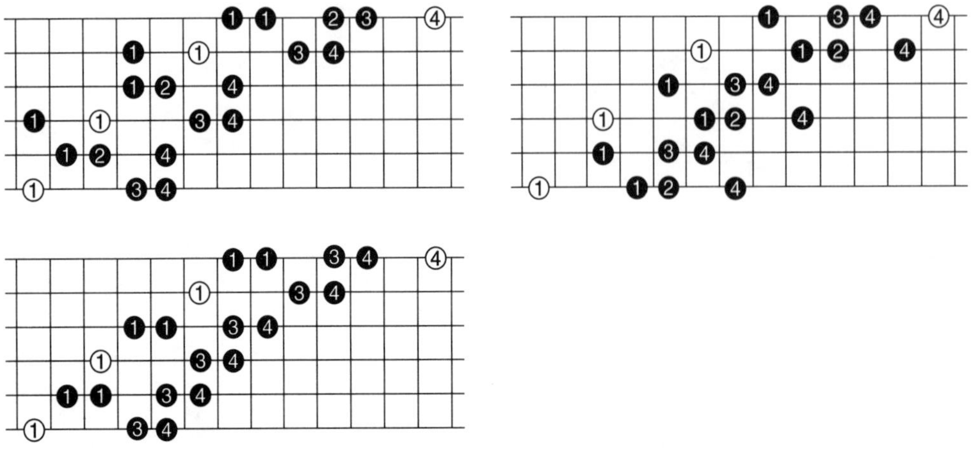

Position-Based Fingerings, Starting on all Scale Degrees

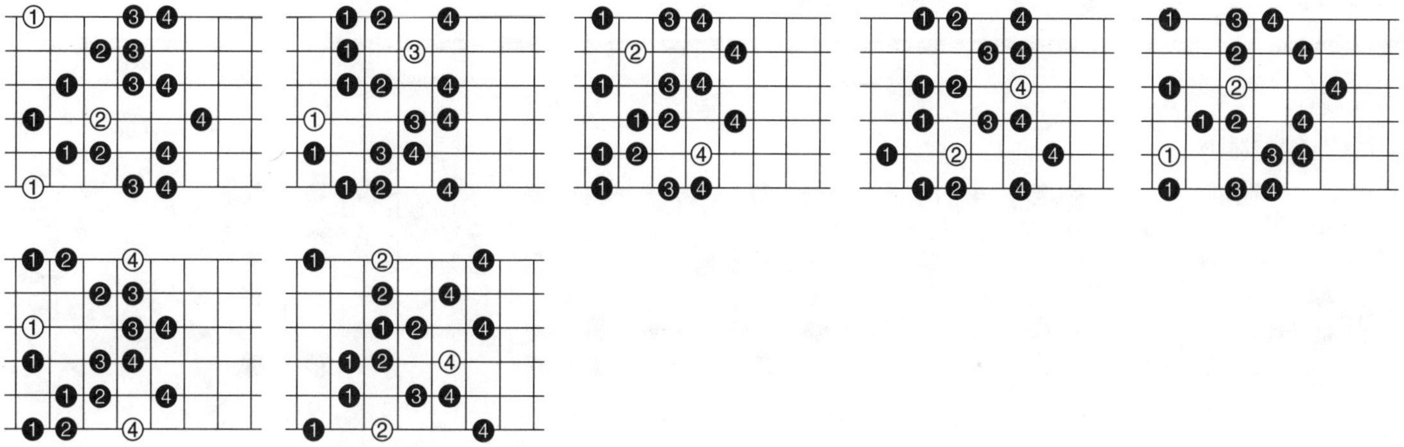

Three-Notes-Per-String Fingerings, Starting on all Scale Degrees

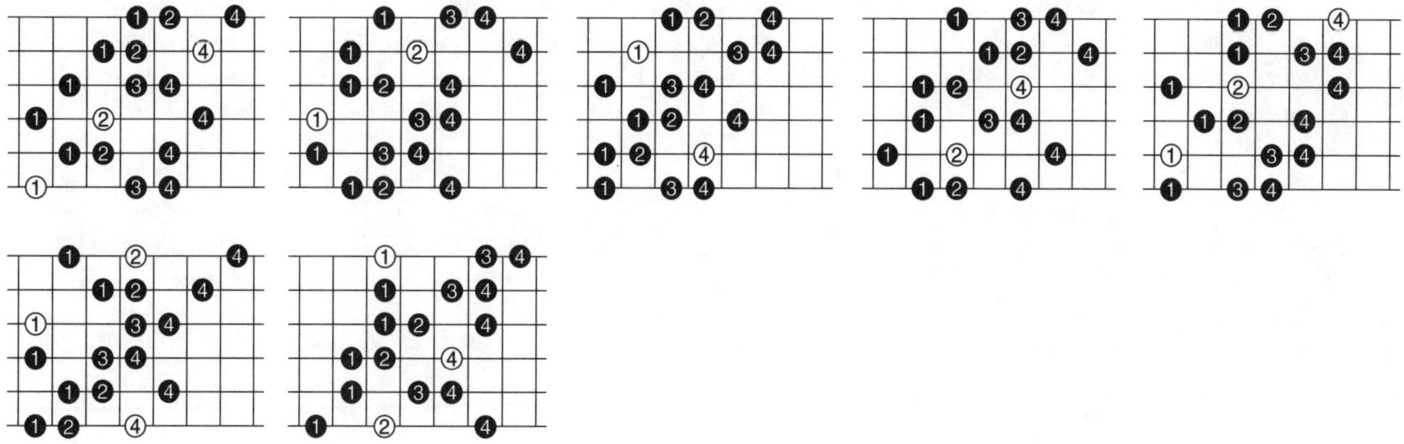

Four-Notes-Per-String Fingerings

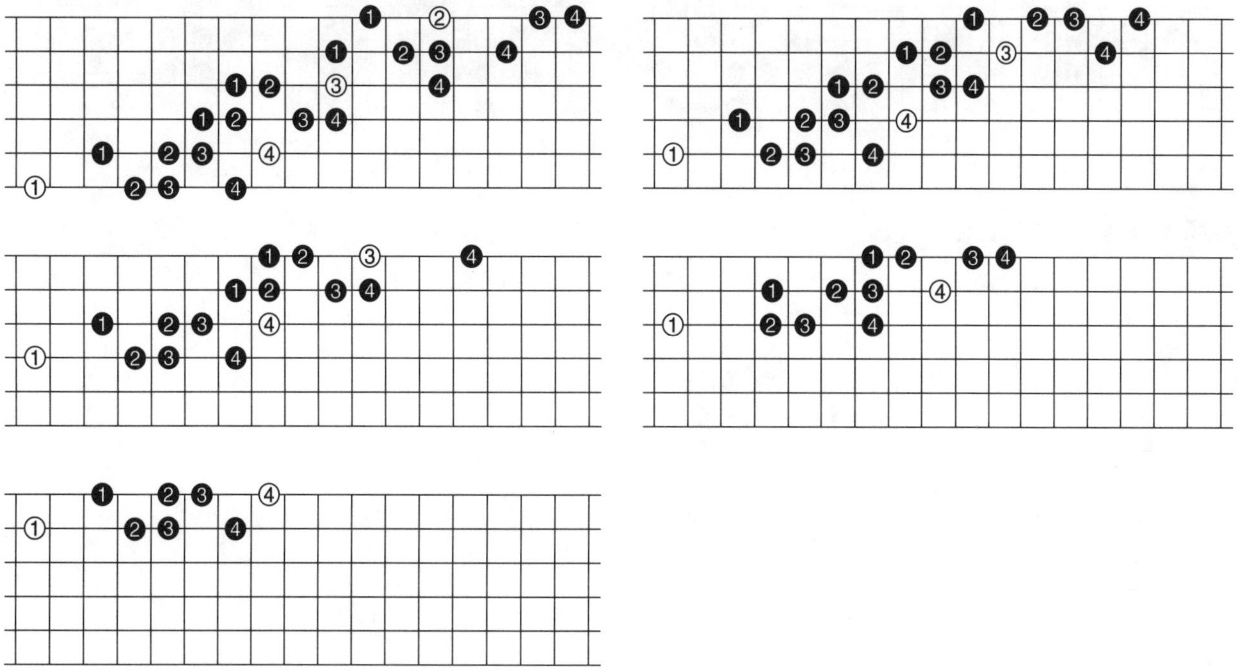

Hungarian Minor

Scale Tones

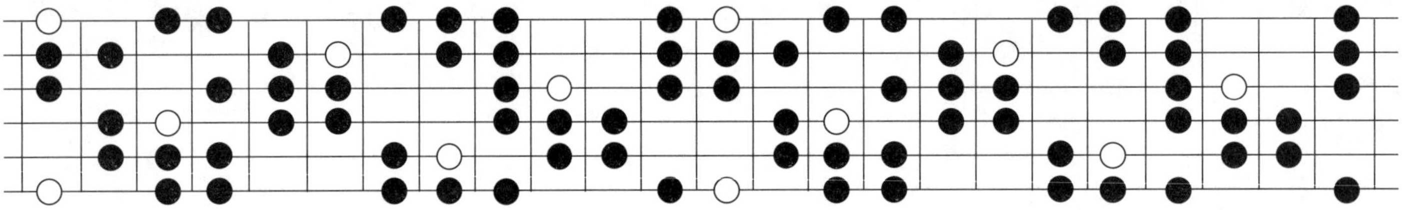

One-Octave Fingerings

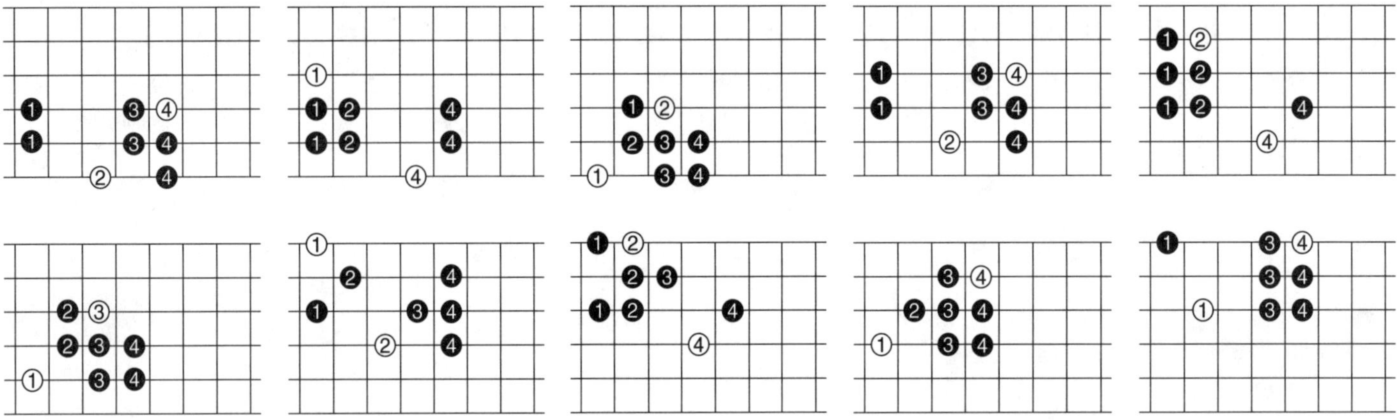

Two-Octave Fingerings

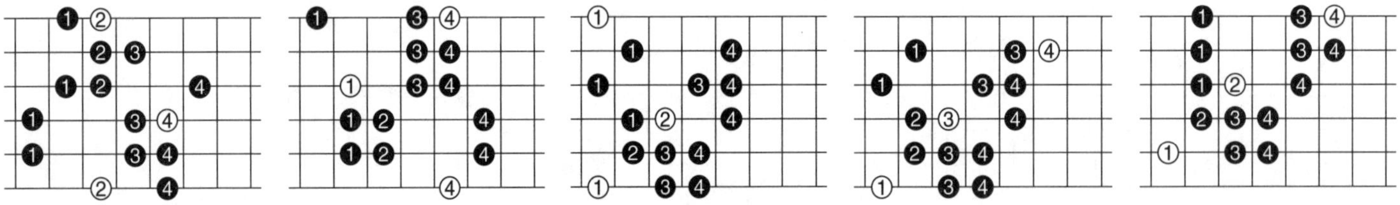

Three-Octave Fingerings

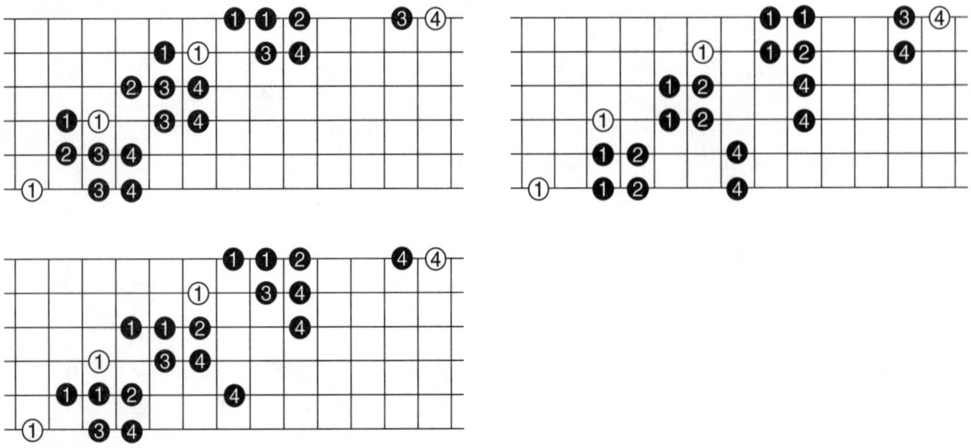

Position-Based Fingerings, Starting on all Scale Degrees

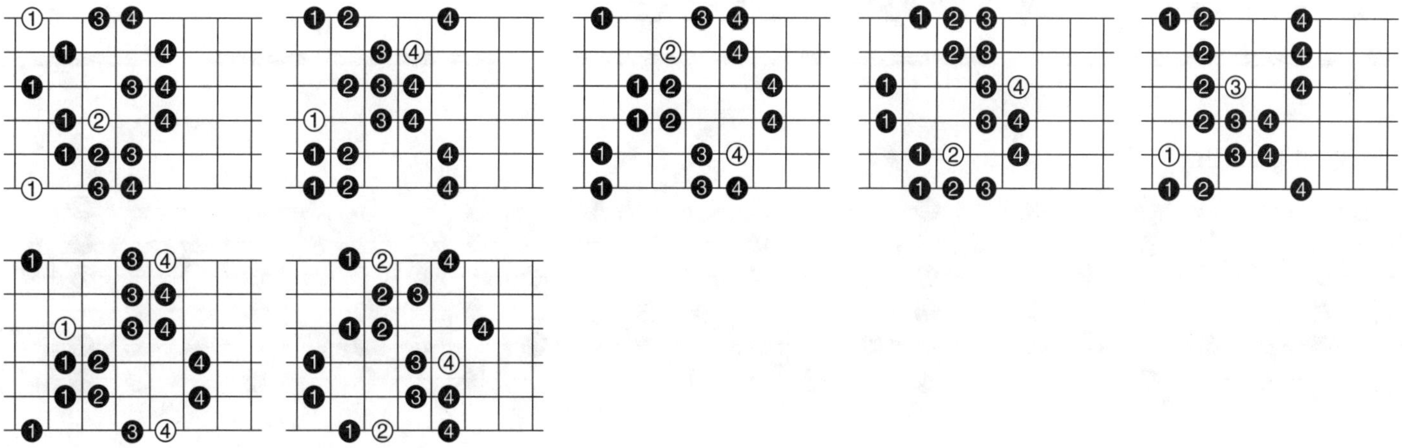

Three-Notes-Per-String Fingerings, Starting on all Scale Degrees

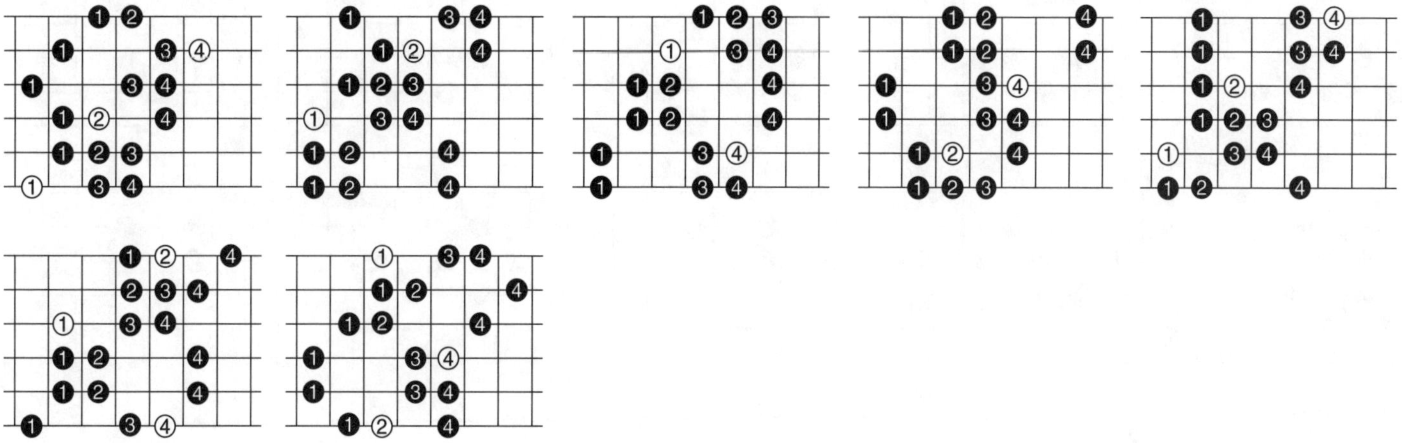

Four-Notes-Per-String Fingerings

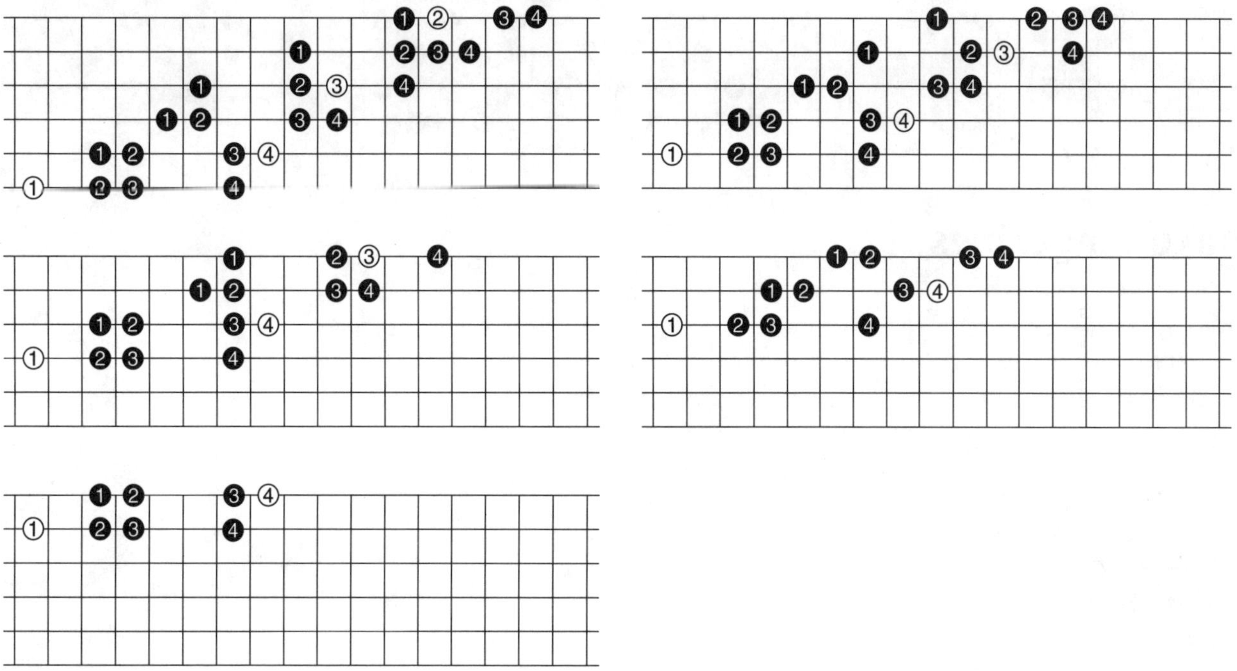

Leading Whole Tone

Scale Tones

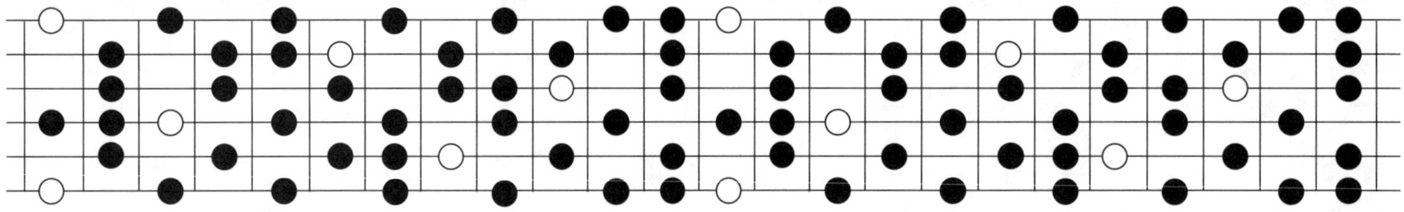

One-Octave Fingerings

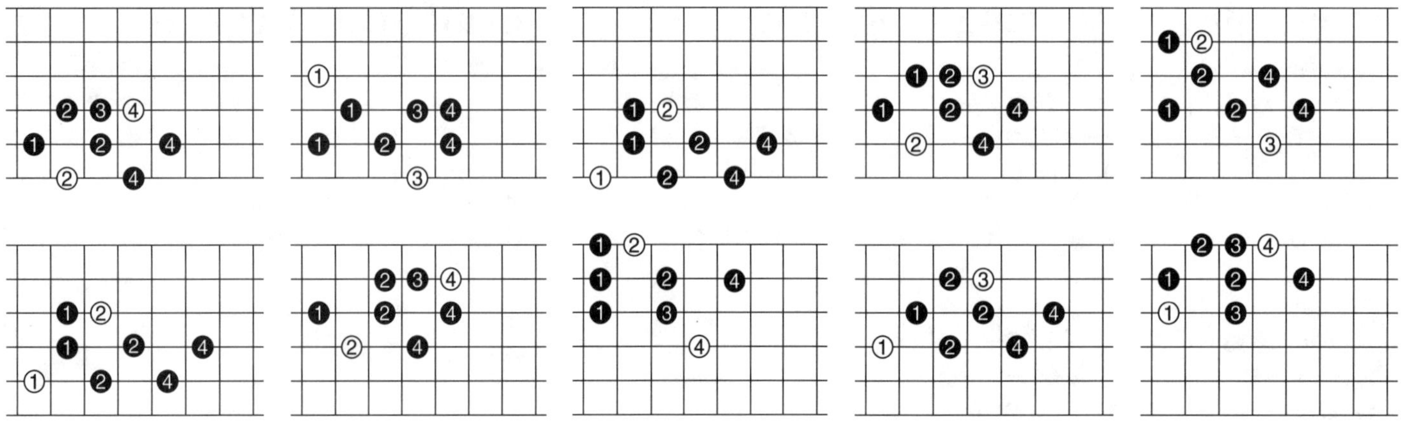

Two-Octave Fingerings

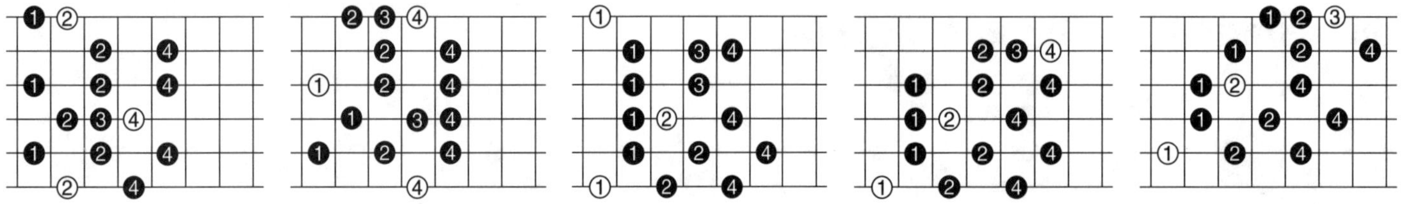

Three-Octave Fingerings

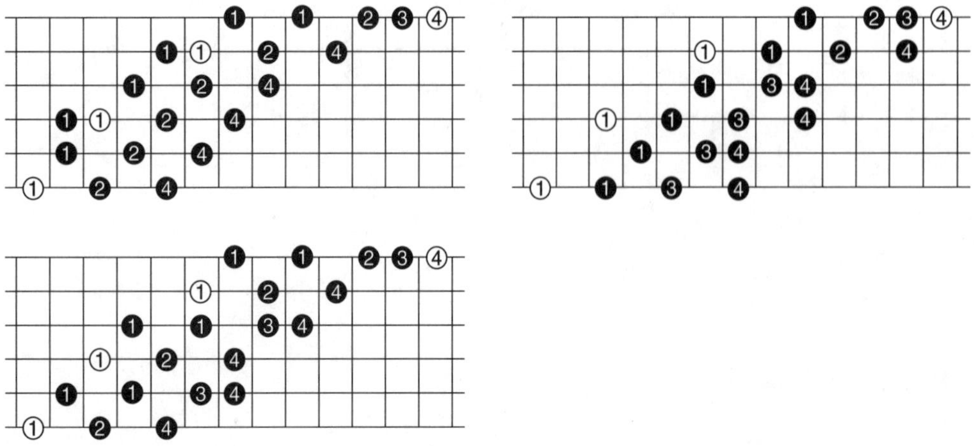

Position-Based Fingerings, Starting on all Scale Degrees

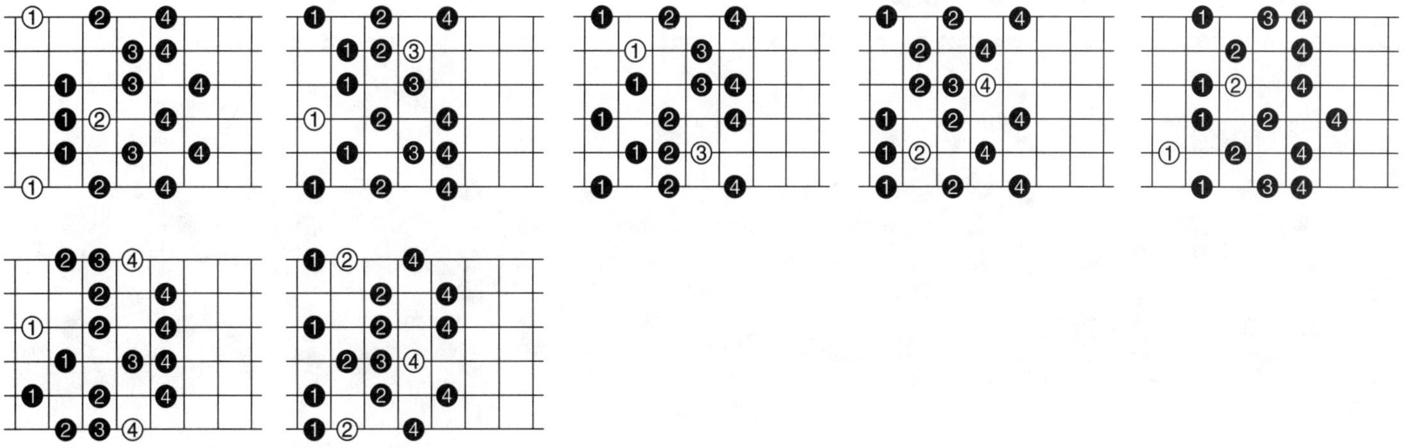

Three-Notes-Per-String Fingerings, Starting on all Scale Degrees

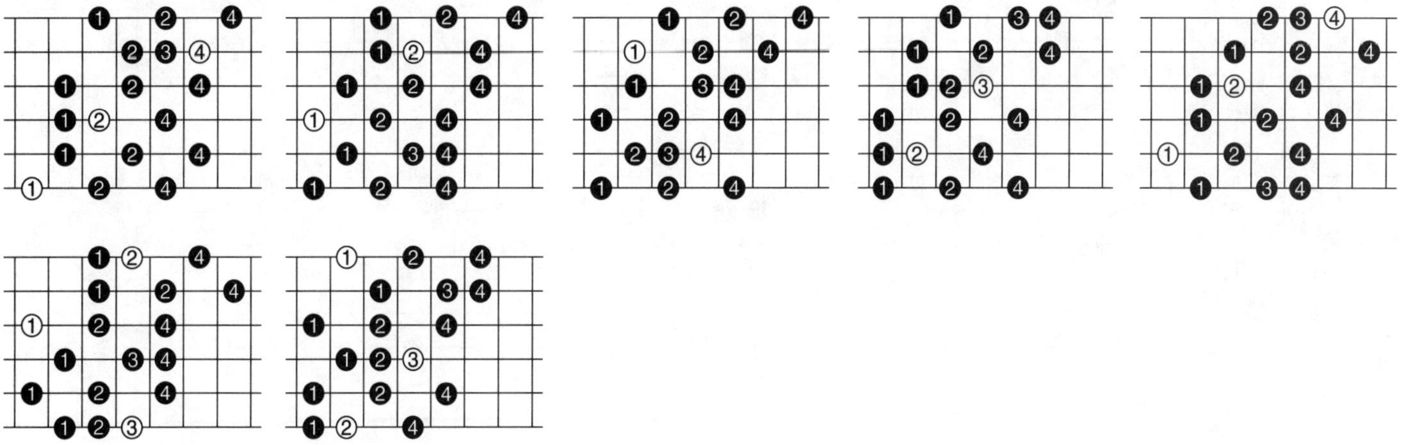

Four-Notes-Per-String Fingerings

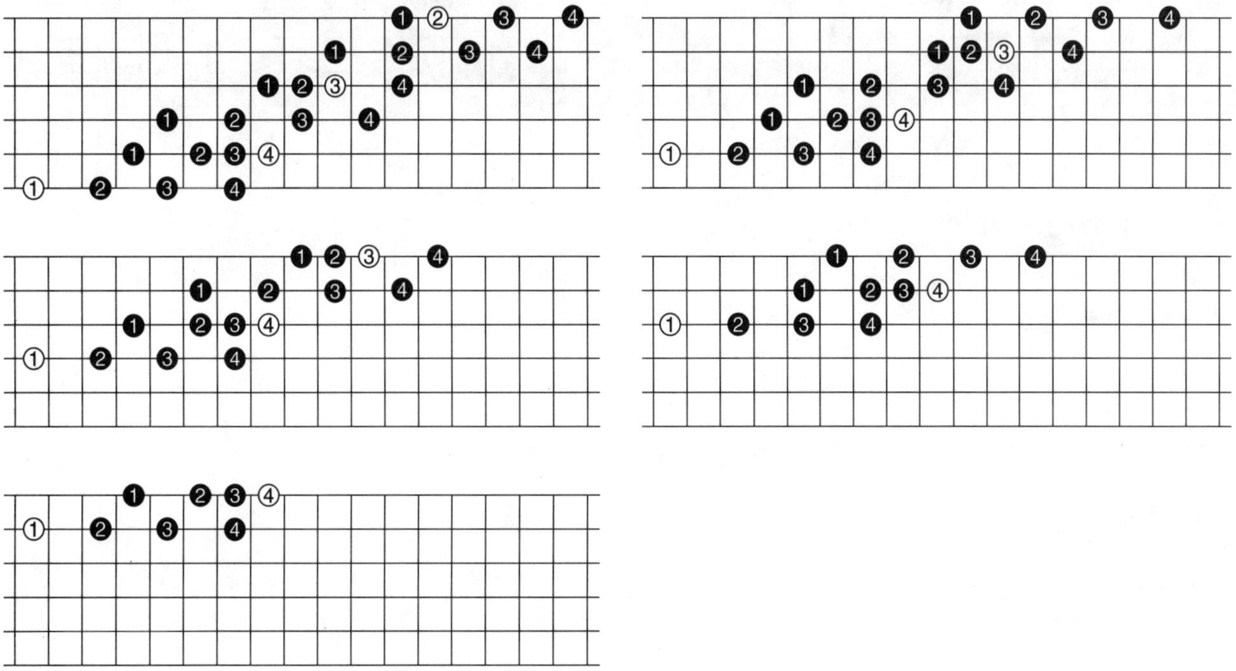

Lydian Minor

Scale Tones

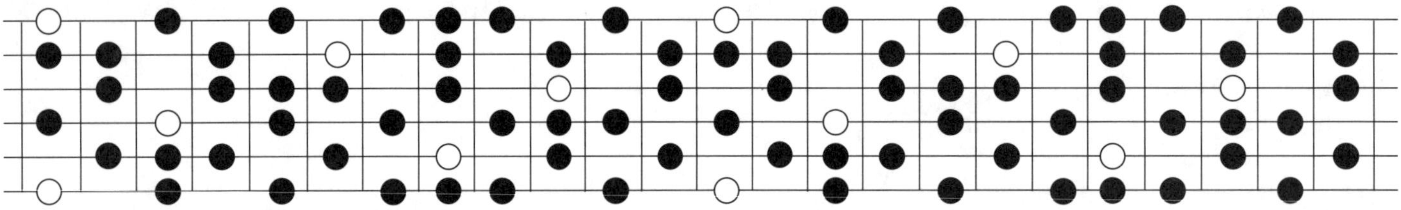

One-Octave Fingerings

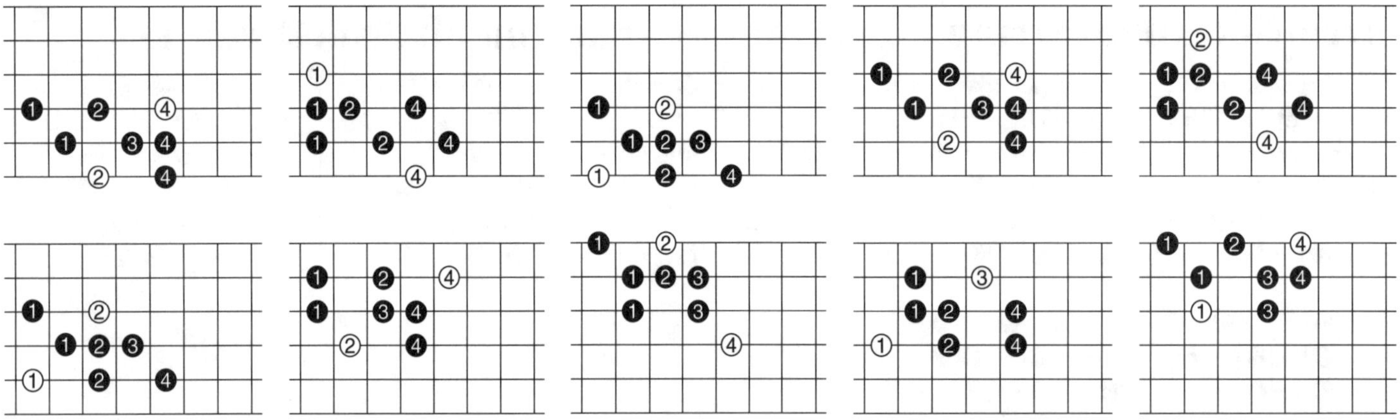

Two-Octave Fingerings

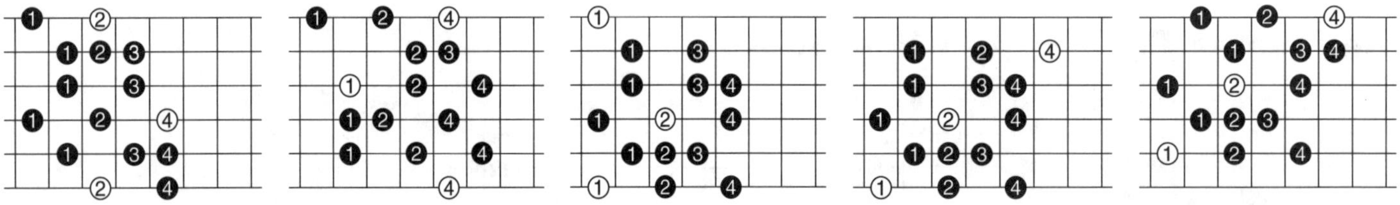

Three-Octave Fingerings

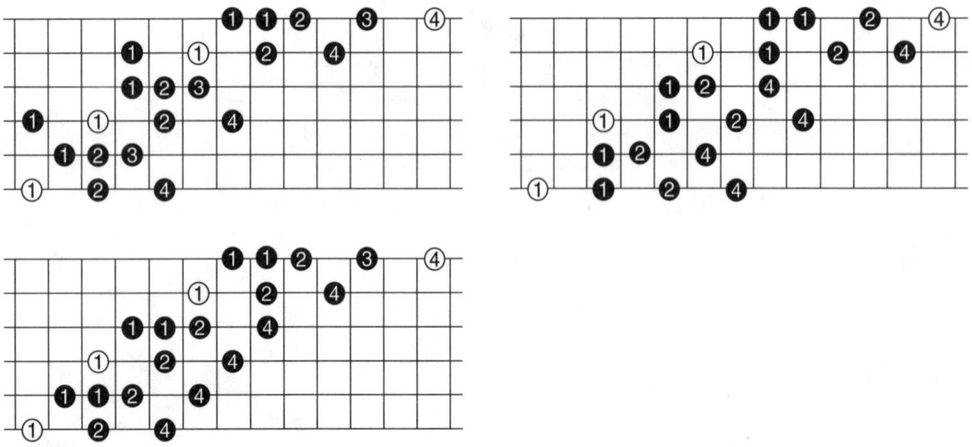

Position-Based Fingerings, Starting on all Scale Degrees

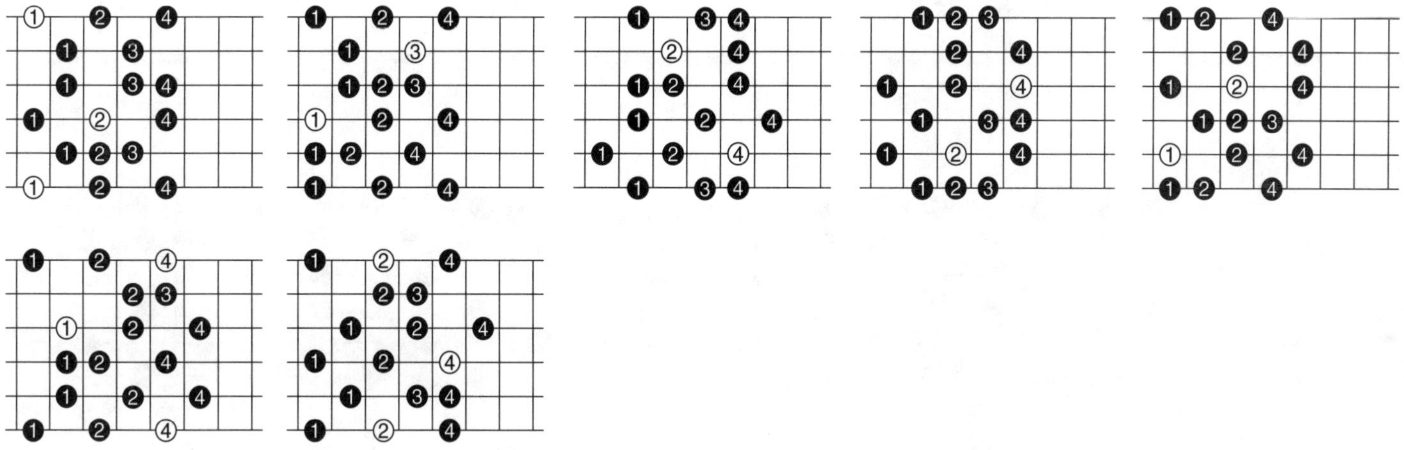

Three-Notes-Per-String Fingerings, Starting on all Scale Degrees

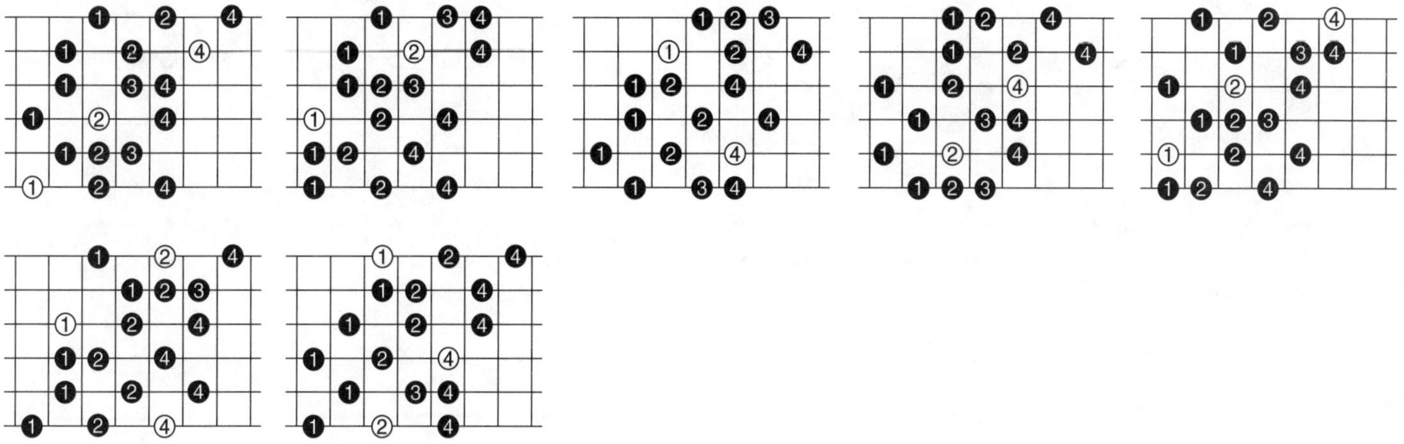

Four-Notes-Per-String Fingerings

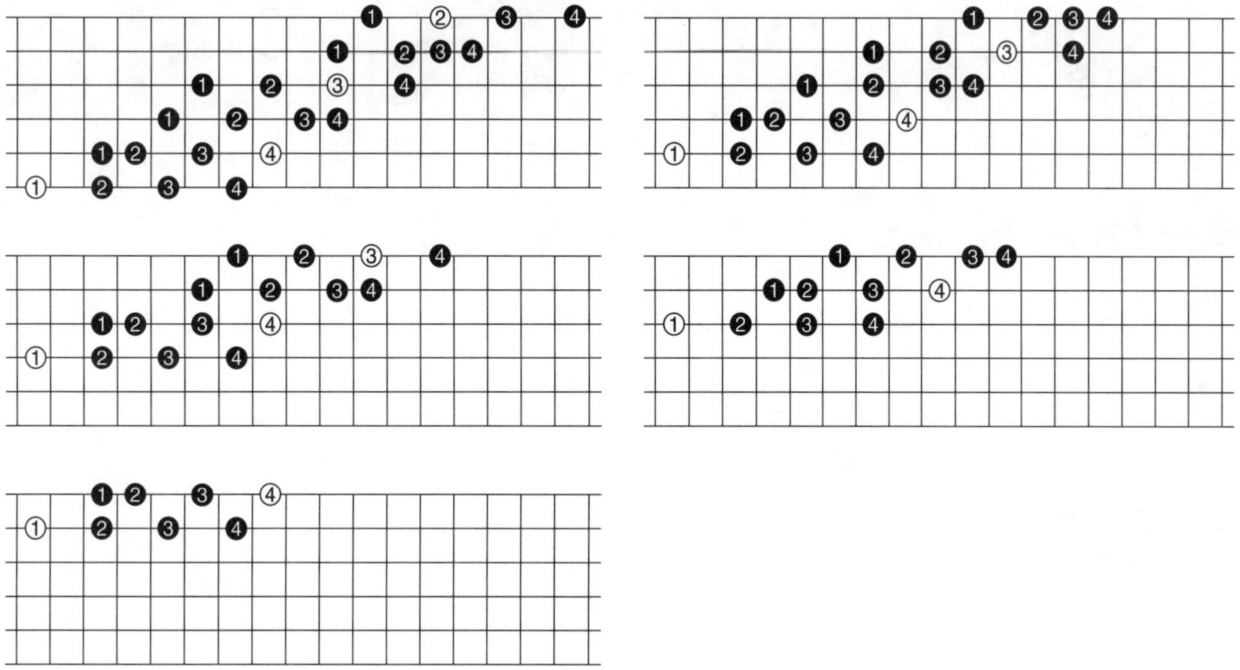

Major Locrian

Scale Tones

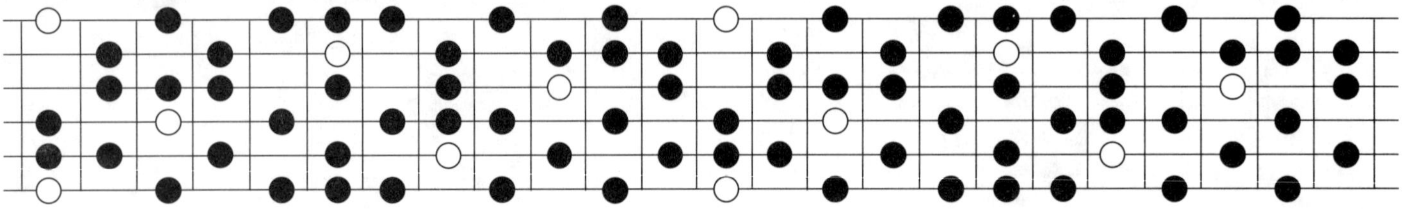

One-Octave Fingerings

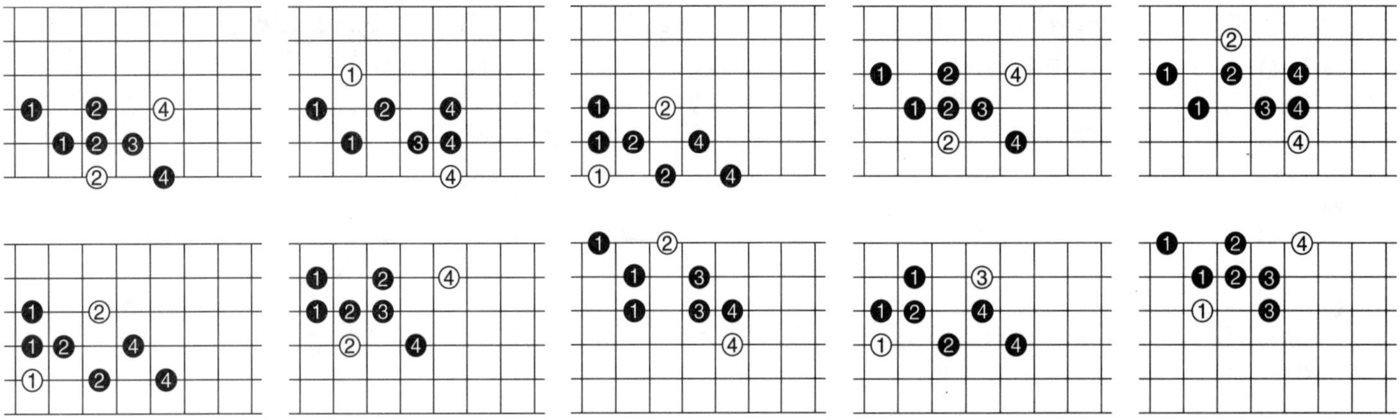

Two-Octave Fingerings

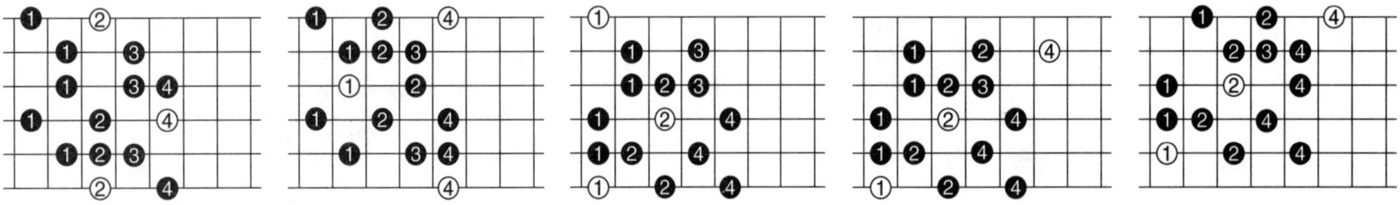

Three-Octave Fingerings

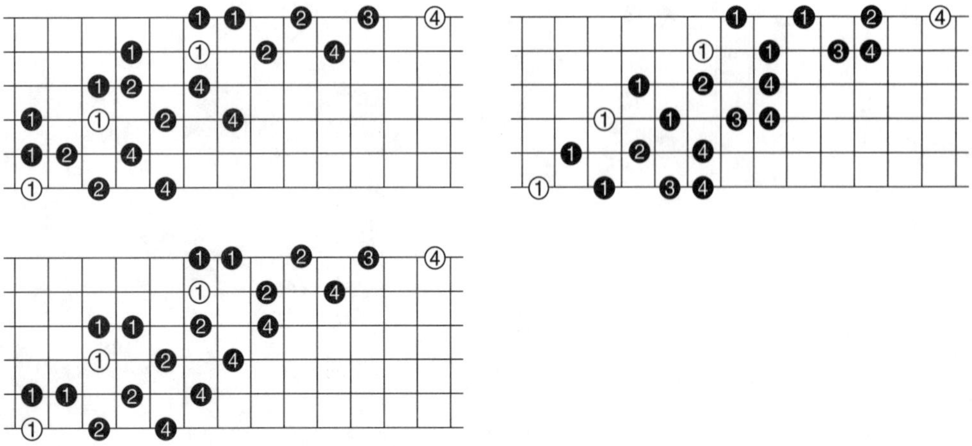

Position-Based Fingerings, Starting on all Scale Degrees

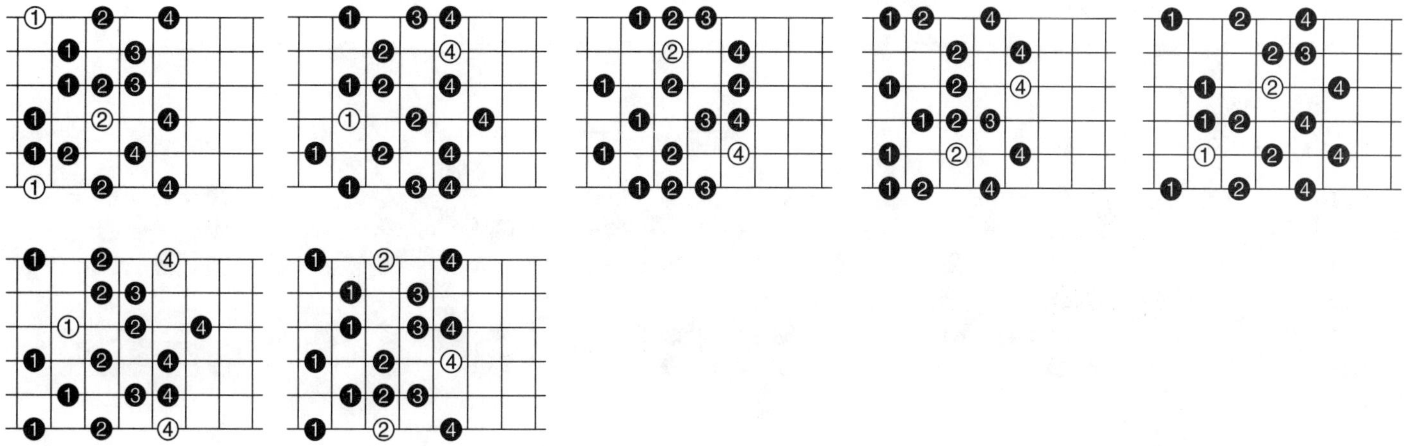

Three-Notes-Per-String Fingerings, Starting on all Scale Degrees

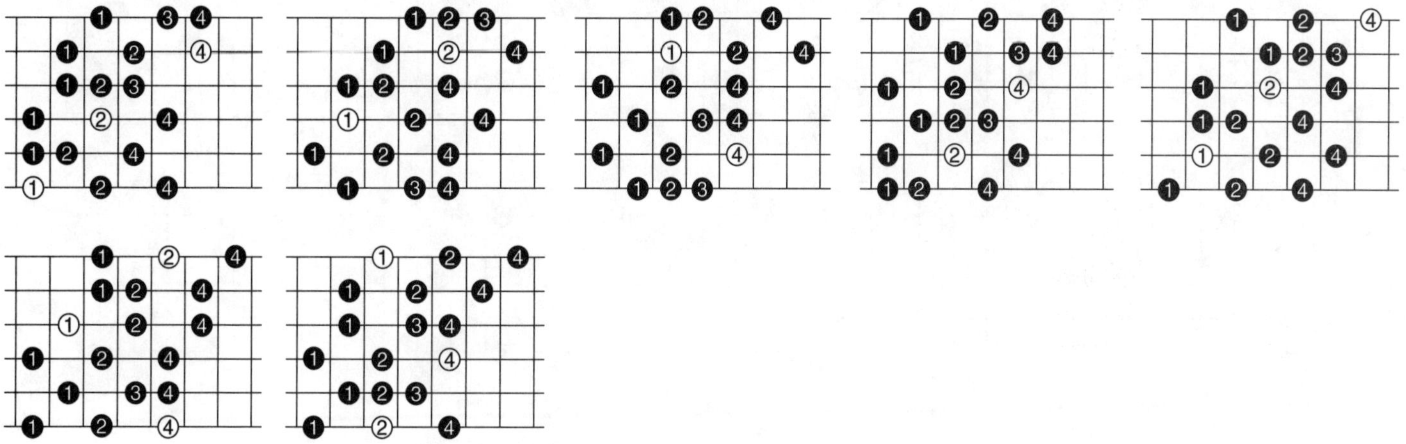

Four-Notes-Per-String Fingerings

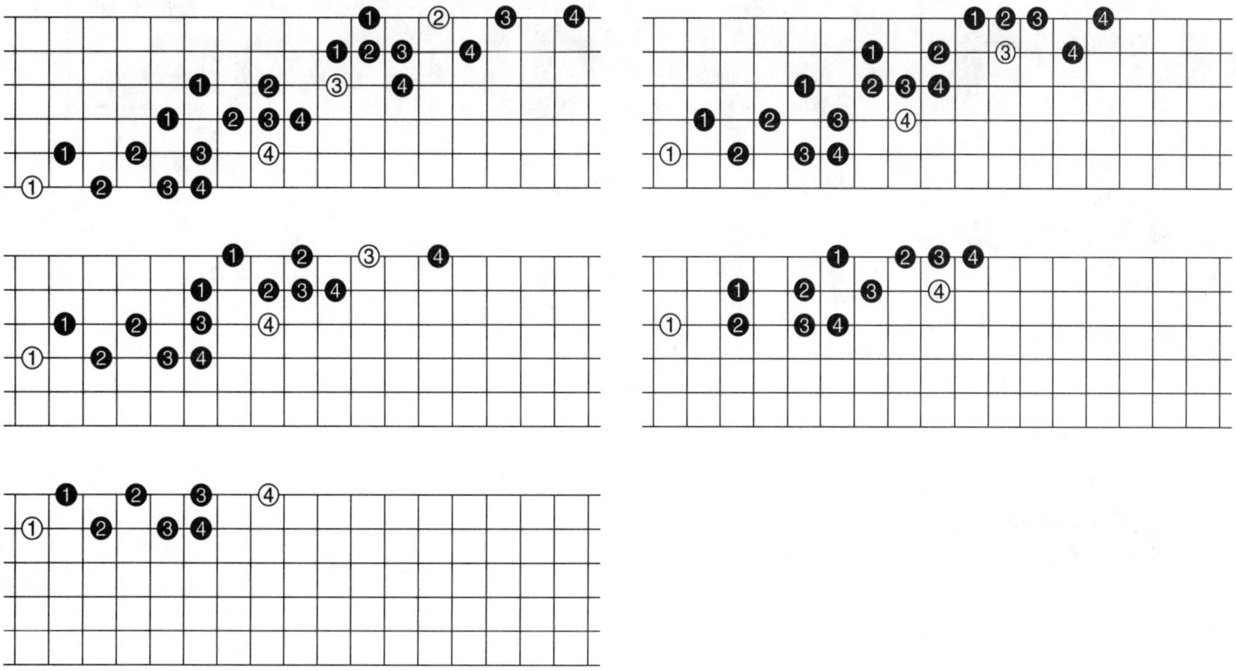

Marwa

Scale Tones

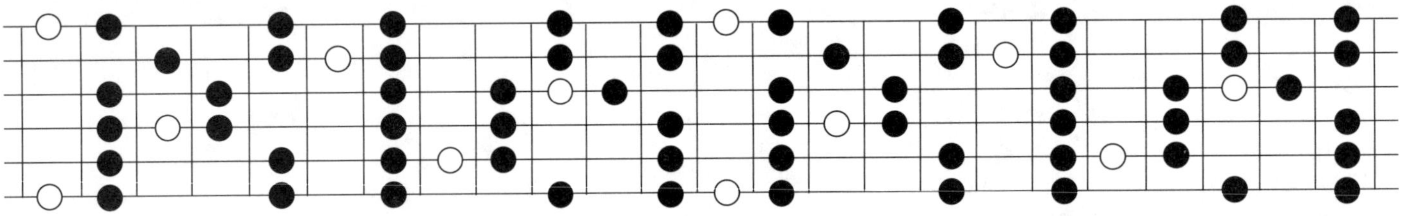

One-Octave Fingerings

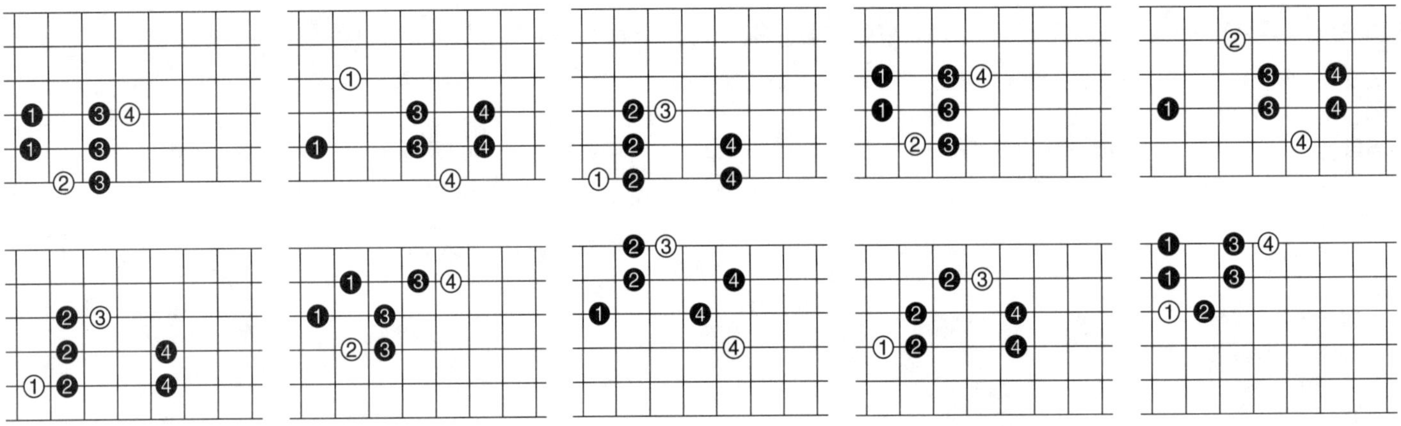

Two-Octave Fingerings

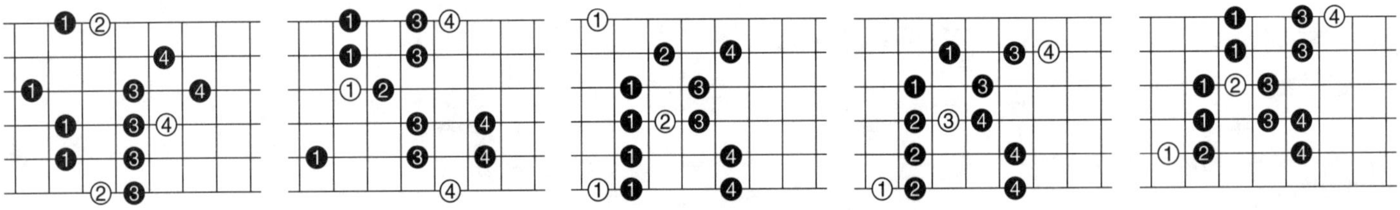

Three-Octave Fingerings

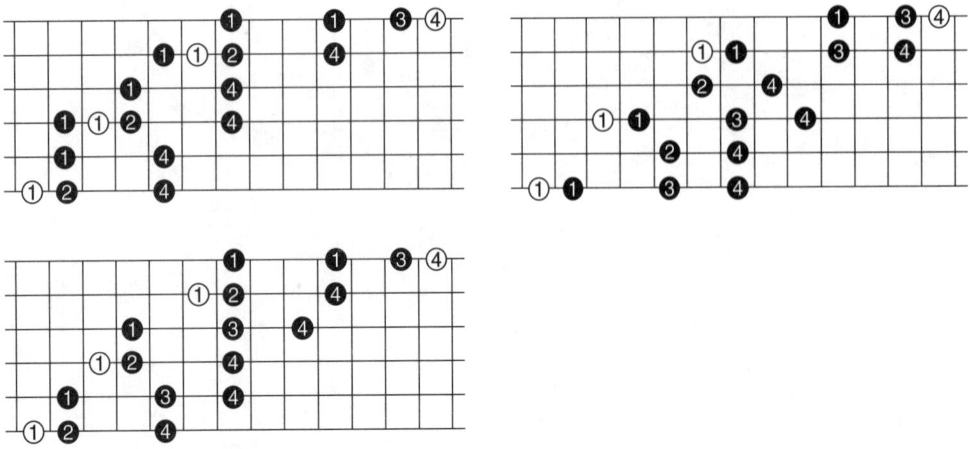

Position-Based Fingerings, Starting on all Scale Degrees

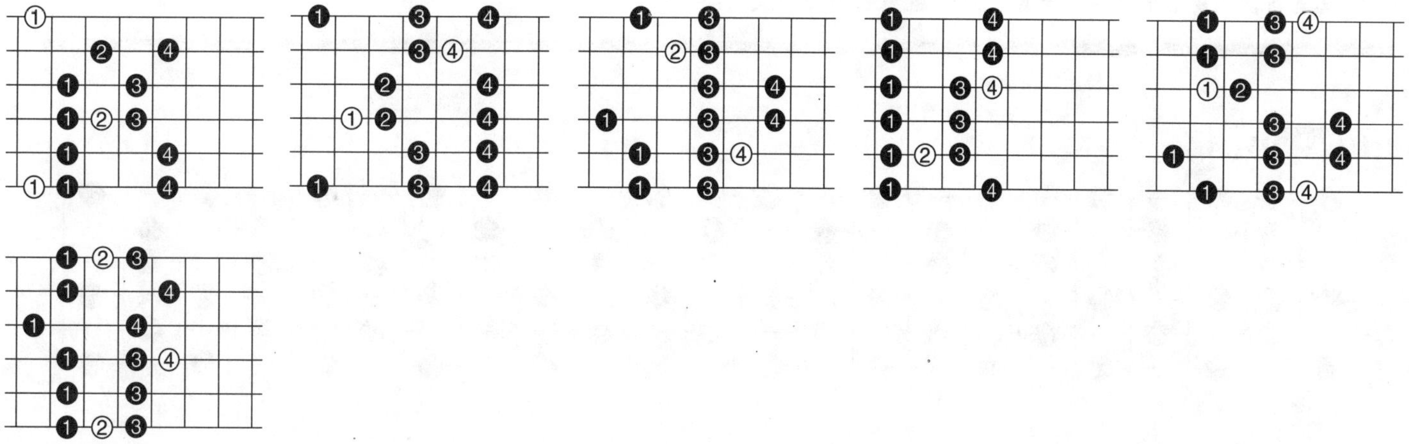

Three-Notes-Per-String Fingerings

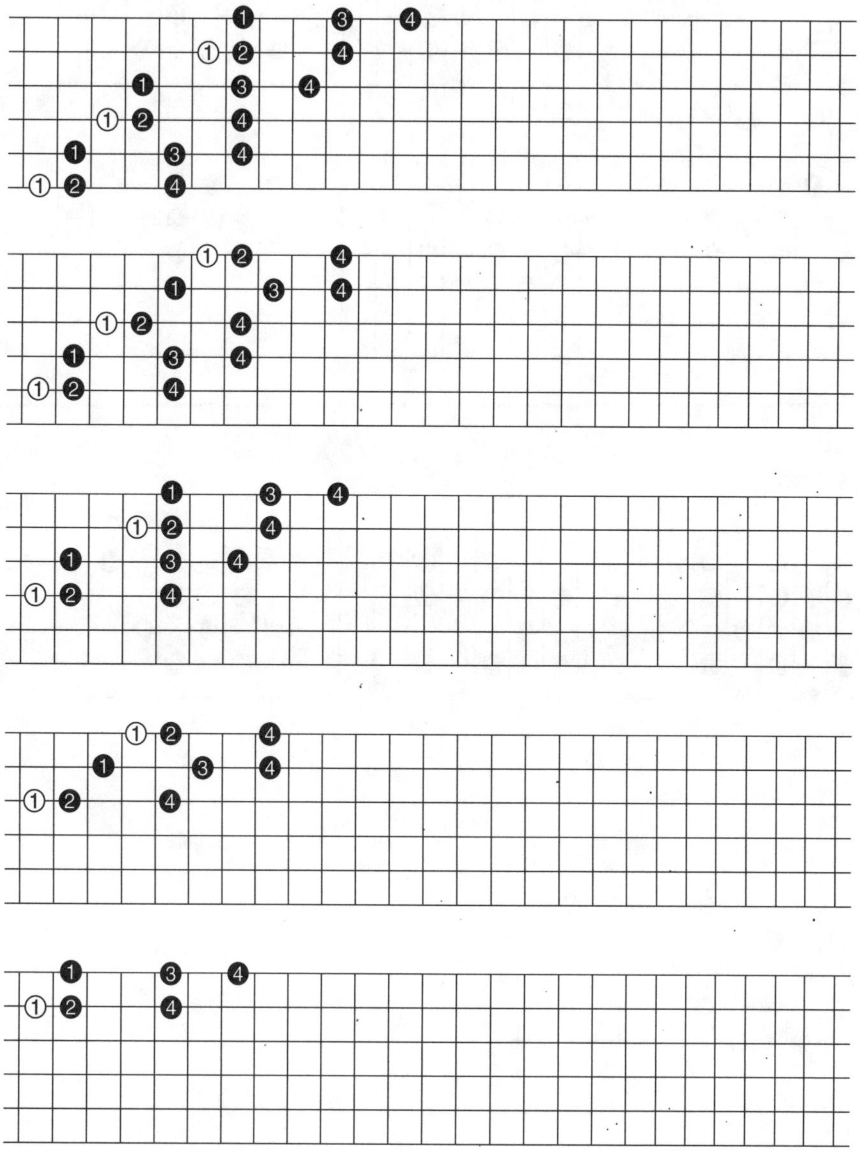

Neapolitan Major

Scale Tones

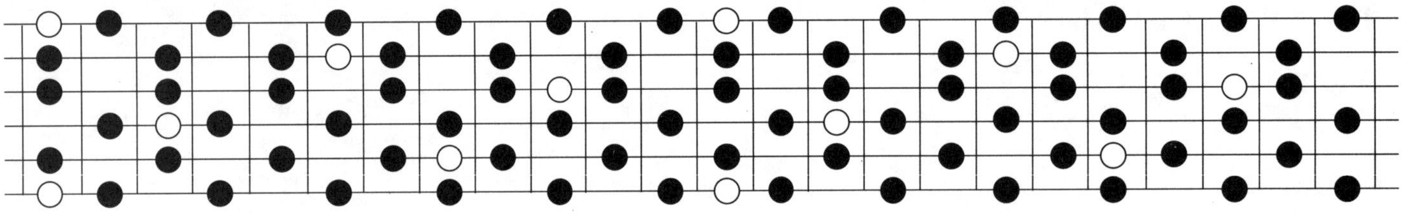

One-Octave Fingerings

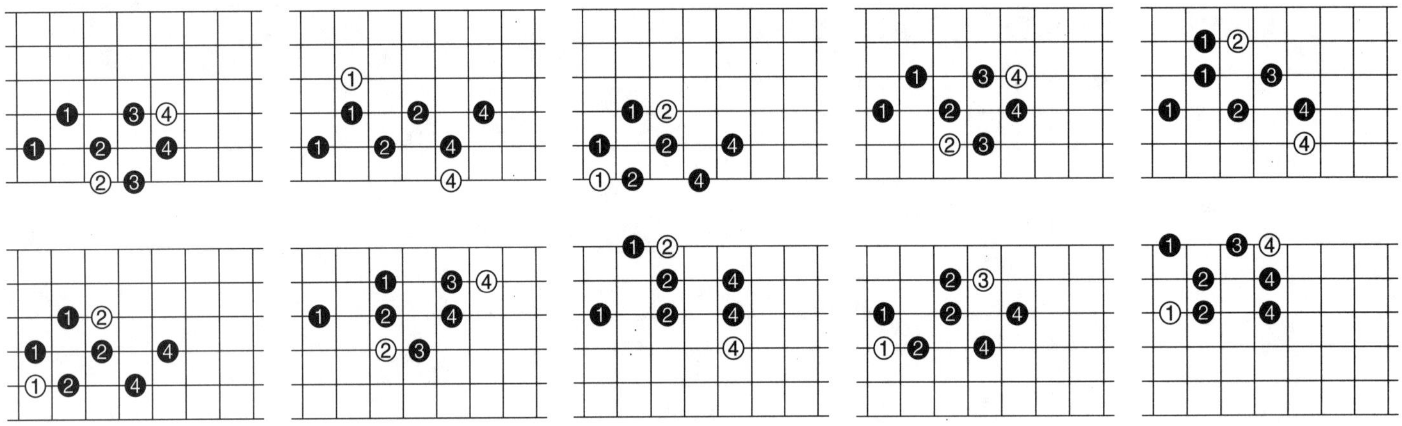

Two-Octave Fingerings

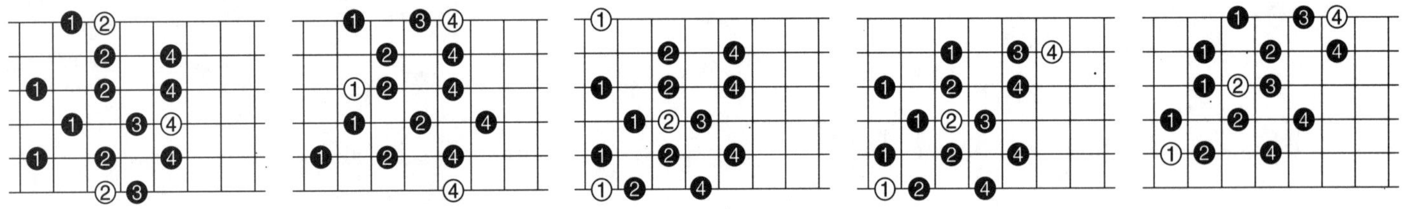

Three-Octave Fingerings

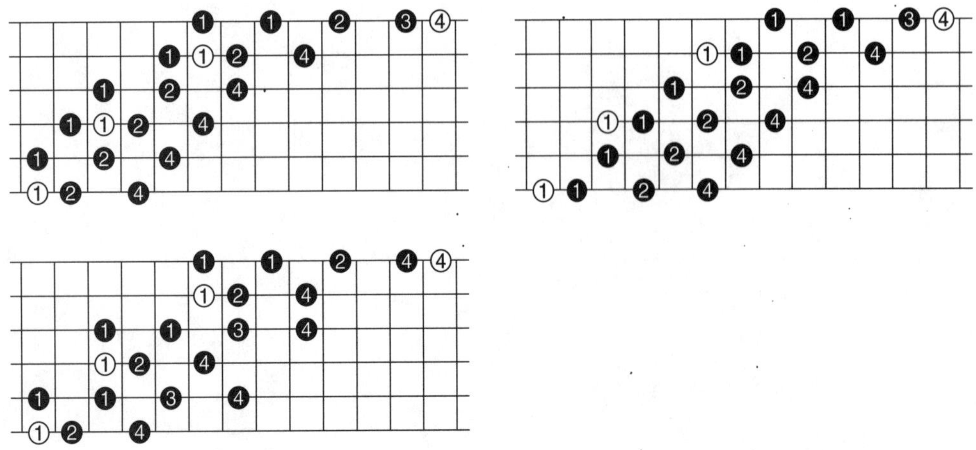

Position-Based Fingerings, Starting on all Scale Degrees

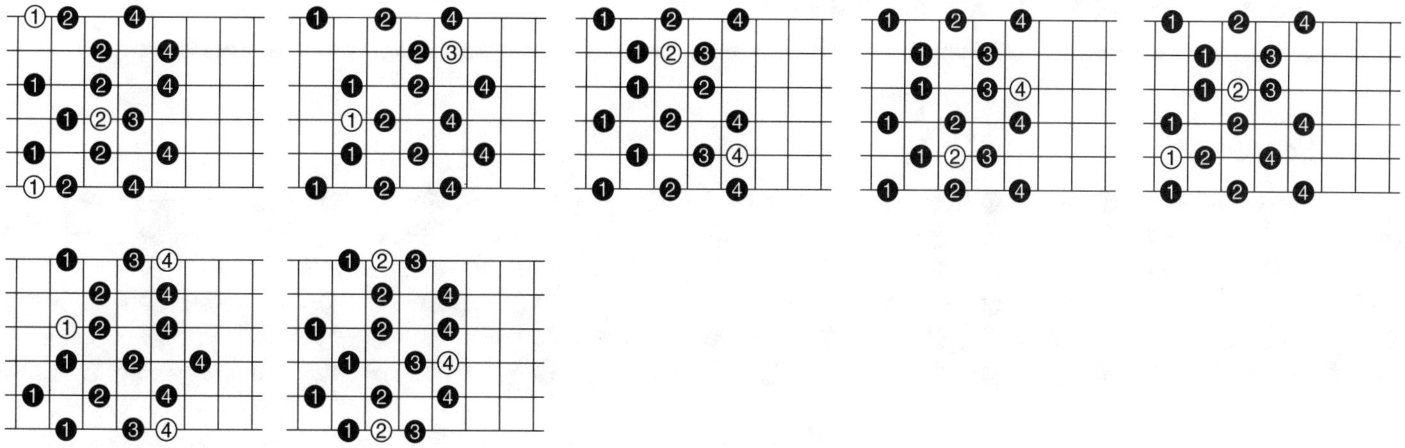

Three-Notes-Per-String Fingerings, Starting on all Scale Degrees

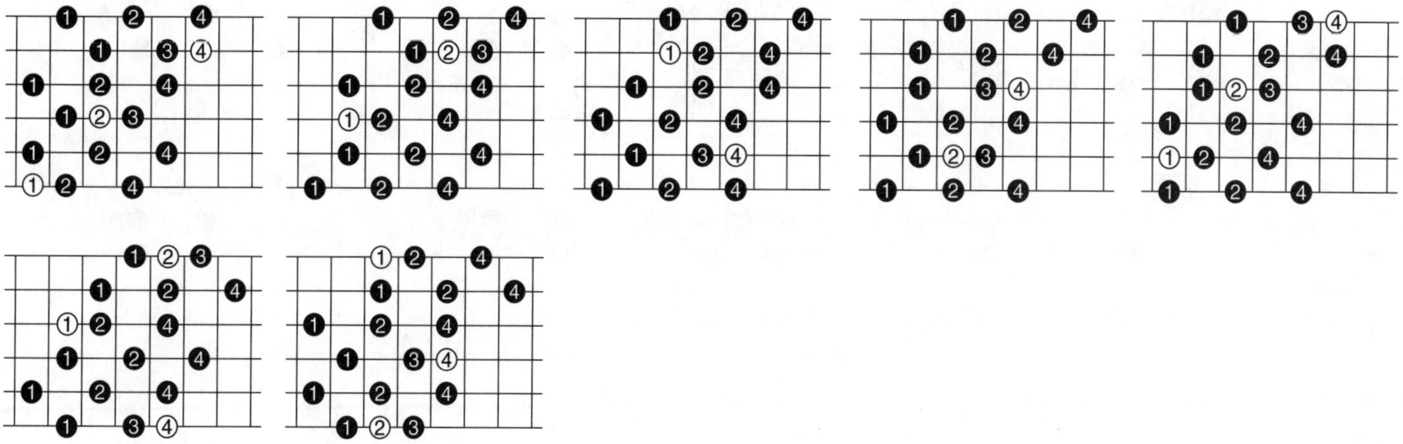

Four-Notes-Per-String Fingerings

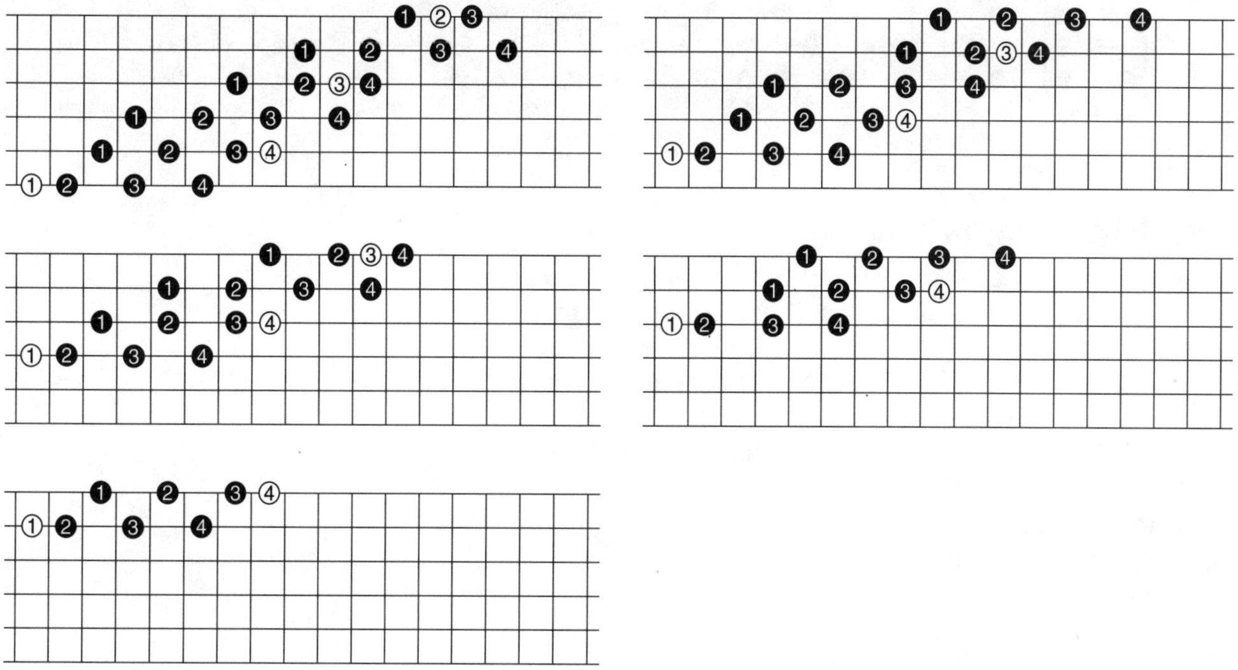

Neapolitan Minor

Scale Tones

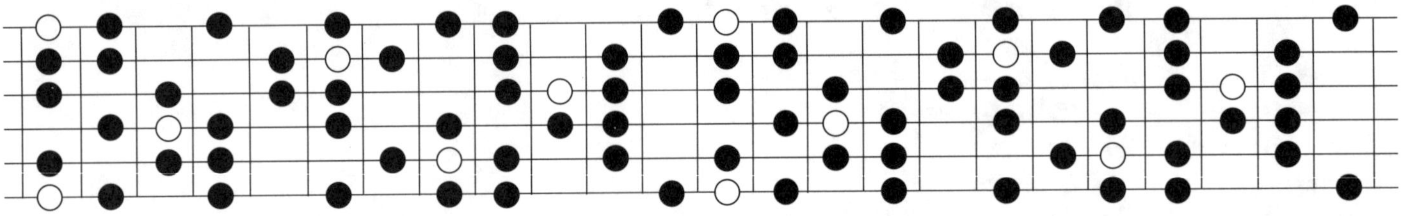

One-Octave Fingerings

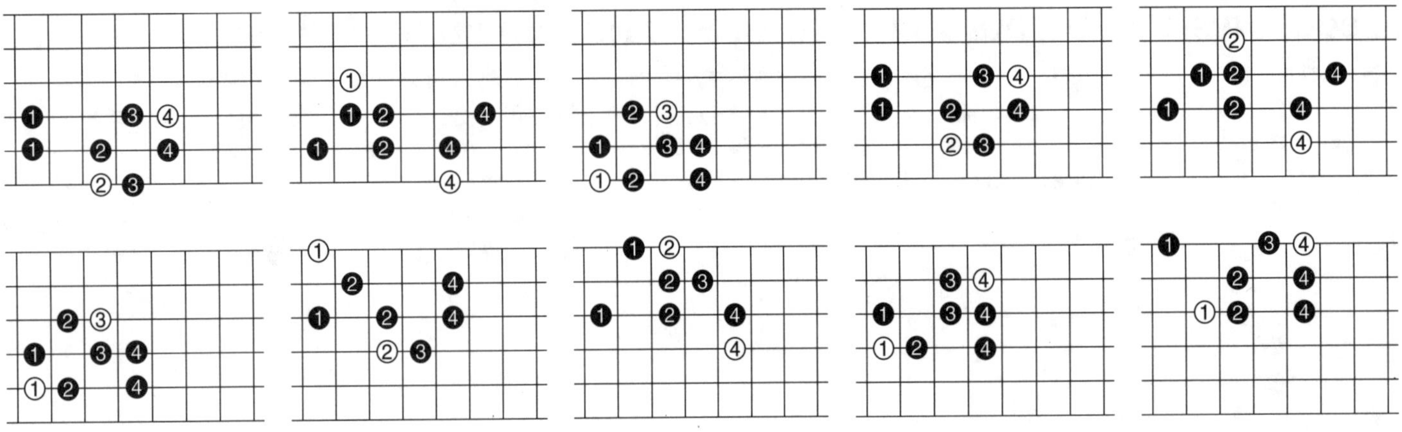

Two-Octave Fingerings

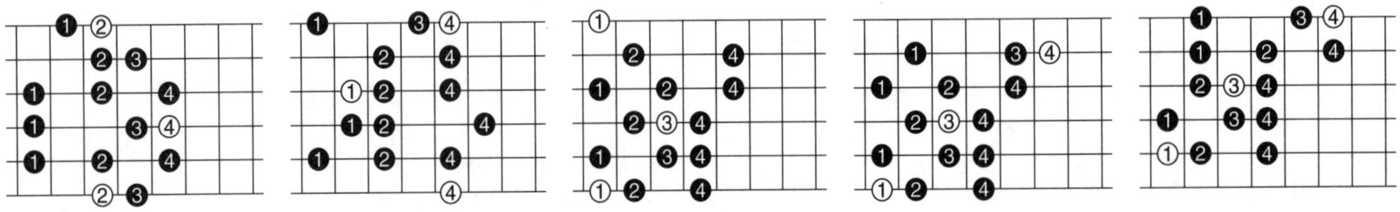

Three-Octave Fingerings

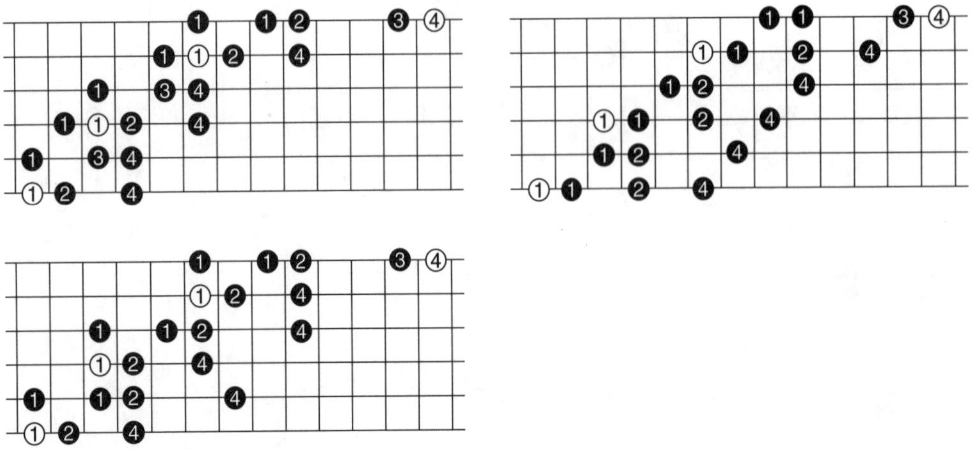

Position-Based Fingerings, Starting on all Scale Degrees

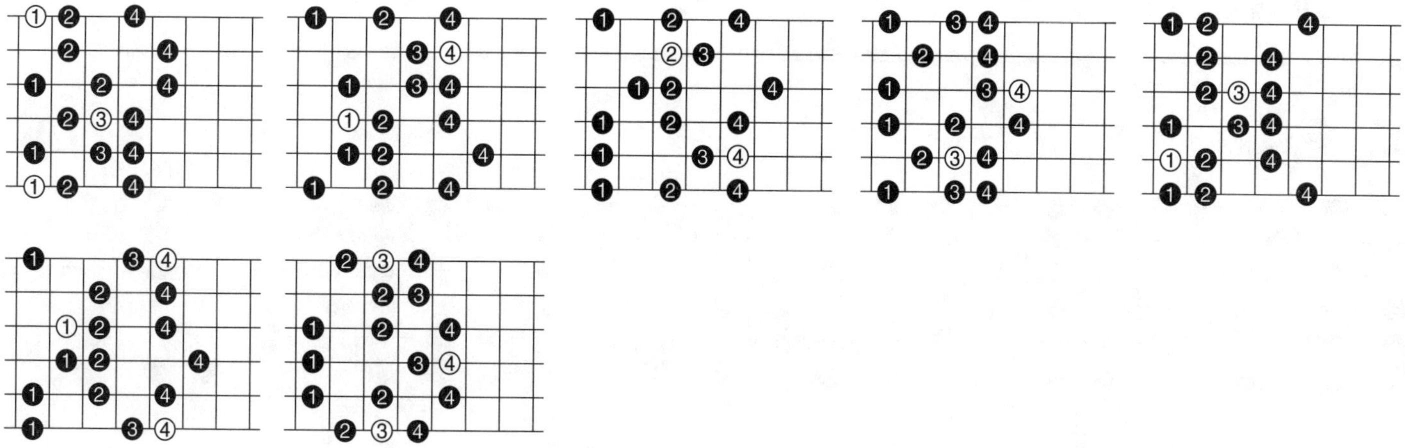

Three-Notes-Per-String Fingerings, Starting on all Scale Degrees

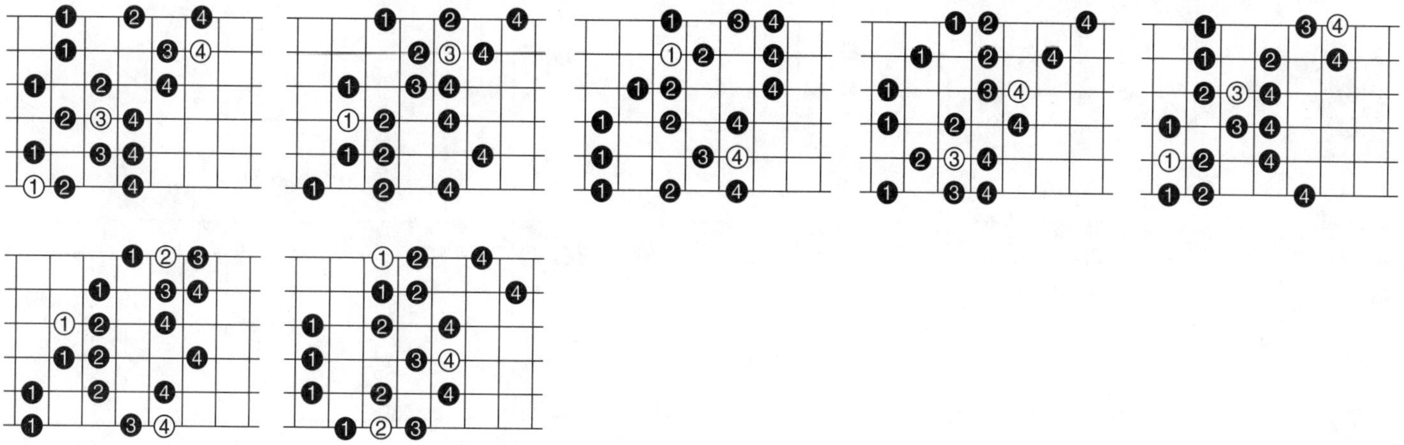

Four-Notes-Per-String Fingerings

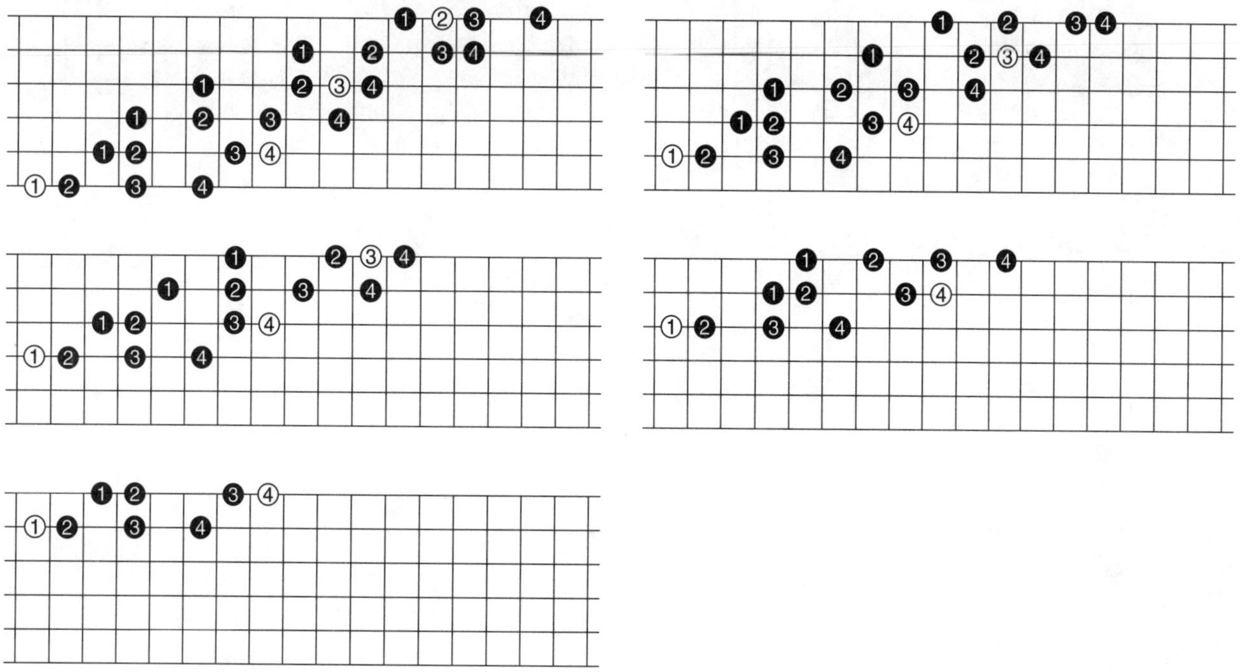

Oriental

Scale Tones

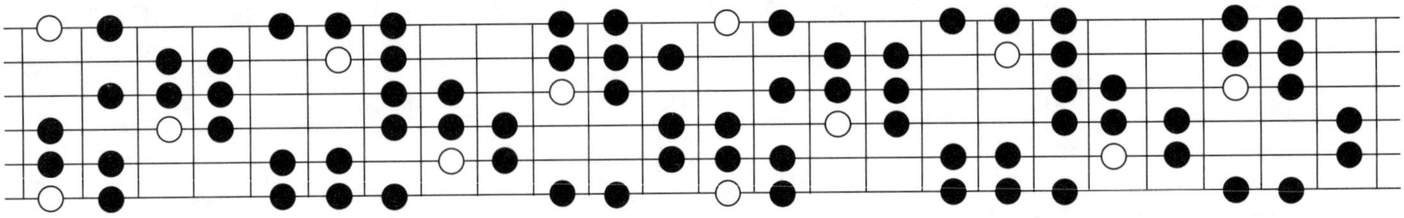

One-Octave Fingerings

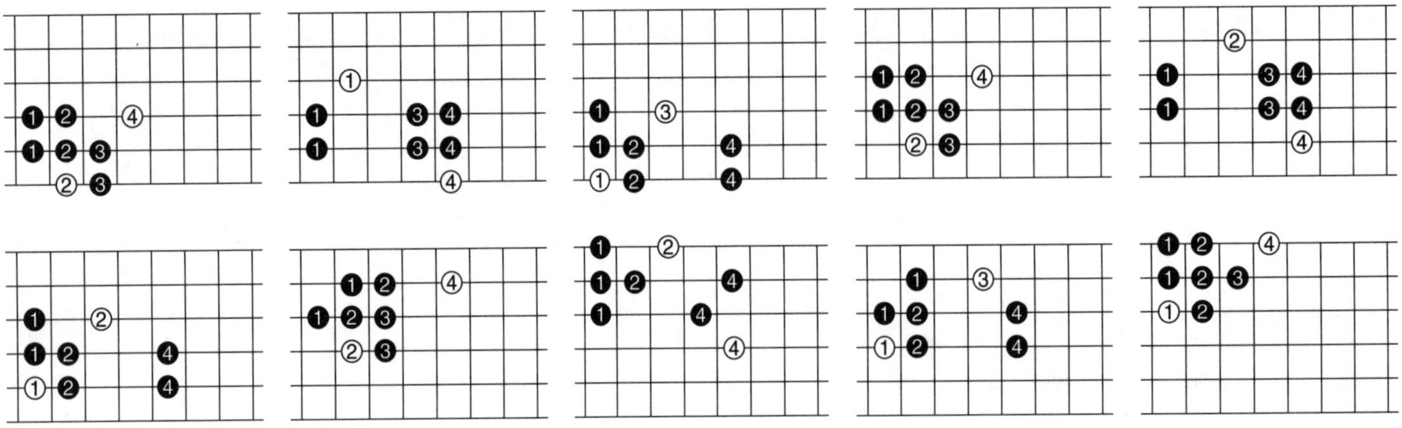

Two-Octave Fingerings

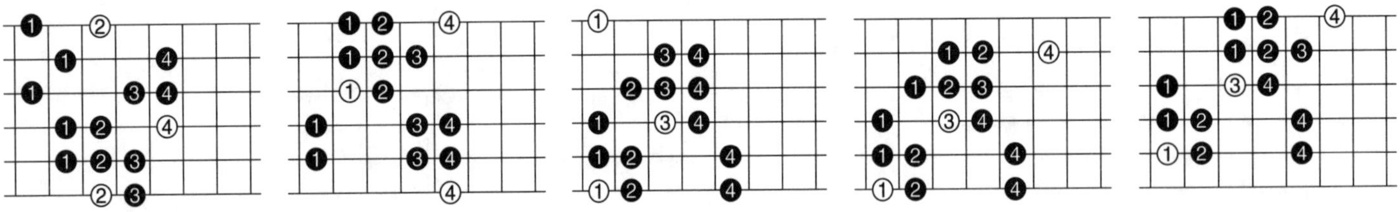

Three-Octave Fingerings

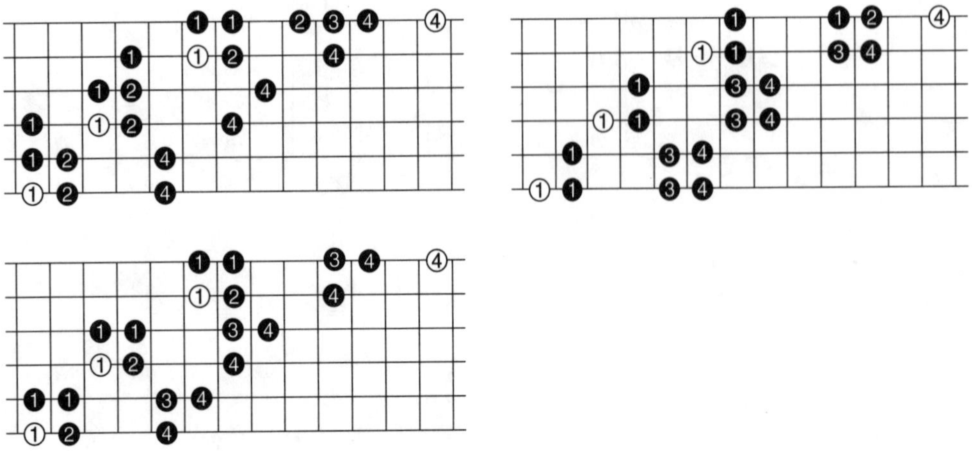

Position-Based Fingerings, Starting on all Scale Degrees

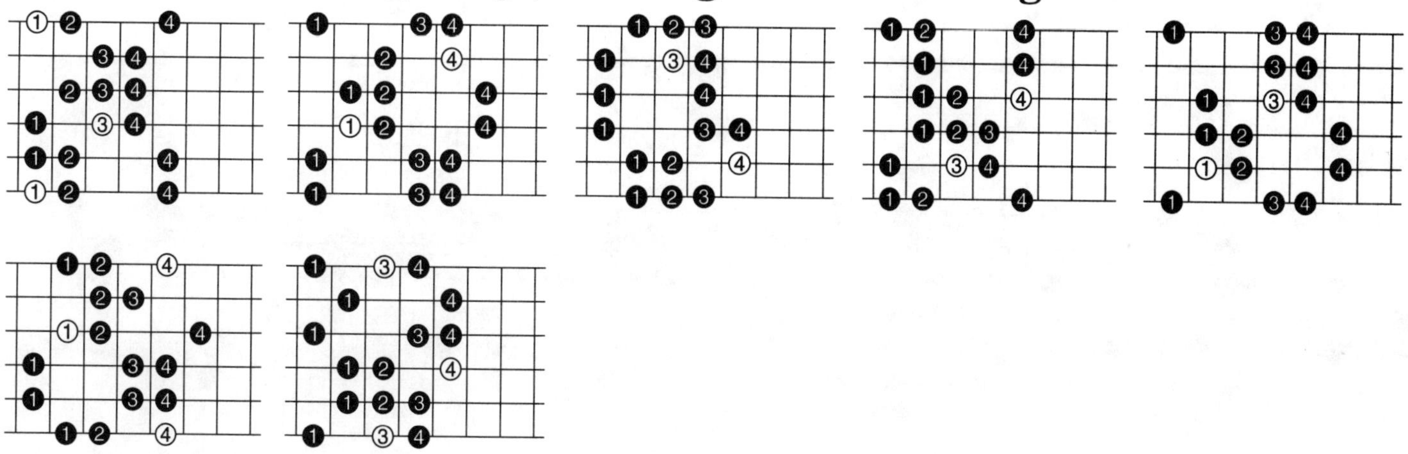

Three-Notes-Per-String Fingerings, Starting on all Scale Degrees

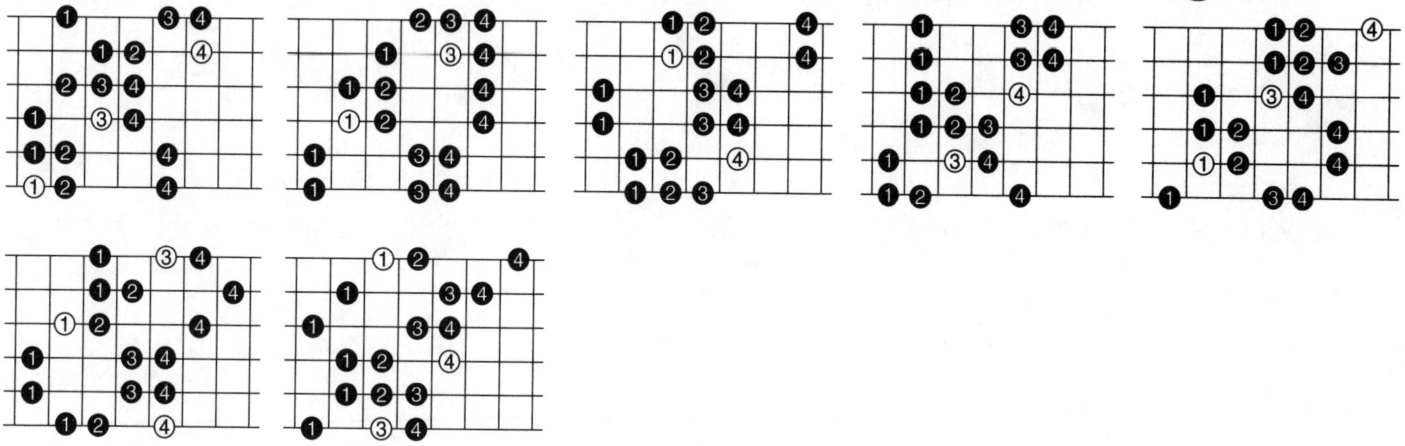

Four-Notes-Per-String Fingerings

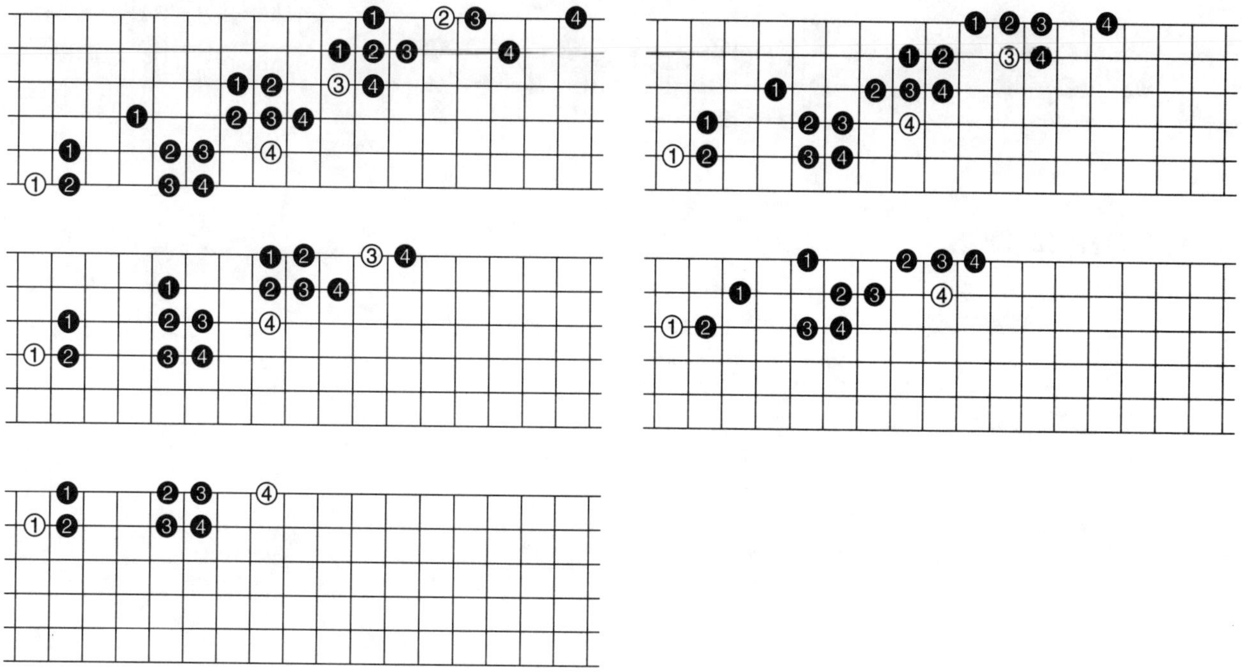

Prometheus

Scale Tones

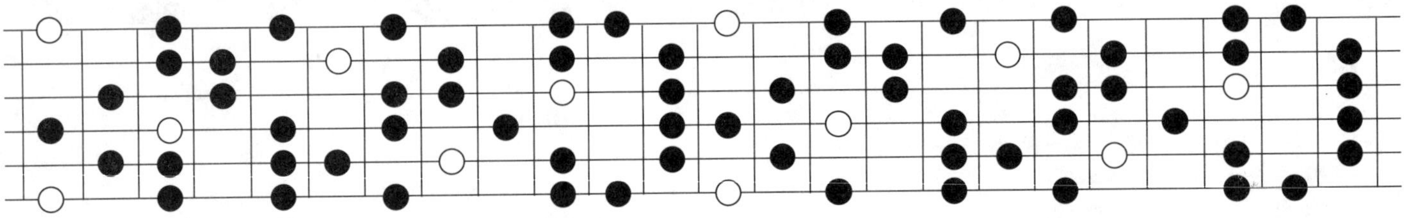

One-Octave Fingerings

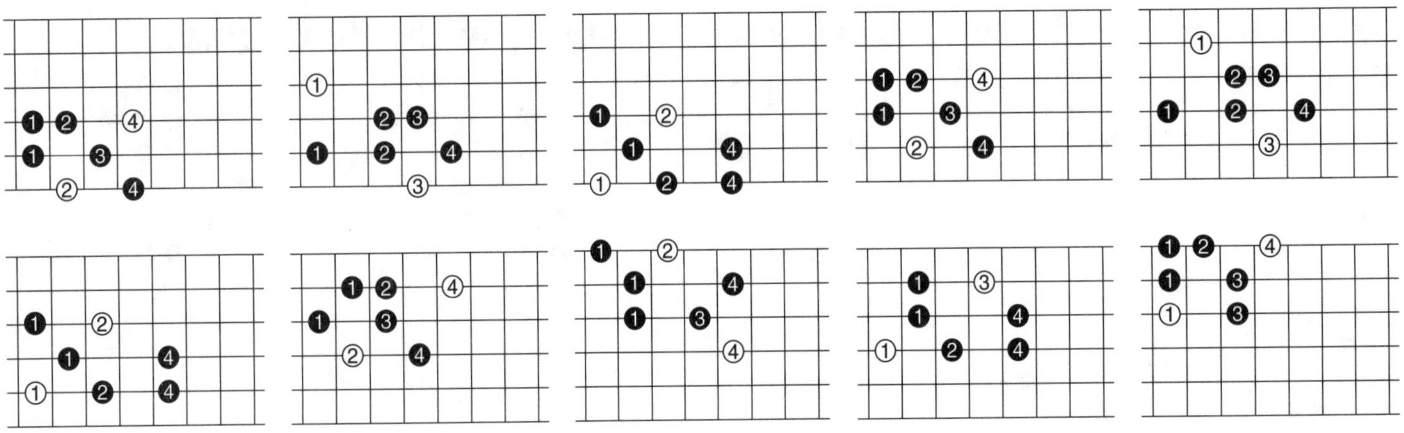

Two-Octave Fingerings

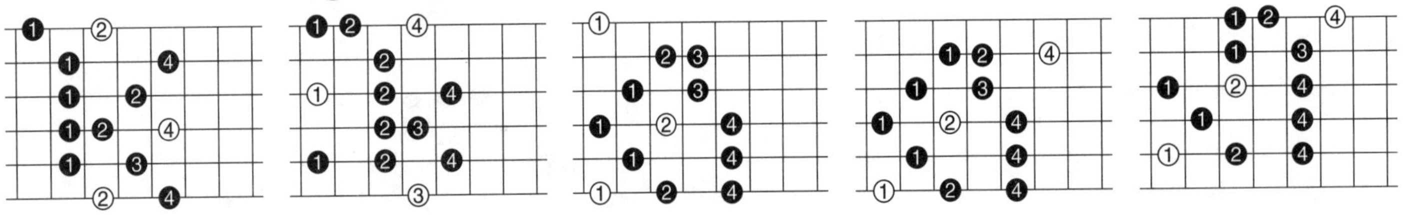

Three-Octave Fingerings

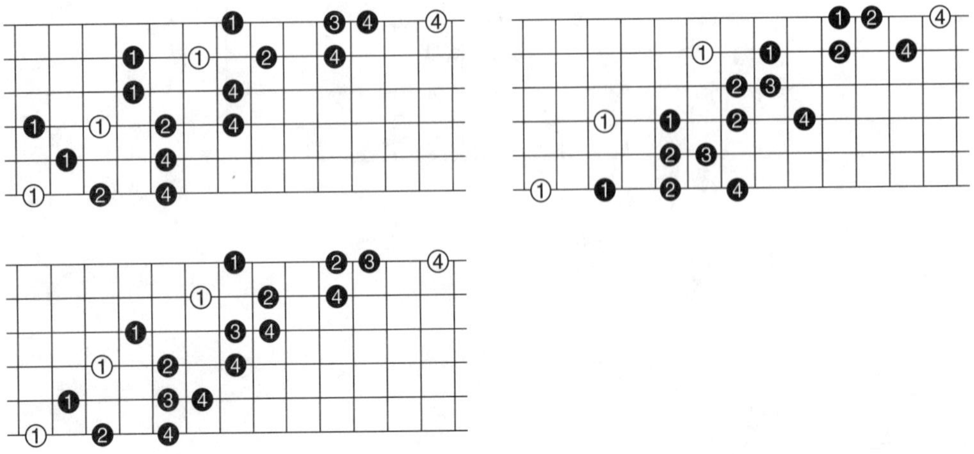

Position-Based Fingerings, Starting on all Scale Degrees

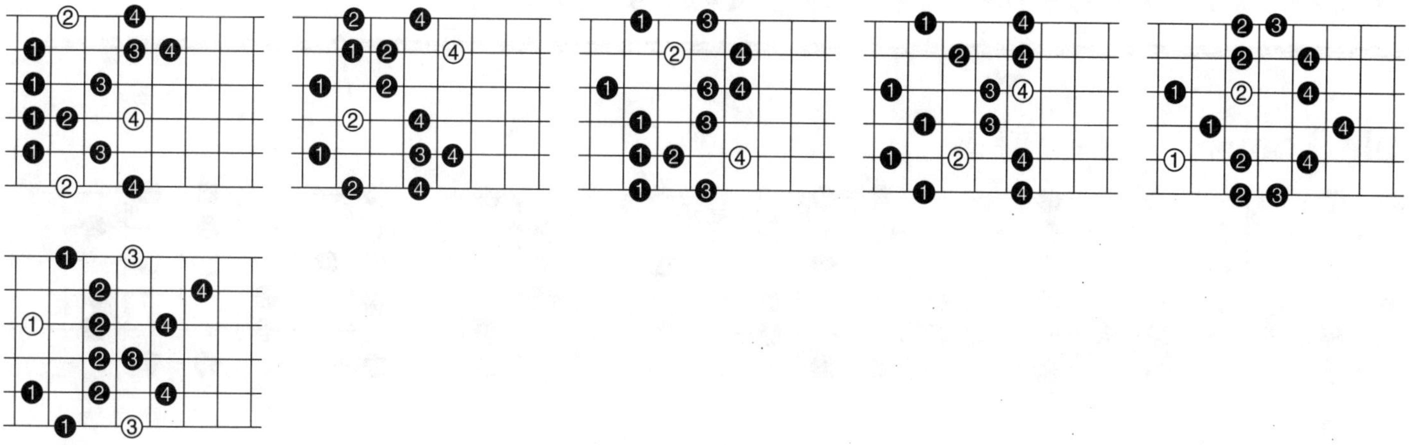

Three-Notes-Per-String Fingerings

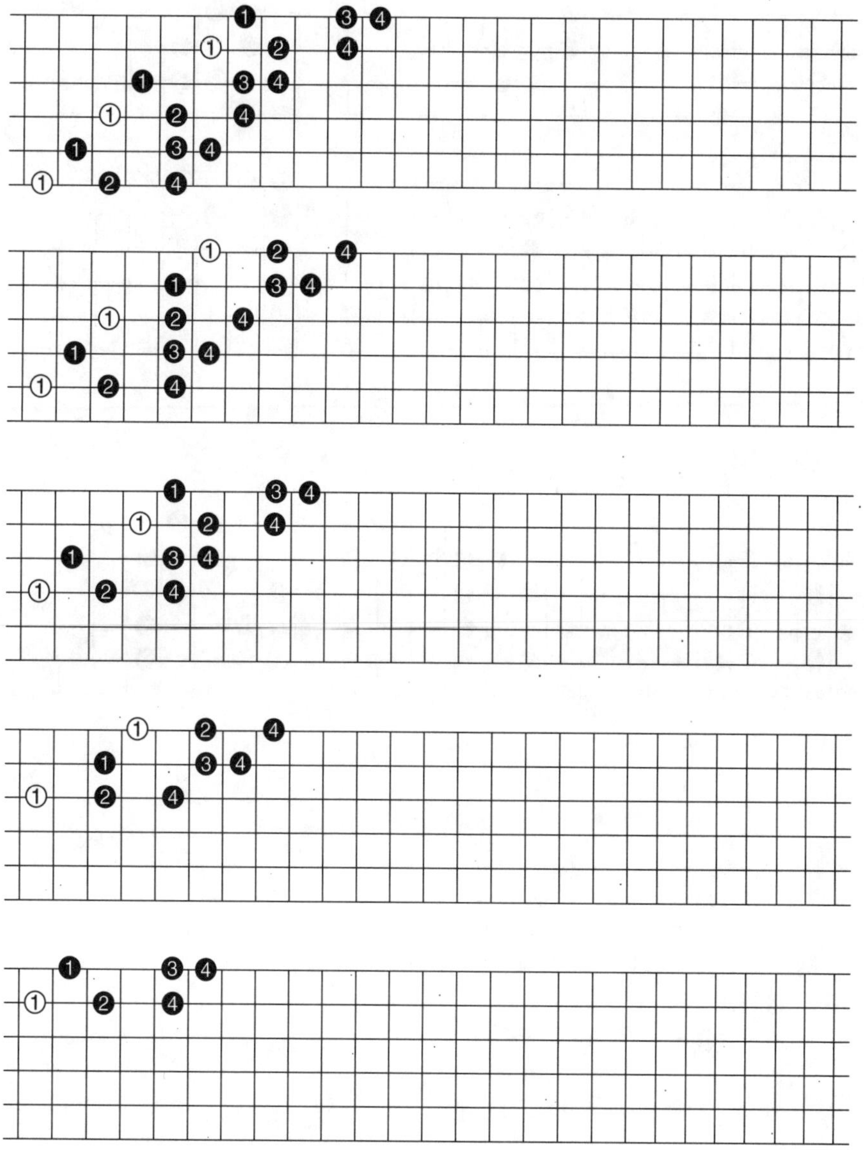

Prometheus Neapolitan

Scale Tones

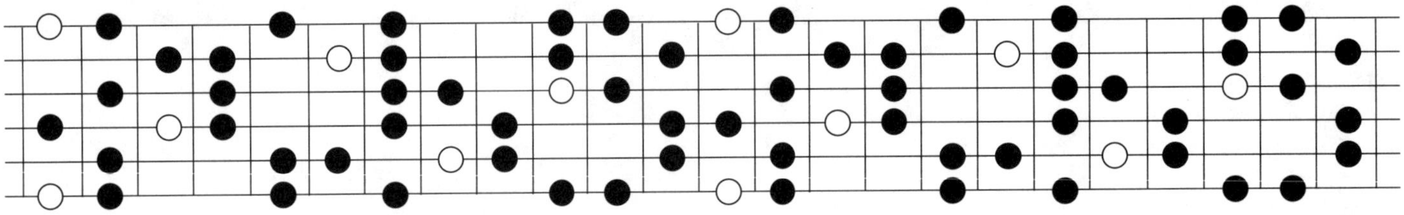

One-Octave Fingerings

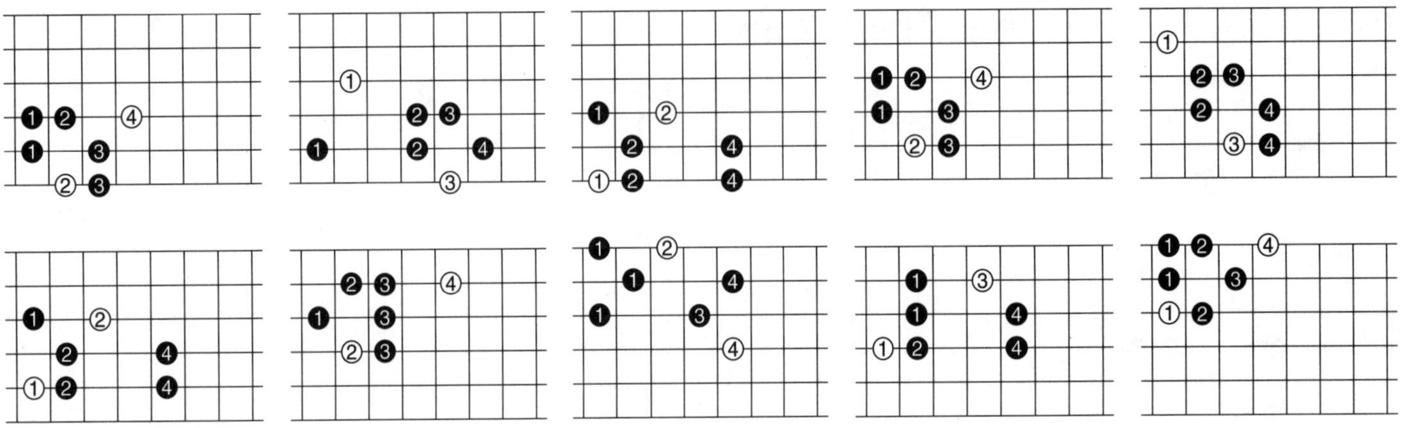

Two-Octave Fingerings

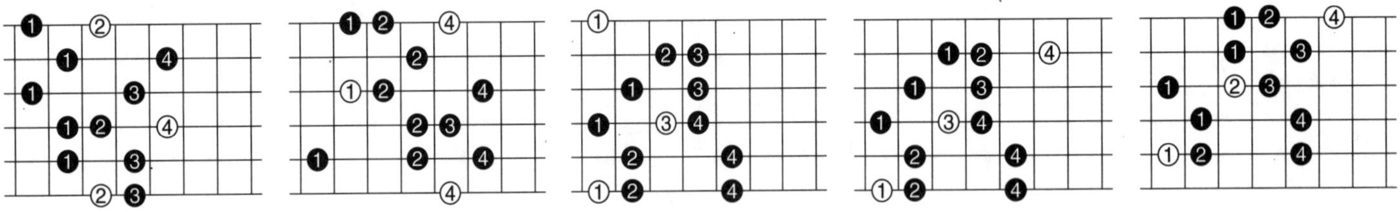

Three-Octave Fingerings

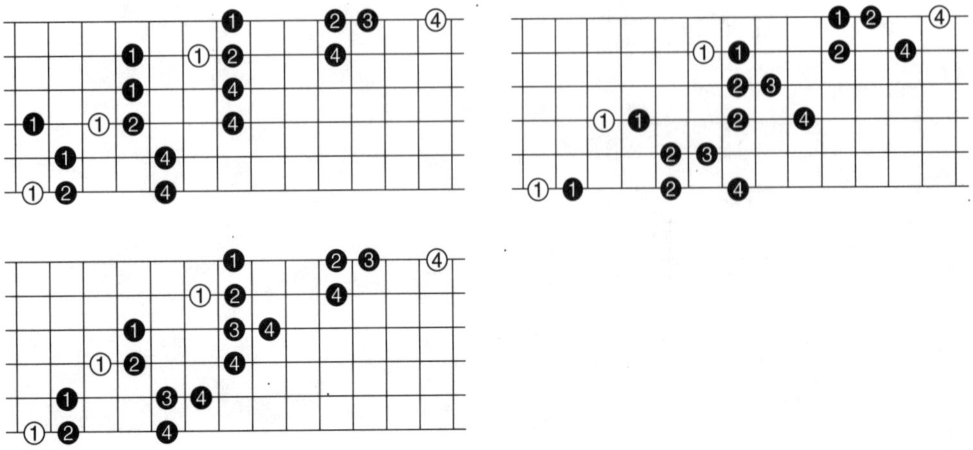

Position-Based Fingerings, Starting on all Scale Degrees

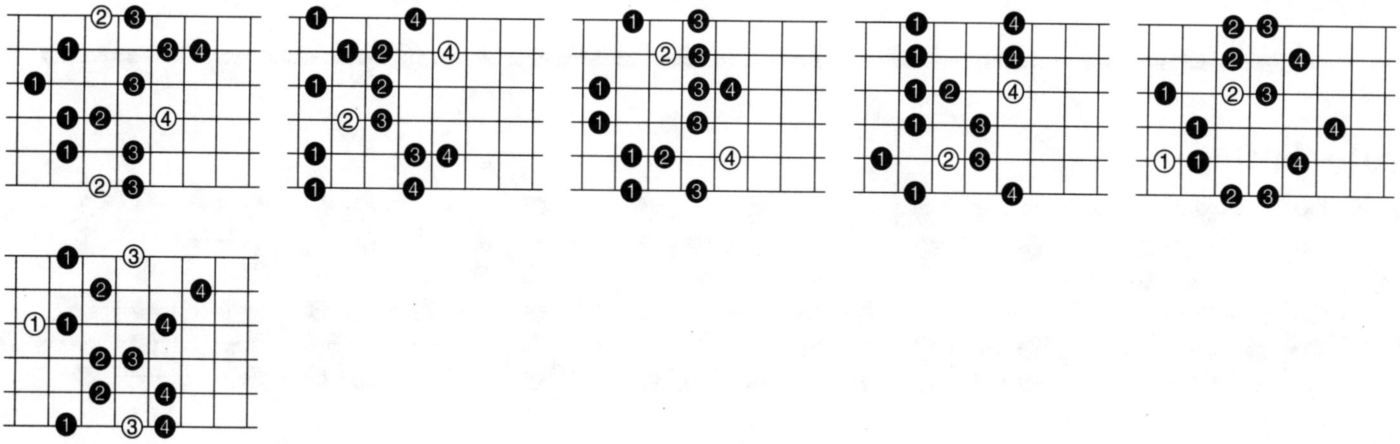

Three-Notes-Per-String Fingerings

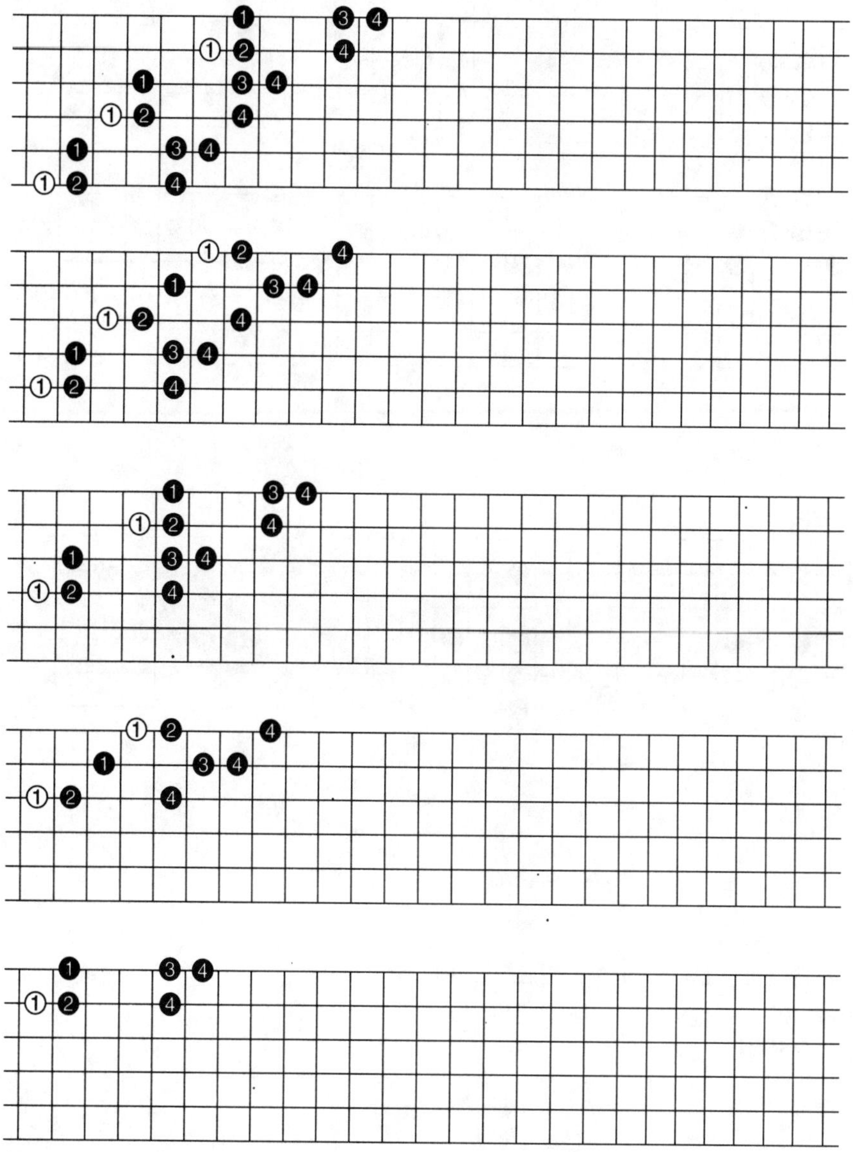

Todi

Scale Tones

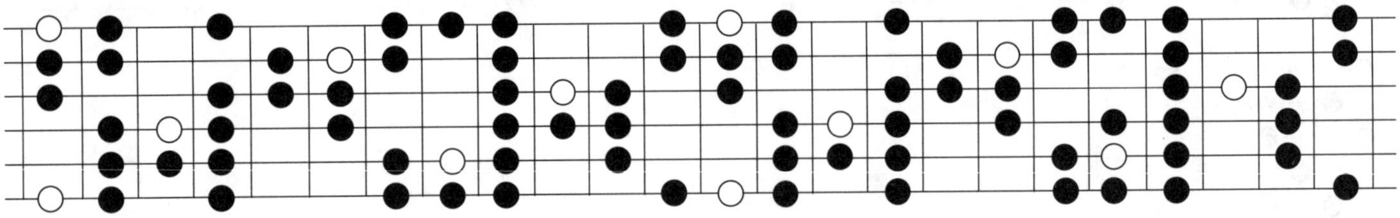

One-Octave Fingerings

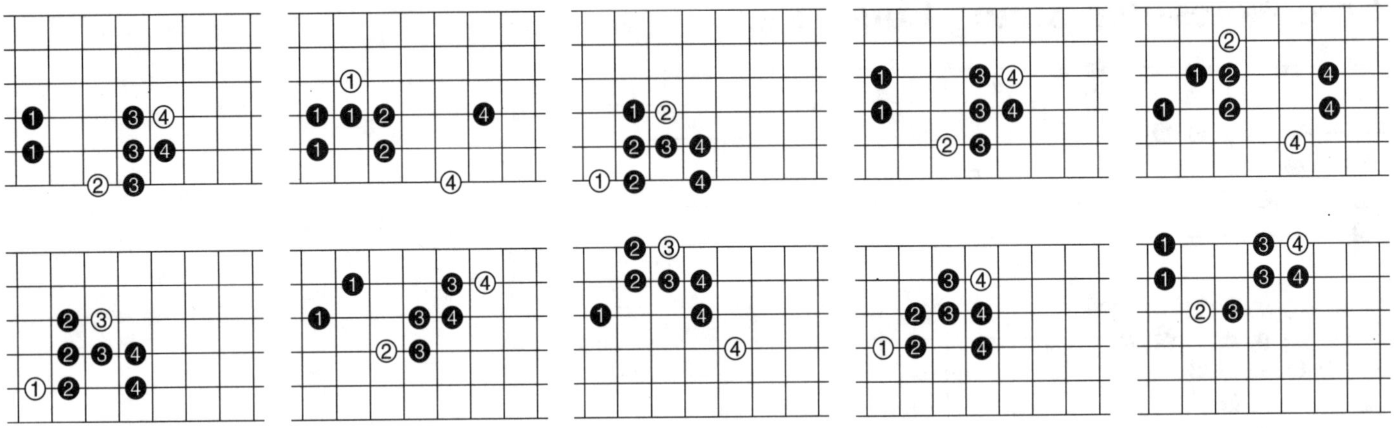

Two-Octave Fingerings

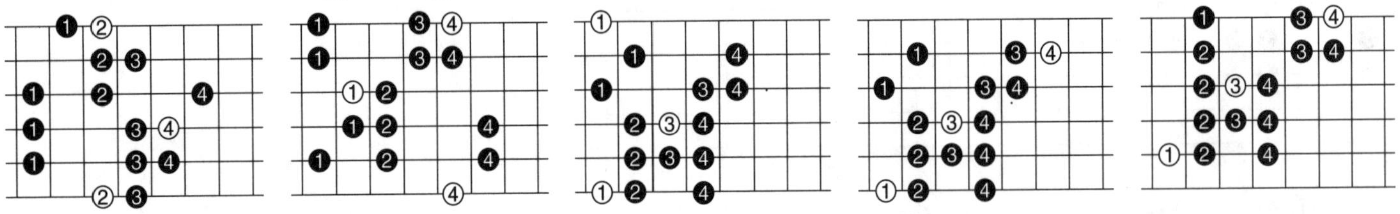

Three-Octave Fingerings

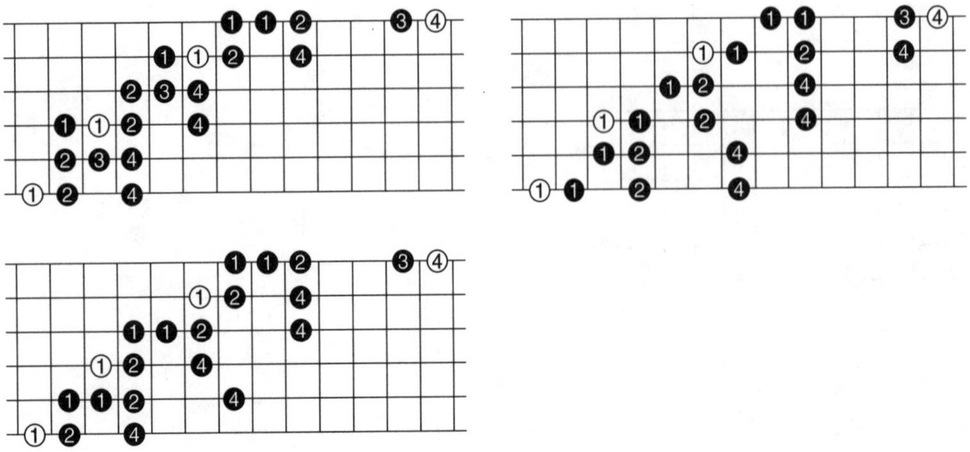

Position-Based Fingerings, Starting on all Scale Degrees

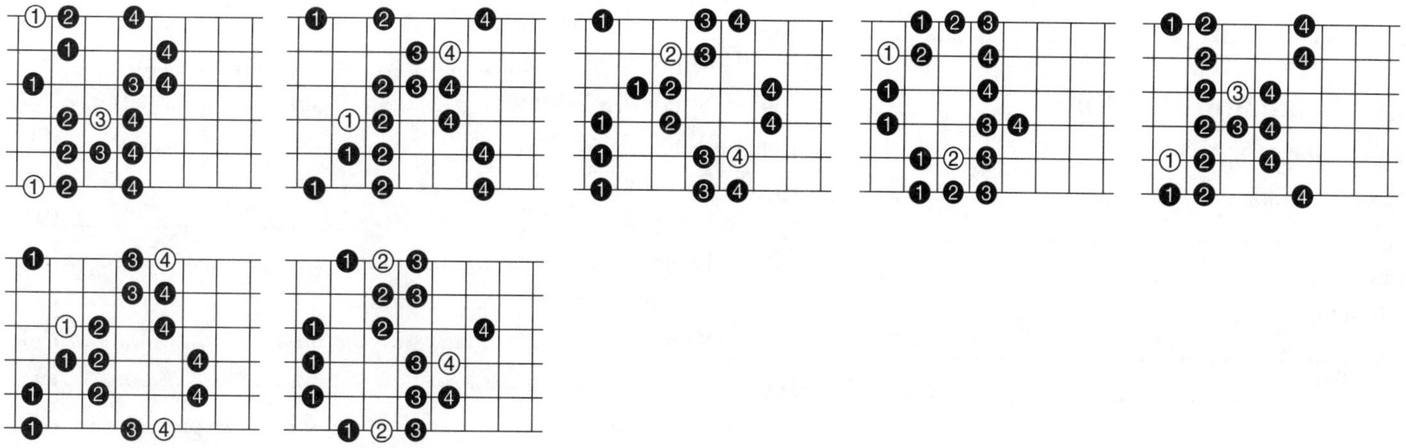

Three-Notes-Per-String Fingerings, Starting on all Scale Degrees

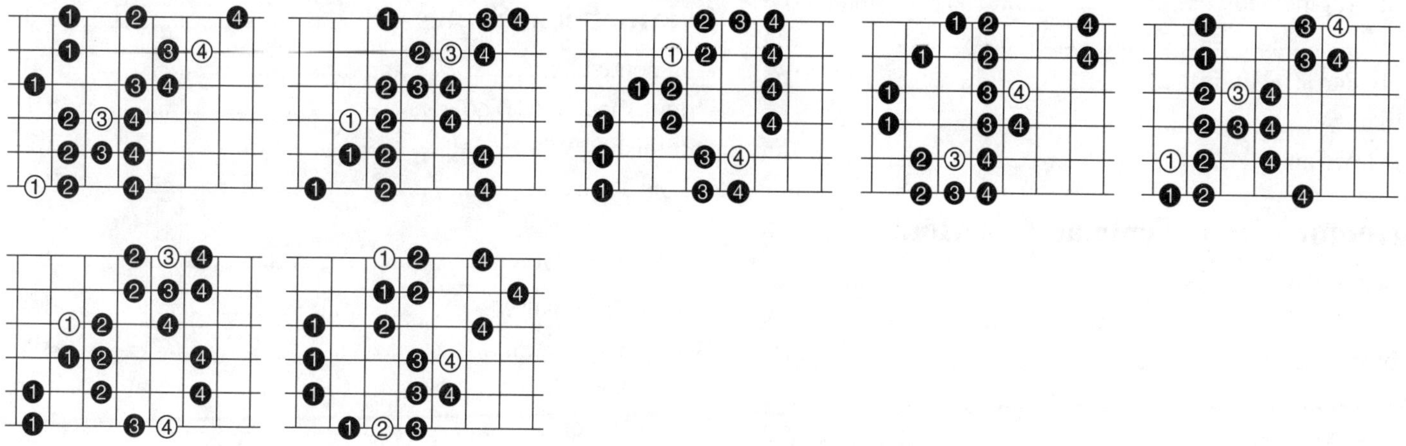

Four-Notes-Per-String Fingerings

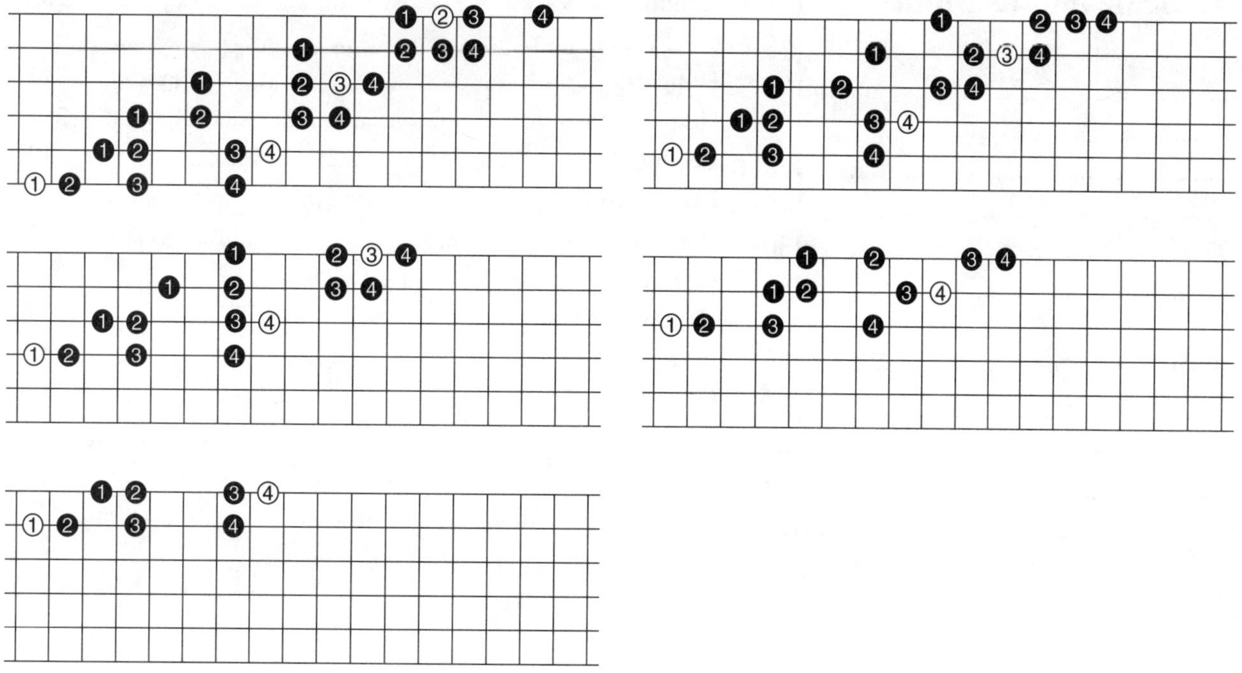

The Scales

Chromatic Scale 153

Major Scale and its Modes 154

Ionian (Major) 154
Dorian 155
Phrygian 156
Lydian 157
Mixolydian 158
Aeolian (Natural Minor) 159
Locrian 160

Melodic Minor Scale and its Modes 161

Melodic Minor 161
Dorian ♭2 162
Lydian Augmented 163
Lydian ♭7 164
Mixolydian ♭6 (Hindu) 165
Aeolian ♭5 166
Super Locrian 167

Harmonic Minor Scale and its Modes 168

Harmonic Minor 168
Locrian ♮6 169
Ionian ♯5 170
Dorian ♯4 171
Phrygian Dominant 172
Lydian ♯2 173
Super Locrian 𝄫7 174

Harmonic Major Scale and its Modes 175

Harmonic Major 175
Dorian ♭5 176
Phrygian ♭4 177
Lydian ♭3 178
Mixolydian ♭2 179
Lydian Augmented ♯2 180
Locrian 𝄫7 181

Pentatonic And Blues Scales 182

Blues 182
Pentatonic Major 183
Pentatonic Minor 184
Major ♭2 Pentatonic 185
Major ♭6 Pentatonic 186
Minor 6 Pentatonic 187
Minor 7♭5 Pentatonic 188
Whole Tone Pentatonic 189
Banshiki-Cho 190
Hirajoshi 191
Iwato 192
Kokin-Chosi 193
Kumoi 194
Naka Zora 195
Pelog 196
Ritsu 197
Ryūkyū 198
Shimo-Chidori 199

Symmetrical Scales 200

Augmented 200
Diminished Half/Whole 201
Diminished Whole/Half 202
Whole Tone 203

Bebop Scales 204

Bebop Dominant 204
Bebop Major 205
Bebop Tonic Minor 206
Bebop Minor 207

Exotic Scales 208

Eight-Tone Spanish 208
Enigmatic 209
Gypsy 210
Hungarian 211
Hungarian Minor 212
Leading Whole Tone 213
Lydian Minor 214
Major Locrian 215
Marwa 216
Neapolitan Major 217
Neapolitan Minor 218
Oriental 219
Prometheus 220
Prometheus Neapolitan 221
Todi 222

Chromatic

1 ♯1 2 ♯2 3 4 ♯4 5 ♯5 6 ♯6 7 H H H H H H H H H H H H

C

D♭

D

E♭

E

F

G♭

G

A♭

A

B♭

B

Ionian (Major)

1 2 3 4 5 6 7 W W H W W W H

C

D♭

D

E♭

E

F

G♭

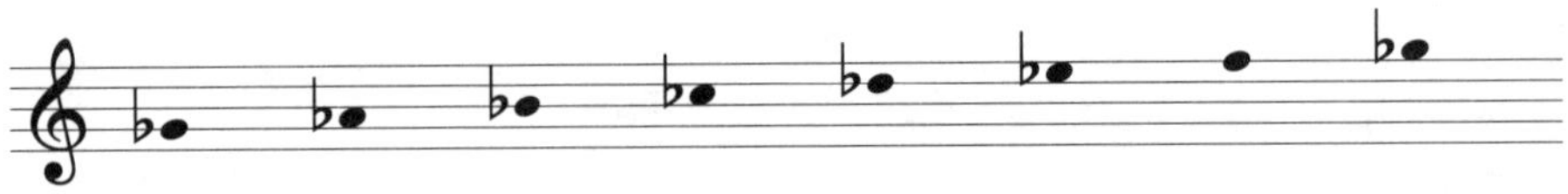

G

A♭

A

B♭

B

Dorian

1 2 ♭3 4 5 6 ♭7 WHWWWHW

C

C♯

D

E♭

E

F

F♯

G

A♭

A

B♭

B

Phrygian

1 ♭2 ♭3 4 5 ♭6 ♭7 H W W W H W W

C

C♯

D

D♯

E

F

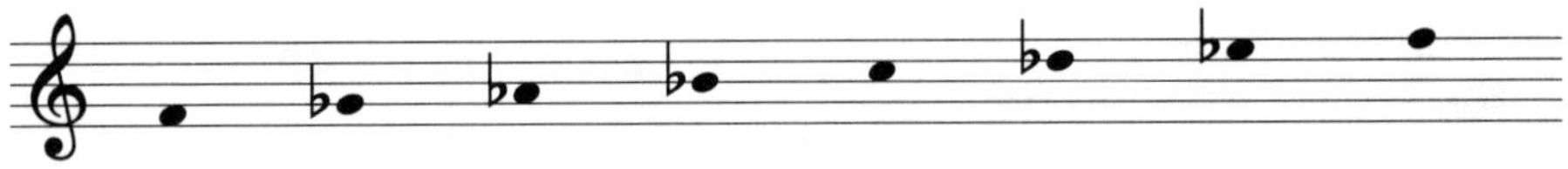

F♯

G

G♯

A

B♭

B

Lydian

1 2 3 ♯4 5 6 7 W W W H W W H

C
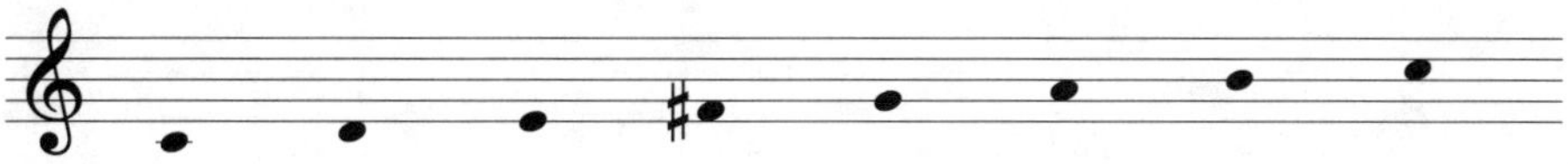

D♭
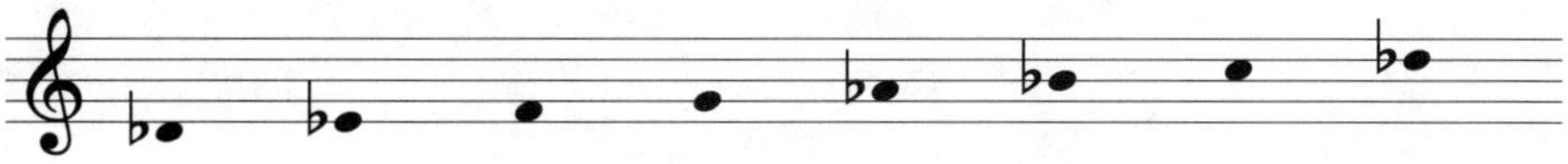

D

E♭

E

F

G♭
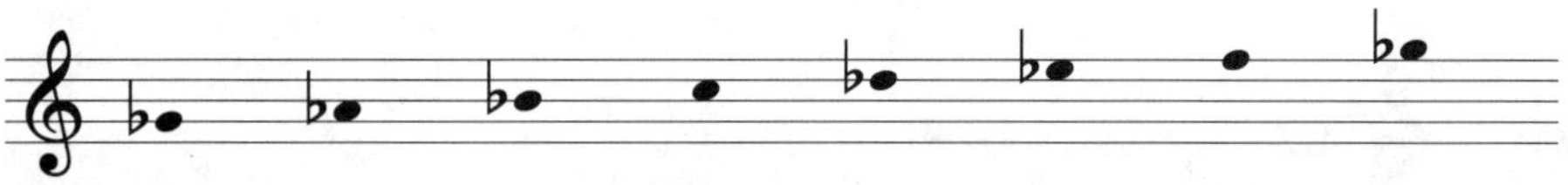

G

A♭

A

B♭

B

Mixolydian

1 2 3 4 5 6 ♭7 W W H W W H W

C

D♭

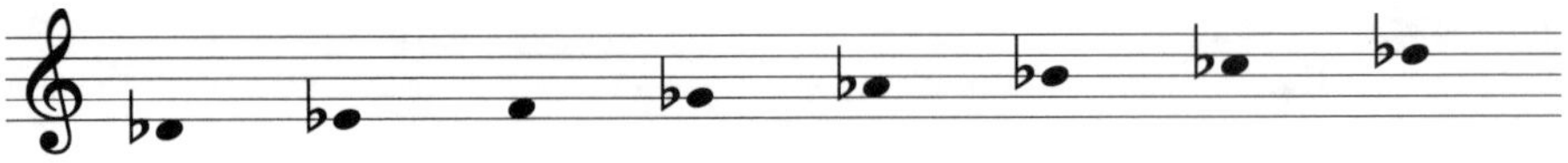

D

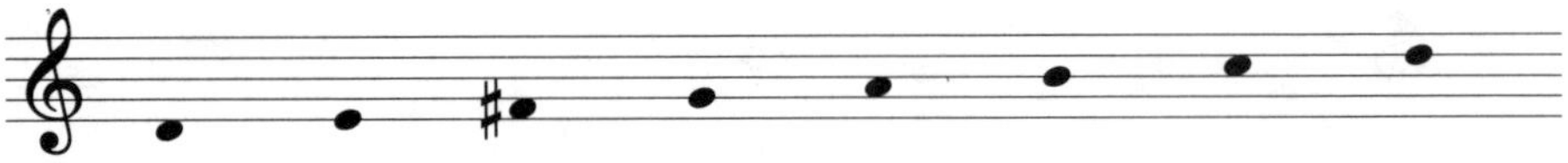

E♭

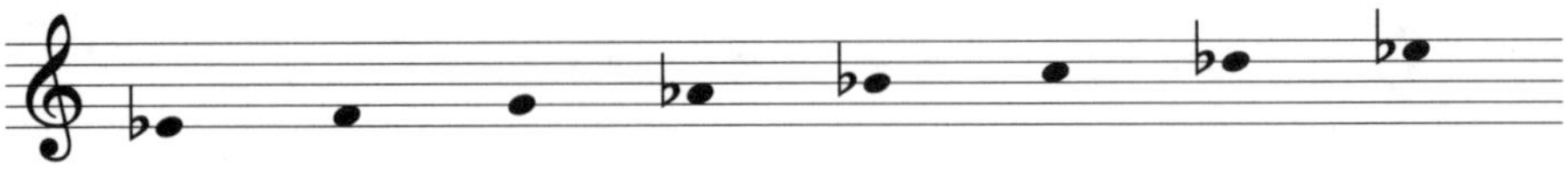

E

F

G♭

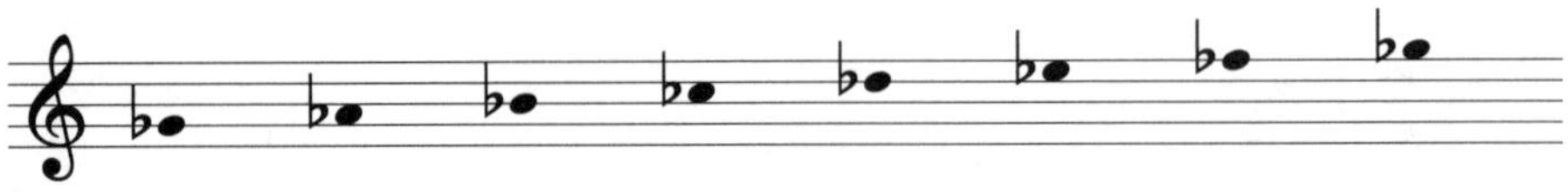

G

A♭

A

B♭

B

Aeolian (Natural Minor)

1 2 ♭3 4 5 ♭6 ♭7 W H W W H W W

C

C♯

D

E♭

E

F

F♯

G

A♭

A

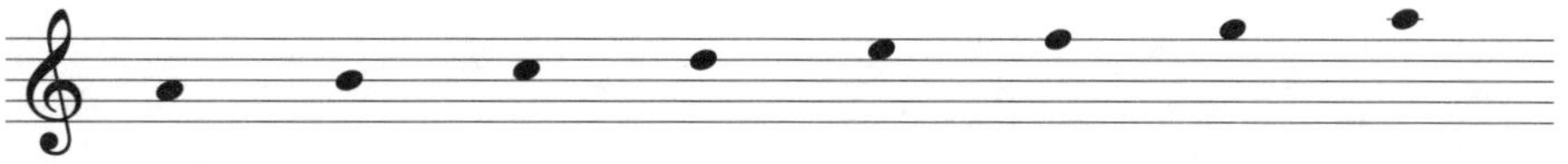

B♭

B

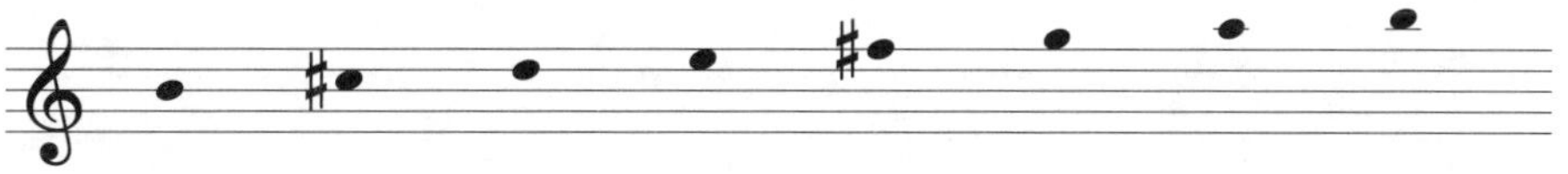

Locrian

1 ♭2 ♭3 4 ♭5 ♭6 ♭7

H W W H W W W

C

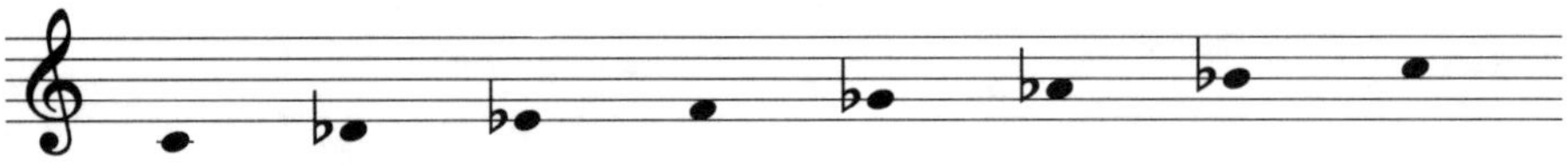

C♯

D

D♯

E

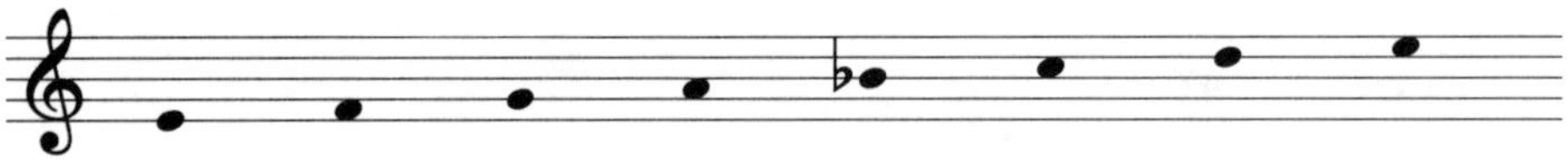

F

F♯

G

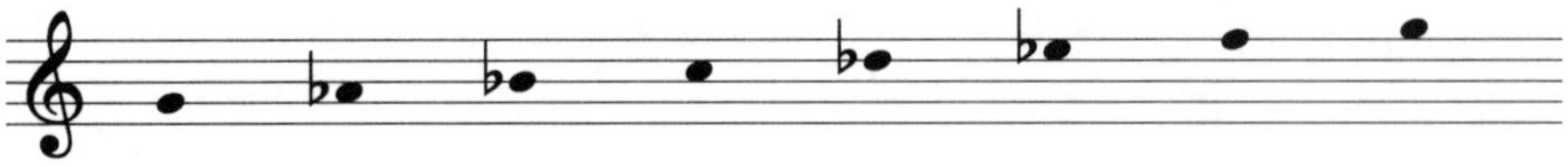

G♯

A

A♯

B

Melodic Minor

1 2 ♭3 4 5 6 7 W H W W W W H

C

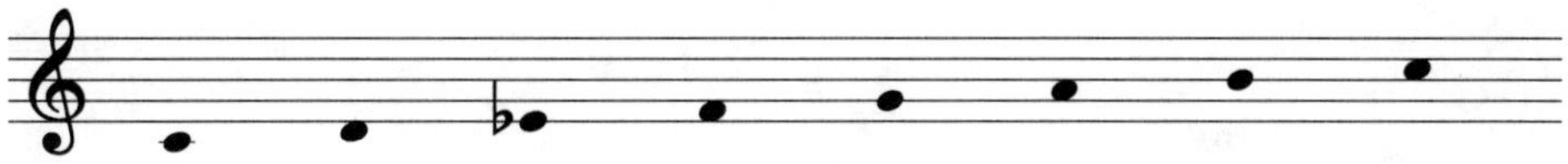

D♭

D

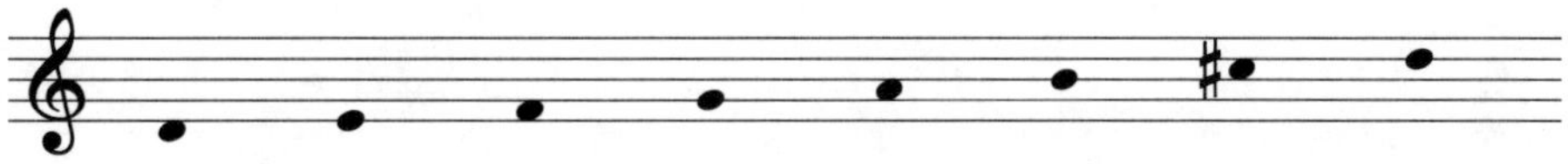

E♭

E

F

F♯

G

A♭

A

B♭

B

Dorian ♭2

1 ♭2 ♭3 4 5 6 ♭7 H W W W W H W

C

C♯

D

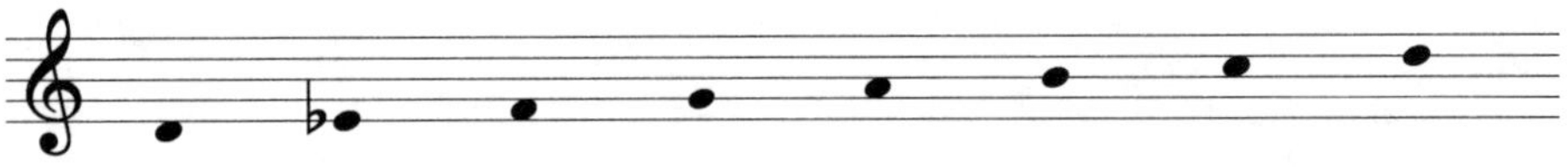

E♭

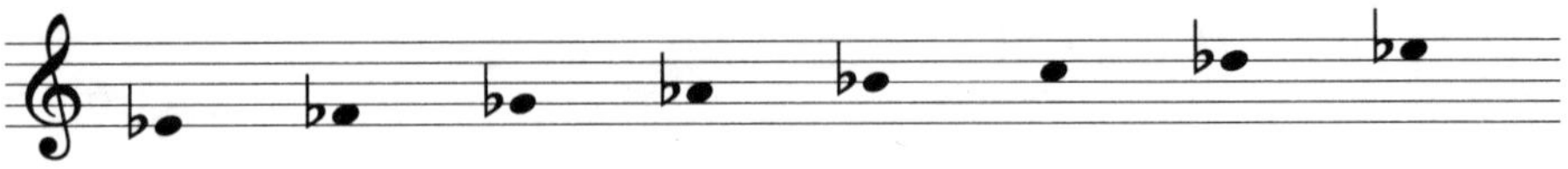

E

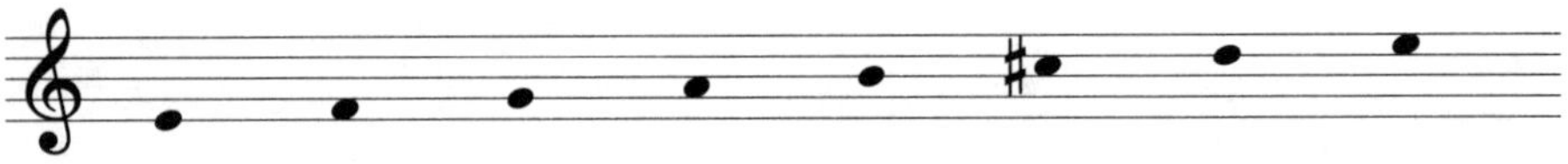

F

F♯

G

G♯

A

B♭

B

Lydian Augmented

1 2 3 ♯4 ♯5 6 7 W W W W H W H

C

D♭
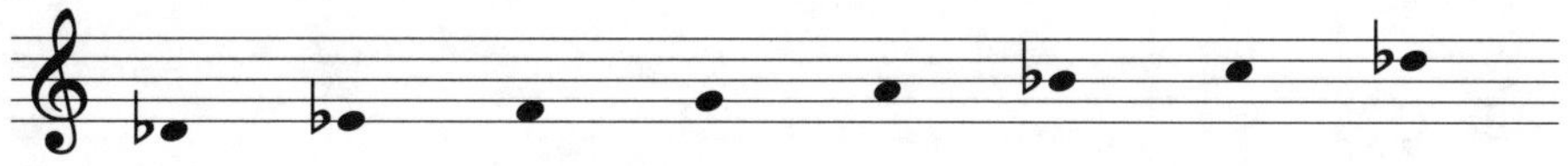

D

E♭

E

F

G♭

G

A♭

A

B♭

B

Lydian ♭7

1 2 3 ♯4 5 6 ♭7 W W W H W H W

C

D♭
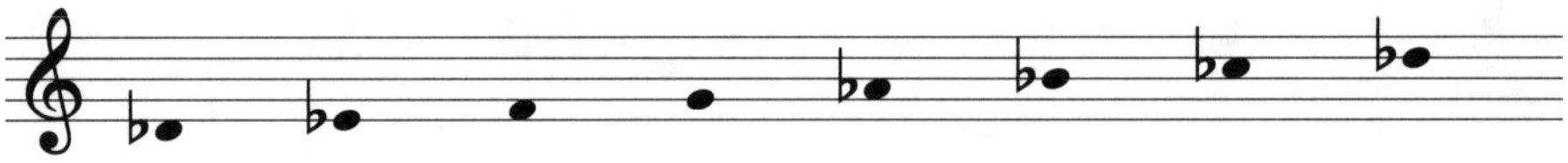

D
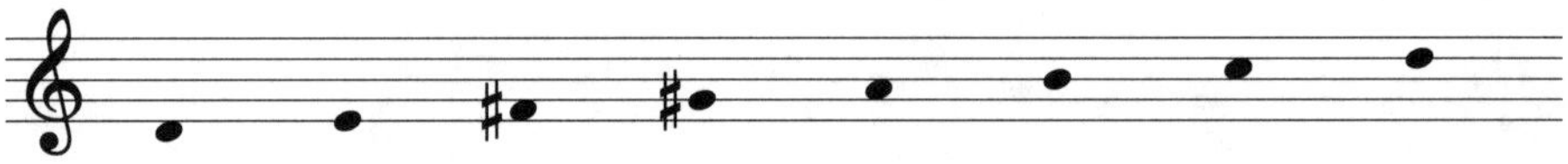

E♭
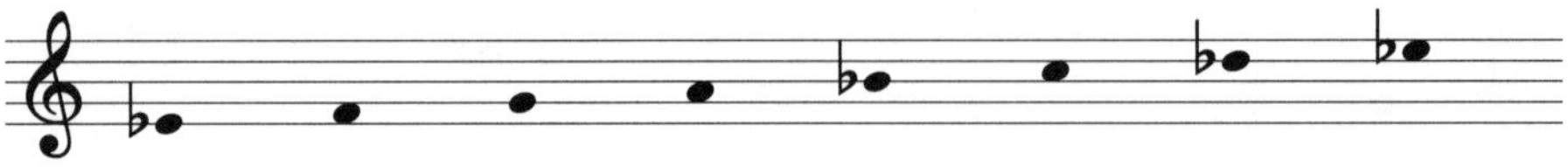

E

F
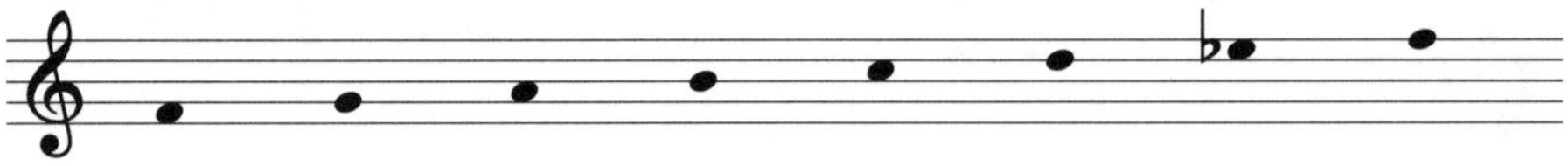

G♭

G

A♭

A

B♭

B

Mixolydian ♭6 (Hindu)

1 2 3 4 5 ♭6 ♭7 W W H W H W W

C

C♯

D

E♭

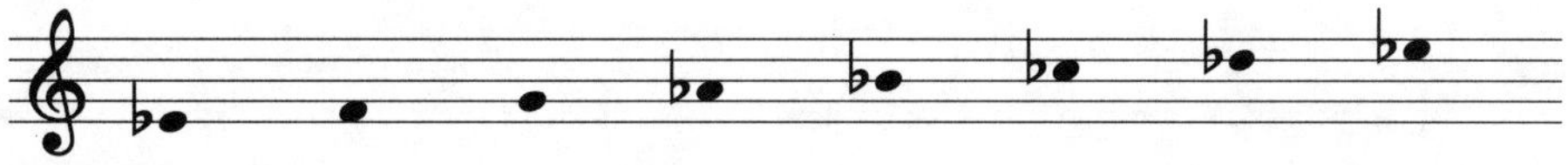

E

F

F♯

G

A♭

A

B♭

B

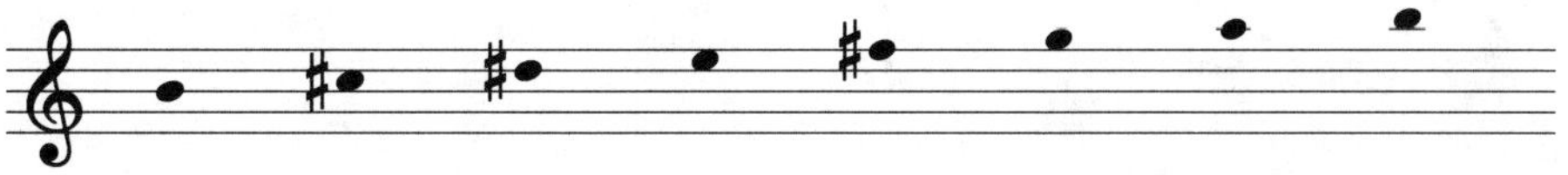

Aeolian ♭5

1 2 ♭3 4 ♭5 ♭6 ♭7 W H W H W W W

C

C♯

D

D♯
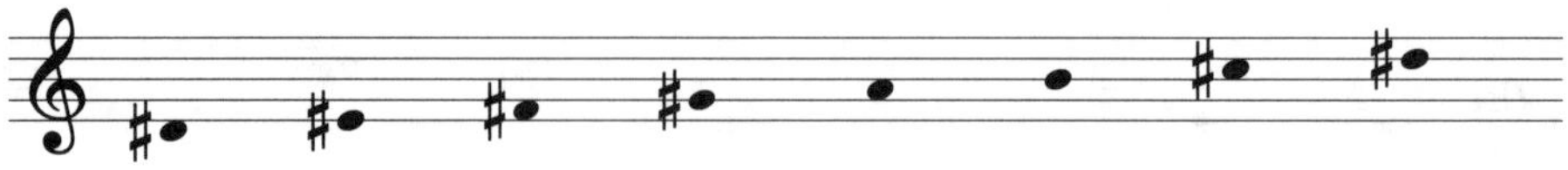

E
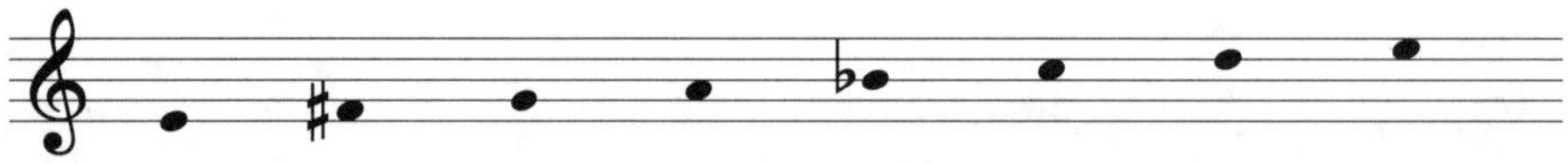

F

F♯

G

G♯

A
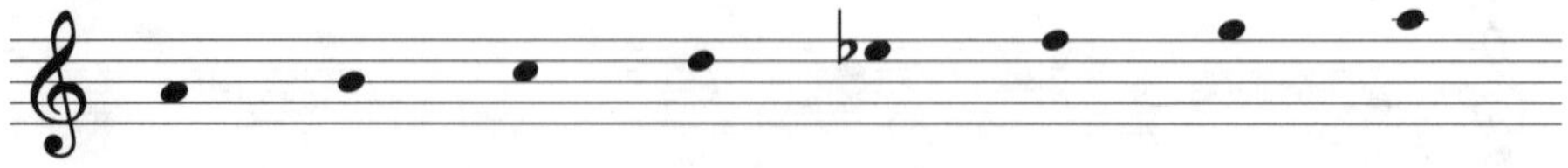

B♭

B

Super Locrian

1 ♭2 ♭3 ♭4 ♭5 ♭6 ♭7 H W H W W W W

C
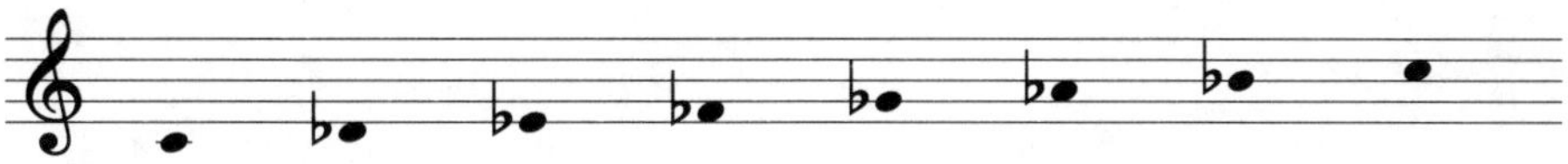

C♯

D

D♯

E

F

F♯

G

G♯

A

A♯

B

Harmonic Minor

1 2 ♭3 4 5 ♭6 7

W H W W H W+H H

C

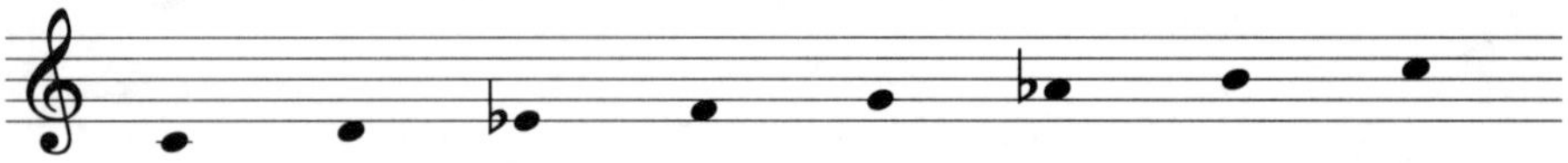

C♯

D

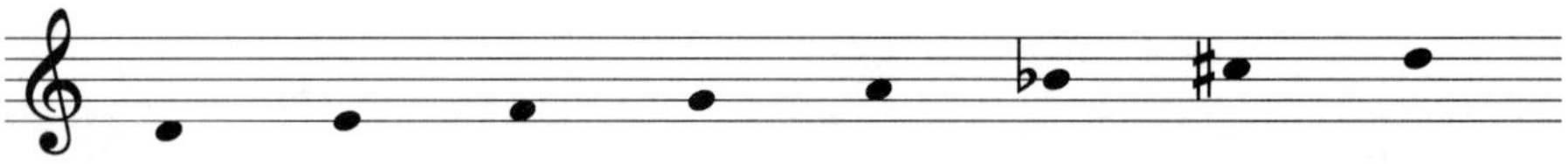

E♭

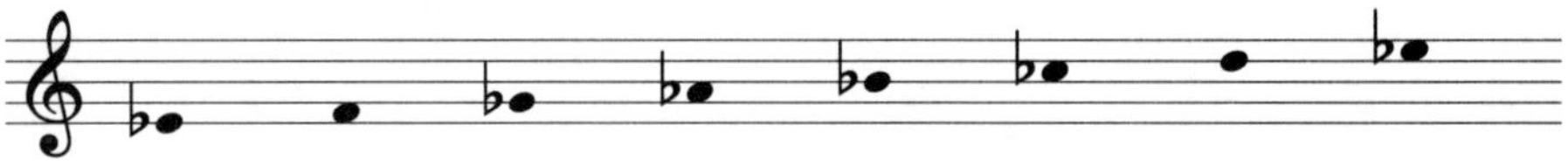

E

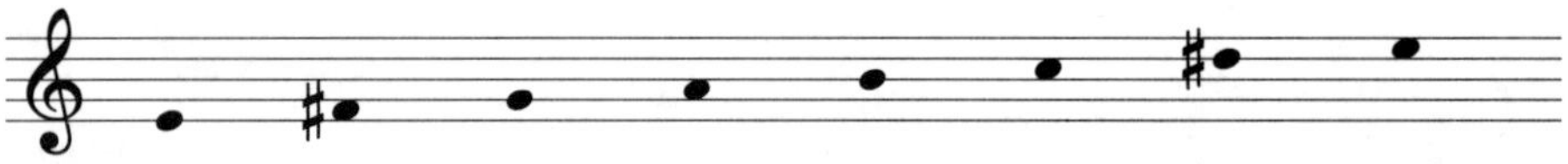

F

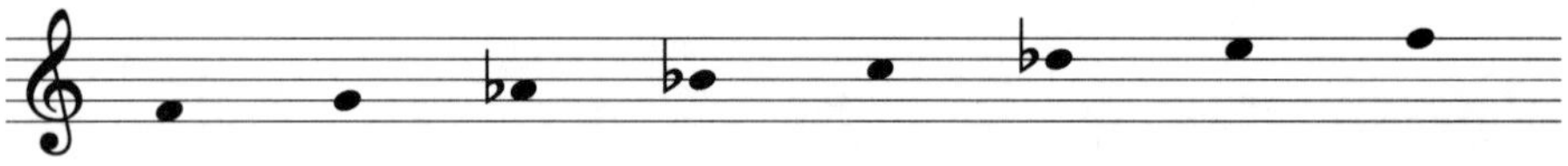

F♯

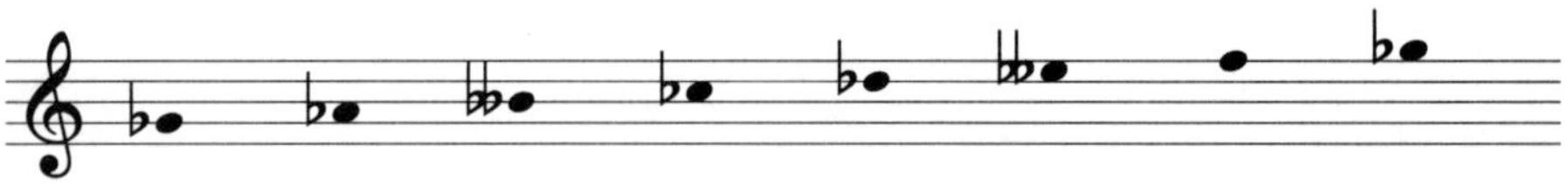

G

A♭

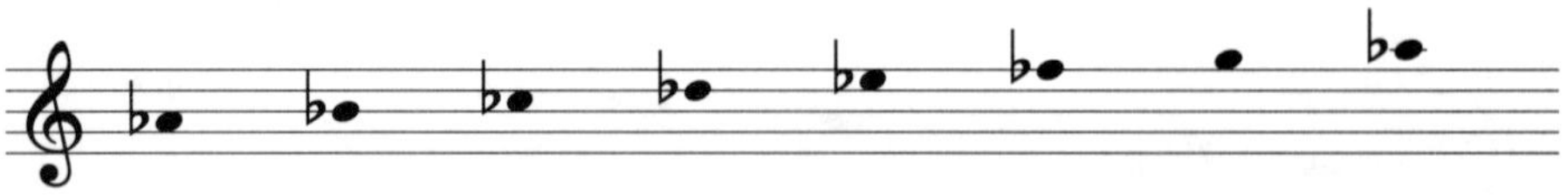

A

B♭

B

Locrian ♮6

1 ♭2 ♭3 4 ♭5 6 ♭7

H W W H W+H H W

C

C♯

D

E♭

E

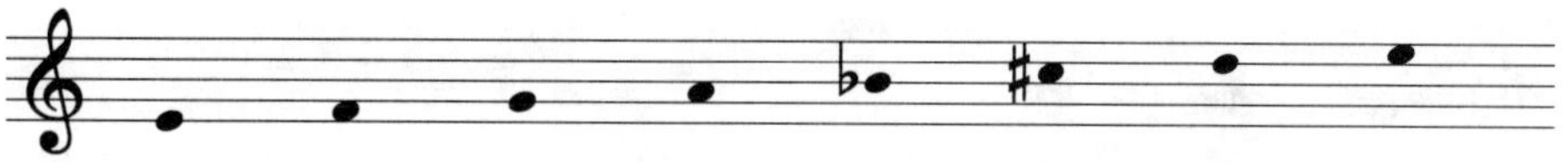

F

F♯

G

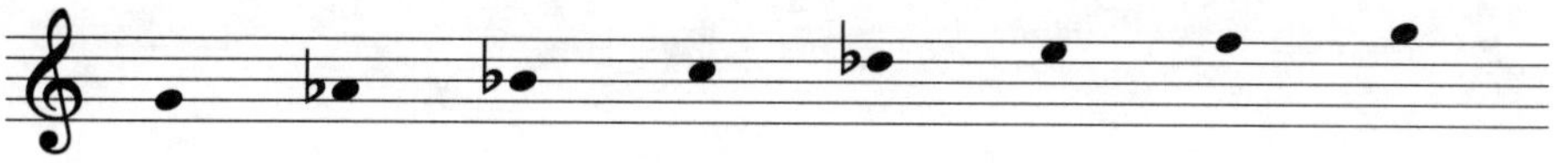

G♯

A

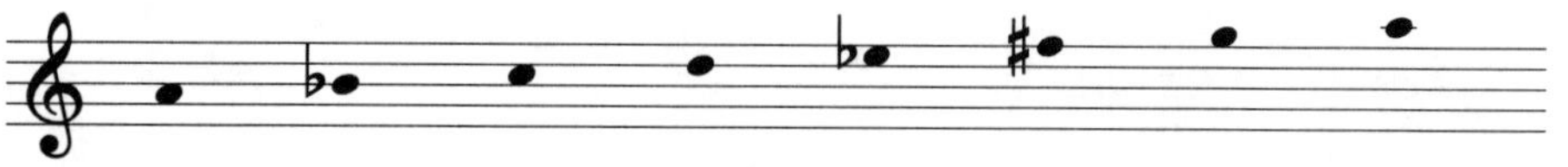

B♭

B

Ionian ♯5

1 2 3 4 ♯5 6 7 W W H W+H H W H

C

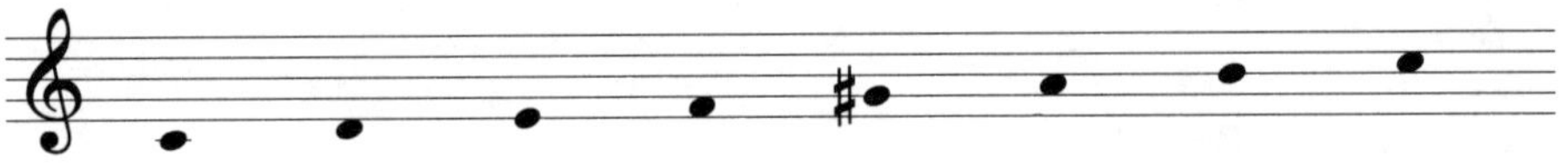

D♭

D

E♭

E

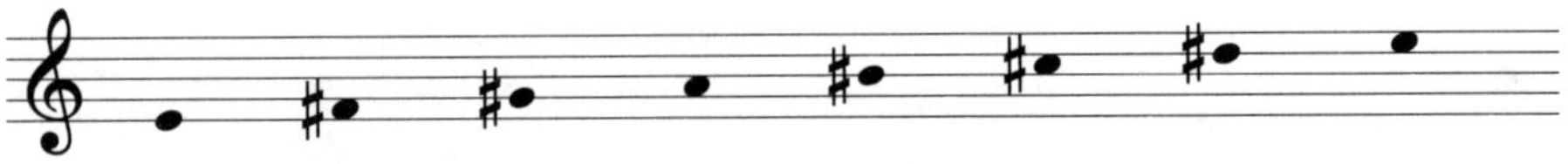

F

G♭

G

A♭

A

B♭

B

Dorian ♯4

1 2 ♭3 ♯4 5 6 ♭7 W H W+H H W H W

C

D♭

D

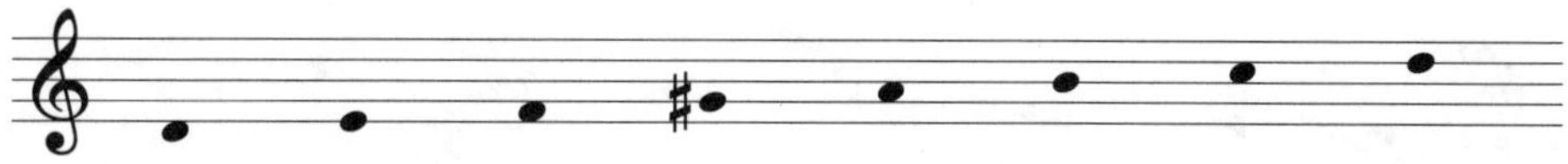

E♭

E

F

F♯

G

A♭

A

B♭

B

Phrygian Dominant

1 ♭2 3 4 5 ♭6 ♭7

H W+H H W H W W

C

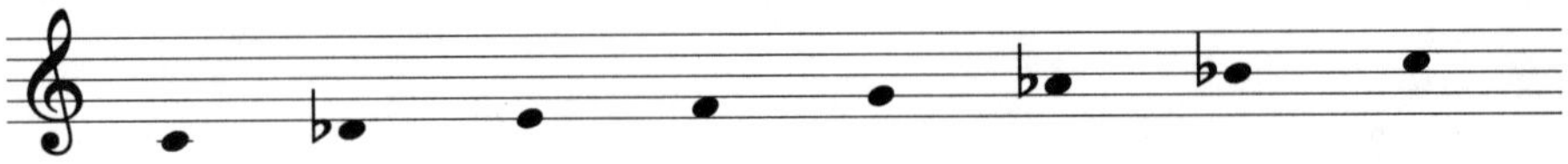

C♯

D

E♭

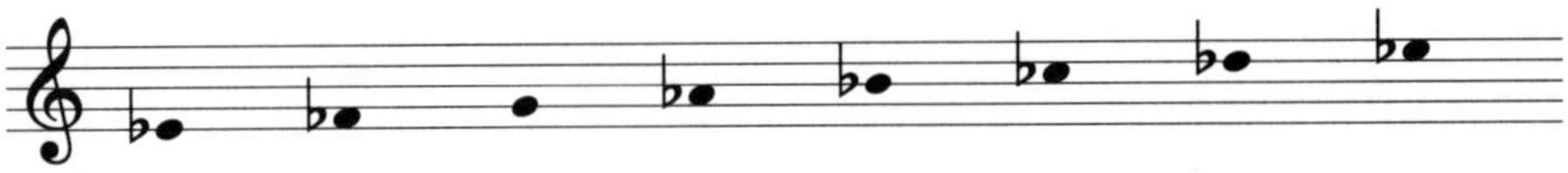

E

F

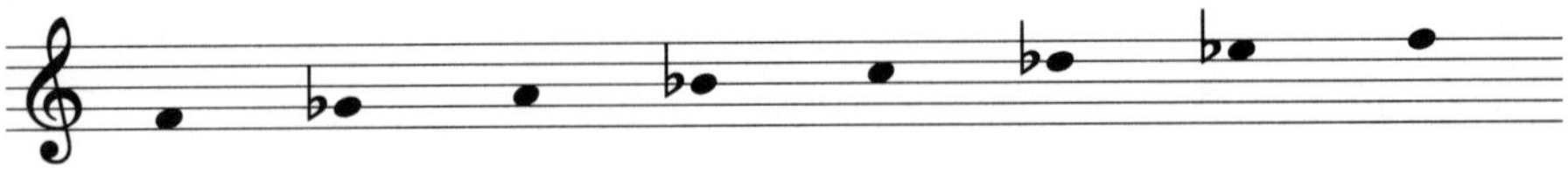

F♯

G

G♯

A

B♭

B

Lydian ♯2

1 ♯2 3 ♯4 5 6 7 W+H H W H W W H

C

D♭

D

E♭

E

F

G♭
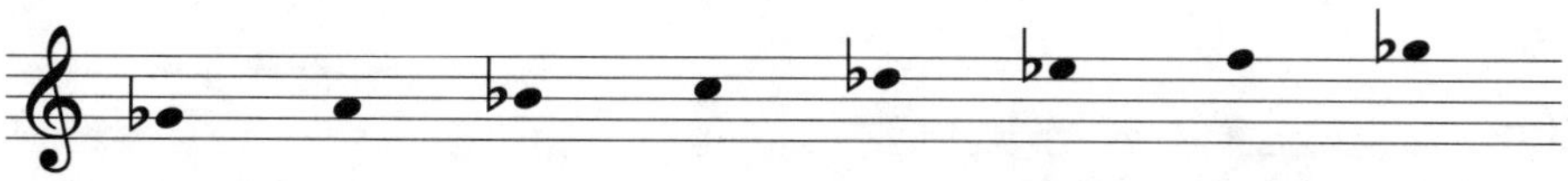

G

A♭
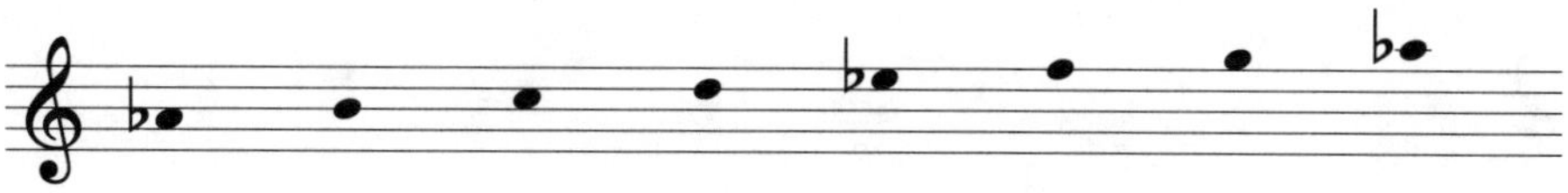

A

B♭
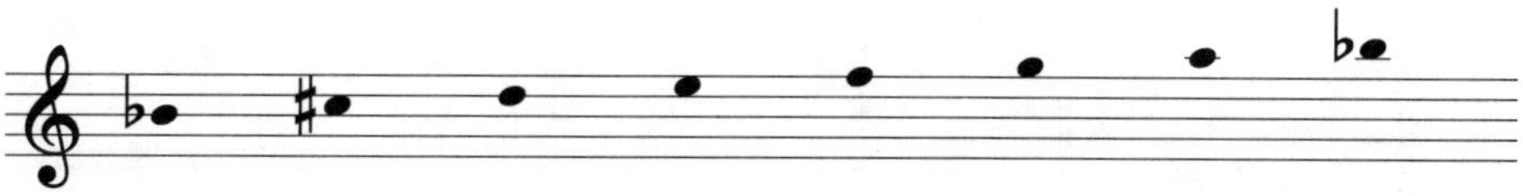

B

Super Locrian 𝄫7

1 ♭2 ♭3 ♭4 ♭5 ♭6 𝄫7 H W H W W H W+H

C

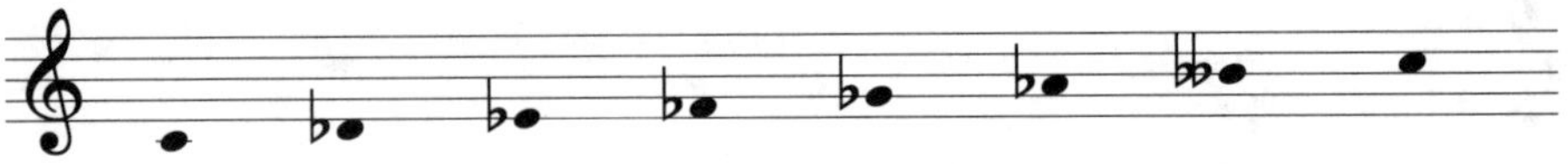

C♯

D

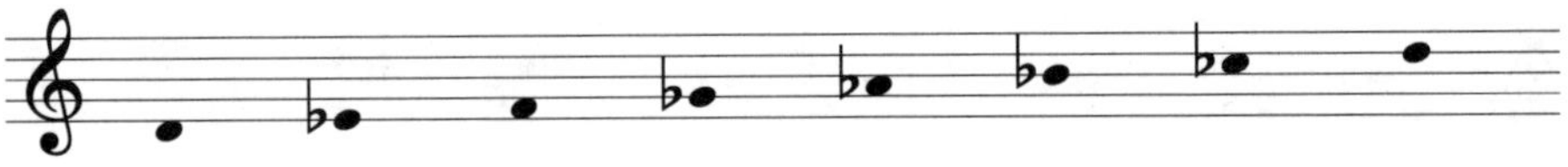

D♯

E

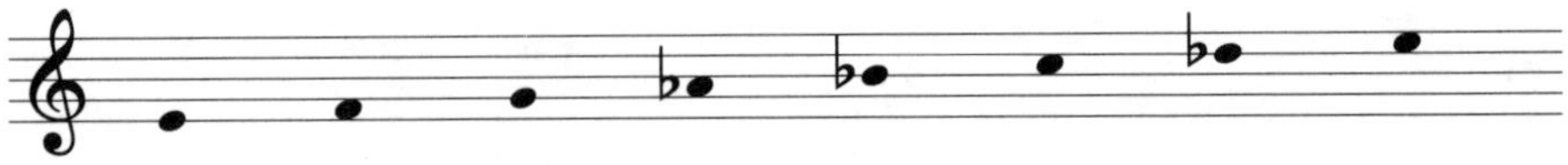

F

F♯

G

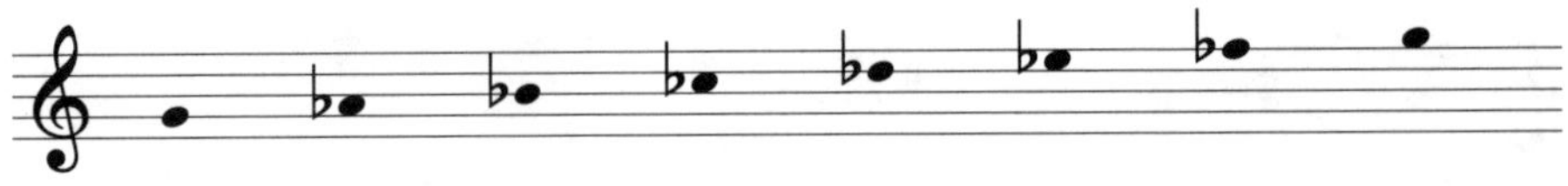

G♯

A

A♯

B

Harmonic Major

1 2 3 4 5 ♭6 7

W W H W H W+H H

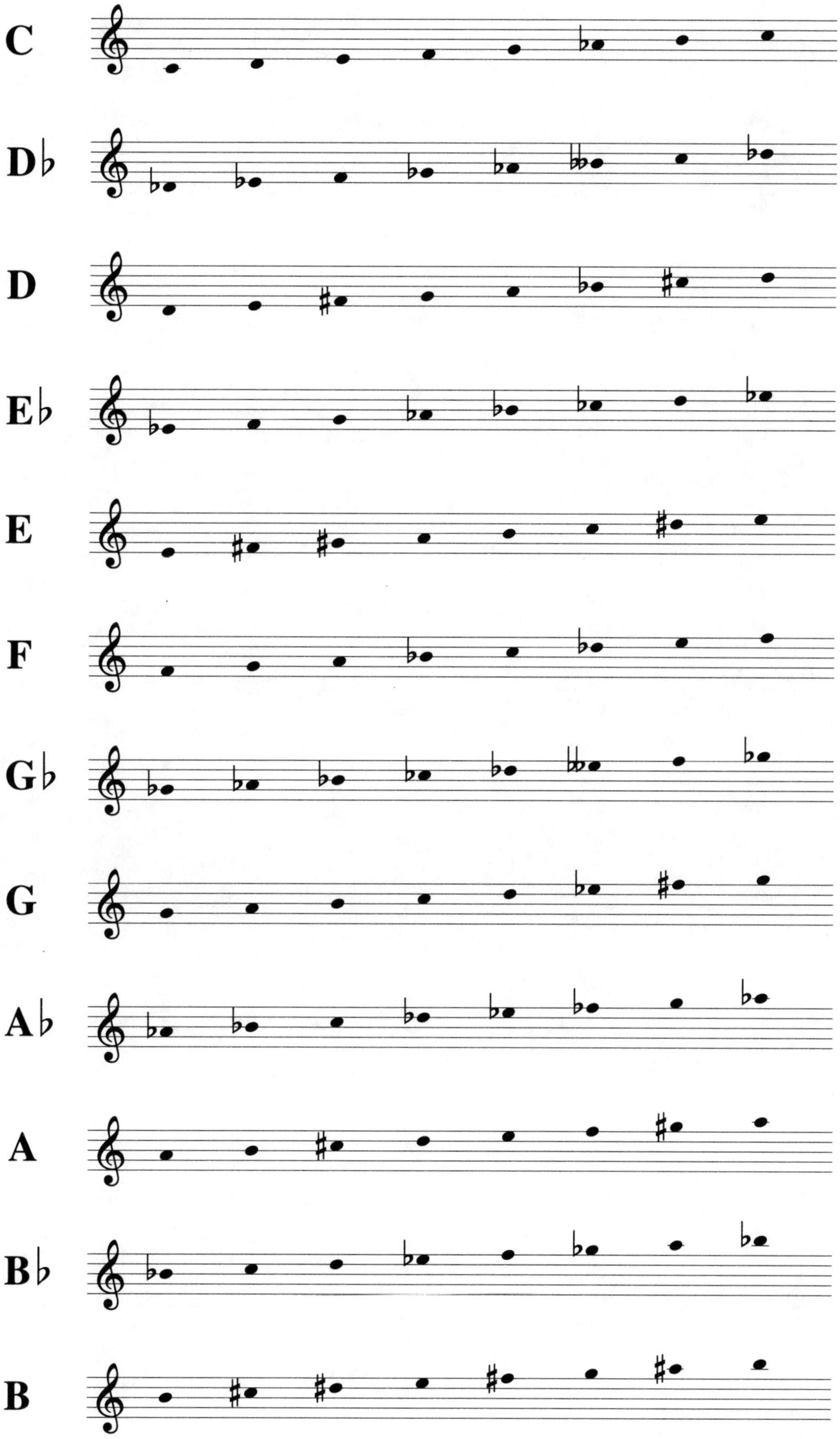

Dorian ♭5

1 2 ♭3 4 ♭5 6 ♭7

W H W H W+H H W

C
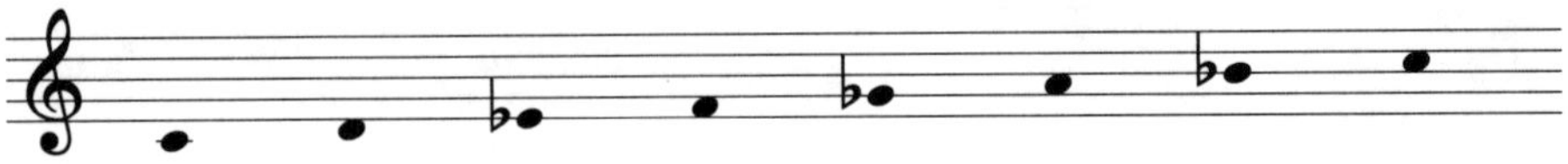

C♯

D
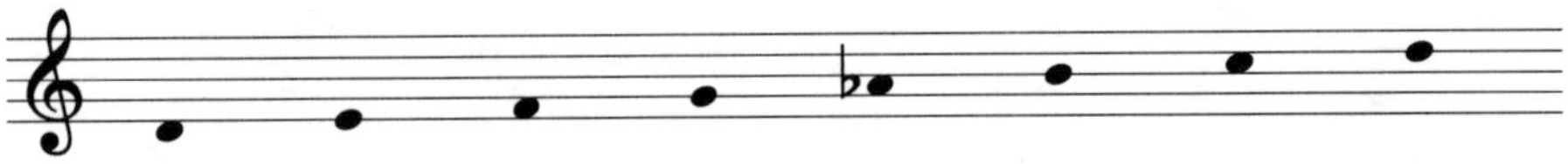

E♭
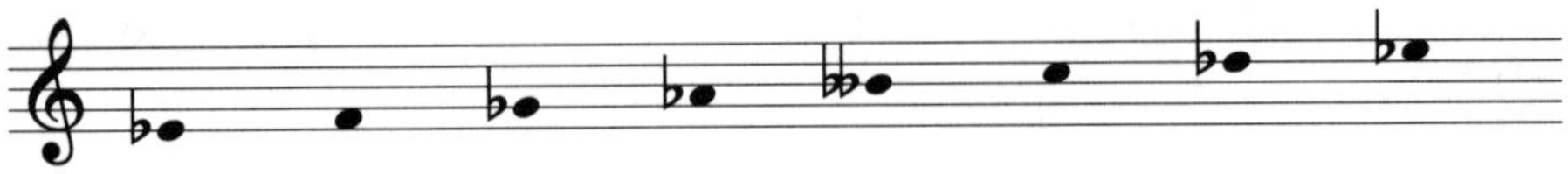

E
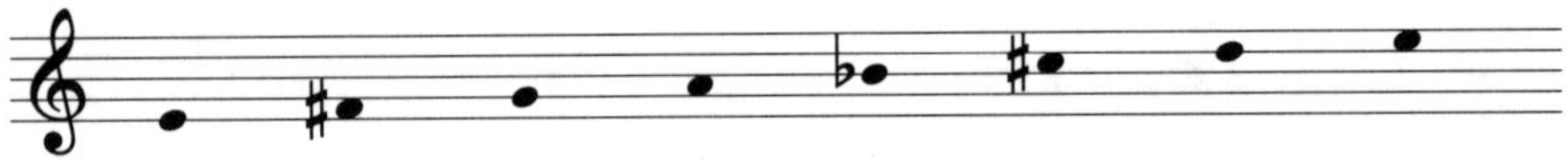

F

F♯

G
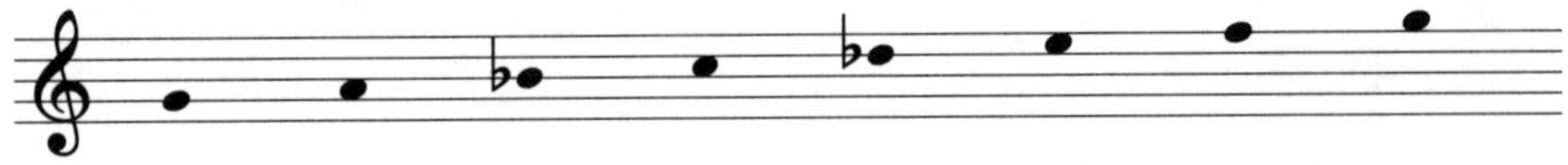

G♯

A
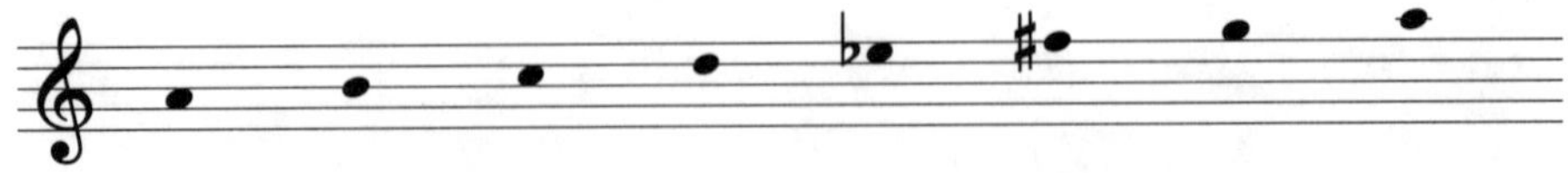

B♭

B

Phrygian ♭4

1 ♭2 ♭3 ♭4 5 ♭6 ♭7 H W H W+H H W W

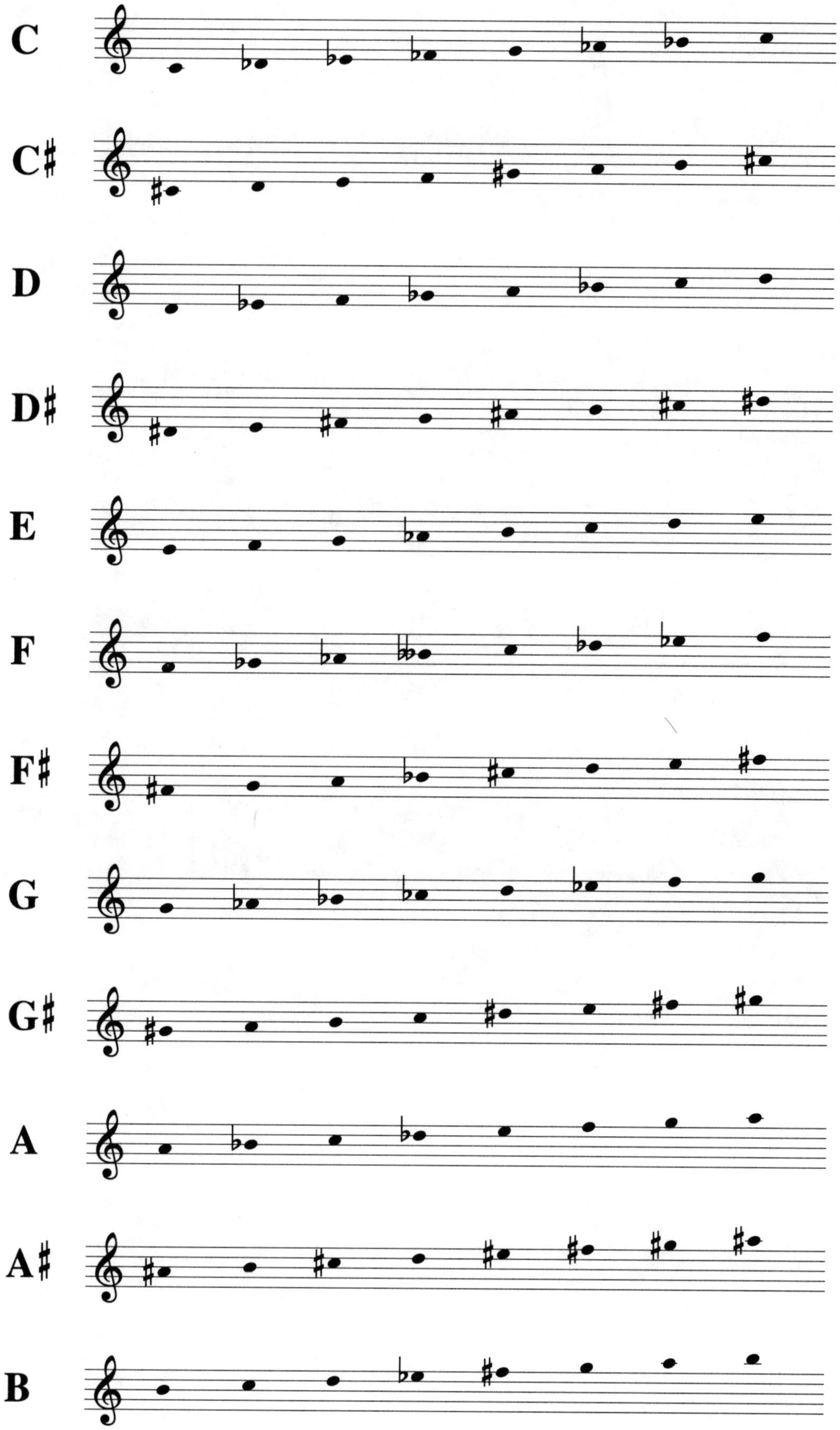

Lydian ♭3

1 2 ♭3 ♯4 5 6 7 — W H W+H H W W H

C

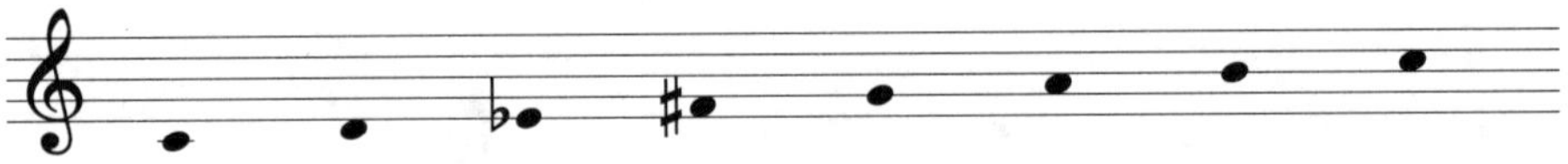

D♭

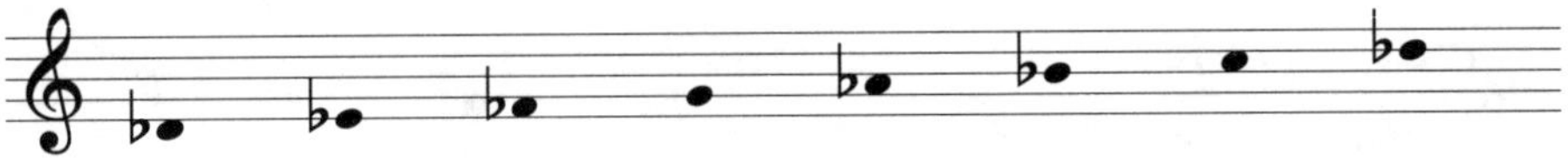

D

E♭

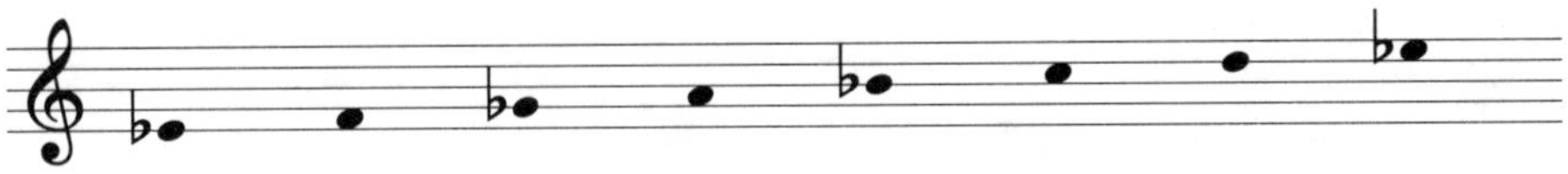

E

F

F♯

G

A♭

A

B♭

B

Mixolydian ♭2

1 ♭2 3 4 5 6 ♭7

H W+H H W W H W

Lydian Augmented ♯2

1 ♯2 3 ♯4 ♯5 6 7 — W+H H W W H W H

Locrian 𝄫7

1 ♭2 ♭3 4 ♭5 ♭6 𝄫7 H W W H W H W+H

C

C♯

D

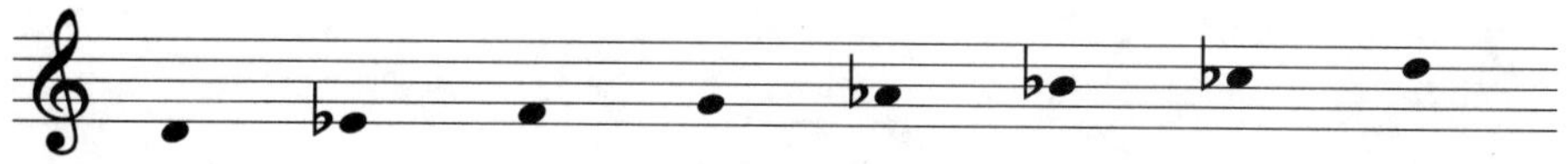

D♯

E

F

F♯

G

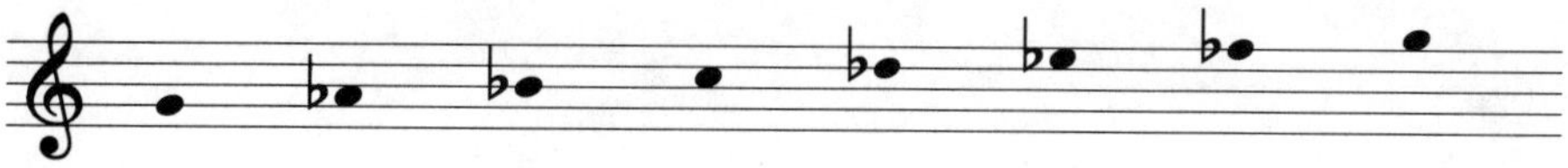

G♯

A

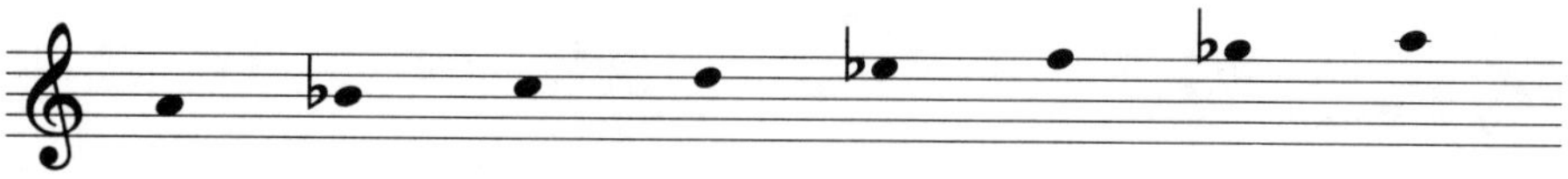

A♯

B

Blues

1 ♭3 4 ♭5 5 ♭7 W+H W H H W+H W

C

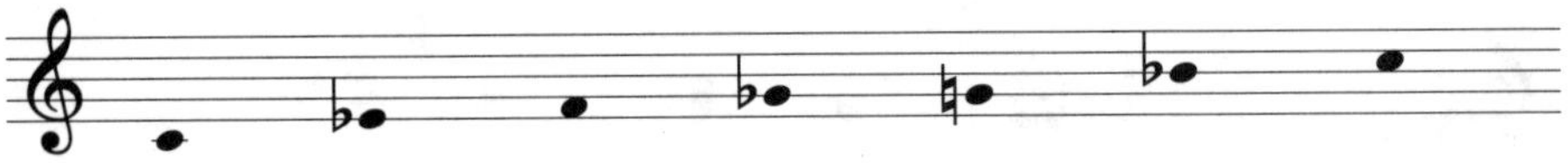

C♯

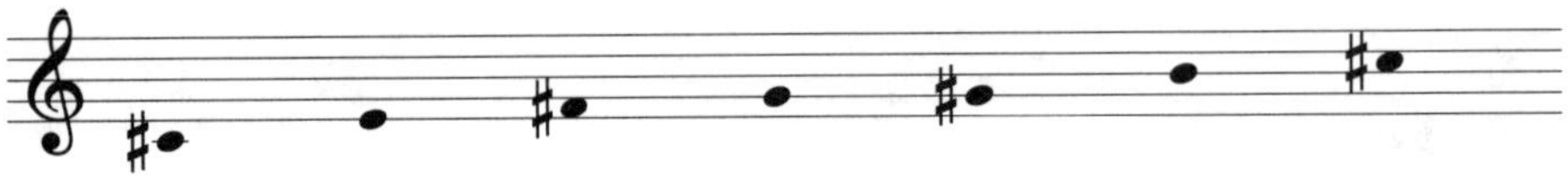

D

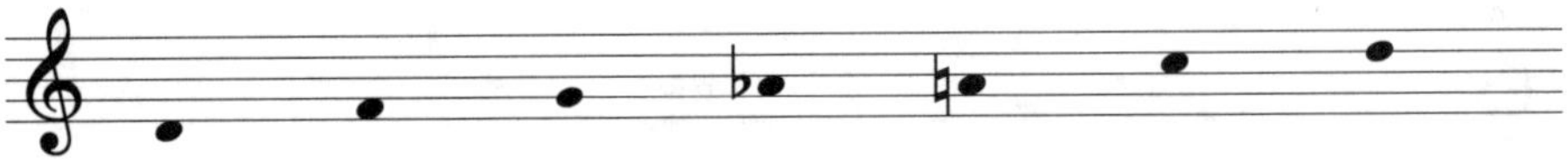

E♭

E

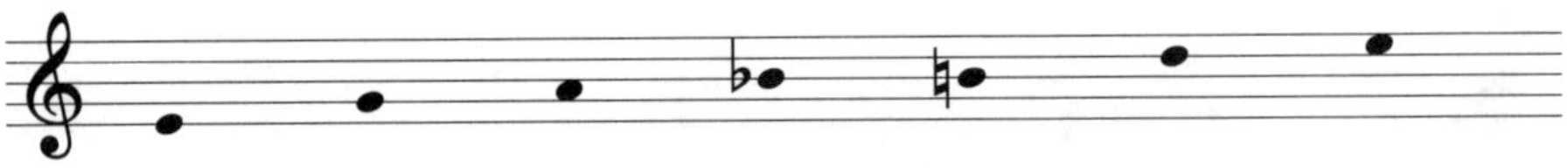

F

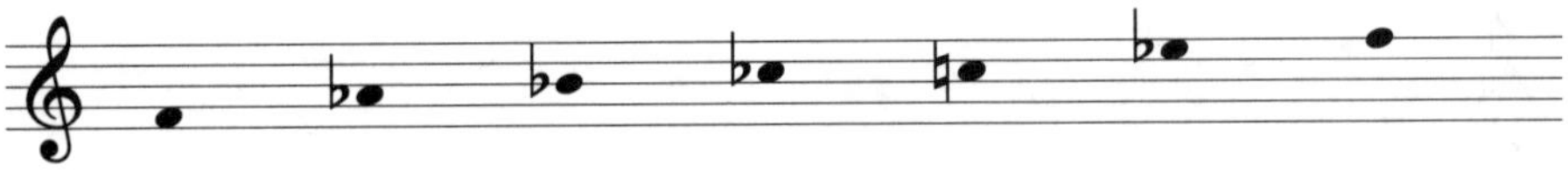

F♯

G

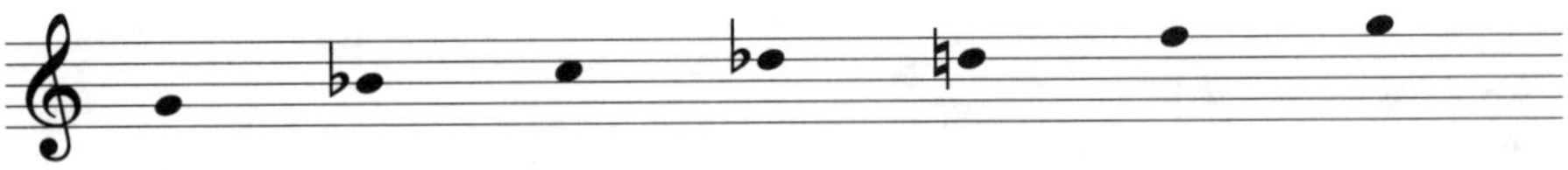

A♭

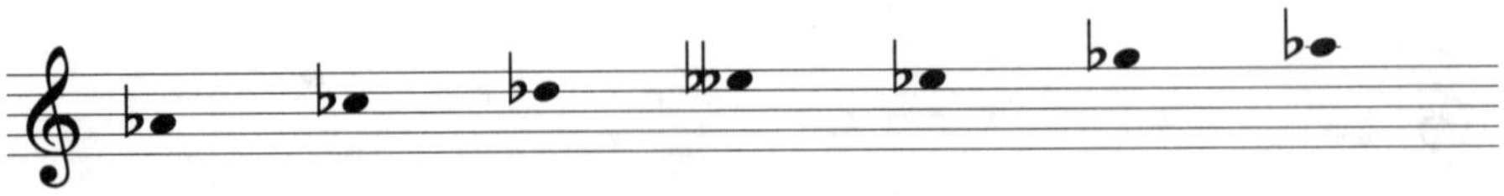

A

B♭

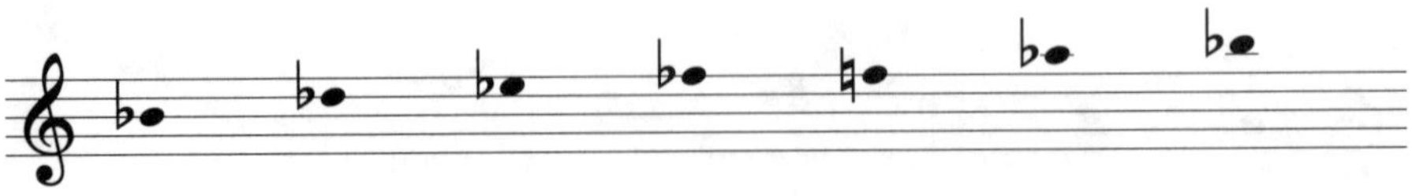

B

Pentatonic Major

1 2 3 5 6 — W W W+H W W+H

C

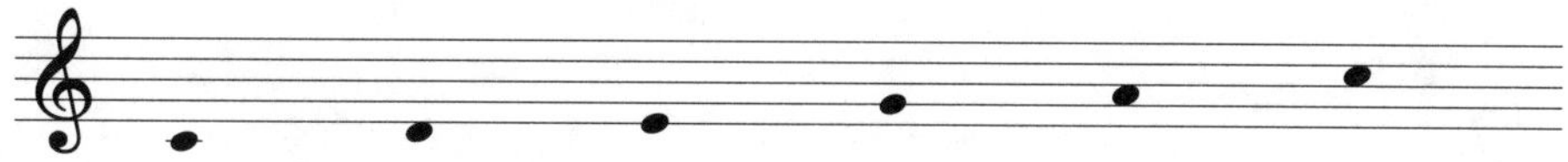

D♭

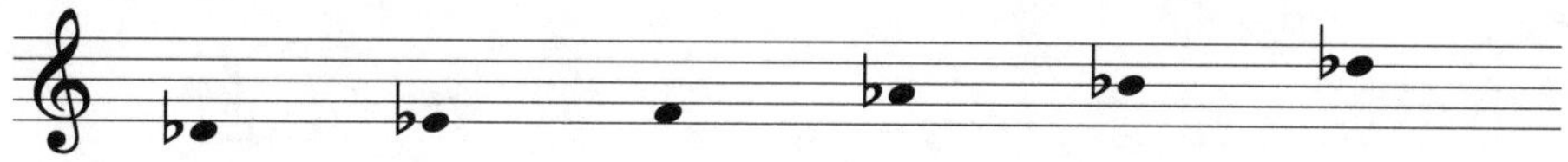

D

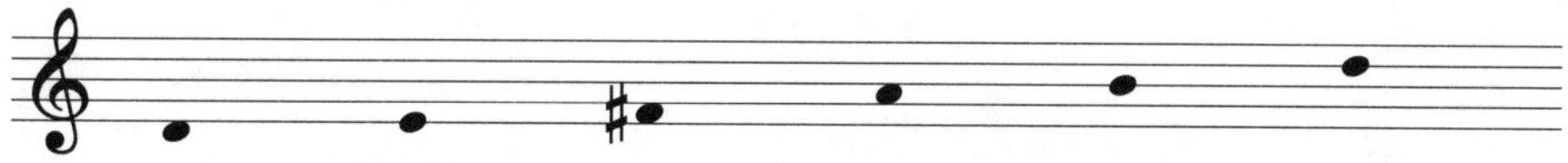

E♭

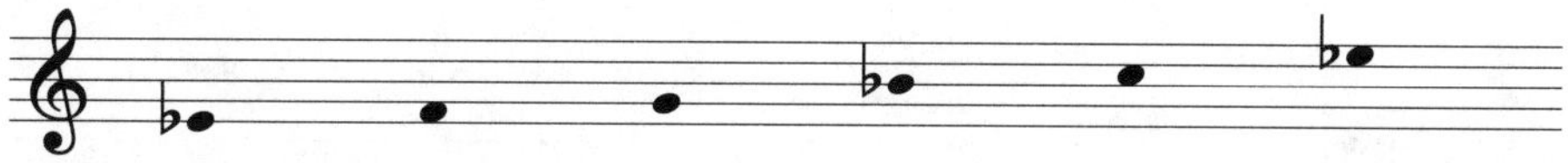

E

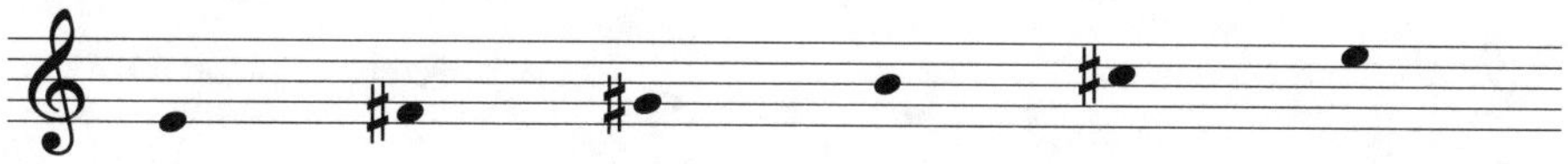

F

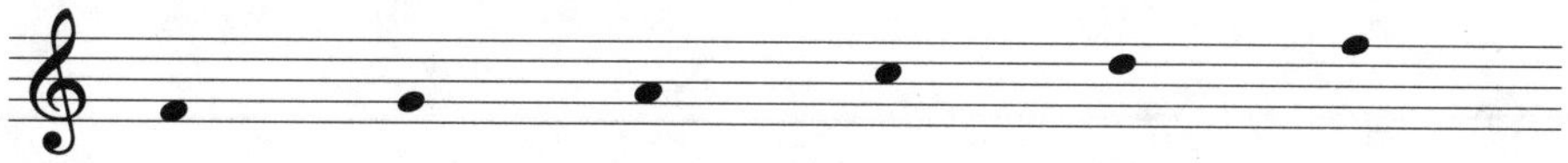

G♭

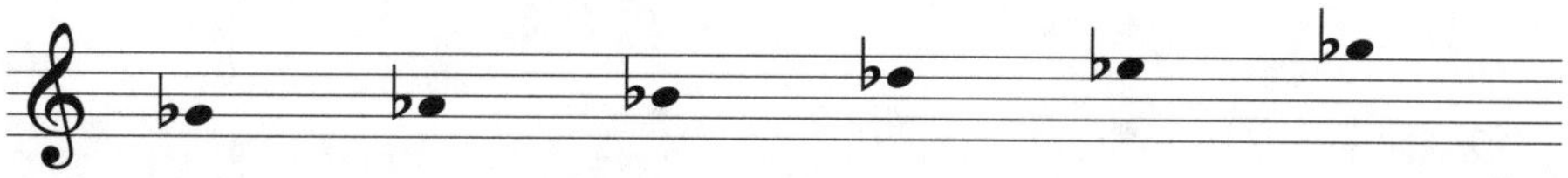

G

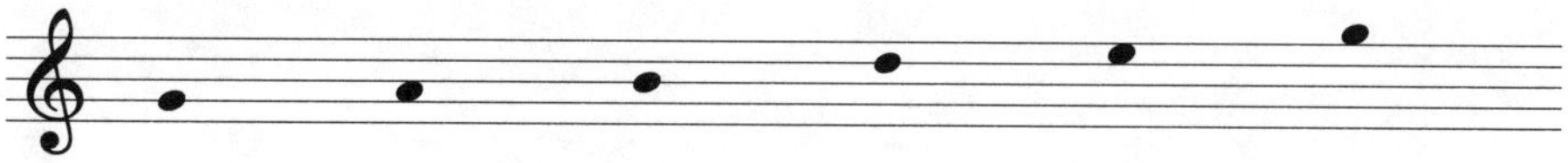

A♭

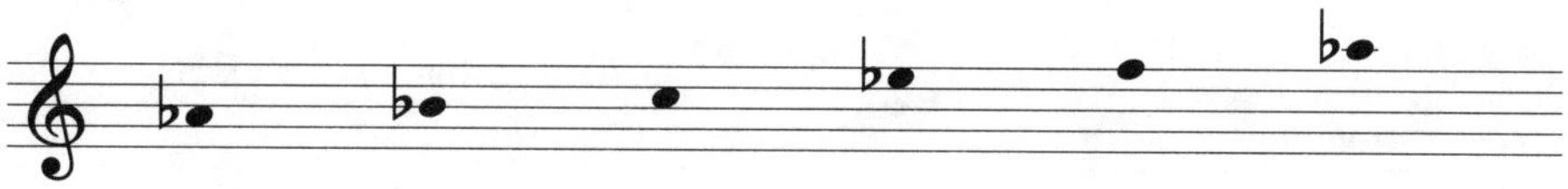

A

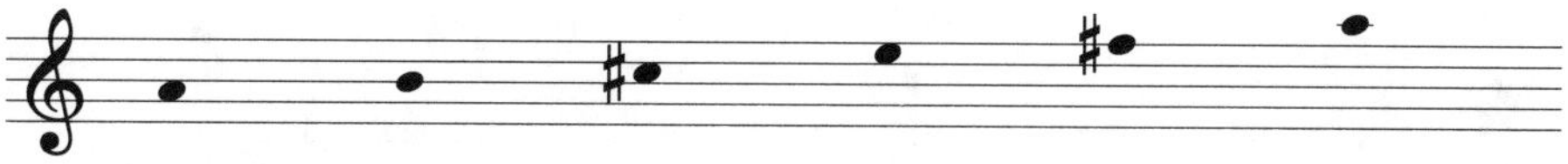

B♭

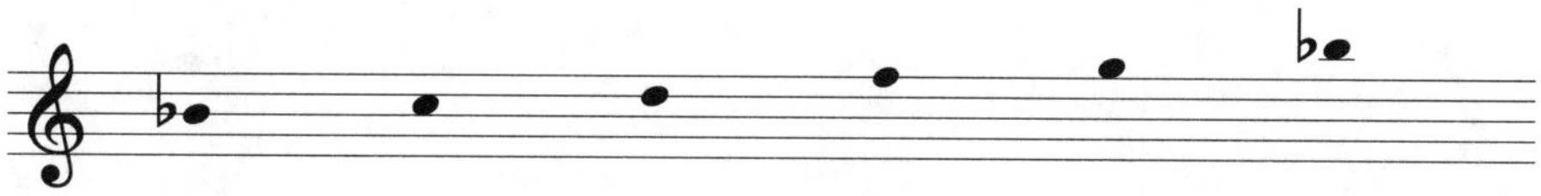

B

Pentatonic Minor

1 ♭3 4 5 ♭7 W+H W W W+H W

C

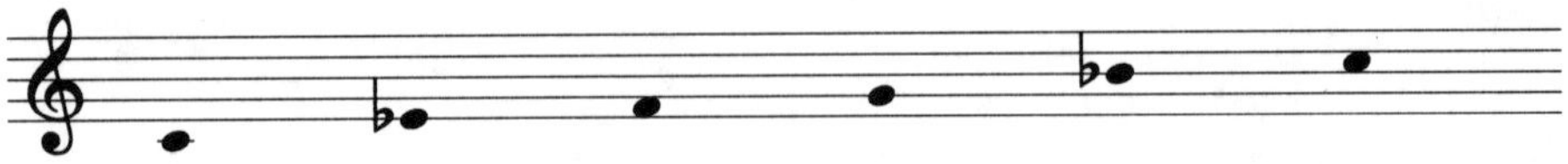

C♯

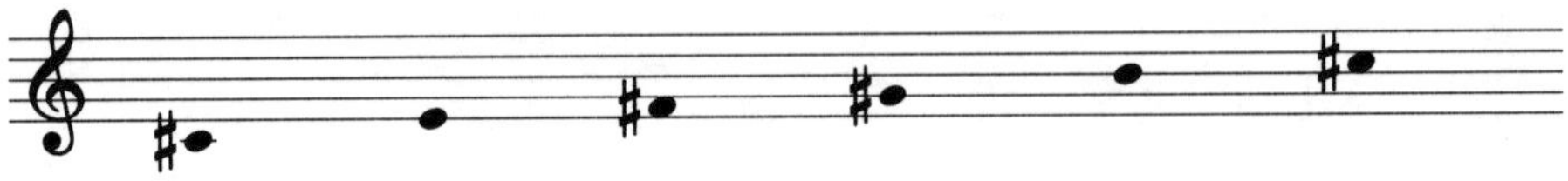

D

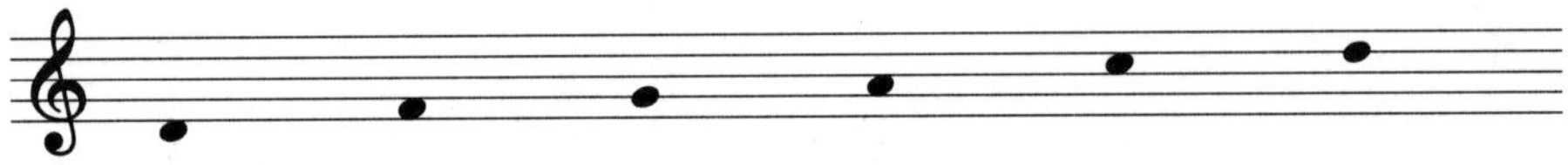

E♭

E

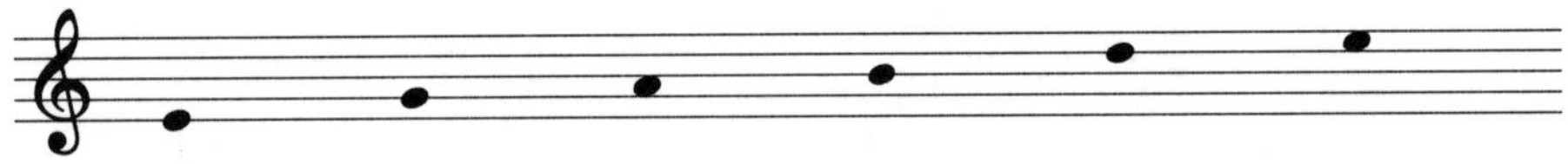

F

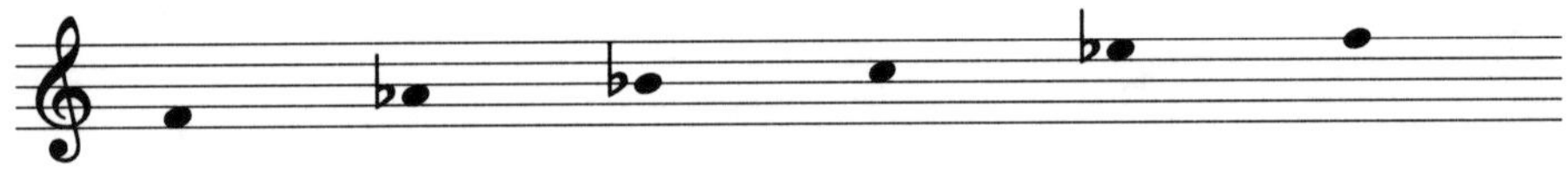

F♯

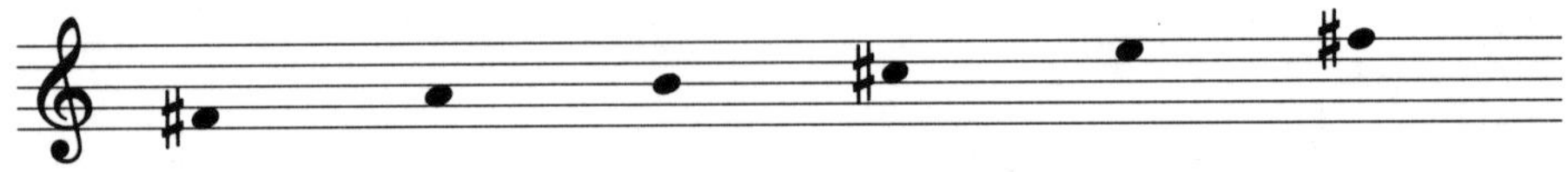

G

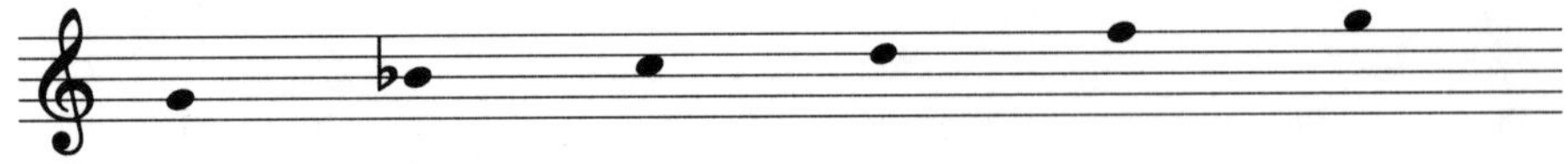

A♭

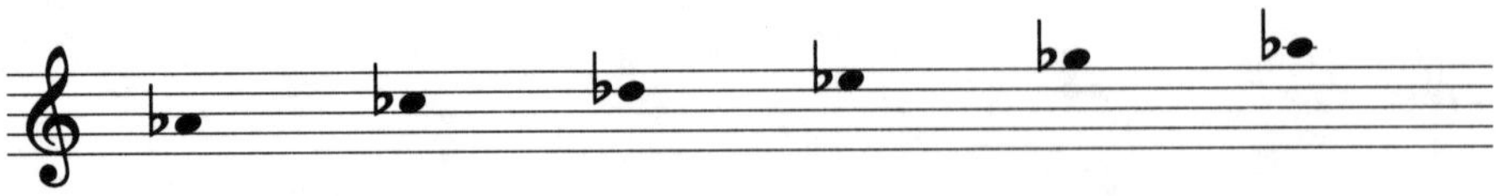

A

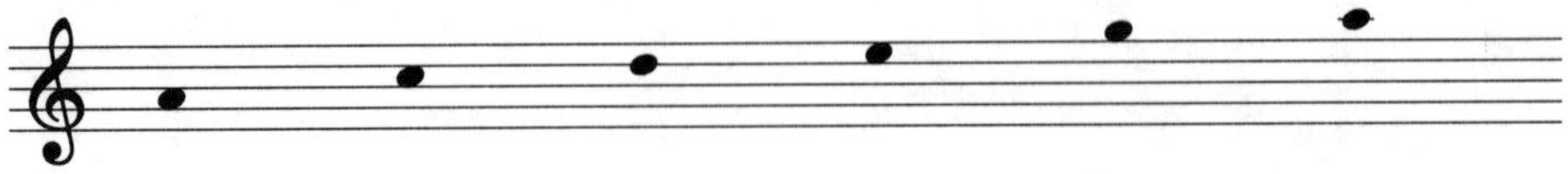

B♭

B

Major ♭2 Pentatonic

1 ♭2 3 5 6 — H W+H W+H W W+H

C

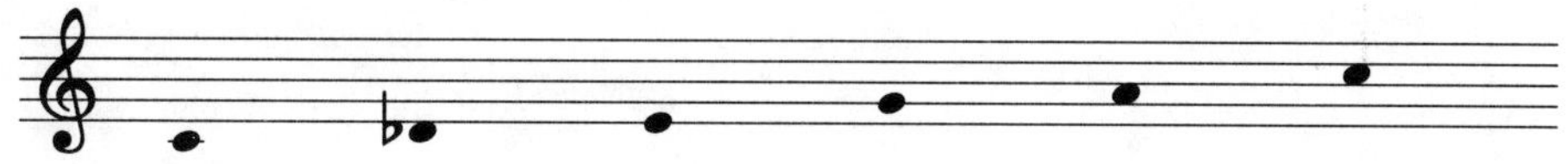

C♯

D

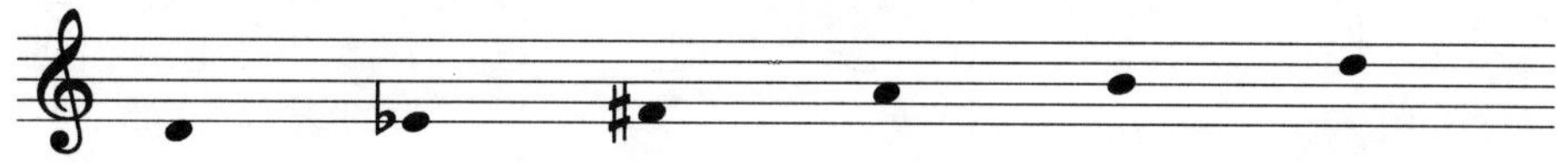

E♭

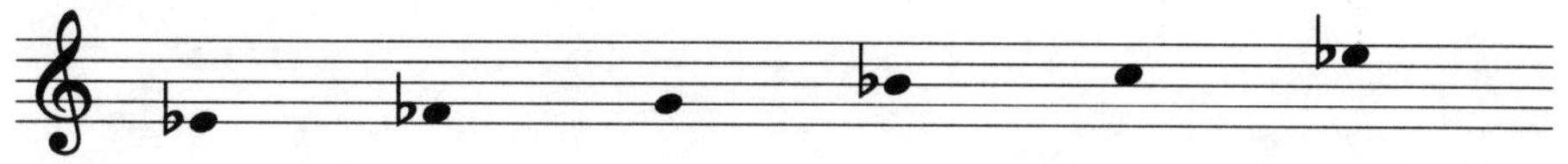

E

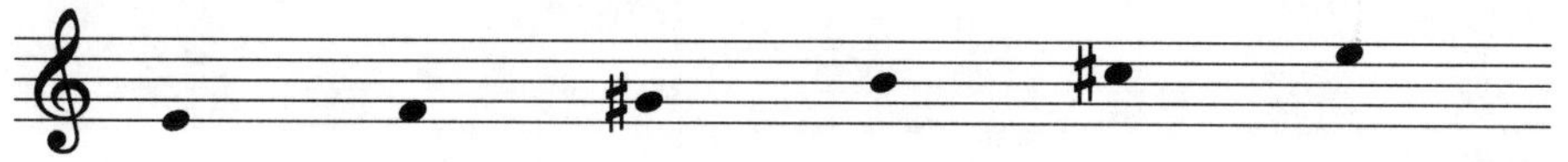

F

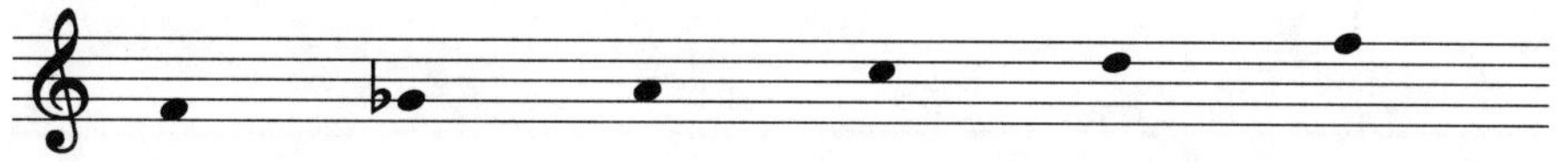

F♯

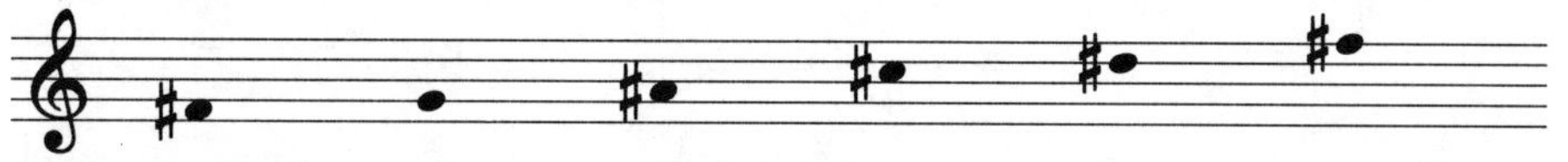

G

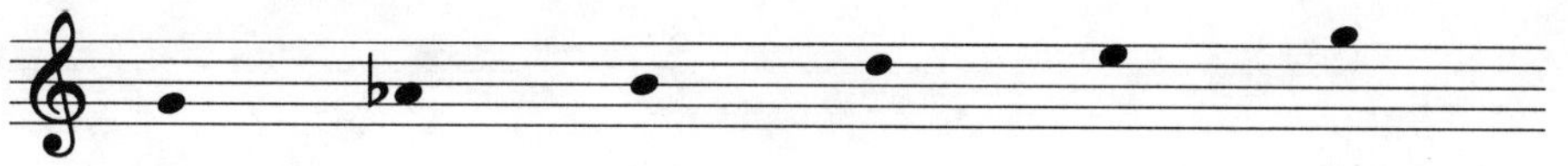

G♯

A

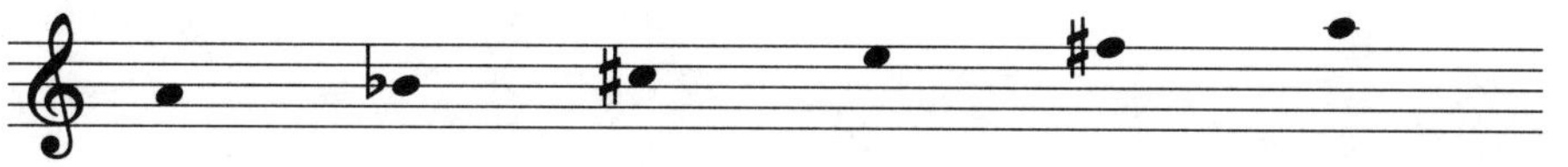

B♭

B

Major ♭6 Pentatonic

1 2 3 5 ♭6 W W W+H H W+W

C
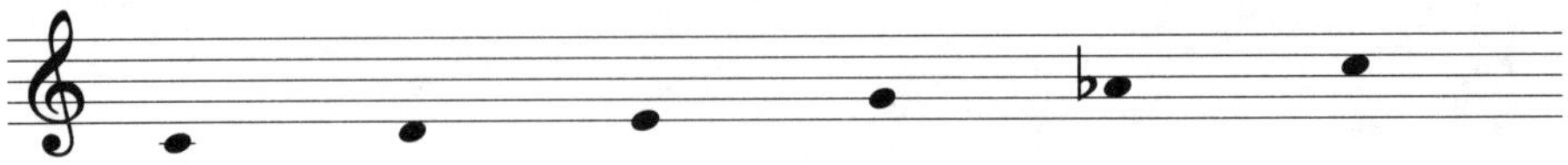

D♭
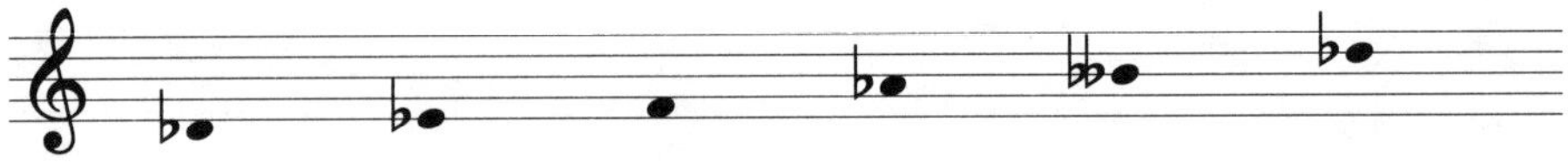

D
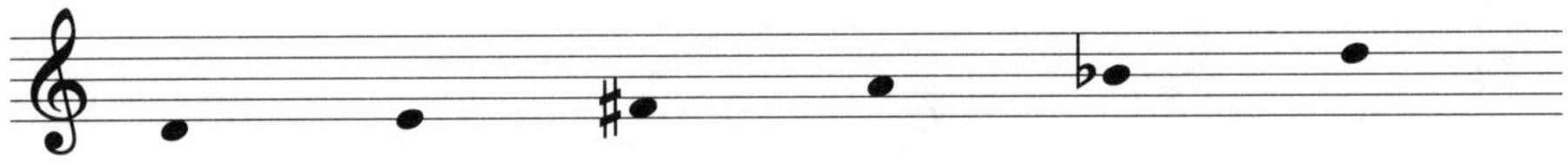

E♭

E
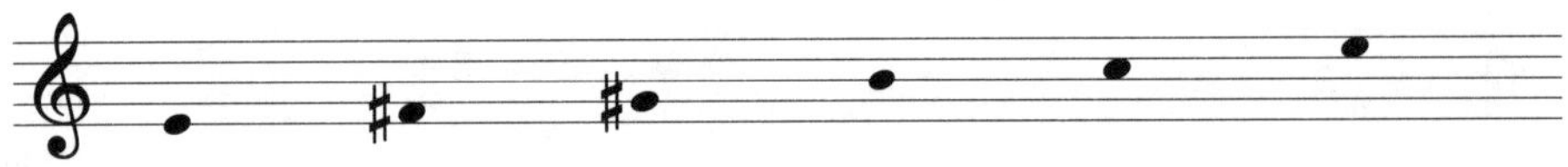

F
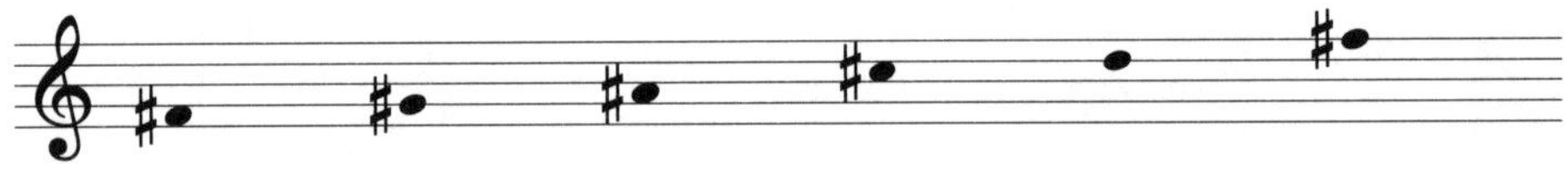

F♯
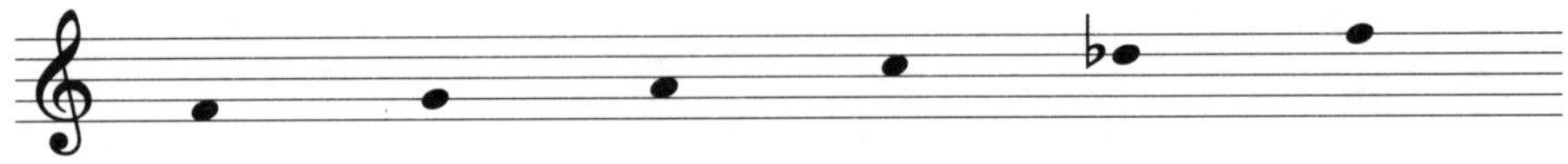

G
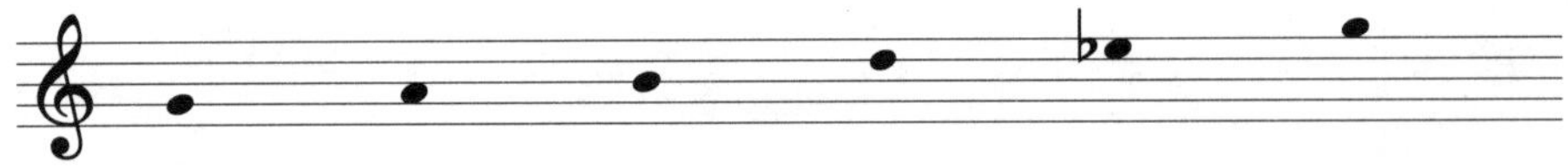

A♭
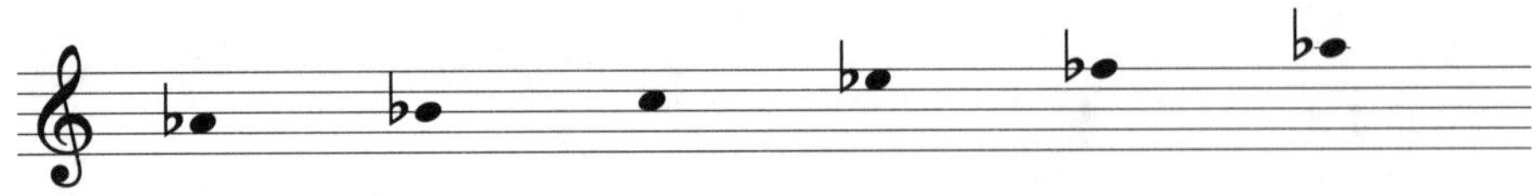

A
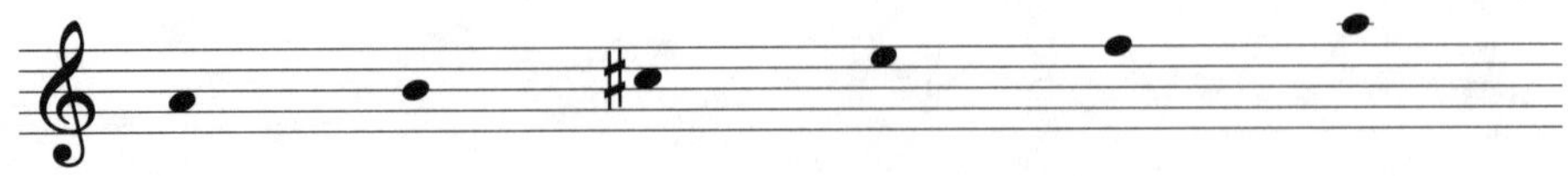

B♭
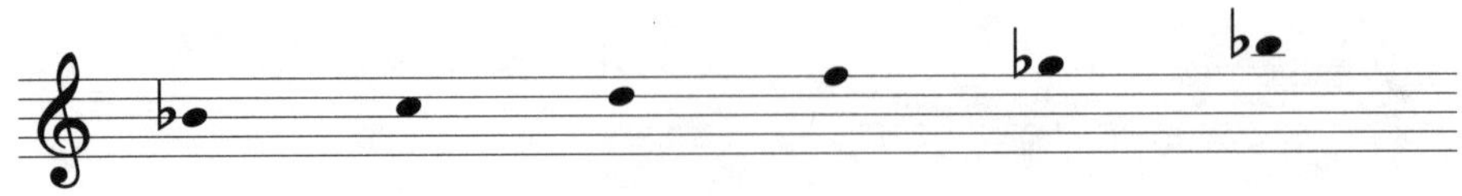

B
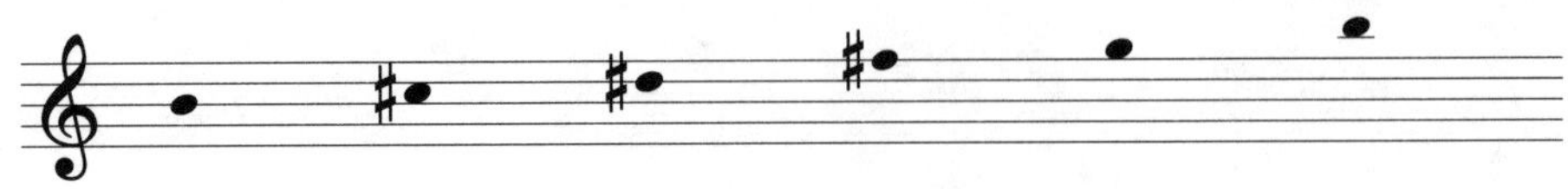

Minor 6 Pentatonic

1 ♭3 4 5 6 W+H W W W W+H

C

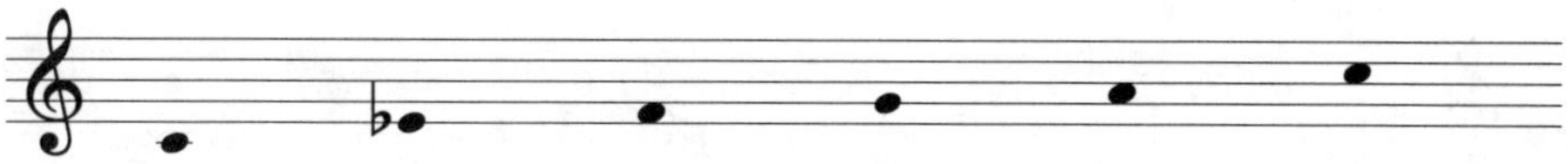

C♯

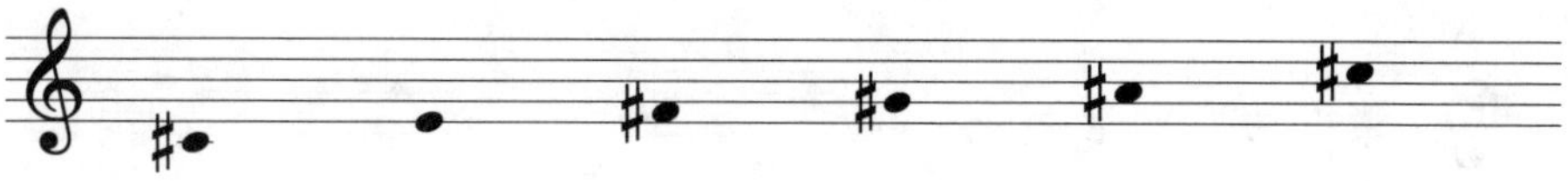

D

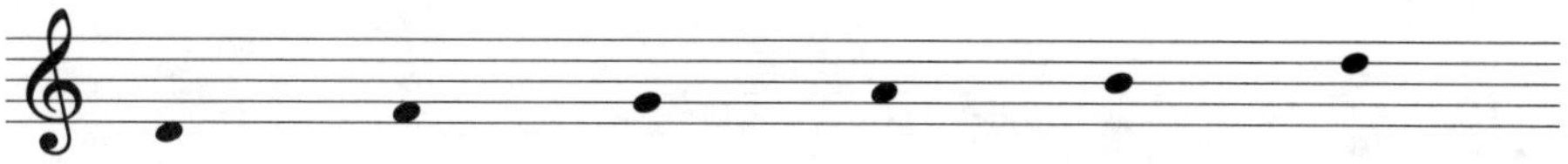

E♭

E

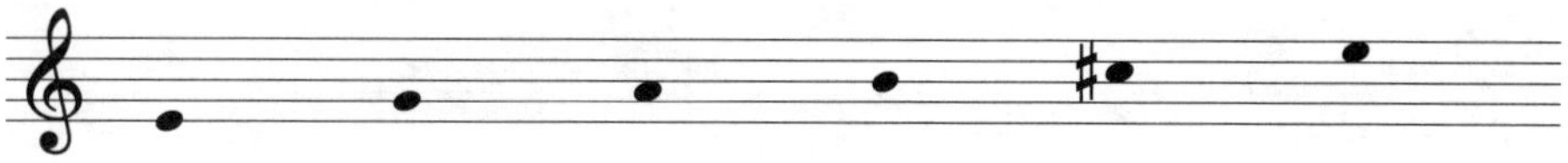

F

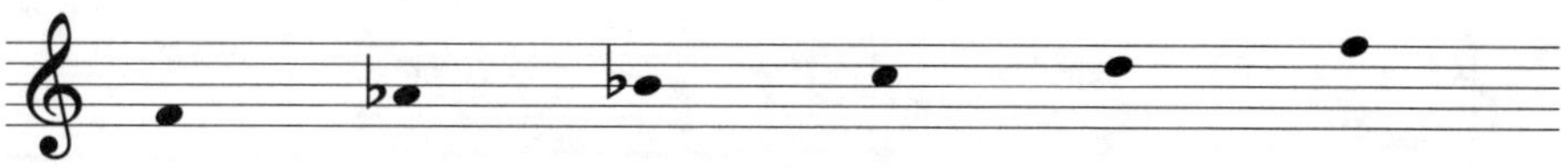

F♯

G

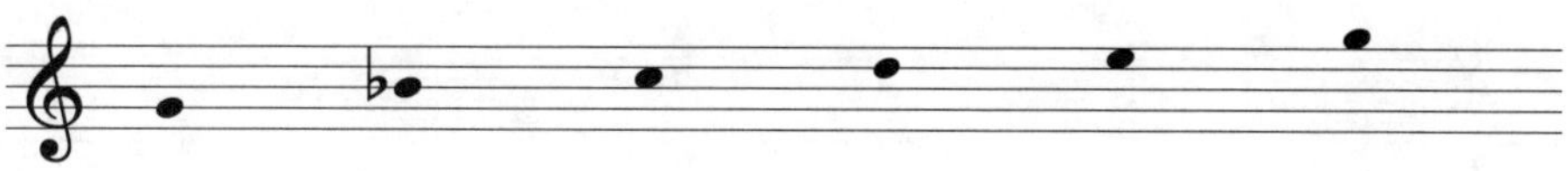

A♭

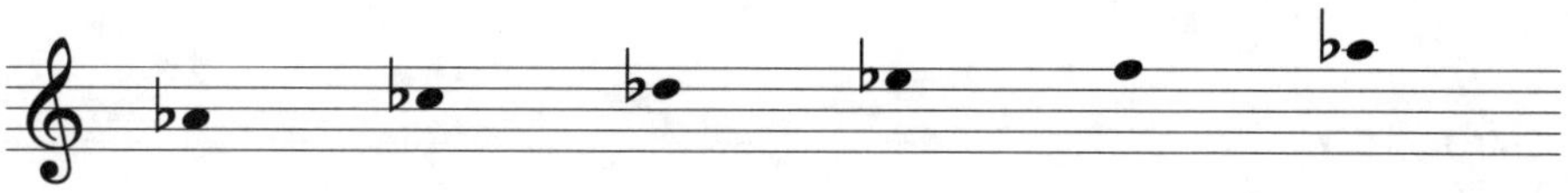

A

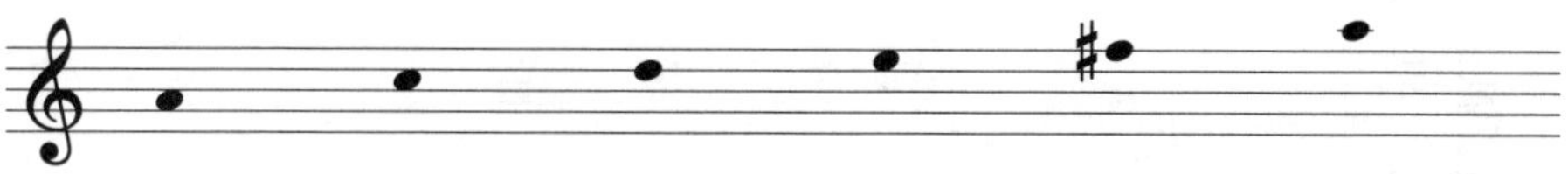

B♭

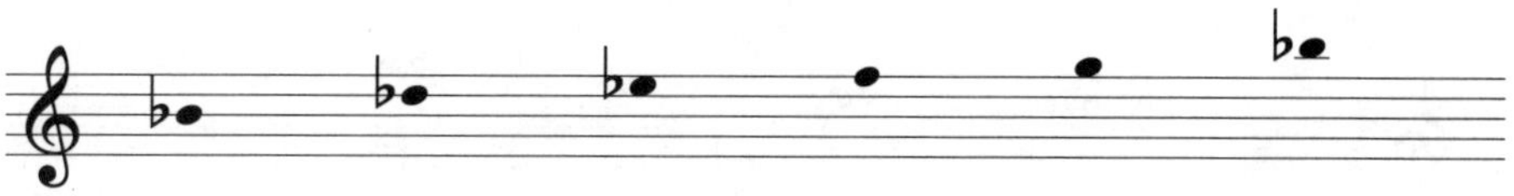

B

Minor 7♭5 Pentatonic

1 ♭3 4 ♭5 ♭7

W+H W H W+W W

C

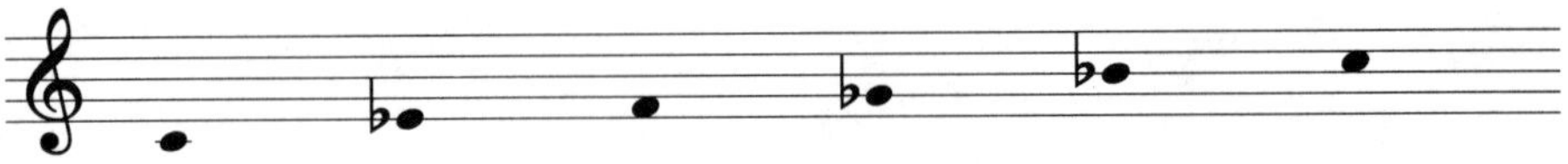

C♯

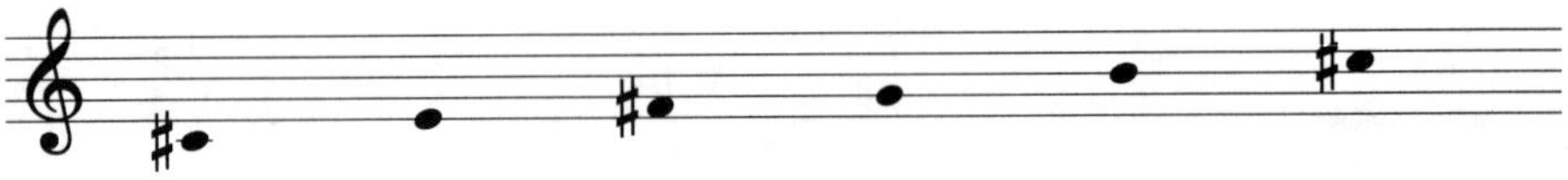

D

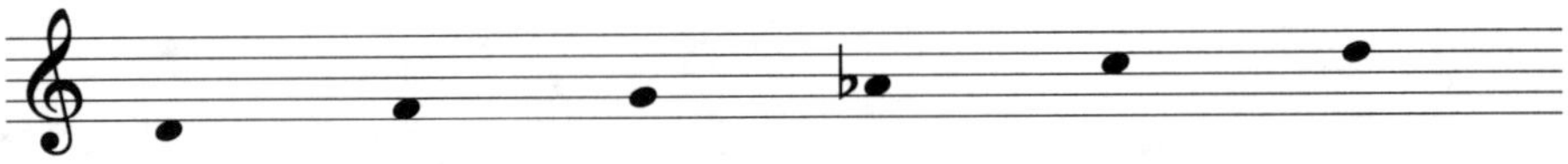

D♯

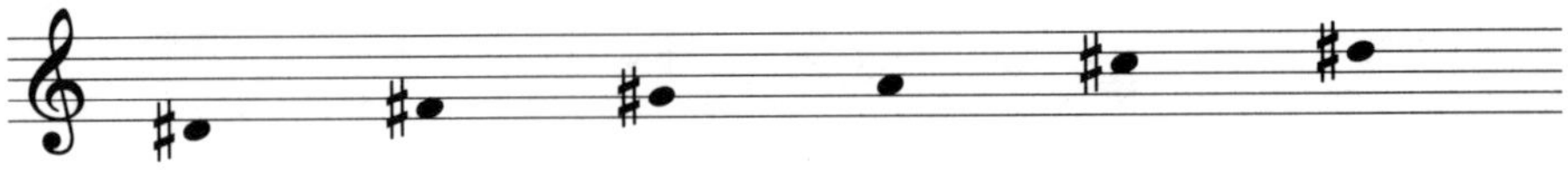

E

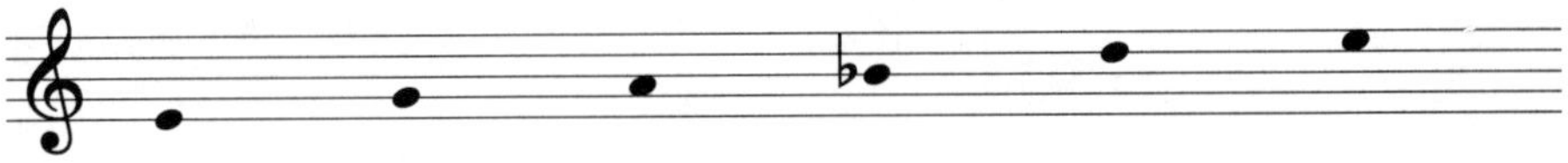

F

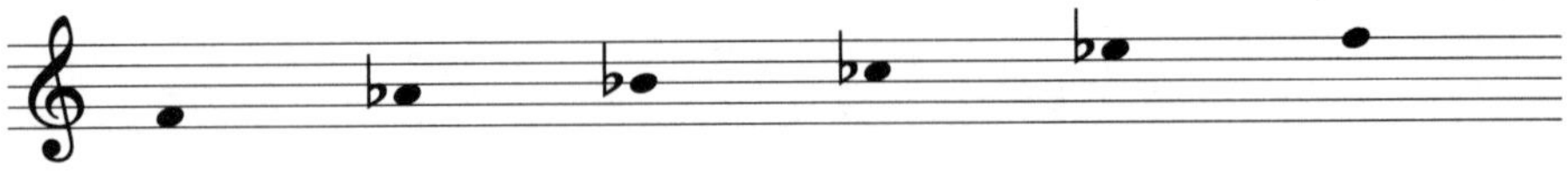

F♯

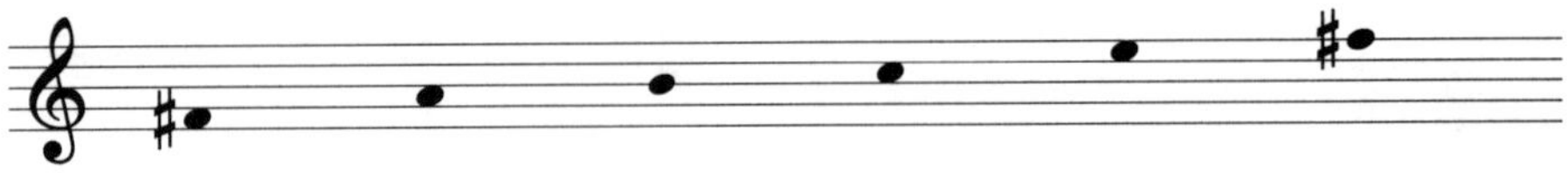

G

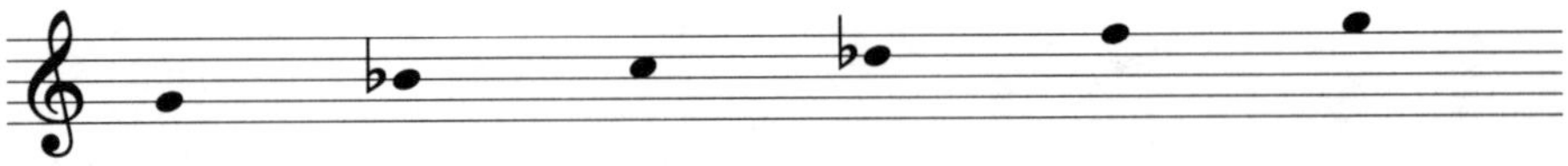

G♯

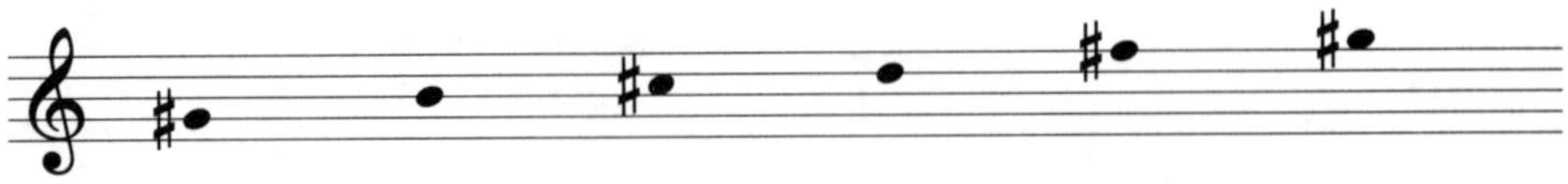

A

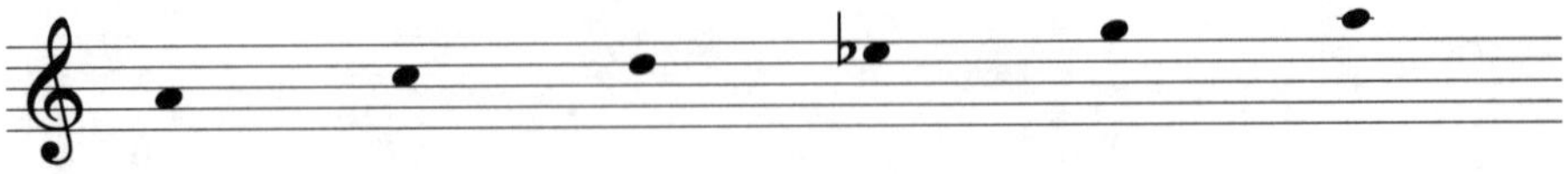

B♭

B

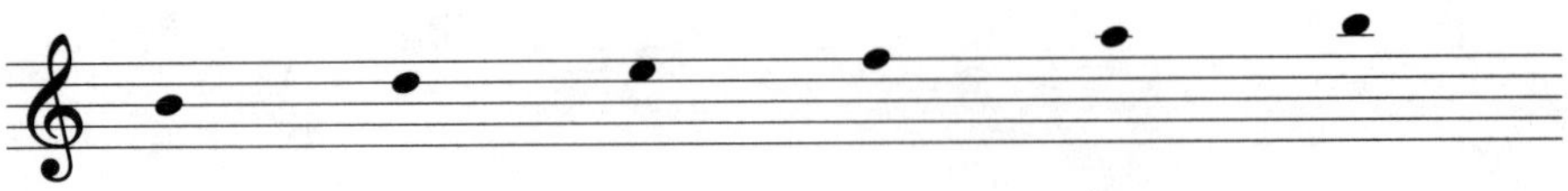

Whole Tone Pentatonic

1 3 ♯4 ♯5 ♭7 W+W W W W W

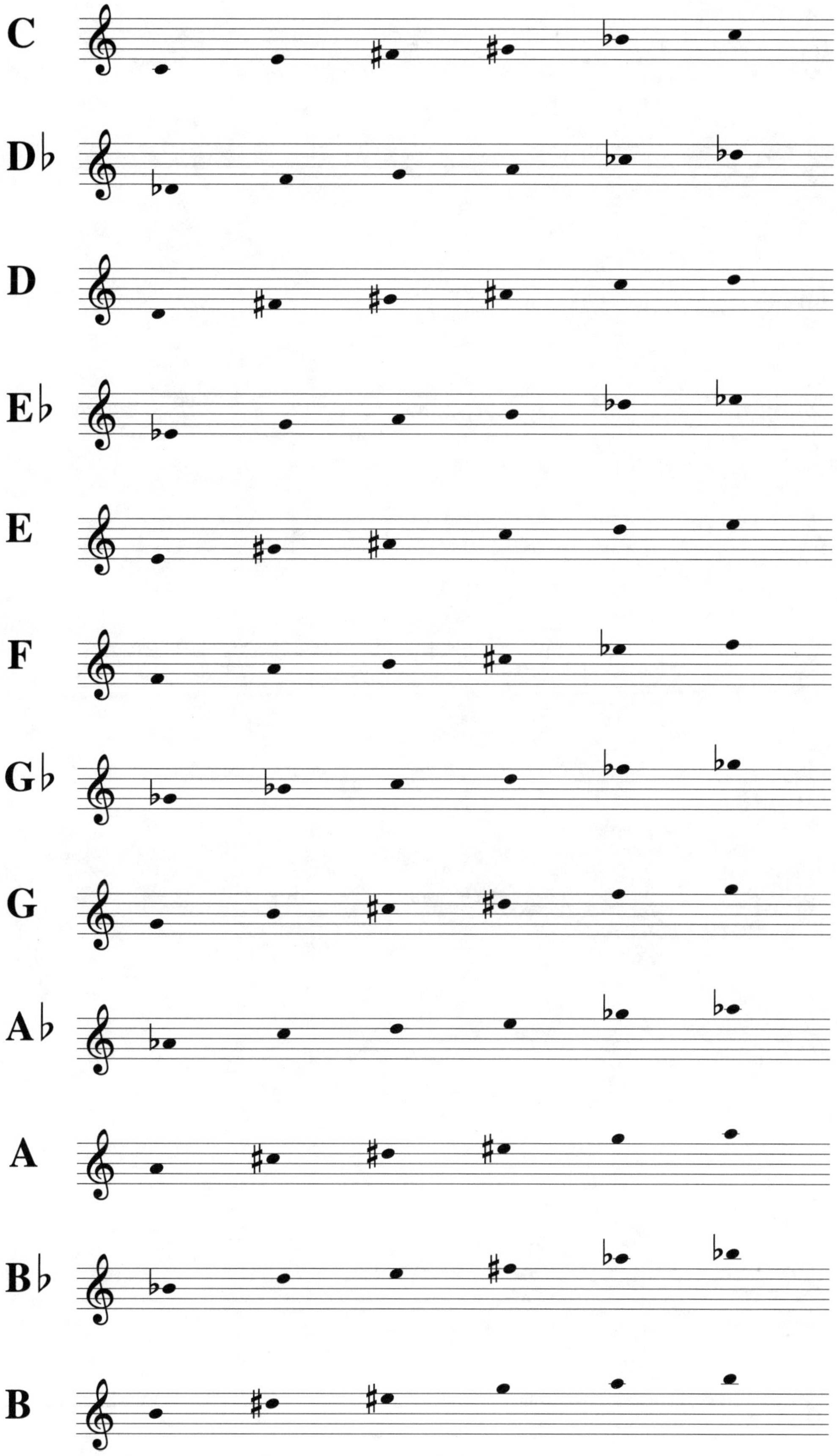

Banshiki-Cho

1 ♭3 4 ♭6 ♭7 W+H W W+H W W

C

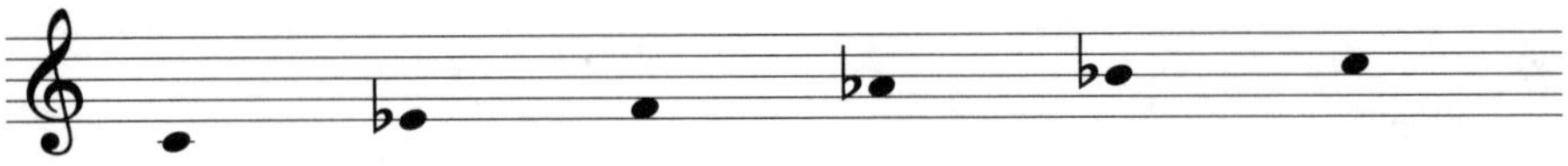

C♯

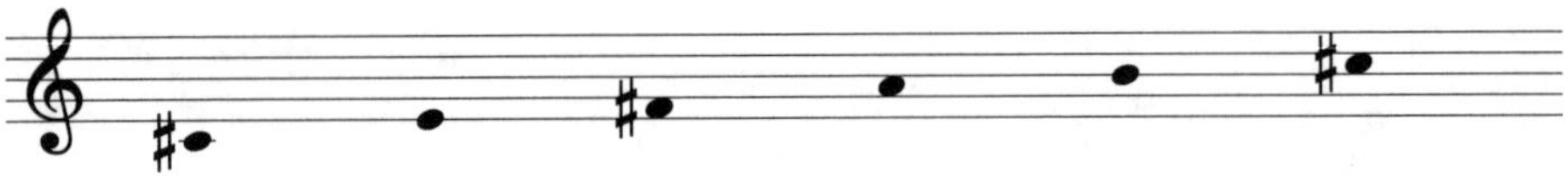

D

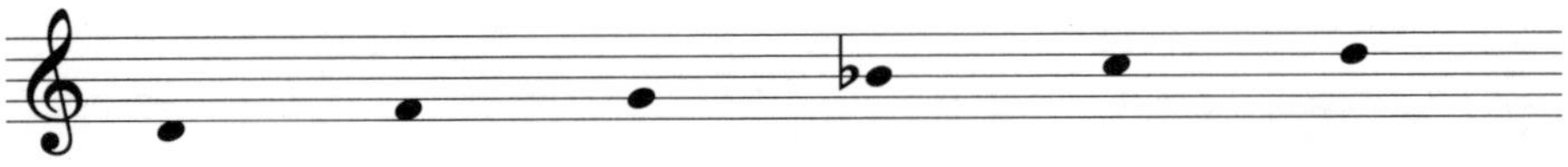

E♭

E

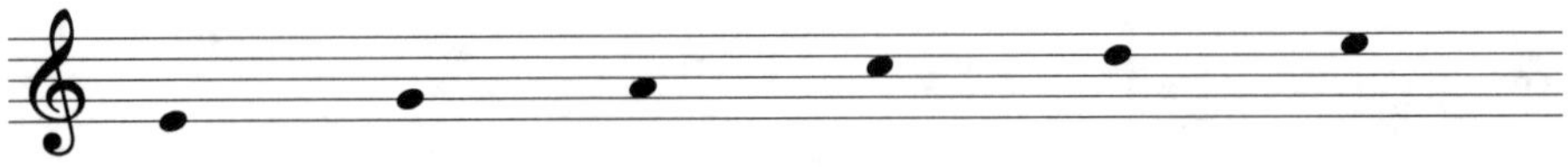

F

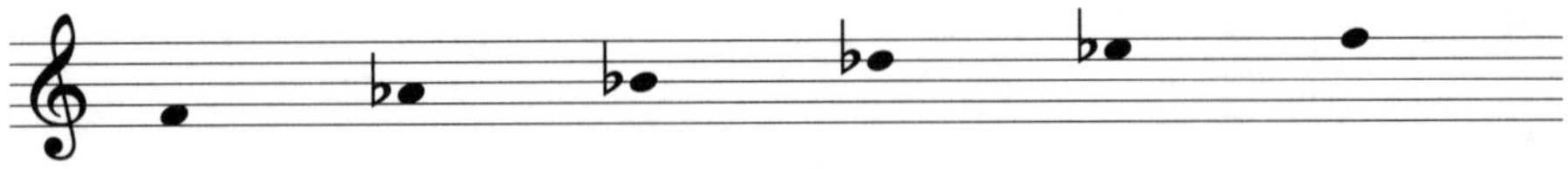

F♯

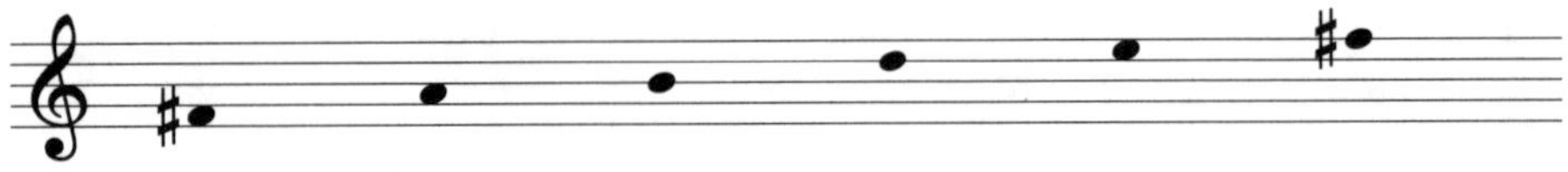

G

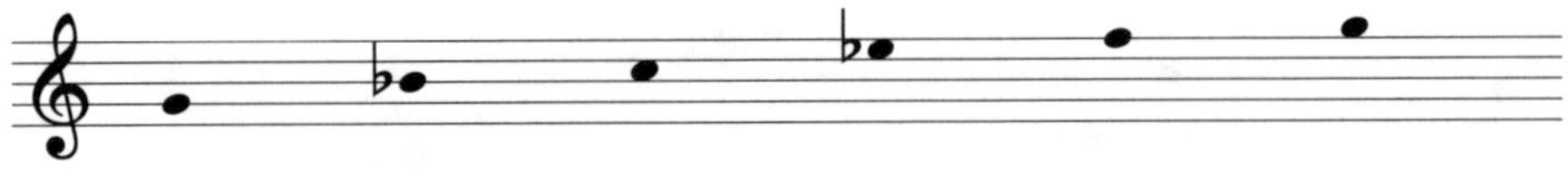

G♯

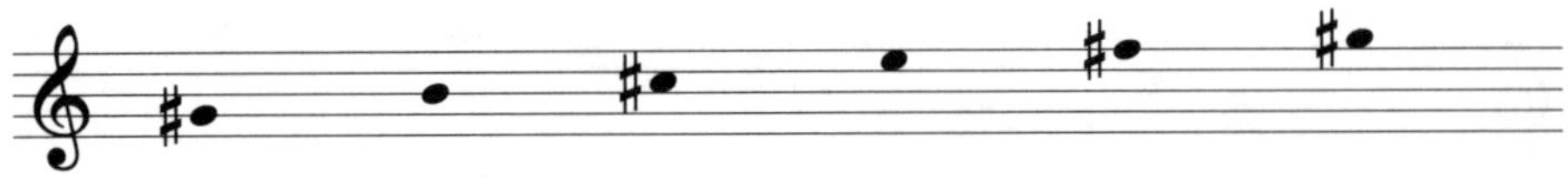

A

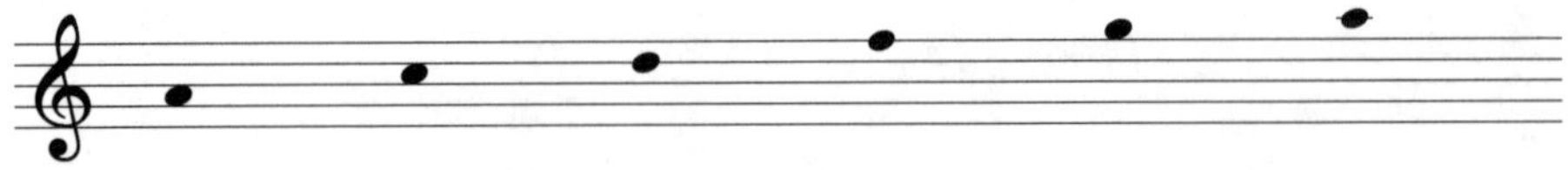

B♭

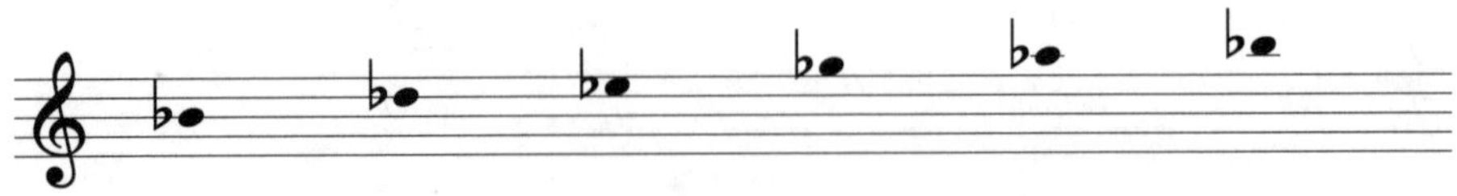

B

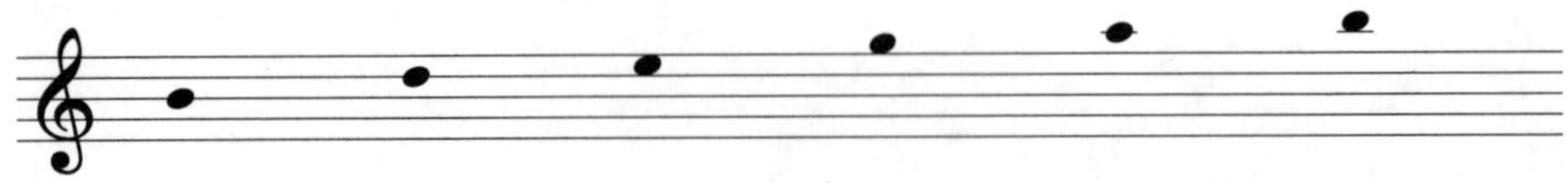

Hirajoshi

1 2 ♭3 5 ♭6 W H W+W H W+W

C

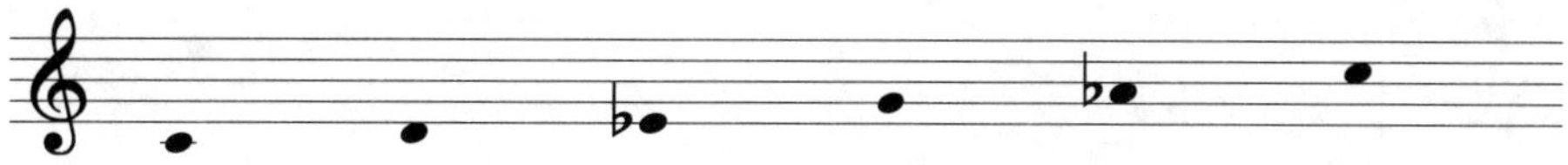

C♯

D

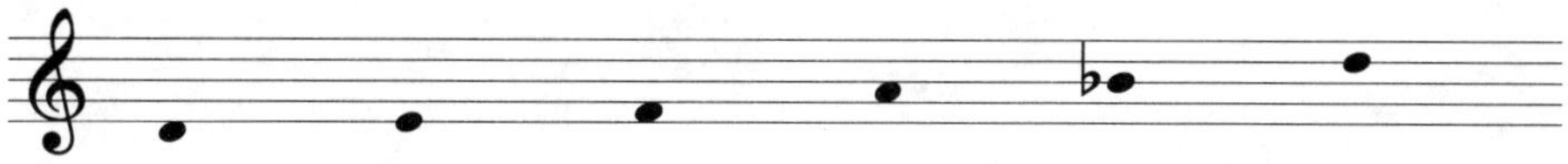

E♭

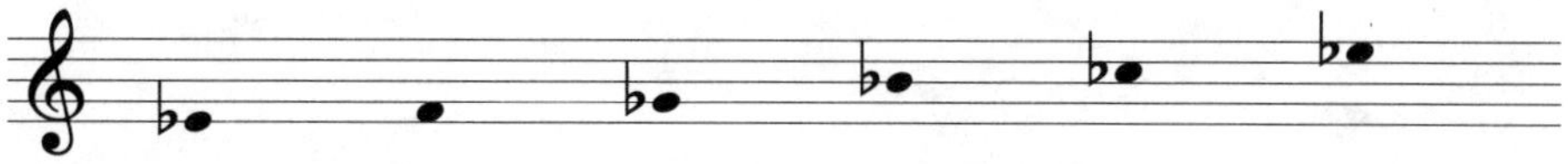

E

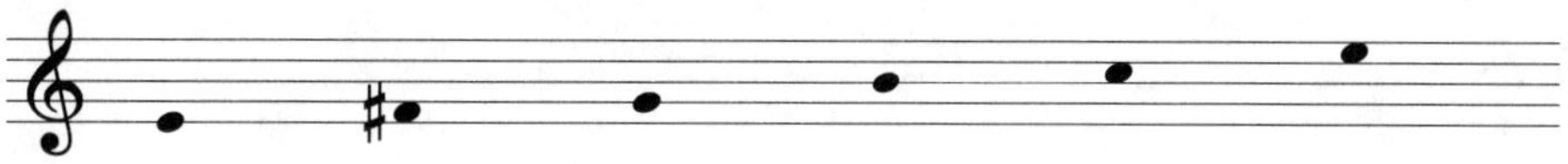

F

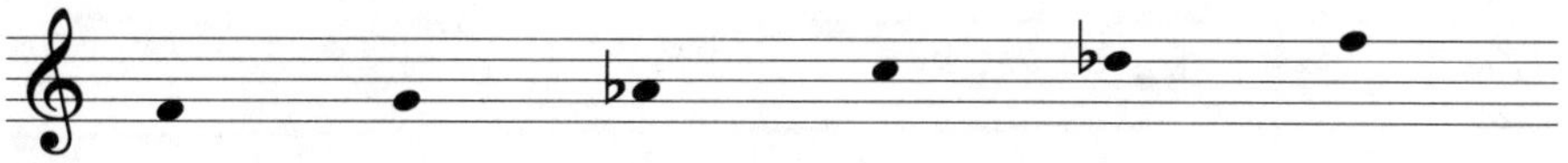

F♯

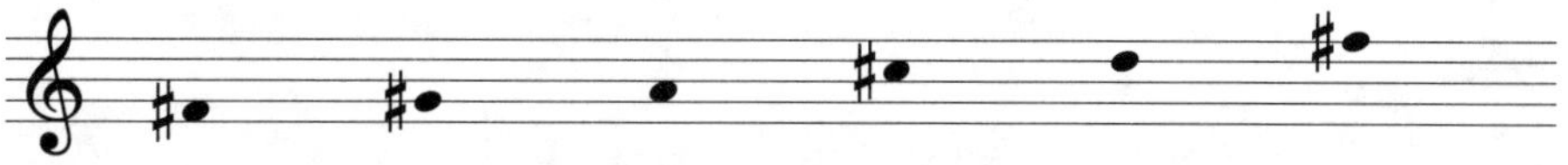

G

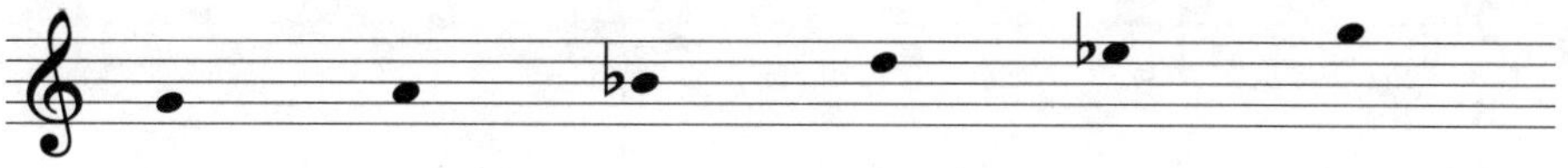

A♭

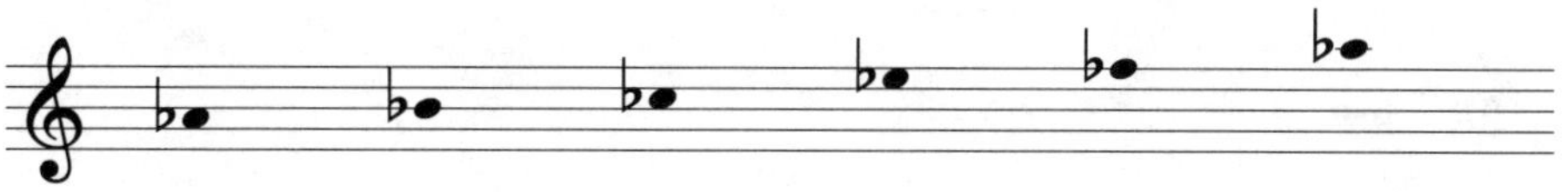

A

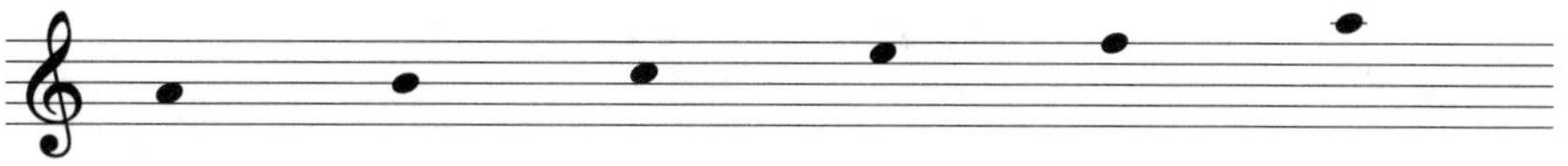

B♭

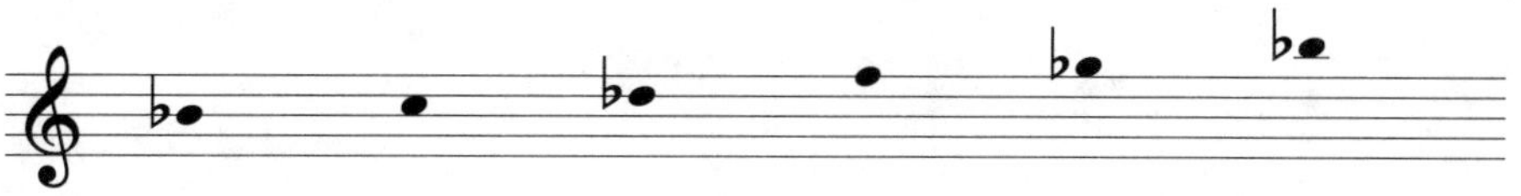

B

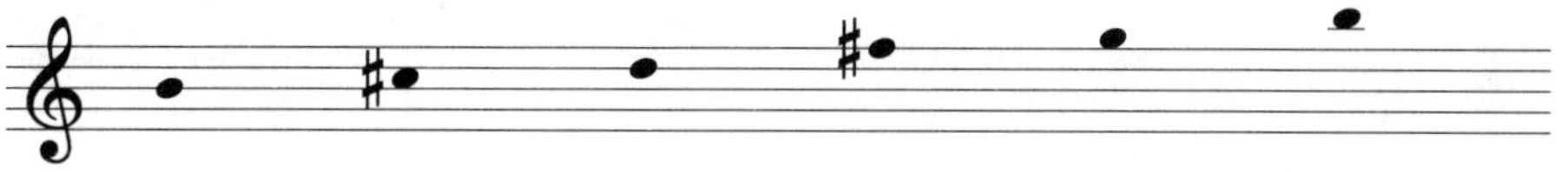

Iwato

1 ♭2 4 ♭5 ♭7 H W+W H W+W W

C
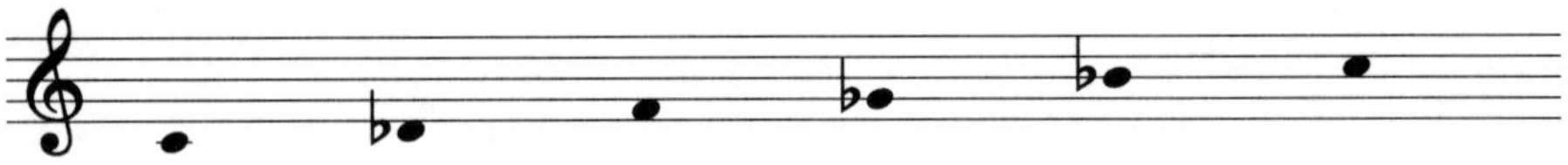

C♯
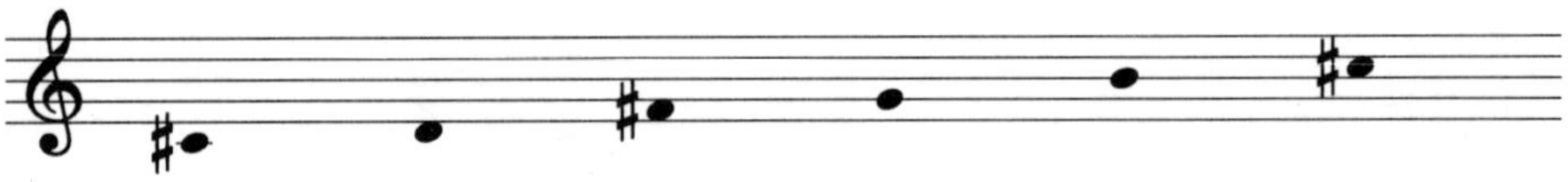

D
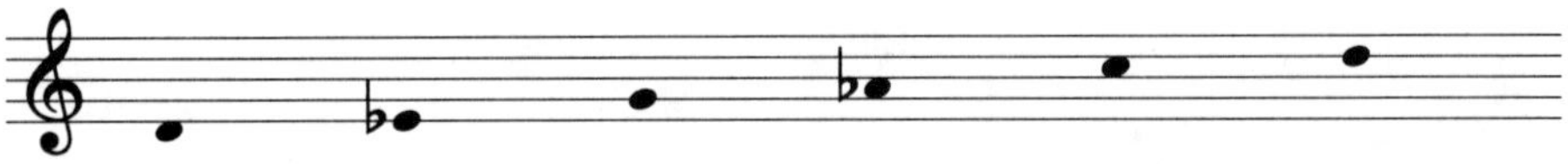

D♯
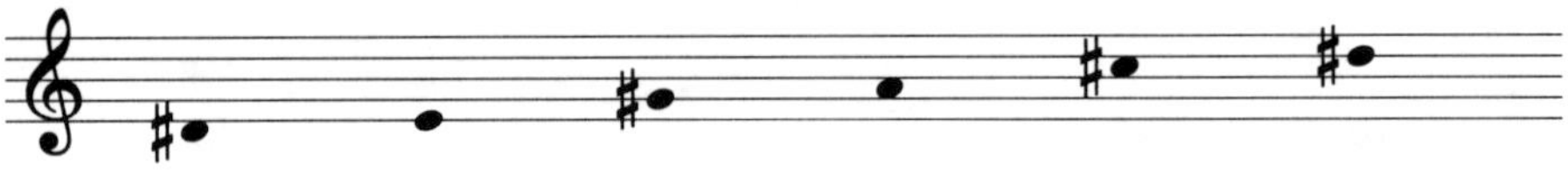

E
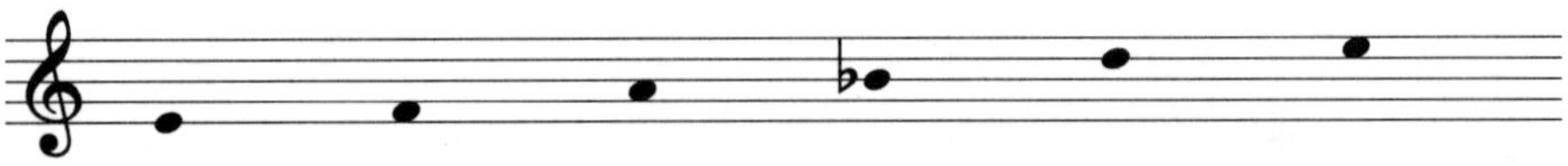

F
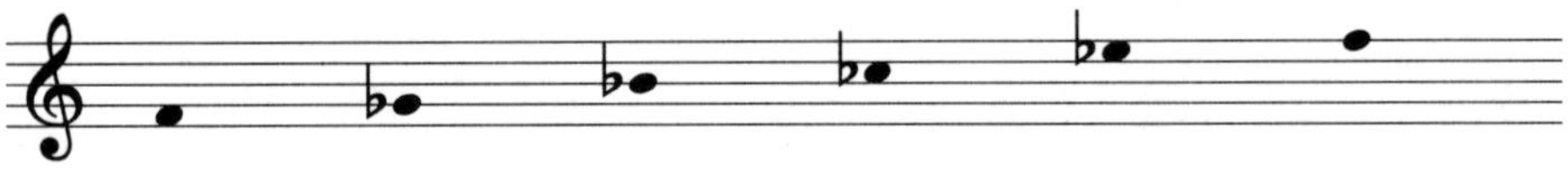

F♯
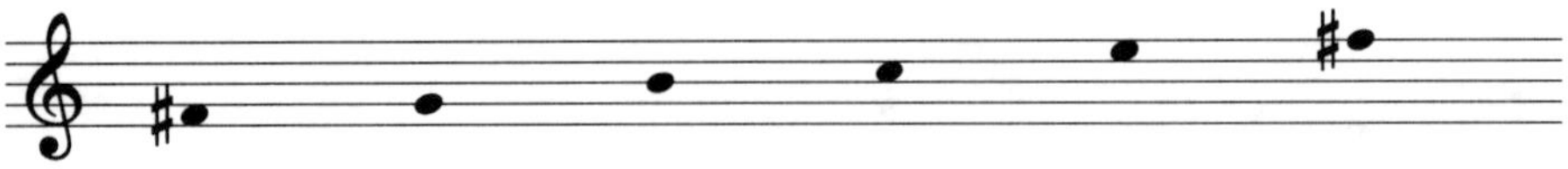

G
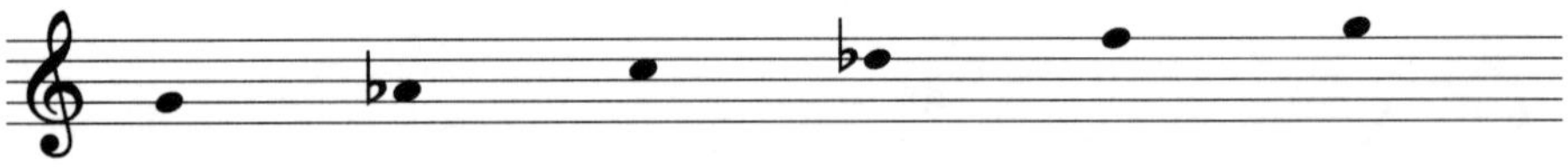

G♯
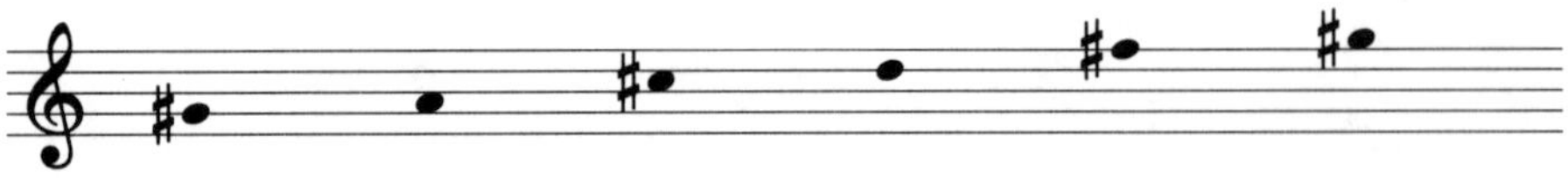

A
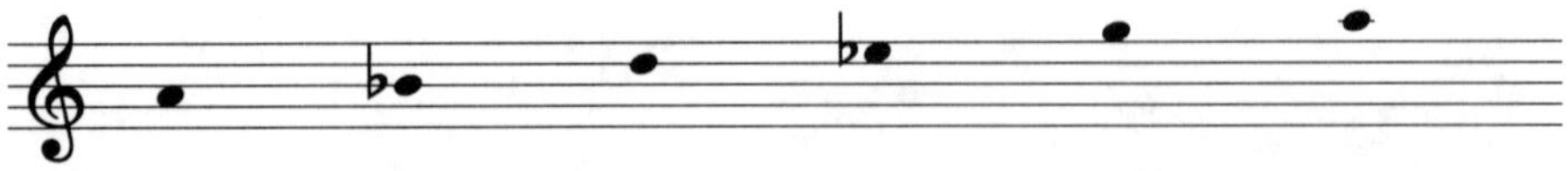

B♭

B
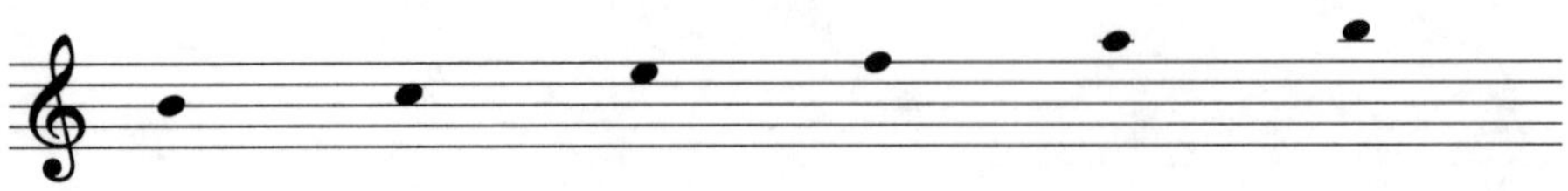

Kokin-Chosi

1 ♭2 4 5 ♭7 H W+W W W+H W

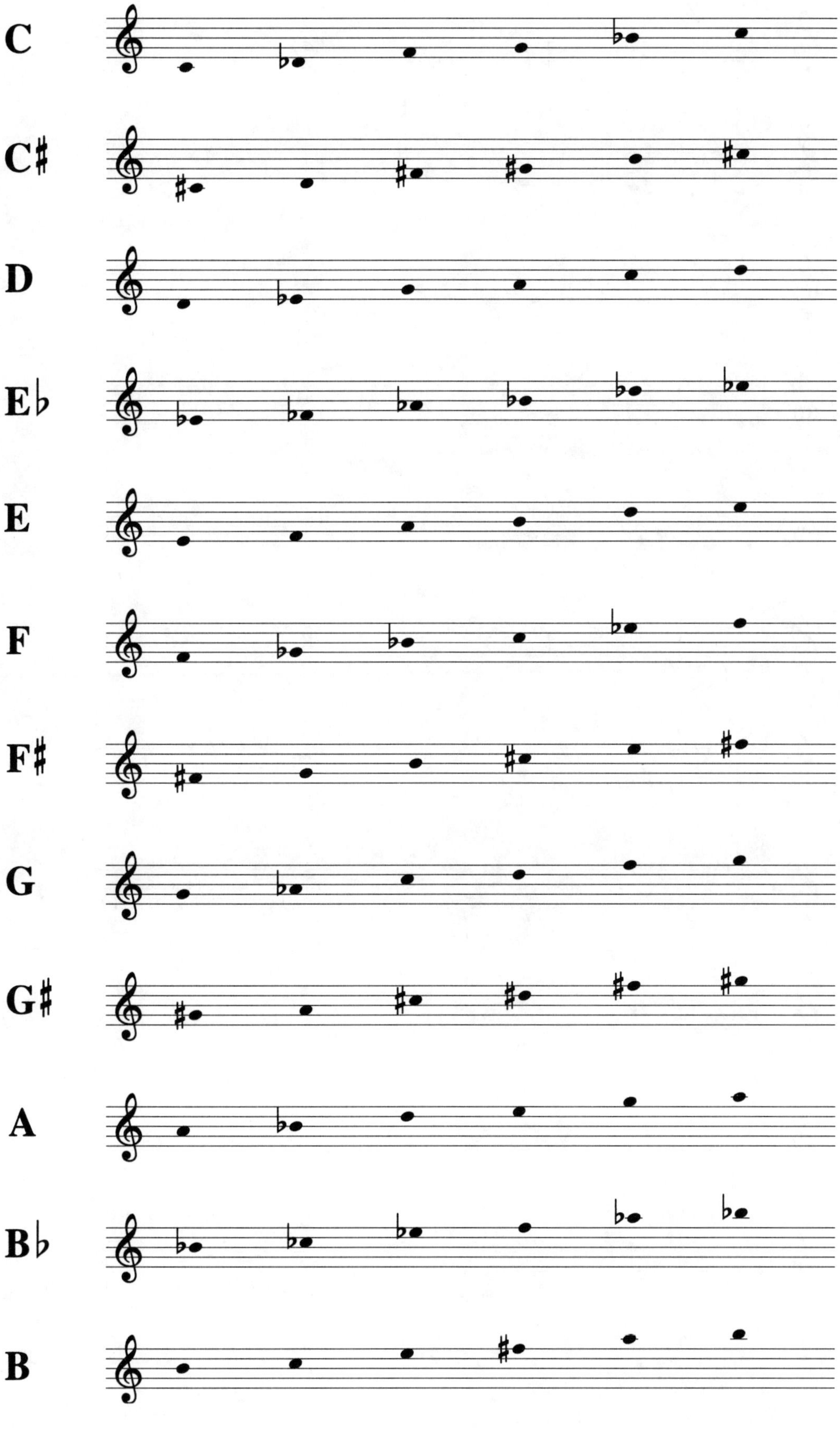

Kumoi

1 2 ♭3 5 6 W H W+W W W+H

C

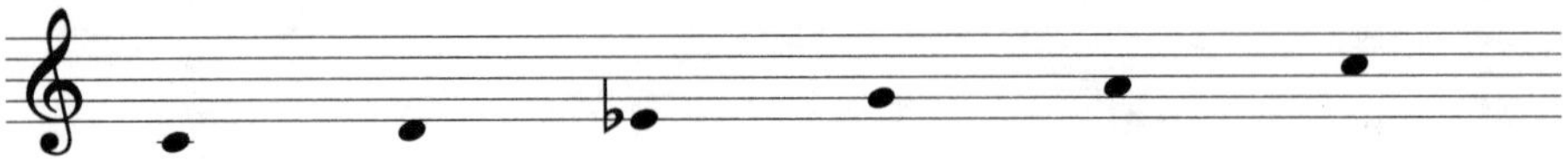

C♯

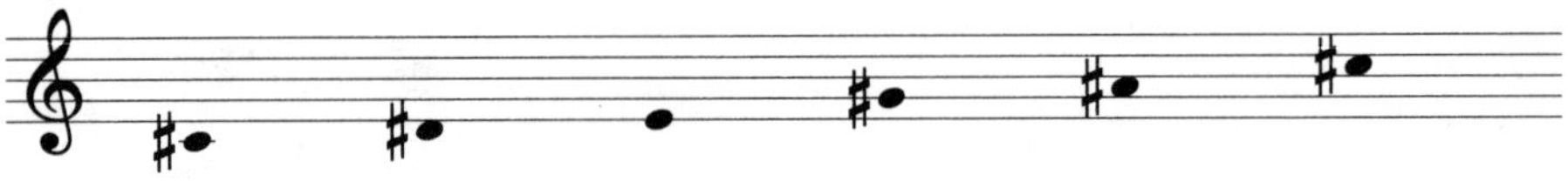

D

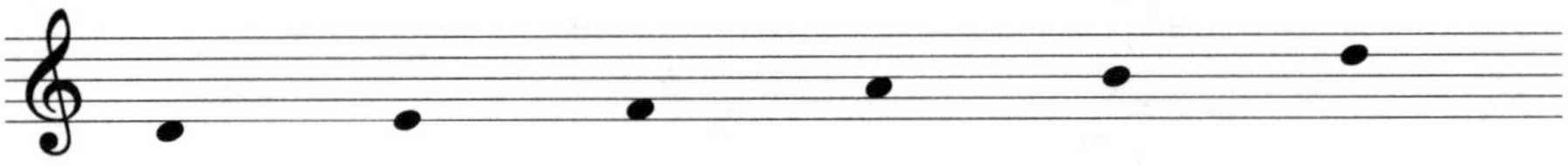

E♭

E

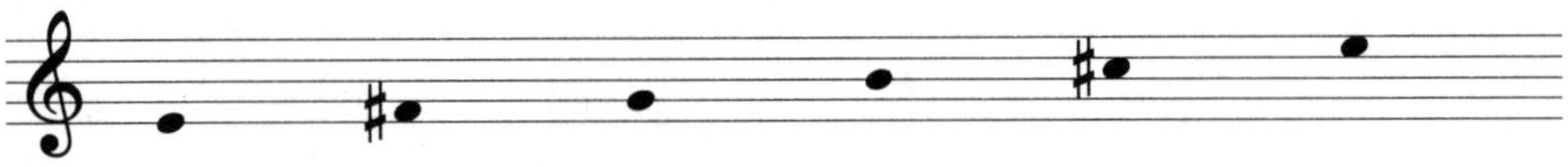

F

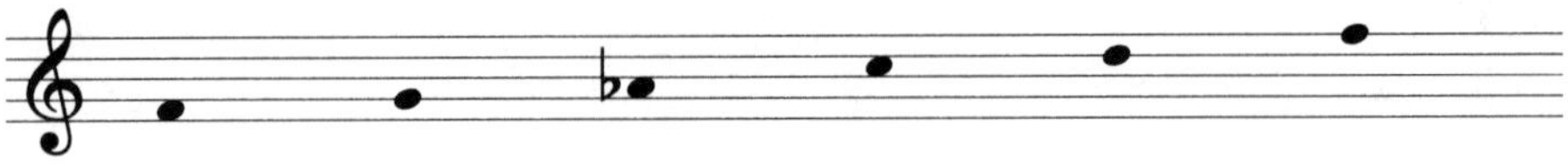

F♯

G

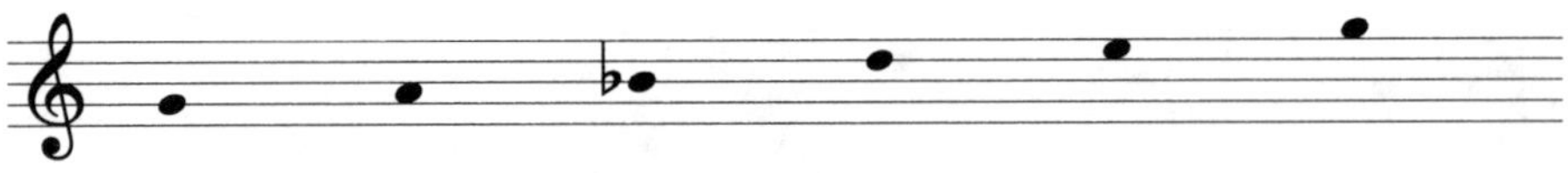

A♭

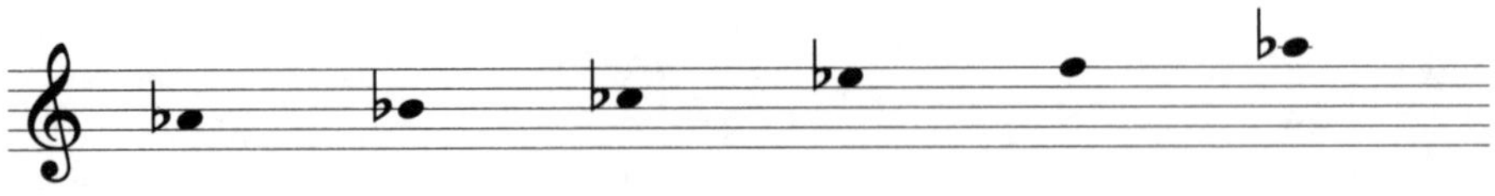

A

B♭

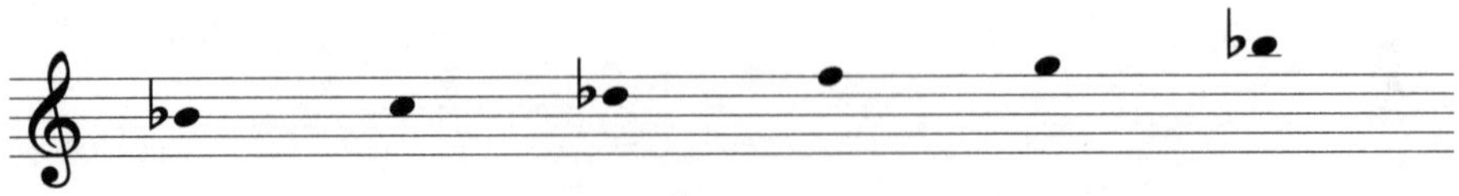

B

Naka Zora

1 ♭2 4 5 ♭6 H W+W W H W+W

C

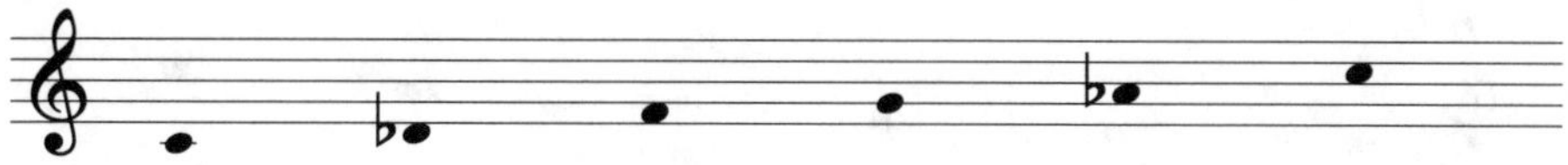

C♯

D

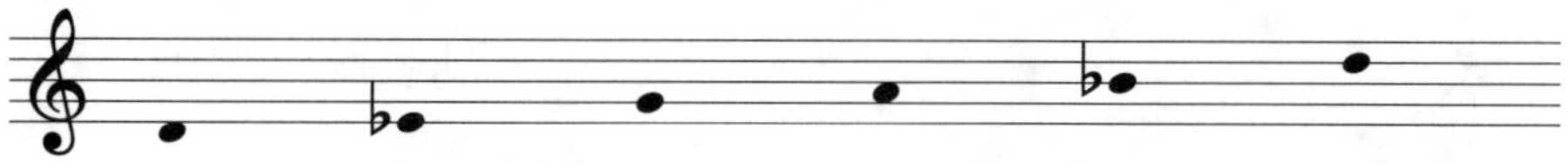

D♯

E

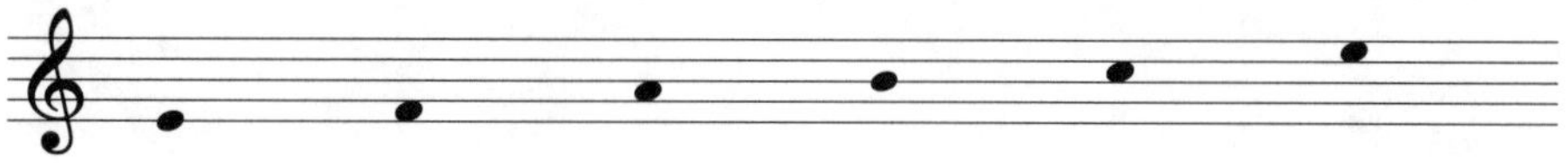

F

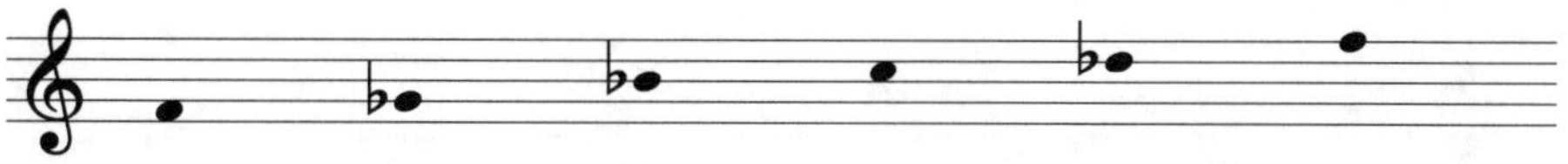

F♯

G

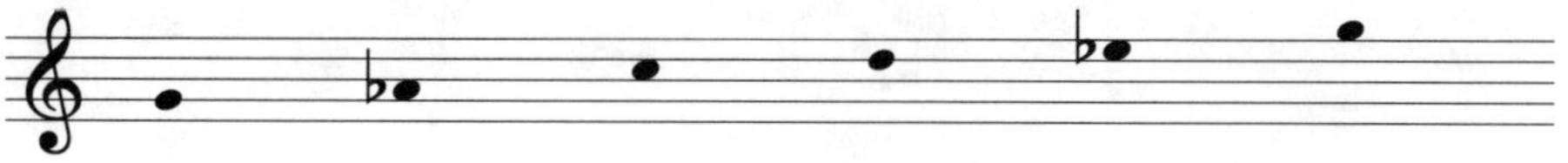

G♯

A

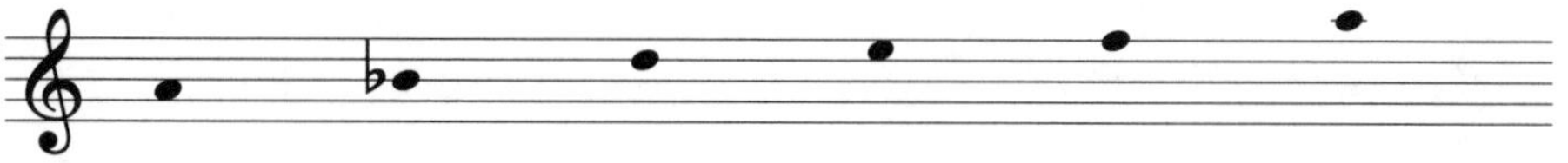

B♭

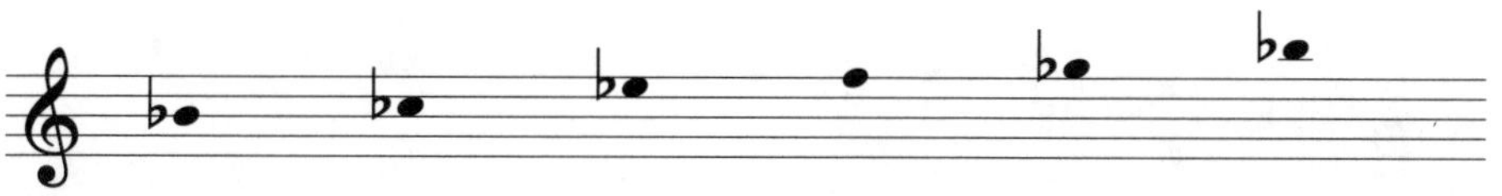

B

Pelog

1 ♭2 ♭3 5 ♭6

H W W+W H W+W

C

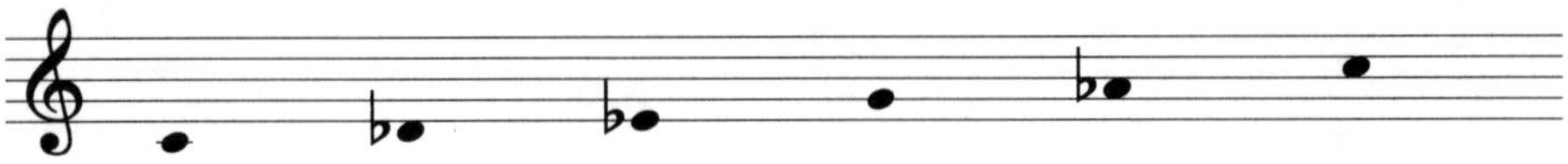

C♯

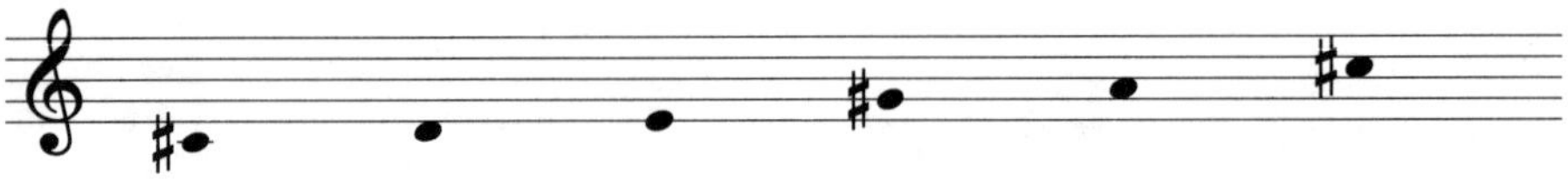

D

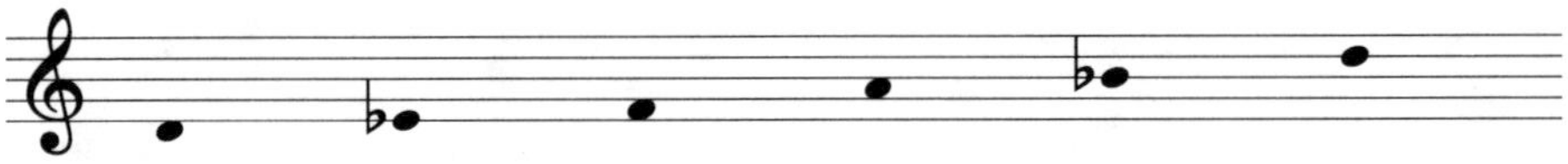

E♭

E

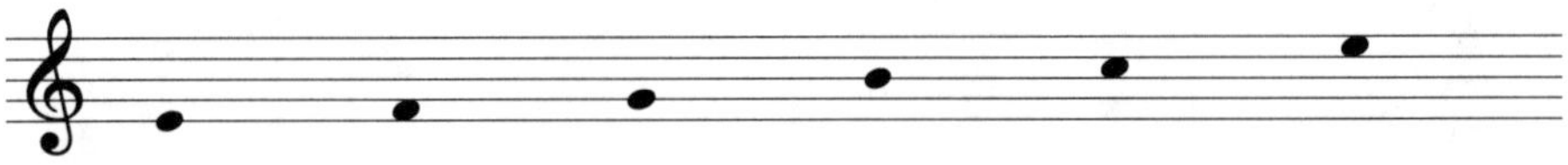

F

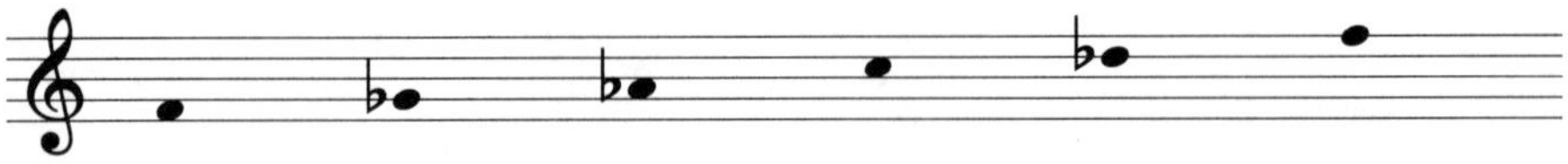

F♯

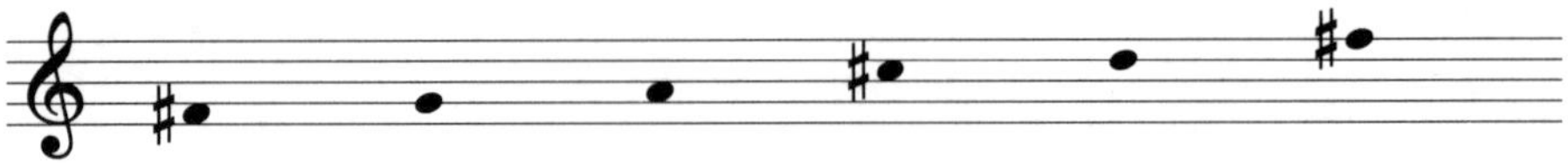

G

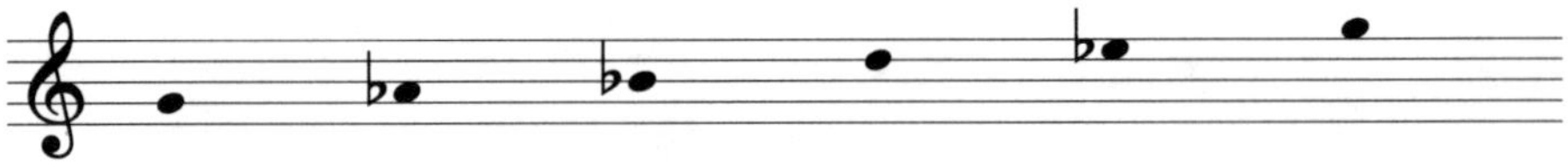

G♯

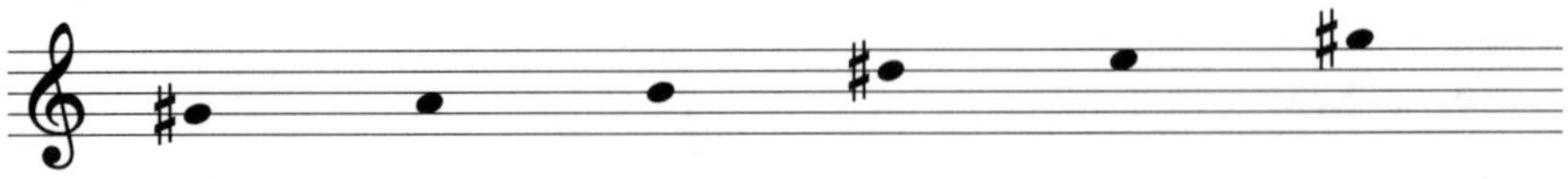

A

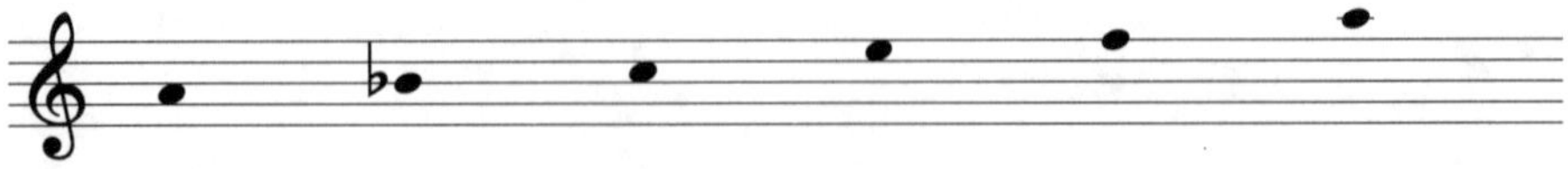

B♭

B

Ritsu

1 2 4 5 6 W W+H W W W+H

C

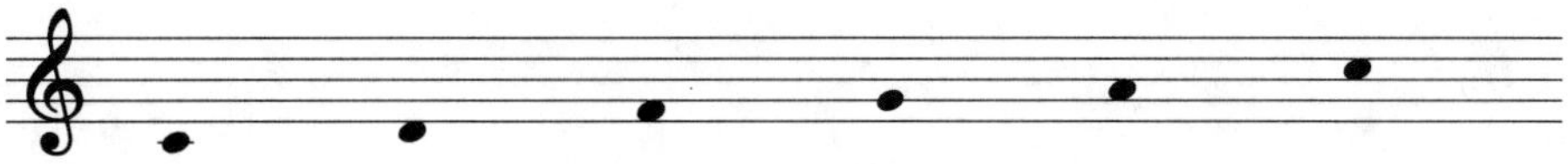

D♭

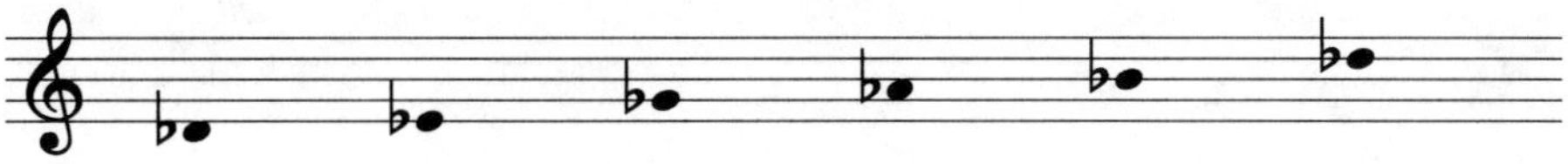

D

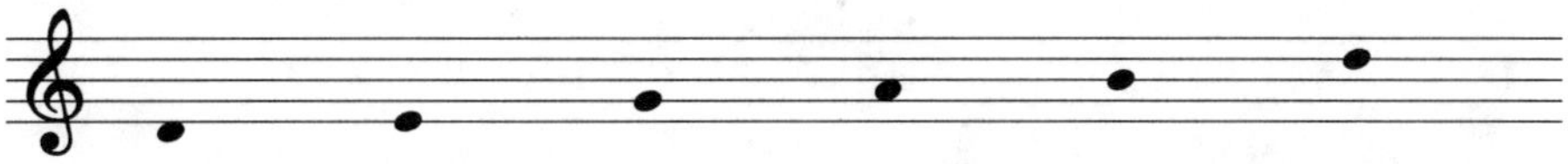

E♭

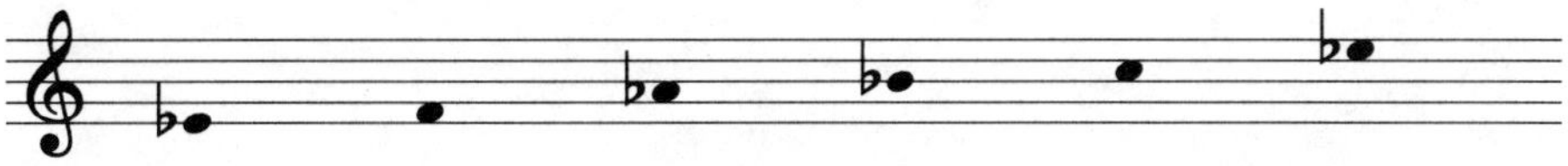

E

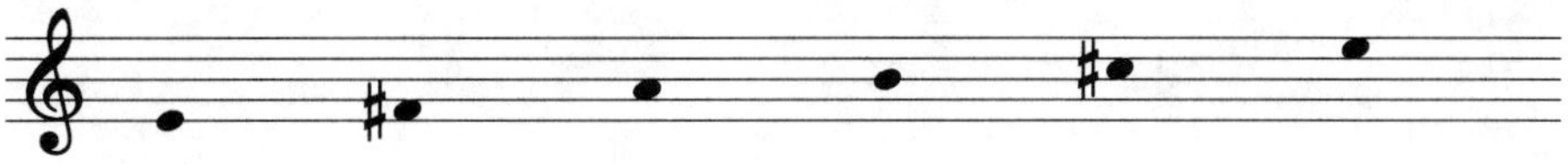

F

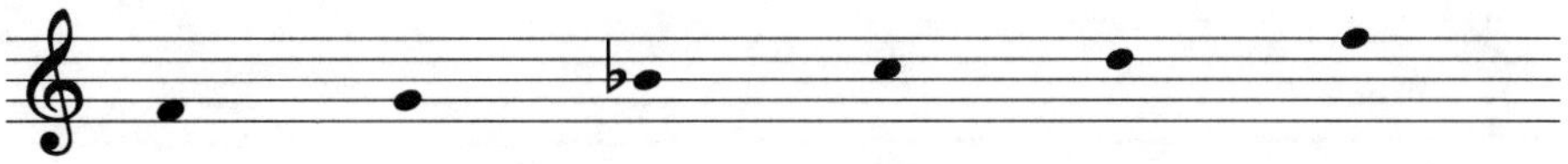

G♭

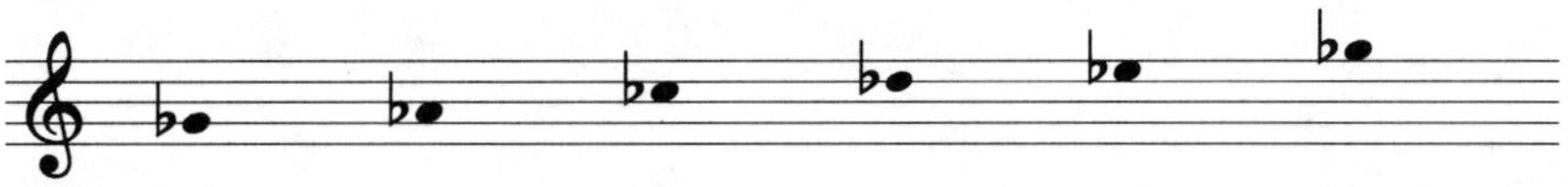

G

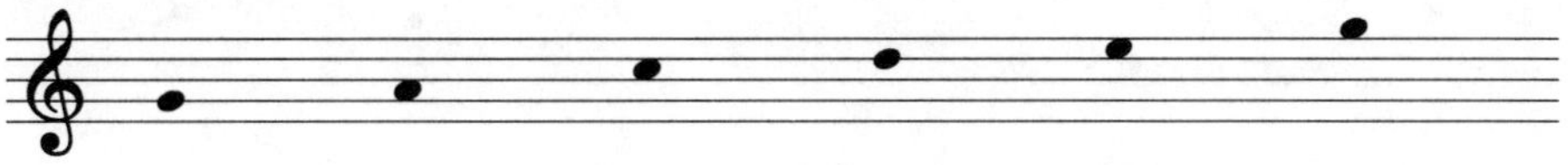

A♭

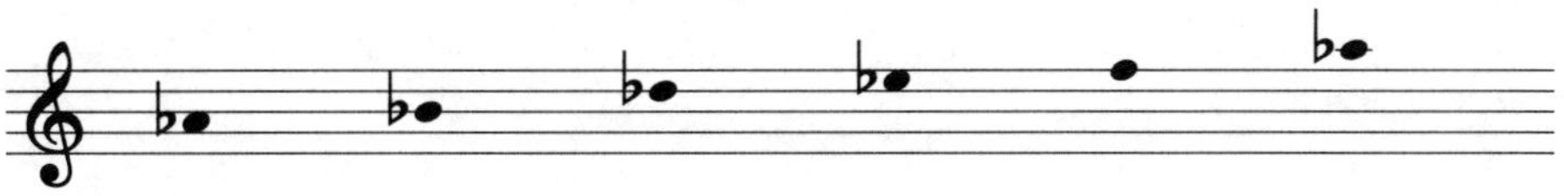

A

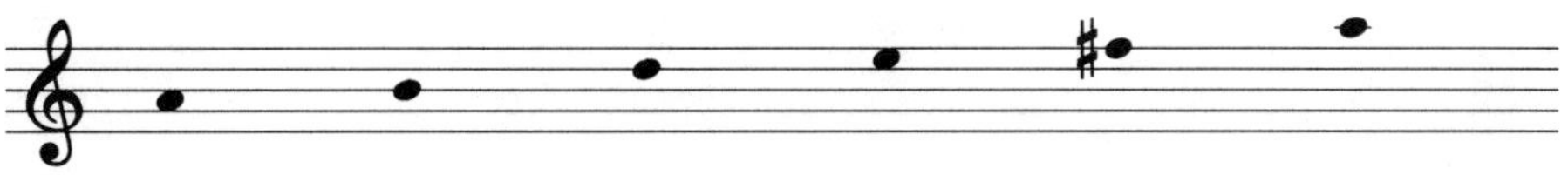

B♭

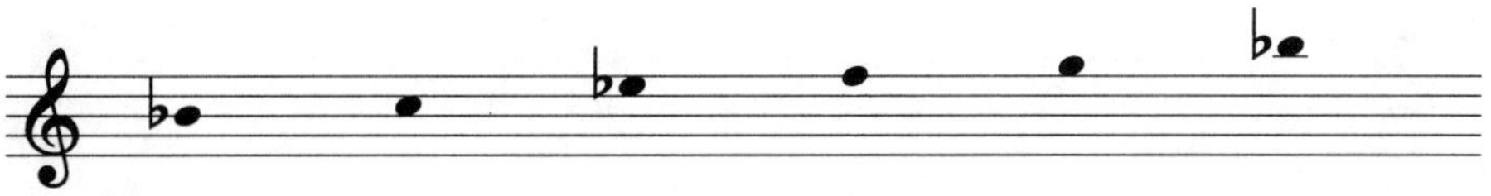

B

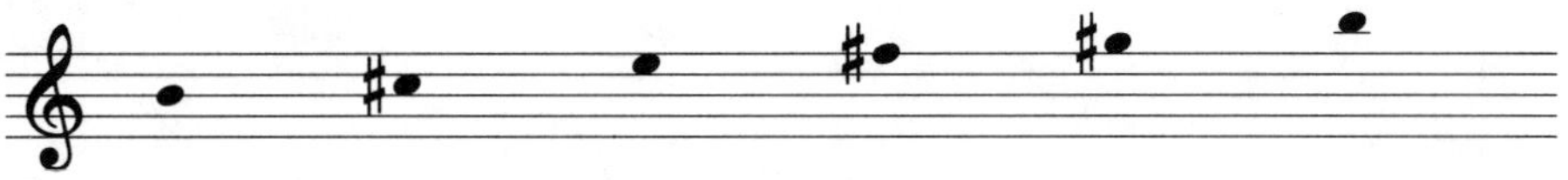

Ryūkyū

1 3 4 5 7 W+W H W W+W H

C

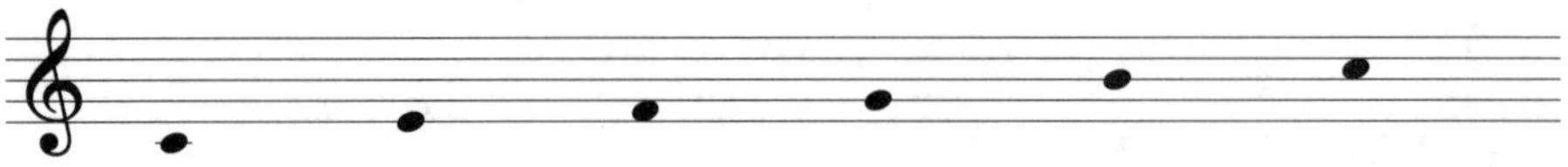

D♭

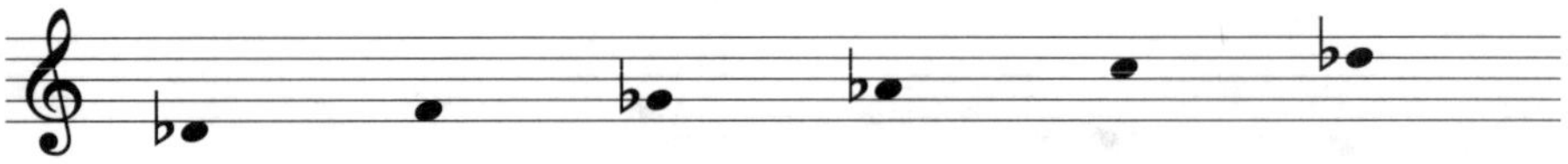

D

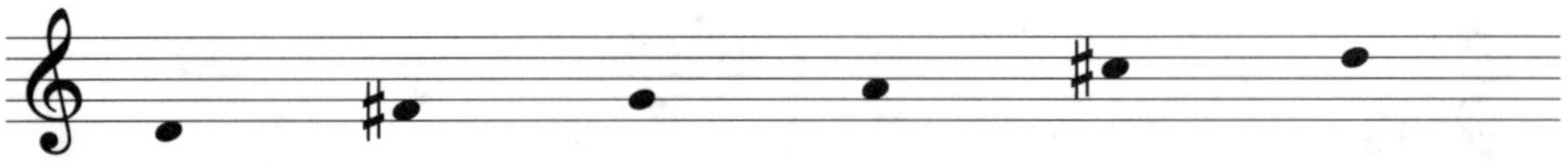

E♭

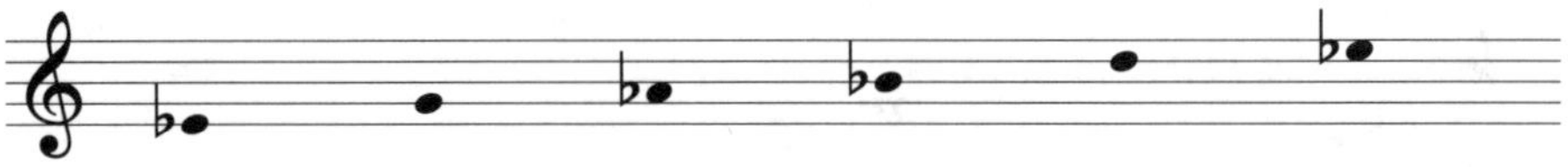

E

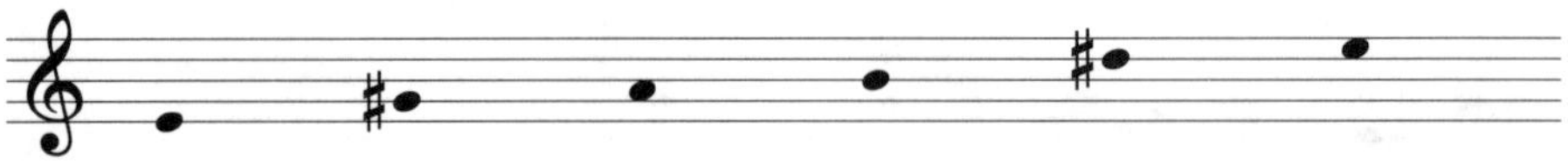

F

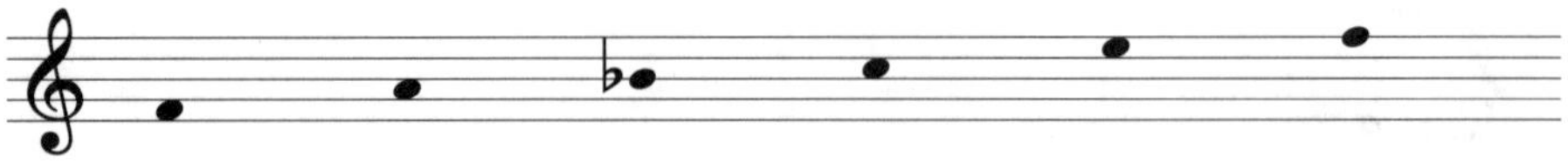

G♭

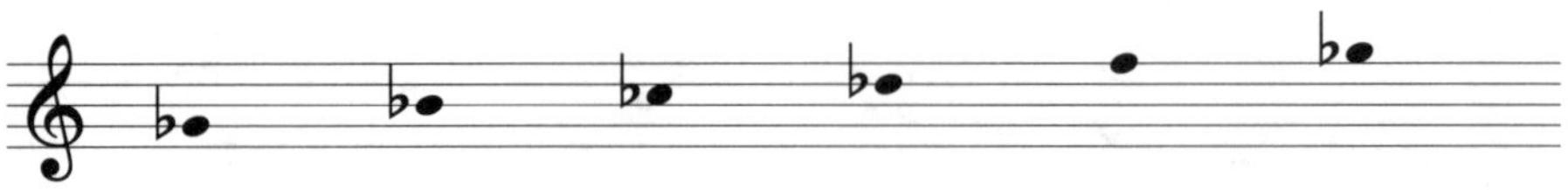

G

A♭

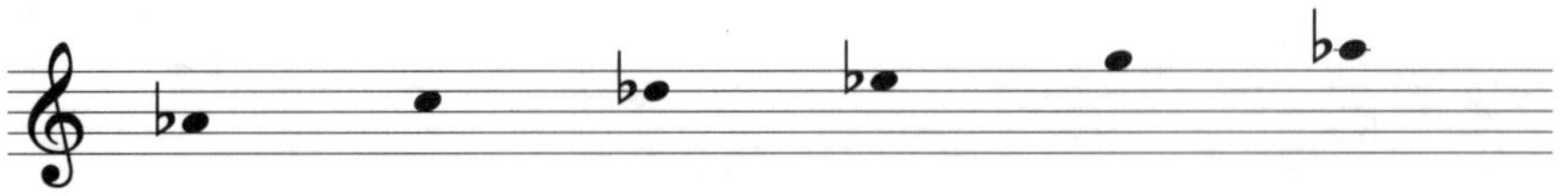

A

B♭

B

Shimo-Chidori

1 3 ♯4 5 7 W+W W H W+W H

C
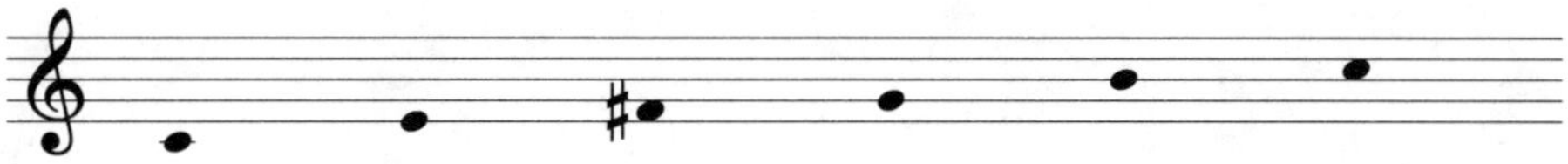

D♭
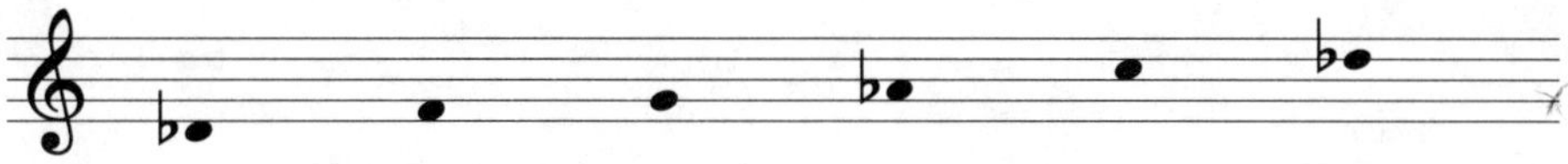

D
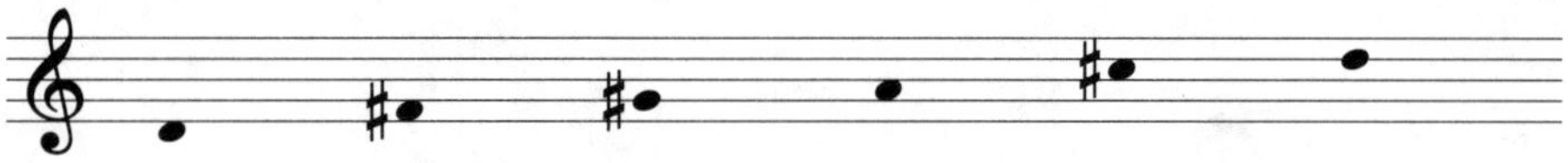

E♭
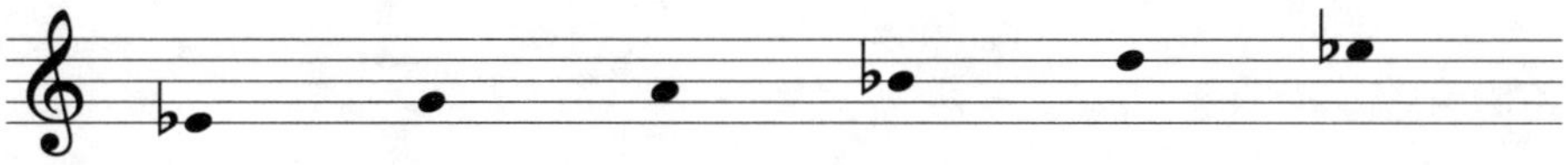

E
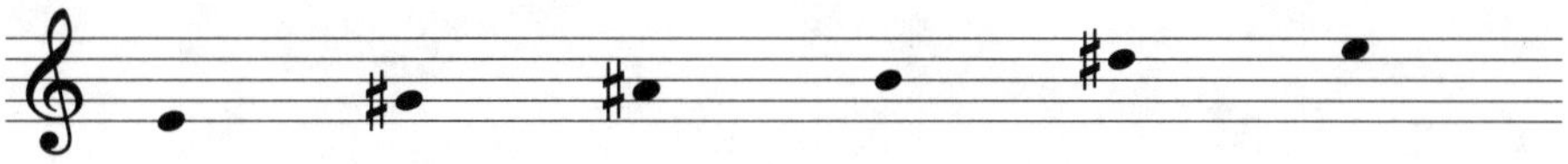

F
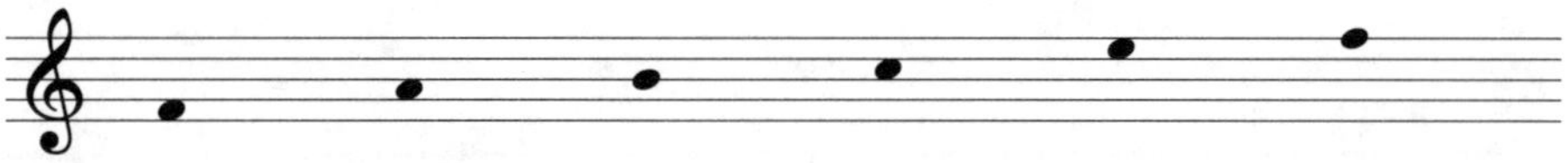

G♭
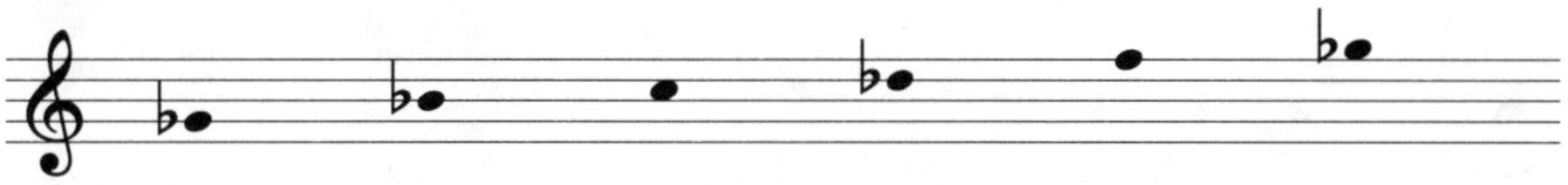

G
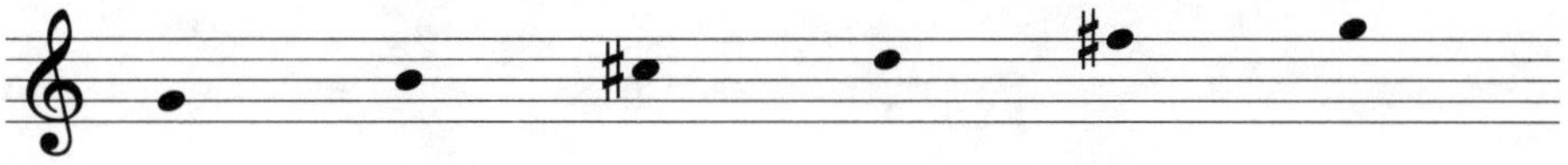

A♭
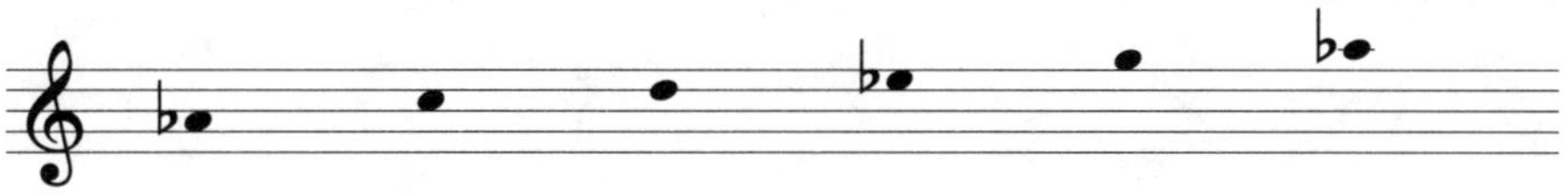

A
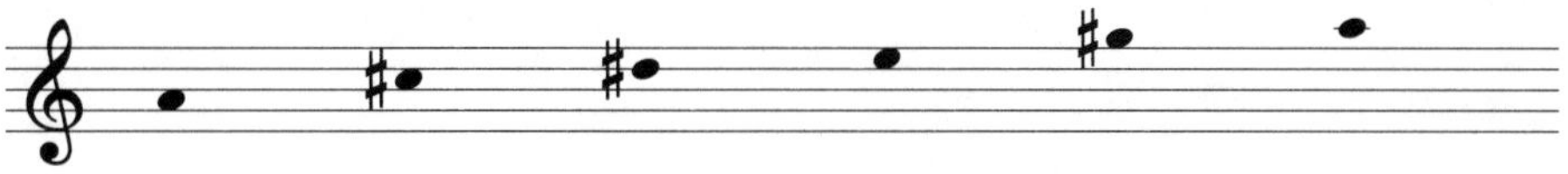

B♭
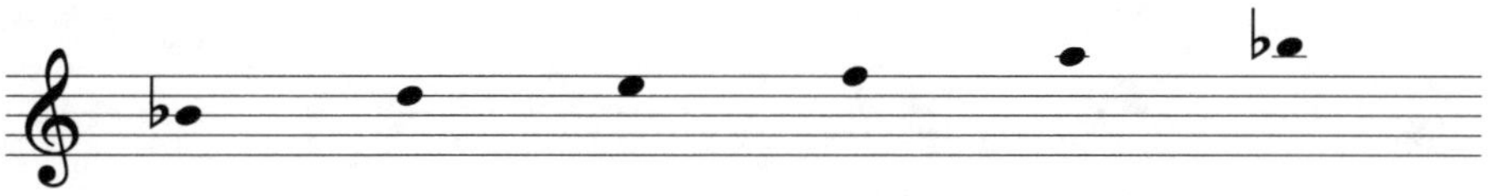

B
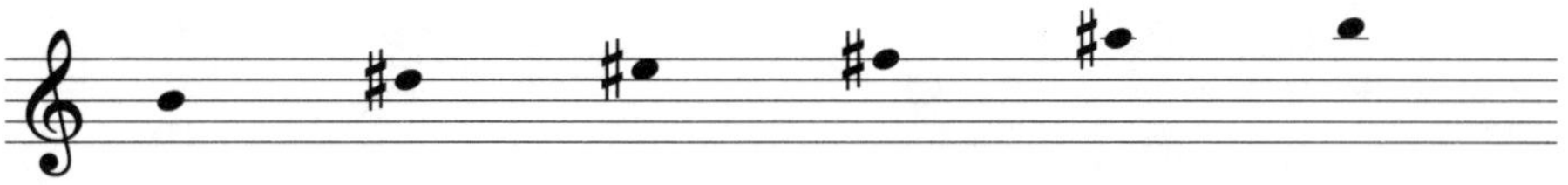

Augmented

1 ♯2 3 5 ♯5 7

W+H H W+H H W+H H

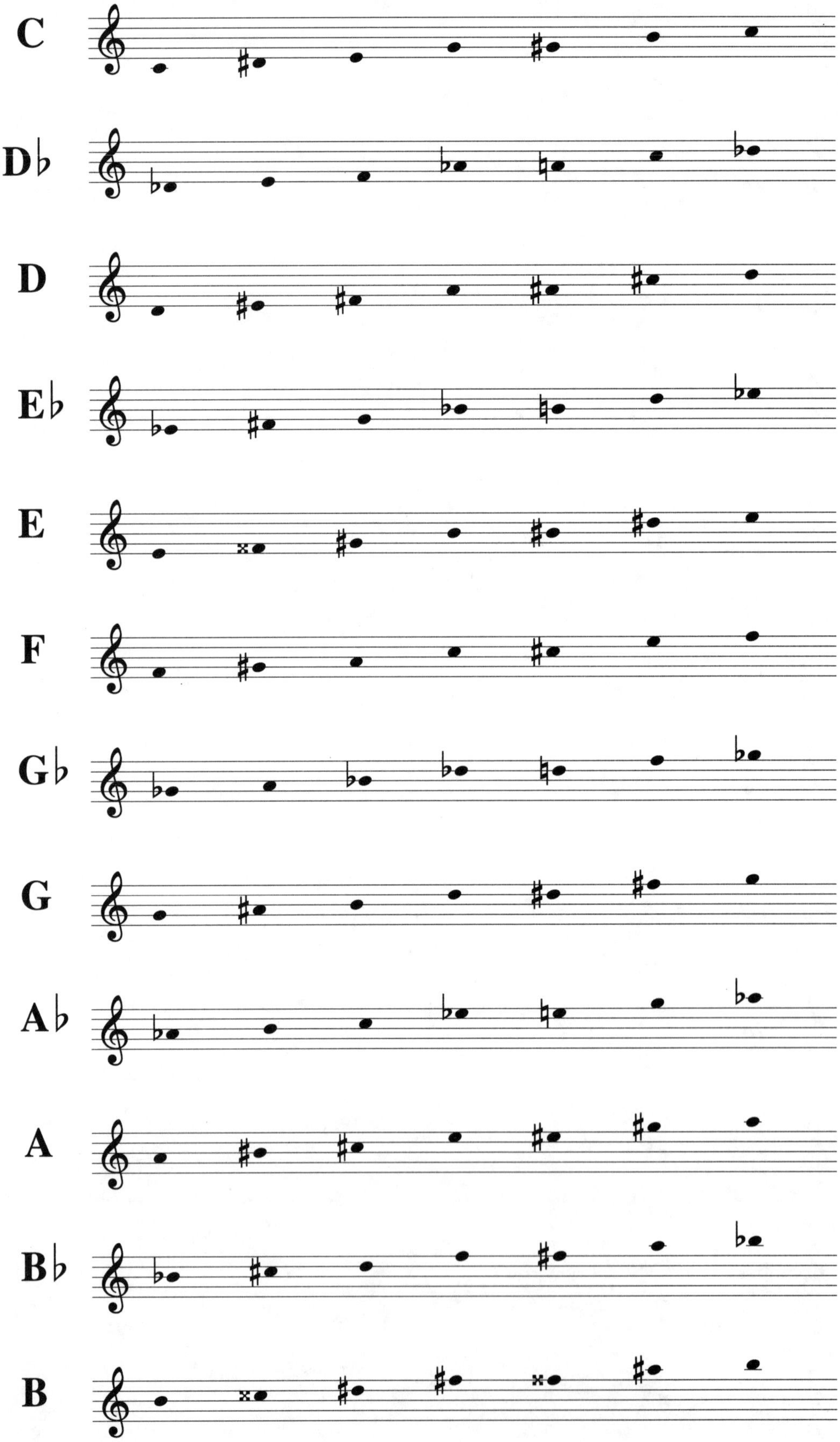

Diminished Half/Whole

1 ♭2 ♯2 3 ♯4 5 6 ♭7 H W H W H W H W

C

C♯

D

D♯

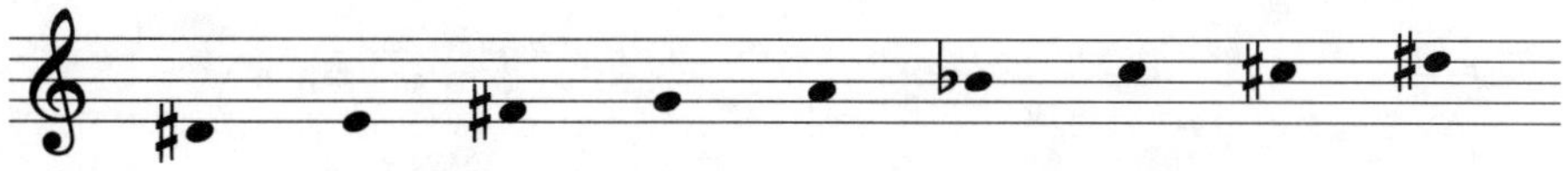

E

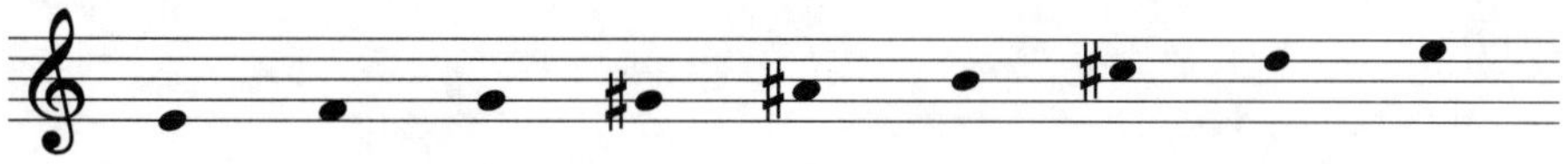

F

F♯

G

G♯

A

B♭

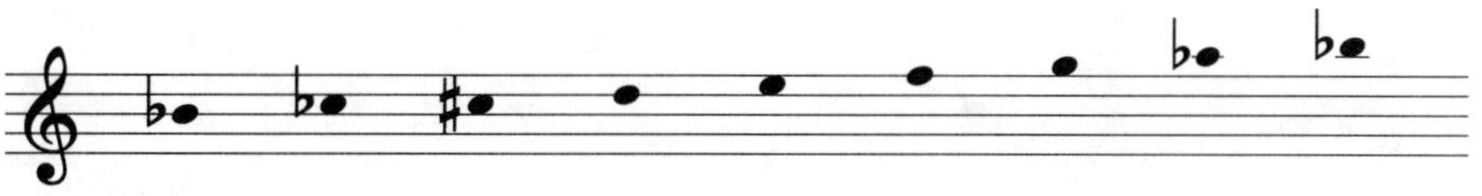

B

Diminished Whole/Half

1 2 ♭3 4 ♭5 ♯5 6 7 W H W H W H W H

C

D♭

D

E♭

E

F

F♯

G

A♭

A

B♭

B

Whole Tone

1 2 3 ♯4 ♯5 ♭7 W W W W W W

C

D♭

D

E♭

E

F

G♭

G

A♭
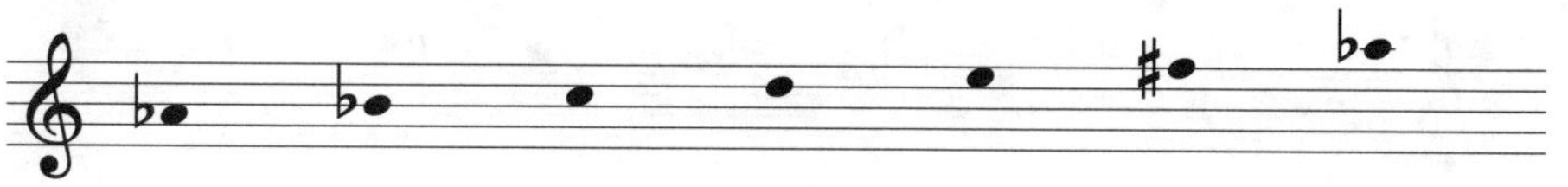

A

B♭
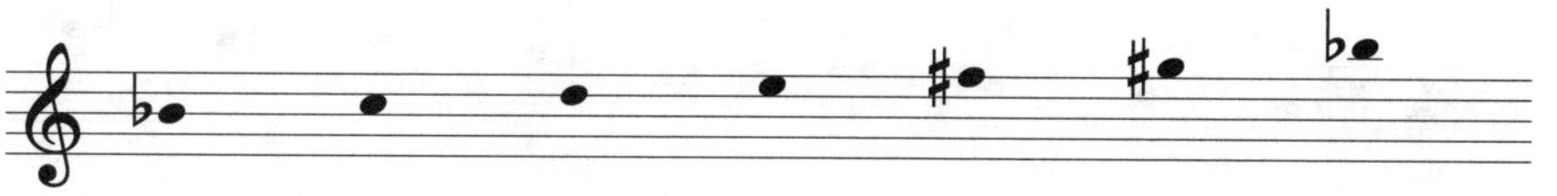

B

Bebop Dominant

1 2 3 4 5 6 ♭7 7 — W W H W W H H H

C

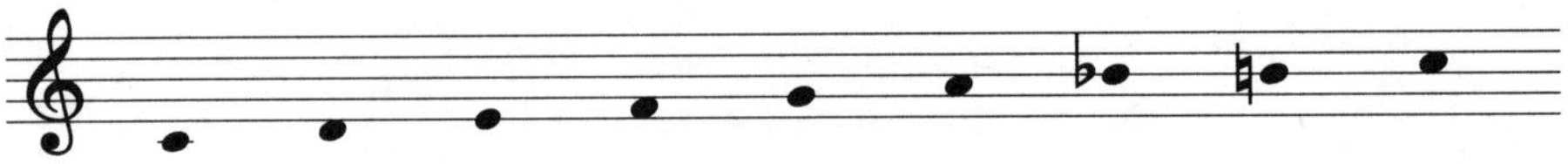

D♭

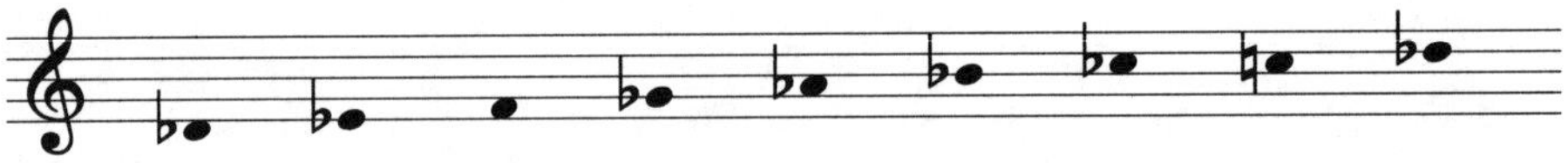

D

E♭

E

F

G♭

G

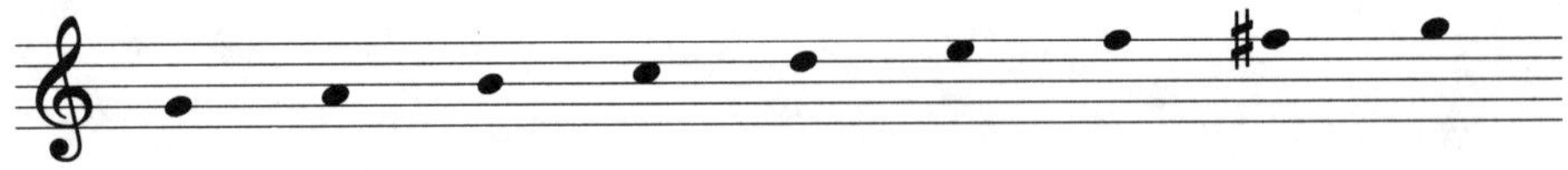

A♭

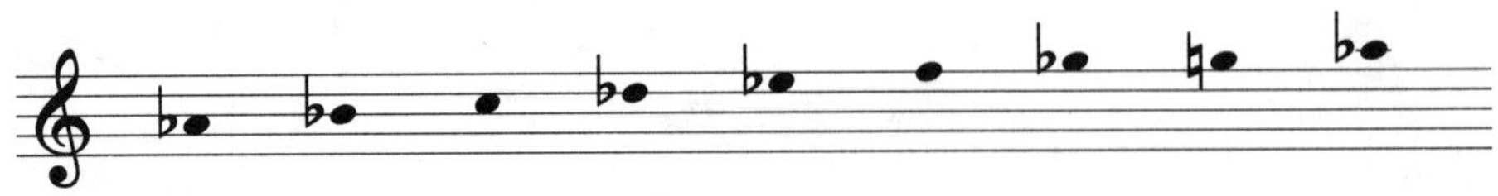

A

B♭

B

Bebop Major

1 2 3 4 5 ♯5 6 7 W W H W H H W H

C
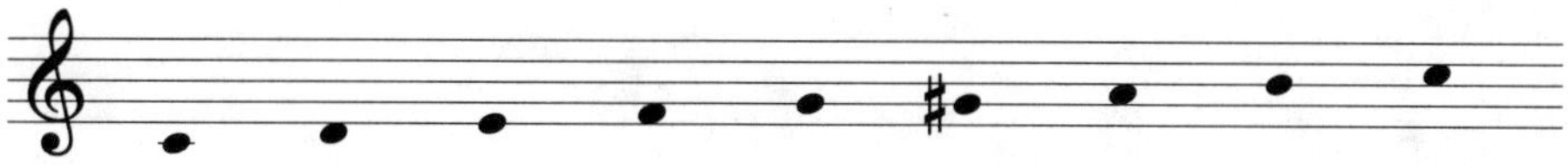

D♭

D

E♭

E
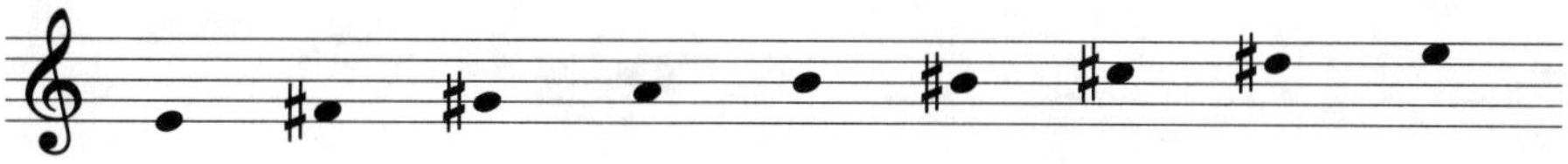

F

G♭

G

A♭

A
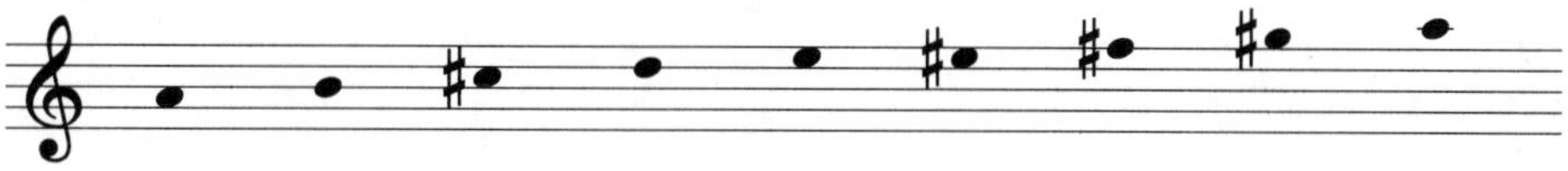

B♭
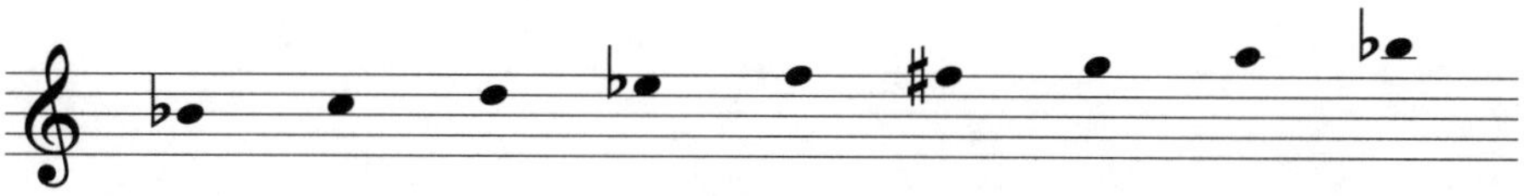

B

Bebop Tonic Minor

1 2 ♭3 4 5 ♯5 6 7

W H W W H H W H

C

D♭

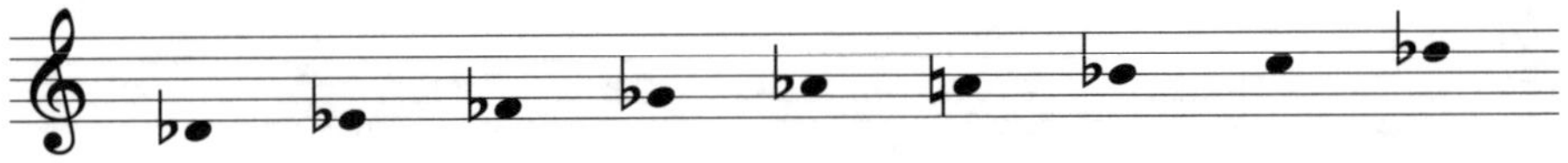

D

E♭

E

F

F♯

G

A♭

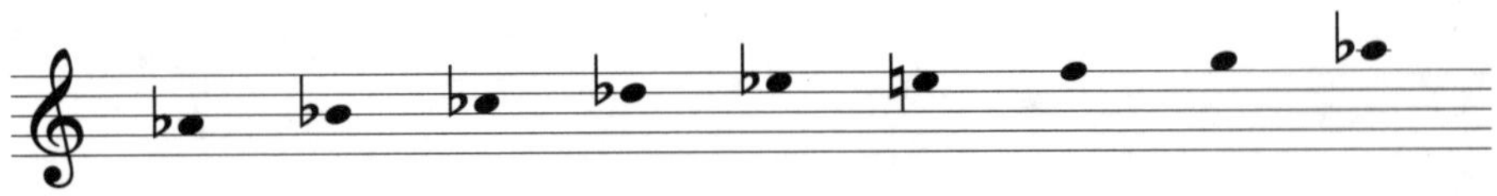

A

B♭

B

Bebop Minor

1 2 ♭3 4 5 ♯5 6 ♭7 W H W W H H H W

C

D♭

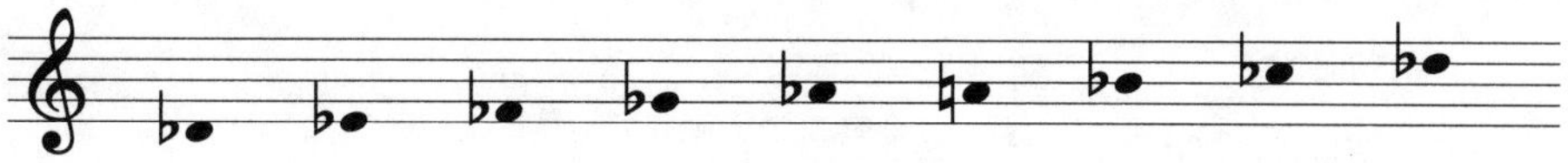

D

E♭

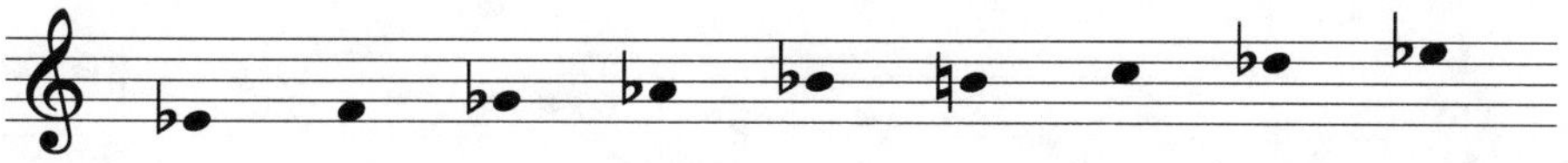

E

F

F♯

G

A♭

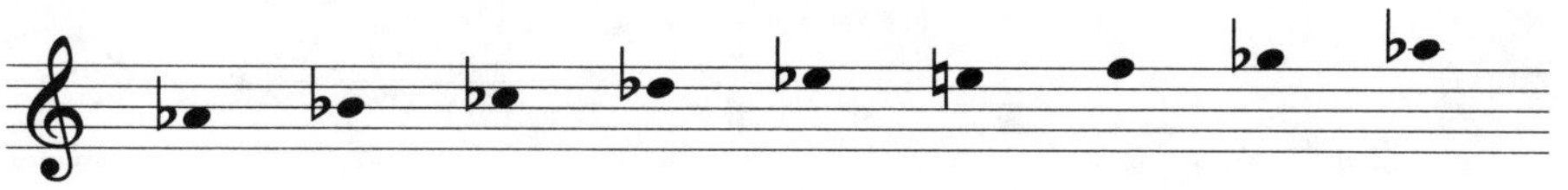

A

B♭

B

Eight–Tone Spanish

1 ♭2 ♭3 3 4 ♭5 ♭6 ♭7 H W H H H W W W

C

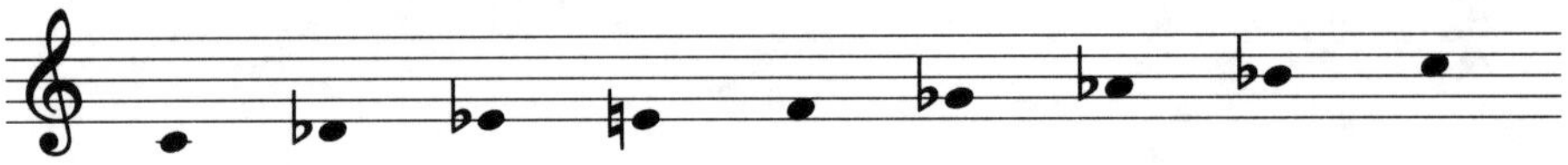

C♯

D

D♯

E

F

F♯

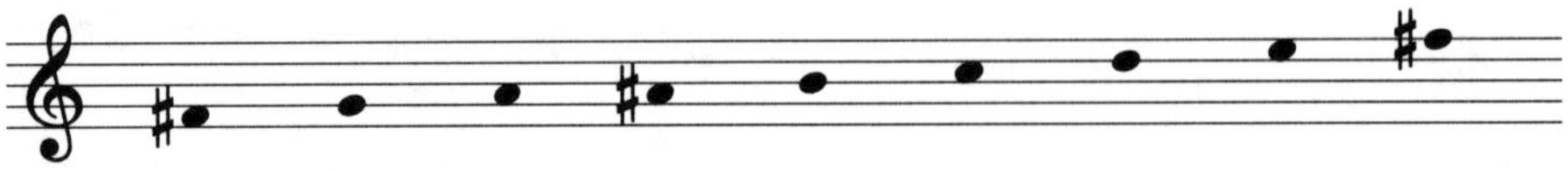

G

G♯

A

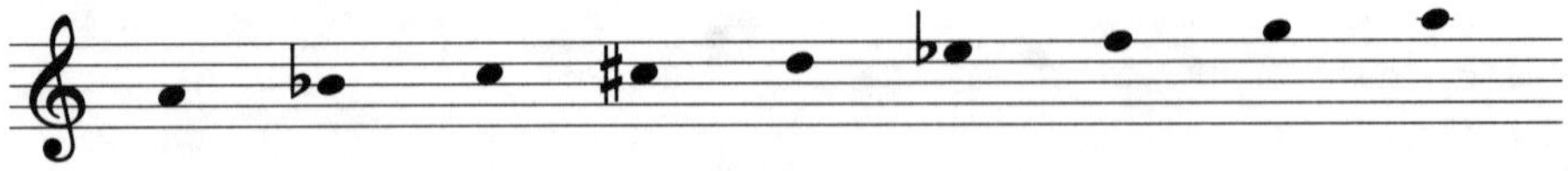

B♭

B

Enigmatic

1 ♭2 3 ♯4 ♯5 ♯6 7 H W+H W W W H H

C

D♭
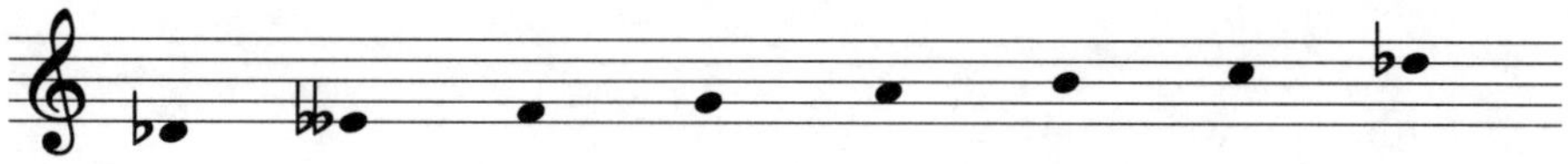

D

E♭

E

F

G♭
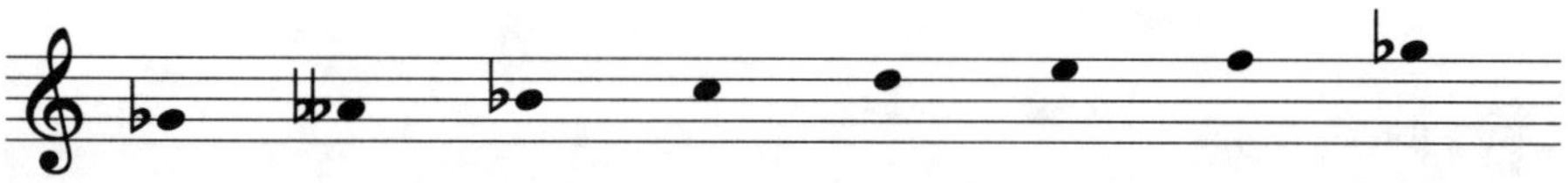

G

A♭

A

B♭

B
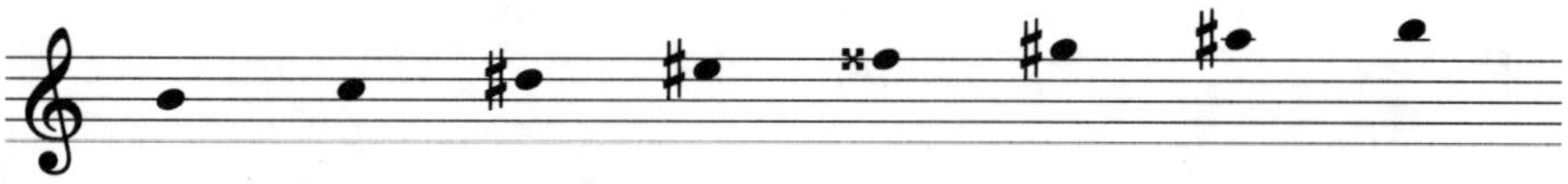

Gypsy

1 2 ♭3 ♯4 5 ♭6 ♭7 W H W+H H H W W

C
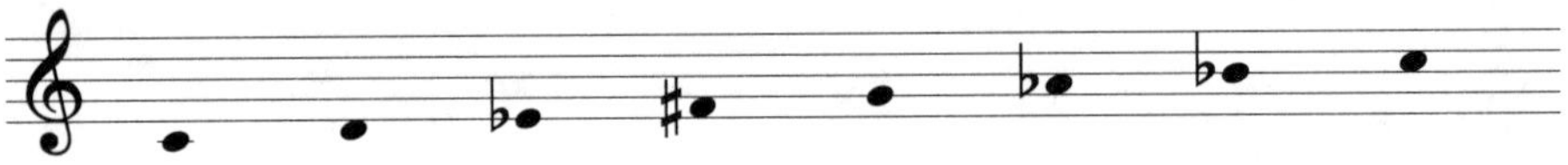

C♯

D
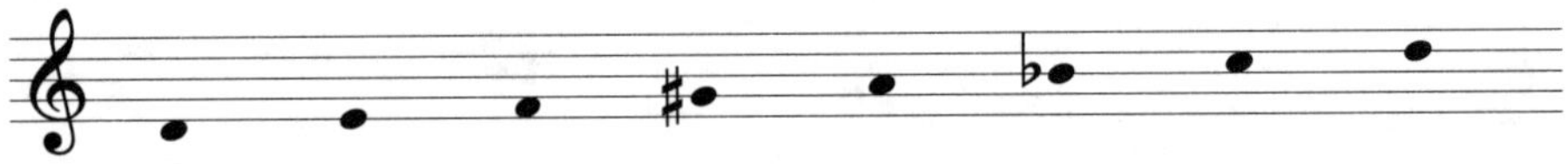

E♭
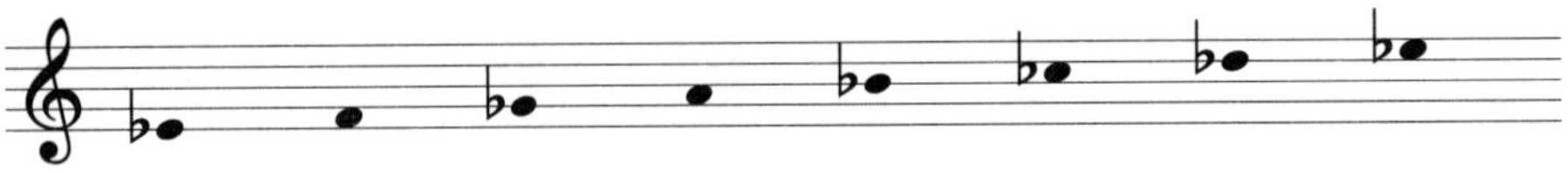

E

F

F♯

G

A♭

A

B♭

B

Hungarian

1 ♯2 3 ♯4 5 6 ♭7 W+H H W H W H W

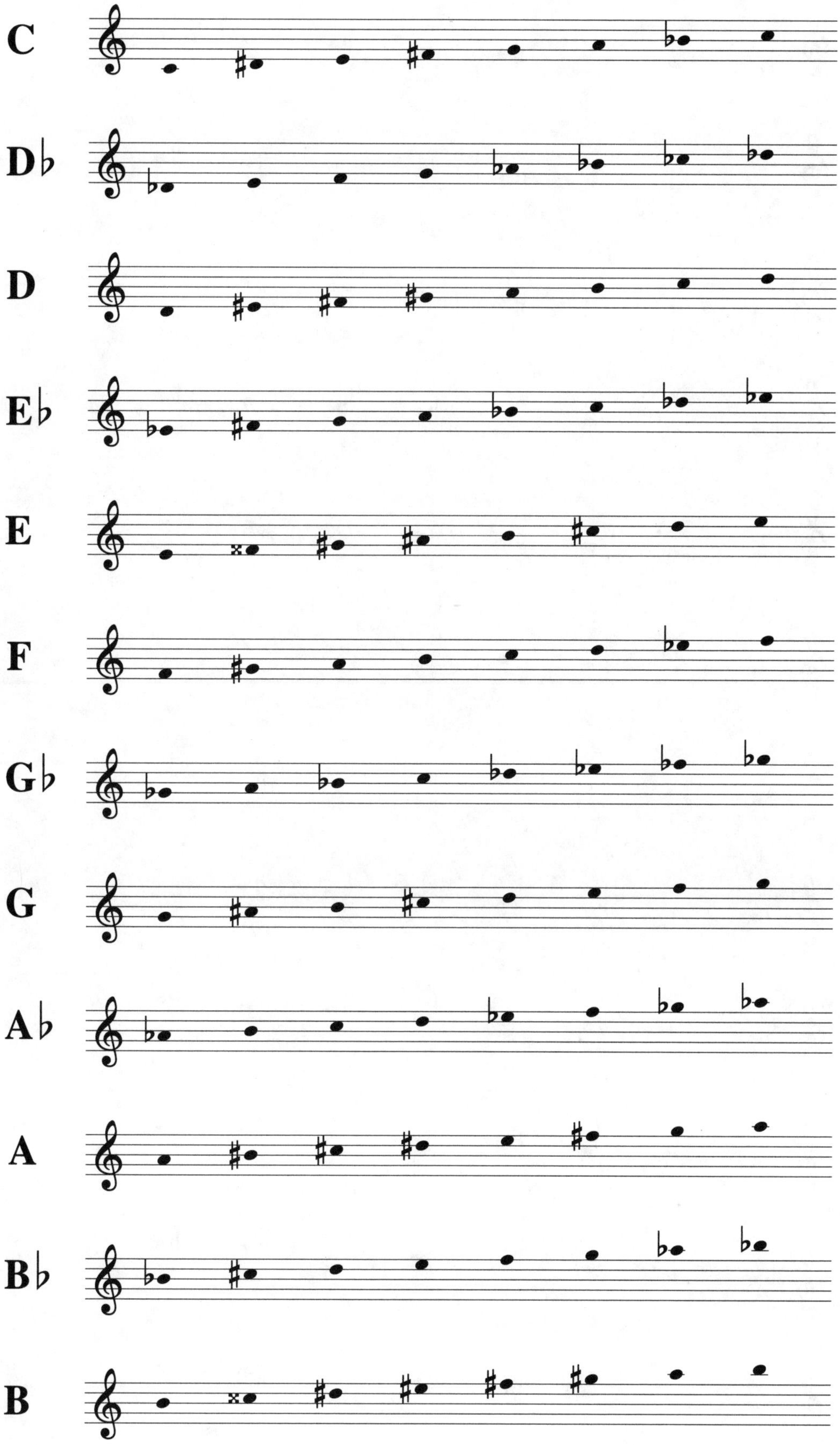

Hungarian Minor

1 2 ♭3 ♯4 5 ♭6 7 W H W+H H H W+H H

C

C♯

D

E♭

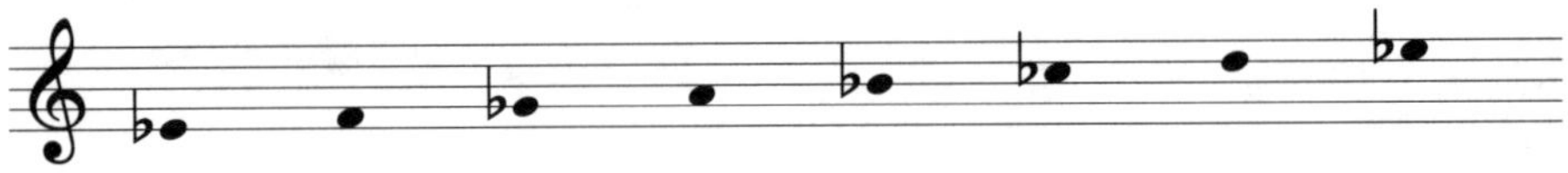

E

F

F♯

G

A♭

A

B♭

B

Leading Whole Tone

1 2 3 ♯4 ♯5 ♯6 7 W W W W W H H

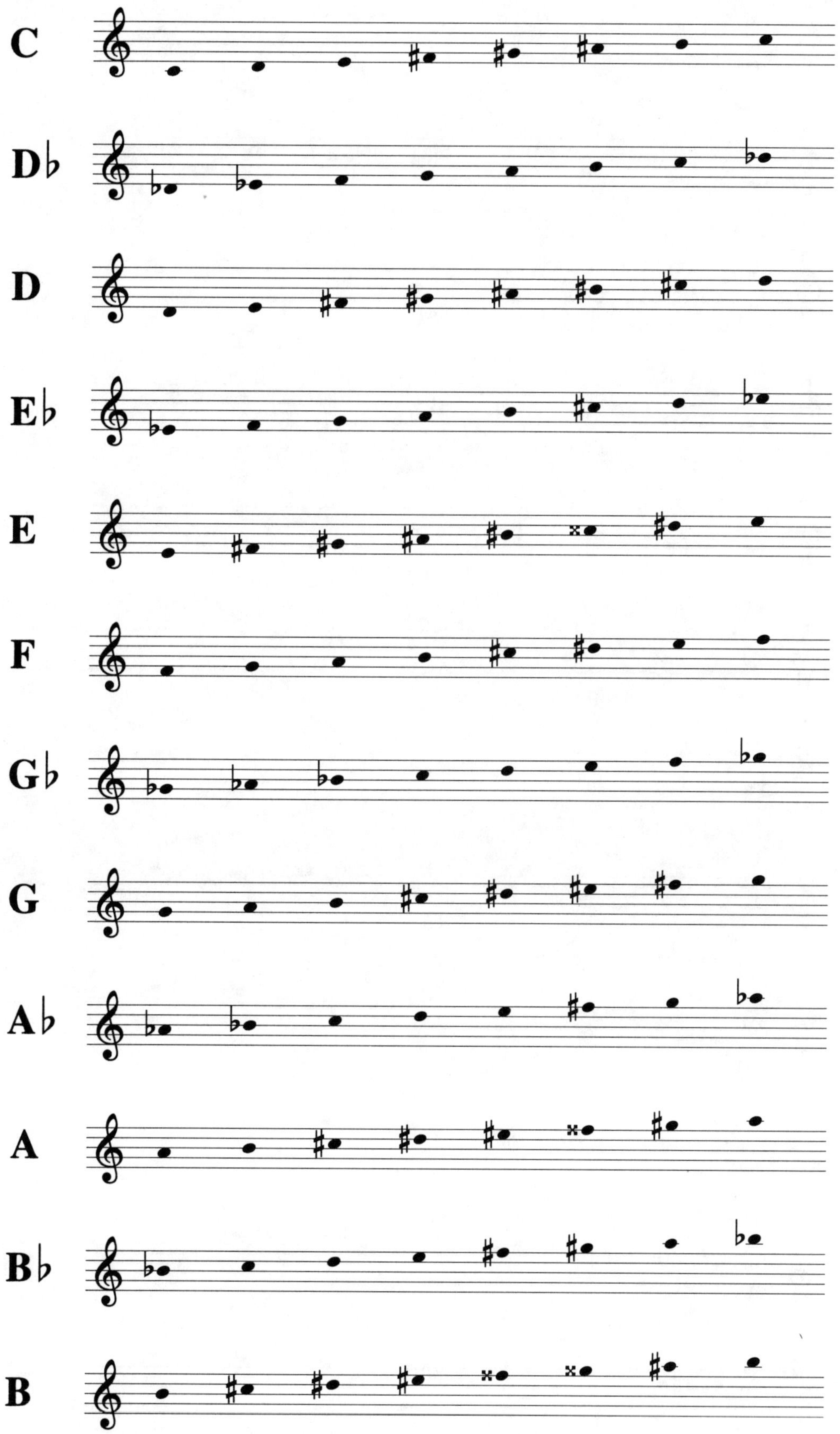

Lydian Minor

1 2 3 ♯4 5 ♭6 ♭7 W W W H H W W

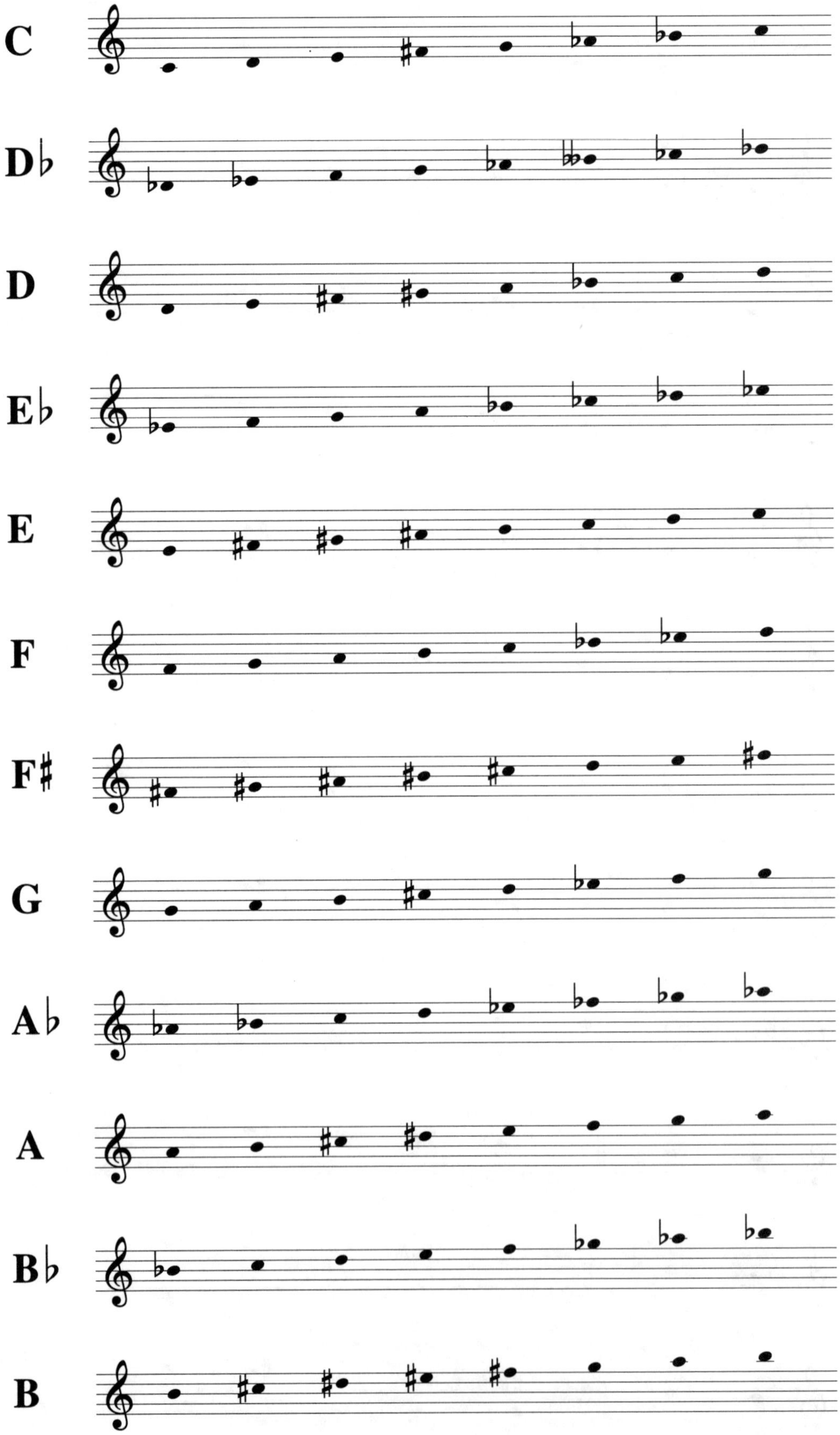

Major Locrian

1 2 3 4 ♭5 ♭6 ♭7   W W H H W W W

C

C♯

D

D♯

E
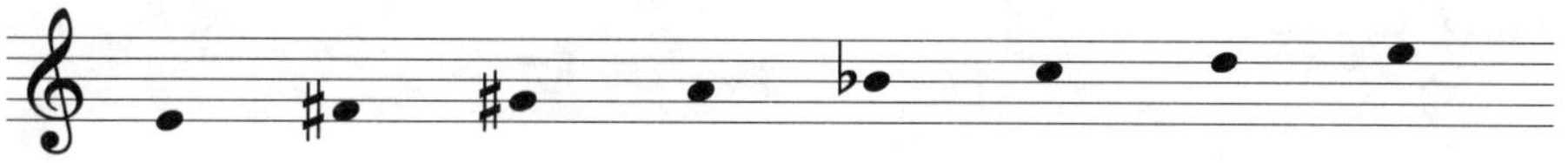

F

F♯

G

G♯

A

B♭

B

Marwa

1 ♭2 3 ♯4 6 7

H W+H W W+H W H

C

C♯

D

E♭

E

F

F♯

G

A♭

A

B♭

B

Neapolitan Major

1 ♭2 ♭3 4 5 6 7 H W W W W W H

C
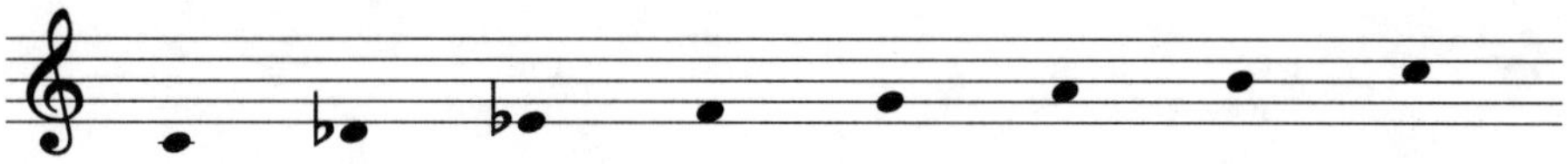

C♯

D
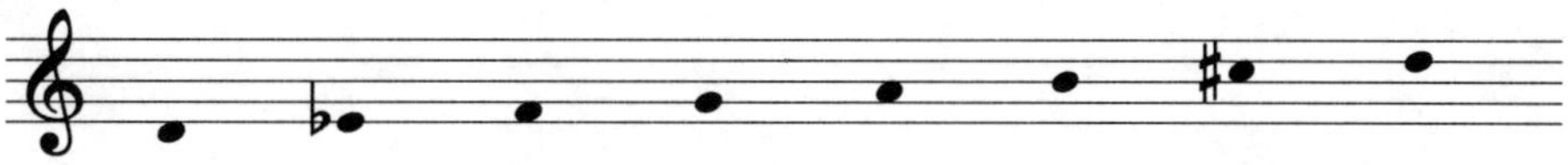

E♭

E

F
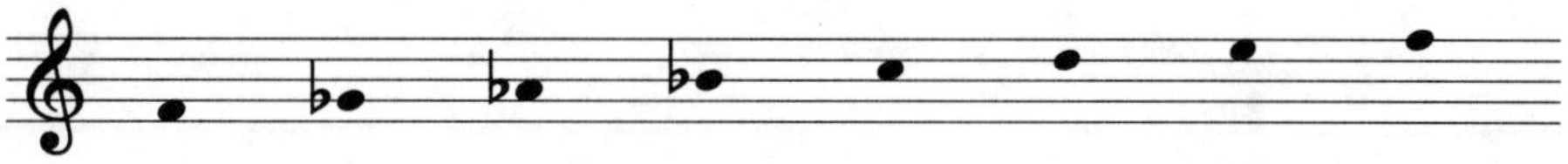

F♯

G
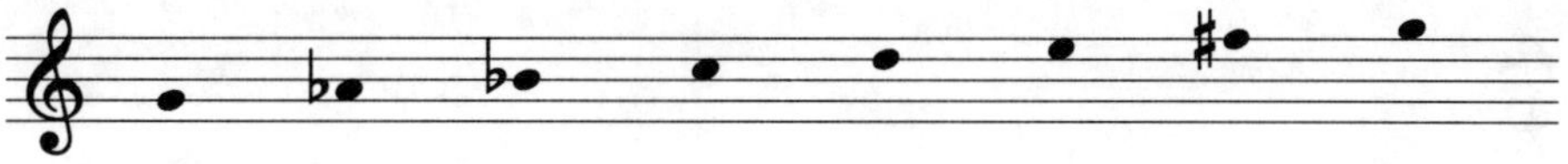

G♯

A

B♭

B

Neapolitan Minor

1 ♭2 ♭3 4 5 ♭6 7

H W W W H W+H H

C

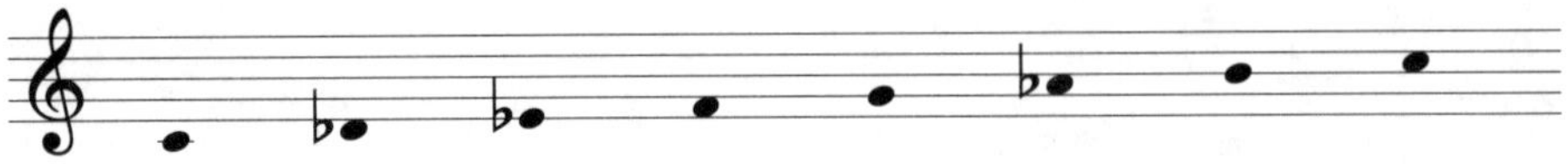

C♯

D

E♭

E

F

F♯

G

G♯

A

B♭

B

Oriental

1 ♭2 3 4 ♭5 6 ♭7 H W+H H H W+H H W

C

C♯

D

E♭

E

F

F♯

G

G♯

A

B♭

B

Prometheus

1 2 3 ♯4 6 ♭7

W W W W+H H W

C

D♭

D

E♭

E

F

G♭

G

A♭

A

B♭

B

Prometheus Neapolitan

1 ♭2 3 ♯4 6 ♭7 H W+H W W+H H W

C

C♯

D
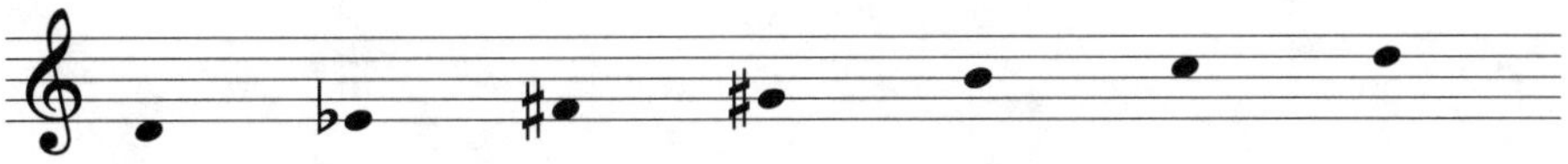

E♭

E

F

F♯

G

G♯

A

B♭

B

Todi

1 ♭2 ♭3 ♯4 5 ♭6 7 H W W+H H H W+H H

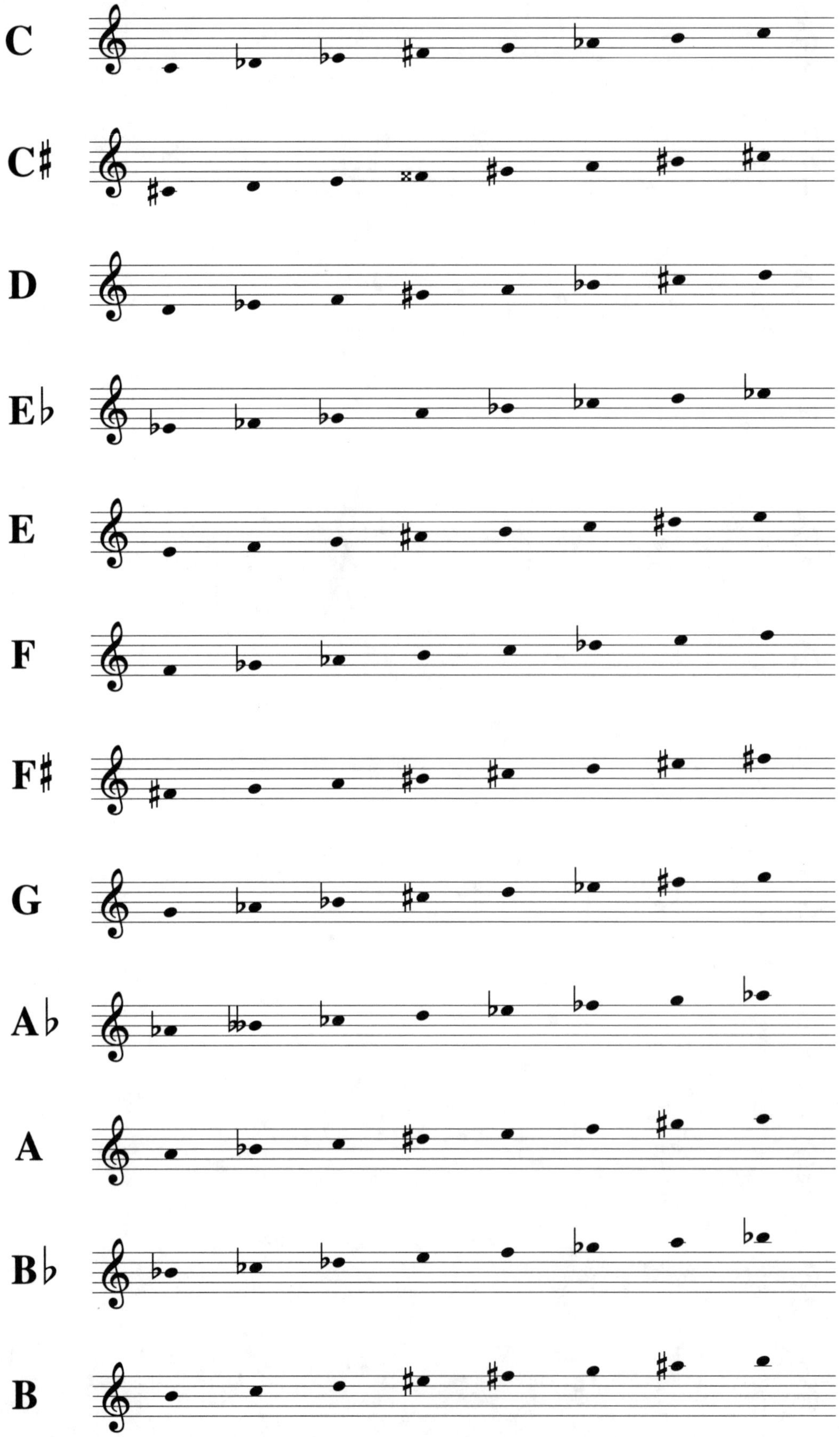

CHERRY LANE™
MUSIC COMPANY

QUALITY IN PRINTED MUSIC